Ninth Edition

D0165122

Ethics
Theory and Practice

Jacques P. Thiroux

Professor Emeritus
Bakersfield College
California State University, Bakersfield

with

Keith W. Krasemann

Professor of Philosophy
and Religious Studies
College of DuPage

PEARSON

Prentice
Hall

Upper Saddle River, New Jersey 07458

Library of Congress Cataloging-in-Publication Data

Thiroux, Jacques P.
  Ethics theory and practice / Jacques P. Thiroux.—9th ed.
    p.   cm.
  Includes bibliographical references and index.
  ISBN 0-13-230213-6 (alk. paper)
  1. Ethics.   2. Ethical problems.   I. Title.
BJ1012.T47 2007
170—dc22

2006018894

Editor-in-Chief: Sarah Touborg
Senior Acquisitions Editor: Mical Moser
Editorial Assistant: Carla Worner
Assistant Marketing Manager: Andrea Messineo
Production Liaison: Marianne Peters-Riordan
Manufacturing Buyer: Christina Amato
Art Director: Jayne Conte
Cover Design: Kiwi Design
Cover Illustration/Photo: Courtesy of the Conway Library,
  Courtauld Institute of Art, London
Director, Image Resource Center: Melinda Patelli
Manager, Rights and Permissions: Zina Arabia
Manager, Visual Research: Beth Brenzel
Manager, Cover Visual Research & Permissions: Karen Sanatar
Image Permission Coordinator: Cynthia Vincenti
Composition/Full-Service Project Management:
  Shiny Rajesh/Integra Software Services
Printer/Binder: R. R. Donnelley & Sons

Credits and acknowledgments borrowed from other sources and reproduced, with permission, in this textbook appear on appropriate page within text.

Pearson Prentice Hall™ is a trademark of Pearson Education, Inc.
Pearson® is a registered trademark of Pearson plc
Prentice Hall® is a registered trademark of Pearson Education, Inc.

Pearson Education LTD.
Pearson Education Singapore, Pte. Ltd
Pearson Education, Canada, Ltd
Pearson Education–Japan
Pearson Education Australia PTY, Limited

Pearson Education North Asia Ltd
Pearson Educación de Mexico, S.A. de C.V.
Pearson Education Malaysia, Pte. Ltd
Pearson Education, Upper Saddle River, New Jersey

10 9 8 7 6 5 4 3 2 1
ISBN: 0-13-230213-6

Dedication

This edition is dedicated to my wife, Emily Thiroux, and Yvonne Demetriff for their support and assistance with the ninth edition.

Family's Dedication

Professor Thiroux completed his final revisions to this text on the day he died. His family believes that he was holding on to life until the revisions were complete. In the nearly 30 years since this text was first published, it has been used around the world and touched many lives. The family hopes that this legacy will continue with this edition.

Contents

Preface

First of all, I want to thank all of the students and professors over the years for having faith in me and my book to find it usable and useful. The book has now been in print for 28 years!—no mean feat for any book, and especially one on ethics. I am very proud and grateful to all of you for helping me make it so.

Each time I have revised it, I have tried to make it more: more all-inclusive, more relevant, and more up to date. This has not always been easy because of the perilous and changing times in which we live. Some of the new material in this edition includes physician assisted suicide, particularly the Terri Schiavo case, non-Western views of environmental issues, and global issues in business. A whole new chapter on Virtue Ethics has been added that includes non-Western as well as Western views. Updated case studies have also been added.

Special features ensure that students new to the study of ethics understand the concepts in the text.

Chapter Objectives at the chapter openings provide students with a summary of complex issues and outline what they can expect to learn in the chapter.

Cases for Study and Discussion illustrate for students how ethical theory and discussion can be specifically applied. Each case is open-ended and encourages the student to examine his or her own ethics and views on how the situation should be handled.

Chapter summaries at the end of each chapter help students to review the concepts discussed in the chapter.

Exercises for Review and Discussion Questions urge students to apply what they have learned to specific problems, such as taking a human life, lying, cheating, stealing, and breaking promises.

Appendices that apply theoretical ethics to eight contemporary ethical problems: Appendices one through eight discuss moral problems in business, medicine, the environment, and more. Each appendix contains a general discussion of the problem and discussions of specific cases. These appendices contain the author's own views on how the various moral issues in the book might be dealt with and resolved. Instructors may assign each appendix with its respective chapter, posing various discussion questions for students to deal with. They may also hold off assigning the appendices until after students have formed their own theories and solutions to the issues and problems discussed.

Supplementary Reading Lists supply resources that make the material more tangible and stimulate further exploration.

INSTRUCTOR SUPPLEMENTS

Instructor's Manual. The instructor's manual contains general overviews of each chapter, class suggestions, sections on key concepts and questions, chapter summaries, and test questions.

ABC News broadcasts on videotape show how ethical issues connect to contemporary situations.

STUDENT SUPPLEMENTS

Companion Website (www.prenhall.com/thiroux): Visit this site when you want to gain a richer perspective and a deeper understanding of the concepts and issues discussed in *Ethics: Theory and Practice.* The Companion Website features chapter review tests learning objectives, and study questions that students can use to assess their comprehension of chapter content.

ACKNOWLEDGMENTS

I would like to thank my editor, Mical Moser; co-author, Keith W. Krasemann, College of DuPage, Illinois, for his significant contributions to the ninth edition; my wife, Emily Thiroux, for helping me with the final copy; and Yvonne Demetriff, for her technical advice. In addition, thanks to Nancy Hudson, California University of PA; Michael R. McVay, Colby Community College; John C. Modschiedler, College of DuPage; and all of the other reviewers who have helped by suggesting changes and appropriate updates.

Ethics continues to be one of more important endeavors. We must continue debating the issues allowing for dissent and using the best ethical reasoning we can muster to deal with the difficult problems of the twenty-first century.

Jacques P. Thiroux
Professor Emeritus
Bakersfield College
California State University, Bakersfield

Chapter

1

What Is Morality?

Objectives

After you have read this chapter, you should be able to

1. Define *philosophy* and explain the relationship of ethics to it.
2. Define key terms concerning ethics or morality.
3. Explain the various approaches to the study of morality.
4. Understand what morality is and how it differs from aesthetics, nonmoral behavior, and manners.
5. Understand to whom morality applies.
6. Have some idea of where morality comes from.
7. Distinguish between morality and the law.
8. Distinguish between morality and religion.
9. Understand why human beings should be moral.

What Is Philosophy and Ethics' Relationship to It?

Philosophy literally means love of wisdom, the Greek words *philia* meaning love or friendship, and *sophia* meaning wisdom. Philosophy is concerned basically with three areas: *epistemology* (the study of knowledge), *metaphysics* (the study of the nature of reality), and *ethics* (the study of morality), which will be our major concern in this book.

Epistemology deals with the following questions: What is knowledge? What are truth and falsity, and to what do they apply? What is required for someone to actually *know* something? What is the nature of perception, and how reliable is it? What are logic and logical reasoning, and how can human beings attain them? What's the difference between knowledge and belief? Is there anything such as "certain knowledge"? From time to time throughout this book, epistemological questions will be discussed, especially in Chapter 5, which deals with absolutes and truth.

Metaphysics is the study of the nature of reality, asking the questions: What exists in reality and what is the nature of what exists? Specifically, such questions as the following are asked: Is there really cause and effect in reality, and if so, how does it work? What is the nature of the physical world, and is there anything other than the physical, such as the mental or spiritual? What is the nature of human beings? Is there freedom in reality or is everything predetermined? Here again, we will deal with some of these questions throughout the book, but especially in Chapter 5—are there any absolutes or is everything really relative?—and Chapter 6, is there any such thing as freedom, or are all things in reality predetermined?

Ethics, our main concern, deals with what is right or wrong in human behavior and conduct. It asks such questions as what constitutes any person or action being good, bad, right, or wrong, and how do we know (epistemology)? What part does self-interest or the interests of others play in the making of moral decisions and judgments? What theories of conduct are valid or invalid, and why? Should we use principles or rules or laws, or should we let each situation decide our morality? Are killing, lying, cheating, stealing, and sexual acts right or wrong, and why or why not?

As you can see, these three areas are related and at times overlap, but each one is worthy of concentrated study in itself. The major concern in this book, as its title suggests, is ethics, and before going any further, it is important to define some key terms used in any discussion of ethics or morality.

Key Terms

Ethical, Moral, Unethical, Immoral

In ordinary language, we frequently use the words *ethical* and *moral* (and *unethical* and *immoral*) interchangeably; that is, we speak of the ethical or moral person or act. On the other hand, we speak of codes of ethics, but only infrequently do we mention codes of morality. Some reserve the terms moral and immoral only for the realm of sexuality and use the words *ethical* and *unethical* when discussing how the business and professional communities should behave toward their members or toward the public. More commonly, however, we use none of these words as often as we use the terms *good, bad, right,* and *wrong*. What do all of these words mean, and what are the relationships among them?

Ethics comes from the Greek *ethos,* meaning character. *Morality* comes from the Latin *moralis,* meaning customs or manners. Ethics, then, seems to pertain to the individual character of a person or persons, whereas morality seems to point to the relationships between human beings. Nevertheless, in ordinary language, whether we call a person ethical or moral, or an act unethical or immoral, doesn't really make any difference. In philosophy, however, the term *ethics* is also used to refer to a specific area of study: the area of morality, which concentrates on human conduct and human values.

When we speak of people as being moral or ethical, we usually mean that they are good people, and when we speak of them as being immoral or unethical, we mean that they are bad people. When we refer to certain human actions as being moral, ethical, immoral, and unethical, we mean that they are right or wrong. The simplicity of these definitions, however, ends here, for how do we define a right or wrong action or a good or bad person? What are the human standards by which such decisions can be made? These are the more difficult questions that make up the greater part of the study of morality, and they will be discussed in more detail in later chapters. The important thing to remember here is that *moral, ethical, immoral,* and *unethical,* essentially mean *good, right, bad,* and *wrong,* often depending upon whether one is referring to people themselves or to their actions.

Characteristics of Good, Bad, Right, Wrong, Happiness, or Pleasure. It seems to be an empirical fact that whatever human beings consider to be good involves happiness and pleasure in some way, and whatever they consider to be bad involves unhappiness and pain in some way. This view of what is good has traditionally been called "hedonism." As long as the widest range of interpretation is given to these words (from simple sensual pleasures to intellectual or spiritual pleasures and from sensual pain to deep emotional unhappiness), then it is difficult to deny that whatever is good involves at least some pleasure or happiness, and whatever is bad involves some pain or unhappiness.

One element involved in the achievement of happiness is the necessity of taking the long- rather than the short-range view. People may undergo some pain or unhappiness in order to attain some pleasure or happiness in the long run. For example, we will put up with the pain of having our teeth drilled in order to keep our teeth and gums healthy so that we may enjoy eating and the general good health that results from having teeth that are well maintained. Similarly, people may do very difficult and even painful work for two days in order to earn money that will bring them pleasure and happiness for a week or two.

Furthermore, the term *good* should be defined in the context of human experience and human relationships rather than in an abstract sense only. For example, knowledge and power in themselves are not good unless a human being derives some satisfaction from them or unless they contribute in some way to moral and meaningful human relationships. They are otherwise nonmoral.

What about actions that will bring someone some good but will cause pain to another, such as those of a sadist who gains pleasure from violently mistreating another human being? Our original statement was that everything that is good will bring some person satisfaction, pleasure, or happiness of some kind, but this statement does not necessarily work in the reverse—that everything that brings someone satisfaction is necessarily good. There certainly are "malicious pleasures."

Excellence. William Frankena states that whatever is good will also probably involve "some kind or degree of excellence."[1] He goes on to say that "what is bad in itself is so because of the presence of either pain or unhappiness or of some kind of defect or lack of excellence."[2] Excellence is an important addition to pleasure or satisfaction in that it makes "experiences or activities better or worse than they would otherwise be."[3] For example, the enjoyment or satisfaction gained from hearing a concert, seeing a fine movie, or reading a good book is due, to a great extent, to the excellence of the creators and presenters of these events (composers, performers, directors, actors, writers). Another and perhaps more profound example of the importance of excellence is that if one gains satisfaction or pleasure from witnessing a well-conducted court case and from seeing and hearing the judge and the lawyers perform their duties well, that satisfaction will be deepened if the judge and the lawyers are also excellent people; that is, if they are kind, fair, and compassionate human beings in addition to being clever and able.

Whatever is good, then, will probably contain some pleasure, happiness, and excellence, whereas whatever is bad will probably contain their opposites: pain, unhappiness, and lack of excellence. I am only stating that there will probably be *some* of these elements present. For example, a good person performing a right action might not be particularly happy and might even find what he or she is doing painful; nonetheless, the recipients of the right action might be made happy by it and the right action also might involve excellence.

Harmony and Creativity. There are two other attributes of "good" and "right" that may add to our definition; they are harmony and creativity on the "good" side and discord, or disharmony, and lack of creativity on the "bad" side. If an action is creative or can aid human beings in becoming creative and, at the same time, help to bring about a harmonious integration of as many human beings as possible, then we can say it is a right action. If an action has the opposite effect, then we can say that it is a wrong action.

For example, if a person or a group of people can end a war between two nations and create an honorable and lasting peace, then a right or good action has been performed. It can allow members of both nations to be creative rather than destructive and can create harmony between both sides and within each nation. On the other hand, causing or starting a war between two nations will have just the opposite effect. Lester A. Kirkendall stresses these points and also adds to what I stated earlier about the necessity of placing the emphasis on what is good or excellent in human experience and relationships:

> Whenever a decision or a choice is to be made concerning behavior, the moral decision will be the one which works toward the creation of trust, confidence, and integrity in relationships. It should increase the capacity of individuals to cooperate, and enhance the sense of self-respect in the individual. Acts which create distrust, suspicion, and misunderstanding, which build barriers and destroy integrity are immoral. They decrease the individual's sense of self-respect and rather than producing a capacity to work together they separate people and break down the capacity for communication.[4]

Two other terms that we should define are *amoral* and *nonmoral*.

Amoral

Amoral means having no moral sense, or being indifferent to right and wrong. This term can be applied to very few people. Certain people who have had prefrontal lobotomies tend to act amorally after the operation; that is, they have no sense of right and wrong. And there are a few human beings who, despite moral education, have remained or become amoral. These tend to be found among certain criminal types who can't seem to realize they've done anything wrong. They tend not to have any remorse, regret, or concern for what they have done.

One such example of an amoral person is Gregory Powell, who, with Jimmy Lee Smith, gratuitously killed a policeman in an onion field south of Bakersfield, California. A good description of him and his attitude can be found in Joseph Wambaugh's *The Onion Field*.[5] Another such example is Colin Pitchfork, another real-life character. Pitchfork raped and killed two young girls in England and was described by Wambaugh in *The Blooding*. In that book Wambaugh also quotes from various psychologists speaking about the amoral, psychopathological, sociopathological personality, which is defined as "a person characterized by emotional instability, lack of sound judgment, perverse and impulsive (often criminal) behavior, inability to learn from experience, amoral and asocial feelings, and other serious personality defects."[6] He describes "the most important feature of the psychopath . . . as his monumental irresponsibility. He knows what the ethical rules are, at least he can repeat them parrot-like, but they are void of meaning to him."[7] He quotes further: "No sense of conscience, guilt, or remorse is present. Harmful acts are committed without discomfort or shame."[8] Amorality, then, is basically an attitude that some—luckily only a few—human beings possess.

All of this doesn't mean that amoral criminals should not be morally blamed and punished for their wrongdoings. In fact, such people are even more dangerous to society than those who can distinguish right from wrong because usually they are morally uneducable. Society, therefore, needs even more protection from such criminals.

Nonmoral

The word *nonmoral* means out of the realm of morality altogether. For example, inanimate objects such as cars and guns are neither moral nor immoral. A person using the car or gun may use it immorally, but the things themselves are nonmoral. Many areas of study (for instance, mathematics, astronomy, and physics) are in themselves nonmoral, but because human beings are involved in these areas, morality may also be involved. A mathematics problem is neither moral nor immoral in itself; however, if it provides the means by which a hydrogen bomb can be exploded, then moral issues certainly will be forthcoming.

In summary, then, the immoral person knowingly violates human moral standards by doing something wrong or by being bad. The amoral person may also violate moral standards because he or she has no moral sense. Something that is nonmoral can neither be good nor bad nor do anything right or wrong simply because it does not fall within the scope of morality.

Approaches to the Study of Morality

Scientific, or Descriptive, Approach

There are two major approaches to the study of morality. The first is *scientific,* or *descriptive.* This approach most often is used in the social sciences and, like ethics, deals with human behavior and conduct. The emphasis here, however, is empirical; that is, social scientists observe and collect data about human behavior and conduct and then draw certain conclusions. For example, some psychologists, after having observed many human beings in many situations, have reached the conclusion that human beings often act in their own self-interest. This is a descriptive, or scientific, approach to human behavior—the psychologists have observed how human beings act in many situations, *described* what they have observed, and drawn conclusions. However, they make no value judgments as to what is morally right or wrong, nor do they prescribe how humans ought to behave.

Philosophical Approach

The second major approach to the study of morality is called the *philosophical* approach, and it consists of two parts.

Normative, or Prescriptive, Ethics. The first part of the philosophical approach deals with norms (or standards) and prescriptions.

Using the example that human beings often act in their own self-interest, normative ethical philosophers would go beyond the description and conclusion of the psychologists and would want to know whether human beings *should* or *ought to* act in their own self-interest. They might even go further and come up with a definite conclusion; for example, "Given these arguments and this evidence, human beings should always act in their own self-interest" (egoism). Or they might say, "Human beings should always act in the interest of others" (altruism), or "Human beings should always act in the interest of all concerned, self included" (utilitarianism). These three conclusions are no longer merely descriptions, but *prescriptions;* that is, the statements are *prescribing* how human beings *should* behave, not merely *describing* how they *do,* in fact, behave.

Another aspect of normative, or prescriptive, ethics is that it encompasses the making of moral value judgments rather than just the presentation or description of facts or data. For example, such statements as "Abortion is immoral" and "Lupe is a morally good person" may not *prescribe* anything, but they do involve those *normative* moral value judgments that we all make every day of our lives.

Metaethics, or Analytic Ethics. The second part of the philosophical approach to the study of ethics is called *metaethics* or, sometimes, *analytic ethics.* Rather than being descriptive or prescriptive, this approach is analytic in two ways. First, metaethicists analyze ethical language (for example, what we mean when we use the word *good*). Second, they analyze the rational foundations of ethical systems, or the logic and reasoning of various ethicists. Metaethicists do not prescribe anything, nor do they deal directly with normative systems. Instead they "go beyond" (a key meaning of the Greek prefix *meta-*), concerning themselves only indirectly with normative ethical systems by concentrating on reasoning, logical structures, and language rather than on content.

It should be noted here that metaethics, although always used to some extent by all ethicists, has become the sole interest of many modern ethical philosophers. This may be due in part to the increasing difficulty of formulating a system of ethics applicable to all or even most human beings. Our world, our cultures, and our lives have become more and more complicated and pluralistic, and finding an ethical system that will undergird all human beings' actions is a difficult if not impossible task. Therefore, these philosophers feel that they might as well do what other specialists have done and concentrate on language and logic rather than attempt to arrive at ethical systems that will help human beings live together more meaningfully and ethically.

Synthesis of Approaches

At this point, I would like to make a commitment that will permeate this book, and that commitment is to a reasonable synthesis. By synthesis I mean a uniting of opposing positions into a whole in which neither position loses itself completely, but the best or most useful parts of both are brought out through a basic principle that will apply to both. There are, of course, conflicts that cannot be synthesized—you cannot synthesize the German dictator Adolf Hitler's love of genocide with any ethical system that stresses the value of life for all human beings—but many can be. For example, later in the book we will see how the views of atheists and agnostics can be synthesized with those of theists in an ethical system that relates to all of them. We will also discover how two major divergent views in normative ethics—the consequentialist and the nonconsequentialist (these terms will be defined later)—can be synthesized into a meaningful ethical worldview.

The point, however, is that a complete study of ethics demands use of the descriptive, the normative, *and* the metaethical approaches. It is important for ethicists to draw on any and all data and on valid results of experiments from the natural, physical, and social sciences. They also must examine their language, logic, and foundations. But it seems to me even more crucial for ethicists to contribute something toward helping all human beings live with each other more meaningfully and more ethically. If philosophy cannot contribute to this latter imperative, then human ethics will either be decided haphazardly by each individual for himself or by unexamined religious pronouncements. My own commitment, then, is to a synthesis of descriptive, normative, and analytic ethics, with a heavy emphasis being placed on putting ethics to use in the human community; that means, in effect, placing a heavier emphasis on the normative.

Morality and Its Applications

What Is Morality?

So far, we have discussed terminology and approaches to studying morality, but we have yet to discover exactly what morality *is*. The full definition of morality, as with other complex issues, will reveal itself gradually as we proceed through this book. In this chapter, however, I will try to make some important distinctions and to arrive at a basic working definition of morality.

Ethics and Aesthetics.   There are two areas of study in philosophy having to do with values and value judgments in human affairs. The first is ethics, or the study of morality—what is good, bad, right, or wrong in a *moral* sense. The second is aesthetics, or the study of art and the artistic, of the beautiful and the nonbeautiful—what is good, bad, right, or wrong in art and what constitutes the beautiful and the nonbeautiful in our lives. There can, of course, be some overlap between the two areas. For example, one can judge Pablo Picasso's painting *Guernica* from an artistic point of view, deciding whether it is beautiful or ugly, whether it constitutes good or bad art in terms of artistic technique. One can also discuss its moral import: In it Picasso makes moral comments on the cruelty and immorality of war and the inhumanity of people toward one another. Essentially, however, when we say that a person is attractive or homely, and when we say that a sunset is beautiful or a dog is ugly or a painting is great or its style is mediocre, we are speaking in terms of aesthetic rather than moral or ethical values.

Good, Bad, Right, and Wrong Used in a Nonmoral Sense.   The same words we use in a moral sense are also often used in a nonmoral sense. The aesthetic use described previously is one of them. And when, for example, we say that a dog or a knife is good, or that a car runs badly, we are often using these value terms (*good, bad,* and so on) in neither an aesthetic nor a moral sense. In calling a dog good, we do not mean that the dog is morally good or even beautiful; we probably mean that it does not bite or that it barks only when strangers threaten us or that it performs well as a hunting dog. When we say that a car runs badly or that a knife is good, we mean that there is something mechanically (but not morally or aesthetically) wrong with the car's engine, or that the knife is sharp and cuts well. In short, what we usually mean by such a statement is that the thing in question is good because it can be used to fulfill some kind of function; that is, it is in "good" working order or has been well trained.

It is interesting to note that Aristotle (384–322 B.C.) argued that being moral has to do with the function of a human being, and that in developing his argument he moved from the nonmoral to the moral uses of good and bad. He suggested that anything that is good or bad is so because it functions well or poorly. He then went on to say that if we could discover what the function of human beings is, then we would know how the term *good* or *bad* can be applied to them. Having arrived at the theory that the proper function of human beings is to reason, he concluded that being moral essentially means "reasoning well for a complete life."

Over the years, many questions have been raised concerning this theory. Some doubt whether Aristotle truly managed to pinpoint the function of humans—for example, some religious sects hold that a human's primary function is to serve God. Others ask whether being moral can be directly tied only to functioning. But the point of this discussion is that the same terms that are used in moral discourse are often also used nonmorally, and neither Aristotle nor anyone else really meant to say that these terms, when applied to such things as knives, dogs, or cars, have anything directly to do with the moral or the ethical.

Morals and Manners, or Etiquette. Manners, or etiquette, is another area of human behavior closely allied with ethics and morals, but careful distinctions must be made between the two spheres. There is no doubt that morals and ethics have a great deal to do with certain types of human behavior. Not all human behavior can be classified as moral, however; some of it is nonmoral and some of it is social, having to do with *manners*, or etiquette, which is essentially a matter of taste rather than of right or wrong. Often, of course, these distinctions blur or overlap, but it is important to distinguish as clearly as we can between nonmoral and moral behavior and that which has to do with manners alone.

Let us take an example from everyday life: an employer giving a secretary a routine business letter to type. Both the act of giving the letter to the secretary and the secretary's act in typing it involve nonmoral behavior. Let us now suppose that the employer uses four-letter words in talking to the secretary and is loud and rude in front of all of the employees in the office. What the employer has done, essentially, is to exhibit poor *manners;* he or she has not really done anything immoral. Swearing and rudeness may be deemed wrong conduct by many, but basically they are an offense to taste rather than a departure from morality.

Let us now suppose, however, that the contents of the letter would ruin an innocent person's reputation or result in someone's death or loss of livelihood. The behavior now falls into the sphere of morality, and questions must be raised about the morality of the employer's behavior. Also, a moral problem arises for the secretary concerning whether he or she should or should not type the letter. Further, if the employer uses four-letter words to intimidate or sexually harass the secretary, then he or she is being immoral by threatening the employee's sense of personal safety, privacy, integrity, and professional pride.

Nonmoral behavior constitutes a great deal of the behavior we see and perform every day of our lives. We must, however, always be aware that our nonmoral behavior can have moral implications. For example, typing a letter is, in itself, nonmoral, but if typing and mailing it will result in someone's death, then morality most certainly enters the picture.

In the realm of manners, behavior such as swearing, eating with one's hands, and dressing sloppily may be acceptable in some situations but be considered bad manners in others. Such behavior seldom would be considered immoral, however. I do not mean to imply that there is *no* connection between manners and morals, only that there is no *necessary* connection between them. Generally speaking, in our society we feel that good manners go along with good morals, and we assume that if people are taught to behave correctly in social situations they also will behave correctly in moral situations.

It is often difficult, however, to draw a direct connection between behaving in a socially acceptable manner and being moral. Many decadent members of societies past and present have acted with impeccable manners and yet have been highly immoral in their treatment of other people. It is, of course, generally desirable for human beings to behave with good manners toward one another and *also* to be moral in their human relationships. But in order to act morally or to bring to light a moral problem, it may at times be necessary to violate the "manners" of a particular society. For example, several years ago, in many elements of our society it was considered bad manners (and was, in some areas, illegal) for nonwhite people to eat in the same area of a restaurant as white people.

In the many sit-ins held in these places, manners were violated in order to point out and try to solve the moral problems associated with inequality of treatment and denial of dignity to human beings.

Therefore, although there may at times be a connection between manners and morals, one must take care to distinguish between the two when there is no clear connection. One must not, for example, equate the use of four-letter words in mixed company with rape or murder or dishonesty in business.

To Whom or What Does Morality Apply?

In discussing the application of morality, four aspects may be considered: religious morality, morality and nature, individual morality, and social morality.

Religious Morality. Religious morality refers to a human being in relationship to a supernatural being or beings. In the Jewish and Christian traditions, for example, the first three of the Ten Commandments (see Figure 1–1) pertain to this kind of morality. These commandments deal with a person's relationship with God, not with any other human beings. By violating any of these three commandments, a person could, according to this particular code of ethics, act immorally toward God without acting immorally toward anyone else.

Morality and Nature. Morality and nature refers to a human being in relationship to nature. Natural morality has been prevalent in all primitive cultures, such as that of the

---

The Ten Commandments

1. I am the Lord, Your God; do not worship false gods.
2. Do not take the name of God in vain.
3. Keep holy the Sabbath Day.
4. Honor your father and your mother.
5. Do not kill.
6. Do not commit adultery.
7. Do not steal.
8. Do not bear false witness against your neighbor.
9. Do not covet your neighbor's spouse.
10. Do not covet your neighbor's belongings.

(Exod. 20:1–17)

Figure 1–1   A paraphrased version of the Ten Commandments.

Native American, and in cultures of the Far East. More recently, the Western tradition has also become aware of the significance of dealing with nature in a moral manner. Some see nature as being valuable only for the good of humanity, but many others have come to see it as a good in itself, worthy of moral consideration. With this viewpoint there is no question about whether a Robinson Crusoe would be capable of moral or immoral actions on a desert island by himself. In the morality and nature aspect, he could be considered either moral or immoral, depending upon his actions toward the natural things around him.

Individual Morality. Individual morality refers to individuals in relation to themselves and to an individual code of morality that may or may not be sanctioned by any society or religion. It allows for a "higher morality," which can be found within the individual rather than beyond this world in some supernatural realm. A person may or may not perform some particular act, not because society, law, or religion says he may or may not, but because he himself thinks it is right or wrong from within his own conscience.

For example, in Greek legend, a daughter (Antigone) confronts a king (Creon), when she seeks to countermand the king's order by burying her dead brother. In Sophocles' (495?–406? B.C.) play, Antigone opposes Creon because of God's higher law; but the Antigone in Jean Anouilh's play opposes Creon not because of God's law, of which she claims no knowledge, but because of her own individual convictions about what is the right thing to do in dealing with human beings, even dead human beings. This aspect also can refer to that area of morality concerned with obligations individuals have to themselves (to promote their own well-being, to develop their talents, to be true to what they believe in, and so on). Commandments nine and ten, although also applicable to social morality, as we shall see in a moment, are good examples of at least an exhortation to individual morality. The purpose of saying "do not covet" would seem to be to set up an internal control within each individual, not even to think of stealing a neighbor's goods or spouse. It is interesting to speculate why there are no "don't covet" type commandments against killing or lying, for example. At any rate, these commandments would seem to stress an individual as well as a social morality.

Social Morality. Social morality concerns a human being in relation to other human beings. It is probably the most important aspect of morality, in that it cuts across all of the other aspects and is found in more ethical systems than any of the others.

Returning briefly to the desert-island example, most ethicists probably would state that Robinson Crusoe is incapable of any really moral or immoral action except toward himself and nature. Such action would be minimal when compared with the potential for morality or immorality if there were nine other people on the island whom he could subjugate, torture, or destroy. Many ethical systems would allow that what he would do to himself is strictly his business, "as long as it doesn't harm anyone else."

The most important human moral issues arise for most ethicists when human beings come together in social groups and begin to conflict with one another. Even though the Jewish and Christian ethical systems, for example, importune human beings to love and obey God, both faiths, in all of their divisions and sects, have a strong social message.

In fact, perhaps 70 to 90 percent of all of their admonitions are directed toward how one human being is to behave toward others. Jesus stated this message succinctly when He said that the two greatest commandments are to love God and to love your neighbor. These fall equally under the religious and social aspects, but observing the whole of Jesus's actions and preachings, one sees the greater emphasis on treating other human beings morally. He seems to say that if one acts morally toward other human beings, then one is automatically acting morally toward God. This is emphasized in one of Jesus' Last Judgment parables when He says (and I paraphrase), "Whatever you have done to the least of Mine [the lowest human beings], so have you done it to Me." Three of the Ten Commandments are directed specifically toward God, while seven are directed toward other human beings—the social aspect taking precedence. In other religions, such as Buddhism and Confucianism, the social aspect represents almost all of morality, there being very little if any focus on the supernatural or religious aspect. Furthermore, everything that is directed toward the individual aspect is also often intended for the good of others who share in the individual's culture.

Nonreligious ethical systems, too, often stress the social aspect. Ethical egoism, which would seem to stress the individual aspect, says in its most commonly stated form, "*everyone* ought to act in his own self-interest," emphasizing the whole social milieu. Utilitarianism in all of its forms emphasizes the good of "all concerned" and therefore obviously is dealing with the social aspect. Nonconsequentialist, or deontological, theories such as Kant's (see Chapter 3) stress actions toward others more than any other aspect, even though the reasons for acting morally toward others are different from those of ethical egoism or utilitarianism. These theories will be dealt with in detail in Chapters 2 and 3. The important thing to note at this point is that most ethical systems, even the most individualistic or religious, will emphasize the social aspect either exclusively or much more than any of the other aspects.

How, then, are we to use these aspects? We may draw upon them as effective distinctions that will allow us to think in the widest terms about the applicability of human ethics. In the spirit of synthesis, however, I would suggest that we hold these distinctions open in unity so that we can accept into a broad human ethics the religious, nature and morality, and individual aspects, recognizing nevertheless that most ethical systems meet in the social aspect. We should, in other words, keep our eyes on the first three aspects while we stand firmly planted in the social aspect, where most human moral problems and conflicts occur.

Who Is Morally or Ethically Responsible? Who can be held morally or ethically responsible for their actions? All of the evidence we have gained to date compels us to say that morality pertains to human beings and only to human beings; all else is speculation. If one wants to attribute morality to supernatural beings, one has to do so on faith. If one wants to hold animals or plants morally responsible for destructive acts against each other or against humans, then one has to ignore most of the evidence that science has given us concerning the instinctual behavior of such beings and the evidence of our own everyday observations.

Recent experimentation with the teaching of language to animals suggests that they are at least minimally capable of developing some thought processes similar to those of humans. It is even possible that they might be taught morality in the future, as humans are now. If this were to occur, then animals could be held morally responsible for their actions. At the present time, however, most evidence seems to indicate that they, as well as plants, should be classified as either nonmoral or amoral—that is, they should be considered either as having no moral sense or as being out of the moral sphere altogether.

Therefore, when we use the terms *moral* and *ethical*, we are using them in reference only to human beings. We do not hold a wolf morally responsible for killing a sheep, or a fox morally responsible for killing a chicken. We may kill the wolf or fox for having done this act, but we do not kill it because we hold the animal *morally* responsible. We do it because we don't want any more of our sheep or chickens to be killed. At this point in the world's history, only human beings can be moral or immoral, and therefore only human beings should be held morally responsible for their actions and behavior. There are, of course, limitations as to when human beings can be held morally responsible, but the question of moral responsibility should not even be brought up where nonhumans are involved.

Where Does Morality Come From?

There has always been a great deal of speculation about where morality or ethics comes from. Has it always been a part of the world, originating from some supernatural being or embedded within nature itself, or is it strictly a product of the minds of human beings? Or is it some combination of two or all three of these? Because morality and ethics deal with values having to do with good, bad, right, and wrong, are these values totally objective—that is, "outside of" human beings? Are they subjective or strictly "within" human beings? Or are they a combination of the two? Let us consider the possibilities.

Values as Totally Objective

There are three ways of looking at values when they are taken as being totally objective:

1. They come from some supernatural being or beings.
2. There are moral laws somehow embedded within nature itself.
3. The world and objects in it have value with or without the presence of valuing human beings.

The Supernatural Theory. Some people believe that values come from some higher or supernatural being, beings, or principle—the Good (Plato); the gods (the Greeks and Romans); Yahweh or God (the Jews); God and His Son, Jesus (the Christians); Allah (the Muslims); and Brahma (the Hindus), to name a few. They believe, further, that these beings or principles embody the highest good themselves, and that they reveal to human beings what is right or good and what is bad or wrong. If human beings want to be moral (and usually they are encouraged in such desires by some sort of temporal or eternal reward), then they must follow these principles or the teachings of these beings. If they don't, then they will end up being disobedient to the highest morality (God, for example), will be considered immoral, and will usually be given some temporal or eternal punishment for their transgressions. Or, if they believe in a principle rather than a supernatural being or beings, then they will be untrue to the highest moral principle.

The Natural Law Theory. Others believe that morality somehow is embodied in nature, and that there are "natural laws" that human beings must adhere to if they are to be moral. (St. Thomas Aquinas, 1225–1274, argued for this as well as for the supernatural basis for morality, and natural law was also central to the ethical theory of Immanuel Kant, 1724–1804.) For example, some people will state that homosexuality is immoral because it goes against "natural moral law"—that is, it is against nature for beings of the same sex to sexually desire or love one another or to engage in sexual acts.

Values as Totally Subjective

In opposition to these arguments, there are those who would argue that morality stems strictly from within human beings. That is, they believe that things can have values and be classed as good, bad, right, or wrong if and only if there is some conscious being who can put value on these things. In other words, if there are no human beings, then there can be no values.

Evaluation of Objective and Subjective Positions

Criticisms of the Supernatural Theory. Albert Einstein (1879–1955), the great mathematician/physicist, said, "I do not believe in immortality of the individual, and I consider ethics to be an exclusively human concern with no superhuman authority behind it."[9]

It is, of course, possible that the supernatural exists and that it somehow communicates with the natural world and the human beings in it. This, however, is only a belief, based on faith, and there is no *conclusive* proof of the existence of a supernatural being, beings, or principle. Also, there are a great number of highly diverse traditions describing such beings or principles. This diversity makes it very difficult to determine exactly what values the beings or principles are trying to communicate and which values, communicated through the many traditions, human beings should accept and follow. All of this does not mean that we should stop searching for the truth or for verification of the possibility of supernaturally based values, but it does mean that it is difficult to establish with any certainty that morality comes from this source.

Criticisms of the Natural Law Theory. On the other hand, we certainly talk about "laws of nature," such as the law of gravity, but if we examine such laws closely, we see that they are quite different from man-made laws having to do with morality or the governing of societies. The law of gravity, for example, says, in effect, that all material objects are drawn toward the center of the earth: If we throw a ball into the air, it will always fall back down to the ground. Sir Isaac Newton discovered that this phenomenon occurred every time an object was subjected to gravity's pull, and he described this constant recurrence by calling it a "law of nature." The key word in this process is described, for so-called natural laws are *descriptive*, whereas moral and societal laws are *prescriptive*.

In other words, the natural law does not say that the ball, when thrown into the air, *should* or *ought to* fall to the ground, as we say that human beings *should not* or *ought not* kill other human beings. Rather, the law of gravity says that the ball *does* or *will* fall when thrown, describing rather than prescribing its behavior.

The question we should ask at this point is, "Are there any natural *moral* laws that *prescribe* how beings in nature should or ought to behave or not behave?" If there are, I do not know what they would be. I mentioned earlier that homosexuality is considered by some to be "unnatural" or "against the laws of nature," a belief that implies the conviction that only heterosexual behavior is "natural." If, however, we examine all aspects of nature, we discover that heterosexuality is not the only type of sexuality that occurs in nature. Some beings in nature are asexual (have no sex at all), some are homosexual (animals as well as humans), and many are bisexual (engaging in sexual behavior with both male and female of the species). Human beings, of course, may wish to *prescribe,* for one reason or another, that homosexual or antiheterosexual behavior is wrong, but it is difficult to argue that there is some "law of nature" that prohibits homosexuality.

Criticisms of Values Existing in the World and Its Objects. Is it feasible or even possible to think of something having a value without there being someone to value it? What value do gold, art, science, politics, or music have without human beings around to value them? After all, except for gold, didn't human beings invent or create them all? It seems, then, almost impossible for values to totally exist in the world and in things themselves.

Criticism of the Subjective Position. Must we then arrive at the position that values are entirely subjective and that the world in all of its aspects would have absolutely no value if there were no human beings living in it? Let us try to imagine objectively a world without any human beings in it. Is there nothing of value in the world and nature—air, water, earth, sunlight, the sea—unless human beings are there to appreciate it? Certainly, whether or not human beings exist, plants and animals would find the world "valuable" in fulfilling their needs. They would find "value" in the warmth of the sun and the shade of the trees, in the food they ate and the water that quenched their thirst. It is true that many things in the world, such as art, science, politics, and music, are valued only by human beings, but there are also quite a few things that are valuable whether human beings are around or not. So it would seem that values are not entirely subjective any more than they are entirely objective.

Values as Both Subjective and Objective—A Synthesis. It would seem that at least some values reside outside of human beings, even though perhaps many more are dependent on conscious human beings, who are able to value things. Therefore, it would seem that values are more complex than either the subjective or the objective position can describe and that a better position to take is that values are both objective and subjective. A third variable should be added so that there is an interaction of three variables as follows:

1. The thing of value, or the thing valued.
2. A conscious being who values, or the valuer.
3. The context or situation in which the valuing takes place.

For example, gold in itself has value in its mineral content and in that it is bright, shiny, and malleable. However, when seen by a human being and discovered to be rare, it becomes—in the context of its beauty and in its role as a support for world finances—a much more highly valued item than it is in itself. Its fullest value, then, depends not only on its individual qualities but also on some conscious being who is valuing it in a specific context or situation. Needless to say, gold is one of those things whose value is heavily dependent on subjective valuing. Note, however, that gold's value would change if the context or situation did. For example, suppose someone were stranded on a desert island without food, water, or human companionship but with 100 pounds of gold. Wouldn't gold's value have dropped considerably given the context or situation in which food, water, and human companionship were missing and which no amount of gold could purchase? This shows how the context or situation can affect values and valuing.

Where Does Morality Come From? A Theory. Values, then, would seem to come most often from a complex interaction between conscious human beings and "things" (material, mental, or emotional) in specific contexts. But how can this discussion help us answer the question of where morality comes from? Any assumptions about the answer to the question of morality's origins certainly have to be speculative. Nevertheless, I believe that by observing how morality develops and changes in human societies, one can see that it has arisen largely from human needs and desires and that it is based upon human emotions and reason.

It seems logical to assume that, as human beings began to become aware of their environment and of other beings like them, they found that they could accomplish more when they were bonded together than they could when isolated from one another. Through deep feelings and thoughts, and after many experiences, they decided upon "goods" and "bads" that would help them to live together more successfully and meaningfully. These beliefs needed sanctions, which were provided by high priests, prophets, and other leaders. Morality was tied by these leaders not only to *their* authority but also to the authority of some sort of supernatural being or beings or to nature, which, in earlier times, were often considered to be inseparable.

For example, as I stated earlier, human beings are able to survive more successfully within their environment in a group than they can as isolated individuals. However, if they are to survive as a community, there must be some prohibition against killing. This can be arrived at either by a consensus of all of the people in the community or by actions taken by the group's leaders. The leaders might provide further sanctions for the law against killing by informing the people that some supernatural being or beings, which may or may not be thought to operate through nature, state that killing is wrong.

It is also possible, of course, that a supernatural being or beings who have laid down such moral laws really exist. However, because most of these laws have in fact been delivered to human beings by other human beings (Moses, Jesus, Buddha, Muhammed, Confucius, and others), we can only say for sure that most of our morality and ethics comes from ourselves—that is, from human origins. All else is speculation or a matter of faith. At the very least, I would argue that morality and moral responsibility must be derived from human beings. Furthermore, I believe that people must decide what is right or good and what is wrong or bad by using both their experience and their best and deepest thoughts and feelings and by applying them as rationally and meaningfully as they can. This brings us to the important distinction between customary or traditional and reflective morality.

Customary or Traditional and Reflective Morality

Customary or Traditional Morality

We are all quite familiar with customary or traditional morality because we are all born into it; it is the first morality with which we come into contact. Morality that exists in various cultures and societies is usually based on custom or tradition, and it is presented to its members, often without critical analysis or evaluation, throughout their childhood and adult years. There is nothing necessarily wrong or bad about this approach to training the young of a society and also its members as a whole.

Many customs and traditions are quite effective and helpful in creating moral societies. As I suggested in the previous paragraph, many moral teachings have arisen out of human need in social interaction and have become customs and traditions in a particular society. For example, in order to live together creatively and in peace, one of the first moral teachings or rules has to be about taking human life because, obviously, if life is constantly in danger, then it is very difficult for people to live and work together. However, in order for customs and traditions to be effective and continuously applicable to the members of a society, they must be critically analyzed, tested, and evaluated, and this is where reflective morality comes in.

Reflective Morality

Philosophers in general demand of themselves and others that every human belief, proposition, or idea be examined carefully and critically to ensure that it has its basis in truth. Morality is no different from any other area of philosophic study in this respect. Philosophers do not suggest that custom and tradition be eliminated or thrown out, but they do urge human beings to use reason to examine the basis and effectiveness of all moral teachings or rules, no matter how traditional or accepted they are. In other words, philosophy requires human beings to reflect on their moral customs and traditions to determine whether they should be retained or eliminated. The great Greek philosopher Socrates (470?–399 B.C.) said, "The unexamined life is not worth living." For morality, a corollary might be, "The unexamined custom or tradition is not worth living by." Therefore, just as people should not accept statements or propositions for which there is no proof or significant logical argument, so they should not accept moral customs or traditions without first testing them against proof, reason, and their experience.

A good example of reflective morality is an examination of the aforementioned Ten Commandments, which many people in Western culture swear by and claim to follow. Interestingly enough, a good many people don't even know what most of them are (with the possible exception of the one against committing adultery, which everyone seems to know!) and often cannot even list them in order or otherwise. Further, how many have examined them in the manner I have suggested earlier and realized that they apply to different aspects of morality? How many people realize that the first three commandments apply only to human beings in relationship to a supernatural being or beings, that commandments four through eight apply to their relationships with others, and that nine and ten basically apply to themselves as individuals?

It is important, then, that all customs, traditions, systems of ethics, rules, and ethical theories should be carefully analyzed and critically evaluated before we continue to accept or live by them. Again, we should not reject them out of hand, but neither should we endorse them wholeheartedly unless we have subjected them to careful, logical scrutiny. As you have seen already, and as you will continue to see throughout the remaining chapters of this book, you are strongly encouraged to become reflective when you are dealing with morality and moral issues.

Morality, Law, and Religion

At this point, it is important that we use reflection to distinguish morality from two other areas of human activity and experience with which it is often confused and of which it is often considered a part: law and religion.

Morality and the Law

The phrase *unjust law* can serve as a starting point for understanding that laws can be immoral. We also have "shysters," or crooked lawyers, who are considered unethical within their own profession. The Watergate conspirators, almost to a man, were lawyers, and the men who tried and judged them were also lawyers. Obviously, morality and the law are not *necessarily* one and the same thing when two people can be lawyers, both having studied a great deal of the same material, and one is moral, whereas the other is not. The many protests we have had throughout history against unjust laws, where more often than not, the protestors were concerned with "what is moral" or a "higher morality," would also seem to indicate that distinctions must be made between law and morality.

Does all of this mean that there is no relationship between law and morality? Is law one thing that is set down by human beings and morality something else that they live by? Is there no connection between the two? A "yes" answer to these questions would be extremely hard to support because much of our morality has become embodied in our legal codes. All we have to do is review any of our legal statutes at any level of government, and we find legal sanctions against robbing, raping, killing, and physical and mental mistreatment of others. We will find many other laws that attempt to protect individuals living together in groups from harm and to provide resolutions of conflicts arising from differences—many of them strictly moral—among the individuals composing these groups.

What, then, is the relationship between law and morality? Michael Scriven points out one important difference when he discusses the differences and distinctions among the

Ten Commandments, which are some of the earlier laws of Western culture believed by Christians and Jews to have been handed down by God. Scriven distinguishes between the laws against coveting and the laws against killing, stealing, and adultery (see Figure 1–1). There is no way a law can regulate someone's desire for another man's wife or belongings as long as the adulterous act or the act of stealing is never carried out. Therefore the statements about coveting contained in the Ten Commandments would seem to be moral admonitions with regard to how one should think or maintain one's interior morality, whereas statements against stealing, killing, and adultery are laws, prohibitions, that are in some way enforceable against certain human acts.[10]

The law provides a series of public statements—a legal code, or system of do's and don'ts—to guide humans in their behavior and to protect them from doing harm to persons and property. Some laws have less moral import than others, but the relationship between law and morality is not entirely reciprocal. What is moral is not necessarily legal and vice versa. That is, you can have morally unjust laws, as mentioned earlier. Also, certain human actions may be considered perfectly legal but be morally questionable.

For example, there were laws in certain parts of the United States that sanctioned the enslavement of one human being by another, despite the fact that freedom and equality for all human beings is a strong basic principle of most ethical systems. It is an important principle in many societies, in theory if not always in action, and it is an important part of the United States Constitution that each individual within the society ought to have a certain amount of individual freedom and a definite moral equality. (This principle will be discussed more fully later on.) If individual freedom and equality are considered to be moral, then laws preventing them must be immoral. To take another example, there is no law against a large chain store's moving into an area and selling products at a loss in order to force the small store owners out of business. But many ethicists would make a case for the immorality of an action that would result in harm to the lives of the small store owners and their families.

Another example of the distinction between law and morality is the recent increase of ethics courses as a significant part of the curriculum in most law schools across the nation. Since scandals such as Watergate, Whitewater, and the Rodney King and O. J. Simpson trials, the public's opinion of lawyers is at an all-time low, but whether lawyers are popular with the public is not the point. Ethics and ethical behavior seem to be missing from many lawyers' activities, to such a degree that law-school faculties have seen an intense need for courses that teach future lawyers the rules of ethical behavior within their profession. Also, many states now require that lawyers who did not have the benefit of a strong ethics course in school take ethics refresher courses. All of this is an indication that to be schooled in the law is not necessarily to be instilled with ethical standards of behavior.

At times, students in my classes have argued that the only thing keeping them from being immoral is fear of punishment, either by the civil authorities or an all-powerful God. I cannot argue with them if they really feel that way, if they have such strong urges to kill, steal, and rape. However, many people that I know, including myself, do not kill, steal, or rape, not out of any fear of punishment but because they believe these acts to be wrong (for any number of reasons). Even if all laws were abolished tomorrow, they still would consider such acts wrong and, wanting to be moral beings, would not commit them.

It should be obvious, then, that morality is not necessarily based on law. In fact, a study of history would probably indicate the opposite—that morality precedes law, whereas law sanctions morality; that is, law puts morality into a code or system that can then be enforced by reward or punishment. Perhaps the larger and more complex the society, the greater the necessity for laws, but it is not inconceivable that a moral society could be formed having no legal system at all—just a few basic principles of morality and an agreement to adhere to those principles. This is not to suggest that law should be eliminated from human affairs, but rather to show that law is not a necessary attribute of morality.

Can law, however, do without morality? It would seem that morality provides the reasons behind any significant laws governing human beings and their institutions. What would be the point of having laws against killing and stealing if there were not some concern that such acts were immoral? Very few laws have no moral import. Even laws controlling the incorporation of businesses, which do not seem to have any direct moral bearing on anyone, function at least to ensure fairness to all concerned—stockholders, owners, and employees. I cannot think of any law that does not have behind it some moral concern—no matter how minor or remote.

We can say, then, that law is the public codification of morality in that it lists for all members of a culture what has come to be accepted as the moral way to behave in that culture. Law also establishes what is the moral way to act, and it sanctions—by its codification and by the entire judiciary process set up to form, uphold, and change parts of the code—the morality that it contains. The corrective for unjust laws, however, is not necessarily more laws, but rather valid moral reasoning carried on by the people who live under the code.

Law is a public expression of social morality and also is its sanction. Law cannot in any way replace or substitute for morality, and therefore we cannot arbitrarily equate what is legal with what is moral. Many times the two "whats" will equate exactly, but many times they will not; and indeed many times what is legal will not, and perhaps should not, completely cover what is moral. For example, most ethicists today seem to agree that except for child molestation and forced sexuality of any kind, there should be no laws governing sexuality among consenting adults. Given this view, one can discuss adult sexual morality without bringing in legal issues. To summarize: It should be obvious that law serves to codify and sanction morality, but that without morality or moral import, law and legal codes are empty.

Morality and Religion

Can there be a morality without religion? Must God or gods exist in order for there to be any real point to morality? If a people are not religious, can they ever be truly moral? And if the answer to these questions is yes, which religion is the real foundation for morality? There seem to be as many conflicts as there are different religions and religious viewpoints.

Religion is one of the oldest human institutions. We have little evidence that language existed in prehistoric times, but we do have evidence of religious practices, which were entwined with artistic expression, and of laws or taboos exhorting early human beings to behave in certain ways. In these earlier times, morality was embedded in the traditions, mores, customs, and religious practices of the culture.

Furthermore, religion served (as it has until quite recently) as a most powerful sanction for getting people to behave morally. That is, if behind a moral prohibition against killing rests the punishing and rewarding power of an all-powerful supernatural being or beings, then the leaders of a culture have the greatest possible sanction for the morality they want their followers to uphold. The sanctions of tribal reward and punishment pale beside the idea of a punishment or reward that can be more destructive or pleasurable than any that one's fellow human beings could possibly administer.

However, because religion may have preceded any formal legal or separate moral system in human history, or because it may have provided very powerful and effective sanctions for morality, does not at all prove that morality must of necessity have a religious basis. It is my contention that for many reasons morality need not, and indeed should not, be based *solely* on religion.

Difficulty of Proving Supernatural Existence. First, in order to prove that one must be religious in order to be moral, we would have to prove conclusively that a supernatural world exists and that morality exists there as well as in the natural world. Even if this could be proved, which is doubtful, we would have to show that the morality existing in the supernatural world has some connection with that which exists in the natural world. It seems obvious, however, that in dealing with morality, the only basis we have is this world, the people who exist in it, and the actions they perform.

One test of the truth of this reason would be to take any set of religious admonitions and ask honestly which of them would be absolutely necessary to the establishment of any moral society. For example, we might make a case for any of the Ten Commandments except the first three (see Figure 1–1 on page 10). The first three may be a necessary set of rules for a Jewish or Christian community, but if a nonreligious community observed only Commandments four through ten, how, *morally* speaking, would the two communities differ—assuming that the religious community observed all ten of the Commandments? (One could probably find reasons for eliminating some of the other seven Commandments, too, but that is another issue.) I do not mean to imply that morality cannot be founded on religion; it is an obvious empirical fact that it has been, is, and probably will be in the future. I am saying that morality *need* not be founded on religion at all, and I would add that there is a danger of narrowness and intolerance if religion becomes the *sole* foundation for morality.

Religious People Can Be Immoral. It is a known fact that some religious people can be immoral, one only needs to look at some priests of the Roman Catholic Church, who even though highly trained in religion and the ethics of their church, nevertheless were guilty of molesting children under their supervision. Also, consider all of the wars and other persecutions by almost every religion in the history of man.

Nonreligious People Can Be Moral. If we can briefly characterize morality in this world as not harming or killing others and generally trying to make life and the world better for everyone and everything that exists (I will attempt to justify this contention later), and if many human beings do not accept the existence of a supernatural world and yet act as morally as anyone who does, then there must be some attributes other than religious belief that are necessary for one to be moral. (I will discuss what I feel these attributes are in a later chapter.) Although it is obvious that most religions contain ethical systems, it is not true that all ethical systems are religiously based; therefore, there is no necessary connection between morality and religion. The very fact that completely nonreligious people (for example, humanist ethicists) can evolve significant and consistent ethical systems is proof of this.

Difficulty of Providing a Rational Foundation. Providing a rational foundation for an ethical system is difficult enough without also having to provide a foundation for the religion that purportedly founds the ethical system. And the difficulty of rationally founding most religious systems is inescapable. It is impossible to prove conclusively the existence of any supernature, afterlife, God, or gods. I will not go into the traditional and modern arguments for the existence or nonexistence of God or gods here, but will merely state that there is no conclusive evidence that such beings do or do not exist.[11]

Therefore, if no evidence is conclusive and none of the arguments' logic is irrefutable, then the existence of a supernatural world, an afterlife, God, or gods, is at least placed in the category of the unproven. This, of course, does not mean that many people will not continue to believe in their existence, basing their belief on faith, fear, hope, or their reading of the evidence, but as a logical foundation for morality, religion is weak indeed except for those who believe.

If one maintains that we are moral (or should be) because a being exists who is all-good or because we will be rewarded or punished in another life, and the existence of these things cannot be proved, then the entire system is based on unproved assumptions. Believing that God or an afterlife exists may make people "feel" better about acting in certain ways. It may also provide powerful sanctions for acting morally or not acting immorally. But it does not provide a valid, rational foundation for morality that can give us reasons, evidence, and logic for acting one way rather than another. Again, as Michael Scriven has stated, "Religion can provide a psychological but not a logical foundation for morality."[12] Can there be any better foundation for morality than religion? Obviously, I think there can be, and I will attempt to present such a foundation later.

Which Religion? Even if religions could be rationally founded, which religion should be the basis of human ethics? Within a particular religion that question is answered, but obviously it is not answered satisfactorily for members of other conflicting religions or for those who do not believe in any religion. Even if the supernatural tenets of religions could be conclusively proved, which religion are we to accept as the true or real foundation of morality? It is certainly true that different religions have many ethical prescriptions in common—for example, not killing—but it is also true that there are many conflicting ones.

Among different sects of Christianity, for example, there are many conflicting ethical statements concerning sex, war, divorce, abortion, marriage, stealing, and lying. How, if they all believe in God and Jesus and their teachings, can there be so many divergent opinions on what is moral or immoral? The obvious answer is that there can be many interpretations of those teachings as set down in the Bible or otherwise passed down through tradition. But what gives a Roman Catholic, for instance, the right to tell a Methodist that his interpretation of Jesus' teachings is wrong? There can be no adjudication here—only referral to passages in the Bible, many of which are open to different interpretations or even to some teachings not held by either of the differing sects. In short, there simply is no rational basis for resolving serious conflicts when they exist.

The difficulty is underscored even more when we consider that people who believe there is no God or supernatural or afterlife (atheists) or people who are not sure (agnostics) are essentially excluded from moral consideration. If such people do not believe, or neither believe nor disbelieve, then how can any of the moral precepts set down within any particular religion have any application to them? They are automatically excluded from the moral sphere created by the ethics of religion. Provisions are, of course, made within each religion for nonbelievers, but these provisions very often involve some sort of eventual conversion to that religion or, frequently, some patronizing statement about loving one's enemies as well as one's friends.

Difficulty of Resolving Conflicts. How do we resolve the conflicts arising from various religiously based ethical systems without going outside of all religions for some more broadly based human system of morality—some wider base from which to make ethical decisions? When such resolutions are successful, it is usually because we have gone beyond any particular religion's ethical system and used some sort of rational compromise or broader ethical system that cuts across all religious and nonreligious lines. I urge that we pursue this approach more strongly and consistently than we have.

Furthermore, I believe that we can establish a system and method by which this can be done. But in order to accomplish this, all people, religious or nonreligious, must be willing to accept an essentially nonreligiously based overall ethical system within which many of their own moral rules and methods can function successfully. My answer to the question of how we resolve moral conflicts without going outside the narrow boundaries of religion is simple—we don't. We must establish a basis for morality from outside religion, but it must be one in which religion is included. This is, I feel, a necessary first step toward a moral society and a moral world. The foregoing statements and questions enable us, at the very least, to see that the relationship between morality and religion is, as Michael Scriven has said, "a very uneasy one indeed."[13]

In summary, then, just what is the connection between religion and morality? The answer is that there is no *necessary* connection. One can have a complete ethical system without mention of any life but this one—no God or gods, no supernatural, no afterlife. Does this mean that to be moral we must avoid religion? Not at all. Human beings should be allowed to believe or disbelieve as long as there is some moral basis that protects all people from immoral treatment at the hands of the religious and nonreligious alike. A religion that advocates the human sacrifice of unwilling participants, for example, would not be moral as it deprives others of their lives. A religion that persecutes all who do not accept its tenets is equally immoral and should not be allowed to exist in that form under a broad moral system. If, however, religions can agree to some broad moral principles and their members can act in accordance with those principles, then they can exist with nonreligious people and still serve their principles meaningfully and well.

One last point about religion and morality is that religion, for most people who are involved with it, is much more than an ethical system. For example, because Jews and Muslims believe that there is a being far worthier of their love than any being in the natural world, it is their relationship with this being that is of uppermost importance to them, rather than how they act within the natural world. In this sense, religion is more than (or other than) an ethical system.

Considering all of the differences that exist among religions and between religionists and nonreligionists, I believe that we should strive all the harder to create a wider-based morality that allows these differences and personal religious relationships to continue and develop, while at the same time allowing for ethical attitudes and actions toward all. What we need is not a strictly religious or a strictly humanist (atheist) ethics but rather what I choose to call a *humanitarian* ethics, which includes these two extremes and the middle ground as well.

Why Should Human Beings Be Moral?

Before going on to discuss ethical or moral systems in greater detail there is one last question that I feel must be dealt with in this chapter, and that is, "Why should human beings be moral?" Another way of putting the problem is as follows: Is there any clear foundation or basis for morality—can any reasons be found for human beings to be good and do right acts rather than be bad and do wrong acts? I want to make it clear at the start that the question I am asking is not "Why should *I* or any one individual be moral?" As Kai Nielsen says in his brilliant essay "Why Should I Be Moral?" these are two different questions.[14] The second one is very difficult to answer with any clear, conclusive evidence or logic, but the first one is not.

I have already pointed out the difficulties involved in founding morality on religion, and especially on religion as a sole factor. However, if a person has religious faith, then he or she does have a foundation for a personal morality, even though this foundation basically is psychological rather than logical in nature. What disturbs me about the use of religion as the foundation of morality is the frequently made assumption that if there is no supernatural or religious basis for morality, then there can be no basis at all. A related, and perhaps deeper, statement is that there can be no real meaning to human life unless there is some sort of afterlife or some other extranatural reason for living. It is obvious that for many individuals this is psychologically true; that is, they feel that their existence has meaning and purpose and that they have a reason for being moral if and only if there is a God, an afterlife, or some sort of religion in their lives. I feel that we must respect this point of view and accept the conviction of the many people who hold it, because that is how they *feel* about life and morality.

It is also obvious, however, that many people do not feel this way. I think it is terribly presumptuous of religious believers to feel that if some people do not have a religious commitment their lives are meaningless, or that such people have no reason for being moral in their actions. But if religion does not necessarily provide a "why" for morality, then what does? Let us assume for the moment that there is no supernatural morality and see if we can find any other reasons why people should be moral.

Enlightened Self-Interest

One can certainly argue on a basis of enlightened self-interest, that it is, at the very least, generally better to be good rather than bad and to create a world and society that is good rather than one that is bad. As a matter of fact, as we shall see in the next chapter, self-interest is the sole basis of one ethical theory, ethical egoism. I am not, however, suggesting at this point that one ought to pursue one's own self-interest. I am merely presenting the argument that if everyone tried to do and be good and to avoid and prevent bad, it would be in everyone's self-interest. For example, if within a group of people no one killed, stole, lied, or cheated, then each member of the group would benefit. An individual member of the group could say, "It's in my self-interest to do good rather than bad because I stand to benefit if I do and also because I could be ostracized or punished if I don't." Therefore, even though it is not airtight (as Kai Nielsen's essay illustrates), the argument from enlightened self-interest is compelling.

Argument from Tradition and Law

Related to the foregoing argument is the argument from tradition and law. This argument suggests that because traditions and laws, established over a long period of time, govern the behavior of human beings, and because these traditions and laws urge human beings to be moral rather than immoral, there are good reasons for being so. Self-interest is one reason, but another is respect for the human thought and effort that has gone into establishing such laws and traditions and transferring them from one historic period and one culture to another. This can be an attractive argument, even though it tends to suppress questioning of traditions and laws—a kind of questioning that is, I feel, the very touchstone of creative moral reasoning. It is interesting to note that most of us probably learned morality through being confronted with this argument, the religious argument, and the experiences surrounding them. Don't we all remember being told we should or should not do something because it was or was not in our own self-interest, because God said it was right or wrong, or because it was the way we were supposed to act in our family, school, society, and world?

Evolution of the Arguments

All of the arguments put forth are compelling and valid to some extent, provided that free questioning of the moral prescriptions that they have established or that they support is allowed and encouraged. I have already pointed out some of the difficulties associated with establishing a religious basis for morality, but problems exist with the other two arguments as well. The self-interest argument can be a problem when other interests conflict with it; often it is difficult to convince someone who sees obvious benefits in acting immorally in a particular situation that it is in his or her self-interest to do otherwise. Morality established by tradition and law is problematic because it is difficult both to change and to question successfully. This lack of questioning sometimes encourages blind obedience to immoral practices. It encourages the belief that because something has been done a certain way for hundreds of years, it must be right. (A good example of the tragic consequences that can ensue from this type of thinking may be found in Shirley Jackson's excellent, frequently anthologized short story "The Lottery.")

Common Human Needs

Are there any other reasons we can give as to why human beings should be moral? If we examine human nature as empirically and rationally as we can, we discover that all human beings have many needs, desires, goals, and objectives in common. For example, people generally seem to need friendship, love, happiness, freedom, peace, creativity, and stability in their lives, not only for themselves but for others, too. It doesn't take much further examination to discover that in order to satisfy these needs, people must establish and follow moral principles that encourage them to cooperate with one another and that free them from fear that they will lose their lives, be mutilated, or be stolen from, lied to, cheated, severely restricted, or imprisoned.

It is my contention, then, that morality has come about because of human needs and through a recognition of the importance of living together in a cooperative and significant way. I am not trying to suggest that all human beings can be convinced that they should be moral, or even that it will always be in each individual's self-interest to be moral. I do believe, however, that the question "Why should human beings be moral?" *generally* can best be answered by the statement that adhering to moral principles enables human beings to live their lives as peacefully, happily, creatively, and meaningfully as is possible.

Significance and Relevance of Ethics

If the reader is not yet convinced of the relevance or significance of ethics, all he or she has to do is to read the papers, watch television, and listen to the radio. Ever since former Vice President Quayle attacked a fictional woman on television for bearing a child out of wedlock and raising the boy herself, the phrase "family values" has fallen "trippingly" off the tongues of politicians, religionists, psychologists, and sociologists. According to these pundits, all of our troubles would be eliminated if every family was heterosexual with the usual 2.5 children—one male, one female, and .5 some sort of combination thereof, I guess. This would seem to be a very oversimplified solution to a rather complex problem.

Also, as I mentioned when discussing law and morality, there has been a marked increase in the teaching of ethics in law schools. The same types of courses have been established at medical schools, and there has been an increase in bioethics and other ethics committees in hospitals and various businesses. For example, James O'Toole has been conducting values-based leadership seminars for CEOs and other managers in business. One might ask, "Does this mean that we are becoming more ethical, or that we will be, as these ethics begin to filter down to the general populace?" Certainly it is admirable that so many—even politicians—are interested in values and in improving the ethical life in America. My major concern is with how superficial all of this is, especially as it comes from politicians trying to get elected. I don't doubt that some of these politicians are sincere, but sometimes I wonder whose values they wish to impose, and also I wonder how much training any of these people have had in ethics.

Yet regardless of how popular, superficially or not, ethics may become, it certainly should be the most important aspect of your life. After all, what could be more important than learning how to live more ethically and improving the quality of your life and the lives of others around you? As Albert Einstein said, "The most important human endeavor is the striving for morality in our actions. Our inner balance and even our very existence depend on it. Only morality in our actions can give beauty and dignity to life."[15]

Hopefully, by the time you have finished this book and others like it, and the ethics course you are taking, you will have a much better background in ethics than most of those who mouth the values without perhaps knowing what they are talking about.

Morality: A Working Definition

I have said a great deal so far in this chapter about what morality or ethics is not, but I have not yet said what it *is*. In setting up a working definition, I would say that morality deals basically with humans and how they relate to other beings, both human and nonhuman. It deals with how humans *treat* other beings so as to promote mutual welfare, growth, creativity, and meaning and to strive for what is good over what is bad and what is right over what is wrong.

In the next two chapters, we will examine two major ethical viewpoints. These contain a number of traditional ethical theories that are concerned not with *why* human beings should be moral, but rather with *how* morality can be attained. There is no point in "starting from scratch" in the study of morality when we can benefit from our own ethical traditions, out of which almost all modern ethical theories have, in one way or another, evolved.

Chapter Summary

   I. Philosophy, and ethics' relationship to it
     A. Philosophy literally means "the love of wisdom."
     B. It is concerned with three areas of study:
       1. Epistemology—the study of knowledge, belief, truth, falsity, certainty, and perception.
       2. Metaphysics—the study of what exists, the nature of what exists, cause and effect, freedom, and determinism.
       3. Ethics—the study of morality, good, bad, right, wrong, human conduct and behavior in a moral sense, and moral issues.

II. Key terms
   A. *Moral* and *ethical* (and *immoral* and *unethical*) are interchangeable in ordinary language.
      1. Moral means what is good or right.
      2. Immoral means what is bad or wrong.
   B. Characteristics of "good, bad, right, wrong."
      1. "Good" or "right" should involve pleasure, happiness, and excellence, and also lead to harmony and creativity.
      2. "Bad" or "wrong" will involve pain, unhappiness, and lack of excellence, and will lead to disharmony and lack of creativity.
      3. The terms good and bad should be defined in the context of human experience and human relationships.
   C. *Amoral* means having no moral sense, or being indifferent to right and wrong.
   D. *Nonmoral* means out of the realm of morality altogether.

III. Approaches to the study of morality
   A. The scientific, or descriptive, approach is used in the social sciences and is concerned with how human beings do, in fact, behave. For example: Human beings often act in their own self-interest.
   B. The philosophical approach is divided into two categories.
      1. The normative, or prescriptive, is concerned with what "should" be or what people "ought to" do. For example: Human beings *ought to* act in their own self-interest.
      2. A second category is concerned with value judgments. For example: "Barbara is a morally good person."
      3. Metaethics, or analytic ethics, is analytic in two ways.
         (a) It analyzes ethical language.
         (b) It analyzes the rational foundations of ethical systems or of the logic and reasoning of various ethicists.

IV. Morality and its applications
   A. In the course of determining what morality is, some distinctions must be made.
      1. There is a difference between ethics and aesthetics.
         (a) *Ethics* is the study of morality, or of what is good, bad, right, or wrong in a moral sense.
         (b) *Aesthetics* is the study of art and the artistic, or of what is good, bad, right, or wrong in art and what constitutes the beautiful in our lives.
      2. The terms *good, bad, right,* and *wrong* can also be used in a nonmoral sense, usually in reference to how someone or something functions.
      3. Manners, or etiquette, differs from morality even though the two are related, in that manners is concerned with certain types of social behavior dealing with taste, whereas morality is concerned with ethical behavior.
   B. There are four main aspects related to the application of morality.
      1. Religious morality is concerned with human beings in relationship to a supernatural being or beings.
      2. Morality and nature are concerned with human beings in relationship to nature.
      3. Individual morality is concerned with human beings in relationship to themselves.
      4. Social morality is concerned with human beings in relationship to other human beings. This is the most important category of all.
   C. Evidence exists to help us determine who is morally or ethically responsible.
      1. Recent experimentation with communication with certain animals reveals that in the future animals could conceivably be taught to be moral.
      2. At the present time, however, humans and only humans can be considered to be moral or immoral, and therefore only they should be considered morally responsible.

V. Theories addressing where morality comes from
  A. There are three ways of looking at values' being totally objective.
    1. Some people believe that values originate with a supernatural being or beings or principle.
    2. Some believe that values are embodied in nature itself—that is, that there are moral laws in nature.
    3. Some believe that the world and the objects in it embody values whether or not there are any human beings around to perceive and appreciate them.
  B. Some hold the theory that values are totally subjective: that morality and values reside strictly within human beings and that there are no values or morality outside of them.
  C. One must evaluate these two conflicting positions.
    1. It is possible to criticize the position that values are objective.
      (a) It is difficult to prove conclusively the existence of any supernatural being, beings, or principle, or to prove that values exist anywhere other than in the natural world.
      (b) There is a difference between "natural laws," which are descriptive, and "moral and societal laws," which are prescriptive; and there is no conclusive evidence that "natural moral laws" exist.
      (c) Is it really possible to think of things of value without someone to value them?
    2. It is possible to criticize the position that values are subjective. Because aspects of the world and nature can be valued whether or not human beings exist, values would not seem to be totally subjective.
  D. Values are both subjective and objective. They are determined by three variables.
    1. The first variable is the thing of value, or the thing valued.
    2. The second is a conscious being who values—the valuer.
    3. The third is the context or situation in which the valuing takes place.
  E. Given the belief that values are both subjective and objective, it is possible to construct a theory concerning the origin of morality.
    1. It comes from a complex interaction between conscious human beings and material, mental, or emotional "things" in specific contexts.
    2. It stems from human needs and desires and is based on human emotions and reason.
VI. Customary or traditional and reflective morality
  A. Customary or traditional morality is based on custom or tradition and is often accepted without analysis or critical evaluation.
  B. Reflective morality is the careful examination and critical evaluation of all moral issues whether or not they are based on religion, custom, or tradition.
VII. Morality and the law
  A. Morality is not necessarily based on law.
  B. Morality provides the basic reasons for any significant laws.
  C. Law is a public expression of and provides a sanction for social morality.
VIII. Morality and religion
  A. Morality need not, indeed should not, be based solely on religion for the following reasons.
    1. It is difficult to prove conclusively the existence of a supernatural being.
    2. Religious people can be immoral.
    3. Nonreligious people can be moral, too.
    4. It is difficult to provide a rational foundation for religion, which makes it difficult to provide such a foundation for morality.
    5. If religion were to be the foundation of morality, which religion would provide this foundation and who would decide?

6. There is a difficulty in resolving the conflicts arising from various religiously based ethical systems without going outside of them.

B. We need a humanitarian ethics that is neither strictly religious nor strictly humanistic (atheistic) but that includes these two extremes and the middle ground as well.

IX. The importance of determining why human beings should be moral
  A. The question is not "Why should any one individual be moral?" but rather "Why should human beings in general be moral?"
  B. Various reasons for being moral have been posited.
    1. Religion, or the supernatural, has been used as the foundation of morality.
    2. It has been argued that enlightened self-interest is the basis for morality.
    3. Tradition and law have been posited as yet another basis for morality.
  C. There are problems with all the reasons given in A and B; therefore, it is my contention that morality has come about because of common human needs and through the recognition of the importance of living together in a cooperative and significant way in order to achieve the greatest possible amount of friendship, love, happiness, freedom, peace, creativity, and stability in the lives of all human beings.

X. A working definition of *morality*. Morality or ethics deals basically with human relationships— how humans treat other beings so as to promote mutual welfare, growth, creativity, and meaning as they strive for good over bad and right over wrong.

Exercises for Review

1. In your own words, define the following terms: *moral, immoral, amoral,* and *nonmoral.*
2. What is the difference between descriptive and normative (or prescriptive) ethics?
3. What is metaethics (or analytic ethics) and how does it differ from descriptive and normative (or prescriptive) ethics?
4. Explain the four aspects of morality.
5. Why is the social aspect the most important?
6. Do you agree that morality is not necessarily based on the law, but that the law gets its real meaning from morality? Why or why not?
7. Give examples of how the law embodies morality.
8. What does it mean to assert that the law provides "sanctions" for morality? How does it do this?
9. Critically examine the Ten Commandments in the following ways:
    (a) Separate them to show how they would fit into any of the four aspects of morality.
    (b) Which commandments do you consider to be absolutely necessary for any society to be moral? Why?
    (c) Which commandments can be enforced legally, and which cannot? Why?
10. Do you agree that what we need is a humanitarian ethics that includes both religious and nonreligious systems? Why or why not?
11. Do you agree with the author's list of the characteristics of "good, bad, right, wrong"? If so, explain why in your own words. If not, explain why not. In either case, provide any additional characteristics that you think these terms possess.
12. What are philosophy, epistemology, and metaphysics, and how do they differ from or relate to ethics?
13. What is the difference between customary or traditional morality and reflective morality?

Discussion Questions

1. Critically examine any ethical system or code (for example, a religious code, or a code or system used in business or any of the professions) and show how each of the do's or don'ts of this code apply to the various aspects of morality.

2. Go to the library or consult other sources at the discretion of your instructor and get a copy of your city's, county's, or state's laws governing a specific area of community activity. Analyze to what extent these laws relate to your community's moral views and standards, and in what ways they do so. To what extent are any of the laws nonmoral or moral in their implications?

3. To what extent do you feel that human beings have an obligation to be moral in their dealings and relationships with nature (excluding other human beings), and for what reasons? Give specific examples of such dealings and relationships, and argue your position fully.

4. Do you think that human beings are essentially good or bad, or a combination of both? Why? In a well-organized essay, argue for and bring evidence to support the position you have taken. How does your position affect your approach to morality—for example, should a moral system be strict, clear, and absolutistic or permissive, flexible, and relativistic? (See Chapter 5 and Glossary for a definition of these terms.)

5. Do you believe that morality should or should not be based *solely* on religion? Why? Is it possible to establish a moral system without any reference to religion? If so, how? If not, why not? What could be the basis of such a system, if not religion? Describe your position in detail.

6. Examine your own life and try to establish as honestly and accurately as possible where your values have come from.

7. Do you feel that you should always be moral? Why or why not? Do you think that human beings in general should be moral? Why or why not?

Notes

1. William K. Frankena, *Ethics*, 2nd ed. (Upper Saddle River, NJ: Prentice Hall, 1973), 91.
2. Ibid.
3. Ibid.
4. Lester A. Kirkendall, *Premarital Intercourse and Interpersonal Relationships* (New York: Julian Press, 1961), 6.
5. Joseph Wambaugh, *The Onion Field* (New York: Dell, 1973).
6. Jean L. McKechnie, ed., *Webster's New Universal Unabridged Dictionary* (New York: Simon and Schuster, 1979), 1454.
7. Joseph Wambaugh, *The Blooding* (New York: Bantam, 1989), 325.
8. Ibid., 341.
9. Mark Winocur, *Einstein, a Portrait* (Corte-Madera, CA: Pomegranate Artbooks, 1984), 96.
10. Michael Scriven, "Rational Moral Education." Speech delivered at Bakersfield College, California, February 18, 1971.
11. See John H. Hick, *Philosophy of Religion* (Upper Saddle River, NJ: Prentice Hall, 1973), 16–17, and John Hospers, *An Introduction to Philosophical Analysis,* 2nd ed. (Upper Saddle River, NJ: Prentice Hall, 1967), 425–90, for a discussion of these arguments from the religious point of view (Hick) and the nonreligious (Hospers).

12. Scriven, "Rational Moral Education."
13. Ibid.
14. Kai Nielsen, "Why Should I Be Moral?" in *Problems of Moral Philosophy*, 2nd ed., ed. Paul W. Taylor (Belmont, CA: Dickenson, 1972), 539–58.
15. Wincour, *Einstein, a Portrait*, 92.

Research Navigator™
(http://www.researchnavigator.com)

This web site offers three research databases: EBESCO's *Content Select Academic Journal and Abstract Database, New York Times* Search by Subject Archive, and *Best of the Web* Link Library. In addition, this site provides helpful advice on how to conduct efficient and productive research from choosing a topic to polishing the final draft. Beginning philosophy students will probably find the *Best of the Web* Link Library the most appropriate place to start their research.

The free access code necessary to employ Research Navigator™ can be found in the Prentice Hall Guide to Evaluating Online Resources. If your text did not come with this guide, please go to *www.prenhall.com/contentselect* for information on how you can purchase an access code.

Consequentialist (Teleological) Theories of Morality

Objectives

After you have read this chapter, you should be able to

1. Define the consequentialist (teleological) and nonconsequentialist (deontological) views of morality.

2. Differentiate psychological egoism from ethical egoism, and explain both theories.

3. Distinguish the three types of ethical egoism.

4. Describe and critically analyze the two main consequentialist theories, ethical egoism and utilitarianism.

5. Distinguish between the two types of utilitarianism.

In the history of ethics, two major viewpoints emerge: the *consequentialist* (based on or concerned with consequences) and the *nonconsequentialist* (not based on or concerned with consequences). Traditionally these have been called the "teleological" and "deontological" theories, respectively, but I will refer to them as consequentialist and nonconsequentialist because these words pinpoint the real differences between them.

The two major consequentialist ethical theories are ethical egoism and utilitarianism. These both agree that human beings ought to behave in ways that will bring about good consequences. They differ, however, in that they disagree on who should benefit from these consequences. The ethical egoist essentially says that human beings ought to act in their own self-interest, whereas utilitarians essentially say that human beings ought to act in the interests of all concerned.

Suppose John has a chance to embezzle some funds from the company for which he works. If he is a consequentialist, he will try to predict the consequences of embezzling and not embezzling. If he is an egoistic consequentialist, he will try to predict what will be in his own best interest; if he is a utilitarian consequentialist, he will try to predict what will be in the interest of everyone concerned. On first learning about ethical egoism, some people immediately assume that if a person like John adheres to this theory he will embezzle the funds, because doing so will give him the money he needs in order to live a good life and so forth. However, it is interesting to note that both ethical egoists and utilitarians might decide, on the basis of their opposite approaches to consequences, not to embezzle the money. Ethical egoists might not think it is in their self-interest to break the law or anger the company and its stockholders or subject themselves to the risk of punishment for their action. Utilitarians, on the other hand, might arrive at the same conclusion, but on the grounds that embezzlement would bring bad consequences to other people involved in the company even though it might bring good consequences to them. Just as egoists and utilitarians might end up acting in the same way for different reasons, so their ethical reasoning also is similar in that they both are concerned with the consequences of any action they are contemplating. It is important now to examine each ethical theory more thoroughly, noting advantages and disadvantages and examining similarities and differences.

Psychological Egoism

Before we discuss ethical egoism in more detail, we should make a distinction between *psychological* egoism, which is *not* an ethical theory, and *ethical* egoism. Some ethical egoists have tried to base their egoistic theories on psychological egoism, so it is important for us to examine whether it is a valid concept and to make sure we know the difference between how people *do* act and how they *should* act. In Chapter 1, I used psychological egoism to point out the difference between the scientific and the normative philosophical approaches to morality; to reiterate, psychological egoism is a scientific, descriptive approach to egoism, whereas ethical egoism is the philosophical-normative (prescriptive) approach.

Psychological egoism may be divided into two forms. The strong form maintains that people *always* act in their own self-interest—that they are psychologically constructed to do so—whereas the weak form maintains that people often, but not always, act in their own self-interest. Neither form can operate as a basis for ethical egoism, however. If the strong form is accepted, then why tell people to do what they cannot help doing? If I am psychologically constructed so as to always act in my own self-interest, what good will it do to tell me that I *should* always act in own self-interest? As for the weaker form, stating that I often *do* act in my own self-interest has nothing in itself to do with what I *should* do. (This is referred in ethics as trying to get "an *ought* from an *is*"—there is no logical argument that conclusively proves that because people *are* behaving in certain ways, they *should* do so or continue to do so.) One might be able to show by means of some rational argument that I should always act in my own self-interest, but that I do so constitutes neither a necessary (absolutely necessary) nor sufficient (enough) argument that I should.

What about the truth of the stronger form of the argument? If human beings must indeed act in their own self-interest and cannot do otherwise, then we are condemned to the egoistic position. Is there any conclusive proof that strong psychological egoism holds true? In order to make an all-encompassing, absolute, universal statement that is used always in connection with human motives and behavior, which are both complex and varied, we would have to be able to examine every single human being's motives and behavior before we could prove such a statement conclusively.

It is presumptuous for psychological egoists to argue that I always act in my own self-interest if I can give them an example of even one time when I have not done so. They certainly can devise a number of ways to show me that everything I do is ultimately related, for one reason or another, to my own self-interest. But I may retort: "Look, when I disregarded my own safety and went after the burglar who robbed the store, I was not motivated by any of the reasons you suggest—I simply did it because I thought that what the burglar did was wrong, and because I like my boss and did not want to see him robbed." The psychological egoists can insist, in turn, that I *probably* wanted to impress my boss or that I wanted to look like a hero to my girlfriend or that I wanted society's or God's or my boss's approval. But if I insist that those motives were not mine, then they are only theorizing, and they cannot parlay such theorizing into an absolutistic theory about all human motives and actions.

Because human beings vary so much in the thoughts, feelings, motives, and reasons for their actions, it is highly presumptuous to assume that everyone "always" thinks, feels, is motivated, or reasons in one way to the exclusion of all others. This theory, like the theory about the existence of a supernatural being, cannot be conclusively proved; indeed, there is some evidence to the contrary.

When all the other arguments fail, as they usually do in the attempted defense of psychological egoism, the psychological egoist, in attempting to prove his or her case, often retreats to the position that people always do what they really want to do. According to the egoist, if people "want" to perform a so-called unselfish act, then they are not really being unselfish because they are doing what they actually want to do. But there are problems with this argument. First of all, how can the psychological egoist deal with the fact that we often do *not* want to act unselfishly, but do so anyway? At times we would really rather do something else but feel we "must" or "have to" do what we don't want to do. Second, the only evidence the psychological egoist can cite in support of the statement "people always do what they want to do" is that the act was done. But all that means is that "everyone always does what he or she does," and this really doesn't give us any information at all about human conduct, nor does it in any way prove that human beings always act only in their own self-interest.

Therefore it seems to me that we can discount psychological egoism as a basis for ethical egoism. In its strong form it would destroy all morality and is lacking both in evidence and in logic; and in either the strong or the weak form it fails to provide a rational foundation for ethical egoism.

Ethical Egoism

What, then, is ethical egoism? It is not necessarily the same thing as selfishness, which could be behavior that is not in the egoist's self-interest at all. That is, if I am always acting selfishly, people may hate me and generally treat me badly, so it might be more in my self-interest not to be selfish. I might even go so far as to be altruistic in my behavior at least some of the time—when it is in my own self-interest to be so, of course. So ethical egoism cannot be equated with selfishness, nor should it necessarily be equated with having a big ego or being conceited. An egoist might very well be conceited; on the other hand, he or she might appear to be very self-effacing and humble.

Ethical egoism can take three possible forms:

1. *Individual ethical egoism,* which states that *everyone* ought to act in *my own* best self-interest.
2. *Personal ethical egoism,* which states that I ought to act in *my own* self-interest, but that I make no claims about what anyone else ought to do.
3. *Universal ethical egoism,* which states as its basic principle that *everyone* should always act in *his or her own* best self-interest, regardless of the interests of others, unless their interests also serve his or hers.

Problems with Individual and Personal Ethical Egoism

There are serious problems associated with individual and personal ethical egoism, in that they apply only to one individual and cannot be laid down for humanity in general. This is a real drawback if one thinks of morality or a moral system as something applicable to all human beings—that is, if one desires to get beyond a strictly individualistic morality, which most moralists do. The problems associated with promulgating (laying out or setting forth) either of these forms of ethical egoism go deeper than their lack of general applicability, however. It probably would not be in the interest of individual or personal egoists to state their theory at all because they might anger other people and thus thwart their own self-interest. For this reason, such egoists might have to appear as other than they really are, or lie about what they really believe, and dishonesty and lying are considered to be questionable moral actions in most moral theories.

We might also ask whether a moral system shouldn't be consistent, and whether it shouldn't be more than just a theory. If a person has to propound one moral theory while knowingly and purposely operating under another, then isn't he or she being inconsistent? And how moral can this system be if it cannot be laid out for others to see? Another problem with such individualistic systems is that they fail to take into consideration the fact that human beings are not isolated from each other, and that the moral and immoral actions of all persons affect other people around them. These two versions of egoism, however, are good only for one person and may not even be beneficial for that individual, especially if anyone else finds out that he or she really is operating under such a system. So these views of egoism are not impossible to hold—indeed, you may find, after we have finished discussing universal ethical egoism, that they are the only ones really possible—but they are highly suspect as valid moral theories.

Universal Ethical Egoism

Universal ethical egoism is the version of the theory most commonly presented by egoists because, like most other ethical theories, it is, as its name states, "universal"—an ethical theory that claims to apply to all human beings. This theory does not state only what *I* should do; rather, it concerns itself with what *all* human beings should do if they want to be moral: They should always act in their own self-interest. Universal ethical egoism has been propounded by Epicurus, Ayn Rand, Jesse Kalin, and John Hospers, among others. These philosophers wish to set up an ethical system for all human beings to follow, and they believe that the most ethical viewpoint is for everyone to act in his or her own self-interest.

Problems with Universal Ethical Egoism

Inconsistency. The most devastating attack on universal ethical egoism was made by Brian Medlin in his essay "Ultimate Principles and Ethical Egoism," which Jesse Kalin attempted to refute in his essay "In Defense of Egoism."[1] Medlin put forth some of the same arguments already described here against individual and personal ethical egoism. For example, he stated that the ethical egoist says that everyone ought to act in his own self-interest. Suppose, however, that Tom is acting in his own self-interest, which is not in the ethical egoist's (let's call him John) self-interest. Then it certainly would not be in John's interest to tell Tom that he should act in his, Tom's, own self-interest; therefore John would be at least reticent to state his ethical system and probably wiser under ethical egoism not to state it at all. Let us suppose that John, the ethical egoist, really means that all people should act in their own self-interest, that the greatest good should be done to all concerned by any ethical action, or, as Medlin states it, that John really wants "everyone to come out on top." Isn't John actually proposing some form of utilitarianism (which states that everyone always should act so that the greatest number of good consequences accrue to everyone concerned by the action) rather than egoism? This may make utilitarians happy, but we don't need two names for one ethical theory.

What Is Meant by Everyone. The problem really becomes critical when we ask exactly what universal ethical egoists mean when they state that *everyone* ought to act in his or her own self-interest. Do they mean that both John and Tom ought to act in their own self-interest when their self-interests conflict? How will this conflict be resolved? Suppose Tom asks John what he should do in the midst of their conflict? Should John tell him to act in his own self-interest even if it means that John will lose out? Universal ethical egoism would seem to advocate this; however, it obviously would not be in John's self-interest to have Tom do so. There is an inconsistency here, no matter what John does, because when self-interests conflict, universal ethical egoism provides for no resolution that will truly be in the best interest of everyone.

Difficulty in Giving Moral Advice. Ethical egoism becomes highly questionable, then, when we talk about giving moral advice. Such advice is inconsistent, in that John should do what is in his own self-interest but must advise Tom to act either in John's interest or in Tom's. If he advises Tom to act in his, John's, interest, then John is retreating to individual egoism; if he advises Tom to act in his own self-interest, then John is not serving his own interest. Either way, it would seem that the purpose behind ethical egoism is defeated.

Jesse Kalin says that the only way to state universal ethical egoism consistently is to advocate that John should act in his own self-interest and Tom in *his* own self-interest. Everything then will be all right because even though the theory is announced to everyone, and even though John will have to advise Tom that Tom should act in his own self-interest, John need not *want* Tom to act in his own self-interest. It is on this point that Kalin feels he has refuted Medlin, who states that universal ethical egoism is inconsistent because what the egoist *wants* is obviously incompatible—he wants himself to come out on top and he wants everyone else to come out on top; but because interests conflict, he obviously has incompatible wants. Kalin uses the example of John and Tom playing chess. John, seeing that Tom could move his bishop and put John's king in check, believes that Tom *ought* to move his bishop but doesn't *want* him to, need not persuade him to, and indeed "ought to . . . sit there quietly, hoping he does not move as he ought."[2] With this statement, the problem that occurred with individual and personal ethical egoism again arises in universal ethical egoism—that what people *ought* to do cannot be promulgated (that is, presented for all to see). In other words, we again have an ethical theory that has to be a secret one; otherwise, it will, by being stated, violate its own major tenet: self-interest.

Blurring the Moral and Non*moral Uses of* **Ought** *and* **Should.** We also must examine how Kalin is using "ought" in his example about the chess game. One of the unintentional outcomes of Kalin's essay seems to be a blurring of the distinction between the *moral* use of *ought* and *should* and a *non*moral use of the two words. In the first chapter, I described the major difference between the scientific and philosophical-normative approaches to morality as being the difference between *is* or *do* and *ought* and *should.* I also pointed out that the last two words are not always used in a moral sense and indeed often may be used in a nonmoral sense.

For example, if the instructions for assembling a toy say you should put two end bolts and nuts together before putting in the other four, there is no moral import at work there. *Should* here implies "if you want this toy to work right and want these two pieces of it to fit snugly." There is no moral imperative unless incorrect assembly of the toy could cost a child his or her life, for example. Rarely do lives depend upon whether games such as chess are won or lost, or whether two sides of a toy fit together well. *Should* in these contexts probably will not have any moral ramifications whatsoever.

Evidently, to Kalin at least, moral rules and advice have such superficial application that *should* and *ought* mean no more than they would mean when applied to a game or the directions for assembling something. It seems that only the oddest of ethical systems would state many do's and don'ts and say that people *ought* to adhere to them but then hope they don't. Consider what it would mean for John to advise Tom, "You should kill me because I stand in the way of your having my wife, and it is in your self-interest for you to do so, but because it is not in *my* self-interest for you to do so, I hope you don't." It certainly is not incompatible with what John *says* he thinks ought to be, but it is a strange moral system that actually states what its advocate really does not want. It is obvious to me that what John really thinks Tom *should* do is leave John and his wife alone. This means, at best, that universal ethical egoism is highly impractical, and, at worst, that it is a theory that seriously brings into conflict the desires of people for good things and that sees the pursuit of happiness as being some sort of intellectual game, the rules of which humans "ought" to be told to follow. Kalin seems to have shown that the egoist need not want to have others practice what he or she preaches. By doing so, however, Kalin raises the specter of an even wider split between what "ought to be" and what "is."

I, at least, am forced back to Medlin's logic: "But is not to believe that someone should act in a certain way, to try to persuade him to do so?" and "Does it make sense to say, 'Of course you should do this, but for goodness' sake, don't?'"[3] Without this logic, ethical systems amount to no more than mere abstract ideals that their proponents hope will not actually be carried out. What this amounts to, if Kalin is correct, is that universal ethical egoism claims to be a moral system that is based on the nonmoral—its rules actually have no more moral import than the rules of a chess game or the directions for assembling a toy.

Inconsistent with Helping Professions. Another criticism of ethical egoism in any of its forms is that it does not provide the proper ethical basis for people who are in the helping professions. It certainly is true that many people are in such professions for their own self-interest to some extent, but the real reason for being a nurse, doctor, social worker, teacher, or minister is to help others, and a highly self-interested attitude would not serve one well in these professions.

These criticisms would support the contentions of some philosophers that egoism in any of its forms is really not a moral system at all, but rather the nonmoral stance from which one asks, "Why should I be moral?"[4] Although not wanting to go that far, I do feel there are a great many problems with ethical egoism that are not easily resolvable. Therefore, it seems to be a highly questionable ethical theory.

Advantages of Universal Ethical Egoism

What conclusions can we draw from this discussion of ethical egoism? Does the theory have any advantages at all?

It's Easier to Determine Self-Interest. One advantage of ethical egoism over theories that advocate doing what is in the interest of others, is that it is much easier for individuals to know what their *own* interests are than it is for them to know what is in the best interest of others. People will not always act in their own self-interest and will certainly make errors in judgment about what is in their self-interest, but they are in a much better position to correctly estimate what they want, need, and should have and do than anyone else is. Also, they have a better chance of assessing their own self-interest than they have of assessing the interests of anyone else.

It Encourages Individual Freedom and Responsibility. Another advantage of universal ethical egoism is that it encourages individual freedom and responsibility. Egoists need only to consider their own self-interest and then take responsibility for their actions. There need be no dependence on anybody else, and one need only seek his or her own self-interest and let others do the same. Therefore, egoists also argue, this means that their theories really fit in best with the United States' capitalist economy.

Limitations to These Advantages. Ethical egoism can work successfully, but it has severe limitations. The theory will work best as long as people are operating in relative isolation, thereby minimizing the occasions for conflict among their self-interests. For example, if everyone could be his or her own self-sufficient community and be almost totally independent, then self-interest would work well. However, as soon as individual spheres begin to touch or overlap, and John's self-interest begins to conflict with Tom's, ethical egoism fails to provide the means of resolving these conflicts in such a way that everyone's self-interest is protected or satisfied. Some principle of justice or compromise must be brought in, and it probably would not be in *everyone's* self-interest. At this point egoists must either become utilitarians and concern themselves with the best interests of everyone involved, or play their nonmoral game by telling people what they should do while hoping they won't in fact do it.

The real and immediate problem with egoism, however, is that we do not live in self-sufficient communities. We live, rather, in increasingly crowded communities where social, economic, and even moral interdependence is a fact of life, and where self-interests conflict constantly and somehow must be compromised. This means that a person's self-interest will be only partially served and, in fact, may not be served at all.

Ayn Rand's Rational Ethical Egoism

The late Ayn Rand (1905–1982), the foremost modern exponent of universal ethical egoism (which she called rational ethical egoism), has said that the self-interests of rational human beings, by virtue of their being rational, will never conflict.[5] I feel that this view is both naive and utopian. No matter how Rand tries to argue away the conflicts of self-interest that continually arise among rational human beings, observation shows us that they do exist and have to be dealt with. For example, Albert Einstein (1879–1955) and Bertrand Russell (1872–1970), both mathematicians and scientists (Russell also was a philosopher), were totally opposed to the development of atomic weapons. On the other hand, Dr. Edward Teller (b. 1908), the renowned physicist responsible for many of the developments of atomic power, advocates its proliferation. These are not mere differences of opinion; Russell, for example, even went to jail in protest of the docking of American nuclear submarines in England. Not only did Russell think that the development and use of atomic weapons were not in his own self-interest, but also he felt that they were not in the interest of human beings in general.

Rand might wish to argue that these men are neither rational nor intelligent, but if so, I would find it difficult to accept her definition of *rational human beings* and *rational self-interest.* Furthermore, it is interesting to speculate, along these lines, why Ayn Rand steadfastly refused to support any of the communities or projects that were set up under her theories. One such was the Minerva Project, an island community to be run without government, and another was Libertarianism, a political party that nominated John Hospers as a presidential candidate in 1972 and has run a candidate in every national election since. Neither endeavor received Rand's blessing. One wonders if she was merely dissatisfied with these particular projects, or if she realized that her theory really was only a utopian ideal that could not function other than in the abstract.

Conclusions

In conclusion, it would seem that people can be ethical egoists with some success only if they advocate some other theory besides ethical egoism, and only if they don't tell people that that is what they're doing! As I stated earlier, this makes for a questionable ethical theory at worst, and an impractical one at best. Given all of these serious problems, we certainly should not settle on ethical egoism until we first have examined other ethical theories.

Utilitarianism

Utilitarianism is an ethical theory whose principal architects were Jeremy Bentham (1748–1832) and John Stuart Mill (1806–1873). It derives its name from *utility,* which means "usefulness." The utilitarian says that an act is right (moral) if it is useful in "bringing about a *desirable* or *good* end."[6] It has been more characteristically stated, however, as "Everyone should perform that act or follow that moral rule that will bring about the greatest good (or happiness) for everyone concerned." The reason for mentioning both acting and following rules is that utilitarianism generally is found in two main forms: *act utilitarianism* and *rule utilitarianism.*

Act Utilitarianism

Act utilitarianism essentially says that everyone should perform that act which will bring about the greatest amount of good over bad for everyone affected by the act. Its advocates do not believe in setting up rules for action because they feel that each situation and each person are different. Each individual, then, must assess the situation he or she is involved in and try to figure out which act would bring about the greatest amount of good consequences with the least amount of bad consequences, not just for himself or herself, as in egoism, but for everyone involved in the situation.

In assessing the situation, the agent (the person who will be acting or is acting) must decide whether, for example, telling the truth is the right thing to do in *this* situation at *this* time. It does not matter that most people believe that telling the truth is generally a good thing to do; the act utilitarian must decide with regard to the particular situation he or she is in at the moment whether or not it is right to tell the truth. For act utilitarianism there can be no absolute rules against killing, stealing, lying, and so on, because every situation is different and all people are different. Therefore, all of those acts that may, in general, be considered immoral would be considered moral or immoral by the act utilitarian only in relation to whether they would or would not bring about the greatest good over bad for everyone in a particular situation.

Criticisms of Act Utilitarianism

Difficulty of Determining Consequences for Others. There are several criticisms of act utilitarianism. One of them has been cited as providing support for ethical egoism, and that is that it is very difficult to ascertain what will turn out to be good consequences for others. Involved in the difficulty of deciding what the consequences will be of any action one is about to take is the problem of deciding what is "good" and "right" for others. What may be a good consequence for you may not be equally, or at all, good for another; and how are you to tell unless you can ask other people what would be good for them? Very often, of course, there is no time to ask anyone anything; we simply must act in the best way we can.

Impracticality of Beginning Anew. Furthermore, there is a certain impracticality in having to begin anew with each situation. In fact, many moralists might question the act consequentialist's belief that each act and each person is completely and uniquely different, claiming that there are many similarities among human beings and their behaviors that would justify the laying down of certain rules. For example, critics of act utilitarianism might say that enough persons value their lives so that there should be some rule against killing, even if it has to be qualified—for instance, by saying "Never kill *except* in self-defense." They might further say that it is a waste of time and even absurd to reassess each situation when there is a choice of killing or not killing; one simply should follow the general rule and any of its valid qualifications. As mentioned earlier, the time factor in moral decision making is often an important one; often a person does not have the time to start from scratch when confronted by each new moral problem. In fact, being forced to constantly begin anew could result in an inability to commit a moral act in time.

The act utilitarian would answer that after experiencing many situations, one learns to apply one's experience to the new situation readily, with a minimum of time-wasting, so that one is really not starting from scratch each time. But when people call on past experience and act consistently in accordance with it, aren't they really acting on the basis of unstated rules? If they have been in a number of situations in which the moral choice is not to kill another human being, and they are now faced with another similar situation, then aren't they really operating under a hidden rule that says, "Never kill another human being in any situation similar to A"? If so, they are rule utilitarians who merely have not announced their rules.

Difficulty of Educating the Young or Uninitiated. One last criticism of act utilitarianism asks how one is to educate the young or the uninitiated to act morally if there are no rules or guides to follow except one: Each person must assess what would be the greatest good consequences of each act for each situation that arises. It would seem that under this ethical system everyone must start afresh as he or she is growing up in seeking to discover what is the moral thing to do in each situation as it occurs. This may be allowable in the estimation of some philosophers, but it is very difficult, if not impossible, to conduct any type of systematic moral education on such a basis.

Rule Utilitarianism

It was to provide an answer to many of the act utilitarian's problems that rule utilitarianism was established. In this form, the basic utilitarian principle is not that "everyone should always *act* to bring about the greatest good for all concerned," but rather that "everyone should always establish and follow that rule or those rules that will bring about the greatest good for all concerned." This at least eliminates the problem of one's having to start anew to figure out the likely consequences for everyone in every situation, and it also provides a set of rules that can be alluded to in the moral education of the uninitiated.

Rule utilitarians try, from experience and careful reasoning, to set up a series of rules that, when followed, will yield the greatest good for all humanity. For example, rather than trying to figure out whether one should or should not kill someone else in each situation where this problem might arise, rule utilitarians might form the rule *Never kill except in self-defense.* Their assumption in stating this rule is that except when it is done in self-defense, killing will bring about more bad consequences than good for all concerned, both now and probably in the long run. Killing, they might add, if allowed in any but the self-defense situation, would set dangerous precedents. It would encourage more people to take others' lives than they now do, and because human life is basic and important to everyone, not having such a rule would always cause more harm than good to all concerned.

Rule utilitarians obviously believe, unlike their "act" counterparts, that there are enough similar human motives, actions, and situations to justify setting up rules that will apply to all human beings and to all human situations. To the rule utilitarian's way of thinking, it is foolish and dangerous to leave moral actions up to individuals without providing them with some guidance and without trying to establish some sort of stability and moral order in society, as opposed to the haphazard, on-the-spot guesswork that seems to be advocated by the act utilitarian.

Criticisms of Rule Utilitarianism

Difficulty of Determining Consequences for Others. Associated with rule utilitarianism are some of the same problems we encountered with the act type, especially in the area of trying to determine good consequences for others. This, as I have already mentioned, is a disadvantage that egoism does not share. How can we be sure, given the vast differences among human beings and human situations, that a rule really can be established that will cover such diversity, much less that it will always and truly bring about the greatest good for all concerned? This difficulty is added to the one shared by the egoist and the act utilitarian, of trying to determine *all* the consequences for not just one action, but all actions and situations occurring under any particular rule. Nonrule moralists argue strongly that there is no rule for which one cannot find at least one exception somewhere along the line, and that by the time you have incorporated all of the possible exceptions into a rule, you really are advocating act utilitarianism. Therefore, they argue, you would be better off without rules, as these cannot possibly apply to all the situations you may face.

For example, can the rule *Never kill except in self-defense* actually cover all of the situations human beings are prone to get involved in? Will it cover abortion, for example? Many antiabortionists think so, stating that in no way can the unborn fetus be considered an aggressor; therefore, it cannot be aborted. Prochoice advocates, on the other hand, either don't consider the fetus to be a human being, or argue for the precedence of the mother's life over the fetus's and believe that there are times when the fetus must be aborted. How, for example, would the rule utilitarian deal with the aborting of the fetus when the mother's life is endangered not specifically because she is pregnant but for some other reason? The fetus cannot be considered an aggressor, so how can it be aborted in self-defense?

I am not trying to say that rule utilitarians would have such a rule, but rather to show how difficult it is to form a rule that will cover all situations without exception. Rule utilitarians can, of course, rate their rules by placing them in primary and secondary categories, but the problem continues regardless of the category in which the rule is found. Act utilitarians do not have this problem; they may have trouble justifying a particular action, but at least they have not committed themselves to acting in just one way in all situations. They may make a mistake in situation A, but when situation B comes along, they have another chance to judge and act anew, without being hampered by any binding rules that tie them to a series of mistakes.

The Cost-Benefit Analysis, or End-Justifies-the-Means, Approach—A Problem for Utilitarianism

There is another problem in both forms of utilitarianism, and that is the difficulty of carrying the "useful" aspect of utility too far. Nonutilitarians may ask, for example, whether it is always right to try to achieve "the greatest good for the greatest number." Doesn't this sometimes end up as the greatest good for the majority with some very bad consequences for the minority? Would science, for example, be justified in taking one hundred children and performing painful and eventually fatal experiments on them if the doctors could guarantee the saving of ten million children's lives in the future? Certainly, by number alone, this would be the greatest good for the greatest number, but many moralists would object, saying that each individual is, morally speaking, unique, and therefore no such experiment should ever be performed regardless of how many individuals will be saved by it.

Yet if we are aiming for the greatest good for everyone, there is the danger of what many call the "cost-benefit analysis," or "end-justifies-the-means," approach to morality; that is, trying to calculate how much effort or cost will bring about the most benefits. This approach also involves us in determining the social worth of individuals in a society, so that those people who are "worth" more to society, such as professional people, are given more benefits (for instance, medical) than those who are not. In other words, sometimes in trying to do the greatest good for the greatest number, we may find ourselves being quite immoral toward a few.

Some moralists, including Immanuel Kant and Ayn Rand, believe that each human being should be considered as an end in himself or herself, never as merely a means. In trying to be fair and just to all members of a society, this would seem to be a more moral approach than merely trying to attain the greatest good for the greatest number. To be sure, there are times when a group of people has to think of the survival of the group rather than of one or two individuals, and then moral decisions have to be made about who gets the "goods" that are in short supply. However, a person who always operates under "the greatest good for the greatest number" ideal very often ignores what is good for everyone.

An example of one of the times when the survival of the group is put before that of a few individuals exists in medicine. During a serious disaster, when medical facilities simply cannot handle everyone who is injured, doctors concentrate on those patients whom they know they can save and not on the "hopeless" cases. Furthermore, an injured doctor or nurse who could be put to work would probably be the first to get medical attention because she or he would be able to help save more of the other injured people than a nonmedical person.

These, fortunately, are unusual circumstances, and they require different priorities from more normal situations. To apply the cost-benefit analysis, or end-justifies-the-means, approach to more normal situations, however, is tantamount to treating human beings as if they were some kind of inanimate "product" in a business where one tries to get the most for one's money and thus discards the inferior product. There have been people who have favored this approach, among them Hitler and some other dictators, but most moralists find this an abhorrent and immoral view of humanity.

Conclusions

In conclusion, then, utilitarianism is an improvement over egoism, in that it attempts to take into consideration all persons concerned by any moral action. At the same time, however, it runs into the difficulty of determining what would be good for others, a difficulty not involved in egoism. In act utilitarianism, the problem is that there are no moral rules or guides to go by; a person must decide what is right for all people in each situation he or she faces. In rule utilitarianism, the problem is to find out which rules really cover all human beings and situations, even though this form of utilitarianism avoids the ambiguity of having to start over in each new situation. The last problem with utilitarianism of either kind is that it lends itself to the cost-benefit analysis type of thinking, which often is the result of "the greatest good for the greatest number" kind of morality. In other words, the notion that any end, and especially any good end, justifies any means used to attain it. There is a question among many moralists as to whether we should concentrate only upon consequences or ends and ignore other things such as means or motives when making moral decisions. This issue will be discussed further when Immanuel Kant's Practical Imperative is presented in the next chapter.

Another advantage utilitarianism has over ethical egoism is that it is far more suitable for people in the helping professions, in that it is concerned with the best good consequences for everyone.

Difficulty with Consequentialist Theories in General

One difficulty inherent in *all* of the consequentialist theories is the necessity of trying to discover and determine as many of the possible consequences of our actions as we can—a difficult task at best. As I have implied, this problem exists both for those who are concerned with self-interest and those who are concerned with the interest of everyone. Obviously, though, it is a greater problem for utilitarians because they have to concern themselves with how consequences affect people other than themselves. The critic of consequentialist theories probably would say that it is very difficult to assess all of the consequences of any of our actions because we cannot see far enough into the future, nor do we have enough knowledge about what is best for ourselves or for all concerned to make such a judgment.

For example, if one is living under the rule of an incompetent leader, the fastest way to remove such a leader would be to assassinate him. But what would the consequence of such an act be, and how can we calculate the number of good as opposed to the number of bad consequences and do this for ourselves or everyone concerned by the action? Obviously one would certainly end this leader's rule by killing him, but who would come to power next? Would this next person be any better, or would he be worse? Suppose we knew who would be next and thought she would be a good leader, but she turned out to be worse than the former leader? And is it worse to suffer for three or four years under an incompetent leader than to give precedent to the act of assassination, so that when people are dissatisfied, rightly or wrongly, with their leader they feel they can use assassination to remove him? In the case of utilitarianism, because we are concerned with *everyone* involved in the situation, can we assess with any precision what effect our killing or not killing the leader will have on the children of the society and even on its future unborn members? Will we ever really know what *all* of the consequences, present and future, of our act will be? If not, then how can we judge each situation well enough to take the right action?

In an example taken from U.S. history, could President Harry Truman have foreseen all of the consequences of his decision to drop the atomic bombs on Hiroshima and Nagasaki during World War II? Obviously he could determine the more immediate consequences, such as the shortening of the war and the saving of American lives. But could he have foreseen the long-range consequences: the cold war, the development of the hydrogen and neutron bombs, the stockpiling of nuclear weapons to the point of "overkill," the radiation fallout and consequent pollution of the atmosphere, and so on? As this example illustrates, the discovery and determination of the consequences of our acts and rules, either for ourselves or others, is no easy task—and it is not one that can always be accurately or precisely accomplished. But what if we were to set up a moral system without having to consider consequences? If we can decide what is right or wrong on some basis other than consequences, perhaps we can avoid some of the difficulties involved in both egoism and utilitarianism. The next chapter will deal with such theories.

Care Ethics

There is a newer theory called "Care Ethics," and sometimes "feminist ethics," which was established by the psychologist Carol Gilligan (1936–) in her book *In A Different Voice* (1982). This theory is generally not considered a consequentialist ethical theory in the formal sense like ethical egoism and utilitarianism, but it would seem to fit under consequentialism more than nonconsequentialism.

Men and Women Are Different When It Comes to Ethical Decision Making

According to Gilligan, men and women think quite differently when it comes to ethics. Another famous psychologist, Lawrence Kohlberg, agrees but concludes that this difference means that women's ethical reasoning is inferior to men's. Gilligan, on the other hand, thinks that women's views on ethics are different from, but should be considered equal with, men's. The difference, according to both these psychologists, is that men's views on ethics have to do with justice, rights, competition, being independent, and living by rules, whereas women's views have to do with generosity, harmony, reconciliation, and working to maintain close relationships.

Kohlberg set up a dilemma where a man's wife is desperately ill and the man cannot afford the medication she needs. Kohlberg then asked two eleven-year-olds, a boy and a girl, if the man should steal the medication. The boy said yes because the wife's life is more important than the rule of not stealing; the girl, however, said no because if the man got caught and went to jail who would look after his sick wife, and also maybe he could ask the pharmacist to give him the medicine and he could pay the pharmacist later. According to Kohlberg, the boy had a clear understanding of the situation because the wife's rights would override the rule of not stealing, that is, the question was all about rights and justice. Further, Kohlberg thought the girl's understanding of the situation was weak. On the other hand, Gilligan thinks that the boy and girl were answering different questions: The boy was answering the question, "Should the man steal the medication or not?" Whereas the girl was answering the question, "Should the man steal the medication or do something else?" The girl was not so much concerned with rights and justice, but with what would happen to the man and his wife and was also considering the possible humaneness of the pharmacist. In other words, she thought in terms of caring. Gilligan sees a tendency of males to focus on an ethics of justice, whereas females focus on an ethics of caring, and she thinks that both views of ethics are advantageous and should be considered different but equally valid. She thinks the ideal situation is that men and women should consider both views of ethics because men could learn about compassion and caring in ethics and women could learn that men always concentrate on rights and justice so that women could recognize their own rights as human beings and not be considered inferior to men simply because they think differently about ethics.

Criticisms of Gilligan's Theory

Some critics think that by accepting Gilligan's theory we may be raising so-called female values far above male values and replacing one unfair ethical system with another unfair ethical system by setting women up as normal and men as inferior. Also, if we say that it's women's nature to be caring and compassionate, are we not pushing them back to where they were before Gilligan? Men (and women) might say that since women can't understand justice, then we can't use them in the outside world and they should return to their homemaking duties, and if a certain job calls for caring qualities, then men can't be hired because they are not good at caring. Therefore, instead of Gilligan's theory giving men and women more opportunities, she may be setting up new categories that could result in excluding women from traditionally men's jobs (for example, engineering) and men from women's jobs (for example, nursing and secretarial). Further, critics say that Gilligan has disrupted the philosophy of gender equality so that a company who wants to hire someone with a good understanding of legal rules, for example, won't hire a women for the job because she has no real sense of justice. In this way, her psychological theory of gender may move from describing gender equality to prescribing a set of rules about who ought to do what jobs.

Chapter Summary

   I. Two major viewpoints of morality
      A. Consequentialist (teleological) morality is based on or concerned with consequences.
      B. Nonconsequentialist (deontological) morality is not based on or concerned with consequences.
  II. Psychological egoism
      A. This is not an ethical theory but a descriptive or scientific theory having to do with egoism.
      B. It appears in two forms, neither of which can operate as a basis for ethical egoism.
         1. The strong form holds that people always act in their own self-interest.
         2. The weak form holds that people often, but not always, act in their own self-interest.
      C. Psychological egoism in its strong form does not refute morality, and in its weak form it does not provide a rational foundation for ethical egoism.
 III. Ethical egoism—a philosophical-normative, prescriptive theory
      A. This appears in three forms.
         1. The individual form maintains that everyone ought to act in my self-interest.
         2. The personal form maintains that I ought to act in my own self-interest, but that I make no claims about what anyone else ought to do.
         3. The universal form maintains that everyone should always act in his or her own self-interest.
      B. The problem with the first and second forms is that they apply only to one individual and cannot be laid down for humanity in general because to do so probably would not be in the egoist's self-interest.
      C. Universal ethical egoism is the most commonly held version of ethical egoism, but it also has its problems.
         1. It is inconsistent, in that it is unclear whose self-interest should be satisfied.
         2. What is meant by *everyone* is unclear.
         3. There is a difficulty in determining how to give moral advice.

4. In answering these criticisms, supporters of egoism tend to blur the moral and nonmoral uses of *ought* and *should*.
5. It does not fit well with the helping professions.

D. Ethical egoism has certain advantages.
1. It is easier for egoists to know what is in their own self-interest than it is for other moralists, who are concerned about more than self-interest, to know what is in the best interest of others.
2. It encourages individual freedom and responsibility and fits in best, according to egoists, with our capitalist economy.
3. It can work successfully as long as people are operating in limited spheres, isolated from each other, thereby minimizing conflicts.

E. Limitations of these advantages.
1. It offers no consistent method of resolving conflicts of self-interests.
2. We do not live in isolated, self-sufficient communities, but rather in increasingly crowded communities where social, economic, and moral interdependence are facts of life and where self-interests conflict constantly and somehow must be compromised.

IV. Utilitarianism

A. Utilitarianism maintains that everyone should perform that act or follow that moral rule which will bring about the greatest good (or happiness) for everyone concerned.

B. Act utilitarianism states that everyone should perform that act which will bring about the greatest good over bad for everyone affected by the act.
1. The act utilitarian believes that one cannot establish rules in advance to cover all situations and people because they are all different.
2. There are difficulties with this theory.
   (a) It is very hard to ascertain what would be good consequences for others.
   (b) It is impractical to have to begin anew with each situation, to decide what would be moral in that situation.
   (c) It is nearly impossible to educate the young or the uninitiated to act morally if they can be given no rules or guides to follow.

C. Rule utilitarianism states that everyone always should follow the rule or rules that will bring about the greatest number of good consequences for all concerned.
1. The rule utilitarian believes that there are enough similar human motives, actions, and situations to justify setting up rules that will apply to all human beings and situations.
2. There are difficulties with this theory.
   (a) As with act utilitarianism, it is difficult to determine what would be good consequences for others.
   (b) It is difficult to see how rule utilitarians can be sure, given the vast differences among human beings and situations, that a rule really can be established to cover such diversity—that they can create a rule that will truly and always bring about the greatest good for all concerned.
   (c) It is difficult to avoid making so many exceptions to rules that the rules cannot really function effectively.

D. Another problem for both forms of utilitarianism is the cost-benefit analysis, or end-justifies-the-means, approach to morality.
1. There is danger here of trying to determine the social worth of individuals.
2. "The greatest good for all concerned" can often be interpreted as "the greatest good for the majority," with possible immoral consequences to any individuals in the minority.
3. Does even a good end justify any means used to attain it, or should we also consider our means and motives?

V. Problems with consequentialist theories
   A. Consequentialist theories demand that we discover and determine all of the consequences of our actions or rules.
   B. This is virtually impossible to accomplish.
   C. Do consequences or ends constitute all of morality?
VI. Care Ethics
   A. Carol Gilligan, a psychologist, has established an ethics called Care Ethics.
   B. She believes that men's moral attitudes have to do with justice, rights, competition, being independent, and living by rules.
   C. Women's moral attitudes have to do with generosity, harmony, reconciliation, and working to maintain close relationships.
   D. These two views are different but equally valid, according to Gilligan.
   E. Criticisms of Gilligan's theory.
      1. Gilligan may be replacing one problematic theory with another.
      2. Instead of her theory describing gender equality, it may be prescribing who ought to do what jobs.

Exercises for Review

1. What is the difference between the consequentialist (teleological) and nonconsequentialist (deontological) views of morality?
2. Explain the difference between psychological egoism and ethical egoism.
3. What are the two forms of psychological egoism? Why do they fail to refute morality or to provide a foundation for ethical egoism?
4. Explain individual and personal ethical egoism. What are the problems with these forms?
5. Why do you think universal ethical egoism is the most commonly held form of ethical egoism? What difficulties does this form present?
6. Why is the universal ethical egoist's interpretation of *everyone* a questionable one?
7. What are the problems associated with Jesse Kalin's criticism of the attack on universal ethical egoism?
8. Describe the advantages and disadvantages of ethical egoism.
9. What do act utilitarians believe? How do their beliefs differ from those of rule utilitarians?
10. What are the difficulties with act and rule utilitarianism?
11. Describe the cost-benefit analysis, or end-justifies-the-means, approach to morality. Why is this a problem in both forms of utilitarianism?

Discussion Questions

1. Analyze the motivations behind some of the decisions you have made and the actions you have taken, and try to determine the extent to which you were motivated by self-interest. Have you ever done what might be called a purely altruistic act? Does this analysis of motivation lead you to believe that psychological egoism is an accurate description of how human beings live their lives? To what extent, and why or why not?

2. On a TV show, an army surgeon performed an unnecessary operation on a battalion commander merely to remove him from battle during the time he would need to recuperate from the surgery. As a result of overaggressiveness the battalion commander had an abnormally high casualty rate among his men, and the surgeon knew that by performing the operation he would probably save the lives of hundreds of soldiers who otherwise would have been victims of the commander's eagerness. A fellow surgeon counseled him that it was unethical to operate on a healthy body even under those circumstances. But the operating surgeon, feeling that more good than bad would come out of his action, performed the operation anyway.

   How does this relate to the cost-benefit analysis approach to morality? To what extent do you feel each surgeon was right in his moral position? Do you feel that in this case the good end justified the means the operating surgeon was using? Why or why not? Is there ever a time when a good end justifies *any* means used to attain it? If so, when? If not, why not?

3. To what extent do you feel that human beings need rules in order to be moral, and to what extent do you feel they should be free to adapt their behavior to different situations? Be specific, giving examples and illustrations.

4. Read Joseph Fletcher's book *Situation Ethics*, and critically evaluate his act utilitarian position. Keeping in mind that Fletcher offers no specific rules for moral behavior, what values and what difficulties do you see in his sole commandment, "Do what is the loving thing to do"? Are there problems with deciding what the loving thing to do is in some situations? If so, what are these problems? If not, why not? Describe a situation in which "the loving thing to do" can be clearly delineated.

5. Read Robert Heinlein's *Stranger in a Strange Land* and critically evaluate the ethical egoism advocated by the author through his main earthborn character. Perform a similar analysis on the protagonists of the author's other books, *The Moon Is a Harsh Mistress* and *I Will Fear No Evil*.

6. Analyze and critically evaluate U.S. national and foreign policies, attempting to determine whether they are based upon egoism in any of its forms or on act or rule utilitarianism. Support your views with examples.

7. To what extent do you feel that Christian ethics is based on egoism or utilitarianism? Give specific examples.

8. Read *The Fountainhead, Atlas Shrugged,* or *The Virtue of Selfishness* by Ayn Rand, and write a critical evaluation of it in relation to ethical egoism.

9. Collect as much information as you can about the Libertarian political party and evaluate what you deem would be the effectiveness or ineffectiveness of its theories if it were the governing party in the United States today.

10. Describe the extent to which you are in any form an ethical egoist or an act or rule utilitarian. Show how these theories have or have not worked for you as you have dealt with specific moral issues and problems.

11. To what extent do you believe that members of your family or your friends are egoists or utilitarians? Describe how these theories work or don't work for them and for those around them.

Notes

1. Both of these essays may be found in William P. Alston and Richard B. Brandt, *The Problems of Philosophy* (Boston: Allyn and Bacon, 1974), 204–19.
2. Ibid., 218.
3. Ibid., 207.

4. For an excellent presentation of this argument, see Kai Nielsen's "Why Should I Be Moral?" in *Problems of Moral Philosophy,* 2nd ed., ed. Paul W. Taylor (Belmont, CA: Dickenson, 1972), 497–517.

5. Ayn Rand, *The Virtue of Selfishness* (New York: New American Library, 1964), 57–67.

6. Paul Taylor, *Problems of Moral Philosophy,* 137.

Research Navigator™
(http://www.researchnavigator.com)

This web site offers three research databases: EBSCO's *Content Select Academic Journal and Abstract Database, New York Times* Search by Subject Archive, and *Best of the Web* Link Library. In addition, this site provides helpful advice on how to conduct efficient and productive research from choosing a topic to polishing the final draft. Beginning philosophy students will probably find the *Best of the Web* Link Library the most appropriate place to start their research.

The free access code necessary to employ Research Navigator™ can be found in the Prentice Hall Guide to Evaluating Online Resources. If your text did not come with this guide, please go to *www.prenhall.com/contentselect* for information on how you can purchase an access code.

Nonconsequentialist (Deontological) Theories of Morality

Objectives

After you have read this chapter, you should be able to

1. Describe nonconsequentialist theories of morality, showing how they differ from the consequentialist theories.

2. Differentiate between act and rule nonconsequentialism and show how they differ from act and rule utilitarianism.

3. Describe and critically analyze act nonconsequentialism, and the Divine Command Theory, Kant's Duty Ethics, Ross' Prima Facie Duties (the main examples of rule nonconsequentialism).

4. Define and analyze such important terms and concepts as *universalizability, Categorical Imperative, reversibility, human beings as ends rather than means, prima facie duties.*

Nonconsequentialist theories of morality are based on something other than the consequences of a person's actions. We have seen that in both egoism and utilitarianism, moralists are concerned with the consequences or outcomes of human actions. Egoists are concerned that people should act in their own self-interest, and utilitarians are concerned that people should act in the interests of all concerned. In these two theories, the goodness of an action is measured by how well it serves the interests of someone, whereas the goodness of a human being is measured by the extent to which he or she performs such actions and actually causes good consequences.

The most important thing to remember when discussing the nonconsequentialist theories is that their proponents claim that consequences do not, and in fact should not, enter into judging whether actions or people are moral or immoral. Actions are to be judged solely on whether they are right and people solely on whether they are good, based on some other (many nonconsequentialists would say "higher") standard or standards of morality. That is, acts or people are to be judged moral or immoral regardless of the consequences of actions. The most obvious example of such a theory is the *Divine Command Theory*. If one believes that there is a God, goddess, or gods, and that He/She or they have set up a series of moral commands, then an action is right and people are good if and only if they obey these commands, *regardless* of the consequences that might ensue.

For example, Joan of Arc was acting under the instructions of what she felt to be voices from God. Egoists probably would consider her martyrdom not to have been in her own self-interest; they would be concerned about the consequences of her actions (her torture and death) in refusing to deny the voices. The Divine Command theorist, however, would state that one should obey a supernatural being and its commandments as relayed to human beings (through voices or any other means) regardless of the consequences *simply* because such a being is all-good and has told us that is what we should do. What is good and what is right is what this being has stated is good and right. That the consequences might involve the loss of life, for example, has nothing to do with the morality or immorality of an act or a person. One simply must accept whatever consequences come about. This is probably the clearest example of a nonconsequentialist theory of morality, but it is not the only one, nor need such a theory be based on the existence of a supernatural being.

Act Nonconsequentialist Theories

Just as utilitarianism falls into two categories (act and rule), so too do nonconsequentialist theories. Remember, however, that the main difference between act and rule utilitarianism and act and rule nonconsequentialism is that the former are based on consequences, whereas the latter are not. Nevertheless, some of the problems and disadvantages of the theories are similar, as we shall see.

Act nonconsequentialists make the major assumption that there are no general moral rules or theories at all, but only particular actions, situations, and people about which we cannot generalize. We must approach each situation individually as one of a kind and somehow decide what is the right action to take in that situation. It is the "how we decide" in this theory that is most interesting. Decisions for the act nonconsequentialist are "intuitionistic." That is, what a person decides in a particular situation, because he or she cannot use any rules or standards, is based upon what he or she believes or feels or intuits to be the right action to take. This type of theory, then, is highly individualistic—individuals must decide what they feel is the right thing to do, and then do it. They are not concerned with consequences—and certainly not with the consequences of other situations, or with people not immediately involved in this particular situation—but they must do what they feel is right given this particular situation and the people involved in it.

This theory is characterized by two popular slogans of the 1960s: *If it feels good—do it* and *Do your own thing.* It also has a more traditional basis in intuitionistic, emotive, and noncognitive theories of morality. What these theories seem to stress is that morality in thought, language, and deed is not based upon reason. Some of these theories even suggest that morality cannot be rationalized because it isn't based upon reason in the same way as scientific experimentation and factual statements about reality are. The "emotive theory," for example, states that ethical words and sentences really do only two things: (1) express people's feelings and attitudes and (2) evoke or generate certain feelings and attitudes in others. This theory will be discussed further in Chapter 5, where we will deal with the meanings of moral propositions. It seems important at this point, however, to discuss the significance of intuition and its relationship to morality.

Intuitionism

Arguments for Intuitionism. In his book *Right and Reason,* Austin Fagothey lists some general reasons for accepting or rejecting intuition as a basis for morality.[1] The general reasons supporting moral intuitionism are (1) any well-meaning person seems to have an immediate sense of right and wrong; (2) human beings had moral ideas and convictions long before philosophers created ethics as a formal study; (3) our reasoning upon moral matters usually is used to confirm our more direct perceptions or "intuitions"; and (4) our reasoning can go wrong in relation to moral issues as well as others, and then we must fall back upon our moral insights and intuitions. Thus these arguments present intuition as a higher form of reasoning indicating humans have deep moral insights which have values in themselves.

Arguments Against Intuitionism. There are at least four strong arguments against moral intuitionism. First, some people have described *intuition* as "hunches," "wild guesses," "irrational inspirations," and "clairvoyance," among other meanings lacking in scientific and philosophical respectability. It is, in short, difficult to define *intuition*, and it is more difficult still to prove its existence. Second, there is no proof that we have any inborn, or innate, set of moral rules with which we can compare our acts to see whether or not they are moral. Third, intuition is immune to objective criticism because it applies only to its possessor and because intuitions differ from one person to the next. Fourth, human beings who do not possess moral intuitions either have no ethics or have to establish their ethics on other grounds.

Criticisms of Act Nonconsequentialism

The greatest problem for act nonconsequentialism would seem to be the third argument listed in the foregoing paragraph, for if intuitions differ from person to person, how can conflicts between opposing intuitions be resolved? All we can say is that we disagree with another person's intuitions; we have no logical basis for saying, "Your intuition is wrong, whereas mine is right." Intuitions simply cannot be arbitrated, as reasons and judgments of evidence can; therefore, any theory of morality based upon intuitions alone, such as act nonconsequentialism, is highly questionable.

Other criticisms of act nonconsequentialism are these:

1. How do we know that what we intuit—with nothing else to guide us—will be morally correct?
2. How can we know when we have sufficient facts to make a moral decision?
3. With morality so highly individualized, how can we be sure we are doing the best thing for anyone else involved in the situation?
4. Can we really rely upon nothing more than our momentary intuitions to help us make our moral decisions?
5. How will we be able to justify our actions except by saying, "Well, I had an intuition that it was the right thing for me to do"?

It would seem to be very difficult to establish a morality of any social applicability here because anyone's intuitions can justify any action he or she might take. An angry person might kill the one who made him angry and then justify the murder by saying, "I had an intuition that I should kill her." But how do we arbitrate the conflict between the killer's intuition and the intense feeling of the victim's family and friends that the act was wrong? This is moral relativism of the highest degree, and absolutely no settlement is possible when the only things we have to go on are the intuitions of a given individual at a particular time.

Another criticism of act nonconsequentialism, similar to the criticism of act utilitarianism, focuses on the questionable assumption that all situations and people are completely different, with none of them having anything in common.

There are, of course, some highly unique situations for which no rules can be set up in advance, but there are many other situations containing enough similarities so that rules, perhaps with some appended exceptions or qualifications, can be stated quite effectively. For example, all situations in which someone is murdered have at least the similarity of there being a killer and a victim; because human life generally is considered to be essentially valuable in itself, rules governing when killing is or is not justified are not difficult to set up. Our legal system, with its different degree charges of murder and manslaughter, is a good example of rules fraught with moral import. These generally work quite satisfactorily by condemning immoral acts while at the same time recognizing extenuating circumstances, thereby attaining a significant degree of justice and fairness for all concerned.

These two criticisms—that each act's being completely dissimilar from every other is simply a false empirical statement and the difficulty of relying solely upon one's individual intuitions—make act nonconsequentialism a questionable ethical system. Even the most active "situationist" of our day, Joseph Fletcher, author of *Situation Ethics*, claims that in all ethical actions there should be at least one unifying factor, namely, Christian love. Because of his religious belief he should probably be classified as an act utilitarian rather than an act nonconsequentialist.

Rule Nonconsequentialist Theories

Rule nonconsequentialists believe that there are or can be rules that are the only basis for morality and that consequences do not matter. It is the following of the rules (which are right moral commands) that is moral, and the concept of morality cannot be applied to the consequences that ensue when one follows the rules. The main way in which the various rule nonconsequentialist theories differ is in their methods of establishing the rules.

Divine Command Theory

As described earlier, the Divine Command Theory states that morality is based not upon the consequences of actions or rules, nor upon self-interest or other-interestedness, but rather upon something "higher" than these mere mundane events of the imperfect human or natural worlds. It is based upon the existence of an all-good being or beings who are supernatural and who have communicated to human beings what they should and should not do in a moral sense. In order to be moral, then, human beings must follow the commands and prohibitions of such a being or beings to the letter without concerning themselves with consequences, self-interest, or anything else.

Criticisms of the Divine Command Theory. The difficulties of the Divine Command Theory are inherent in the lack of rational foundation for the existence of some sort of supernatural being or beings and the further lack of proof that the support of such a being or beings is enough to make rational and useful the ethical system in question (see Chapter 1).

Even if one could prove conclusively the existence of the supernatural, how could one prove that any supernatural being is morally trustworthy? The rules themselves might be morally valid, but the justification for following them regardless of the consequences is weak indeed. Furthermore, of what validity are the rules if a person does not believe in any kind of supernatural existence? And even if we were to accept the existence of this supernatural being and its commandments, how could we be sure we were interpreting them correctly? Interpretations of the Ten Commandments vary and often conflict. Must there not be some clearer and generally more acceptable basis for rules than the existence of the supernatural?

Kant's Duty Ethics

Another famous rule nonconsequentialist theory, often called "Duty Ethics," was formulated by Immanuel Kant (1724–1804) and contains several ethical principles.

The Good Will. Kant believed that nothing was good in itself except a good will, and he defined *will* as the uniquely human ability to act in accordance with moral rules, laws, or principles regardless of interests or consequences.

Establishing Morality by Reasoning Alone. After establishing good will as the most important human attribute, Kant then argued that reason was the second most important human attribute and that it therefore was possible to set up valid absolute moral rules on a basis of reason alone, not by reference to any supernatural being or by empirical evidence but by the same kind of logical reasoning that establishes such indisputable truths in mathematics and logic as $2 + 2 = 4$, "No circles are squares," and "All triangles are three-sided."

Kant's first requirement for an absolute moral truth is that it must be logically consistent; that is, it cannot be self-contradictory as the statement "A circle is a square" would be. Second, the truth must be universalizable; that is, it must be able to be stated so as to apply to everything without exception, not just to some or perhaps even most things. This is exemplified by the statement "All triangles are three-sided," for which there are no exceptions. Triangles may be of different sizes and shapes, but they are by definition indisputably and universally three-sided. If moral rules could indeed be established in this same manner, as Kant thought, then they too would be indisputable and therefore logically and morally binding upon all human beings. Of course, some people might disobey these rules, but we could clearly brand such people as immoral.

In some ways, Kant's ideas were brilliant. For example, he could establish the fact that living parasitically would be immoral because it also would be illogical. He could say that the commandment "Always be a parasite, living off of someone else" is illogical because if all people lived like parasites, then off whom could they live? It is easy to see that it is in conflict with the principle of *universalizability* that causes the inconsistency here. Obviously some people can be parasites, but not all. Now, if one could find such *moral* absolutes, then a completely irrefutable system of ethics could be established, and the obeying of the rules of this system would be what is moral, regardless of the consequences to oneself or to others. The major way that Kant gave us to discover these moral absolutes was by means of his Categorical Imperative.

The Categorical Imperative. The Categorical Imperative may be stated in several ways, but basically it asserts that an act is immoral if the rule that would authorize it cannot be made into a rule for all human beings to follow.[2] This means that whenever someone is about to make a moral decision, he or she must, according to Kant, ask first, "What is the rule authorizing this act I am about to perform?" and, second, "Can it become a universal rule for all human beings to follow?" For example, if a lazy person is thinking, "Why should I work hard in order to live; why don't I just steal from everyone else?" and if this person is aware of Kant's requirement, he or she will have to ask him- or herself what the rule is for this contemplated action. The rule would have to be, "I shall never work, but steal what I need from other human beings." If the person then attempts to universalize this statement, it will read: "No human being should ever work, but all human beings should steal what they need from each other." But if no one worked, there would be nothing to steal. How then would human beings live? Who would there be to steal from? It is obvious that *some* human beings can steal from others, but that not *all* human beings can do so. According to Kant stealing must therefore be immoral because it cannot be applied to all human beings.

Another, more crucial example, concerns killing another human being. Kant argued that one could not kill another human being without violating a moral absolute because in order to do so one would have to establish a rule that would be self-contradictory: "Everyone must kill everyone else." Because the meaning of life is to live, then everyone killing everyone else would contradict that meaning and would therefore violate the Categorical Imperative and fail to universalize. Killing, then, is immoral, and one should not kill.

The Practical Imperative. Another important principle in Kant's ethical system is that no human being should be thought of or used merely as a means for someone else's end, that each human being is a unique end in himself or herself, morally speaking at least. This principle sometimes is referred to as Kant's "Practical Imperative." It certainly seems to be an important principle if we consider fairness and equal treatment to be necessary attributes of any moral system. Incidentally, this principle also can operate as an antidote to the "cost-benefit analysis," or "end-justifies-the-means," problem that I mentioned in connection with both forms of utilitarianism in Chapter 2.

Let's take an example of how this Practical Imperative might work in practice from the field of medical ethics in the area of human experimentation. Kant would oppose using a human being for experimental purposes "for the good of humanity" or for any other reason that would lead us to look upon a human being as merely a "means" to an "end." Thus, in the case I described in Chapter 2 concerning the experimentation on one hundred babies now to save ten million children's lives in the future, Kant definitely would brand such experimentation as immoral. On the other hand, if an experimental procedure were the only way to save a child's life and it also would furnish doctors with information that might well save lives in the future, Kant probably would allow it because in this case a human being would not merely be used as a means to an end but considered an end in him- or herself. That is, the experimental procedure would be therapeutic for the human being involved—in this case, the child.

Duty Rather Than Inclination. Kant next spoke about obeying such rules out of a sense of duty. He said that each human being is inclined to act in certain ways. That is, each of us is inclined to do a variety of things such as give to the poor, stay in bed rather than go to work, rape someone, or be gentle to children. Because inclinations, according to Kant, are irrational and emotional and because we seem to be operating upon a basis of whim rather than reason when we follow them, people must force themselves to do what is moral out of a sense of duty. In other words, we have many inclinations of various sorts, some of which are moral and others immoral. If we are to act morally, however, we must rely on our reason and our will and act out of a sense of duty.

Kant even went so far as to say that an act simply is not fully moral unless duty rather than inclination is the motive behind it. A person who is merely *inclined* to be kind and generous to others is not to be considered moral in the fullest sense in which Kant uses the word. Only if this person, perhaps because of some unexpected tragedy in his life, no longer is inclined to be kind and generous toward others, but now forces himself to be so out of a sense of duty, only then is he acting in a fully moral manner. This strikes most people as being a very harsh approach, but it does reveal Kant's emphasis on his concept of duty as it pertains to following clearly established and absolute moral rules.

After Kant felt that he had established moral absolutes, it seemed obvious to him that to be moral one should obey them out of a sense of duty.

Summary and Illustration of Kant's System. With the last point established, it appears we finally have an airtight moral system, one that cannot be successfully attacked in any way. We have "proved" that there are absolute moral rules that can be established irrefutably by reason, that one should obey them out of a sense of duty in order to be moral, and that all persons must be considered to be unique individuals who are never to be used for anyone else's purposes or ends. But let us continue.

In order to show how Kant carried his theory into practice, it is important to present here one of his several "illustrations." Kant describes a man who, in despair yet still in possession of his reason, is contemplating suicide. Using Kant's system, the man must discover whether a maxim of his action could be made into a universal law for all human beings, so he frames the maxim as follows: "From self-love I should end my life whenever not ending it is likely to bring more bad than good." Kant then states that this cannot be universalized because it is contradictory to end life by the very feeling (self-love) that impels one to improve it. Therefore the maxim cannot possibly exist as a universal law for all human beings because it is wholly inconsistent in itself and with the Categorical Imperative.

It also violates Kant's Practical Imperative—that every human being is an end in himself or herself—because if the man destroys himself in order to escape from painful circumstances, he uses a person merely as a means to maintain tolerable conditions up to the end of his life. However, Kant maintains that people are neither things nor means for anyone else's ends but are ends in themselves; therefore, the suicidal man cannot destroy a person (whether it be himself or another) without violating this principle.[3]

Criticisms of Kant's Duty Ethics

Consistency and Conflicts of Duties. As you might suspect, there are several significant criticisms of Kant's system. He did show that some rules, when made universal, would become inconsistent and, therefore, could be said to be immoral because of their inconsistency. However, this does not tell us which rules are morally valid. Kant promulgated several Ten Commandment-like moral prohibitions based upon his moral system, such as "Do not kill," "Do not steal," "Do not break promises."

He argued, for example, that one should not break a promise because it would be inconsistent to state, "I promise that I will repay you in 30 days, but I don't intend to keep my promise." Also, Kant reasoned, you cannot universalize the rule "Never break promises except when it is inconvenient for you to keep them," because promises then would have no meaning—or at least we wouldn't know when they did or did not. Kant asked what meaning a contractual agreement would have if after having said, "I promise to do 1, 2, 3, and 4," clause 5 read, "But I can break this agreement any time at my convenience."

Suppose, however, that not breaking a promise would result in someone's being seriously injured or even killed. According to Kant, we have to keep the promise, and because consequences do not matter, an innocent person would simply have to be hurt or killed. But which is, in fact, more important: keeping a promise, or preventing an innocent person from being injured or killed? One of the problems here is that Kant never tells us how to choose between conflicting duties so as to obey different but equally absolute rules. We have a duty not to kill and a duty not to break promises, but which takes precedence when the two duties conflict?

Another criticism of universalizability and consistency, as criteria of morality, is that many rules of questionable moral value can be universalized without inconsistency. For example, is there anything inconsistent or nonuniversalizable about "Never help anyone in need"? If a society were made up of fairly self-sufficient individuals, there would be nothing immoral about not helping anyone. But even if there were people in need, what would establish the necessity of helping them? If 100 people in a group were self-sufficient and 15 were in need, would it be inconsistent or nonuniversal for the 100 to keep what they had and survive, allowing the other 15 to die? It might not be moral under some other kind of rules or principles, but it would not be inconsistent to state such a rule.

The Reversibility Criterion. Kant answered this type of criticism by introducing the criterion of *reversibility;* that is, if an action were reversed, would a person want it to be done to him? This is otherwise known as "the Golden Rule concept." For instance, Kant would ask of the rule "Never help anyone in need," what would you want done to or for you if you were in need? You would want to be helped; therefore such a rule, although universalizable, would not be morally universalizable, because it would not meet the reversibility (would-you-want-this-done-to-you) criterion. This criterion helps to eliminate further what seem to be immoral rules, but isn't it a rather cagey way of smuggling in consequences? Isn't Kant really saying that although "Never help anyone in need" is universalizable, it isn't morally acceptable because the *consequences* of such a rule might backfire on the person stating it? This of course is no problem for the consequentialist (the rule utilitarian who would be the closest to Kant's theory were it not for the fact that the utilitarian considers consequences important), but Kant has said that absolute moral rules, not consequences, are the basis of morality. Isn't it inconsistent of him—especially because he has made such an issue of consistency—to allow consequences to creep into his theory?

Qualifying a Rule versus Making Exceptions to It. Another criticism of the concept of absolute rules is that it leaves open to question whether a qualified rule is any less universalizable than one that is unqualified. Kant never distinguished between making an exception to a rule and qualifying that rule. For example, if the rule is stated, "Do not break promises, but I feel that *I* can break them any time *I* want to," I would be making an unfair exception of myself to the rule. Kant felt that one should not make an exception to a general rule, and certainly not for one's self alone. However, what if the rule is *qualified* so that it applies to everyone: "Do not break promises *except* when not breaking a promise would seriously harm or kill someone"? Here the exception applies to the rule itself rather than to some individual or individuals. Kant certainly had a strong point to make about not making exceptions; after all, what good is a rule if one can make an exception of one's self at any time one wants to? However, "Do not kill except in self-defense" is not any less universalizable than "Do not kill," and the former rule would seem to relate to the history of human values and also to a doctrine of fairness much better than the latter.

Duties versus Inclinations. There is still another criticism having to do with the inclination-duties conflict that Kant described, and that is, what happens when your inclinations and duties are the same? For example, what if you are *inclined* not to kill people, a tendency that fits well with Kant's rule "Do not kill," which it is your duty to obey. Does this mean that because you are not inclined to kill, you are not a moral person because your duty is not pulling you away from your inclinations? Many moralists disagree with the idea that people are not moral merely because they are inclined to be good rather than always struggling with themselves to be so. Kant did not believe that a person who acts morally from inclination is immoral, but he did believe that such a person is not moral in the truest sense of the word.

It is true that on many occasions the real test of personal morality comes when human beings must decide whether to fight against their inclinations (for example, to steal money when no one can catch them) and act out of a sense of duty (they should not steal because it is wrong or because they would not want someone else to steal from them). But is this any reason to consider people as being not fully moral if they lead a good life, do no harm to others because they do not want to, *and* also think it is their duty not to? Which type of person would you feel safer with, the person who is inclined not to harm or kill others, or the person who has a strong inclination to kill others but restrains himself merely out of a sense of duty? It would seem that society has a better chance of being moral if most people in it have become inclined to be moral through some sort of moral education. One other inconsistency in Kant's Duty Ethics is that he was strongly against killing and yet he was in favor of capital punishment.

Ross' Prima Facie *Duties*

Sir William David Ross (1877–1940) agreed with Kant that morality basically should not rest on consequences, but he disagreed with the unyielding absolutism of Kant's theories. One might place Ross somewhere in between Kant and the rule utilitarians, in that he believed that we have certain *prima facie* duties that we must always adhere to *unless* serious circumstances or reasons tell us to do otherwise. In such exceptional circumstances an individual's *actual* duty might be different from one's *prima facie* duty. In other words, he did not believe that consequences make an action right or wrong, but he did think that it is necessary to consider consequences when we are making our moral choices.

Prima Facie *Duties.* The term *prima facie* literally means "at first glance" or "on the surface of things." A *prima facie* duty, then, is one that all human beings must obey in a general way before any other considerations enter into the picture. Some of Ross' *Prima Facie Duties* are the duties of

1. Fidelity (or faithfulness): telling the truth, keeping actual and implied promises, and meeting contractual agreements.
2. Reparation: making up for the wrongs we have done to others—in other words, making reparation for wrongful acts.

3. Gratitude: recognizing what others have done for us and extending our gratitude to them.

4. Justice: preventing the improper distribution of good and bad that is not in keeping with what people merit or deserve.

5. Beneficence: helping to improve the condition of others in the areas of virtue, intelligence, and happiness.

6. Self-improvement: the obligation we have to improve our own virtue, intelligence, and happiness.

7. Nonmaleficence (noninjury): not injuring others and preventing injury to others.[4]

Thus, Ross, like Kant, thought that there are rules all human beings should adhere to because it is their moral obligation to do so. He also improved on Kant a great deal in the area of what to do when duties (especially *Prima Facie* Duties) conflict.

Principles to Resolve Conflicting Duties. Ross established two principles that we may call upon when attempting to deal with the conflict of *Prima Facie* Duties: (1) Always do that act in accord with the stronger *prima facie* duty; and (2) always do that act that has the greatest degree of *prima facie* rightness over *prima facie* wrongness.[5]

Criticisms of Ross' Theory

Clearly, there are some *"prima facie"* problems with Ross' theories.

Selecting **Prima Facie** *Duties.* How are we to decide which duties are indeed *prima facie?* Ross did list some of these duties for us, but on what basis did he do so, and what justification either in evidence or reasoning has he given us? When confronted with questions as to how we should select *prima facie* duties, Ross said that he was

claiming that we *know* them to be true. To me it seems as self-evident as anything could be, that to make a promise, for instance, is to create a moral claim on us in someone else. Many readers will perhaps say that they do *not* know this to be true. If so I certainly cannot prove it to them. I can only ask them to reflect again, in the hope that they will ultimately agree that they also know it to be true.[6]

What Ross actually is basing this selection of such duties on, then, is intuition; that is, there is no logic or evidence to justify his choices, but we are to accept what he says on the basis of intuition. If we do not have the same intuitions as he, then we are to keep trying until we do! This, of course, is both highly speculative and vague in its application with all of the attendant problems we encountered when discussing and evaluating the intuitive basis for act nonconsequentialism.

Deciding Which **Prima Facie** *Duty Takes Precedence.* A second problem arises when we look at the way in which Ross tries to resolve the decision-making difficulty of choosing the correct *prima facie* duty when it conflicts with another. Both of Ross' principles are difficult to apply. He does not really tell us how we are to determine when one obligation is stronger than the other. Further, he does not give us a clear rule for determining the "balance" of *prima facie* rightness over wrongness. Therefore, there seems to be no clear criteria either for choosing which duties are *prima facie* or for deciding how we are to distinguish among them after they have been established.

General Criticisms of Nonconsequentialist Theories

The criticism of nonconsequentialist theories in general is this: Can we, and indeed should we, really avoid consequences when we are trying to set up a moral system? In addition, rule nonconsequentialist theories raise the following problems.

1. Why should we follow rules if the consequences of following them could be bad even for a few, but also, in some cases, for all concerned?
2. How can we resolve conflicts among rules that are all equally and absolutely binding?
3. Is there such a thing as a moral rule with absolutely *no* exceptions, given the complexities of human behavior and experience? If so, what is it?

First, even Kant, who fought against consequences, seems to have smuggled them in by means of his reversibility doctrine. But even without this doctrine, when one pushes any ethical system back far enough, asking why one should do the things prescribed, won't one's answers have to bring in consequences for oneself, others, or all concerned? For example, in the Divine Command Theory, isn't it really possible to justify the more immediately applicable and practical commandments as being ethical necessities, whether or not one believes that a supernatural being gave them to human beings? One could ask why such a being is so wise in having stated that human beings should not kill, steal, or commit adultery, and answer that the consequences of not having some rules in those areas would be much worse. If killing were freely allowed, then people's lives would be in danger constantly, human growth would not be able to take place, and there would be no moral systems or cultures, only constant battles to avoid being killed. These commandments and others like them help all human beings to respect the rights of their fellows and bring some stability and order into a social system that otherwise would be in a constant state of chaotic upheaval.

Second, it is true that Kant starts without *officially* using consequences, by beginning with logical inconsistency, but are consequences really very far behind? What is the real point of any moral system if not to do good for oneself or others or both and if not to create a moral society in which people can create and grow peacefully with a minimum of unnecessary conflict? I cannot think of one system of morality that is not concerned with consequences somewhere along the line. Many systems may try to justify their imperatives by stating, "You should do this simply because it is right [or because some supernatural being said so, or because to do otherwise would be logically inconsistent]." But despite these justifications, the moral prescriptions of each system are calculated to bring about some good consequences, usually for most, if not all, human beings.

Fourth, Ross at least attempted to answer the question of whether there really are any absolute moral rules. And yet many people, especially in the twenty-first century, when so many of what were once considered absolutes have been shown to have exceptions, insist that there are either no absolutes or so few that one can hardly state them. Some moralists—moral relativists—state that everything is relative and that there are no absolutes. Others, such as Joseph Fletcher, state that there is but one absolute—love—and that everything else is relative to it. Regardless of whether their arguments are cogent (the problem of absolutes will be discussed more fully in Chapter 5), there is a serious problem with all nonconsequentialist theories in that the selection of moral rules and duties seems to be arbitrary and often destructive of creative argument. One cannot argue that killing may sometimes be justified if a nonconsequentialist has stated simply that in order to be moral one must not kill.

A good example of this type of dead-end reasoning is the antiabortionist argument that under no circumstances may a life be taken and that life begins at conception. How can one argue for the saving of the mother's life, or consider the kind of life either mother or baby will live if such absolutes already have been established? On the other side of the coin, how can one argue for the value of the life of a fetus if the prochoice advocate has taken as an absolute a woman's right over her own body, regardless of what that body contains? What justification can either arguer give for the validity of these absolutes and for why there can be no exceptions to them under any circumstances?

When people are arguing consequences, they may at least be able to show that one action will have more good consequences than another, but when they are merely presenting arbitrary absolutes, there can be no counterarguments made that will serve to justify exceptions. If we simply adopt an arbitrary, nonconsequentialist, absolute moral rule, then all arguments both from consequentialists and others are simply excluded. Closing off debate in this fashion is destructive to the search for truth and understanding in other areas, such as science, but it is disastrous in the sphere of morality, where the need to arrive at right answers is more crucial than in any other area of human experience.

Conclusions

In summary, then, the nonconsequentialist theories of morality have certain advantages. First, they do not necessitate the difficult task of computing consequences for a moral action. Second, they provide, in their rule form, a strong set of moral guides—unlike those of the act moralists of both the consequentialist and nonconsequentialist approaches to morality. Third, nonconsequentialists are able to found their system on something other than consequences, thereby avoiding the pitfall of a cost-benefit analysis approach to morality.

On the other hand, as difficult as computing consequences may be, nonconsequentialists really seem to avoid the whole point of morality—certainly social morality—by trying to ignore the consequences of their rules or acts. Although it is helpful to have a series of strong rules and guides to go by, rule nonconsequentialism makes it difficult to decide which rules these will be and how to rank them in order of importance or otherwise resolve conflicts when absolutes oppose each other. Furthermore, rule nonconsequential-ism provides for no open discussion of moral quandaries because it has closed the door by arbitrarily stating what is right and what is wrong, without any possibility of exception. And what is right and wrong is based either upon the supposed commands of a super-natural being or beings whom no one is allowed to question or upon a theory of logical consistency that can show that human beings should not be inconsistent but can give very few other reasons why one should follow one rule rather than another.

The nonconsequentialist theories do not seem any more satisfying than the con-sequentialist—to many people, probably even less so. What are we to do, then? Should we retreat to consequentialist theories with their attendant problems, or adopt the nonconsequentialist approach as being the "lesser of two evils"? I believe there is a value in trying to synthesize the best of these systems while deemphasizing the worst. We shall examine the possibilities of such a synthesis in Chapter 8. First, however, it is important that we tackle three problem areas that vitally affect the setting up of a moral system: absolutism versus relativism, freedom versus determinism, and reward and punishment.

Chapter Summary

I. Nonconsequentialist (deontological) theories of morality
   A. The basic assumption of these theories is that consequences do not, and in fact should not, enter into our judging of whether actions or people are moral or immoral.
   B. What is moral and immoral is decided upon the basis of some standard or standards of morality other than consequences.
II. Act nonconsequentialist theories
   A. The act nonconsequentialist's major assumption is that there are no general moral rules or theories, but only particular actions, situations, and people about which we cannot generalize.
   B. Decisions are based upon "intuitionism"; that is, what is right and wrong in any particular situation is based upon what people feel (intuit) is right or wrong—this is, therefore, a highly individualistic theory.
   C. There are several criticisms of act nonconsequentialism.
      1. How can we know, with no other guides, that what we feel will be morally correct?
      2. How will we know when we have acquired sufficient facts to make a moral decision?
      3. With morality so highly individualized, how can we know we are doing the best thing for everyone else involved in a particular situation?
      4. Can we really rely upon nothing more than our momentary feelings to help us make our moral decisions?
      5. How will we be able to justify our actions except by saying, "Well, it felt like the right thing for me to do"?
III. Rule nonconsequentialist theories
   A. The major assumption here is that there are or can be rules that are the only basis for moral-ity and that consequences do not matter—following the rules, which are right moral commands, is what is moral, not what happens because one follows the rules.

B. According to the Divine Command Theory, an action is right and people are good if, and only if, they obey commands supposedly given to them by a divine being, regardless of consequences. There are some criticisms of this theory.
   1. The theory does not provide a rational foundation for the existence of a supernatural being and therefore not for morality either.
   2. Even if we could prove conclusively the existence of a supernatural being, how could we prove that this being was morally trustworthy?
   3. How are we to interpret these commands even if we accept the existence of a supernatural?
   4. Rules founded upon the Divine Command Theory may be valid, but they need to be justified on some other, more rational basis.

IV. Kant's Duty Ethics
   A. Kant believed that it is possible by reasoning alone to set up valid absolute moral rules that have the same force as indisputable mathematical truths.
      1. Such truths must be logically consistent, not self-contradictory.
      2. They also must be universalizable.
   B. According to the Categorical Imperative, an act is immoral if the rule that would authorize it cannot be made into a rule for all human beings to follow.
   C. The Practical Imperative, another important principle in Kant's moral system, states that no human being should be thought of or used merely as a means for someone else's end, but rather that each human being is a unique end in himself or herself.
   D. Once moral rules have been discovered to be absolutes, human beings must obey them out of a sense of duty rather than follow their inclinations.
   E. There are criticisms of Kant's system.
      1. Although Kant showed that some rules would become inconsistent when universalized, this does not tell us which rules are morally valid.
      2. Kant never showed us how to resolve conflicts between equally absolute rules, such as "Do not break a promise" and "Do not kill."
      3. Kant did not distinguish between making an exception to a rule and qualifying a rule.
      4. Some rules, such as "Do not help anyone in need" can be universalized without inconsistency yet still have questionable moral value.
         (a) Kant answered this criticism by means of the reversibility criterion, that is, the would-you-want-this-done-to-you, or Golden Rule, idea.
         (b) However, the reversibility criterion suggests a reliance upon consequences, which goes against the grain of everything Kant set out to do in his system.
      5. Kant seems to have emphasized duties over inclinations, in stating that we must act from a sense of duty rather than from our inclinations. However, he gave us no rule for what we should do when our inclinations and duties are the same.

V. Ross' *Prima Facie* Duties
   A. Ross agreed with Kant as to the establishing of morality on a basis other than consequences but disagreed with Kant's overly absolute rules. He falls between Kant and rule utilitarianism in his approach to ethics.
   B. He established *Prima Facie* Duties that all human beings must adhere to, unless there are serious reasons why they should not.
   C. He listed several *Prima Facie* Duties, those of
      1. Fidelity
      2. Reparation
      3. Gratitude

4. Justice
5. Beneficence
6. Self-improvement
7. Nonmaleficence (noninjury)

D. He offered two principles for use in the resolution of conflicting duties.
   1. Always act in accord with the stronger *prima facie* duty.
   2. Always act in such a way as to achieve the greatest amount of *prima facie* rightness over wrongness.

E. There are criticisms of Ross' theory.
   1. How are we to decide which duties are *prima facie*?
   2. On what basis are we to decide which take precedence over the rest?
   3. How can we determine when there is sufficient reason to override one *prima facie* duty with another?

VI. General criticisms of nonconsequentialist theories

A. Can we, and indeed should we, avoid consequences when we are trying to set up a moral system?

B. Is it entirely possible to exclude consequences from an ethical system?

C. What is the real point of any moral system if not to do good for oneself, others, or both and if not to create a moral society in which people can create and grow peacefully with a minimum of unnecessary conflict?

D. How do we resolve conflicts among moral rules that are equally absolute? This problem is peculiar to rule nonconsequentialist theories.

E. Any system that operates on a basis of such rigid absolutes as does rule nonconsequentialism closes the door on further discussion of moral quandaries.

Exercises for Review

1. What, essentially, are nonconsequentialist (deontological) theories of morality? How do they differ from consequentialist (teleological) theories?
2. What do act nonconsequentialists believe? How do they differ from act utilitarians?
3. What do rule nonconsequentialists believe? How do they differ from rule utilitarians?
4. Describe and critically analyze the Divine Command Theory.
5. Explain and critically analyze Kant's Duty Ethics, responding as you do so to the following questions:
  (a) What are absolute moral truths, according to Kant, and how can they be arrived at?
  (b) Explain the difference between duties and inclinations. Why did Kant believe that people ought to act out of a sense of duty rather than from inclination?
  (c) Explain the Categorical Imperative.
  (d) What does *universalizability* mean, and why is it important to Kant's moral system?
  (e) What is the reversibility criterion? What are the problems associated with it?
6. Explain Kant's Practical Imperative. Do you agree or disagree with this principle? Why?
7. What are *Prima Facie* Duties? What problems do they raise? Can you think of any moral duties that might be *prima facie*? What are they?
8. In your opinion, can a moral system really function without taking account of consequences? How or how not?

9. Explain the problems that are peculiar to rule nonconsequentialist theories of morality.
10. Comment on the problem of arbitrariness when dealing with moral problems as it relates to creative argument and moral problem solving.
11. What are the problems associated with discovering who the ideal virtuous person is?

Discussion Questions

1. The act nonconsequentialist theory allows one greater freedom in making moral decisions than do other theories because it leaves moral decisions completely up to each individual's own feelings. How free do you think individuals should be in their moral decision making? To what extent does this theory appeal or not appeal to you, and why?
2. The rule nonconsequentialist theories essentially state that there are certain moral absolutes that should never be violated (for example, rules against killing, mutilating, stealing, and breaking promises). To what extent do you agree or disagree with this idea? Are there certain do's and don'ts to which human beings should always adhere? If so, why should they be adhered to and what are they? If not, why not?
3. One of the advantages of rule nonconsequentialist theories is that they clearly state do's and don'ts, thereby lending a great deal of stability and order to morality. Adherents describe the benefits of this when they say, "We know just where we stand with this type of morality, and it gives us a great deal of security when compared to relativistic morality." To what extent do you feel that this advantage is an important one? Why? What are its strong points and its drawbacks?
4. To what extent do you believe that Christians, Jews, and Muslims use the Divine Command Theory approach rather than egoism or act or rule utilitarianism as a basis for their ethical systems? For example, do you believe that most Christians follow their religion's moral rules because they believe that those rules were established by a supernatural being or for other reasons? Answer in detail.
5. To what extent do you believe that a consideration of consequences can safely be eliminated from any moral system?
6. Reread discussion question 2 in Chapter 2. To what extent do you feel that the surgeon is justified in using the battalion commander as a means toward what he deems to be a "good" end, that is, saving soldiers' lives? To what extent is the other surgeon justified in his nonconsequentialist rule that doctors should never knowingly perform unnecessary operations?
7. To what extent do you think it is important to rank moral rules in order of importance (for example, Ross' *Prima Facie* Duties)? Show how you would rank your own ethical rules, or those of any other system of which you are aware.
8. To what extent are emotions or feelings important to a moral system? Be specific, and explain how you think emotions or feelings relate to morality.
9. How much importance do you think duty ought to have in relation to morality? Explain your answer.
10. Rule nonconsequentialist theories stress consistency in their moral systems and codes, whereas the act nonconsequentialist theory seems to imply variety and inconsistency. How important do you think it is for a moral system or code, or for a person, to be consistent?

Notes

1. Austin Fagothey, *Right and Reason,* 8th ed., rev. Milton A. Gonsalves (St. Louis: C. V. Mosby, 1985), 114–15.
2. Kant's actual formulation may be found in *Problems of Moral Philosophy,* 2nd ed., ed. Paul W. Taylor (Belmont, CA: Dickenson, 1972), 219. The version given here is a paraphrase.
3. Immanuel Kant, *Fundamental Principles of the Metaphysics of Morals,* trans. H. J. Paton (New York: Harper & Row, 1957), Sections I, II, and III.
4. William D. Ross, *The Right and the Good* (New York: Oxford University Press, 1930), 21–22.
5. Ibid., 41–42.
6. Ibid., 24.

Research Navigator™
(http://www.researchnavigator.com)

This web site offers three research databases: EBSCO's *Content Select Academic Journal and Abstract Database, New York Times* Search by Subject Archive, and *Best of the Web* Link Library. In addition, this site provides helpful advice on how to conduct efficient and productive research from choosing a topic to polishing the final draft. Beginning philosophy students probably will find the *Best of the Web* Link Library the most appropriate place to start their research.

The free access code necessary to employ Research Navigator™ can be found in the Prentice Hall Guide to Evaluating Online Resources. If your text did not come with this guide, please go to *www.prenhall.com/contentselect* for information on how you can purchase an access code.

Chapter

4

Virtue Ethics

Objectives

After you have read this chapter, you should be able to

1. Describe Virtue Ethics theories showing how they differ from consequentialist or nonconsequentialist ethical theories

2. Define and analyze such important terms and concepts as *virtue, the virtues, vice*, and *vices.*

3. Describe Aristotle's *Nichomachean Ethics* and how the virtues are central to living a good life.

4. Describe the ethics of Confucius in the *Analects* and explain the virtues in light of the Confucian notion of self-cultivation.

5. Explain the advantages and disadvantages of virtue ethics in the context of an overall theory of ethics.

Another moral theory that has become significant to many contemporary ethicists is known as "Virtue Ethics." It certainly is not a new theory, for it is typically associated with the Greeks and especially with Aristotle in the fourth century B.C. although its origins in Chinese philosophy are even more ancient. Essentially, this theory differs from all of the previous ones we have discussed in that it focuses not upon consequences, intuitions, or rules, so much as the development within human beings of a moral or virtuous character by means of doing what a good or "virtuous" person would do.

Definition of Terms

The dictionary defines *virtue* as "the quality of moral excellence, righteousness, and responsibility . . . a specific type of moral excellence or other exemplary quality considered meritorious; a worthy practice or ideal."[1] It further lists the "cardinal" or "natural" virtues as "justice, prudence, fortitude, and temperance."[2]

A dictionary of philosophy describes the term *virtue* as it is employed in Aristotle's philosophy as being "that state of a thing which constitutes its peculiar excellence and enables it to perform its function well . . . in man [it is] the activity of reason and of rationally ordered habits."[3]

As you can see, the emphasis is on the good or virtuous character of human beings themselves, rather than on their acts or the consequences of their acts, or feelings, or rules. In other words it is the development of the good or virtuous person that is important in this moral theory, not abstract rules or consequences of acts or rules except as they derive from a good or virtuous person or cause that person to be good or virtuous.

Aristotle's Nichomachean Ethics

Virtue Ethics derives from Aristotle's *Nichomachean Ethics* (named for his son, Nichomachus). Such ethics are teleological in character (that is, aim toward some end or purpose). As Aristotle put it: "Every art and every inquiry, every action and choice, seems to aim at some good . . . [and] the good has rightly been defined as that at which all things aim."[4] For example, a doctor's art aims at health, seamanship aims at a safe voyage, and economy aims at wealth. He goes on to say that the end of human life is happiness, and the basic activity of human beings is reason—a virtuous activity; therefore, the aim of human beings, according to Aristotle, is to reason well for a whole or complete life.

Emphasis on Goodness of Character

Aristotle is concerned with action, not as being right or good in itself, but as it is conducive to human good. In ethics he starts from the actual moral judgments of human beings, and says that by comparing, contrasting, and sifting them, we come to the formulation of general principles. Notice how this differs from the Divine Command Theory and the theories of Kant and Ross, as to the way in which principles are established. In the latter three theories, ethical principles are objective to, or outside of, human beings and are established by the supernatural or by abstract reason itself. Aristotle presupposes that there are natural ethical tendencies implanted in human beings, and that to follow them with a general attitude of consistent harmony and proportion constitutes an ethical life.

Development of the Good or Virtuous Human Being

Aristotle describes his ethical system as being eminently common-sense-based, for the most part, founded as it is on the moral judgments of the ideal human being, who based upon reason, is considered good and virtuous. He states that humans begin with a capacity for goodness, which has to be developed by practice. He says we start by doing acts that are objectively virtuous, without a knowledge that the acts are good and without actively or rationally choosing them ourselves. As we practice these acts, we come to realize that the virtue is good in and of itself. For example, a child is taught to tell the truth (objectively a virtue) by her parents, and she does so because they have taught her she should. Eventually she recognizes that truth telling is a virtue in and of itself, and she continues to tell the truth because she knows that it is virtuous to do so.

This process would seem to be circular, except that Aristotle makes a distinction between those acts that create a good disposition (such as telling the truth without knowing this to be a virtue) and those that flow from the good disposition once it has been created (such as telling the truth because a person has come to know it to be a virtue). Aristotle further states that virtue itself is a disposition that has been developed out of a capacity by the proper exercise of that capacity.

What Is Virtue and How Does It Relate to Vice?

According to Aristotle, virtue is a mean between two extremes, both of which are vices—either excess or deficiency (or defect). Moral virtue, then, is defined by Aristotle as being "a disposition to choose by a rule . . . which a practically wise man would determine" to be the mean between the two extremes of excess or deficiency.[5] And, according to Aristotle, practical wisdom is the ability to see what is the right thing to do in any circumstance. Therefore, a person must determine what a "practically wise, virtuous man" would choose in any circumstance calling for moral choice, and then do the right thing. Obviously, Aristotle attaches much more importance to an enlightened conscience than to prior theoretical rules (again differing from the Divine Command theorist, Kant, or Ross).

How to Determine the Proper Mean

What is the mean between excess and deficiency, and how does one determine it? According to Aristotle, the mean in ethics cannot be determined mathematically. Rather it is a mean "relative to us" or to whoever is trying to determine the right thing to do. For example, if ten pounds of food are too much (excess) and two are too little (deficiency or defect), then six pounds, which is the mean between these two extremes, still may be too much for some and too little for others; therefore, one must choose the appropriate mean between the two extremes, relative to himself or herself.[6]

Some examples of means between two extremes, established by Aristotle and tabulated by Sir William David Ross (who established the ethical theory of *Prima Facie* Duties), are in the following table. This partial list will give you some idea of what Aristotle means by the mean between two extremes, but it doesn't really show what the mean "relative to us" would actually be. It does, however, provide us with some general guidelines that we can refer to as we attempt to determine the mean "relative to us."

Feeling or Action	Excess	Mean	Defect
Confidence	Rashness	Courage	Cowardice
Sensual Pleasure	Profligacy	Temperance	Insensibility
Shame	Bashfulness	Modesty	Shamelessness
Giving Amusement	Buffoonery	Wittiness	Boorishness
Truth Telling About Oneself	Boastfulness	Truthfulness	Self-depreciation
Friendship	Obsequiousness	Friendship	Sulkiness[7]

Confucian Moral Self-Cultivation

At the heart of Chinese theories of moral self-cultivation is the concept of virtue. The Chinese term *de*, "virtue," can be traced back to the Shang dynasty in the twelfth century B.C. where it was understood to be "a kind of power that accrued to or resided within an individual that acted favorably toward a spirit or another person."[8] In later etymologies the term *de*, "virtue," meant to "have a hold upon" someone, but this power over others was such that it could not be used to manipulate others in order to satisfy one's own self-interest.[9] *De* is the inherent power or tendency to affect others and is hence most commonly translated as either "virtue" or "power."

But it was believed that *de* could be cultivated and developed in ways that would lead to a self-transformation necessary to live an ethically fulfilled life. The lives of such transformed individuals would in turn have a positive, dramatic and powerful affect upon others. The term thus carries the sense of self-realization in that it signifies all that a person can do or be as a member of a community. As such the term "excellence" might be a better translation of *de*. It connotes an individual excelling at becoming all that one can be in the sense of doing the best with what one has. That which each person has inherently is *de*, but the excellence is to develop it fully in the context of one's life and society.

From the time of the Zhou dynasty in approximately the eleventh century B.C. virtue was intimately connected with statecraft. The ancient sage kings governed through ritual propriety and customs (*li*) and not by law and force, for good rulers displayed heart-felt reverence for their past and were concerned to look after the material and spiritual well-being of the people and to maintain harmony between heaven and earth. Proper cultivation of royal virtue or *de* was necessary to accomplish this in the proper way because it allowed the ruler to gain the endorsement of heaven, attract and retain good and capable ministers, and ensure the respect and loyalty of subjects.

Kongzi or "Confucius" (551–479 B.C.) said: "Governing with excellence (*de*) can be compared to being the North Star: The North Star dwells in its place, and the multitude of stars pay it tribute."[10] It was by way of the proper cultivation of *de* that an excellent leader was enabled to exert such a powerful and sweeping effect on society. It was Confucius and his followers who worked out the foundations for a comprehensive program of moral self cultivation.

The Confucian Analects

No thinker has influenced the ethics of Asia more than Confucius. He is China's greatest teacher and his lessons are profoundly humanistic, emphasizing the responsibilities people have to each other for the purpose of producing and maintaining a just and orderly society. Confucius lived during a time of political upheaval and chaos known as the Warring States Period and his moral insights prevailed and became the basis for China's long stability as both a civilization and a nation.

For Confucius, human beings are fundamentally social in nature. One is born into a family and is a member of a community and a nation that was regarded as an extended or "big" family. In other words, one's identity is at all times tied to the group and one's relationships within the social order. As a relational self the individual occupies certain social roles that carry corresponding responsibilities. In a Chinese world the fundamental unit is the family while the state is, in effect, the family WRIT LARGE. Enmeshed in, and a part of, this social structure one is expected to exercise mutual consideration in all human relationships. In Confucianism there are five cardinal relationships, chiefly patriarchal and hierarchical in nature that specify duties and privileges. It is within the structure of these relationships that the virtues and attitudes that would enhance daily life were carried out.

The Five Confucian Cardinal Relationships

- Ruler and subject
- Father and son
- Husband and wife
- Elder brother and younger brother
- Friend and friend

We discussed the relationship between ruler and subject earlier in our presentation of royal virtue (*de*) and ritual propriety and customs (*li*). In the *Analects* Confucius puts it this way:

> Lead the people with administrative injunctions (*zheng*) and keep them orderly with penal law (*xing*), and they will avoid punishments but will be without a sense of shame. Lead them with excellence (*de*) and keep them orderly through observing ritual propriety (*li*) and they will develop a sense of shame, and moreover, will order themselves.[11]

Confucius sees a clear difference between doing the right thing and being a good person.

All the Confucian relationships are governed by the practice of *shu*, "reciprocity." The father is to care for the son, give protection, and provide education. In return the son is to practice filial piety, accept instruction, guidance, and direction from the father and care for him in old age. In addition, the eldest son was to conduct the burial ceremony according to customary procedures and to honor ancestors.

As husband, the man is to head the household and take care of family duties and provide for his wife and family. Moreover, he was to be honorable and faithful. The wife's position is subordinate to her husband. She is to look after the home and be obedient to her husband. There is an old saying in China: "The husband sings and the wife harmonizes." Additionally, the wife is expected to meet the needs of her husband and care for children. The elder brother is to set an example of good behavior and cultivate refinement for the younger children. The younger brother in turn shows respect to the elder brother because of his experience and character.

Friendship is a reciprocal relationship of respect among equals. It is the only cardinal relationship that is not hierarchical. The nature of the Confucian relationships tells us that while we must show respect equally to all, not everyone is equal. There is a place for legitimate authority and it is proper to show deference to that position of authority. Over time the relationships and their corresponding roles and responsibilities change—the elder son becomes a husband and father and children become parents. In the Confucian relationships each person understands his or her place in relation to others and virtue only makes sense within interpersonal relationships. The Confucian virtues thus are decidedly social in nature.

Confucian Harmony

A study of Chinese thought suggests that its aim is to achieve a grand harmony. In light of this notion of harmony we will discuss the two chief Confucian virtues, namely, *ren*, translated variously as "human-heartedness," "benevolence," "goodness," or "humaneness" and *li*, "rites," "ritual propriety," or "appropriateness."

Ren etymologically referred to "members of a clan" as opposed to those outside of the clan or aliens. Within the clan it referred to the forbearance toward other members that was not extended to those outside the clan. Their behavior was humane and eventually became a general term for human being, thus, distinguishing the "human" from the "animal" and suggesting conduct worthy and befitting of a human as distinct from brutes. It is characterized by the Confucian Silver Rule: "Not to do to others as you would not wish done to yourself."

Ren is the chief Confucian virtue and highlights and enhances the natural relationship between the individual and the community. In fact, the term *ren* is actually composed of two Chinese characters: The first represents the individual person and the second is the character for the number two. Hence, the ideogram for *ren* is "one-being-with-others."[12] The Chinese self is a relational-self. One is an "individual" only in relation to others and those relationships constitute one's identity. Confucian scholar Roger Ames puts it this way:

> The community is a project of disclosure. This inseparability of personal integrity and social integration collapses the means/end distinction, rendering each person both an end in himself or herself and a condition or means for everyone else in the community to be what they are. The model is one of mutuality.[13]

Ren attempts to harmonize individual interests with the good of the community. However, in all cases primacy is extended to the common good. This last point leads logically to a consideration of *li*.

Li, "ritual propriety," is the Confucian virtue that must be cultivated if one is to be a full participant in the community, which by way of *li* is itself ritually constituted. *Li* refers to all meaning-invested roles and life forms within the community that are transmitted by way of custom and tradition from generation to generation. If the cultivation of the virtue *ren* results in the proper dispositional attitude that, as a human being, one brings to human relationships, then *li* makes it possible for the individual to exhibit appropriate conduct in any specific situation from conducting oneself in the presence of a ruler, to dress, table manners and etiquette, patterns of greeting, to graduations, weddings, funerals and ancestor worship. "*Li* is the concretized expression of humanness."[14] *Li* is the personal appropriation of the tradition and hence of the community in a way that is not merely formal and perfunctory but also authentic heartfelt and personal. *Li* brings social stability to a society and allows it to run well without excessive imposition of laws and threats of punishment.

Confucius' disciple Mengzi or "Mencius" (391–308 B.C.) presented an idealized Confucianism and argued that human beings are innately good. That is, people have a natural disposition toward goodness. As such moral self-cultivation involves the development and bringing forth of one's true nature. Like "sprouts" virtue needs to be tended and cultivated into full bloom. However, an equally great figure in the Confucian tradition, Xunzi (310–219 B.C.), offered what he considered a realistic rendering of Confucian thought. Master Xun taught that human nature is evil. Human nature is evil because people are not, as Mengzi taught, naturally disposed to goodness but are inclined to self-interest. Since goods are limited and people desire the same things there will be conflict and evil. Thus, virtuous conduct that leads to a stable and good society involves disciplined cultivation. In contrast to Mencius who describes moral self-cultivation utilizing the agricultural metaphor of tending sprouts, Xunzi describes moral cultivation in terms of the metaphorically severe processes of straightening crooked wood and sharpening metal on a grindstone. That is to say, becoming virtuous is nonnatural, but strictly conventional.

In any case, all Confucians agree that the virtues are developed through moral self-cultivation until they become habits and attitudes of character. This process is a process of not only becoming a good person but also, in fact, of becoming fully human. This moral ideal is embodied in the person of the *junzi*, "superior person," or "cultivated individual" (similar in some respects to Aristotle's "practically wise, virtuous man"). In Confucian thought moral self-cultivation is always an exercise in, and refinement of, social virtuosity.

Contemporary Analysis of Virtue Ethics

Contemporary theories of Virtue Ethics are primarily a reaction against moral theories that attempt to fit our moral experience into an *established* system of rules or preestablished ideals.

That is to say, contemporary theories of virtue ethics stand in opposition to the moral theories that have come to dominate the modern world, specifically consequentialism and Kantianism. Suggestions have been made that modern moral philosophy is bankrupt, misguided, overformalized, and incomplete. Proponents of virtue ethics hold that a consideration of character provides a more adequate and comprehensive understanding of moral experience because it more adequately captures the issues and concerns of ordinary life. There is a wide variety of contemporary theories of virtue ethics and although most draw heavily from the ideas of Aristotle, these theories are chiefly concerned with overcoming the perceived weaknesses of modern moral theory based largely on rules. There has been increased interest in, and a revival of, Confucian views of ethics too.

Alasdair MacIntyre's Analysis of Virtue Ethics

Probably the most significant and prominent contemporary analysis of Virtue Ethics, especially Aristotle's version of it, may be found in Alasdair MacIntyre's book *After Virtue.* In analyzing Aristotle's intentions, MacIntyre states that virtues are dispositions not only to act in particular ways but also to *feel* in particular ways, which obviously emphasizes the creation of a virtuous character in oneself, not merely the following of rules or the calculation of good consequences. One must create virtuous feelings or inclinations within oneself, not merely act virtuously. MacIntyre stated further that to act virtuously is not to act against inclination (as Kant thought), but rather to act from inclinations that have been formed through the cultivation of the virtues.[15] The idea, then, is to decide what the practically wise and virtuous human being would do in any situation involving moral choice, and then do likewise. As MacIntyre says, human beings must know what they are doing when they judge or act virtuously, and then they should do what is virtuous merely because it *is* so.[16]

Advantages of Virtue Ethics

Creating the Good Human Being. Virtue Ethics attempts to create the good or virtuous human being, not just good acts or rules and not just a robot who follows preestablished rules or a person who acts on whim or tries to achieve good consequences. It seeks to inculcate virtue by urging human beings to practice virtuous acts in order to create the habitually virtuous or good person who will then continue to act virtuously. Many ethicists see this as constituting one of our major problems today: We have rules and laws and systems of ethics, but we still do not have ethical or virtuous human beings. These ethicists believe that until we create ethical or virtuous people, our chances of creating a moral society will remain minimal. After all, they say, we have had rules, laws, and regulations for at least several millennia and have even more nowadays, but still badness, immorality, viciousness, cruelty, and vice seem to be getting worse rather than better. It is generally agreed that virtues are beneficial to individuals and the community.

An example of this debate may be drawn from the passing of laws against racial discrimination. When President Harry Truman proposed the racial integration of the

U.S. military, some argued that "you cannot legislate morality"; that is, you may pass laws that force people to behave in certain ways or to act differently than they want to or have done in the past, but laws cannot change the way people feel inside. Until you change their feelings, they said, you will never really change people's morals. This idea has its point; however, many people's moral views *did* change when racial integration became the law of the land. Many others' views, of course, still haven't changed, and critics of this view ask: "Isn't it too idealistic to think you can change people's morality to the point where everyone becomes a virtuous person?" Also, they add that rules and laws often do help to create virtuous people, or at least force them to act virtuously, and perhaps that's the best we can do.

Unifying Reason and Emotion. Both act nonconsequentialism and Kant's theories attempt to separate reason from emotion or feelings. Virtue Ethics, on the other hand, attempts to unify them by stating that virtues are dispositions not only to *act* in certain ways but also to *feel* in certain ways—virtuously in both cases. The purpose again is to use reasoning (practical wisdom) to cause people to do what is virtuous, while at the same time inculcating that virtuousness *within* so that humans not only reason virtuously but also begin and continue to feel virtuous. None of the other theories attempt to do this.

Kant eschews acting on inclination almost to the point of absurdity so that the critical question to be propounded against his theory is, "What if people *are inclined* to be virtuous? Shouldn't they *act* upon those inclinations?" Kant seems to say that such people wouldn't be as moral as they would have been if they had acted virtuously against their bad inclinations. On the other hand, the act nonconsequentialist says that we should act only on a basis of emotion—that is, what feels right or virtuous at any particular moment or in any particular situation. Aristotle, like Kant, would be aghast at such a theory of morality because he believed that human beings' major activity was to reason well so as to achieve a complete life; however, he tried much more than Kant did to integrate emotion or feelings with reason, without excluding the former.

Emphasizes Moderation. Virtue Ethics, at least Aristotle's version of it, gives us a way to achieve moderation between excess and deficiency. Many ethicists believe, along with the Greeks, that "moderation in all things" is what human beings ought to strive for. As you will discover in Chapters 9 through 16, I often present the moderate point of view, and Humanitarian Ethics often goes along with that view. Aristotle attempts to set up means to achieve moderation by codifying what constitutes excess, defect, and the mean between them, as described in Ross' table shown earlier. He also encourages freedom by allowing individuals to decide upon the appropriate mean relative to themselves. Again he seems to encourage an integration between feeling and reason by urging individuals to use both their reason and their feelings to decide upon the appropriate mean for them. For Confucius the virtues contribute both to harmony between reason and feelings and harmony between the individual and society.

Disadvantages or Problems

Do Human Beings Have an End? One of Aristotle's first assumptions is that all things have a purpose or end at which they aim. He then goes on to say that the end of human life is happiness, and that all human beings aim at that. First, is it true or proven that all things have an end or purpose? Many people argue that they do, but many also argue that it is not clear that they do. For example, some argue that the world and everything in it has occurred by chance or randomly, and that it is not at all clear that anything in such a universe aims toward any end except its own death or dissolution. Even if we assume that everything has an end toward which it aims, what proves that the end of human life is happiness? Couldn't it just as well be knowledge, spirituality, death, suffering, or other things? Aristotle's assumption is just that—an assumption. Many would also argue that happiness is not an appropriate end for human life but that something more "noble" is appropriate, such as love of God and the hope of being with Him. Furthermore, some argue that "to reason well for a complete life" might be a philosopher's view of what the human aim is, but why couldn't it be other things as well? Again, Aristotle has made another assumption, but religionists might argue that being spiritual is the human aim, and other philosophers might argue that feelings or emotions are the aim. Many contemporary proponents of Virtue Ethics do not agree with Aristotle that the ultimate aim is happiness, but something else, for example, responding well to the "demands of the world" as a matter of disposition. It is appropriate to question Aristotle's assumption about the ultimate end for human beings, but the challenges to Aristotle's view do not present a fatal flaw for Virtue Ethics.

Are Morals Naturally Implanted? A second major assumption by Aristotle is that the tendency to be moral is naturally implanted in human beings. What evidence is there to support that claim? Many would argue that morality is not some innate characteristic or idea, but rather something that is taught and learned from experience. The only tendency humans have is to be able to reason, and reason in and of itself does not necessarily imply morality, although it is thought by many, Aristotle included, to be its basis. Is it really true, however, that human beings have a natural, innate tendency to be moral? Some argue in the affirmative and some argue the opposite, but there is no clear evidence or proof that Aristotle's assumption is true. The Confucian scholar Xunzi, as we saw earlier, made the opposite assumption as the basis of his account of virtue and moral self-cultivation.

What Is Virtue and What Constitutes the Virtues? One of the most significant problems with this theory, however, centers around the following questions: What is virtue, what are the virtues, and what is the ideal, or who is the virtuous human being we are supposed to emulate when choosing our virtues? Some, including Aristotle, argue that all we need to know and provide is an account of what human flourishing and well-being consist of; then the virtues can be adequately characterized as those qualities needed to promote such flourishing and well-being. According to MacIntyre, however, there have been, and still are, deep conflicts as to what is involved in human flourishing and well-being.[17]

He goes on to say that different periods in history and historical figures from those periods present us with several sets of virtues:

1. In ancient Homeric Greece, a man was what he did; that is, a man and his actions were considered to be identical. Morality and social structure were one in heroic societies; the ideal virtuous man was the warrior, and the virtues were strength and courage.

2. For Aristotle, Aquinas, and the New Testament, virtue is a quality that enables one to move toward the achievement of a specifically human end (natural or supernatural). For Aristotle, this was rationality and the ideal virtuous man was the Athenian gentleman. For Aquinas and the New Testament, the virtues are faith, hope, charity (or love), and humility, and the ideal virtuous man is the saint.

3. For Benjamin Franklin, virtue is a quality that has utility in achieving earthly and heavenly success. His concept of virtue was teleological, like Aristotle's, but utilitarian in character. To Franklin the virtues were cleanliness, silence, industry, and chastity, among many.[18]

Who Is the Ideal Virtuous Person?

Finally, because Aristotle states that we ought to decide what a virtuous act or person is by modeling ourselves after the ideal virtuous person, how do we determine who and what that person is? I'm sure we could each name an ideal person we feel we ought to emulate, but wouldn't we come up with a lot of different ones, depending upon our own backgrounds, experiences, and desires? For example, the Homeric ideal of a virtuous human being would appeal to some people, as would the humble saint to others, or the person of intellect to still others, but wouldn't we all act differently depending upon what traits we admired? I'm not saying we couldn't agree upon some sort of composite virtuous person, but I do argue that it wouldn't be easy. How would we be able to say that we ought to act in connection with such an ideal when it would be just that: an abstract ideal of a human being? Also, how would we know that we had come up with the truly virtuous ideal person?

Certainly one of the goals of the teaching of ethics would seem to be the creation of a virtuous or ethical person; however, it is one thing to try to get people to act ethically and another to assume that they will do ethical acts because they are already virtuous. It hasn't worked successfully to hold up certain public figures and say, "Here is the ideal virtuous person; now act as he or she does." History has shown that many of our so-called heroes have had feet of clay, or at least not always acted virtuously. Look at the number of corrupt "scholar–officials" who have characterized much of China's long history. These men received extensive training in the Confucian classics as a requirement for public service. Look at how many of our nation's famous founders owned slaves, for instance. Look at how many presidents have not been perfect in their private and their public lives. Many of them have still done some good for the country and the people in it, but they have not necessarily fit any pattern of the "ideal virtuous person."

Some contemporary theorists of Virtue Ethics, such as Christine Swanton, argue that the requirements for virtue are not set by one standard, for example, that attainable by Aristotle's "practically wise, virtuous man" or Confucian *junzi*. Standards for virtuous conduct, she holds, should reflect the human condition marred by assorted troubles and the difficulty of attaining (full) virtue. Her view is that virtue is a concept that must always be understood and applied contextually. "A *virtue*," Swanton says, "is a good quality of character, more specifically a disposition to respond to, or acknowledge, items within its field or fields in an excellent or good enough way."[19] Now the notion of a "good enough way" is vague and thus problematic. For Swanton it means that one's response must appropriately meet the demands of the world in a particular situation in which virtue applies. In Aristotelian terms one might say that between the extremes of excess and deficiency there is a range of possible responses that may be considered virtuous relative to a particular situation.

Virtue Ethics helps us see that an overall theory of ethics must provide an understanding of moral character. Clearly, modern moral philosophy has failed to do this and thus is incomplete. But, theories of Virtue Ethics are also incomplete in the opposite way because they do not tell us what we should *do* in specific situations. That is, virtues do not provide specific directives for right conduct. Furthermore, theories of Virtue Ethics do not help us analyze moral issues or to effectually engage in moral reasoning. This last point is especially important because the world in which we live is becoming increasingly nontraditional. Moreover, the world is driven by high-speed technological and social change that creates issues of increasing novelty and complexity. The ability to reason well about complicated ethical issues and to think through global moral problems and multicultural contexts should be a primary concern of moral education. What we need is rational moral education (not indoctrination into a specific ethical code) that will enable people to learn what moral issues are and how to deal with them. With such an education, hopefully they will at least know *how* to act virtuously and ethically. To provide such an education is the main purpose of this book and especially of Chapter 8.

Vice and Virtue

Vices such as cowardice, jealousy, envy, greed, gluttony, and spite are examples of undesirable character traits. These traits become imbedded in an individual's life through the indulgence of degrading appetites, lack of self-discipline and education, and the habitual practice of immoral conduct. Because of vice the possessor is rendered base and ignoble. Such a person is ruled, not by reason, but by impulse. The vicious person is discontent and anxiety ridden and lives a life tormented by inner tension and chaos. This stormy inner life manifests itself in conduct that is corrupt, ignoble, and immoral. Some hold the life of the vicious person is defective.

In contrast, virtues are "human excellences." They consist of those traits of character that should be fostered in human beings, such as honesty, loyalty, courage, wisdom, moderation, civility, compassion, tolerance, and reverence. This is only a partial list. The life of the virtuous person is characterized by inner strength, contentment, happiness, and purpose.

St. Augustine's Vices

St. Augustine is one of the great Christian philosophers in the Western tradition. In "The Depths of Vice," St. Augustine looks at the anatomy of evil. In his discussion he lists a number of vices and describes the various manifestations of these vices:

> pride imitates loftiness of mind . . .
>
> what does ambition seek, except honor and glory . . .
>
> the cruelty of the mighty desires to be feared . . .
>
> the caresses of the wanton call for love . . .
>
> curiosity pretends to be a desire for knowledge . . .
>
> ignorance itself and folly are cloaked over the names of simplicity and innocence . . .
>
> sloth . . . seeks rest . . .
>
> luxury of life desires to be called plenty and abundance . . .
>
> prodigality casts but the shadow of liberality
>
> avarice desires to possess many things
>
> envy contends for excellence . . .
>
> anger seeks vengeance . . .
>
> fear shrinks back at sudden and unusual things threatening what it loves . . .
>
> sadness wastes away over things now lost in which desire once took delight . . .
>
> (and), the soul commits fornication then it is turned away from you (God).[20]

Franklin's Thirteen Virtues

Perhaps no American made the most of what he had than Benjamin Franklin (1706–1790). A true "universal man"—philosopher, scientist, political sage, printer, business and civic leader, musician, and inventor—Franklin desired to achieve moral excellence. In order to fulfill his purpose he chose, from among the many enumerations of the virtues that he had encountered in his personal reading and study, thirteen virtues. To each he annexed a short precept that he felt fully expressed the extent he assigned to its meaning. The names of Franklin's virtues and their precepts are

1. TEMPERANCE

   Eat not to dullness; drink not to elevation.

2. SILENCE

   Speak not but what may benefit others or yourself:

3. ORDER

   Let all your things have their places; let each part of your business have its time.

4. RESOLUTION

Resolve to perform what you ought; perform without fail what you resolve.

5. FRUGALITY

Make no expense but to do good to others or yourself; that is, waste nothing.

6. INDUSTRY

Lose no time; be always employed in something useful; cut off all unnecessary actions.

7. SINCERITY

Use no hurtful deceit; think innocently and justly and, if you speak, speak accordingly.

8. JUSTICE

Wrong none by doing injuries, or omitting the benefits that are your duty.

9. MODERATION

Avoid extremes; forbear resenting injuries so much as you think they deserve.

10. CLEANLINESS

Tolerate no uncleanness in body, cloths or habitation.

11. TRANQUILITY

Be not disturbed at trifles, or at accidents common or unavoidable.

12. CHASTITY

Rarely use venery but for health or offspring, never to dullness, weakness, or the injury of your own or another's peace or reputation.

13. HUMILITY

Imitate Jesus and Socrates.

Franklin's plan was to make each of the thirteen virtues a habit by focusing his attention on only one at a time until he had achieved mastery. With that aim in mind Franklin arranged the virtues in the order they appear above.

Conclusions

Virtue Ethics has the advantage of seeking to develop the moral person from within as well as from without, but it is based upon a number of assumptions that are difficult to prove, such as human beings having an end or purpose and what that purpose is; that morality is innate; and what virtue, the virtues, and the virtuous human being are.

Virtue Ethics theories do not seem any more satisfying than the consequentialist or nonconsequentialist—to many people, probably even less so. What are we to do, then? Should we retreat to consequentialist theories with their attendant problems, or adopt the nonconsequentialist or the Virtue Ethics approach as being the "lesser of two evils"? I believe there is a value in trying to synthesize the best of these systems while deemphasizing the worst. We shall examine the possibilities of such a synthesis in Chapter 8. First, however, it is important that we tackle three problem areas that vitally affect the setting up of a moral system: absolutism versus relativism, freedom versus determinism, and reward and punishment.

Chapter Summary

I. Virtue Ethics
   A. Virtue Ethics is not a new theory, having had its beginnings with the Greeks and especially Aristotle in the fourth century B.C. although its origins in Chinese philosophy are even more ancient. It has become significant to many contemporary ethicists.
   B. *Virtue* is defined as "moral excellence, righteousness, responsibility, or other exemplary qualities considered meritorious."
   C. Emphasis is on the good or virtuous character of human beings themselves, rather than on their acts, consequences, feelings, or rules.
   D. Aristotle's *Nichomachean Ethics* is based upon the following tenets:
      1. Reality and life are teleological in that they aim toward some end or purpose.
      2. The end of human life is happiness, and reason is the basic activity of humans; therefore, the aim of human beings is to reason well so as to achieve a complete life.
      3. Aristotle begins with the moral judgments of reasonable and virtuous human beings and then formulates general principles, as opposed to the nonconsequentialists—Divine Command theories, Kant, and Ross—who begin with abstract ethical principles.
      4. Human beings have a capacity for goodness. This has to be developed by practice based upon an emulation of the moral decision making of the ideal virtuous human being.
      5. What is virtue and how does it relate to vice?
         (a) Virtue is a mean, relative to us, between the two extremes of excess and deficiency (or defect).
         (b) In the feeling of shame, for example, modesty is the mean between the excess of bashfulness and the defect of shamelessness.
   E. Confucian Moral Self-Cultivation
      1. The Chinese term *de*, "virtue," is the inherent power or tendency to affect others in a positive, dramatic, and powerful way for good.
      2. In a Confucian world one's identity is at all times tied to the group and one's relationships within the social order. The Confucian virtues thus are decidedly social in nature.
      3. All Confucian virtues are carried out within the context of Five Cardinal Relationships that are all governed by the practice of *shu*, "reciprocity."
      4. *Ren*, translated variously as "human-heartedness," "benevolence," "goodness," or "humaneness," is the chief Confucian virtue and highlights and enhances the natural relationships between the individual and the community. The ideogram for *ren* is "one-being-with-others."

    5. *Li*, "ritual propriety," is the Confucian virtue that must be cultivated if one is to be a full participant in the community and makes it possible for an individual to exhibit appropriate conduct in specific situations.

    6. Idealist and Realist Conceptions of Confucianism

       (a) Mengzi or "Mencius" held that human beings have a natural disposition toward goodness, and virtue is cultivated, metaphorically, as the watering of "sprouts."

       (b) Xunzi taught that humans are not naturally disposed toward goodness, but human nature is evil and must be overcome in the manner one straightens crooked wood or sharpens metal on a grinder.

F. Contemporary Analysis of Virtue Ethics

    1. Contemporary theories of Virtue Ethics are primarily a reaction against moral theories that attempt to fit our moral experience into an a priori system of rules or preestablished ideals, specifically, consequentialism and Kantianism.

    2. Most contemporary theories of virtue ethics draw heavily from Aristotle, although they do not necessarily accept all of his assumptions.

G. Alasdair MacIntyre provides a contemporary analysis of Virtue Ethics.

    1. The virtues are dispositions both to act and to feel in particular ways, and one must create virtuous feelings within oneself, not merely act virtuously.

    2. One must then decide what the practically wise and virtuous human being would do in any situation and then do the virtuous act that such a person would do.

H. There are several advantages to Virtue Ethics.

    1. It strives to create the good human being, not merely good acts or rules.

    2. It attempts to unify reason and emotion.

    3. It emphasizes moderation, a quality prized by many ethicists.

I. It also has disadvantages.

    1. Do human beings have an end or purpose? If so what is it, and how can we prove any of this?

    2. Are morals naturally implanted, or are they learned through experience?

    3. What is virtue, and what constitutes the virtues? There seems to be a wide variety of opinions on this, so how can we decide what virtue really is and which virtues are really virtues?

    4. Who is the ideal virtuous human being, and how are we to determine or prove this?

J. Vice and Virtue

    1. Vices such as cowardice, jealousy, envy, greed, gluttony, and spite are examples of undesirable character traits that become imbedded in an individual's life through the indulgence of degrading appetites, lack of self-discipline and education, and the habitual practice of immoral conduct.

    2. The vicious person is ruled, not by reason, but by impulse and lives a life tormented by inner tension and chaos.

    3. Virtues are "human excellences" and consist of those traits of character that should be fostered in human beings, such as honesty, loyalty, courage, wisdom, moderation, civility, compassion, tolerance, and reverence.

    4. The life of the virtuous person is characterized by inner strength, contentment, happiness, and purpose.

    5. In fashioning an anatomy of evil, St. Augustine lists a number of vices and their manifestations.

    6. Benjamin Franklin presents a method for mastering the virtues. He selects thirteen virtues and to each annexes a precept that is both action guiding and expresses the extent of the meaning assigned to the virtue.

Exercises for Review

1. What essentially is Virtue Ethics and where did it originate?
2. How does it differ from both consequentialist and non consequentialist theories of ethics?
3. What are the advantages of Virtue Ethics?
4. What are the disadvantages of Virtue Ethics?
5. What are the problems associated with discovering who the ideal virtuous person is?

Discussion Questions

1. Do you know anyone whom you think of as being an "ideal virtuous person"? Who? Why? Describe that person's character and what it is about him or her that you think makes him or her "ideal."
2. Make your own list of the virtues you think everyone should possess and explain each. Like Benjamin Franklin, annex a precept to each virtue.
3. Do you believe that human beings are teleological, that is, have a purpose? Is there only one purpose that all human beings share, or do different human beings have different purposes? Explain your answer.
4. What makes people virtuous? Are they born that way, or do they have to be taught? If you believe they are born that way, what evidence or proof can you cite in support of your belief? If people must be taught to be virtuous, what methods should be used to make them so?
5. Do you believe that moderation is always a virtue? Should people always strive to reach the mean between two extremes? Why, or why not? How about people with strong beliefs, such as advocates of the prolife or prochoice positions on abortion?

Notes

1. William Morris, ed., *The American Heritage Dictionary of the English Language* (Boston: Houghton Mifflin, 1978), 1432.
2. Ibid., 203.
3. Dagobert D. Runes, *Dictionary of Philosophy* (Totowa, NJ: Littlefield, Adams and Co., 1968), 332.
4. Richard McKeon, ed., *Introduction to Aristotle* (New York: The Modern Library, 1947), 308.
5. Ibid., 340.
6. Ibid., 339.
7. Sir David Ross, *Aristotle* (London: Methuen and Co., 1964), 203.
8. Philip J. Ivanhoe, *Confucian Moral Self Cultivation*, 2nd ed. (Indianapolis, IN: Hackett Publishing Company, Inc., 2000), ix.
9. Ibid.
10. Roger T. Ames and Henry Rosemont, Jr., trans., *Analects*, 2.1, in *The Analects of Confucius: A Philosophical Translation* (New York: The Ballantine Publishing Group, 1998), 76.
11. Ibid, 2.3, 76.
12. Michael C. Brannigan, *Ethics Across Cultures: An Introductory Text with Readings* (Boston: McGraw-Hill, 2005), 296.

13. Roger T. Ames, "Rites as Rights: The Confucian Alternative," in Leroy S. Roumer, ed., *Human Rights and the World's Religions* (Notre Dame, IN: University of Notre Dame Press, 1988), 201.

14. Brannigan, *Ethics Across Cultures*, 298.

15. Alasdair MacIntyre, *After Virtue* (Notre Dame, IN: University of Notre Dame Press, 1984), 149.

16. Ibid., 154.

17. Ibid., 162.

18. Ibid., 182–85.

19. Christine Swanton, *Virtue Ethics: A Pluralistic View* (New York: Oxford University Press, 2003), 19.

20. St. Augustine, "The Depths of Vice," in Keith W. Krasemann, ed., *Quest for Goodness: An Introduction to Ethics* (Needham Heights, MA: Simon & Schuster, 1998), 312.

Research Navigator™
(http://www.researchnavigator.com)

This web site offers three research databases: EBSCO's *Content Select Academic Journal and Abstract Database, New York Times* Search by Subject Archive, and *Best of the Web* Link Library. In addition, this site provides helpful advice on how to conduct efficient and productive research from choosing a topic to polishing the final draft. Beginning philosophy students probably will find the *Best of the Web* Link Library the most appropriate place to start their research.

The free access code necessary to employ Research Navigator™ can be found in the Prentice Hall Guide to Evaluating Online Resources. If your text did not come with this guide, please go to *www.prenhall.com/contentselect* for information on how you can purchase an access code.

Absolutism Versus Relativism

Objectives

After you have read this chapter, you should be able to

1. Define the following terms: *absolutism, relativism, proposition, truth, falsity*, and *states of affairs.*

2. Know the so-called anthropological "facts" about absolutism and relativism, and understand the criticism of these "facts."

3. Describe different types of propositions and show how truth and knowledge relate to them.

4. Understand that absolutes exist and show how human beings can relate them to their moral lives.

5. Understand how basic principles, as "near" or "almost" absolutes, are important to morality.

Two extremes in ethical reasoning have become very obvious in the twentieth and twenty-first centuries. One side (usually that of the rule nonconsequentialist moralists) believes that there are absolutes in the world, especially moral absolutes, which, once discovered, must be adhered to. That is, they believe that if "Do not kill" is a real absolute, it never changes either because it is logically irrefutable or because it has come from some absolute being (e.g., God); it applies for all time and to all human beings everywhere. The other side has become cynical about the existence of any absolutes, mainly because modern science has exploded so many former "absolutes" and because there does not seem to be anything that can be *conclusively* proved to be absolute in any area of our experience with the possible exception of logic and mathematics, neither of which can encompass the entirety of human experience.

The moral relativist says that there are no absolutes and that morality (that is, what is moral and what is immoral) is *relative* only to a specific culture, group, or individual. We have all heard sayings such as "What's right for me may not be right for you" or "What's right for Americans may not be right for Asians." Furthermore, anthropological studies prove that cultures do differ. However, such studies also show that there are some similarities. Traditional morality stresses absolutes, whereas the so-called "new morality" stresses such concepts as "doing your own thing," "if it feels good, do it," or, in a milder form, "as long as you can fulfill the Christian commandment to love, then anything goes."

The Meanings of *Absolute*

In one sense, the word *absolute* means "perfect in quality, and complete"; in another, it means "not limited by restrictions or exceptions"; in still another, it means "not to be doubted or questioned—positive, certain, and unconditional."[1] The word has been, and is used, to describe a supernatural being, "laws" of nature, propositions concerning truth and falsity, and law and morality. The question of whether an absolute supernatural being exists, and the difficulty of proving its existence conclusively, have already been discussed in Chapters 1 and 3.

It is also difficult to prove conclusively the assumption that there are certain absolutes ("laws") in nature. One of the problems with so-called scientific natural laws is that although they have held for as long as we can remember and as often as we have observed them, they are still only probable (although very strongly probable), rather than certain. For example, the law of gravity would seem to be an absolute "law" of nature, but its validity still depends upon our ability to see it verified again and again. In other words, we don't know for certain whether the law of gravity will still hold in the next minute until we have lived through this time and observed it holding. Putting it more specifically, we don't know whether a ball will fall back down to the ground until we have thrown it up in the air and tested the "law" once again. This doesn't mean, of course, that there are no absolutes in nature, but it does mean—especially because our empirical knowledge of nature and of the universe is limited—that we don't know *conclusively* that any exist.

Even harder to prove or discover is the basis for any sort of "natural moral laws." Our discussion of the possibility of such laws in Chapter 1 revealed to us the difficulty of discovering any such moral laws, and brought out the importance of distinguishing between them and descriptive natural laws. It would seem that there is no clear basis or justification for holding that natural moral laws exist.

The Meaning of *Relative*

Relativism states that there are no absolute values at all and that all values are relative to time, place, persons, and situations. In other words, there are no values that cut across all cultures and peoples; all are relative to the specific place in which they are held, according to the relativist. In its milder forms, relativism merely states that morality varies from culture to culture and from individual to individual and that we ought to respect each other's moral views. In its extreme form, relativism means that anything goes; whatever anyone asserts is moral is definitely moral and we cannot dispute or refute his or her morality. This means that if one person thinks it's all right to kill other people and the rest of us don't, we cannot argue with this morality—he or she is as moral as those of us who don't believe that killing is moral.

Cultural Relativism and Cultural Absolutism

Cultural Relativism

Are there any anthropological "facts" that prove conclusively that either cultural relativism or cultural absolutism is true? If so, what are they? Those anthropologists who believe in cultural relativism cite the following empirical "facts":

1. Studies of both primitive and modern cultures reveal an extreme variation in customs, manners, taboos, religions, moralities, daily habits, and attitudes from culture to culture.
2. The moral beliefs and attitudes of human beings are absorbed essentially from their cultural environments, and people tend to internalize—at least a great deal of the time—what is socially accepted or sanctioned in their cultures.
3. People in different cultures tend to believe not merely that there is only one true morality, but also that that one true morality is the one *they* hold.

Cultural Absolutism

Cultural absolutism, on the other hand, is the view that says ultimate moral principles do not vary from culture to culture. This does not mean that all cultures have the same moral rules and standards, which obviously would be a false empirical statement; what it does mean is that the ultimate principles underlying all of the varying rules and standards are the same. For example, the cultural absolutist might argue that in all cultures there is some principle concerning the value of human life, but that there are many different rules and standards when it comes to protecting it or authorizing its destruction.

With this distinction in mind, cultural absolutists cite the following "facts" to support their theory:

1. Similar moral principles exist in all societies, such as those concerning the preservation of human life, governing sexual behavior, prohibiting lying, and establishing reciprocal obligations between parents and children.
2. People in all cultures have similar needs, such as the need to survive, to eat and drink, and to have sex.

3. There are a great many similarities in situations and relationships in all cultures, such as having two parents of opposite sexes, competing with brothers and sisters, and participating in the arts, languages, religion, and family.

4. There are a great many intercultural similarities in the areas of sentiment, emotion, and attitude, as with jealousy, love, and the need for respect.

Evaluation of These Theories

Essentially, what do these so-called facts really prove? What are their implications for moral absolutism or relativism?

Evaluation of Moral Relativism. First, just because cultures differ as to what is right and wrong does not mean that a particular belief of any culture is right or wrong. For example, suppose that a certain culture believes the world is flat, whereas another believes the world is round. It is obvious that what cultures believe has no *necessary* connection with what is true. Second, just because a belief is learned from or accepted by a culture does not mean that it is true or false, or that truth is relative only to specific societies.

Evaluation of Moral Absolutism. First, just because moral principles are similar in all societies does not mean that they are valid or absolute. Second, even if people have similar needs, sentiments, emotions, and attitudes, there is still a question of whether these *should* or *should not* be satisfied. And finally, just because there are similarities in cultural situations and relationships does not mean that these are the only morally correct situations and relationships in existence, or that they are morally correct at all.

What this boils down to is that merely because things, situations, and people exist or behave in certain ways, there is no necessary connection between what *is* or what people *do*, and what *should be* or what they *ought to* do. We have returned again to the distinction made in Chapter 1 between descriptive and prescriptive approaches to morality. Anthropologists have given us important information about human and cultural behavior, but they have not proved conclusively that everything is either relative or absolute, nor have they shown what is or is not moral.

How, then, are we to resolve this controversy of absolutism versus relativism? It would seem that if relativism exists, then absolutism cannot, certainly not for all people. An individual can accept or set up for himself a code of morality, but if relativism holds, it will apply only to that person and to no one else, unless another individual or group of individuals also chooses the same code. In any case, if moral relativism holds true, there are no absolutes binding any human being to any moral point of view and—to choose an extreme case—we must accept Osama Bin Laden's value system as well as Jesus', for how can we condemn any human being or culture for doing anything wrong if there are no absolutes by which we can measure their morality? We cannot say, "What they are doing is wrong"; we can only say, "What they are doing is different from what we would do," and then either condemn them for the difference and stop them by force or allow them to continue and hope that both sides do not destroy each other.

On the other hand, if we accept certain moral rules as absolutes and another individual or group accepts conflicting rules as absolutes, then we are confronted by the great difficulty of trying to resolve the conflicts that arise from two sets of opposing absolutes meeting head-on. How, when two conflicting moral absolutes collide, can we possibly resolve the ensuing controversy? There is no conceivable way of doing this other than by declaring one of the absolutes to not really be an absolute. This brings up the knotty question of how we can know if there are any absolutes, or what they might be.

Propositions and Truth

Propositions and States of Affairs

As far as morality is concerned, however, the most important way in which the term *absolute* is used is in connection with propositions as they relate to truth and falsity. Propositions are meaningful statements describing states of affairs, and they must be either true or false. A state of affairs is an occurrence, an event, or a happening. It is neither true nor false; it either occurs or it does not occur. A proposition describes a state of affairs and if it is true, then it describes a state of affairs that did occur (past tense: "It rained yesterday"); that is occurring (present tense: "It is raining right now"); or that will occur (future tense: "It will rain tomorrow"). When a proposition is false, then it describes a state of affairs that did not occur, is not occurring, or will not occur. Only propositions are true or false, never states of affairs.[2]

Are There Any Absolute Truths?

The question that concerns us is this: "Are there any absolute truths or falsities, or are truth and falsity always relative?" Let's take an example. Suppose that on January 1, 2006, I state the proposition "It will rain tomorrow, January 2, 2006, in Los Angeles, California." In order to discover whether truth and falsity are relative or absolute, we need to ask what the status of this proposition is on the day I stated it (January 1, 2006). There are a number of possibilities. At the time I state it, is it true until proven false, or false until proven true? Is it true to me because I believe it and false to someone else because he or she doesn't believe it? Is it false or true because no one knows on January 1, 2006, whether it actually will rain on the following day? Or is it really neither true nor false because January 2, 2006, isn't here yet?

Let us now suppose that it *is* January 2, 2006, and that it is raining in Los Angeles. Looking back to the proposition stated on January 1, wasn't it actually true when I stated it? On the other hand, if it doesn't rain on January 2 in Los Angeles, then wasn't the proposition false when I stated it on January 1? In other words, the proposition had to be *either* true *or* false when I stated it on January 1; we just didn't *know* at the time which condition applied to it.

The point I am trying to make is that truth does not slip around because of time, or because of what anyone believes or even knows. Let us suppose that I believe the proposition to be true (after all, I stated it), but Mary does not. What difference does this make as to whether it is actually true or false? Also, on January 1 neither one of us *knows* it is either true or false, but, again, what difference does that make? None whatsoever—whether the proposition is true or false is based upon whether or not the state of affairs actually occurs.

Truth and falsity, then, are indeed absolute. They do not shift around depending upon belief, time, feelings, or even knowledge. Propositions, carefully and accurately stated, are not just true or false when they are stated but are in fact true or false for all time. We may not *know* which propositions are true and which are false, but that really has nothing to do with whether propositions really *are* true or false.

Types of Propositions

The real problem associated with the search for absolute moral truths, however, seems to be centered upon the area of knowing. There may be absolute truths, moral or otherwise, but do we know of any for sure? At this point it is important that we distinguish among different types of propositions.

Analytic Propositions. First there are analytic propositions, such as "No circles are squares," "*A* is *A*," "Everything is either *A* or not *A*," "Nothing can be both *A* and not *A*," "All triangles are three-sided," "All bachelors are unmarried," and so on. To deny the truth of this type of proposition would be to contradict oneself; therefore, given the definitions of the words and the meaning of these propositions, they are absolute truths, and we know they are. For example, given the definitions of a circle and a square, it is not logically possible that one could be the other. Also, assuming that *A* stands for anything, it is a basic and ultimate truth (called a "law" or "principle of logic") that whatever else may or may not be said truly about anything, a thing must by its very definition be what it is (a car is a car, a dog is a dog, a table is a table). Therefore, any analytic proposition is a truth that is known to be absolute.

Internal Sense Propositions. There are also propositions that human beings assert about their own internal senses or states (feelings, moods, emotions), such as "My head hurts," "I feel sick," "I am in a bad mood," "I believe in God," "I am frightened." Such propositions also are always true (assuming that they are honestly spoken) because we alone truly know our own internal states. A doctor can talk all day about how there is no reason or cause for you to have a headache, but he or she cannot deny that you have one. Only you know whether you do or not, and when you do have one, merely having it is enough for you to state unequivocally, "I have a headache." You are simply describing what you feel, and you need no further evidence. These two types of propositions, then, state truths that we know are absolute. These propositions can be known to be true in what John Hospers calls "the strong sense of knowing," if the latter fulfills the following requirements:

1. I must believe that the proposition is true.
2. The proposition must actually *be* true.
3. I must have absolutely conclusive evidence that it is true.[3]

In order for us to know that the two types of propositions discussed are true, in the first type we need no evidence other than our knowledge of the definitions of words and the meanings of sentences, and in the second type no evidence other than our actual experience of the internal state we are describing.

Empirical, or External Sense, Propositions. Another type of proposition, an empirical, or external sense, proposition, is different from the first two, in that it describes a state of affairs that occurs in the external world of which we have evidence through our senses (sight, touch, hearing, smell, taste) or, indirectly, through our reasoning. "Her hair is brown," "There is a table at the front of this room," "There is life on other planets," and "Man has landed on the moon" are examples of empirical propositions. The question of whether empirical propositions can ever be known to be absolutely true has been a source of controversy in philosophy throughout the ages. I happen to agree with Norman Malcolm (1911–1990) and other like-minded philosophers that some empirical propositions can be known to be absolutely true or false. For example, if the light is good, if your eyes are normal, if you understand what the words you are using mean, and if you have carefully examined an object in front of you and have found it to be a table, then the statement "This is a table here before me" would seem to be an absolutely true proposition that you know to be true. So, for the purpose of this book, at least, I will assume that some empirical propositions can be known to be true—and therefore, that there are some empirical propositions that are absolutely true.

Moral Propositions. A fourth type of proposition is a moral proposition, or a proposition that has moral import. Some examples of this type of proposition are "Human beings should never kill other human beings," "You should not treat people badly," "Martin Luther King was a good man," "Abortion is evil." This type of proposition differs from the other three types we have discussed, in that it contains value judgments as to the morality of human actions or character. It also contains such key words as *good, evil, wrong, right, bad, should,* and *ought,* among others. The first distinction is the most important because many propositions containing the words just cited have no moral import at all.[4] One example of such a proposition is "You should make a right turn at the next corner." There can be, of course, situations in which making a turn when asked *could* have moral import, but something other than the use of *should* and *right* would have to be involved. In short, making or not making the turn would have to have some moral implication, such as that if you did not make the turn, you would run down a child.

The Emotive Theory

The questions now confronting us are these: "Are moral propositions ever absolutely true, and, further, can any human being know whether they are or not?" As mentioned in Chapter 3, in our discussion of the basis of act nonconsequentialism, some philosophers have stated that moral propositions have only "emotive," or "noncognitive," meanings; that is, they express only feelings or attitudes. For example, when people utter a moral proposition, such as "Tom is a good man" or "One should never steal," they are either voicing their approval or disapproval of an entity, trying to evoke certain feelings or attitudes in others, or perhaps both. Proponents of this theory, called the "emotive theory," maintain that unlike other types of propositions, such as "Tom is six feet tall" or "If you steal my car, I will be unhappy," moral propositions have no real basis in fact.

General Problems with the Emotive Theory. In *Human Conduct*, John Hospers points out some discrepancies inherent in this theory that raise some serious questions about its assumption that moral propositions are only emotive.[5] Hospers does not deny that moral propositions are used emotively; he does, however, question the theory that they have *only* that use or meaning. He sees moral propositions as having three aspects:

1. The purpose or intention of the person who utters them.
2. The effect the propositions have on their hearers.
3. The actual meaning of the propositions.

These three aspects should be carefully distinguished from one another because they all may be present in a particular moral proposition. For example, even though a moral proposition I state may express approval or disapproval, or may be intended to evoke certain feelings or attitudes, it may *also* have a meaning separate from those other two aspects or functions. Hospers further argues that even though we use moral propositions for emotive purposes we don't *always* use them in that way.[6]

Like other theories we have discussed, such as psychological egoism in its strong form and the theory that there are natural moral laws, the emotive theory exaggerates its claims. For example, if one examines the moral proposition "It was wrong of Brutus to kill Caesar," it becomes clear that there is no way the proposition can be said to evoke a feeling in Brutus that he should not kill Caesar because the act already has been committed.[7] Even if one tries to translate this proposition into the generalization "Human beings shouldn't kill other human beings," there is a difficulty: One cannot necessarily infer the second proposition from the first. True, one can say that the speaker is expressing his disapproval of Brutus's act, but must the speaker always be doing this when he makes the statement? Might not the speaker simply mean, "Look what followed historically from Brutus's action," a statement that expresses neither approval nor disapproval?

Moore's Naturalistic Fallacy. If we try to state that moral propositions are no different from empirical propositions, we run into the "naturalistic fallacy" problem (so named by the philosopher G. E. Moore, 1873–1958): the problem of "getting an *ought* from an *is*." We discussed this problem in Chapter 1 when we dealt with the difference between the descriptive or scientific, approach to ethics and the prescriptive or philosophical-normative, approach. Moore states that a proposition such as "I will be angry if you steal my wife," which can be considered to be factual (because it describes an actual state of affairs that will take place in the future), has no *necessary* connection to the proposition "You *should* not steal my wife." That is, if the person I am talking to wishes to say, "So you'll be angry; so what? I still think I should steal your wife," how can I logically say, "Therefore, you shouldn't"? However, aren't some moves from the descriptive *is* to the prescriptive *ought* clear and logical, such as, "AIDS is a sexually transmitted fatal disease; therefore, people ought to practice safe sex if they don't want to get sick and die"? I would agree that you can't get an *ought* from an *is*, but I do feel that careful examination of a series of pertinent facts surrounding a moral situation may lead us to some significant moral propositions about good, bad, right, and wrong and also enable us to prescribe what people should do in various situations in which morality is at stake.

Moral Propositions as Types of Empirical Propositions

These assumptions lead me to propose a third alternative that is at least worthy of examination and argument, even though it is not conclusively provable. This alternative is the position that moral statements are indeed propositions of the empirical type, except that they contain either value judgments or moral prescriptions. Let's examine this alternative as objectively as we can.

Normative Moral Statements. Normative moral statements, such as "He is a good man" or "What she did was right," could conceivably be considered to be propositions much like "That is a green table" and "She cleaned her house." There is a greater problem in establishing what *good* and *right* mean than what *green* and *cleaned her house* mean, but if we can set up some standards as to what it means for a person to be good and an act to be right, we ought to be able to say, at least in theory, that these are propositions having moral import.

Prescriptive Moral Statements. However, what about those moral statements that are prescriptive, such as "Human beings should never kill other human beings except in self-defense" and "A woman ought to have an abortion for any reason she thinks valid"? They certainly assert something about reality, even though they include a value judgment as part of that assertion, but can they ever be known to be true or false? As I pointed out in Chapter 2, while discussing Jesse Kalin's defense of ethical egoism, there are prescriptive propositions that are nonmoral and could nonetheless certainly be considered to be propositions. That is, they are meaningful statements that assert something about reality and that are either true or false.

If you remember Kalin's chess-game example, John sees that Tom *ought to* move his bishop in such a way so as to put John's king in check. The proposition here is simply, "Tom ought to move his bishop to position A." This also can be stated as, "According to the rules for playing chess, Tom's next move ought to be to move his bishop to position A." This means that within the confines of chess-game rules, to state that "Tom ought to move his bishop to position A" is to state a true proposition. To say the opposite, that "Tom ought not to move his bishop to position A," would be a false proposition, again within the structure of chess-game rules. Of course, there could be times when the former proposition might be false—for example, under the condition that if Tom won the game, his opponent would kill him, having threatened to do so previously. However, this would be an extenuating circumstance outside the confines of the chess game itself. In this case, therefore, the proposition would be based upon more than chess-game rules.

Proposition Against Killing Human Beings. Can we now make the same kind of case as in the foregoing for the proposition "Human beings should never kill other human beings" because it is similar in structure although moral rather than nonmoral? It is obvious that we can set up rules for moral behavior as well as for chess games and that within the framework of that set of rules we can state true and false propositions about what human beings or chess players should or ought to do. But can evidence be brought forth to conclusively show that such a proposition can be known to be true, as in the propositions "All triangles are three-sided," "This table is green," and "I have a headache"? Let's examine this type of moral proposition and its implications.

First, by *kill* I mean "taking another human being's life against his will." Perhaps *murder* would be a more accurate term, because *kill* means "to put to death, slay, deprive of life, put an end to or extinguish," whereas *murder* means "the unlawful killing of one human being by another, especially with malice aforethought."[8] Second, given the way in which this proposition is worded, it applies only to killing or murdering other human beings, even though there are ethical codes (pacifism and Jainism to name two) that believe in the sanctity of all life, not just human life. Now is there any evidence that this proposition can be known to be true? If we look to our experience of the world and especially of human life, we must come to the conclusion that life, or being alive, is the one basic thing we all have in common. Furthermore, there can be no real morality or immorality involved in dealing with a human being who is no longer alive. Even when we are opposed to the mutilation or cannibalism of dead human bodies, it is out of respect either for the human being that once was or for the feelings of other human beings still alive.

Because all the qualities we attribute to human beings are based upon their being alive, then life or "aliveness" is a fundamental necessity for any moral system. There can be no human beings, moral or immoral, if there is no human life; there can be no discussion of morality, a setting up of codes, or even concern about what is or is not moral if there are no live human beings around. We cannot possibly state that "all human beings should kill each other" because (in true Kantian fashion) this would end up being inconsistent and illogical in much the same way as is the statement "Everyone should always be a parasite." There would be no human beings left to follow the rule encompassed by the statement.

All of this, however, merely proves that life, or being alive, is a necessary precondition of morality. Are there any other reasons why human beings ought not to kill one another? First, the social and natural sciences have proved that human beings have a strong drive for survival, and one of the best ways to survive is to "let live," or not to put one's own life in jeopardy by threatening the lives of others. Second, most human beings seek to attain some peace, happiness, and stability in their lives, and they cannot attain any degree of these qualities if human life in general and their lives in particular are constantly being threatened. Third, experience seems to indicate that human beings have a potential for being good and doing right, as well as a potential for being bad and doing wrong, so we can be sure that there is within us at least a partial urge to be and do good.

And indeed, when it is accompanied by our desires for survival, peace, happiness, and stability, the urge to do and be good seems to be stronger in most of our lives than the impulse toward evil. It also seems to be a good thing most of the time that human beings not kill other human beings because if they do, they will deprive those whom they kill of any possible good they might attain while alive (this in addition to the basic and obvious good of continuing to possess life itself). Therefore, if life is basic to human beings, to their morality, their drive for survival, their desire for peace, happiness, and stability, and their urge to be and do good, then to destroy life is tantamount to destroying the ultimate basis of human-ness, which includes morality. "Human beings should never kill other human beings" can therefore be seen as a true proposition, and it can be known to be true because the evidence for it can be observed and we can reason consistently from that evidence.

Problems with Moral Propositions. It is generally assumed by reasonable human beings that if we know certain propositions to be true, then we will seek to live our lives by them. Following up this assumption, we can say that human beings who kill other human beings are not living their lives in accordance with a true proposition. They may, of course, not be aware of the proposition, or they may be aware of it but disregard it. We do this many times with other propositions. We know, for instance, that "if you drive too fast and recklessly on a crowded freeway, you will endanger human life" is a true proposition, yet some people drive recklessly anyway. Here we have another moral problem, the matching of propositions that are known to be true with human actions. Many people know that propositions having to do with not killing or not lying or not raping, for example, should be adhered to, but some people still do not act in accordance with such propositions. Of course, that people do not act in accordance with propositions has nothing to do with whether or not they are true. Still another problem arises when propositions conflict—when, for instance, the absolute "Do not kill" conflicts with the absolute "Do not lie." We must have a way of choosing not only between true and false propositions but also between propositions that conflict.

Furthermore, we must distinguish between the term *absolute* as it is used to imply the existence of moral laws outside of human beings (see Chapter 1), and moral absolutes (moral laws), which human beings establish based upon reason and evidence. I do not suggest here that these arguments have proved conclusively that there are moral propositions that can be known absolutely to be true or false. I believe I have shown, however, that we can discover and present evidence for the existence of such propositions and, in reasoning from that evidence, perhaps arrive at some *near or almost* absolutes (if there can be such things) and establish basic moral principles similar to Ross' *Prima Facie* Duties. It is also important to recognize that no moral system or code can exist without at least one basic principle (near or almost absolute). Every ethical theory we have examined so far has had one or more basic principles; even total relativism is based upon at least one near or almost absolute: That there are no absolutes!

Near or Almost Absolutes

The greatest problem raised in the absolutism-versus-relativism controversy is how to introduce stability, order, and security (absolutism) into morality and moral systems, while still allowing for individual and group freedom and creativity (relativism). This problem is important because the very crux of a moral system is its ability to match the tremendous complexity of human thoughts, feelings, and actions with absolute moral propositions. The way in which we can do this is by setting up basic moral principles that are near or almost absolutes. We will try to observe these principles as absolutes in every case we can, but we will realize that there may be some justifiable exceptions to the principles. The term *justifiable* is a key one here, because it means that if we intend to make an exception to a near or almost absolute, then we must fully justify that exception.

I have already argued for the validity of one proposition: that we should never kill other human beings. True pacifists will adhere to this proposition even when their lives are threatened; they will lose their own lives rather than take another's. In so doing they will be acting as consistently as possible with their principles. However, given the complexity and variety of human experience, if life is basic, as the proposition states, then one's own life and the lives of innocent people who are the intended victims of some killer are also basic. Therefore, as many ethical systems state it, one has the right to and should protect one's own life and the lives of other innocent people from someone who is threatening to take them, even if it means that someone must take the life of the killer and thus become a killer himself.

The absolute "Human beings should not kill other human beings" thus becomes the basic moral principle "Human beings should not kill other human beings except in self-defense or in the defense of other innocent human beings." Although there is still the problem of defining *self-defense* and *innocent*, the absolute has been qualified by the phrases concerning "self-defense" and "defense of the innocent," thus justifying some exceptions to the proposition "Do not kill." There may be other exceptions, but they will also have to be justified very strongly because they are exceptions to an absolute that is basic to all human morality. The arguments necessary for these exceptions, and for other basic principles and their exceptions will be dealt with in Chapter 8 in the discussion of how a system of morality can be set up. For now, it is enough to say that basic moral principles can indeed be set up so as to govern most human actions, and that exceptions can be provided for by means of careful and strong justifications in each case.

Conclusion

Relativism

In addition to citing the argument that just because values differ that does not necessarily make them right in one culture or another, critics also argue that relativism is really impractical, especially in its extreme form. It certainly is important to allow for cultural and individual freedom when deciding what values people should be allowed to follow, but is anyone really a full-blown relativist in practical living situations? Are any of us willing to say that people should be allowed to do whatever they want to do as long as they think it is right? If we ask ourselves that question, won't we discover that we definitely want to qualify it by adding, "as long as they don't harm anyone else" or "as long as they don't interfere with anyone else's rights"?

In stating such a qualification we may not be setting up absolutes, but neither are we totally accepting the theory that values are entirely relative. Doesn't this felt need to qualify relativism suggest that there must be certain guidelines or limits within which all humans should behave? It would seem, therefore, that the practicality of living itself will not allow us to adopt a totally relativistic point of view.

Absolutism

What about absolutism? It would seem that there are such things as absolutes in both the nonmoral and the moral sphere. Some absolutes, however, are too general to be of use in the specific situations in which we find ourselves, so they become the basis for establishing basic principles that may have exceptions. Such exceptions must however be fully justified because the principles *are* basic; to make unjustified exceptions is to act immorally. These principles, in turn, serve as a means to enable human beings to act as closely as possible in accordance with known true propositions. That a proposition is true is no guarantee that people will act in accordance with it, but the proposition remains true whether they do or not.

To repeat: There are absolutes in the sense of absolutely true propositions that we can know. Some of them are analytic, some are internal sense statements, and others are empirical propositions with or without moral import. From these absolutes we derive near or almost absolutes in the form of those basic moral principles that form the cornerstone of any human ethical system. All normative moral systems rest upon the absolutes that are proposed by whoever sets up these systems. Yet this does not mean that morality is relative, for many absolutes are founded upon propositions that are known to be true by means of evidence gained through the senses and logical argument supplied through reasoning.

Chapter Summary

I. Two extremes in ethical reasoning
   A. Absolutism maintains that there are absolute truths and, especially, absolute moral truths to which all human beings must adhere if they are to be moral.
   B. Relativism maintains that there are no absolutes of any kind, but that everything, especially morality, is "relative" to specific cultures, groups, or even individuals.

II. Meaning and application of *absolute* and *relative*
   A. *Absolute* essentially means "perfect in quality; complete; not limited by restriction or exceptions; not to be doubted or questioned—positive, certain, unconditional." We apply this word to supernatural beings (for example, gods); to laws of nature; to propositions; to law and morality; and, most important, to propositions, truth, and falsity.
   B. *Relative* essentially means that there are no values that cut across all cultures and peoples that are not relative to the specific place or person in and by which they are held.

III. Anthropological "facts"
   A. Some anthropological facts are cited in support of cultural relativism.
      1. There is extreme variation in customs, manners, taboos, religions, and so on, from culture to culture.
      2. Moral beliefs and attitudes of human beings are learned essentially from their cultural environments.
      3. People in different cultures tend to believe that their morality is the one true morality.
   B. Other such facts are cited in support of cultural absolutism.
      1. Similar moral principles exist in all societies.
      2. People in all cultures have similar needs.
      3. There are a great many similarities in situations and relationships existing in all cultures.
      4. There are a great many similarities in sentiments, emotions, and attitudes.
   C. Anthropological facts are open to criticism.
      1. Just because cultures differ about what is right and wrong does not mean that one culture is right whereas another is wrong.
      2. Just because a belief is learned from or accepted by a culture does not mean that it is true or false or that truth is relative only to specific societies.
      3. Just because moral principles are similar in all societies does not mean that they are valid or absolute.
      4. Even if people have similar needs, sentiments, emotions, and attitudes, there is still a question of whether these should or should not be satisfied.
      5. Just because there are similarities in cultural situations and relationships does not mean that these are the only morally correct situations and relationships in existence or that they are morally correct at all.

IV. Propositions and truth
   A. Truth applies to propositions that are meaningful statements describing states of affairs (occurrences, events, or happenings). Propositions are either true or false.
      1. A true proposition describes a state of affairs that was, is, or will be occurring.
      2. A false proposition describes a state of affairs that did not occur, is not occurring, or will not occur.
      3. Only propositions are true or false, never states of affairs—they either occur or do not occur.
   B. Truth is absolute and not relative to belief, knowledge, person, place, or time. If propositions are stated accurately, this will always hold.
   C. There are several types of propositions.
      1. Analytic propositions are truths that are *known* to be absolute ("All triangles are three-sided") because we know the definitions and meanings of words.
      2. Internal sense or internal state propositions are propositions we know to be true merely because we have the experience—we alone truly know our own internal states ("I have a headache").
      3. Empirical, or external sense, propositions describe a state of affairs that occurs in the external world of which we have evidence through our external senses. There is a controversy in philosophy as to whether such propositions can be known to be true, but my own assumption is that some empirical propositions can be known to be absolutely true ("There is a table at the front of this room").
      4. Moral propositions are propositions about morality or those that have moral import ("Human beings should never kill other human beings").
         (a) These are empirical and rational in form.
         (b) They are found in the larger class of propositions called "empirical."

(c) Some philosophers say that moral statements are not propositions at all, maintaining instead that they are merely emotive utterances. Some say that moral statements are propositions, but that they cannot be known to be true or false because they are not based on fact. A third alternative, not conclusively provable, is that they are empirical propositions with moral import that can be known to be true or false.

(d) We still are confronted by the problem of matching propositions with the complexity of human thoughts, feelings, and actions; to do this, we must move from the concept of absolutes to that of "near or almost absolutes," or "basic principles."

(e) A basic principle, or near or almost absolute, because it is based upon an absolute moral proposition, should be adhered to unless some strong justification can authorize an exception to it.

Exercises for Review

1. Define and explain the terms *absolutism, relativism, proposition, truth, falsity,* and *state of affairs*.
2. What are the anthropological "facts" cited in support of cultural absolutism and relativism, and what are the problems associated with basing moral theories upon these facts?
3. What are the different types of propositions, and how do they differ? Give your own example of each type.
4. Is truth absolute, or is it relative to knowledge, belief, people, places, and times? Explain your answer in detail.
5. Can we know for certain (in the "strong" sense of "know"—define this) that any propositions are true? If so, which types can we be sure of? If not, why not?
6. Are there moral absolutes, or is morality strictly relative? What are the implications of your viewpoint on this issue for your own moral attitudes, beliefs, and code?
7. What are the basic principles of each of the ethical theories you have studied? To what extent are they absolutistic or relativistic?
8. What are moral propositions, and how are they similar to and different from other types of propositions? Explain your answer.
9. Basing your answer upon your own observations and studies, to what extent do you think cultural absolutists or cultural relativists (in the field of anthropology) are correct in their assumptions? Explain your answer.
10. Are there any absolutes outside of truth and falsity? If so, what are they? If not, why do you believe there are none?

Discussion Questions

1. Under the moral system espoused by Adolf Hitler and the Nazi party, property was stolen and destroyed; countries were invaded, looted, and pillaged; and millions of innocent people were raped, mutilated, experimented upon, tortured, and murdered. Discuss the extent to which you feel that such a system is moral or immoral, basing your answer upon whether you feel morality is relative or absolute.
2. Read Jean Anouilh's play *Antigone* and evaluate the moral positions of Creon and Antigone from the point of view of the absolutism-versus-relativism controversy.

3. Analyze any religious code of ethics (for example, that of Judaism, Christianity, Islam, Buddhism)—preferably one with which you are familiar. Indicate to what extent the code of ethics you have chosen is absolutistic or relativistic, and discuss the problems created by its position in this controversy.
4. Read Chapter 11 of John Hospers's *Human Conduct* and Chapter 7 of Paul Taylor's *Problems of Moral Philosophy*; then write a paper that deals with the problem of verifying moral reasoning and the relationship between values and facts.
5. Discuss the extent to which you believe the rule "Adults should *never* sexually molest children" is absolute. Do you feel it can ever be right to violate this rule? If not, why not? If so, under what conditions? Is this a real absolute moral rule?
6. Discuss the extent to which you think the rule "Rape is always wrong" is an absolute. Can there be any exceptions to this rule? Why, or why not?
7. To what extent is it possible "to get an *ought* from an *is*"? What does this phrase actually mean? Answer in detail. Read Chapter 1 of G. E. Moore's *Principia Ethica* (see the listing in Supplementary Reading).

Notes

1. William Morris, ed., *The American Heritage Dictionary of the English Language* (Boston: Houghton Mifflin, 1975), 5.
2. This is John Hospers's description of truth and propositions, which is the clearest and most meaningful I have read. It appears on pages 114–21 of *An Introduction to Philosophical Analysis*, 2nd ed. (Upper Saddle River, NJ: Prentice Hall, 1967).
3. Ibid., 151.
4. Refer to Chapters 1 and 2 and to the chess-game example in this chapter, which points out the nonmoral uses of *should* and *ought to*.
5. John Hospers, *Human Conduct: An Introduction to the Problems of Ethics*, 2nd ed. (New York: Harcourt Brace Jovanovich, 1982), 526–93.
6. Ibid., 559–66.
7. Ibid., 564–65.
8. Morris, *American Heritage Dictionary*, 720, 863.

Research Navigator™
(http://www.researchnavigator.com)

This web site offers three research databases: EBSCO's *Content Select Academic Journal and Abstract Database, New York Times* Search by Subject Archive, and *Best of the Web* Link Library. In addition, this site provides helpful advice on how to conduct efficient and productive research from choosing a topic to polishing the final draft. Beginning philosophy students probably will find the *Best of the Web* Link Library the most appropriate place to start their research.

The free access code necessary to employ Research Navigator™ can be found in the Prentice Hall Guide to Evaluating Online Resources. If your text did not come with this guide, please go to *www.prenhall.com/contentselect* for information on how you can purchase an access code.

Chapter

6

Freedom Versus Determinism

Objectives

After you have read this chapter, you should be able to

1. Define the following terms: *freedom, determinism, universal causation, fatalism, predestination,* and *indeterminism*.

2. Understand the differences between hard and soft determinism, fatalism, and indeterminism.

3. Understand the various arguments for and against determinism presented by natural and physical scientists, historians, economists, psychologists, and religionists.

4. Understand the arguments for freedom and free will.

5. Come to some conclusions concerning the freedom-versus-determinism controversy, and apply those conclusions to moral responsibility.

We have already seen, in the previous chapter, how important the controversy concerning absolutism versus relativism is to morality. There is, however, yet another question related to this controversy that affects morality and especially moral responsibility. This question is whether human beings are free to make moral decisions and to act upon them, or whether they are "determined" by forces both outside and within them over which they have no control, so that what they think are free decisions and actions are in fact not so.

The problem of freedom and determinism as such is really not a moral problem but, rather, a metaphysical one (having to do with the nature of reality). However, the questions concerning whether human beings are free or not, and to what extent they are or not, have very important implications for whether humans can be held morally responsible or even set up moral systems for themselves.

The Meaning of *Determinism*

What exactly does *determinism* mean? It means the same thing as *universal causation*; that is, for every result, effect, and event that occurs in reality, a cause or causes exist. Putting this in another way, we can say that there is no such thing as an uncaused result, effect, or event. One example of a moral problem arising from a deterministic point of view was discussed in Chapter 2 in connection with the theory of psychological egoism. To quickly reiterate, how can we tell human beings what they should or should not do, if—because they are "determined" by forces they can't control—they can follow only one type of ethical system: egoism? If they must always act in their own self-interest because that is simply the way they are made, then there is no use in telling them that they should or should not act in their own self-interest. Even ethical egoism is absurd if all human beings already have been programmed to act at all times in their own self-interest.

A related problem inherent in determinism is this: What is the point of holding people morally responsible—blaming, praising, rewarding, or punishing them—for what they do or fail to do if they cannot help what they do?

As you can see, the freedom-versus-determinism controversy has powerful implications for morality and moral responsibility, and we will explore these implications in greater detail later.

Types and Theories of Determinism

The various arguments and theories supporting determinism go far back in time, but they have become increasingly compelling as they have extended their reach into the twentieth and twenty-first centuries. These arguments and theories arise out of all aspects of human endeavor and concern: from religion; from the physical and natural sciences; and from history, economics, and psychology. Let's examine the arguments for determinism that have arisen from each of these areas.

Religious Determinism—Predestination

Religious determinism, or predestination, is derived from the attributes assigned, especially in the chief Western religions (Judaism, Christianity, and Islam), to some supernatural being. These attributes are omnipotence (being all-powerful) and omniscience (being all-knowing). According to such religions, because such a being created the universe and everything in it, including human beings, it has the power to do anything and knows everything that has happened, is happening, and will happen. Because of these attributes, then, everything in the world's history—past, present, and future—can be seen as being predestined and foreknown.

If, for example, this being has decided that I will lead a good life and "go to heaven," then I will; if, on the other hand, it has decided I will lead a bad life and "go to hell," then I will do that instead. I have absolutely no say over what I or anyone else does because everything has been predestined, programmed, "predetermined" by an almighty supernatural being. This theory, for reasons that soon will become evident, is not generally accepted by the three major Western religions, although it has been held to be true by some theologians. The theory of predestination was most strongly presented by the Protestant minister and theologian John Calvin (1509–1564), who said that individuals can do nothing to ensure their own salvation.

There are several problems with this theory. There is the difficulty, which I discussed in Chapter 1, of proving the existence of a supernatural being and, even if we could, of proving that it created the world, that it is indeed all-powerful and all-knowing, and, last, that it predestined everything so that it would happen in a certain way. Even if we take all of the preceding on faith, however, the theory of predestination still presents some real difficulties with regard to the characteristics of the supreme being, the world, and human beings.

First, if the universe and everything in it was created by a supernatural being, then it must also have created evil, and this constitutes a definite problem for theologians holding to the predestination viewpoint. Most theologians are not willing to assign the responsibility for evil to this being, even though the problem of evil's existence, given an all-powerful and all-good supernatural being, is a real moral dilemma.[1]

Second, such a being seems to be a very strange indeed—especially in view of the emphasis the three major Western religions place upon salvation—if it predetermines that some humans will be good and some will be bad—then punishes and rewards them for something over which they have no control! Such a characterization of the supernatural being's relationship with its creatures certainly does not square with the image of an all-merciful, all-just being that the three religions also accept. Furthermore, the concept of salvation doesn't really mean much if it cannot be assumed that human beings are free to choose to do the good rather than the evil act. None of these problems, of course, actually refutes the theory of religious determinism, but all do indicate why the theory is generally not held, at least in any extreme form, by any of three Western religions. There is, I would add, no conclusive proof or argument that indicates that this theory is anything but one based upon very weak assumptions indeed.

Scientific Determinism

Because the physical and natural sciences depend upon experiments, constancy, and prediction in their search for truth, they must accept universal causation. This has led many scientists to presume further that such causation means that there is absolutely no freedom in the universe at all. I stress that not all scientists accept this extreme point of view, although I also hasten to add that the strongest arguments and evidence for determinism have arisen in the twentieth and twenty-first centuries from the natural and physical sciences, especially as these have affected modern psychology.

Physical Science and Physical Determinism. The greatest exponent of physical determinism was Sir Isaac Newton (1642–1727). He believed that the entire realm of nature and the universe is governed by natural laws (for example, the law of gravity), and that there is, therefore, no such thing as freedom. Because everything observable—even things unobservable to the naked eye, such as atoms and molecules—is physical in nature, then everything that occurs to these things and everything they do is caused by one or another physical law or event. According to Newton, because human beings also are physical in nature, they are subject to physical causes both within and outside them; for them, freedom is simply an illusion. This argument is a very compelling one, for even though, as pointed out in the last chapter, the law of gravity, for example, does not state a certainty but rather a probability, has anyone ever observed any exceptions to what the law states?

Despite the attractiveness of the theory of physical determinism, there is a problem in assuming that because natural physical laws hold, there can be no freedom. Critics of Newton argue that humans are not merely physical but are also mental (and/or spiritual) beings, and that because they are more than physical they are able to "transcend" physical laws. Furthermore, the discoveries of modern physics, exemplified most pertinently by Werner Heisenberg's (1901–1976) quantum theory of physics, have raised serious doubts about Newtonian views of nature and the universe. The door has been left open for the possibility of freedom even for nonconscious entities such as atoms and molecules.

Biological and Genetic Determinism. Biological determinism is best exemplified by Charles Darwin's theory of natural selection, which he presented in his most famous work, *The Origin of Species*. Darwin (1809–1882) believed that various species in nature evolve at different stages in the history of the world and that only the fittest survive. For example, even though some prehistoric animals (dinosaurs, for example) were extremely large and powerful, their brain capacity and mental ability were so limited that they did not survive, whereas smaller and more intelligent beings, such as humans, did. Darwin suggested that this process of natural selection essentially has nothing to do with freedom. He believed that it is nature that governs, through its various processes, the makeup, strength, and survival potential of the various species, and that the species that emerge as dominant are determined by the stage along the evolutionary scale at which they appear.

A more modern and sophisticated version of this theory is concerned with genetic makeup, especially that of human beings. None of us has any say over the identity of our parents, from whom we inherit our genes; and because our genes determine so much of our makeup—our sex, mental potential, and eye, hair, and skin color—how can we be said to be free in any real sense of the word?

Yet the problem with biological determinism is identical to the problem with physical determinism, in that both theories tend to limit human beings strictly to their physical and biological makeup and structure, ignoring the possibility that a mental or spiritual side may exist.

Social-Cultural Determinism

Historical, or Cultural, Determinism. Georg W. F. Hegel (1770–1831) developed a deterministic theory that was based upon history. He believed that the various periods of the world's history are manifestations of an "absolute mind" that is trying to realize itself in a state of perfection. He also believed that the basic nature of reality and the world is rational and mental, and that the physical is merely a manifestation of the absolute mind's intellectual growth toward perfection. The implications of his theory are that we are neither responsible for nor able to control the period of history or the culture into which we are born. Rather, the character and actions of all individuals are determined by their own culture and all preceding cultures and historical events. Furthermore, because history is a manifestation of an absolute mind that exists in the universe and is attempting to realize itself, then we too are a result, or manifestation, of that absolute mind.

Obvious problems exist with this theory, too. First, it would be difficult at best to prove that any such absolute mind exists and, furthermore, that a mind can exist without a body. Second, even though a rational and evolutionary theory of history has some plausibility, no conclusive proof exists to support it; there are many other theories of history and culture that are equally plausible, if not more so. Third, even though human beings are influenced by their culture and past history, this does not necessarily mean that their development is totally determined or governed by this influence.

Economic or Social Determinism. Karl Marx (1818–1883), following in Hegel's theoretical footsteps, believed that our characters and actions are not so much historically determined as they are economically and socially determined. Marx's theory, called "dialectical materialism," states that human beings are determined by an evolutionary economic class struggle. According to Marx, this evolutionary process has led from early agrarian economics, through monarchies and feudalism, through the rise of the middle class and industrialism, to capitalism and eventually to socialism. He believed that although people can't control the economic class into which they are born, their natures are determined in every way by this event. He further believed—much like Hegel—that there is an inevitable force in nature (economic rather than historical) that human beings cannot control and that will eventually lead to the ultimate goal, a classless society.

The problems with this theory are similar to those raised by Hegel's theory. First, dialectical materialism is based upon unproved assumptions, and there are other theories of economics that are just as plausible and yet do not espouse determinism. Second, even though there is no doubt that people are influenced by their individual economic status and that of their society, there are, as we have seen, many other influences that affect economics as well as human beings. For example, scientific and technological developments have a great deal of influence on the economic status of cultures and their members— probably more than economics itself has upon science and technology. Also, economic influence is not the only influence that affects human beings; in fact, one could argue that human beings affect or determine changes in economics, at least to some extent.

Psychological Determinism—Freudianism and Behaviorism. Some of the most convincing of the arguments developed in the twentieth century in support of determinism, especially determinism as it affects human beings, have come from the field of psychology. In the nineteenth century, Sigmund Freud (1856–1939), the founder of psychoanalysis, put forth the theory that human beings are determined, even prior to birth in the womb, by their unconscious minds and by various natural drives that their society's mores and customs required them to repress. For example, one of Freud's theories is that all sons are basically in love with their mothers (Oedipus complex) and all daughters basically in love with their fathers (Electra complex). Because incest is forbidden in most societies, these unconscious yet natural drives must be repressed, causing human beings to be affected in different ways. Therefore, if mothers or fathers give too much, too little, or the wrong kind of love to their sons or daughters, the entire mental and emotional lives of the children can be affected to the point where they become neurotic or psychotic.

This theory has been used many times in defending criminal killers—when, for example, the defense claims that a certain man who has raped and killed a number of women has done so because they all resembled his mother and that his unconscious hatred of her compelled him to commit the crimes. Just as this man was "determined" by his unconscious drives of love and hate for his parents to perform terrible acts, so, a Freudian would argue, all human beings are determined by inner drives and unconscious motivations to behave in the ways they do.

The major criticism of Freud's theories is that they are too generalized to have any real basis in fact. That is, he has taken his experiences with a few abnormally disturbed patients as a basis for establishing theories that apply to all human beings. It certainly may be true that some sons are in love with their mothers and that some daughters are in love with their fathers, and further, that these emotions have caused them a great deal of difficulty in their lives. There is, however, little conclusive evidence to show that these problems affect *all* human beings and therefore that their lives can be said to be determined by such influences.

In the twentieth century, psychological determinism has been most significantly argued not from the point of view of the inner psyche, as in Freudianism, but, rather, from the point of view of behaviorism. This approach is best exemplified by the work of B. F. Skinner (1904–1990), who described his theories in two books, *Science and Human Behavior* and *Beyond Freedom and Dignity*, and in his utopian novel, *Walden II*. Skinner based his work upon that of Ivan P. Pavlov (1849–1936), the Russian physiologist who first developed the concept of "conditioned reflex." In his experiments with dogs, Pavlov discovered that they would react to the sound of a bell by salivating if he conditioned them to do so by ringing the bell every time he gave them food. Once the dogs had been conditioned, Pavlov could ring the bell without giving them food and they would begin to salivate nonetheless. This led him to posit the theory that all animals, human beings included, could be conditioned to act in certain ways—and in fact were and are conditioned by various external forces.

Skinner's theory is more involved and complex than Pavlov's in that he believes that human beings are totally physical beings and that the behavior they exhibit is strictly the result of years of haphazard conditioning from their environments, both physical and social or cultural. Skinner feels that all traditional statements about soul, psyche, self, or mind are merely superstitious, outdated concepts based upon a lack of scientific knowledge. He further theorizes that freedom is an illusion, and that once this illusion has been abandoned, human beings will be able to eliminate all of the problems (for example, poverty, violence, war, cruelty) that now plague humanity. Even though human beings have been totally and haphazardly conditioned down through the ages, Skinner maintains that now that we have a complete science of human behavior, we can create the perfect society.

There are several problems with this theory, the most important of which is that its very basis is a thoroughgoing materialism. That is, Skinner believes that human beings are strictly material, or physical, beings, possessing no mind, self, soul, or ego. This theory reduces mind to brain and body, a reduction that will not work because mental events do differ from physical events in that the former are private and not locatable in space, whereas the latter are public and easily locatable in space.[2] I will discuss the importance of mind and consciousness to human freedom a little later on. Another problem with Skinner's theory is that, as is also true of Freud's theories and the concept of psychological egoism, it carries essentially sound premises too far. Skinner is quite right in stating that people can be conditioned by various methods so as to make them behave in certain ways or to change certain aspects of their behavior. Weight-, smoking-, and alcohol-control clinics, among others, are perfect examples that this can be done.

The fact that conditioning works under some circumstances does not mean, however, that human beings merely react to external stimuli all the time, or that conditioning always works or even that it should be applied in all instances. Many of Skinner's critics are not overly concerned about whether his theories are accurate portrayals of what does and can happen in the realm of human behavior; what truly disturbs them is that he completely denies the existence of human freedom and wants to apply conditioning to everyone in an acculturation process that will alter their behavior. Behavior-control techniques probably should be applied in certain instances and to certain people, but—his critics state—not to a total population in an attempt to attain a utopian society of the behaviorist's design. This latter ideal is especially disturbing to his critics, because his theories are based upon a questionable, if not totally false, premise (materialism). Further criticisms of Skinner's theories will be discussed in the last section of this chapter, in which we will examine arguments for the existence of human freedom.

Summary. In the foregoing sections, we have seen that there are many arguments in favor of determinism, coming from almost all areas of human endeavor: religion, the natural and physical sciences, and the social sciences. But before we accept the arguments for determinism, let us look more deeply into what determinism means and what it implies for morality.

Fatalism and Hard and Soft Determinism

For the sake of clarity, let me redefine *determinism.* Determinism is the same thing as universal causation. Stated positively, universal causation means that for every result, effect, or occurrence there is a cause or causes; stated negatively, it means that there is no such thing as an uncaused event. Before going on to discuss hard and soft determinism, it is important that we make a distinction between fatalism and determinism.

Fatalism

Fatalism is the view that all events are irrevocably fixed and predetermined, that they cannot be altered in any way by human beings, that the future is always beyond our control. In wartime, human beings have expressed this view by saying, "If there's a bullet or bomb with my name on it, then I'll die; if not, then I won't. There's nothing I can do about it." Certainly it is true that many events are outside of human control. For example, even when people have taken the precaution of getting into a foxhole or bomb shelter, they still may receive a direct hit from a bullet or bomb and die. Are not their chances of being killed increased, however, if they merely stand up in the street or on the battlefield, doing nothing to protect themselves? Therefore, it does not seem to be true—certainly not in all cases—that it makes no difference what a person does; that "whatever will be, will be."

There are very few true fatalists (if any at all); otherwise, people would not "be careful" or "take precautions" against getting hurt or killed. True fatalists would never worry about stop signs or hesitate to play Russian roulette; they would never take medications when they were sick or protect themselves when confronted by a dangerous situation. This may not be a total refutation of the theory of fatalism, but it does illustrate the theory's impracticality. It is important to realize that the determinist, especially the soft determinist, is not really saying the same thing as the fatalist, for to say that everything has a cause is not the same as to say that every single thing that happens is completely and irrevocably outside of human control.

Hard Determinism

Hard determinism essentially maintains that if all events are caused, then there can be no such thing as freedom or free will. That is, if you trace causes back far enough in history or in any person's life, you will find that the basic causes are not within human control. Hard determinists are not saying exactly the same thing as the fatalists here: They do not maintain that humans cannot change the future. They are saying, rather, that certain causes that are not within human control have determined both the way human beings are and the way they act. Hard determinists do not maintain that humans can affect nothing; rather, they say that the way humans affect things is caused by their personal makeup and environment and that these, in turn, are caused by factors over which human beings have no control. In presenting their position, hard determinists will use evidence and arguments from every aspect of human existence.

For example, let us say that Mary Smith is born in the 1930s to a middle-class working family, during the Great Depression. Already she has no control over the century or culture into which she is born, the depression her country is in, her economic class, or, most important, the genetic makeup inherited from her parents. She could be born crippled, blind, or quite normal; she has no control over this, either. Let us say that she is born blind and that her father is an alcoholic and her mother a child abuser. Let us also assume that, due to these factors, she endures a miserable childhood that leads to a miserable adult life.

Mary may react, out of anger at her lot, by becoming a criminal, resorting to violence against both men and women in an attempt to avenge herself for the treatment she received from her mother and father. On the other hand, she may lead a blameless life. In this case, freedom advocates would point out that Mary, who had a terrible childhood and was born blind, overcame all of this, whereas her sister Elaine, for example, who was not blind but who also had an unhappy childhood, became a drug addict and prostitute. They would argue that both women had at least some say in determining the outcome of their lives.

Hard determinists would answer, however, that neither Mary nor Elaine was responsible for the way she turned out. There must have been some important differences in the women's genetic makeup or in the way they were treated by their parents, or, hard determinists would argue, some other influence from outside—perhaps a teacher who encouraged Mary or a prostitute who influenced Elaine's choice of career. The fact that hard determinists cannot trace all of the causes doesn't refute their theory. On the contrary, they would argue, the mere fact that there are causes and that many, if not most of them, are outside the control of Mary and Elaine would indicate that we cannot, and indeed, should not hold the two women morally responsible for the courses their lives take.

What the hard determinist is saying, then, is that if every event, action, result, effect—everything—has a cause, then everything, including human desires, feelings, thoughts, choices, decisions, and actions, is "determined." The hard determinist says further that if human beings are born into a world that has been determined by prior causes over which they have no control, that if their genetic makeup is not theirs to choose freely, and that if their early environment is governed by physical events and human actions over which they have no say, then none of us can be said to be free. He argues that if you keep pushing back far enough in analyzing any human action or choice, you will eventually arrive at a cause that is outside the control of the person who is choosing or acting.

Because human beings have no control over their genetic makeup or their early environment, they cannot be responsible for their original character, nor can they control what desires they have. They are, in effect, programmed to choose and act in certain ways because of these earlier forces, as well as the present forces of their environment, which are also determining them at every turn. The heart of the hard determinist's argument is summed up by John Hospers as follows:

> "We can act in accordance with our choices or decisions," he will say, "and we can choose in accordance with our desires. But we are not free to *desire*. We can choose as we please, but we can't please as we please. If my biological or psychological nature is such that at a certain moment I desire A, I shall choose A, and if it is such that I desire B, I shall choose B. I am free to choose either A or B, but I am not free to desire either A or B. Moreover, my desires are not themselves the outcomes of choices, for I cannot choose to have them or not to have them."[3]

Soft Determinism

Soft determinists maintain that there is universal causation, but, unlike hard determinists, they believe that some of this causation originates with human beings, thus giving meaning to the phrase "human freedom." If human beings can be said to cause some of their actions by means of their own minds and wills, then they can be said to have some free-dom. It is important to note that when we use the word *freedom* here, we mean freedom in a limited sense. No one is completely free. We cannot freely act on all of our desires. We cannot, for example, change ourselves into other beings or live without oxygen or snap our fingers and make people disappear; nor is it necessary that a human being have the freedom to perform such actions in order to be morally free. If there is freedom, we have to recognize that it is by nature limited. That is one reason why the soft determinist can argue that not only within causation but because of it, human beings are free. If human beings can be shown to be the originators of some causes, then—the soft determinist argues—there is human freedom within universal causation, and this is all we can hope to attain and indeed all we really need.

The strongest criticism of soft determinism comes, of course, from the hard determinists. They ask how any causes can be said to originate with human beings when the series of causes leading up to a particular effect can be traced back to factors outside of a particular human being's control. The hard determinists do not make the claim that human beings *never* cause anything to happen, but they do maintain that ultimate causes are always beyond an individual's control. Another criticism of soft determinism comes from a group calling themselves "indeterminists," and we will examine their theories before discussing determinism in more detail.

Indeterminism

Indeterminists hold that there is a certain amount of chance and freedom in the world—that not everything is caused and that there is a real pluralism in reality. Furthermore, the indeterminist believes that most of the freedom or chance that exists can be found in the area of human deliberation and choice, especially moral deliberation and decision making. William James (1842–1910), the noted American psychologist and philosopher, is the most prominent exponent of this view. James desires that there be novelty and spontaneity in the world, allowing human beings to exercise their faculties of choice and creativity. He suggests that "our first act of freedom, if we are free, ought in all inward propriety to be to affirm that we are free."[4] Our strivings for good and our regrets over bad deeds are, he feels, indications that there is freedom, for if a bad act, for example, were fully predeter-mined, then there would be no point in feeling regret.[5] James further maintains that because we can't always predict in advance whether a human being is going to take path A or path B, then chance and spontaneity evidently play at least some part in the nature of reality, and such freedom does therefore exist, at least to some extent.

The hard determinists offer several strong criticisms of the theory of indeterminism. First, isn't James's theory really based on wishful thinking rather than actual evidence or logic? Wanting to be free or wanting the world to be spontaneous does not make it so, any more than wanting the earth to be the center of the universe makes it so. Evidence and logic, say the hard determinists, point toward the conclusion that universal causation rather than indeterminism accurately describes the way things are. Hard determinists have to admit that there is no absolutely conclusive evidence for determinism, but they maintain, nevertheless, that the evidence points overwhelmingly toward universal causation rather than chance. What would an uncaused event be like, they ask—can we even describe such an event?

One criticism offered by both hard and soft determinists is that indeterminism really will not help to solve the problem of human freedom and moral responsibility in any case because if an act is not caused, then it is not caused by anyone, including the moral person. Again, this means that we would have to say that all moral acts are accidents for which we cannot assign responsibility to human beings and for which we cannot give praise, blame, reward, or punishment. Therefore, indeterminism is not only empirically doubtful but also does not support the argument for human freedom in any way. Indeterminism, in short, could only guarantee accident or chance, not human freedom. Let us now return to criticisms of hard determinism to see if we can uncover any support for the concept of human freedom.

Criticisms of Hard Determinism and Arguments for Freedom

We could argue against hard determinists that because morality is not possible given their viewpoint and because we do have morality, hard determinism does not hold. We also could argue that because human beings feel free some of the time, they must therefore *be* free. However, hard determinists would counter both of these arguments with the "facts" of universal causation; they would assert that both morality based upon freedom and the feeling that we are free are illusions, not facts.

When we are bad or good, they would argue, it is because we have been determined to be so by forces outside of our control. Even the actions of praising, blaming, rewarding, and punishing are useless, unless we can change someone's behavior programming; that is, unless we either strike a "goodness" chord that is already embedded in the person's original character or override some earlier determining factor by means of a stronger one.

What we are doing, hard determinists would say, is not getting people to freely respond and make moral decisions but merely changing the way in which they are determined. The intimation is that we would not be able to do even this if their characters were not set up in such a way as to cause them to acquiesce to such determinism. Hard determinists might advocate reward and punishment if they felt that such means could stop someone from killing people, for example. However, they would feel that it is really impossible to *morally* blame people for the way they act because they are, after all, determined. One can try to change the way in which a person is determined, but one cannot morally blame someone for acting in a way in which he or she has been determined to act. From the hard determinist's viewpoint, there is no moral responsibility in the experience of human beings; there is only the illusion of it.

Hospers agrees with the hard determinist that people very often fall victim to inner urges and desires that they do not want and cannot escape from, but he argues very effectively in rebuttal that nevertheless, to a very *limited* extent (varying considerably from person to person) and *over a considerable span of time*, we *are* free to desire or not to desire.

We can choose to do our best to get rid of certain desires and to encourage other ones; and to a limited extent we may be successful in this endeavor. People who greatly desire alcohol sometimes succeed, by joining Alcoholics Anonymous or by other means, in resisting the temptation to drink until finally they no longer desire to do so. So, it is not true that we are never free to desire or that we are always the victims of whatever desires we happen to have.[6]

Inaccurate Use of Language

Hospers also argues effectively against the hard determinists' inaccurate use of language, claiming that they tend to push words such as *freedom* right out of the context in which they make sense. For example, according to Hospers, the hard determinist maintains the impossible position that if human beings aren't completely free in an unlimited sense, then there can be no freedom at all. The hard determinist argues that in order for human beings to be free, they must have control over their own genetic makeup, their early childhood, and their "original character." This type of argument, says Hospers, simply puts too great a strain upon language. He agrees with the hard determinists that we cannot have caused our original characters, but he goes on to examine the logical fallacies that they have built around this belief. In order to cause our original characters, we would have to already have existed, and how could we exist without an original character? Hospers concludes that this whole argument is in fact self-contradictory.[7]

Human Complexity

I agree fully with Hospers's criticisms of the hard determinists' misuse of language. I also feel, however, that hard determinism does not account for the complexity of the nature of human beings, especially of human minds and consciousness; rather, it tends to oversimplify and reduce everything to the lowest common denominator. Earlier, we discussed the psychological egoist's belief that all human actions are performed by human beings in their own self-interest, regardless of the altruistic motives they may claim to have. All we require in order to refute this claim is one case of someone's stating that he or she truly performed an action strictly in someone else's interest. In the same way, we must show that human beings have enough control over causation so that they can be said to originate some causes themselves. Then we can speak of freedom, at least in the limited sense mentioned earlier.

Levels of Differences

Rocks, Plants, and Animals. When talking about universal causation, we must first take into consideration the great complexity of the human mind. A rock is dependent upon outside forces for its movement, change in shape, and change in color. Plant life is subject to forces outside and within it, and a plant grows, changes, and dies in reaction to these forces, which, as far as we can determine, operate at all times on a basis of some sort of biological (or botanical) instinct. Animals, too, although closer to human beings in their bodies and minds, are often governed by instinctual actions programmed down through the years by hereditary and genetic changes.

As we move along the evolutionary scale from inanimate to animate beings and from vegetative to animalistic beings, we see the element of freedom increase with each step. The rock, which has no freedom at all, is drastically different from the plant, which is affected by its own internal workings as well as by outside forces. Animals are much more mobile than plants, have a greater observable consciousness, and can even be said to make some limited choices. For example, if a forest is on fire, the instinct to survive will cause an animal to attempt to escape by running away from the fire. Assuming that the fire is covering the 180 degrees of ground behind the animal, then there are 180 degrees in front of him. Because he has a 180-degree range of directions in which to run, what makes him choose a particular direction? There may be obstacles that narrow the number of possible directions, but even within the narrow range of possibilities, doesn't the animal, in a limited sense at least, "choose" a pathway of escape?

Human Beings. When, on the evolutionary scale, we reach human beings, who have a much more sophisticated consciousness and whose minds and emotions are developed far beyond those of any other observable beings, then the possibility of freedom increases greatly. It is the area of consciousness, or the human mind and its power of reason, upon which most soft determinists and indeterminists base their arguments for human freedom.

Existentialism and Human Consciousness. One of the best arguments for freedom comes from the existentialists, especially the philosopher Jean-Paul Sartre (1905–1980).[8] Sartre believed that there does exist a limited determinism in that people cannot help that they are born, how they are born, in what century or to which parents they are born; but he also believed that people can help to determine how they live. Sartre maintained that human beings have freedom because human perception is open-ended. He agreed with the philosopher Edmund Husserl (1859–1938) that consciousness is directional and creative. (The word Husserl used is *intentional*, in the sense that consciousness "intends" things rather than merely passively receiving them.) In other words, a person may drive along the same route from work every day for a year, yet each trip will be different in the sense that the person's mind notices different objects along the way. Naturally, some of the external objects along the route change from day to day, but even if they didn't, the human mind could direct itself in different ways, selecting among the objects and thus, in a sense, *create* its own experience. If the possibilities are open-ended, there is a myriad to choose from; because the human mind can select and direct itself differently, there are many more possibilities of choice available to the human being than there are to the forest animal with the fire at its back. The level of sophistication of choices is also, of course, much higher.

If the human mind can, even in part, create its own experience, then experience is not just waiting in a deterministic sense to impinge itself upon human consciousness. As Sartre pointed out, you may have been born crippled or blind, and you were not free to choose otherwise, but you are free with regard to how you choose to live with your infirmity. You are determined in your physical limitations, you are even determined by the culture, economic level, and family into which you are born, but you are not completely determined—unless you *choose* to be—with regard to how you live out your life, even though it has been influenced, in part, by all of these factors. Building upon the Hospers example cited earlier, we can see that this means that although I may have been born with a physical or psychological lack or urge that causes me to become addicted to alcohol when I drink it, I may become aware of this lack or urge and—with or without help—override this deterministic factor in my life.

One might say that my consciousness is directing itself to a new life experience, one free from addiction to alcohol and all of its attendant difficulties. I, then, to some extent create that life experience for myself, even though I have, in my physical and psychological nature, formerly been determined very strongly toward the completely different life experience of a person addicted to alcohol. Almost all of the groups that have been successful in helping people to overcome the various drug addictions have stated that all they can really do is to try to make people strong enough so that they can make the choice for nonaddiction themselves, and then to support them at every point along the way; the choice, however, has to be the addicts'. And until they actively choose the new life experience, their lives probably will not change very much. This argument should convince us that there *is* such a thing as human freedom. And once we have accepted that it does exist, it is only logical to assume that it applies to morality as well as to choosing what clothes we will wear or where we will spend this year's vacation.

Conclusion: Soft Determinism

It would seem, then, that the only tenable position in this controversy is soft determinism, which views universal causation as being a strongly supported theory of reality that is still compatible with human freedom. At least, this is the position that I support. Our freedom is limited, and there are many times when our actions are not within our control. We may be suffering from a psychological compulsion such as kleptomania and therefore cannot be held morally responsible for stealing because our compulsion to steal is beyond our control. We may be forced at gunpoint to do something that we know is morally wrong, or we may be constrained in such a way that we cannot do something morally right. We may be powerfully affected by the way we were treated by our family, by our genetic deficiencies, by the century in which we were born, by the culture and economic level into which we were born: All of these things may determine our characters to a great degree. But—to paraphrase Hospers—nevertheless, to some extent (varying considerably from person to person) and over a considerable span of time, we *are* free to desire or not to desire, to choose or not to choose, to act or not to act.

Upon acceptance of this viewpoint, then, it does make sense to assign moral responsibility to human beings when appropriate, and it also makes sense to praise, blame, reward, and punish them for their actions. We certainly should be careful to ascertain that people are not acting from uncontrollable compulsions or constraints before we assign praise or blame to them. Having ascertained, however, that they have acted in freedom, it does make sense to talk of moral responsibility and its attendant rewards and punishments.

Chapter Summary

I. Freedom versus determinism
  A. *Determinism* means the same thing as *universal causation*; that is, for every effect, event, or occurrence in reality, a cause or causes exist. There is no such thing as an uncaused event.
  B. The theory of determinism holds serious implications for morality.
    1. How can we tell people what they should or ought to do if they are programmed or predetermined to act in the ways they do?
    2. How can we praise, blame, reward, and punish if people cannot help acting in the ways they do?

II. Types and theories of determinism
  A. Religious determinism—predestination—is the theory that if God is all-powerful and all-knowing, then He must have predestined everything that occurs.
    1. There is a problem here in proving that there is such a being and, if He does exist, that He is all-powerful and all-knowing and has predestined everything.
    2. Most theories of salvation make no sense if human beings are not free to make choices between good and evil.
  B. There are several types of scientific determinism.
    1. Physical determinism arose from discoveries in the physical sciences.
      (a) Sir Isaac Newton theorized that everything in reality is basically material, or physical, in nature and is therefore completely determined by natural laws, such as the law of gravity.
      (b) There are problems with this theory.
        (1) Natural laws state probabilities, not certainties.
        (2) Modern physics has raised serious doubts about Newtonian physics.
    2. Advances in the natural sciences gave rise to biological and genetic determinism.
      (a) Charles Darwin's theories—that species evolve by means of natural selection and that only the fittest survive—led to a belief that nature determines human beings.
      (b) A more sophisticated form of this theory states that human beings are totally determined by their genetic makeup, over which they have no control.
    3. The problem with both forms of scientific determinism is that they reduce human beings strictly to the physical, disregarding the possibility of a mental or spiritual side.
  C. Historical, or cultural, determinism arose from the theories of Georg Hegel.
    1. Hegel maintained that an absolute mind is trying to realize itself in perfection and manifest itself through the history of the world, and that human beings therefore are completely determined by their past and present history and cultures.
    2. There are problems with this theory.
      (a) It is difficult to prove the existence of both an "absolute mind" and a mind that can exist without a body.
      (b) Other theories of history are just as plausible, if not more so.
  D. Economic or social determinism arose from the theories of Karl Marx.
    1. Marx says that human beings are determined by economic class struggles that inevitably will lead to a classless society.
    2. The problems with this theory are similar to those raised by Hegel's.
      (a) Marx's theory is based upon unproved assumptions, and other theories of economics are equally plausible.
      (b) Even though human beings are influenced by economics, other influences exist, such as science, technology, and human beings themselves, that affect economics.

E. Psychological determinism arose out of the work of Freud and the behaviorists.

1. Freudian psychology maintains that human beings are affected by their unconscious drives and their attempts to repress them to the extent that their early childhood determines the course of their adult lives. The main criticism of this theory is that it is too generalized to have any real basis in fact.

2. The type of psychological determinism espoused by the behaviorists, particularly B. F. Skinner, maintains that human beings are completely physical beings whose development is totally determined by those external stimuli provided by their physical and cultural environments.

3. There are problems with this theory.

   (a) It is based on a completely materialistic view of human beings, which does not stand up to evidence or argument.

   (b) Like Freud's theories, it goes too far in its claims, using the validity of operant conditioning in some instances as a basis for claiming its validity in all instances.

III. Fatalism and hard and soft determinism

A. Fatalism is the belief that all events are irrevocably fixed and predetermined so that human beings cannot alter them in any way.

1. Sometimes events are outside of our control, but it does not make sense to act as if all events were outside of human control.

2. This is an impractical theory by which few people, if any, really attempt to live their lives.

B. Hard determinism is the theory that if all events are caused, then freedom is incompatible with determinism.

C. Soft determinism is the theory that all events are caused, but that some events and causes originate with human beings. The hard determinist criticizes the soft determinist by questioning how human beings can be said to originate any events when, if one traces causes back far enough, they end up being outside of the control of human beings.

IV. Indeterminism

A. Indeterminists maintain that there is a certain amount of chance and freedom in the world, and that not everything is caused.

1. William James says that he desires that there be novelty and spontaneity in the world, allowing human beings to be free and creative.

2. James feels that our strivings for good over the bad and our regrets over our bad deeds mean that we must be free.

B. There are problems with this theory.

1. It seems to be based upon wishful thinking rather than upon evidence or logical argument.

2. There is little evidence to suggest that uncaused events exist.

3. If some events are totally uncaused, then they are not caused by anything or anybody; therefore, indeterminism is no guarantee of human freedom, only of chance.

V. Criticisms of hard determinism and arguments for freedom

A. Hard determinists push language out of context.

B. Their arguments do not account for the complexity of the nature of human beings. Like the psychological egoist, they try to reduce what is in fact really complex to something simple, and this reductionism will not work.

C. Human minds and human perception are open-ended and creative—humans create their experience of the world. They are not mere passive receivers of sense experience, but active seekers and creators.

D. Soft determinism seems to be the only tenable position. Acceptance of this position allows us to assign moral responsibility to human beings and to praise, blame, reward, and punish them when and if it is justifiable to do so.

Exercises for Review

1. Define and explain the terms *determinism, indeterminism, fatalism, predestination, universal causation*, and *freedom*.
2. Differentiate between hard and soft determinism, indeterminism, and fatalism. What are the problems associated with each theory?
3. Discuss whether you believe human beings are free or determined. If they are free, to what extent are they free? If they are determined, what difficulties does this raise for morality?
4. How does the existentialist view of human consciousness relate to the argument for human freedom?
5. Research any of the following men and their work and explain in full the extent to which you think their theories are valid or invalid where freedom and determinism are concerned: Calvin and predestination; Newton and scientific determinism; Darwin and biological determinism; Hegel and historical determinism; Marx and economic determinism; Freud and psychological determinism; Skinner and behaviorism; William James and indeterminism; Sartre and freedom.

Discussion Questions

1. Analyze any act you have committed about which you have strong feelings (for example, of regret or of pride), and argue to what extent you feel that this act was freely done by you or determined by forces working within or outside you. Be specific.
2. Read any of the following literary works, and discuss the extent to which the main characters are free or determined: Albert Camus's *The Stranger*; Herman Melville's *Bartleby the Scrivener*; Stephen Crane's *The Open Boat*; Joan Didion's *Play It as It Lays*; Fyodor Dostoyevsky's *Crime and Punishment*; Arthur Miller's *Death of a Salesman*.
3. Research the background of some great men or women (for example, Albert Einstein, Eleanor Roosevelt, John F. Kennedy, Golda Meier, Florence Nightingale, Bill Clinton, Dwight Eisenhower, Martin Luther King Mary Cassatt, Pablo Picasso) or some infamous men or women (for example, Charles Manson, Lee Harvey Oswald, Ma Barker, Sadam Hussein, the Boston Strangler, Mata Hari, Lizzie Borden, Adolf Hitler), and discuss the extent to which their goodness or badness was determined by forces over which they had no control (for example, genetic makeup, early childhood, economic or cultural deprivation).
4. Read any of the following books and discuss both how the authors view determinism and freedom and what you think of the societies depicted in these books: Aldous Huxley's *Brave New World, Brave New World Revisited*, and *Island*; George Orwell's *1984* and *Animal Farm*; Plato's *The Republic*; B. F. Skinner's *Walden II*; Ray Bradbury's *Fahrenheit 451*; Robert Heinlein's *The Moon Is a Harsh Mistress*; Jean-Paul Sartre's *No Exit* and *Nausea*.
5. When you examine the world around you, to what extent do you believe that human beings are subject to the same types of determinism as plants and animals are? Be specific.

Notes

1. See John Hick, *Philosophy of Religion*, 3rd ed. (Upper Saddle River, NJ: Prentice Hall, 1983), 36–43, and John Hospers, *Introduction to Philosophical Analysis*, 2nd ed. (Upper Saddle River, NJ: Prentice Hall, 1967), 461–76, for a full discussion of this problem.
2. See Hospers, *Introduction to Philosophical Analysis*, 378–91.
3. See John Hospers, *Human Conduct: An Introduction to the Problems of Ethics* (New York: Harcourt Brace Jovanovich, 1961), 508.
4. William James, *The Will to Believe and Other Essays in Popular Philosophy* (New York: Longmans, Green, 1912), 146.
5. Ibid., 161–62.
6. Hospers, *Human Conduct*, 508–9.
7. Ibid., 513–17.
8. Mary Warnock, *Existentialism* (New York: Oxford University Press, 1970), 113–24.

Research Navigator™
(http://www.researchnavigator.com)

This web site offers three research data bases: EBSCO's *Content Select Academic Journal and Abstract Database*, *New York Times Search by Subject* Archive, and *Best of the Web* Link Library. In addition, this site provides helpful advice on how to conduct efficient and productive research from choosing a topic to polishing the final draft. Beginning philosophy students probably will find the *Best of the Web* Link Library the most appropriate place to start their research.

The free access code necessary to employ Research Navigator™ can be found in the Prentice Hall Guide to Evaluating Online Resources. If your text did not come with this guide, please go to *www.prenhall.com/contentselect* for information on how you can purchase an access code.

Chapter

7

Reward and Punishment

Objectives

After you have read this chapter, you should be able to

1. Understand the relationship between reward and punishment and justice.
2. Understand the meanings and differences among the three theories of reward and punishment: retribution, utilitarianism, and restitution.
3. Identify and understand the many criteria for rewarding and punishing.
4. Identify and understand the arguments for and against all three theories.
5. Describe John Rawls' Theory of Justice.

Definition of Key Terms

Retributive Justice.   Probably the oldest form of justice, retributive justice is best expressed in the biblical saying, "an eye for an eye and a tooth for a tooth" (Exodus 21:24–25). This kind of justice means that people should get what they deserve, either by way of reward or punishment, regardless of the consequences.

Distributive Justice.   Distributive justice concerns itself essentially with the equitable distribution of good and bad to human beings on a just and fair basis.

Reward.   Reward is something given or received for worthy behavior, usually on the basis of merit, deserts (what people deserve), or ability.[1]

Punishment.   Punishment is the act of penalizing someone for a crime, fault, or misbehavior; a penalty for wrongdoing.[2]

Retribution (Deserts Theory).   Retribution is the act of giving people what they deserve, regardless of the consequences—in punishment sometimes referred to as the "eye for an eye, tooth for a tooth" or "revenge" or "just deserts" theory.

Utilitarianism (Results Theory).   Utilitarianism advocates rewarding or punishing based upon the results of the act and whether or not it brings about the greatest good consequences for the greatest number of people.

Restitution (Compensation Theory).   Restitution is the act of somehow compensating a victim for harm or wrong done to him or her; such compensation usually is required to be made to the victim by the perpetrator of the harm or wrong.

Reward and Punishment in Relationship to Justice

Nowhere does the issue of being just or fair arise more powerfully than in the matters of reward and punishment, and especially punishment. One element missing from the ethical theories as I have described them thus far is a discussion of what to do with those who seriously violate one or more of the basic ethical tenets. Should the same principle of justice be applied to grievous wrongdoers as well as to those who follow an ethical system faithfully, or are the transgressors beneath this principle because of their unethical actions and behavior? What I shall attempt to do in this chapter is to discuss reward and punishment as aspects of justice and to present the various theories of distributing reward and punishment in order to see whether we can discover which would be the most just.

Elements of Justice

Several elements of justice in general apply specifically to reward and punishment.

What Justice Involves

Just as ethics or morality involves the "treatment" of human beings by other human beings (see the working definition of ethics in Chapter 1), justice as an aspect of ethics involves the same thing. When we talk about being just or fair, we are talking about being just or fair to other human beings, and reward and punishment have to do with the way in which one human being treats another. What we are discussing here, then, is the notion of *distributive justice*, or how we can dispense good and bad or reward and punishment on a just and fair basis.

Concern with Past Events

Justice basically is concerned with past rather than future events in that we reward or punish people for what they *have done*, not for what they *will do*. It is certainly unfair and even unrealistic to reward or punish people for what they *might do* even though incentives sometimes are given with an eye to future accomplishments and even though—as you will see when we discuss the utilitarian theory—to some extent the future can be considered when one is rewarding or punishing.

Individualistic Rather Than Collectivistic

Justice should be individualistic in its application, not collectivistic. It is individuals rather than groups who are deserving of reward and punishment. If we punish groups or individuals because they are a part of a larger group, then our punishment will be collectivistic, or we will be guilty of *mass punishment*, as it is sometimes called. This type of punishment is a source of a good deal of the injustice in our society. It is very closely related to discrimination by race, religion, sex, age, and mental or physical handicap, and it tends to unjustly punish individuals simply because they are members of some group against which many people are prejudiced.

The military, among other institutions in our society, often is guilty of collective punishment. If one serviceman does not keep his area clean, his bed made, or his uniform up to snuff, then everyone in his barracks is punished by being denied passes or other privileges. The military's purpose in doing this is to prod the nonwrongdoer into pressuring the wrongdoer to correct his ways, but the punishment as it is meted out to include the innocent is unjust. The offending serviceman should alone be punished, and not his obedient peers.

Comparative Justice

Comparative justice deals with the way in which a person is treated in relation to another person. For example, if two people have committed murder under similar circumstances and one gets out of prison in ten years but the other is executed, this might be considered as comparative, but not collectivistic injustice, depending, of course, upon the circumstances, extenuating or otherwise, surrounding each crime.[3]

Reward

Reward is one method of distributing on a fair and just basis the good that we are concerned with. There are basically four ways in which the good or rewards can be distributed:

1. As equally among people as possible without regard to their abilities or merits.
2. According to people's abilities.
3. According to what they merit, or deserve.
4. According to their needs.

We will examine these as well as other criteria.

Criteria for Rewarding People

Egalitarian Criterion or Equal Distribution of Goods and Rewards. Wouldn't it be most just and fair to distribute good things and rewards equally among people, regardless of their merits, abilities, needs, or what they produce? An example that shows the significance of distributing good and bad equally among people concerns the scarcity of certain medical resources.

For example, in 1962 there were not enough kidney machines to dialyze (see Glossary for definition of dialysis) the kidneys of people who were in various stages of kidney failure. When there is not enough to go around of something as important as this, an ethical question arises: how to make a decision that will be just or fair to everyone concerned. Swedish Hospital in Seattle, Washington, was the first hospital to deal with this problem in connection with kidney patients, and it attempted to solve the problem by establishing two committees: a medical panel, to select those people capable of being medically assisted by dialysis, and a panel of mostly nonmedical people who would then decide who, out of those medically qualified for dialysis, would actually get the treatment. In 1963, the second panel was composed of a lawyer, a clergyman, a housewife, a banker, a labor leader, and two physicians. The medical panel had narrowed the 30 patients needing dialysis to 17, and the nonmedical panel was asked to consider the following factors: age; sex; marital status and number of dependents; income; net worth; emotional stability (especially in the sense of being able to accept treatment); education; occupation; past performance and future potential; and references.

The committee soon realized that making fair decisions was a nearly impossible task. Which factors should be considered seriously and in what order of importance: Whether the person was educated or uneducated? Whether the person was a professional, a laborer, or an office worker? Whether the person was religious or not? Whether the person was male or female? Whether the person had good, mediocre, or only poor references as to his or her character, potential, or past performance? Such difficulties proved to be insurmountable, and the decisions were terribly agonizing for this panel of extremely well-meaning people. A much more complete description of the committee and its problems may be found in Paul Ramsey's *The Patient as Person*,[4] but what follows will illustrate a few of the difficulties.

> What happens when we get two men with the same job, the same number of children, the same income, and so forth? Between a man with three children and a man with an older wife and six children we must, for the sake of the children, reckon the surviving widow's opportunity to remarry. In estimating "worth to society," how much chance would an artist or a composer have before this committee in comparison with the needs of a woman with six children? Finally, if a patient is given a place in a kidney dialysis program because he "passed" a comparative evaluation of his worthiness in terms of broad social standards of eligibility, the needs of his dependents, or his potentiality for contribution to humanity, one can ask whether he should be removed from the program when his esteemed character changes. . . . As Dr. George Schreiner said, "You should be logical and say that when a man stops going to church or is divorced or loses his job, he ought to be removed from the programme and somebody else who fulfills these criteria substituted."[5]

Again, the question is how one is to distribute this "good" (dialysis) to people on a just and fair basis. We can, in this instance at least, rule out need because the patients all "need" the dialysis. If we go by abilities, how are we to distinguish justly between a house-wife and mother, a lawyer, a doctor, an executive, a member of the clergy, a teacher, and a laborer, all of whom may be very able in their particular jobs? If we go by what people deserve or merit, then how are we to distinguish among these people, who all may be deserving of the treatment in the sense that they are productive human beings in their own fields and within their own families and communities? If we are going to rank people by merit, then what are the criteria to be, and how can they be just? For example, will we place a very clever and intelligent lawyer at the top and a rather simple but hardworking laborer at the bottom? These distinctions, of course, can be worked out on a quite arbitrary basis, as indeed they have been in various totalitarian societies, but then we must question whether being arbitrary is just and fair.

The most ideal solution is to gain enough resources so that everyone who needs them can have them, but this probably will never happen in all areas of need because there are so many needs and a definite limitation on available resources. Therefore, how are we to choose justly? Evidently, the "let the better person live" notion that we have just been discussing will not work too well, or at least will fall far short of distributing the resources fairly. We can also consider the alternative "all should die," as Ramsey does, but who would deem it fair to let all 17 people die when we are certain that 10 of them can live—who wants to "throw out the baby with the bathwater"?[6] The other alternative, which is the approach I would argue for, is the "drawing of straws" approach.[7] After having witnessed the agonies undergone by the Swedish Hospital committee, many other committees or dialysis units throughout the country used a lottery method once the medical decisions had been made.

This alternative—that the lives of people must be decided by a lottery—may not be palatable to many people, but how else can you be just and fair toward all 17 people? Would you, as a kidney patient, rather be denied dialysis because you are not thought to be as worthy, able, or deserving as someone else, or because you did not win a fairly conducted lottery? At least, we would have to admit that everyone was treated fairly and justly by the latter means. It seems, then, at least in this situation, that this egalitarian way of determining justice is the most ethical, just, and fair.

Problems with Equality of Distribution. And yet, there are problems with the egalitarian method of distribution. By definition, it ignores other criteria deemed important by their advocates and by people in general, such as merit, ability, need, productiveness, and effort, in its attempt to be fair and egalitarian in its approach to rewarding. Second, in what ways and to what extent are people equal? Is a doctor with long years of training equal to a janitor who learned the trade in a few weeks or months on the job? Should a beginning pianist and a fully trained concert pianist both be given equal chances to perform at Carnegie Hall? Should students be allowed to depose a fully trained, credentialed teacher and conduct class in the teacher's place? As you can see, it doesn't take many examples to point out the inequalities among people, jobs, and professions. So in what sense should they all be rewarded the same?

Perhaps they should all be given equality of consideration *if* they have other attributes or fulfill other qualifications that are necessary to certain jobs or professions, for example. People certainly should not be denied opportunities because of race, sex, religion, age, or handicap, but what if a job requires a great deal of physical strength and stamina? Unless women, senior citizens, or handicapped people can muster these attributes, should they be given equal opportunity for such a job along with those who can?

Finally, can we really ignore all of the other criteria used to determine reward, such as what people produce; effort extended; ability; need; long and expensive training; expensive equipment; physical danger; and unpleasantness of job? Shouldn't these at least be considered, and when they are, isn't equality as a basis of reward weakened? It would at least seem that we must examine these other criteria before settling upon an egalitarian approach to reward.

Production, or What People Produce. One criterion for rewarding is based upon what people produce, achieve, or accomplish through their own efforts, regardless of the amount of effort or the time taken. For instance, if a student has done exceptional work in a class, by this criterion she is entitled to a grade of A even if she had to put out very little effort or time because, for example, she has an excellent mathematical imagination and above-average ability. That another member of the class raised himself from failing work to a C by the end of the semester, by expending a great deal of time and effort, doesn't mean he gets an A, too. He still has produced only C work through his efforts.

This production can be based upon quantity or quality, or both. For example, fruit or vegetable pickers are paid mostly on a piecework basis; that is, the more potatoes or peaches they pick in a day, the more they get paid. Others are paid basically for the quality of their work: for having creative ideas that improve the quality of a company's product, efficiency, or image. Probably most employers will reward on a basis both of quality and quantity. The worker who can produce a high-quality product in large quantity is more highly paid than one who produces quality goods in small quantity, or one who produces a lot of goods of only mediocre or sometimes even poor quality. Therefore, based upon this criterion, people are rewarded solely on what they deserve, or merit, in view of what and/or how much they have produced; little account is taken of effort, ability, or need in determining whom to reward. The problems inherent in this method will be discussed as we proceed.

Effort. Another standard for rewarding, which was hinted at in the previous section, is effort. This criterion would reward effort regardless of the quantity or quality of what is produced, achieved, or accomplished. In a classroom situation, those who put out the greatest effort according to their abilities would be rewarded the most. In a work situation, each employee would be required to put in eight hours of his greatest effort, and each would be paid the same wage.

There are certainly problems with this notion in that, for one thing, those who have contracted to do a job (for example, building contractors) and who are being paid so much for the job, are being paid not for how much time and effort they put in but solely for what they produce: a finished job. And how can effort be measured? Some people will work harder if given some incentive to do so, and others will make only an average effort no matter what they are offered. Third, suppose a fairly dull-witted person and a very bright person both work for eight hours at top capacity. Should they both receive the same consideration for wages and promotions? Which one would you want as a foreman or executive, for example: the one who is brighter or the one who is duller, given that they both make a full effort every day? The difficulty in determining effort, and the problem that effort alone does not necessarily make a person deserving of reward, causes this criterion to be a weak one, at least when taken by itself.

Ability. Some people think that reward should be made on a basis of ability. But first, we must distinguish between natural and acquired abilities. Some people, such as the A student I described earlier, have superior natural abilities in certain areas. However, is merely having natural abilities ever enough? Should people be rewarded simply because they have certain abilities through no responsibility of their own? What if people choose not to put their abilities to use, owing to laziness or procrastination? If they are indeed more able than others but choose not to employ their abilities, should they be rewarded over people who do not have such abilities but who work hard and produce more and better?

Acquired abilities are different in that people have had to put out time, effort, and money to get them. For example, certain professionals, such as doctors and lawyers, must expend a great deal of time and money in order to acquire the abilities of their profession. Such abilities, once acquired, would be more significant than natural ones as far as rewarding is concerned. Of course, not using these skills remains as much of a problem as it does with natural abilities. It would seem, then, that abilities alone, whether natural or acquired, would not constitute a good criterion for reward—some combination with effort and production would have to be included in order to measure the use of and achievement attained by such abilities.

Need. Some argue that good things and rewards should be handed out on the basis of need; that is, people who have the greatest needs should be given the most good things or should be "rewarded" for their need. Let us first distinguish between two types of need: private and public.

Private need is concerned with what individuals need as a result of being poor or out of work. Many people argue that we should help the poor and needy among us and that we should give them some of or the same goods as the rest of us possess. From a humane point of view, of course, helping the needy would seem to be an honorable ideal. However, to what extent do they deserve to be rewarded on the basis of need alone? For example, should we hire only the needy, regardless of qualifications or abilities? As John Hospers points out, people who need jobs most are often those who have no employable skills, and should employers load their businesses with unskilled workers and pay them the same as they would skilled workers?[8] What would happen to their businesses if they did, and what incentives would skilled workers have to continue to work for such employers?

The questions pertaining to need often arise in academic situations when financial aid or scholarships are to be awarded. Should they be awarded to the most needy, the brightest, or both? It would seem that the ideal situation would be one in which those who have the highest academic potential and the highest need should be the ones to get these rewards, but often the most needy are not as academically successful as the less needy. And what about the consistently high-scoring student whose need isn't as great as the more needy student's, or who has little or no need? Many such students feel that recognition for their outstanding academic achievement is being overshadowed by the needs of those who are average or only slightly-above-average students. One of the biggest problems with rewarding on the basis of need, both in the academic and the business world, is that it eliminates the incentive to make an effort or develop abilities. If students or others are going to be rewarded on a basis of need alone, then why try to do anything other than be needy? Second, this criterion obviously is not just or fair to talented and hardworking people. Helping the needy, then, is an admirable goal, but to reward them, in the fullest sense of the word, on the basis of need alone, would seem to be neither just nor fair to those who fall into other categories.

Public need is somewhat different than private need in that here rewarding is done on the basis of people's contribution to or fulfilling of public needs. For example, doctors often are rewarded because they fulfill a need that everyone has for health care. On the other hand, nurses, who fulfill the same need in different but extremely important ways, are not rewarded the same as doctors. In fact, some nurses feel they are penalized rather than rewarded for what they are doing. This points out the difficulty of determining which needs are the most important, and how the suppliers of those needs should be rewarded. How will we rate farmers, plumbers, jewelers, teachers, police, and entertainers as to their relative importance in supplying public needs? Sometimes people who supply less important needs get much greater rewards for their efforts than those who supply more important ones. Some entertainers and athletes, for example, are much more munificently rewarded than police officers, firefighters, or nurses, all of whom risk their lives or try to protect human life every day. How we should reward public need, then, is a difficult problem to resolve.

Other Criteria. Five other criteria should be mentioned before we enter into our discussion of the two major theories dealing with reward.

1. *Long and expensive training in a profession.* For example, it often takes three or four years beyond the bachelor's degree to become a lawyer, and more beyond it to become a doctor—shouldn't this be rewarded in some way? On the other hand, teachers who get degrees beyond the B.A., which may take them two to five years, depending upon the degree, often aren't paid as much as entry-level skilled laborers, who may never have had to finish high school, much less go on to college. In other words, rewarding on this basis seems to be uneven, to say the least. Also, should incompetent doctors or lawyers be rewarded for the length and cost of their training without regard to ability or effort?

2. *Job or profession requiring expensive equipment.* Some feel that those who are required to purchase and maintain expensive equipment should also be rewarded. Doctors and dentists, who require very expensive equipment, would be rewarded more than others, according to this criterion. Perhaps this is fair or just, but how much more should they be rewarded than practitioners in professions that don't require

expensive equipment but do require a lot of education and training or skills or hazardous duty? And to what extent should their rewards continue after the equipment is essentially paid off, for as long as they practice their professions?

3. *Physical danger.* Should members of bomb squads and other hazardous duties be paid extra or given higher wages because of the nature of their duties? Extra pay often is allotted to such professions in the military with its combat, flight, and special duty pay, but very often it is not at all commensurate with the dangers or hazards faced. Again, police officers, firefighters, and nurses are seldom given any extra pay, and often their regular pay does not really compensate or reward them for all the risks to their and others' lives.

4. *Unpleasantness of job.* Another of the "other" criteria is that of rewarding people for the unpleasantness of their jobs; for example, paying garbage collectors high wages because what they do is necessary, fulfills a public need, and because few people want to do such jobs. The main difficulties here are, how are we to decide which jobs get the greater reward because of their unpleasantness, and how much reward are the people doing them to be given?

5. *Seniority.* Many institutions and businesses reward on the basis of seniority. The argument here is that those who have shown loyalty and perseverance through long years of service to a specific organization should be rewarded. Often when people are in jobs for too long a time, however, they may become ineffective or even burned-out. If such people are no longer effective workers, should they continue to be promoted and rewarded over those who may be junior to them in seniority but who are more skillful as workers? Only if qualifications and abilities are equal can seniority be a fair way of rewarding people for their efforts.

Theories of How to Reward

Two major theories dealing with reward also deal with punishment, as you will see in the next section of this chapter. These are the *retributivist*, or *deserts*, theory and the *utilitarian*, or *results*, theory.

Retributivist, or Deserts, Theory

The first theory concerns itself strictly with what people deserve, or merit, for what they have done in the past. These theorists feel that people ought to be rewarded for what they have done, not for what the consequences of what they have done may be, or what kind of future good consequences may be derived from rewarding them. Retributivists generally focus on rewarding people for their efforts. They are not concerned with the utility of rewarding people—such as incentives to do more and better work, or what is in the public good—but rather on what effort people have expended rather than what they have done as a result of that effort. Therefore, two people who put out their best efforts on the job for eight hours a day would, according to this theory, be rewarded in the same way or paid the same wage because they deserve it regardless of any future consequences.

Obviously, one such future consequence might be that a brighter and more productive worker would seek employment elsewhere, where he or she could be rewarded for abilities as well as effort, and then the company might lose its better workers and put out a product of less quality and in less quantity. Also, people would not seek dangerous or unpleasant work because there would be little or no incentive for them to do so. Such an approach might affect not only a particular business alone but also, if applied on a widespread basis, an entire economy. The retributivist would argue that at least all people would be getting what they deserve and that they should be rewarded on that basis alone. The utilitarian would argue that although this might be just, still the utility, or "usefulness" of rewarding in this manner would not be in the best interests of everyone.

Utilitarian, or Results, Theory

As we discovered in Chapter 2, utilitarians base their ethical theories upon good consequences for everyone affected by acts or rules. Unlike the retributivists, they emphasize the future results of rewarding rather than merely respond to past efforts. The utilitarian would argue that rewards should be given only upon a basis seeking to bring about good consequences for everyone, so that if rewarding a worker in a certain way will give him or her an incentive to do better and work harder or encourage more people to do the same, then the proper reward to accomplish all of this should be given.

The utilitarian definitely would be in favor of paying higher wages or giving extra pay for dangerous or unpleasant jobs because the good consequences that would derive from doing so would be to attract people to these jobs who might not otherwise have been willing to do them. Utilitarians also would believe in rewarding workers who are brighter or who produce more and better results regardless of the effort they put in because in the long run doing so will bring about the best consequences not only for these particular workers but for the company and the economy in general.

One of the problems with the utilitarian theory is that instead of rewarding hard work and conscientiousness, it essentially rewards production. For example, if a flamboyant, playboy type of employee who makes little or no effort can bring in more business than a hardworking, conscientious, but somewhat dull employee, then the former would be rewarded more than the latter even though the latter might be more deserving. This would be discouraging to the hard worker, who might quit. The retributivist would argue, of course, that the hard worker is not getting what he deserves, whereas the playboy is getting more than he deserves because he has put in much less effort than the hardworking employee.

Another problem with the utilitarian approach is that if good consequences alone are the criterion for reward, then it is possible to reward a totally undeserving person. For example, suppose a boss knows that one of his workers, Tom, is totally incompetent but is extremely well liked by his fellow workers. Thinking of good consequences—the morale and happiness of the workers—and not of what Tom deserves, he might give Tom a promotion and a raise. This is possible under a strictly utilitarian results-theory approach to reward. As you can see, the difficulty of whom and how to reward is a real problem.

John Rawls and His Theory of Justice

American philosopher John Rawls (1921–2002) has developed an influential theory of "Justice as Fairness." In this chapter the ideas of Rawls are contrasted with those of an equally prominent American philosopher, Robert Nozick (1938–2002).

Natural Rights versus Rights of a Just Society

John Locke (1632–1704) and the more contemporary philosopher, Robert Nozick, believe that human rights are natural rights, that is, they somehow exist in human beings through nature.

According to these two philosophers, these rights are life, liberty, and property. According to Thomas Jefferson, in the Declaration of Independence, they are life, liberty, and the pursuit of happiness. These rights, according to Locke and Nozick, cannot be violated by any governmental laws, for example, government invasion of property, government-mandated affirmative action, or government-mandated payments to the poor, especially by taxation of the wealthier members of society. One of the more immediate problems with this theory is where do natural rights come from? Some have said from God, but this theory has all of the attendant problems of proving the existence of God and that such rights were indeed God given.

Rawls, on the other hand, believes that such rights are given to human beings by a just society in which no one has an unfair advantage over others. In other words, Rawls believes we must adopt principles of social justice which we would agree upon behind what he calls a "veil of ignorance." That is, we must know how such principles would shape society without knowing our specific position in that society. We must establish such principles, then, without regard to anyone's position in the society. Behind this veil of ignorance, Rawls' "original position," we then could set up principles for fairness and justice for all without regard for anyone's specific talents, inclinations, social status, political ideology, or any other accidental features of their lives. One might say that the veil of ignorance is a way of looking at society in a neutral manner without regard to individual characteristics of anyone.

Rawls' Two Basic Principles

The Equality Principle. Each person has equal rights to maximum liberty compatible with the same amount of liberty for everyone else. In other words there must be freedom for all.

The Difference Principle. Any inequality is permissible to the extent that it is to everyone's advantage, including people at the bottom of society's ranks, and that it arises under conditions of equal opportunity. For example, doctors are necessary for the health and well-being of everyone in a society, so doctors receive more pay and advantages than blue-collar workers because they have spent a great deal of time and money achieving their medical degrees, and having good doctors is advantageous to everyone in the society. However, everyone must also have equal access to medical schools regardless of race or gender, for example. Therefore, such inequality is permitted in a just society.

The first principle gives members of society the freedom advocated by Locke and Nozick. However, the second principle gives people many more individual rights not among their so-called natural rights; for example, people at the bottom of the economic scale have the right to a minimum income which must be supplemented by government taxes on others. Rawls believes that justice as fairness requires the distribution of wealth to all members of society, and the rule governing the distribution of wealth must give no member of society unfair advantage over other members. Rawls believes that we can guarantee a just and fair outcome by requiring the rule be acceptable to all members of society without their knowing how the rule will work out for them, that is, they will know how wealth will be distributed among different segments of society without knowing to which segment they will belong. They must be willing to accept the rule no matter what their segment will be. This, of course, would violate Locke's and Nozick's natural rights theory. Rawls would accomplish the distribution of wealth by what is known as a transfer of payments, that is, he would tax those nearest the top ranks of wealth to supplement the income of the poor.

Difference between Nozick and Rawls

Nozick, who is a libertarian, seeks to maximize individual liberty and minimize or even eliminate any violation of liberty by government or others. He believes that the wealth of society is the sum of individuals' wealth. Rawls, on the other hand, who is considered a welfare liberal or welfare capitalist, believes that the wealth of society is society's wealth and that all members of society cooperate in creating that wealth by making it possible for individuals to earn the wealth they do because of mutually agreed upon fundamental rules of society.

Advantages and Disadvantages of Rawls' Theory

The first advantage of his theory is it seems to fit in with the ideals of the liberal capitalist structure of democratic nations like the United States. It allows for individual freedom but still allows for a fair and equitable distribution of wealth to all members of society. It also provides for a way to arrive at a just set of rules and principles by using the veil of ignorance as a method. It tries to balance individual rights and freedom with the good of everyone. Whether it succeeds or not is another story.

One of its disadvantages is it does not fit in with the strong individual rights theories of conservative members of our society who believe that all people have the rights to their earned and inherited wealth and property and should not have to share them with other members of society unless they wish to. We know that many wealthy members of society will voluntarily share their wealth with the poor or underprivileged, and the government gives them an incentive to do so by allowing them charitable tax deductions, but critics of Rawls believe that people should not be coerced or forced in any way to share their wealth either earned or inherited through mandatory government taxation. Secondly, can members really operate out of a veil of ignorance? Do they want to? It's an interesting idea, but how many people really want to set up principles of justice without considering where they will fit into the overall scheme of things? How does Rawls' theory fit in with the exorbitant amounts of money acquired by entertainers or sports figures as opposed to teachers, for example? It's true that such people provide entertainment for all, but is the service they provide worth the millions and billions they make over one year or more? It is true that such people are taxed, but there are also loopholes for them to pay less. I'm not saying that Rawls would approve of such exorbitant incomes, but doesn't his theory lend itself to such excesses? Last, is Rawls' theory of justice with its equality of distribution the best theory? Before we seek some kind of solution to problems of justice, let's look at the moral issue of punishment, which is even more thorny than reward because it involves doing harm or injury to people, raising the question of whether it can be ethically justified at all.

Punishment

Anyone can decide to punish anyone else. For example, when children misbehave, their parents have the authority to punish them—short of child abuse and battering—by "grounding" them, spanking them, speaking harshly to them, depriving them of fun or social activities, or sending them to their rooms. A husband who cheats on his wife can be punished by her by being thrown out of the house and not being allowed to see his children easily. There are many ways in which people can be punished by others for real or imagined offenses. However, in our discussion of punishment in this chapter, we will be talking about that which is meted out for a violation of a duly constituted moral rule or criminal or civil law.

Requirements of Punishment

There are four requirements that punishment should meet:

1. It must involve unpleasantness of some sort. It would hardly be punishment if it did not, and this is one of its dangers, in that usually it imposes harm or injury upon someone. Therefore, it requires special justification and should be administered only if and when a person has seriously violated the rights of others by injuring or harming them.
2. Punishment must be given or done *for* something. It should not be imposed for no reason at all (what sense would that make?) or because the person doling it out gets pleasure from doing it, for example. This would be unfair to the recipient.
3. It should be imposed by some person or group that has been given "duly constituted" moral or legal authority to punish and should not merely be left up to the whim or caprice of individuals.
4. It must be imposed according to certain rules or laws that have been violated by the offender. This is why it is important for each ethical system to have some theory or rules concerning the punishment of violators of that system.[9]

Given these requirements, it would seem that the best context in which punishment should be administered is the legal system because, first of all, individuals often are concerned with vengeance, not justice, whereas the state is concerned (at its best) with the opposite. The state can provide a more objective arena in which to administer punishment than when the atmosphere is filled with the anger and hurt of the aggrieved victim or victims. In other words, by the authority of the state and its laws, violators should be punished for disobeying the laws within an *institutional* rather than a *vengeful* context.

There are several reasons why punishment on a basis of law is more ethical and just than that carried out through individual vengeance. First of all, when punishment is done according to law, the matter is ended; that is, once the appropriate punishment has been meted out by duly constituted authority, no more punishment is given for the violation. This is not so with the concept of vengeance—it can go on and on, sometimes decimating whole families, tribes, and societies. For example, in longstanding feuds, if a person of family A is killed, then vengeance requires that a person from family B should be killed to "even the score" or "exact justice," and then, of course, another person from family A must be killed to bring justice to family B, and so on. Punishment often is never-ending when individual vengeance is its context.

Second, as I mentioned previously, law can be more unbiased than individuals can. Lawyers, judges, and juries usually are not personally involved with either the offender or the victim, and they also have to operate within a set of strict rules, procedures, and laws rather than on a basis of whim or caprice. The entire situation and the people involved in the crime—including extenuating circumstances and other special issues—can be presented and adjudged as fairly as possible. Hurt and angry victims are often incapable of being unbiased and objective—no one really expects them to be. Therefore, despite the failures of our legal system, it is still the more just way to deal with violations of our ethical and legal rules and laws and with the punishment of such violations.

Theories of Punishment

Retributive, or Deserts, Theory

The first and probably the oldest theory of punishment is the retributive, or deserts (based upon what people actually deserve), theory, which states that punishment should be given only when it is deserved and only to the extent that it is deserved. In this sense, the retributivist theory is concerned with the past, not the future. Punishment is imposed not *in order to* do or accomplish anything, such as deter offensive behavior in society. This, as we shall see, is the utilitarian point of view. Rather it should be imposed solely *because of* an offense or crime a person has committed; that is, the punishment must actually be deserved and not be administered solely in order to bring about good consequences. F. H. Bradley, a nineteenth-century philosopher, stated this point of view succinctly:

> Punishment is punishment, only when it is deserved. We pay the penalty because we owe it, and for no other reason; and if punishment is inflicted for any other reason whatever than because it is merited by wrong, it is a gross immorality, a crying injustice, an abominable crime, and not what it pretends to be.[10]

Why Crime Requires Punishment.

Crime requires punishment for two reasons, according to retributivists. First, punishment is required in order to reestablish the balance of morality, which is disturbed when someone violates laws or moral rules. Such laws and rules are established in order to achieve a balance in a given society between individual rights and the common good, and when a crime is committed, the balance is upset and must be restored. According to the retributivist, punishment is the only way to correct this imbalance.

Second, the benefits that a society brings to its members carry with them the burden of self-restraint, and anyone who alleviates himself of this burden acquires an unfair advantage. According to the retributivist, this advantage must be eliminated and the burden of self-restraint restored. For example, in our society two of the benefits that we are all supposed to enjoy are freedom from bodily harm or injury and a noninvasion of privacy. Both require the burden of self-restraint on the part of all of us to see that such benefits are maintained. If a man rapes a woman, however, these benefits are denied her because the man failed to restrain himself; therefore, the unfair advantage he gained of having power over another and gaining benefits to which he was not entitled needs to be righted in some way. The guilty party must be punished, according to the retributivist, in order to eliminate the unfair advantage he gained by raping the woman.

Problems with Determining What People Deserve.

In many ways, punishing on the basis of what people deserve seems to be the most just approach: people violate a moral rule or societal law, and they are given punishment for it only because they deserve it for what they did. However, there are several problems with this theory. First of all, how are we to decide what it is that people actually deserve? What if a crime cries out for life imprisonment or execution, but the person who committed it is old and sick?

For example, in a Florida case, a man was convicted of murder for shooting his wife because she had Alzheimer's disease and osteoporosis (softening of the bones). He stated that he felt she wanted to die but was unable to kill herself because of her illness. He was 75 years old, and in Florida, a person guilty of murder must serve a minimum of 25 years before being considered for parole. Many people argued, first of all, that he shouldn't have been tried for murder because what he did was an act of mercy, prompted by love for his wife. Second, they argued that the sentence was not what he deserved because he was old and not well himself and 25 years in prison would probably hasten his death. The sentence surely would mean that he would die in prison—after all, how many people live to be 100 years old? Many people, including his daughter, begged for mercy for him, asking that he be pardoned or paroled or that his sentence be commuted (that is, reduced). Whatever one may think about the man's guilt or reasons for doing what he did, critics of retributivism could ask, "Shouldn't his age and state of health be considered?"

Another example points up the problem of punishing on the basis of deserts alone. What if a man committed a crime several years earlier but was never caught until now and since that time has lived an exemplary life, doing a lot of good for humanity? Should he now be made to pay for that crime? The answer, based strictly upon the deserts theory, would be yes. He committed the crime, and he still deserves to be punished for it, the deserts theory having no need to concern itself with any concept of mercy or forgiveness based upon what he has or has not done since the crime.

Problem of Mercy. Can mercy play a part in the deserts theory of punishment, and if so, how? To whom and under what conditions should mercy be given to criminals? If retributivists wish to temper punishment with mercy, then how are they to do this? If they give one criminal less punishment than another one owing to considerations of mercy, then will their actions be just to victims of the crime or to the other criminal? This problem has caused many retributivists to hold to the idea that retributive justice is enough; a person should be punished only because he or she deserves it, with any application of mercy serving only to dilute justice.

Problem of Determining Seriousness of Offenses and Punishment. The general rule applied by the retributivist to punishment is, "The more serious the crime, the more severe the punishment." But how does one determine which offenses are the most serious and which punishments are the most severe? People differ with regard to these two issues. For example, most people feel that the killing of a human being is the most serious of crimes, but a rape victim may wish that she *had* been killed rather than have to live with the physical and emotional injuries she has sustained as a result of being raped. In some cultures, stealing is punishable by death, but is theft a serious enough crime for which to be executed?

Even when people generally agree about the seriousness of a crime, which is the proper punishment? Some people advocate life imprisonment or life imprisonment without parole for the taking of another's life; others adamantly urge the death penalty. Which is most deserved? In some Middle Eastern countries, thieves have one hand cut off if they are caught stealing once, and the other if they are caught again. What happens if they are caught a third time? Is this piece-by-piece mutilation just, or would a determinate sentence in prison (as generally prescribed in the West) be more so?

"An Eye for an Eye and a Tooth for a Tooth." The retributivist presents two views based on the retributivistic saying in the Old Testament that reads as follows: "An eye for an eye, and a tooth for a tooth." The first, which states that the punishment should be given in the same degree or severity as the crime, is sometimes called the *mirror-image theory.*[11] In this view, the punishment should mirror the crime exactly both in seriousness and severity. For example, if someone kills another, then the killer should also be killed. This is the viewpoint of people who support capital punishment, as we shall see in Chapter 9.

But can one death actually mirror another? Suppose the victim was first tortured or raped and then killed—should the criminal also receive the same treatment? Many people who argue for capital punishment will often feel that the criminal should be put to death painlessly, and, of course, those who are against it do not feel that it is appropriate at all but rather that it is barbaric, outmoded, and inappropriate according to the two-wrongs-don't-make-a-right argument. And what about stealing, rape, or child molestation? Should we *steal* from thieves? Should we rape the rapist or molest the children of the child molester (the latter may have already done so!)? The mirror-image theory, therefore, does not seem to be very feasible.

The second view, based on the Old Testament saying, is that punishment should be suitable or appropriate to the crime; but this is even more vague than the first view.

What is a suitable punishment in the case of stealing—six months in jail, one year, three years—and how are we to determine this? Is life imprisonment more suitable than execution or vice versa? It seems that when punishment is based solely upon what violators actually deserve, determining the appropriate punishment is a real problem that is difficult to solve. Finally, can we ever find an appropriate punishment for crimes such as murder, rape, or child molestation? Can a lengthy prison sentence, or even death, ever eradicate the scars of the victims and their families, or balance the scales of justice? What type of deserved punishment will be sufficient to accomplish any of this?

Utilitarian, or Results, Theory

The utilitarian theory differs from the retributivist theory in that it is future-oriented—that is, it looks forward to the results and consequences that might conceivably accrue from punishing someone. The utilitarian would not punish *because* of a crime, as in retributivism, but *in order that* something good could result from the punishment. Jeremy Bentham, one of the founders of utilitarianism, stated that punishment should always have as its aim the good of society.

He went on to describe two types of sanctions meant to discourage or eliminate criminal behavior: (1) internal sanctions, which are brought about by the development of conscience in children and others in order to mobilize feelings of guilt and shame; and (2) external sanctions, which usually are established by laws providing penalties to be imposed for immoral or criminal behavior.[12] Laws or rules providing penalties and punishment for offenses or crimes can function at both levels to some extent. That is, punishment for certain offenses can provide both forms of sanctions, the penalties helping to form people's consciences while at the same time punishing the actual offenses.

Therefore, in consonance with the utilitarian ideal as described in Chapter 2, that one should strive to bring about the best good consequences for everyone by means of acts or rules, punishment is justified if and only if it brings about better consequences than some other treatment of the offender. There is no point to punishment, according to the utilitarian, if it doesn't produce good consequences or prevent harmful ones. The utilitarian would ask three questions concerning the punishment of any offender: (1) Will the wrongdoer be deterred from future crimes and become a better person or member of society? (2) Will others in the society be deterred from committing crimes because of the wrongdoer's punishment? and (3) Will society be protected from such criminals? If these three questions cannot be answered in the affirmative, then according to the utilitarian, punishment is not morally justified. To punish people just because they deserve it, unless it brings about the preceding good consequences, would not be moral or just.

Consequences for the Offender. The question of whether or not punishment will bring about good consequences for offenders is a difficult one. According to the utilitarian, the purpose behind punishment of offenders is to rehabilitate and reform them so that they are deterred from committing the same offense or any others in the future. Second, punishment should make them better persons and therefore better members of society. It is obvious that capital punishment, or the executing of offenders for a serious offense, will certainly deter them from committing future crimes, but it is also obvious that killing them will not rehabilitate or reform them in any way.

What about other types of punishment, short of execution, such as imprisonment for determinate or indeterminate periods of time or for life. Life imprisonment—if it really is life imprisonment, that is, without parole—would deter offenders from committing more crimes out in society (not necessarily within prison), but would it rehabilitate or reform them? And if it truly did foster reform, then would it be just or fair to keep such offenders in prison? What about lesser sentences? Would the punishment while in prison deter offenders from future wrongdoing, and would it rehabilitate and reform them so that they could return to society as moral members? The answer depends in part upon what is to be done with offenders while they are imprisoned. Most experts argue that our whole belief that imprisonment rehabilitates and reforms offenders is at best a bad joke. Very few are rehabilitated by being sent to prison, where they will be associating with habitual criminals who usually are guilty of worse crimes than first offenders ever thought of committing. How can such associations and such an atmosphere rehabilitate or reform?

Utilitarians and others dissatisfied with the prison system have often argued for incarceration not as a punishment, but for purposes of psychiatric treatment, hoping that the proper psychiatric and psychological techniques and therapies may rehabilitate and reform offenders when imprisonment alone cannot. However, such an approach of treatment rather than punishment is also often ineffectual for several reasons: (1) Prisoners often resent mandatory treatment—they "don't want shrinks messing with their minds," which they often feel are just fine and not in need of adjustment of any kind; (2) therapists all have different approaches and different ways of measuring results, and there are no clear general standards of treatment by which to operate or cure; (3) therapists may have too much power over offenders in that often the alternatives to psychiatric or psychological treatment are further penalties within the prison system, such as solitary confinement for those offenders who will not cooperate; (4) therapists also have the power over release dates in that sentences for treatment may be indeterminate, whereas regular sentences usually are determinate. In the play *Nuts*, by Tom Topor, Claudia, a woman who is fighting a "legally insane" designation so that she can be tried for the crime of first-degree manslaughter, states this problem quite well when asked by her attorney what the sanity hearing means for her future:

> If I lose today, I'm committed for a year. . . . Sixty days before the year is up, the hospital can ask to retain me. If I lose again, the hospital can keep me for two years. From then on, the hospital can apply to hold me every two years until two-thirds of the maximum sentence on the highest charge in the indictment. Two-thirds of twenty-five years is seventeen years. . . . But you guys aren't done yet. If the commissioner of the hospital—this is the hospital I've been sitting in for seventeen years—if he decides I'm still mentally ill and need some more treatment, he can apply to get an order of certification. . . . If they do it right, they can lock me up in a hospital for the criminally insane, then they can lock me up in a run-of-the-mill loony bin. And they don't ever have to let me have a trial. That's what it means.[13]

Finally, psychology and psychiatry are such inexact sciences that few therapists can really be certain that one of their patients has been sufficiently cured so that he or she is quite certain not to commit another crime or endanger anyone in society. One of the most frustrating and discouraging things about societal punishment is that studies have revealed that no matter whether offenders have simply been locked up, locked up with punishment, or locked up with treatment, their recidivism rates (return to crime and prison) are the same. No way of punishing offenders seems to work better than any other. This problem certainly weakens the utilitarian's position of at least trying to find a method of punishment that will actually bring about good consequences for the offender and for society's protection as well.

Consequences for Potential Offenders—Deterrence. Another way that utilitarians have of measuring the future good consequences of punishment is seeing whether or not it deters people from committing crimes or being immoral; that is, to what extent does punishing a criminal, or at least having punishment available, deter former criminals or noncriminals from committing offenses? From the utilitarian standpoint, if punishment could do this, it certainly would be worthwhile. The assumption behind this type of deterrence is that if people see or hear of offenders being punished for crimes they have committed, then they themselves will be deterred from committing crimes. In this sense, punishment operates as that external sanction of which Jeremy Bentham wrote.

There are several problems with the deterrence theory, however. First of all, there is no conclusive proof or evidence that the punishment of one person deters anyone else from committing crimes. For one thing, not all people know of punishment when it is meted out; but even if they did, there is still no evidence that the knowledge deters. In early England, thieves used to be hanged publicly, and pickpockets worked their way through the crowds while the hangings were taking place! Also, none of our capital punishment executions are seen by the public; they only hear or read about it on radio, on television, or in the newspapers. So how or why should they be deterred?

Moreover, to punish for purposes of deterrence is to use a person as a means to an end, which is unjust according to many. For example, remember that Kant in his Practical Imperative (see Chapter 3) stated that no person should be used merely as a means to an end but should be considered as a unique end in him- or herself. This is one of the retributivist's strongest criticisms of the utilitarian theory: That people may be punished, not because they deserve it, but rather because they should be "made an example of" or because their punishment will deter others. The retributivist argues that offenders should be punished if and only if they deserve it, not for some other future-good-consequences reason.

This problem only gets worse when we realize that if deterrence works or is thought to work, then it could be accomplished just as well by punishing the wrong or innocent person. Many tyrants in history have used this technique to instill fear in their subjects, with the people who were punished not having to be guilty of anything. Suppose that a particular heinous crime has been committed—such as the rape, torture, and murder of a little girl—and that the public is highly outraged by this crime. Such a public's cry for justice may well be satisfied by punishing the wrong person as well as the right one, as long as someone is caught and punished for the crime. If we thought it was unjust to use real criminals as means to the end of deterrence, then what of using the wrong or innocent person and the harm that would do to the person and his or her family?

We can see, then, that there are some serious problems with the deterrence argument for punishment. John Hospers states that a legal system that is strong and pervasive and relatively free from corruption—where "at all times the police, the courts, and the jails are in operation, and there is always a good chance that they will catch violators of the law"—probably deters most people from committing crimes, rather than seeing to it that a particular criminal or even criminals are punished.[14]

Effect on Society at Large—Protection. The last area from which good consequences may derive is the protection of society in general by means of the punishment of criminals. Almost everyone will agree that the major reason for punishing criminals, particularly for imprisoning or executing them, is to protect society in general from their actions, which may be dangerous, harmful, and even fatal to its members. There is no doubt that executing criminals or keeping them out of the mainstream of society by imprisonment certainly counts as good consequences, but even here we encounter problems. First of all, as has been mentioned, when should we let these offenders back into society, and what will they be like after having been subjected to the deeply criminal atmosphere of most of our prisons? Will they be worse or better members of society after they come out? Nobody can tell—neither psychiatrists, psychologists, sociologists, parole board members, wardens, nor even the prisoners themselves.

For example, I know of two cases in which ex-convicts should have been able to work their way back into society perfectly, and indeed they did so—for a while. One ex-convict I knew of was a good writer and even had a job waiting for him on the outside at a newspaper. He was allowed to leave prison to take college courses in journalism, and generally he did well during this period, writing articles (which were considered quite good) for the school and local newspapers. When he got out, he continued to do well for a while—and then was involved in a fight that resulted in a murder and was sent back to prison.

In the second case, a man who had served eight years for dealing and using drugs was released. He returned to college, learned a skilled trade, and even did well enough to open his own business and become bonded. When he had marital problems, however, he again resorted to drugs, lost his business, attempted to kill someone, and very nearly lost his life. This does not mean that some ex-convicts don't make it on the outside and no longer threaten society in any way, but it does raise the question of how effective punishment really is in protecting society, at least over the long run.

Another criticism of this theory of punishment is that some crimes are crimes of passion, and the persons who commit them will probably never commit a crime again. For example, a husband who comes home, catches his wife with a lover, and in a fit of passion kills them both, is not any more dangerous to society after the murder than someone who has not committed a crime, according to many psychologists. The retributivist would say that he should be punished because he deserves it, but from a utilitarian point of view, if his punishment would not protect society, in that he is no longer a danger, should he be punished? Many would point to the fact he demonstrated an inability to stop himself from committing such a heinous crime, then doesn't that provide at least some evidence that society should be protected from him? Further, how can we know for certain that he won't kill again if he is put into another similarly stressful and emotional situation?

Problem with Justice. The last and major criticism leveled against the utilitarian theory of punishment is that it doesn't concern itself with the *justice* of punishment, as retributivism attempts to, but rather only with its utility. Utilitarians are accused of being interested in social engineering rather than in justice. Some utilitarians admit to their interest in social engineering but argue that justice is really an old-fashioned concept and that social engineering for the common good is morally superior.

This problem associated with the search for justice—the danger of utilitarianism degenerating into a cost-benefit analysis, or end-justifies-the-means, approach to morality—was first discussed in Chapter 2, so it is not surprising that it again rears its ugly head when we are dealing with the matter of punishment.

We have seen that the utilitarian theory of punishment avoids some of the problems associated with the retributivist theory, but there are problems with the utilitarian theory that raise issues of the justness of punishment from the point of view of utility. Before we discuss any possible synthesis of the two theories and their associated problems, one other and newer theory must be presented.

Restitution, or Compensation for Victims, Theory

The restitution, or compensation for victims, theory holds that justice is served only if victims are provided with restitution for the crimes committed against them. For example, if someone steals from a man, then what is stolen should be paid back in some way, either by returning his property in its original form or by furnishing him with some sort of compensation for what he has lost.

Crime Against the State, not the Individual. The crimes-against-the-state theory has come about because of a change in the views about whom a crime really wrongs. Prior to the American Revolution, crimes were considered to be violations committed against individuals, but in contemporary society, crimes are considered to be violations committed against the state; therefore, restitution has not been a major concern until recently. If someone murders another, the murderer has legally committed a crime against the state; therefore, the state, through its judicial system, will seek to bring the murderer to trial and to punish him or her for the crime if found guilty. Of course, the perpetrator has in actuality murdered a person, not the state, and the survivors of the victim have been made to suffer because of the crime.

Given this view, perhaps it is easier to understand why so many survivors demand the death penalty for killers. They feel that the crime was committed against them and the person they lost and that taking the criminal's life is the only way to attain justice. The state, on the other hand, sees this as being a crime against the state that may or may not require the death penalty.

The restitution theory, then, has been established in order to counteract the emphasis on crimes being committed against the state, for this has tended to ignore compensation or restitution to the victims of the crime. Whatever other kind of punishment of the criminal is being considered, this theory requires that some sort of compensation or restitution to the victim or the victim's family be included. For example, if a woman kills the husband and father of a family, part or all of her punishment may be to work most or all of her life to support that family because in this case she has eliminated its major source of financial support. She also can be ordered to pay medical and hospital bills where injury or harm has ensued and to provide some sort of compensation for injuries sustained as determined by a court of law.

It is important that restitution not be decided by the victims themselves because often they are too emotionally involved to be fair in their demand for compensation; therefore, it must be reached through the judicial process. In this way criminals can either compensate victims with money or be put to work for the victims' advantage, either at their home or place of business. If not, then criminals can be forced to work in some state-supervised job, all the earnings from which will go to their victims.

Restitution's Relationship to the Retributivist and Utilitarian Theories. Restitution fits in well with the retributivist theory in that it takes into consideration not only the deserts of the criminal, but also those of the victims. It provides a more meaningful punishment to satisfy these two types of deserts, and the retributivist can avoid criticisms of punishment for punishment's sake.

Utilitarians, on the other hand, may be happier with this type of punishment because they will see it as more useful and bringing about more good consequences than, say, locking up criminals to do nothing for the rest of their lives or killing them. Utilitarians may feel that good, honest work for criminals will be rehabilitative, whereas some good consequences will also accrue to the victims of the crime in that they will be compensated to some degree for the crimes against them.

Problems with Restitution. Although the idea of compensation and restitution for victims sounds good, there are several problems with this approach to punishment. To begin with, there is really no restitution possible for the crime of murder. How much money will compensate for the taking of a human life? Because each life is unique and basically irreplaceable, how can one put a price on it? Further, such heinous crimes as rape and child molestation are not much more easily compensated. How can you give people back their privacy once you've invaded it, or their dignity once you've taken it away? How can you ever make restitution to children for taking away their childhood and affecting them adversely forever?

If restitution is made in monetary form, which it mostly is, such punishment or restitution will be uneven; that is, the richer criminals will be able to afford it, whereas the poorer will not. How can punishment under such circumstances be just? Would you make the rich pay more and the poor pay less? If so, victims will not be compensated evenly, and rich criminals will still get off with less punishment than poor ones.

Further, if criminals are old or sick, how can they compensate by their labor or in any other way? We cannot expect a man who is seriously ill or dying, for example, to hold down a job or even to come up with money. And what if he becomes too old or sick to work after the restitution has been made for a while? Can we expect him to continue somehow? And won't the victim be denied restitution if any of this happens?

Finally, the most serious problem is that restitution does not distinguish between intentional and unintentional injury or harm. What if, for example, an accident in which someone is seriously injured or killed occurs because a car's brakes fail and the driver didn't know they were faulty? Should she be required to make restitution to the same degree as one who intentionally robbed, raped, molested, and murdered his or her victim? There is still a victim, and the victim is still due restitution or compensation under this theory, but would this be fair to the unintentional perpetrator of the injury or harm?

As a matter of fact, this kind of case where harm occurs, but the people causing it are really without fault, presents problems for all three theories of punishment. For example, people who are unknown carriers of injurious or fatal diseases certainly can be the cause of injury, harm, or death, but to what degree should they be punished? Are there really any criminal deserts from the retributivist's point of view? It would certainly seem not; therefore, why should carriers be punished? And yet quarantining or isolating is after all a form of punishment, isn't it? The strict view of the retributivist, that punishment should be deserved, then, presents a problem in such cases. As far as the utilitarian is concerned, perhaps quarantining or isolating the person is good for society in general, but it certainly would not bring about good consequences for the carrier—in other words, not for everyone concerned. And as I mentioned earlier, why should such people have to make restitution to or compensate victims when they are not essentially at fault?

The AIDS (acquired immune deficiency syndrome) crisis is a good example of this problem. There has been so much bumbling and confusion in the handling of the crisis at so many levels and for such a long time that many people who had the virus, but not the overt disease, could infect others with the virus long before they knew they had it. Most of these carriers engaged in activities (sexual intercourse, drug use, and intravenous blood donation) that transmitted it to others. Some who were warned that what they were doing was dangerous did change their lifestyles, but some paid no attention to the warnings and continued to engage in activities that would infect others. Should all AIDS carriers be punished in some way, or only the latter group who disregarded warnings? Is it even fair to punish the latter group, given the fact that we didn't know for sure that people were carriers unless they had full-blown AIDS or until a test had been developed to detect the AIDS virus in the bloodstream (not until 1985—the infection has been thought to have begun as early as 1976)?

There were a few carriers who seemed intentionally set on transmitting the disease, and scientists and doctors were quite upset with them for being so careless in their lifestyles, but the attempt to stop them forcefully was really impossible. The so-called Patient Zero, Gaetan Dugas, described in Randy Shilts's fascinating book on the AIDS crisis, *And the Band Played On*, was one of these people.[15] He was thought to have been the first person to bring AIDS into the United States, and because of his multiple sexual contacts he may have infected as many as 2,000 people! When told of this problem, he refused to accept any responsibility or change his lifestyle in any way. Should he have been punished in some way? How? No matter how angry we are with such people, imposing punishment under any of the three theories would be extremely difficult.

Is a Synthesis Possible?

Because all three theories have their disadvantages and because difficulties exist if we try to apply them singly to the problems of reward and punishment, perhaps a compromise or a reasonable synthesis might work.

From Retributivism. From the retributivist theory we certainly could consider what people deserve or merit before rewarding them, at the same time recognizing that we don't have to settle on this criterion alone. In relation to punishment, we could use the idea that no one who is innocent should be convicted or punished no matter how many good consequences might come about from doing so (general deterrence, for example). We would have as a basic principle that in order for people to be punished, they must truly deserve punishment and that the punishment must "fit the crime" and not be excessive. We also could adopt from the retributivist the principle that in general more serious crimes require more severe punishment and vice versa.

From Utilitarianism. After we had adopted these preceding basic principles, we then could modify or moderate the distribution of rewards and punishments, or suspend sentences, based on what would be useful, especially in cases where retributivism might seem to border on the unjust or unfair. In other words, we could insert the idea of *utility* into our deliberations on rewarding or punishing. We could say, for example, "This man deserves to be punished because he has committed a serious crime," but then ask ourselves what useful purpose would be served in severely punishing a sick 80-year-old man? In this way we could temper what is at times deemed to be overly severe or unfair punishment with a consideration of usefulness—if a particular punishment would not bring about the best good consequences or at least do more good than not punishing or punishing less, then retribution could be tempered by the utilitarian approach to reward and punishment.

From Restitution. Actually, the theory of restitution can fit nicely into the utilitarian theory of reward and punishment because it certainly can bring about good consequences for the victim of a crime while at the same time helping to move the criminal toward a more worthwhile and noncriminal life.

From the point of view of the retributivist, not only would criminals get what they deserve, but compensating victims might also be seen as a more just type of desert for the criminals than many of the useless types of punishment, such as putting them in solitary confinement or executing them. Further, the innocent and most deserving victims of crimes also would be rewarded to the best extent possible by being compensated at least in part for the harm done to them.

Some Other Possibilities for the Distribution of Good or Rewards

In addition to synthesizing the preceding three theories, we could also try to synthesize the four major ways and other criteria for distributing good, or rewarding people (mentioned earlier in this chapter). We could begin on a basis of distributing as equitably as possible and with respect to need, and then we could temper these considerations where applicable with the notion of what people deserve, or merit, as a result of their abilities or other factors, such as their productivity, effort, and the stress, danger, or unpleasantness of their jobs. A synthetic approach, then, might be the best one to use. Whether the problems inherent in all three theories could be resolved enough to make such an approach work remains to be seen.

Another important variable in deciding how and to whom to distribute good and bad would have to be the situation or context in which the distribution is to take place. For example, in the kidney dialysis situation previously described, need was a given in that all patients with kidney failure need dialysis or they will die. Also, the committee had determined that all of them basically deserved to be dialyzed. The problem arose when the committee tried to determine the individual and comparative worth of their lives. In this case, then, a system that distributed good *and* bad equally, without regard to desert or merit or ability, seemed to be the most just approach to this problem, and so the lottery or chance method of distribution was used.

It is quite possible that a situation could arise in which an exception could be made to this egalitarian approach. Suppose, for example, that one of the patients needing dialysis was a world-renowned doctor, a *nephrologist* (a specialist in kidney diseases) working to expand the availability of dialysis machines and kidneys for transplantation. Might it not be advantageous to the other and future patients with kidney failure to allow him to be dialyzed, even if he didn't win the lottery? Further, if the president of the United States were in need of dialysis, shouldn't he be given preferential consideration considering that what happens to him affects everyone under his jurisdiction? Other issues have arisen since these decisions were made. Some nephrologists have required that patients who are to receive dialysis must stay on their required regimen (a very strict one for kidney patients) in order to receive dialysis, the idea being that if the patients are not going to do what is necessary to help themselves, then dialysis is essentially wasted on them and would be better utilized with patients who will cooperate with their own health care.

In some cases, we would not use the egalitarian method of distribution at all. For example, it is not required that in order to be fair, all of us should have the same security and protection as the president. Because of his ability, the dangers of his exposure, and the good of all people for whom he is responsible, he deserves and merits such protection, whereas the rest of us don't, unless our situation is such to require it (for example, our lives have been threatened by an escaped criminal at whose trial we were key witnesses).

In conclusion, it would seem that some type of synthetic approach could be brought to bear in both reward and punishment, utilizing those principles from the three major theories—retributivism, utilitarianism, and restitution—and taking into consideration the situations and contexts in which distribution of good and bad is to take place, but never losing sight of the significance of need and an egalitarian method of distribution wherever possible. In the next chapter, the principle of justice or fairness will be presented, justified, and discussed, and this issue of fair and just distribution will again arise. Further, in Chapter 9, the moral issue of capital punishment will be presented and discussed, to which this chapter will be applied in a more specific way.

Chapter Summary

I. Key terms

    A. *Retributive justice*: People should get what they deserve either in reward or punishment, regardless of the consequences.

    B. *Distributive justice*: The distribution of good and bad on a just and fair basis.

    C. *Reward*: Something given or received for worthy behavior.

    D. *Punishment*: The act of penalizing someone for a crime, fault, or misbehavior—a penalty for wrongdoing.

    E. *Retributivism* (deserts theory): The act of giving people what they deserve, regardless of the consequences.

    F. *Utilitarianism* (results theory): The act of rewarding or punishing based upon its consequences.

    G. *Restitution* (compensation theory): The act of compensating victims for harm or wrong done to them.

II. Reward and punishment in relationship to justice

    A. Reward and punishment are both aspects of distributive justice.

    B. Elements of justice are defined.

        1. Justice, as ethics in general, involves the treatment of human beings by other human beings.

        2. It is concerned basically with past rather than future events.

        3. It should be individualistic rather than collectivistic in application.

        4. Comparative justice is different from collectivistic injustice in that the former has to do with the way a person is treated in relation to another person.

III. Reward

    A. Four basic ways in which good and bad can be distributed:

        1. As equally among people as possible.

        2. According to people's abilities.

        3. According to what they deserve or merit.

        4. According to their needs.

    B. Equal distribution of goods and rewards.

        1. Scarce-medical-resources problem (kidney dialysis issue is a good example of this). The lottery or chance method of distribution would distribute good and bad equally.

        2. Problems with this theory:

            (a) It ignores other criteria that are deemed important.

            (b) It is difficult to determine in what ways and to what extent people are equal.

            (c) Can we really ignore all of the other criteria?

    C. Production, or what people produce or achieve, is often used but ignores effort, ability, or need.

    D. Effort also is used but also has several problems:

        1. Those who have contracted to do a job are paid not for time and effort but for the finished job.

        2. It is difficult to measure effort.

        3. How does one distinguish between bright and dull-witted people if they are being rewarded only for effort?

    E. Ability

        1. Natural ability. People can't help having the abilities they come by naturally: Should they be rewarded for these?

    2. Acquired ability. This type may be more significant where reward is concerned because often a great deal of money, time, and effort goes into acquiring skills.

    3. One problem with both 1 and 2 is the possibility that people may not use their abilities or may not use them well.

  F. Need. There are two types of need:

    1. *Private need* is a term used to describe the personal, material needs of individuals who are poor or out of work. Should such people be rewarded regardless of their abilities or qualifications? Often these people are the most unskilled in our society.

    2. *Public need* refers to the system by which people are rewarded for fulfilling the needs of the general public; but *which* needs—individual or collective—are the most important, and how are we to decide?

  G. Other criteria:

    1. Long and expensive training in a profession. Trying to reward on this basis would be uneven, and what if the professionals are incompetent? Should they still be rewarded for this?

    2. Job or profession requiring expensive equipment. How much more should such people be rewarded in this case, and should they continue to be rewarded for it even after the equipment has been paid for?

    3. Physical danger. It would seem that people who are in such professions should be rewarded, but how much and for what dangers?

    4. Job unpleasantness. How do we decide which jobs get the greater reward because of their unpleasantness, and how much should be given?

    5. Seniority.

IV. Two major theories of how to reward

  A. Retributivist, or deserts, theory states that people should be rewarded strictly on a basis of what they deserve or merit for what they have done in the past.

    1. This theory is not concerned with the future good consequences that might arise out of people's actions.

    2. It also tends to reward efforts rather than achievement, productivity, or consequences.

  B. Utilitarian, or results, theory would reward on the future good consequences of rewarding.

    1. This theory would definitely be in favor of paying higher wages or giving extra pay for dangerous or unpleasant jobs.

    2. It would reward production and achievement rather than hard work or effort.

    3. Another problem is that if consequences are the only criteria, then it is possible to reward a totally undeserving person.

V. John Rawls and His Theory of Justice.

  A. Natural rights (life, liberty, and property), according to Locke and Nozick, somehow exist in human beings through nature or God.

  B. Rawls believes such rights are given to humans by a just society, developed behind a "veil of ignorance."

  C. Rawls' two basic principles.

    1. Equality principle: Each person has equal rights to maximum liberty compatible with the same amount of liberty for everyone else.

    2. Difference principle: Inequality is permissible if it's to everyone's advantage.

  D. Difference between Nozick and Rawls.

    1. Nozick is a libertarian who believes in individual rights and freedom without interference of government or others.

    2. Rawls is a welfare liberal or welfare capitalist who believes that the wealth is society's, not the individual's, wealth.

E. Advantages and disadvantages of Rawls' theory.
1. It seems to fit in well with the capitalism of democratic societies.
2. It allows for freedom but also for a just and fair distribution of wealth.
3. It provides a way to arrive at a just set of rules by the veil of ignorance.
4. It tries to balance individual rights and freedom with the good of everyone.
5. One disadvantage is not fitting in with the more conservative views of rights.
6. Another questions whether people really can operate out of the veil of ignorance.
7. Does the difference principle really operate successfully, for example, given the high salaries of entertainers and sports stars.
8. Lastly, Rawls ignores other theories of fair distribution of wealth.

VI. Punishment
A. Four requirements of punishment:
1. It must involve unpleasantness of some sort.
2. It must be imposed or endured for some reason.
3. It should be imposed by some person or group that has "duly constituted" moral or legal authority.
4. It must be imposed according to certain rules or laws.
B. Given these requirements, punishment should be administered from within a duly constituted legal system for several reasons:
1. Under law, once punishment has been done or given, the matter is ended, as opposed to vengeance or whim, which can go on indefinitely.
2. Law can be more unbiased and objective than individuals can.

VII. Theories of punishment
A. Retributive, or deserts, theory, which states that punishment should be given only when it is deserved and only to the extent that it is deserved, is concerned with the past rather than the future.
B. Why crime requires punishment:
1. To reestablish the balance of morality that has been disturbed when someone has violated laws or moral rules.
2. Benefits carry with them the burden of self-restraint, and anyone who alleviates himself or herself of this burden acquires an unfair advantage; according to the retributivist, this must be eliminated and the burden of self-restraint restored.
C. Problems with this theory:
1. It is difficult to determine what people deserve.
2. It is difficult to utilize mercy in this theory.
3. It is also difficult to determine the seriousness of offenses and punishment.
4. What is meant by "an eye for an eye"?
   (a) The mirror-image view says that the punishment should mirror the crime exactly, but how can this be accomplished with exactness without arriving at absurdity (e.g., should we steal from the thief?).
   (b) The second view states that the punishment must be suitable or appropriate to the crime, but this also is difficult to calculate.
   (c) Can we ever find appropriate punishment for murder, rape, or child molestation?
D. Utilitarian, or results, theory is future-oriented and given *in order that* . . . rather than *because of* . . . as in retributivism.
1. Bentham stated that punishment should always have as its aim the good of society.

2. Two types of sanctions are meant to discourage or eliminate criminal behavior:
    (a) Internal sanctions, which are brought about by the development of conscience in children and others.
    (b) External sanctions, which are established by laws providing penalties to be imposed for criminal behavior.
    (c) Laws or rules providing penalties and punishment for offenses or crimes could function at both levels.
3. Three questions the utilitarian would ask about the punishment of any offender:
    (a) Will the wrongdoer be deterred from future crimes and become a better person or member of society?
    (b) Will others in society be deterred from committing crimes because of the criminal's punishment?
    (c) Will society be protected from such criminals?
E. Consequences for the offender bring up the problems of rehabilitation and reform.
    1. Imprisonment, in which first-time offenders usually are lumped together with habitual criminals, is not conducive to rehabilitation and reform.
    2. Psychiatric or psychological treatment, rather than punishment, also is ineffectual for the following reasons:
        (a) Prisoners often resent and resist mandatory treatment.
        (b) There are no general standards of treatment.
        (c) Therapists may have too much power over offenders because of the unattractive alternatives to treatment (e.g., solitary confinement).
        (d) Therapists also have power over release dates for offenders.
        (e) Psychology and psychiatry are inexact sciences; therefore, therapists can never be certain that patients have been cured.
F. Consequences for potential offenders, or deterrence, also have several problems:
    1. There is no conclusive proof or evidence that punishment of one person deters anyone else from committing crimes.
    2. To punish for deterrence is to use a person as a means to an end, which is considered unjust by many moralists.
    3. It is even worse when we see that it is possible to punish the wrong person for deterrence reasons.
G. Its effect on society at large, or protection, is probably the major reason for punishing criminals, particularly by imprisonment or execution, but this reason has its problems also:
    1. When should we allow criminals back into mainstream society?
    2. Some crimes are crimes of passion, and the perpetrators may never commit them again; so from a utilitarian point of view, why punish them?
H. The last major criticism of the utilitarian theory is that it doesn't concern itself with the justice of punishment, as retributivism attempts to do, but rather only with its utility and with social engineering.
I. The restitution, or compensation-for-victims, theory holds that justice is served only if victims are granted restitution for the crimes committed against them.
    1. This theory has come about because the older attitude that a crime is committed against an individual has given way to the newer attitude that all crimes are committed against the state. The restitution theory has been established in order to counteract this point of view and to provide compensation to victims.

2. Restitution should be decided not by victims but through the judicial process.
3. Restitution can fit in well with both the retributivist and utilitarian theories.
   (a) For the retributivist, it considers both the deserts of the criminal and the victim and may provide a more meaningful punishment, helping the retributivist to avoid the criticism of seeking punishment for punishment's sake.
   (b) The utilitarian may see restitution as being more useful and bringing about more good consequences, to both the criminal and the victim.
4. Problems with restitution:
   (a) There is really no restitution for such crimes as murder, rape, or child molestation.
   (b) Restitution in monetary form will be uneven for rich and poor criminals and for their victims as well.
   (c) If criminals are old or sick, how can they compensate victims?
   (d) The most serious problem is that restitution does not distinguish between intentional and unintentional injury or harm—this is actually a problem with all three theories.

VIII. Synthesis
   A. With retributivism we could consider what people deserve or merit before rewarding them, at the same time realizing that we needn't use this criterion alone.
      1. No one who is innocent should be convicted or punished despite any good consequences that might be derived from the punishment.
      2. People must truly deserve any punishment they get, and the punishment should fit the crime and not be excessive.
      3. More serious crimes would require more severe punishment.
   B. With utilitarianism we could modify or moderate the distribution of rewards and punishments or suspend sentences based on what would be useful.
   C. Because restitution could fit in with both retributivism and utilitarianism, it could function to modify their excesses and problems while providing the additional reward or punishment of compensating victims of crimes.
   D. We also could try to synthesize the four major ways and other criteria for distributing good and bad.
      1. We could start with a basis of distributing as equitably as possible and with respect to need.
      2. We could then temper that approach by considering what people deserve or merit through their abilities, productivity, effort, and other criteria, such as stress, danger, and unpleasantness of their jobs.
      3. The situation or context would be another important variable; for example, the egalitarian method of distributing good and bad would work well in the kidney dialysis situation but not in others.
   E. In conclusion, a synthesis might just work out but only if it were carefully organized.

Exercises for Review

1. Describe and explain the relationship between reward and punishment and justice.
2. What are the elements of justice, and to what extent do you agree with them?
3. What are the four major ways of distributing good, and which of them do you think is or are the most fair and just?

4. What do you think of the other criteria for distributing good: production, effort, ability, need (both private and public), long and expensive training, expensive equipment, physical danger, unpleasantness of jobs? Which ones do you think are the most important and which least important? Why?

5. Describe and explain retributivism and utilitarianism as theories of reward or distributing good. Which do you think is most valid? Why?

6. Do you agree with the requirements of punishment? Why or why not? To what extent do you agree that punishment should be meted out within the legal system?

7. Describe and explain the three theories of punishment. Which do you think is most valid? Why?

8. Which is the more important principle in punishing: giving people what they deserve or punishing only if you can bring about good consequences? Why?

9. What should be emphasized in punishment: the deterrence and rehabilitation of the offender, the deterrence of others, or the protection of society? Why?

10. To what extent should restitution to or compensation of victims be a part of any system of punishment? Answer in detail.

Discussion Questions

1. Whenever you have had occasion to reward or punish someone, which of the three theories have you drawn upon, and why?

2. How do we in America generally reward, punish, or distribute good or bad, and which theories do you think we basically follow? Give specific examples and illustrations to support your main points.

3. How effective do you feel our judicial and penal systems are in punishing or rehabilitating criminals? Why? Again, give specific examples and illustrations.

4. To what extent do you feel that the purpose of punishment is to (a) protect society, (b) punish criminals, or (c) rehabilitate and reform criminals? Why? Answer in detail.

5. When you have had occasion to distribute good or bad to others, which of the many ways described have you used? Why? Have you found yourself using different ways for different situations and people? Which, and why? Answer in detail.

6. What method of reward and punishment is used in your family, and how does it fit in with the three theories? Does it work? Be specific.

7. Analyze any group or institution of which you are or have been a member (e.g., church, school, the military, sports team, honorary club or society in school or out of it), and describe what theories are or have been used in distributing good and bad and in rewarding and punishing. Do you believe that the methods are fair and just? Why or why not?

8. To what extent do you feel that as a country and a people we should take care of our less fortunate and "needy" members, and why? How should this be done—through private donations, government support, or both? If private donations are not sufficient, should we through government taxation ensure that these people are cared for? Why or why not?

Notes

1. William Morris, ed., *The American Heritage Dictionary of the English Language* (Boston: Houghton Mifflin, 1978), 113.
2. Ibid., 1060.

3. I am heavily indebted to John Hospers, *Human Conduct: An Introduction to the Problems of Ethics*, 2nd ed. (New York: Harcourt Brace Jovanovich, 1982) 306–8, for these elements.
4. Paul Ramsey, *The Patient as Person* (New Haven, CT: Yale University Press, 1970), 239–52.
5. Ibid., 246–47.
6. Ibid., 259–66.
7. Ibid., 252–59.
8. Hospers, *Human Conduct*, 321–22.
9. Ibid., 328–30.
10. Francis H. Bradley, *Ethical Studies* (London: Oxford University Press, 1876), 26–27.
11. Hospers, *Human Conduct*, 341.
12. Ibid., 331.
13. Tom Topor, *Nuts* (New York: Samuel French, 1981), 66–67.
14. Hospers, *Human Conduct*, 334.
15. Randy Shilts, *And the Band Played On* (New York: St. Martin's Press, 1987), Chapter 13.

Research Navigator™
(http://www.researchnavigator.com)

This web site offers three research databases: EBSCO's *ContentSelect Academic Journal and Abstract Database, New York Times* Search by Subject Archive, and *Best of the Web* Link Library. In addition, this site provides helpful advice on how to conduct efficient and productive research from choosing a topic to polishing the final draft. Beginning philosophy students probably will find the *Best of the Web* Link Library the most appropriate place to start their research.

The free access code necessary to employ Research Navigator™ can be found in the Prentice Hall Guide to Evaluating Online Resources. If your text did not come with this guide, please go to *www.prenhall.com/contentselect* for information on how you can purchase an access code.

Chapter

8

Setting Up a Moral System: Basic Assumptions and Basic Principles

Objectives

After you have read this chapter, you should be able to

1. Identify, define, and explain the major conflicting general moral issues in setting up a moral system.

2. Present, describe, and discuss basic assumptions about what characteristics or attributes any meaningful, livable, and workable moral system or theory should contain.

3. Try to resolve the central problem areas of morality—which are how to attain stability, unity, and order without eliminating individual freedom by the establishment of basic ethical principles.

4. Establish and justify the priority in which the five basic principles should be applied.

At this point in a course in ethics or in most texts on ethics, students usually throw up their hands in frustration, saying, "If all of the ethical theories and systems are so full of problems, then perhaps there is no such thing as a workable and meaningful moral system. Perhaps morality is relative to whoever sets it up and to no one else." Too often teachers of ethics courses and authors of ethics books do very little to alleviate these frustrations, except to say that perhaps students ought to take another course or simply try to do the best they can with the "broken" theories or systems to which they have been exposed. I believe, however, that we can attempt to show the way toward building a moral system that is workable not only for many individuals, but also for most, if not all, human beings.

In order to do this, we need to point toward the reasonable synthesis mentioned in Chapter 1. We must try to combine what is best in all of the ethical systems and theories we have examined—religious, nonreligious, consequentialist, nonconsequentialist, individualistic, and altruistic—to arrive at a common moral ground, while at the same time dealing with or eliminating their problems and difficulties. We must search for a larger meeting ground in which the best of all these theories and systems can operate meaningfully and with a minimum of conflict and opposition.

Before doing this, however, it is important to state the two reasons I had for writing this chapter. My first motivation was to develop my own ethical system as an important part of my own philosophy of life. Second, I wanted to try to show readers how they might go about constructing their own ethical systems, given all of the information they have received in Chapters 1 through 7. It is important that readers realize that I am not suggesting they must follow my ethical system or accept it in any way. But I think it is important that they see that it is possible to construct their own systems rather than become frustrated by the problems associated with the other systems. Readers may choose one of the theories in Chapters 2, 3, or 4, or some combination of them, or my system if it appeals to them, or their own system. I do not intend this chapter to be a form of indoctrination, and students, instructors, and other readers are free to be critical of anything I have written here. Now that I have made this clear, we may proceed to examine conflicting moral issues, some ethical assumptions (which again are mine), and basic ethical principles.

Conflicting General Moral Issues

In dealing with traditional ethical theories in Chapters 2, 3 and 4, we discovered several general moral issues that must be resolved or synthesized in some way before we can begin to set up a moral system of our own. They are the issues of consequentialism versus nonconsequentialism, self- versus other-interestedness, act versus rule, and emotion versus reason.

Consequentialism versus Nonconsequentialism

In order to set up a moral system, it is important to decide first to what extent it will be based on consequences and to what extent it will be nonconsequentialist. In presenting the criticisms at the end of Chapter 3, I arrived at the conclusion that I simply cannot be moral without taking into consideration the consequences of moral decisions, acts, or rules.

At the same time, I was definitely made aware of the difficulty of considering only conse-quences or ends without regard to means or motives. The cost-benefit-analysis, or end-justifies-the-means, problems brought this home to me, and Kant's Practical Imperative pointed to a way out of this problem. My own synthesis of this conflict is to have a basic concern with consequences in my moral system and yet be aware that the end, even a good end, does not always justify the means or motives leading to it. How these two atti-tudes are to be synthesized will be shown later in the chapter, after I have presented my own moral system.

Self- versus Other-Interestedness

Although I feel that people certainly are justified when they consider themselves as a vital factor in any moral system they may establish, I do not feel, for the reasons stated in Chapter 2, that ethical egoism, or self-interest, will provide a workable basis for a valid moral system because of its many disadvantages. Therefore, I feel I must go along with the utilitarian viewpoint of always striving to bring about the best good consequences for everyone, which, of course, includes myself. Given the necessary modifications, I feel that there is a greater chance of maximizing good consequences and attaining justice and fair-ness with this approach.

Act versus Rule

Another problem in establishing a moral system is how to allow for the greatest amount of individual freedom while still incorporating stability, security, and order. The act approach allows for the most freedom; the rule approach imposes certain constraints on freedom, yet provides for greater stability. As you will see, I attempt to bring in the best of both approaches by establishing rules that nevertheless include a strong element of freedom within them.

Emotion versus Reason

The issue of emotion versus reason will be discussed largely as a part of the justification for the first assumption that follows, but the synthesis here will be to base my moral sys-tem on reason without excluding emotions, which are a definite part of morality; that is, it is natural to feel very strongly about most moral issues, and these feelings should con-tribute to the formation of a moral system. However, it is my contention that ultimately a viable moral system should be based upon reason.

Basic Assumptions

First, it is important to clearly delineate several basic assumptions concerning what consti-tutes a workable set of standards for morality. I will list these assumptions and then try to argue why they should be a part of any moral system.

In order for a moral system to be tenable and viable, I believe it ought to have the following characteristics:

1. It should be rationally based and yet not be devoid of emotion—this was implied in my criticism of a religiously based morality and of an intuitionally based act nonconsequentialism.

2. It should be as logically consistent as possible, but not rigid and inflexible—this was implied in my criticisms of egoism, especially universal ethical egoism, and of the rule nonconsequentialist theories.

3. It must have universality or general application to all humanity, and yet be applicable (in a practical sense) to particular individuals and situations—this I implied in my criticisms of both act consequentialist and act nonconsequentialist theories, as well as individual and personal ethical egoism (for their highly individualistic approach to morality) and rule nonconsequentialist theories (for their failure to be applicable to practical situations).

4. It should be able to be taught and promulgated—this was implied in my criticism of all forms of ethical egoism and all act theories of morality.

5. It must have the ability to resolve conflicts among human beings, duties, and obligations—this was implied in my criticisms of both universal ethical egoism and Kant's Duty Ethics.

Including the Rational and Emotional Aspects

Human Nature—Rational and Emotional. It is an obvious empirical fact that human beings are both feeling (emotional or affective) and reasoning (rational or cognitive) beings, and that in order to establish any sort of system that can be applied to everyone, we have to take these two human aspects into consideration. However, if we rely only upon our emotions when we are making moral decisions, we can run into severe problems in resolving conflicts that may arise from the very different and individual feelings we have. Also, if we are thrown back solely upon feelings as the basis of our moral decisions, then there is no common ground for arbitration between what A feels is right and what B feels is right, for anyone's feelings are as good as anyone else's. How can we argue against the way I feel or the way you feel if feelings are our sole basis for deciding what is right and wrong?

Emotion. Just because feelings are difficult to work with when we are making moral decisions does not mean that morality must be a completely cold, calculating, and unemotional affair. After all, moral issues are some of the most emotional ones we face; therefore, it is too much to expect that we will not feel strongly about them. However, as a sole basis for making moral decisions, feelings are too unreliable and individualistic, and some other basis that is fairer and more objective is needed. That basis is reason.

Reason. The word *reason* implies giving "reasons" for a decision or an action, and such an activity already involves more than merely expressing feelings. Further, reason, which is an ability, should be differentiated from *reasoning*, which is an activity; reason is a power that human beings *have*, whereas reasoning is something they *do*. All humans have the ability to reason in varying degrees, but there are formal rules for reasoning that can be taught to all and can thereby form the basis for our understanding each other and for supporting any decisions or actions we make or perform.

Reasoning implies several things:

1. Logical argument, which includes supplying empirical evidence in support of one's position.
2. Logical consistency, which involves avoiding fallacies and making sure that one's argument follows smoothly from one point to the next until it arrives at a logical conclusion.
3. A certain detachment from feelings; this springs from reasoning's formality, which forces one to consider the truth and validity of what the individual and others are thinking and saying.
4. A common means by which differences in feelings, opinions, and thoughts can be arbitrated.

At this point, let me briefly cite an example from the controversy over abortion, which is covered in much greater detail in a later chapter. Suppose that Tom says he "feels" abortion is always wrong, and Barbara says she "feels" abortion is always right. We have two sets of opposing feelings; and if feelings are our only basis for deciding what is right and wrong, where can we go from there? True, Tom can attempt to refuse to let his wife have an abortion, or he can lobby for legislation to prevent any woman from getting one, whereas Barbara can have an abortion herself or encourage other women to have one, or lobby for legislation opposed to Tom's. However, how will any of us, including Barbara and Tom, know whose position is the correct one? All we can know is how the two of them feel and that their feelings differ radically. If Barbara and Tom were the only two people involved, then perhaps we could live with their conflicting feelings; however, also involved are the lives of fetuses and of other people affected by the results of their feelings, decisions, and legislation.

If we ask Barbara and Tom why they feel the way they do, the process of reasoning has already begun. Tom might give the following "reasons":

1. All human life is precious, including that which is yet unborn, and only God has the right to decide which life should begin or end and when.
2. Human life begins at conception.
3. Women do not have absolute rights over their own bodies when those bodies contain another life.
4. Once a woman has become pregnant, she has a moral obligation to carry the fetus to term regardless of any and all reasons to the contrary.

On the other hand, Barbara might give the following reasons:

1. A person who is already born has a greater right to life than one who is yet unborn.
2. Only a woman can decide whether she ought or ought not bear a child because she has absolute rights over her own body.

3. Human life does not begin until viability (about the twenty-eighth week of pregnancy) or until the child actually is born.

Once we have been given reasons to work with, we can begin to examine the basis for Barbara's and Tom's feelings, bring evidence and facts to bear on their reasons, and test these bases with rational and logical arguments. We can, for example, examine all of the biological, sociological, and psychological evidence that is available concerning the issue of when human life can actually be said to begin. We also can examine all of the arguments and evidence for the existence or nonexistence of God, and we can consider if He exists, whether He is the lord of life, or whether He has delegated the authority for life-and-death decisions to human beings. Next, we can examine the reasons for terminating a pregnancy and see if any evidence can be shown to justify any such termination. Then we can look into how we might compare the worth of an already existent human being with one yet unborn. The main point here is that whereas, earlier, Barbara and Tom were merely spouting their strong feelings, they are now in a position to critically evaluate and analyze those feelings by bringing evidence and reasoning to bear upon them. In this way, we have built up a broader and less arbitrary basis upon which we can grapple with the difficulties associated with each position on abortion.

Logical Consistency with Flexibility

It is important that any ethical system be logically consistent so that there will be some stability to our moral decision making. A moral system that says that in situation A1 we should kill a person but in similar situation A2 we should not, gives us neither a guide nor stability, only capricious whim. On the other hand, if a moral system says that we can *never* in *any* situation kill anyone and still be moral, then all of the complexity and diversity that comprise humanness has become rigidly boxed in, with no possibility of justifying ourselves by means of the extenuating situations we often face. We must, instead, strive to be as logically consistent as we can in our morality and yet allow enough flexibility so that our system will remain truly applicable to the complexity and variety of human living.

Including Universality and Particularity

Universality. Any morality that attempts to help all human beings relate to each other meaningfully must strive to possess a universal applicability; if, like individual or personal ethical egoism, a moral system applies only to one person, then all remaining human beings are essentially excluded from it. Also, if it depends upon a belief in a certain supernatural being and a set of dogmatic "truths" that have no conclusive evidential or rational basis, then those who do not believe at all, or who believe only in part, are also excluded. Therefore, it is very important that any moral system apply to human beings in general, which means that it must be broadly enough based not to exclude anyone who is striving to be good, and to include as many meaningful and workable moral systems as possible.

Particularity. In its universality, however, one's moral system should not become so generalized and abstract that it cannot be applied to particular situations and individuals.

Morality, after all, always takes place at particular times, in particular places, in particular situations, and between or among particular individuals; it never takes place in the abstract.

Morality may be theorized about or discussed in the abstract, but decisions, actions, or failures to act always occur in concrete, everyday situations. That is why, for example, universal pronouncements, such as "Abortions are never justified," although they do sound highly moral and certainly apply to all people at all times, fail to take into consideration the many serious implications for all those involved in the situation surrounding an abortion. Such pronouncements never provide us with any real criteria for weighing one human life (the mother's) against another (the fetus's) when one is definitely threatened by the other. The particular situation may be that the expectant mother has a family of little children and a young husband, all of whom need her very badly. Yet if she herself feels bound by the abstract absolutism of the abortion pronouncement thus cited, she is almost forbidden to consider that one life has to be sacrificed, either hers or that of her unborn child. In short, the particular situation is often much more complicated than the abstract generalization allows for; therefore, in such cases the generalization is virtually unusable.

Ability to Be Taught and Promulgated

If any moral system is to be applied to more than one person, it must be able to be promulgated, that is, laid out for people to see and understand. It also should be teachable so that others can learn about it regardless of whether they wish to accept or reject it. If, as with egoism, teaching or promulgating one's moral theory violates the very basis of that theory, then it must be kept secret, and therefore it can have no real applicability to anyone other than the individual who holds it. Furthermore, if there is really nothing to teach except, for example, the concept that one should act on the basis of what one feels to be right without considering what those "right feelings" really amount to, then the moral system is questionable because it cannot be passed on to anyone in a meaningful way. These problems are very serious because the greatest emphasis for morality is the social emphasis. If a moral theory is not teachable or cannot be promulgated, then how can it be applicable to society or any part of it beyond the one person who holds it?

Ability to Resolve Conflicts

A final consideration is that a workable moral system must be able to resolve conflicts among duties and obligations, and even among its participants. In universal ethical egoism, for example, if it is not possible to decide whose self-interest should be served when self-interests conflict, then the entire theory is thrown into doubt, for it states, on the one hand, that everyone's self-interest should be served, and yet, on the other hand, it does not say how that can be done when there is a conflict of interests.

Further, if any moral theory or system proposes a series of duties or obligations that human beings ought to perform or be responsible for, yet fails to tell people what they should do when these conflict, then again the system is unworkable. For example, if a system proposes that it is wrong to lie and also wrong to break promises, yet does not tell its adherents which of the two wrongs takes precedence when these conflict, then how can one know what to do if one has promised to protect the lives of some friends but must tell a lie to a killer who is in search of them? Simply to say that both actions are wrong or right will not help us when confronted with an actual moral decision. People must know, when clashes between or among moral commandments occur, *how* they can choose the action that will be most moral. Any system that does not provide for the resolution of such conflicts may be abstractly or theoretically meaningful, but, again, in the concrete moral situation it will be of very little use to human beings who are striving to do the right thing. A system such as Sir William David Ross' *Prima Facie*, Duties, even with its problems, might be helpful as a guide to resolving conflicts.

Keeping these assumptions in mind, then, the most important question we have to face is how we can go about setting up a moral system that is rationally based and yet not unemotional; logically consistent, but not rigid or inflexible; universal, and yet practically applicable to particular individuals and situations; can be taught and promulgated; and can effectively resolve conflicts among human beings, duties, and obligations.

In Chapters 5 and 6, we looked at the problems having to do with absolutes and freedom, and we arrived at two conclusions: (1) There are moral absolutes that can be known, and (2) although their freedom is limited, human beings can be said to be free in a very real sense. We also concluded that because of the variety, diversity, and complexity of human beings, we must move from absolutes to "near" absolutes, which I labeled basic principles. It now seems that the problems of morality center essentially in these two areas: that of working with basic principles in order to avoid the chaos of situationism and intuitionism, while at the same time allowing for the freedom that individual human beings and groups require if they are to work with such basic principles in a meaningful, practical, and creative fashion. The way this can best be accomplished is to discover those principles that are indeed truly basic and necessary to almost any moral system or theory and to be sure that individual freedom is one of them. I intend to show how this can be done in the remainder of this chapter.

Basic Principles, Individual Freedom, and Their Justification

What we need first is a basic principle or principles. If we remember the ethical systems described so far, we will note that each of them has at least one basic principle and that some have more. In ethical egoism, the basic principle is self-interest; in utilitarianism, it is the interest of all concerned; in Kant's system it is the Categorical Imperative, the emphasis upon duty rather than inclination, the reversibility criterion, and the principle that each human being is an end and not a means only. Even the ethical system that advocates rules the least and stresses particular situations the most—situation ethics—still has one basic principle, which is love.

Is there any way that we can cut across all of these ethical systems to arrive at basic principles with which they all might agree? I am not referring here to agreement in the sense of how these basic principles are carried out or acted on; rather, I am concerned with agreement as to the ultimacy of principles necessary to the formation of any ethical system that will successfully apply to human morality.

Choosing Principles

Number of Principles. One must first decide on how many principles the system will have. One principle does not seem to be enough, and yet in the interest of simplicity, neither does one want too many. In my experience, one principle will not cover everything that is needed in a system. For example, Michael Scriven states that the equality principle ("Everyone has equal rights with you in moral matters until they prove otherwise") is the only one needed in his moral system. This principle is certainly admirable in that it sets up individual freedom, but it doesn't state any other values (freedom *from* what, to *do* what?), nor does it specify exactly what "until they prove otherwise" means.

The Golden Rule. One of the most popular rules or principles people put forth when asked what they base their ethics on is the Golden Rule, or what Kant called "the reversibility criterion." It can be stated many ways, but the usual way is, "Do unto others as you would have them do unto you." In other words, if you want to find out what the moral thing to do is in any situation, you should ask yourself what you would like done to or for you if you were going to be the recipient of your own moral action. There is nothing really wrong with putting oneself in the other person's shoes, as the saying goes, but as a primary and especially *only* principle on which to base a moral system, it is not very adequate.

First of all, in applying the Golden Rule, we are assuming that what the other person will want or need is the same as what we will want or need, and this is not always true. For example, some people might thrive on physical contact that could cause minor or sometimes major injury. Some people feel their weekend is not complete until they have had at least one fistfight. Such people, going only by the Golden Rule, may figure that's what they would want done to them, and therefore that's what they should do to others. Perhaps this example is somewhat exaggerated, but it does point out at least one problem with making the Golden Rule one's only principle.

Second, the Golden Rule doesn't really tell us what we should do: It only gives a method for testing what we have chosen to do, against how it would affect us if we were to be the recipients of a certain act. That we would consider what we think to be the wishes of others, before we commit ourselves to any action, is in itself admirable, but it does not tell us what we actually should do and thereby fails to provide a realistic basis for choosing among acts that will affect others.

Too often, such principles as the Golden Rule are chosen solely on the basis of custom or tradition. But reflection will reveal that we need to ask ourselves, "What are the important things in life, and which principles will protect and enhance them?" if we are to construct a significant basis for morality. In attempting to do just that, I will first suggest certain principles and show how almost all ethical systems adhere to them, either explicitly or implicitly. Next, I will provide evidence and rational argument in an attempt to prove that these principles are absolutely vital to any meaningful, workable, and livable system of human ethics.

The Value of Life Principle

The first principle we shall discuss is the Value of Life principle. This principle can be stated in several ways, but I prefer to state it as follows: "Human beings should revere life and accept death." As I argued in Chapter 5, no ethical system can function or persist without some statement, positive or negative or both, that reflects a concern for the preservation and protection of human life. It is perhaps the most basic and necessary principle of ethics because, empirically speaking, there can be no ethics whatsoever without living human beings. This does not necessarily mean that no one may ever be killed, or that people should never be allowed to die, or that no one can ever commit suicide or have an abortion. Each ethical system could differ in many of these areas for logical reasons, but there must be some sort of concern for human life arising out of pragmatic considerations alone.

However, I think more justification than that of "no human life, no ethical system" can and should be given. Most ethical systems have some sort of prohibition against killing: the "Thou shalt not kill" of Judeo-Christian ethics; the "Never kill" of Kant; the prohibitions against killing in Buddhism, Hinduism, and humanism, to name but a few. In fact, even the most primitive of societies have had something to say about killing in general. All of these systems do allow killing under some circumstances, but usually they contain very strong commandments against the destruction of human life in general. Many systems extend the not-killing ideal beyond human life to all living things, but all concern themselves with some sort of preservation of human life. Even the least ethical systems, such as Sadam Hussein's, concern themselves with the value of *some* life (for example, its leaders' lives only).

Justification of the Value of Life Principle. It is my assumption, as stated earlier in this chapter, that morality should be based upon reason and empirical evidence, but it remains to be shown whether the principles proposed here can be so supported. I believe that I have already given sufficient evidence and argument to support the Value of Life principle at the end of Chapter 5. This principle is empirically prior to any other because without human life there can be no goodness or badness, justice or injustice, honesty or dishonesty, freedom or lack of it. Life is a basic possession, the main possession of each individual human being. It is the one thing that all living human beings have in common, yet each individual experiences life uniquely—no one else can truly share or live another's life.

Therefore, individuals (as Kant maintained) should never be treated merely as means, but rather as unique and individual ends in themselves. This does not mean that the ending of a human life can never be justified. In fact, it is precisely because such an occurrence sometimes is justified that I have formulated the Value of Life principle as "Humans should revere life and accept death." This means that although we recognize life as basic and important, we also realize that no human life has been everlasting and that none is ever likely to be. All of us must die sometime; therefore, "life at all costs" is not what the principle stands for, nor does it stand for the quantity of life over its quality. It merely proposes that no life should be ended without very strong justification.

One of the important adjuncts of this last statement and the statement about the uniqueness of an individual's life is that an individual's right to his own life *and* death is a basic concept; that is, decisions about whether a person should or should not live should not be made without the person's informed consent unless the justification is very great. This means that it is morally wrong to take people's lives against their will unless great justification can be brought forward for doing so; it also means that it is morally wrong to interfere with their death or dying against their will without similar justification. The four other principles enforce the value of life here. I see these principles as being mutually supportive at various points, as being flexibly able to act and react with each other so as to form the unity that a universal ethical system needs. But before discussing their justification, let me reiterate that the Value of Life principle is justified as a near or almost absolute because life is held both in common and uniquely by all human beings, and it has to constitute that empirical starting point for any morality or humanity whatsoever.

The Principle of Goodness or Rightness

The second principle implied in every ethical system I have ever heard of is the Principle of Goodness or Rightness. This principle sometimes is presented as two separate principles (see Ross' *Prima Facie* Duties in Chapter 3, for example): (1) the Principle of Beneficence, which states that one should always do good, and (2) the Principle of Nonmaleficence, which states that one should always try to prevent and avoid doing badness or harm. We shall see how these relate to each other when we list what the Principle of Goodness or Rightness demands of us. If morality means what is "good" or what is "right," then every system of morality must clearly imply, whether it is stated or not, the Principle of Goodness or Rightness. That is, all ethical systems are based on the idea that we should strive to be "good" human beings and attempt to perform "right" actions; and, conversely, that we should try both *not* to be "bad" human beings and to avoid performing "wrong" actions. By the very definition of the terms *morality* and *immorality* we are concerned with being good and doing right. In actuality, the Principle of Goodness or Rightness demands that human beings attempt to do three things:

1. Promote goodness over badness and do good (beneficence).
2. Cause no harm or badness (nonmalfeasance).
3. Prevent badness or harm (nonmalfeasance).

Ethicists may differ over what they actually consider to be good and bad or right and wrong, but they all demand that human beings strive for the good and the right and avoid and prevent the bad and the wrong. Ethical systems embody this principle by implying, "If human beings are to be good (moral), then they should do so-and-so" (for example, act in their own self-interest).

Justification of the Principle of Goodness. Unless one wants to argue the question "Why be moral?" (see Chapter 1 for references to this), when one accepts morality, one also accepts goodness because that is essentially what the first term means. In Chapter 1,

I defined *morality* as being goodness or rightness, and *immorality* as being badness or wrongness. When we speak of a moral person, life, or action, we mean a good person, a good life, and a right action; when we speak of an immoral person, life, or action, we mean a bad person, a bad life, and a wrong action. I also defined *good* and *right* as involving happiness, pleasure, excellence, harmony, and creativity, and *bad* and *wrong* as involving unhappiness, pain, lack of excellence, disharmony, and lack of creativity. How these characteristics are to be defined by individuals, however, is not so clear because they are subject to the same truths and facts as the Principle of Individual Freedom—that is, they will mean different things to some extent because each individual is by nature different from every other one.

Despite all of these differences, however, it is possible to discover some "goods" that human beings have generally been able to agree upon. These include life, consciousness, pleasure, happiness, truth, knowledge, beauty, love, friendship, self-expression, self-realization, freedom, honor, peace, and security. There is no doubt that people rank these "goods" differently or even omit one or two from their list of "good things," but most people, after careful discussion, probably will include many of these. Some moralists hold that there is only one thing (for instance, happiness) that is intrinsically good (good in itself); this view is called *monism*. However, as you might guess, because I have stressed freedom and individuality and uniqueness so much and also have stressed a synthesis of ethical approaches, my view would be that there are many "goods"; this view is called *pluralism*.

Having defined *good* and *right*, and having shown that both of these must be manifested in human experience and in human interpersonal relationships, the question is whether we can justify the Principle of Goodness: Human beings should always do good and avoid or prevent what is bad.

There is not one ethical system that advocates that a person do what is bad and avoid what is good. But this in itself is not justification; it is merely an empirical fact. If a person thinks that human beings ought to be moral, then he or she thinks that they ought to do good and avoid or prevent bad. If, however, a person thinks that people need not strive for the good and avoid or prevent bad, then his or her concern lies outside of morality, and the question "Why should I be moral at all?" has to be answered. Because this question is nonmoral and cannot be answered within morality, the Principle of Goodness is simply an ultimate principle for morality of any kind and cannot be justified any further than was done in Chapter 1. The Principle of Goodness is *logically* prior to all other principles, just as the Value of Life principle is *empirically* prior. This distinction will be clarified at the end of this chapter.

The Principle of Justice or Fairness

The third principle is the Principle of Justice or Fairness. This concerns itself essentially with the distribution of good and bad on a just and fair basis. It says that human beings should treat other human beings fairly and justly when distributing goodness and badness among them. It is not enough that people should try to be good and to do what is right; there also must be some attempt made to distribute the benefits of being good and doing right. Ways in which "distributive" justice can be considered have been discussed fully in Chapter 7 and should be referred to at this point.

It is difficult to find an ethical system that does not include some concern for justice. Even ethical egoism, which one might think would have no concern for justice because its major aim is self-interest, does in its most accepted form—universal ethical egoism—want everyone to act in his or her own self-interest. Isn't this asking, in essence, that everyone be treated justly? Egoists would be strongly opposed to some versions of distributive justice, but they at least advocate that *everyone* should act in his or her own self-interest. Kant's Duty Ethics—with its universal applicability, the Categorical Imperative, reversibility criterion, and regard for all human beings as ends rather than means—has justice at its core. Utilitarianism, whether it be act or rule, advocates a general concern for justice because it attempts to deal with the happiness of all concerned, not just self and not even just other people. Judaism and Christianity, in their Ten Commandments—which stress not killing, not stealing, not committing adultery, and not coveting—are concerned with justice, and the urgings of Jesus to "love thy neighbor as thyself" and "love even your enemies" emphasize justice and fairness, among other things.

Justification of the Principle of Justice. I would argue that it is another empirical truth that there are many human beings in the world and that very few, if any, live in complete isolation; in fact, most of our actions and lives are performed and lived in the company of others. In such a situation, should one bring goodness only to oneself and do absolutely nothing for others? Very few strong egoists would accept such behavior as being in one's self-interest, and it certainly would not be in the interest of others or of all concerned.

If one accepts the concept that good should be shared, the next issue to be considered is who should get the benefits resulting from good human actions and how should they be distributed. Because there are very few occasions when an individual's moral action does not affect anyone other than her- or himself, the good or bad resulting from this action must inevitably fall upon other people. One could, of course, merely let the consequences fall where they may, but we are attempting to work with a rationally based morality, and reason dictates that there should be some order to any distribution of good or bad.

All human beings have common characteristics, as we have said, and yet each human is unique, so how do we distribute goodness and badness with these truths in mind? What does it mean when we say that we should try to distribute goodness and badness fairly and equally among all human beings? If, for example, we return to the dialysis case described in the previous chapter, it means that everyone gets an equal chance at both the good and the bad in the situation. Presuming that, for people with kidney failure, receiving kidney dialysis is a good and not getting it is a bad, then by the lottery method we make it possible to distribute this good and this bad equally among the 17 patients. Some will have to receive the bad, but all will have an equal chance of obtaining the good.

Does this mean that we must share each other's property, families, jobs, or money? Not necessarily. There are, for example, exceptions to the equal distribution ideal in a *triage*, a medical emergency situation in which the patients greatly outnumber the medical personnel and facilities. Choices have to be made, and the lottery method may not, and probably will not, be the fairest or most effective way of dealing with the situation. Because so many need medical attention and so few are able to give it, then under the circumstances, medical personnel who can be put back into service after receiving medical attention should have first priority, and the patients who can with some certainty be saved should be next.

These emergency situations are rare exceptions for the most part, but what about using the lottery method to determine who gets money, property, and jobs? This view of justice, of course, would be absurd; however, everyone must have an equal opportunity to *acquire* these things if they desire them. Not everyone has the persistence or intelligence to become a doctor or lawyer, for example, but everyone who has the necessary qualifications ought to have an equal opportunity to apply for and to be accepted at medical and law schools.

It is almost too obvious to state that no one should be denied this opportunity because of his or her skin color, sex, religious belief, age, or beauty or lack thereof, nor should anyone be denied the opportunity to earn as much money as anyone else for these or other reasons that have nothing to do with fair qualifications for obtaining a position. In this way we recognize the common equality of human beings as human beings and yet allow for individual differences when attempting to distribute goodness and badness fairly. We must have the Principle of Justice, then, in order to be moral toward other people because they are inevitably affected by our actions.

The Principle of Truth Telling or Honesty

The fourth basic principle is almost a corollary to the Principle of Justice or Fairness; however, I think that it is important enough in its own right to be a separate principle of equal status with the other four described in this chapter. This is the Principle of Truth Telling or Honesty. It is extremely important, if for no other reason than to provide for meaningful communication, which is an absolute necessity in any moral system or in any moral relationship between two or more human beings. How, indeed, can any moral system function if its participants can never know whether anyone is telling the truth? How, with the stress placed on teaching and promulgating, can moral theories be communicated if no one can be sure whether the communicators are lying or telling the truth? One of the basic criticisms I leveled at individual and personal ethical egoism was that such egoists undoubtedly would have to lie or be dishonest in order to satisfy their own self-interests; that is, they would believe in one ethical theory but would have to pretend they actually believed in another. If they did not do this, they probably would not be operating in their own self-interests.

Further, all of morality depends upon agreements between human beings, and how can agreements be made or maintained without some assurance that people are entering into them honestly and truthfully? Therefore, it would seem that truth telling and honesty are important and basic cornerstones of morality. Most ethical systems have some prohibition against lying. In Judeo-Christian ethics, the commandment "Thou shalt not bear false witness" makes it clear that lying is wrong. Kant states that lying cannot be made into a maxim for all humanity without being inconsistent, and most other ethical systems contain at least a general prohibition against lying even if they allow for many exceptional instances in which lying would be "the lesser of two evils." Lying will be discussed in more detail in Chapter 12.

Justification of the Principle of Truth Telling or Honesty. I have already argued that a basic agreement to be truthful is necessary to the communication of a moral theory or system, but such an agreement also is extremely important in establishing and maintaining vital and meaningful human relationships of any kind, moral or nonmoral. Human beings need to enter into relationships with each other with a sense of mutual trust, believing that whatever they say or do to one another will be as honest and open an expression of their thoughts and feelings as possible. This principle may be the most difficult of all the principles to try to live with because human beings are essentially very vulnerable in the area of human relationships, and in order to protect this vulnerability may have built up defenses against exposing themselves to others. This is especially true in a modern, crowded, and complex civilization such as ours.

Because of such obvious vulnerability, this very demanding principle is open to many carefully justified exceptions. Basically, however, it still must be adhered to wherever possible. It is not true that people will never lie to one another, and not even true that lying or dishonesty might not be justified; however, it is true that a strong *attempt* must be made to be truthful and honest in human relationships because morality, in the final analysis, depends upon what people say and do.

For example, suppose that A borrows money from B and agrees to pay it back but then does not. When B asks A for the money, A says that he does not intend to pay it back and never did. Now, when the money was borrowed and loaned, there was a mutual sense of trust involved in that B was going to help A out by loaning him money, and A was going to pay her back in gratitude for the help. When B discovers that A has not only defaulted but also never intended to pay back the money, the sense of mutual trust is broken, not only for this one transaction and relationship but also, perhaps, for any future relationships that B might have with A or with other people.

The problem is that the basis of human relationships is communication, and when communication is eroded by lying or dishonesty, that basis is destroyed, and meaningful human relationships—especially those in the moral sphere—become impossible. Therefore, because all human relationships are based upon communication and because—to my way of thinking—morality is the most important of all human relationships, it is absolutely necessary that truth telling and honesty be considered as fundamental and basic to any theory or system of morality.

The Principle of Individual Freedom

The fifth and last basic principle is the Principle of Individual Freedom, or the equality principle, sometimes referred to as the Principle of Autonomy. For Michael Scriven, this is the ultimate moral principle; in fact, he defines *morality* as "equal consideration, from which all other moral principles (justice, and so on) can be developed" and as the recognition that "people have equal rights with you in moral matters until they prove otherwise."[1]

He goes on to stress that this does not mean that they are equal in height or weight or intelligence, but rather that they are equal in moral matters. This principle means that people, being individuals with individual differences, must have the freedom to choose their own ways and means of being moral *within the framework of the first four basic principles*. This last stipulation is, of course, mine and not Scriven's because I do not believe that the equality principle in itself is enough of a basis upon which to develop an ethical system. In fact, I have presented this principle last so that it is understood that individual moral freedom is limited by the other four principles: the necessity of preserving and protecting human life; the necessity of doing good and preventing and avoiding bad; the necessity of treating human beings justly when distributing goodness and badness; and, finally, the necessity of telling the truth and being honest.

It seems to be a powerful necessity, if one considers the tremendous variety of human desires, needs, and concerns, that people be allowed to follow the dictates of their own intelligence and conscience as much as possible. Most people will agree with this statement, especially in a definitely pluralistic society such as ours; but they also will want to stipulate that this principle is valid only as long as it does not interfere with someone else in any serious way.

Because no person is exactly like another and no situation is exactly like another, there must be some leeway for people to deal with these differences in the manner best suited to them. However, neither freedom itself nor moral freedom is absolute. For example, just because one man wants the freedom to rape a woman or desires to kill someone, does not mean he ought to have the freedom to do so, nor should he have the freedom to steal someone's new car just because he has the freedom to wish he could have it. The limitations of one's freedom, then, should be established by the other four principles.

It is important to distinguish between this principle and the second one in that the second principle has to do with the equal *distribution* of goodness and badness, whereas the Principle of Individual Freedom has to do with the equality of human beings *themselves* when it comes to moral matters. When Kant stated that each human being ought to be considered an end in himself or herself and not a means for anyone else's end, he implied the equality principle. The Golden Rule says that one ought to consider other people in the same way that one considers oneself—that is, as one's equals insofar as moral choices and treatment are concerned. When Jesus was asked, "But who is my neighbor?" in relation to His commandment "Love thy neighbor as thyself," He answered with the parable of the Good Samaritan, indicating that all people are to be considered as moral equals despite any belief that they might not be one's intellectual, social, religious, or economic equal. One person should not condemn another for the way he or she lives, no matter how great are the differences in lifestyle, as long as both people adhere to the principles of goodness, justice, value of life, and honesty.

Justification of the Principle of Individual Freedom. I have already argued, in Chapter 6, that human beings have freedom in a limited but real sense to make decisions and choices, including, of course, moral decisions and choices. The important question is to what degree they should be allowed such freedom in their dealings with other human beings. The Principle of Individual Freedom resolves the problem of instilling flexibility within a moral system—a flexibility it needs owing to the very real diversity that exists among human beings.

I justify the Principle of Individual Freedom on the basis that there are many human beings to be considered when one is attempting to establish a human morality, and although they have common characteristics (bodies, minds, feelings, and so forth), each person is, nevertheless, unique. Human beings are at different stages of development, have different talents and abilities, and possess different feelings, wants, and needs, and if we are not to completely obliterate these differences, we must recognize and allow for them. The only way to allow for them is to let individuals live out their lives in whatever unique and different ways they choose.

What I am saying is that there is no possible way that one human life can be lived by anyone other than the person who is living it; therefore, we must accept each human being for the true individual he or she is. This acceptance amounts to granting to all individuals the freedom to live their lives in ways best suited to them, thereby recognizing what is actually a natural and empirical truth about human beings: That they are in fact different and unique. Freedom, like life, then, is "built into" the human structure, both empirically and rationally.

Nowhere is freedom more important or significant than in morality. As stated in Chapter 6, morality could not exist if human beings were not to some extent free to make moral choices and decisions. There is no point in assigning moral responsibility, in praising or blaming, or in rewarding or punishing, if human beings are not somehow free to be responsible, praiseworthy, or blameworthy. Therefore, it seems that freedom must be built into any moral system if such a system is to function properly.

It is even more important, however, if a system is to work for all human beings who are trying to be moral, that they be allowed the greatest latitude possible when making moral choices and decisions. It is important not only because of the obvious diversity among human beings, which has already been recognized, but also because the basic principles are only *near or* almost absolutes, and every opportunity must be given human beings to follow these principles in the way that best suits their individuality, their lives and life situations, and their relationships with other human beings. The Principle of Individual Freedom, then, is extremely important to any moral system in that it can encourage the widest possible expression of moral preferences, choices, and decisions within the structure of the other four principles, thus allowing for the combination of flexibility and stability that all livable and workable moral systems need.

Priority of the Basic Principles

One of the problems associated with any set of basic principles is the priority in which they are to be used. For example, is the Value of Life principle always inviolable even though it may bring about badness rather than goodness? Must we be concerned about the distribution of goodness and badness even where such distribution seriously violates someone's freedom? Further, must we always tell the truth even if it will bring badness, not goodness? As I have already said, our five basic principles—the value of life;

goodness, or rightness; justice, or fairness; truth telling, or honesty; and individual freedom—are not absolutes, but *near* or *almost* absolutes, and they can be violated so long as there is sufficient justification to do so. But what, for example, constitutes sufficient justification to violate the Value of Life principle?

Even though, as the reader might suspect, I have presented and have attempted to support these principles in the order in which I feel they should be followed, that order and any other considerations of priority that are to be made remain to be justified. First, there are two important ways in which the priority of the basic principles may be determined:

1. A general way, in which the five principles are classified into two major categories based upon logical and empirical priority.
2. A particular way, in which priority is determined by the actual situation or context in which moral actions and decisions occur and in which all basic principles must inevitably function.

A General Way of Determining Priority—Two Categories

The Primary Category. Under the general way of classifying the five basic principles, the first two are logically and empirically prior to the other three and, therefore, fall into the first major category. *Logical priority* means the way in which logic determines the order in which the principles must occur, or in which logical thinking forces us to place them. *Empirical priority* means that priority which is established by evidence gained from observation through the senses. Logical reasoning plays a part here, too, but the emphasis is on evidence derived through the senses.

Logically speaking, the Principle of Goodness comes first. What this means is that in establishing any moral system, one immediately has to assume the ultimate moral principle: goodness. After all, *morality*, as I have already said, means the same thing as *goodness*, so when speaking of morality, one can assume that this ultimate moral principle is *logically* prior to any other.

As I also have argued, however, in an empirical sense one cannot have human morality unless one first has human life. If there are no human beings, then there can be no human morality—this is an obvious empirical fact. These two principles, then, are logically and empirically necessary to morality, and because of this necessity they take precedence over the other three principles and must be placed in the first, or primary, category.

The Secondary Category. The other three principles fall into the secondary category in the following order: The third principle is that of justice or fairness, because in most human actions more than one person is involved, and some kind of distribution must be established. The fourth principle is that of truth telling or honesty, because it follows from the need to be fair and just in dealings with others. This principle also is very important, as we have seen, because it is basic to human communication and human relationships, which underlie all morality. Last, but certainly not least, is the fifth principle, that of individual freedom, which is important because each individual is unique and in many cases is the only person capable of successfully determining what is good for him- or herself.

By putting five principles into these two major categories, I do not mean to imply that principles from the secondary category will not, under certain circumstances, take precedence over those in the primary. For example, at many moments in history, human beings have willingly given up their lives so as to preserve their freedom and the freedom of others. The two categories merely give human beings a priority to follow in a *general* sense; in general, the Value of Life principle and the Principle of Goodness strike us as being more important than the other three principles because the former are absolutely essential to any moral system or theory.

Another justification for placing the five principles in categories is that principles one and two are often interchangeable with each other in terms of priority, whereas principles three through five are also interchangeable among themselves. For example, it is wrong or bad to take a person's life against his or her will, but if this person is violating the first two principles by aggressively seeking to take the lives of innocent people, one's own included, then one might have the right to attempt to stop the person from doing bad by any means one can, including killing him if no lesser means can be used. In this case, the Principle of Goodness may take precedence over the Value of Life principle.

As an example of the fact that the second three principles are at times interchangeable, consider the following. If any decision involves freely consenting individuals but does not seriously affect others, then the Principle of Individual Freedom may override the Principle of Justice. The implication is that people ought to be able to do what they want as long as it does not interfere with others in any serious manner. This is why most sexual activity between freely consenting adults may not be governed by the Principle of Justice so much as by the Principle of Individual Freedom. Here, the latter may take precedence over the former.

Rape, child molestation, and sadistic acts performed upon unwilling victims are, of course, violations of the Principle of Justice, but sexual activity agreed upon by consenting adults may not be. Offense to others' taste may not be a sufficient reason to invoke the Principle of Justice unless other people are being forced into such acts. For example, just because I may feel that group sex is wrong for and distasteful to me does not mean I can impose my own feelings upon other freely consenting adults. (These issues and others will be discussed in much more detail in Chapter 13.) To sum up: The principles may overlap, depending upon the particular situation, but basically and generally the first two principles should be stressed and should be seen as interchangeable in terms of priority, whereas the last three should be given lesser status and should also be seen as being interchangeable among themselves in terms of priority.

The Particular Way of Determining Priority: Situation or Context

In discussing the second, and particular, way in which priority is determined, it is important to note that morality and moral decision making do not occur in the abstract but in concrete, everyday-life situations. Because morality or immorality occurs in *particular* situations or contexts, such situations and contexts must be observed and analyzed carefully. Any theories or rules or ethical principles that cannot be applied to actual human situations in a meaningful manner should definitely be questioned and probably be discarded as worthless.

This does not mean that one cannot generalize from these particular situations, especially where they are sufficiently similar; on the contrary, it means that generalizations must be made from the particular whenever possible so that the generalizations will be supported with as much real and actual evidence as one can master. It is for this reason that I am opposed to a strictly nonconsequentialist approach to ethics—because I believe that all actions have consequences and that moral or immoral actions have the most serious of all consequences for human beings. This is also why I am opposed to a strictly "rules" approach to ethics; too often rules are so broad and general that there can be no disputing them until one tries unsuccessfully to apply them to a particular situation. It is at this point that people discover that rules may sound and even be moral but simply do not tell people how to act in particular situations A and B.

Nevertheless, because I advocate five basic principles that I have stated should not be violated without strong justification, I obviously do not think that simply waiting to see what happens in each situation is the most meaningful way of going about being moral. I feel that we must start from some broad yet humanly applicable basic principles so that we will have some foundation for acting morally and avoiding immorality and so that the profusion of different situations we face in life will not confuse our thinking when it comes to making moral decisions. For these reasons, my approach to ethics is eclectic (that is, made up from what I consider to be the best aspects of many different systems). It also can be called "mixed deontological," or what I would describe as a combined consequentialist-nonconsequentialist and rules-act approach to ethics—in other words, yet another reasonable synthesis.

This means that one enters all situations with a reverence for human life and an acceptance of human death; with the idea of doing good and avoiding and preventing bad; with the hope of justly distributing the good and bad that result from situations; with the desire to be truthful and honest; and with the idea of granting individual freedom and equality to everyone involved in the situations as long as doing so does not violate the other four principles.

Then each situation will help human beings to determine how these principles will be adhered to or carried out. The particular situation will help them to determine whether a life should be taken or not; how much freedom should be allowed or denied; what is the right or wrong act to perform; and what is the fairest way to act toward everyone. In this way, the unity that human beings need will be provided by the basic principles of morality, whereas the diversity that also is required will be provided by the individual interpretation and carrying out of these principles in particular situations involving moral decisions.

For example, it is quite easy to state that one should not steal from another person under the principles of goodness, justice, honesty, and individual freedom. That is, *generally*, it is not right to steal from another because stealing violates a person's freedom to earn and own property; it does not bring satisfaction to the person stolen from (although it may bring satisfaction to the thief); it is not an action with any excellence in it (although a particular thief may be a clever and "excellent" one); it does not create harmony because one should, if one is able, earn one's own property; and it is not fair to the other person, who has worked hard to acquire what she or he owns.

We could say, then, that people who steal merely because they like to or because they would rather not work, are performing a dishonest and immoral action. However, let us suppose that your sister is searching diligently for her gun in order to kill someone who has made her angry. You certainly would be justified in stealing your sister's gun so that she would not be able to violate all five of the principles by doing something bad, by taking a life, by encroaching on someone else's freedom, and by not being fair or honest to the person who made her angry. Because the Value of Life and the Goodness principles are more crucial to morality than the other three, you are justified in stealing in this situation because you may save a life and prevent badness by doing so.

Another example actually occurred when a plane with missionaries aboard crashed in the Amazon jungle of South America. The only survivor was the missionaries' daughter, who attempted to make her way to a village or city to save herself. At one point in her wanderings, she arrived at a river where she found a boat. Following to the letter the Judeo-Christian commandment against stealing, she refused to take the boat and went on wandering through the jungle. She adhered to a moral rule very strictly, but would she have been immoral if she had not? Under the system I have proposed, she would not have. She might have waited to see if the boat was abandoned, but after a while, when she was fairly sure that it was and that there was no one around to either use the boat or help her, she would have been justified under the Value of Life principle in violating the rule against stealing.

Let us also note, however, that she was not *obligated* to take the boat; in her own individual freedom, she could choose—as she did—not to steal, at the risk of losing her life. She could have reasoned further that whoever had left the boat would know the jungle much better than she and would therefore be better able to survive. She also could have marked the spot where she took it, and as soon as she arrived at the first village, she could have sent some villagers back to find the boat's owner, thus being as fair as she could under the circumstances. Therefore, the situation or context in which we have to act does, indeed, have a bearing on how we interpret and use the five basic principles as we go about making our moral decisions; however, the principles do remain the basis for deciding or acting at all.

How the System of Humanitarian Ethics Works

Before we conclude this chapter, let's examine two human events involving moral issues and run them through the five principles to see how the system works. The two events I will apply the principles to are (1) two young adults living together without benefit of marriage, and (2) rape.

Living Together Without Marriage

Let's say that a young man and woman, age 18, want to live together, enjoying the full benefits of a live-in relationship. Both sets of parents object strenuously to their doing so. Is what the young people are seeking to do immoral? Let's apply the five principles.

Value of Life Principle. There doesn't seem to be a violation of the Value of Life principle in that no one's life is threatened by this contemplated action. If the woman becomes pregnant, the problem of abortion may arise, but we can presume that the couple will utilize contraception or will have something else moral set up in the event of pregnancy.

Principle of Goodness. It's difficult to see any significant violation of the Principle of Goodness unless one applies some specific standard of a particular religion, for example, one specifically stating that such a relationship is immoral. If, however, the couple does not adhere to this religion, even though their parents may, then such a standard cannot be forced on them. The couple evidently feels that living together will bring about goodness for themselves, whereas their parents feel it will not. The parents also may feel that this will not bring about goodness for themselves; that is, it will make them worry, embarrass them in front of family and friends, and generally upset them.

Principle of Justice. The Principle of Justice really seems to be the only principle that would affect the parents. That is, is the distribution of goodness fair if the parents are not made happy by this arrangement? In other words, the man and woman feel that they are being fair to each other and their parents, but the parents feel that their children are not being fair to their families. What their children are doing is offensive to them—to their taste and to their belief in the sanctity of marriage.

Two questions arise: "Is this sufficient reason for not allowing the couple to live together and to brand their actions as immoral?" and "For how long must children conform to their parents' lifestyle or values?" Is not 18 an age at which young people should have the right to live their own lives and take responsibility for what they do?

Principle of Honesty and Truth Telling. There seems to be no violation of the Principle of Honesty and Truth Telling because the young people are quite open about their intentions.

Principle of Individual Freedom. The question really centers upon the Principle of Individual Freedom. If there is no serious violation of the other four principles, then according to this ethical system, individual freedom should be allowed. I do not feel that any of the principles can be clearly shown to have been seriously violated; therefore, although what the couple is doing may be offensive to some people's (obviously their parents') tastes, this in itself should not deny these young consenting adults the right to live together if they want to as long as they are moral toward each other. This, of course, is another area where the principles should be applied and constitutes a separate issue. We presume that the young people have agreed to be moral toward one another. Serious breaches of morality in their relationship toward one another would, of course, alter the conclusion concerning the morality of their living together. On the face of it, however, there would seem to be no reason not to allow them to live together.

Rape

Suppose a man wants to rape a woman. Would this ever be a moral act?

Value of Life Principle. The Value of Life principle would certainly be violated whether or not the woman were killed because her life and its quality would be threatened by the act of rape. She would be sexually violated and also violated in other ways, both physically and psychologically.

Principle of Goodness. Obviously, there is nothing good for the woman in the act of rape. The only possible good in the act would be the pleasure the rapist might get, but that pleasure is certainly to be classed as malicious because it totally disregards the pain and unhappiness of his victim.

Principle of Justice. There is no way the rapist's act could be considered to be just or fair to the woman because he would be forcing himself on her against her wishes and without her permission, committing the greatest invasion of her privacy and her life.

Principle of Honesty and Truth Telling. The Principle of Honesty and Truth Telling may or may not come into the picture, depending upon whether or not the rapist lies to the woman in order to get her into a situation where the rape can take place.

Principle of Individual Freedom. Because rape violates all of the first four principles, it can never be considered as moral, and, therefore, no man or woman should ever have the freedom to rape another.

Conclusion

We now have five fairly well-established principles under which any ethical system can operate. These principles are broad enough to take cognizance of all human beings and their moral treatment, and as such they are near or almost absolutes, in that exceptions to these principles can be made only if they can be completely justified through empirical evidence and reasoning. Generally, however, these principles will take precedence over all other ethical concerns.

My contention, then, is that if we recognize the value of human life; always attempt to do good and avoid or prevent bad; attempt to distribute good and bad fairly and justly; try to be honest and tell the truth; and still allow for the fullest possible amount of individual freedom and for equal consideration within the limits of the other four principles, we will have an ethical basis upon which many varied individual and group ethical systems can function without serious conflict or the need to eliminate one system because it conflicts with another.

I maintain that the five principles described here are extremely essential to a morality that will relate effectively to all human beings everywhere and yet will allow them the individual freedom to manifest these basic principles in their own individual ways, suitable to their cultural, social, and personal situations. What I envision as the ideal universal moral system, out of which many individual moral systems can successfully be formulated without serious conflict, is one that stresses "unity in diversity." The unity is provided by the first four basic principles, which are not absolutes, but near or almost absolutes, and which, therefore, should not be violated without careful and well-documented justification. The diversity is provided by the fifth principle, which not only allows but also encourages all human beings to seek out the best ways to carry out the other four principles. This means that as long as the five principles are adhered to—with the exceptions being fully justified—whether people are religious or nonreligious, consequentialist or nonconsequentialist, "rule" or "act" in their approach to ethics, they should be able to pursue their own lives within the limitations of the principles without hindrance.

For example, religious and nonreligious ethical systems can easily flourish side by side if the five basic principles are adhered to by both. A particular religion may wish to make certain other moral demands on its members, such as having them worship a god and requiring their participation in its religious activities, but it cannot in any way impose such demands on any human beings outside of the religion itself. Similarly, it cannot take any immoral action against nonreligious persons that would violate the five principles, such as harming or killing them because they do not accept its religious tenets. On the other hand, nonreligious ethicists must allow for the free religious worship of others as long as those others observe the five basic principles. By the same token, nonreligious ethicists are not free to violate any of the principles simply because they do not like what the particular religion believes in or does.

It is even acceptable that a particular religion demand greater moral requirements of its members than those set down in the five principles. For example, Jainists and Quakers have more stringent stipulations against taking human life, and indeed all life, than those encompassed in the Value of Life principle.

This system, which I call Humanitarian Ethics, allows for the greatest amount of diversity and variety, while at the same time providing enough stability and order to protect all human beings while they explore their diverse ethical possibilities.

In the search for the greatest and widest possible morality, I also wish to stress that the views of all ethical systems should be allowed to be set forth and to be openly, honestly, and freely discussed and argued. It is not wrong for one ethical system to attempt to convince others to accept its views as long as this is done by reasonable argument rather than by force, and as long as the five principles are carefully observed in the process. The principles, then, can provide the framework for all ethical systems.

Chapter Summary

I. Conflicting general moral issues
   A. Consequences versus non-consequences. We must consider the consequences of our decisions, acts, and rules, but at the same time be aware of and avoid the end-justifies-the-means problem.

    B. Self- versus other-interestedness. There are problems associated with a totally self-interested basis for morality; therefore, I agree with the utilitarian approach of doing what is in the best interest of everyone.

    C. Act versus rule. In a moral system, we require freedom (act) and yet also stability and order (rule).

    D. Emotion versus reason. A moral system should be based upon reason without excluding emotion.

II. Basic assumptions concerning what constitutes a workable and livable moral system

    A. It should be rationally based and yet not devoid of emotion.

    B. It should be as logically consistent as possible but not rigid and inflexible.

    C. It must have universality or general application to all humanity and yet be applicable in a practical way to particular individuals and situations.

    D. It should be able to be taught and promulgated.

    E. It must have the ability to resolve conflicts among human beings, duties, and obligations.

III. Basic principles, individual freedom, and their justification

    A. The problems of morality center essentially upon two areas.

        1. How to attain unity and order by working with basic principles so as to avoid the chaos of situationism and intuitionism.

        2. How to allow individual and group freedom to work with such principles meaningfully.

    B. The Value of Life principle states that human beings should revere life and accept death.

    C. The Principle of Goodness or Rightness is ultimate to any moral system, and it requires that human beings attempt to do three things: promote goodness over badness and do good; cause no harm or badness; and prevent badness or harm.

    D. The Principle of Justice or Fairness

        1. The type of justice referred to here is *distributive*, meaning that human beings should treat other human beings justly and fairly when attempting to distribute goodness and badness among them.

        2. Theories about, and ways of distributing, good and bad have been fully described in Chapter 6.

    E. The Principle of Truth Telling or Honesty provides for meaningful communication.

    F. The Principle of Individual Freedom states that people, being individuals with individual differences, must have the freedom to choose their own ways and means of being moral within the framework of the first four basic principles.

IV. Two ways of establishing the priority of the five moral principles

    A. In the first, or general, way, the principles are classified into two major categories based upon logical and empirical priority.

        1. The Value of Life principle (because without life there can be no morality whatever) and the Principle of Goodness (because it is the ultimate principle of any moral system) form the first category because they are logically and empirically prior to the other three principles.

        2. The other three principles fall into the second category: the Principle of Justice or Fairness (because in most human actions more than just one person is involved, and some form of distribution of goodness and badness must be established), the Principle of Truth Telling or Honesty (because it follows from the need to be fair and just in one's dealings with others), and the Principle of Individual Freedom (because each individual is the only one truly able to decide what is good for himself).

    B. In the second, or particular, way, priority is determined only by referring to the actual situation or context in which moral actions and decisions occur.

V. Importance of the situation and context of moral problems and basic principles.
   A. The situation or context is important because morality always occurs in particular situations to particular people, never in the abstract.
   B. We must start from a broad yet humanly applicable, near-absolute principle so that there will be some basis for acting morally and avoiding immorality.
   C. Humanitarian Ethics is an eclectic approach, a "mixed deontological," or combined consequentialist-nonconsequentialist and act-rule, approach to morality.

Exercises for Review

1. Explain and analyze the five attributes that the author says must be present in order for any moral system to be livable and workable. With which of these do you agree, and why? With which do you disagree, and why? Can you suggest any others?
2. Do you agree that the central problem of morality is how to attain unity and order in a moral system without denying individual freedom? Why or why not? If you think another problem is more important, explain and discuss it.
3. Explain in detail the five basic principles presented by the author.
4. Would you eliminate any of these five principles as not really basic? If so, which ones and why? If not, why not?
5. Are there any other principles you think are important enough to be added to or to replace any of the five given in this chapter? If so, present them in detail and support your contention with as much argument and evidence as you can.
6. In what order of priority should the five basic moral principles be applied? Distinguish between the general and particular ways of establishing such priority.
7. What is the respective importance of (a) considering the situation or context in which moral problems occur and (b) establishing moral principles, rules, or guidelines?
8. How many of the basic principles does the moral system that you yourself believe in ascribe to? Which ones are they, and why?
9. How have you chosen to resolve the four general moral issues, and why?

Discussion Questions

1. Examine a system of ethics or moral code with which you are quite familiar (for example, your religion's code of ethics, your family's code of ethics, or your desired profession's code of ethics), and describe the extent to which any or all of the five basic principles described in this chapter are found in that system or code. What other principles are found there? Is the addition of these principles an improvement over Humanitarian Ethics? Explain your answer.
2. To what extent do you believe that the United States as a nation follows the five basic principles? Does it follow any other principles? Does the addition of these other principles (if there are others) constitute an improvement over Humanitarian Ethics? Why or why not? Answer all parts of this question in detail.
3. What is your personal moral system or code of ethics? On what principle or principles is it based? Justify that principle or those principles in detail. How does your system make allowances for individual freedom and yet maintain order and stability? Develop your answer fully.

Note

1. Michael Scriven, speech on "Rational Moral Education" and also *Primary Philosophy* (New York: McGraw-Hill, 1966), 232.

Research Navigator™
(http://www.researchnavigator.com)

This web site offers three research databases: EBSCO'S *Content Select Academic Journal and Abstract Database*, *New York Times* Search by Subject Archive, and *Best of the Web* Link Library. In addition, this site provides helpful advice on how to conduct efficient and productive research from choosing a topic to polishing the final draft. Beginning philosophy students probably will find the *Best of the Web* Link Library the most appropriate place to start their research.

The free access code necessary to employ Research Navigator™ can be found in the Prentice Hall Guide to Evaluating Online Resources. If your text did not come with this guide, please go to *www.prenhall.com/contentselect* for information on how you can purchase an access code.

The Taking of Human Life

Objectives

After you have read this chapter, you should be able to

1. Understand further the importance of having basic principles, rules, or guidelines on which to base an approach to dealing with moral issues.

2. Show how basic principles can be applied to the general and significant problem of the taking of human life.

3. Show how basic principles are used to deal with the specific moral problems of suicide, defense of the innocent, war, terrorism, and capital punishment, and know the arguments for and against these issues.

Some of the basic arguments for and against the taking of human life in certain instances (for example, suicide and war) will be examined in this chapter and the next two, and some cases will be laid out for readers to try to solve through their own ethical systems, considering the problems and issues that must be faced. Also, if instructors and students are interested, there is a special appendix for each chapter that explains how Humanitarian Ethics (the system I have proposed in Chapter 8) would attempt to solve the problems being presented. In this way readers are not subjected, unless they want to be, to my system of dealing with moral issues but will still have the moral issues presented to them as such. If they wish, however, they may use the Humanitarian Ethics solutions for critical discussion and evaluation. The Humanitarian Ethics discussion for this chapter may be found in Appendix 1, for the next chapter in Appendix 2, and so on.

The Taking of Human Life

One of the worst possible moral offenses that a human being can commit is the taking of another human's life. As I stated earlier, the Value of Life principle is empirically the most important of the five, inasmuch as morality itself depends on it; therefore, one must revere life and accept death. Does this mean that human life may never be taken? We will examine different types of situations involving the taking of human life and see how basic principles can be applied to them.

Suicide

Definitions of Suicide

In Chapter 5, I presented definitions of killing and murder. To reiterate, *killing* means "to put to death, slay, deprive of life," whereas *murder* means "the unlawful killing of one human being by another, especially with malice aforethought." *Suicide* is defined in the same dictionary as "an intentional taking of one's own life."[1] Under this definition, the act of suicide certainly involves both killing and the taking of a human life, but it is extremely difficult to justify the argument that it involves murder. Furthermore, suicide is not generally considered civilly or criminally unlawful in most states and countries because it involves the taking of one's own life, not the life of another; it is a decision made by people about their own lives based upon their own thoughts and feelings.

Arguments Against the Morality of Suicide

The Irrationality of Suicide. One of the most common arguments against the morality of suicide is the one that suggests that *all* people who attempt or commit suicide are irrational or mentally or emotionally disturbed, a viewpoint characterized by the statement "No one in his right mind would commit suicide." This argument states further that because suicide is *never* a rational act, it can never be considered as anything but immoral. The problem with this assumption is that it is too all-encompassing, as are the theories of psychological egoism (see Chapter 2) and hard determinism (see Chapter 6). How can a person who maintains this point of view prove that *all* people who attempt or commit suicide are irrational when they perform these acts? It certainly would be empirically true to say that *some* people have been driven by a mental imbalance to attempt or commit suicide; evidence for this exists both in suicide notes and in the explanations of those who have failed in their attempts. However, there is also some evidence to suggest that many suicide attempts and suicides are carefully thought out and rationally decided upon.

Many people who intend to commit suicide often leave calm, well-written letters explaining why they decided to commit suicide. It also has been noticed, by many of the families after the suicide has occurred, that there was calm and contentment just before the person committed suicide. In fact, families often are surprised, given the fact that the suicidal person was emotionally and mentally troubled and upset for most of his or her life, that just before he or she committed suicide that person seems to have been at peace. This might suggest that the suicidal person had found what he or she deems a "rational" way of solving his or her problems. Is this so irrational even if one does believe suicide to be wrong?

In another example, Socrates, who was condemned to death by his peers, was urged to escape and had every opportunity to do so. Instead, he chose to drink hemlock, a poison. Before he committed this act, he rationally discussed his decision with his students and friends, a conversation dramatized in Plato's dialogue *Crito*. Anyone who reads this dialogue will be hard put to say that Socrates was irrational in any sense of the word. One may not agree with Socrates' arguments or with his final decision, but it would be difficult to question the soundness of his mind. In any case, the argument that suicide is an irrational act, though sometimes valid, cannot be used to declare all suicides immoral, for it cannot be proven to be true in all cases.

The Religious Argument. Various religions are opposed to suicide because they believe that only God has the authority to give and take away life; human beings are only loaned their lives to be lived as well, morally and religiously, as they can. Religions certainly are entitled to this belief, and they may require that their members adhere to it by not committing suicide, but in no way can this view be imposed upon nonmembers, religious or nonreligious, without some violation of the principles of Freedom and Justice. Furthermore, there are real problems with this view of God and life, whether one is religious or not, and they are carefully pointed out by Daniel Callahan in his book *Abortion: Law, Choice and Morality*:

> [This view] presupposes that God intervenes directly in natural and human affairs as the primary causative agent of life and death. Not only is this theologically dubious, it also has the effect of obscuring the necessity that human beings define terms, make decisions and take responsibility for the direct care of human life. Moreover, to say that God is the ultimate source of the "right to life," which is less objectionable theologically, still does not solve the problem of *how* human beings ought to respect that right or how they are to balance a conflict of rights.[2]

This theological problem applies to all aspects of the taking of human life, not just suicide; therefore, it would be good to keep this problem in mind as we deal with the other issues in this area.

The Domino Argument. People who hold to "the domino argument" believe that if you allow human life to be taken in some instances, you open the door to its being taken in other instances and, eventually, in all instances. Like the religious argument, the domino argument also applies to areas of the taking of human life other than suicide. Furthermore, it is a good argument to be aware of when we are discussing any moral issue, because it forces us to be concerned about the effects of our moral decisions or laws. For example, if we argue that suicide is moral, then we should be concerned with where this will lead us: Will murder be made moral next? Or if suicide is all right, then why not mercy killing and abortion?

Even though it is important for us to try to gauge the effects of our rules and actions, where there is no definite or conclusive proof that one thing necessarily leads to another, we cannot use this argument as the *sole* reason for not allowing an act or person to be declared moral or immoral. And there is no conclusive proof that if suicide is allowed, murder soon will be allowed as well. As I have said, most states and countries have laws against capital punishment, abortion, mercy killing, and of course, murder.

The Justice Argument. Probably the most effective case against the morality of suicide is made by those who argue that the people who survive a person who has committed suicide pay an unjust penalty. A husband or wife may leave behind a despondent and destitute spouse and grief-stricken children; sons and daughters may leave guilt-ridden parents; society may be denied the important contributions that could have been made by the person who killed himself. This is an argument that must be carefully considered, for it involves the Principle of Justice, which, in the matter of suicide, conflicts with the Principle of Individual Freedom. This is a conflict that must be dealt with as one attempts to decide whether suicide is moral.

Argument for the Morality of Suicide

The basic argument in favor of suicide as a moral act has to do with a person's rights over his or her own body and life. It also is concerned with the freedom of a person to make decisions affecting his or her own body and life. Life is important, but to whom? Mostly to the person to whom it belongs, of course. Because suicide is an individual decision made by a person about his or her own life, it cannot be described as taking a life against a person's will. Therefore it does not fully violate the Value of Life principle except in the sense that one ought to think carefully about the importance of life before one commits the act. When individuals decide that they would rather die than live, however, no one else, according to this argument, has the right to tell them otherwise.

The Principle of Individual Freedom is important here, of course, and so is the Principle of Goodness. Suicide is such a private act that only the person who is considering it can know to any degree whether continuing to live would bring her more satisfaction, excellence, or harmony than ending her life. This argument stresses that individuals are unique and that only they know whether or not their lives are worth living; therefore, only they should be able to make decisions concerning whether they live or die. According to this argument, a decision to commit suicide may be considered rational, provided that a person's reasoning faculties are not impaired by severe mental or emotional disturbances. Even when they are in perfect mental health, however, people who successfully commit suicide should not be blamed for being immoral, nor should people who attempt suicide be blamed or punished in any way.

The main criticism of this argument, other than those presented in the arguments against suicide we have already discussed, is that it tends to imply that people have absolute rights over their own bodies and lives. In other words, it suggests that the Principle of Individual Freedom has no limitations, an implication that can raise some difficult problems.

For example, if a man has a highly contagious disease and doesn't want to be placed in quarantine because it will limit his freedom over his own body and life, his freedom must nevertheless be restricted; otherwise, he could be responsible for the sickness and death of many other innocent people. That is, because of the priority of the first four basic principles, his freedom to do what he wants with his body and his life must be curtailed. In a similar manner, when a person's contemplated suicide will definitely affect the lives and welfare of others (for example, his dependents), then questions must at least be raised concerning the possible limits of the person's freedom over his own body and life.

Generally speaking, neither the arguments for nor those against the morality of suicide advocate the taking of one's own life, and most people on either side probably would urge the use of all possible means to prevent people from killing themselves. The side supporting the morality of suicide, however, probably would allow for greater freedom for individual decision making. For example, those who feel suicide is always immoral might advocate the imposition of physical and legal restraints upon people who are known to be suicidal, whereas people who believe that suicide can be a moral act will try to prevent people from committing suicide but will not use force in attempting to deny them the freedom to make their own rational decisions.

The matter of assisted suicide will be discussed in the next chapter.

CASE 1 Terminal Cancer

William, 60, has had inoperable cancer for several months, and it is now in the terminal stages. Unwilling to go to a hospital or a hospice, he lives unhappily at home. Everything about living has lost its savor: He no longer enjoys eating, drinking, smoking, or any of his other former pleasures. He has made a will and taken care of all unfinished business. Finally he confronts his wife and two teenage children with his wish to commit suicide—to die with dignity, as he expresses it, rather than linger on and become increasingly ill. His wife and children don't like the idea, but they agree with him that the choice is his. He shoots himself and dies.

CASE 2 Teenage Suicide

Joan, 18, has lived in one foster home after another ever since she was born. She has been in and out of mental institutions, having been treated for extreme depression. She has used drugs but is not using them now. Having twice become pregnant, she has had two abortions. She feels she has no real friends, she has no parents to relate to, and she can't concentrate on school or work. Although she has talked to several psychiatrists and psychologists, she doesn't feel any better about herself or her life. She finally decides, calmly, that she is tired of living. She takes an overdose of barbiturates without leaving a suicide note or telling anybody what she is going to do, and dies.

Defense of the Innocent (the Self Included)

Argument Against Killing in Defense of the Innocent

There is really only one argument against killing in defense of the innocent, and that is based on the assumption—held by the adherents of a few ethical systems (Pacifists, Jainists, Kantian Duty Ethicists)—that the taking of human life is always wrong. This position is the most consistent one possible in terms of the Value of Life principle because it respects human life at all costs. According to this argument, all human life is to be revered and no one may ever be killed for any reason, even if one's life is threatened by another. In such a case, one who is being threatened may try everything short of violence or killing to prevent being killed, but he or she may not kill another, even in self-defense or in defense of other innocent people.

To refrain from killing any humans is, of course, an admirable ideal, and it is one to which most people are able to adhere throughout their lives. The main criticism of this point of view is that it does not take into consideration all the complexities of human existence, especially the fact that some humans—fortunately a relatively small number— do not respect the lives of others. If all humans would respect human life completely, then maybe everyone could completely adhere to the ideal of not killing other humans under any circumstances. This ideal certainly is put forth in Christianity in Jesus's teachings of "Love thy enemies" and "Turn the other cheek." However, very few Christians or other human beings are willing to adhere to such an ideal; they simply do not feel that it is good, fair, or just for innocent people to lose their lives to killers who violate this ideal, and who often cannot be stopped in any other way than by being killed themselves.

Argument for Killing in Defense of the Innocent

The argument for killing in defense of the innocent generally rests upon two assumptions: First, even though the Value of Life principle advocates a reverence for all human life, people have a right and, indeed, a moral obligation to protect any innocent lives, their own included, when it becomes clear that another human being no longer recognizes the value of other people's lives. Second, the good of defending the innocent far outweighs the bad of killing a person who is threatening to kill or who actually kills innocent people. The essence of this argument is that by threatening to kill or by killing others, killers in a sense forfeit their right to have their lives considered as valuable, especially when their acts cannot be stopped unless they themselves are killed. This argument qualifies the Value of Life principle by stating that one should never kill other humans *except* when defending innocent people, including oneself.

The main criticism of this argument is that violence tends to breed more violence, and that once the killing of humans has been allowed, even in defense of the innocent, no one knows where the violence will end (the domino argument again). The religious argument also applies here, adding the criticism that only God can create or take away life, and that, in His infinite wisdom, He will duly punish the killer in some way. Killing, in any case, is not the right of other humans under any circumstances. The religious argument is open to the same criticism as that presented in the discussion of suicide.

Cases for Study and Discussion

CASE 1 Burglar

Hearing a noise at the back of his house one afternoon, Ed picks up his loaded automatic pistol from a drawer in his desk and goes to investigate. He surprises an 18-year-old man in the act of going through his dresser drawers. The man has no weapons in his hands or in view. Ed asks what he is doing there, and the young man runs for the back door. Ed points the gun at his retreating back, fires three shots, and kills him. Is Ed morally justified in killing the young man?

CASE 2 Assault on Woman

Mary, 22, returns home fairly late one evening from a party. As she enters her bedroom, a man jumps at her from behind the door, pins her down with one arm, and covers her mouth with the other. He wrestles her to her bed, and as she attempts to scream, he hits her several times in the face and on other parts of her body. She somehow manages to push him off the bed and onto the floor, and while he is recovering his equilibrium, she gets a loaded pistol out of the bedside table drawer. As the man stands up again, ready to lunge at Mary, she fires several shots and kills him. Is Mary's action justifiable?

CASE 3 Sniper

The scene is a crowded outdoor shopping mall that has a clock tower at its center. Rifle shots ring out from the tower and several people, including children, drop to the ground—three are seriously injured and three are killed. Police try for several hours to get the sniper to throw down his weapon and come out, but he continues to fire his rifle into store windows, into a nearby parking lot, and into a nearby street. One of the officers, a sharpshooter with a high-powered rifle, manages to maneuver himself into a position where he can get a perfect shot, but only at the sniper's head. He does so, killing the sniper instantly. Was the officer justified in killing the sniper?

War

Arguments Against the Morality of War

The Standard College Dictionary defines *war* as "an armed conflict openly carried on between nations or states, or between different parties in the same state." The dictionary could have added, "and in which people, many of them completely innocent, are killed, usually violently." Because of the wholesale killing that almost inevitably accompanies any type of war except a so-called *cold* one, war is a powerful threat to the Value of Life principle and should be avoided by every human effort possible. The arguments against war have increased during the twentieth and twenty-first centuries because of our advanced military technology, especially the nuclear capability of various nations, which could lead to world destruction. The chances of a world war occurring seem to have diminished, and at least the larger nations have begun to see the futility of a nuclear war that would destroy everything and everybody. However, small wars would seem to have increased in various parts of the world, and even though they do not involve nuclear weaponry, their destructiveness to life and the environment in each respective location is still unacceptable to peace-loving people and nations. Further, such small wars inevitably attract the involvement of the larger nations with nuclear capability, which makes any war a danger to world peace.

The main argument against the morality of war is that it is a direct and massive violation of the Value of Life principle. War doesn't just involve the killing of one human being by another; rather, it involves a mass killing of up to millions, depending upon the scale of the war. Furthermore, especially because of modern military techniques, war necessitates the useless killing of a great number of innocent noncombatants, many of them children. Those who take an antiwar stance maintain that, in the long run, so little is gained by war and yet so much is lost in terms of human life and human possessions that it has to be considered an immoral act—in fact, the most immoral act human beings can perform.

This point of view was held widely during the Vietnam War era, when there was a tremendous rise in the number of conscientious objectors and outspoken pacifists. Pacifists have argued that war in all its aspects should be banned worldwide, and that violence and aggression should never be met with similar force but rather with nonviolence and nonaggression. They would argue, for example, that every peaceful effort must be exerted to avert war, but that even if a country is invaded, its citizens should try to pacify their violent invaders rather than resort to violence. This extreme form of the antiwar argument is held by a minority of the world's population, even though it has grown in popularity because of the many destructive wars that have occurred since 1900. Many more people hold a moderate view: a general policy of nonaggression toward other people or countries.

Arguments for the Morality of War

Even though I believe few people advocate war openly as a general solution to human problems, there are some traditional arguments in favor of war that should be examined.

War as the Best Controller of Overpopulation. The view that sees war as being the best controller of overpopulation is based upon the fact that the population of the world is increasing at too rapid a rate. Therefore, war, which effectively decreases the population, helps to solve this problem very efficiently. The argument is, of course, morally weak because alternate solutions are available, especially in our scientifically and technologically oriented society. In addition, one could argue effectively that the quality of population control achieved by war is very poor because it is the youth, the best hope of all societies, that generally suffer the greatest casualty rate. In any case, many countries have found alternate methods for reducing their populations without resorting to the destruction and decimation of war.

War as the Mother of Invention. The argument has been advocated that war is the only way in which societies can develop and experiment with advanced technology. There is no doubt that many technological advances that were developed for military purposes have also been used in a peaceful way. Some of these advances are directly dependent upon war; for example, the development of advanced surgical techniques, prosthetic devices, and plastic surgery techniques that occurred during the Korean War. These certainly could have been developed without war, but perhaps it would have taken much longer to do so. Obviously, one has to consider the price that must be paid for such "invention." Furthermore, it certainly is true that technological development can occur without war (for example, by means of the space development program) even though peacetime development may be slower or more expensive.

War as a Boon to Economic Gain and National Unity. Many argue that nothing unifies a people more than working together to achieve a national goal, such as winning a war. Furthermore, it is argued, such unification, which often involves the production of war machines and matériel, creates an upsurge in economic well-being and prosperity. This argument became particularly popular during and after World War II, especially in the United States. Nothing had ever unified the nation to the extent that the "war effort" did, and, despite wartime shortages, the nation achieved an economic prosperity that continued even after the war was over. The country mass-produced planes, tanks, weapons, and other matériel on a greater scale than ever before, and after the war, factories produced great numbers of peacetime goods—cars, homes, appliances—which the entire population desired after four years of deprivation. After two more wars, however, the divisive aspects of war became obvious, and people began to recognize that the cost of achieving economic prosperity through war is too high. As a matter of fact, though not the only factor in our economic problems, waging our current war on terror is certainly a contributing factor and therefore not a boon to our economy. Since World War II, countries have been able to unify and to achieve economic well-being without wartime production, and this fact encourages most people to seek alternative means of attaining these national goals.

War as a "Necessary Evil"—The Just War Argument. Probably the most morally significant argument for war is that although war generally is immoral, there is such a thing as a "morally just war" under certain conditions. One example of such an argument can be found in Roman Catholic teachings. Before discussing this argument, I would like to stress that it applied essentially to nonnuclear warfare; also, it would be incorrect to assume that this is the position presently held by the Roman Catholic Church. With these disclaimers in mind, the following conditions might be considered to describe a morally just war:

> . . . that it shall be undertaken by the lawful authority; that it shall be undertaken for the vindication of an undoubted and proportionate right that has certainly been infringed; that it shall be a last resort, all peaceful means of settlement having been tried in vain; that the good to be achieved shall outweigh

the evils that war will involve; that there shall be a reasonable hope of victory for justice (a war undertaken in face of certain failure is, however heroic, irrational, and therefore indefensible); there must be a right intention, that is, to right the wrong and not simply to maintain national prestige and influence or to enlarge territory (territory is not a just cause of war), nor may war be waged as part of a scheme for converting the heathen to Christianity; and the methods of warfare must be legitimate, i.e., in accordance with international agreements, with our nature as rational beings and with the moral teachings of Christianity.[3]

The Catholic Encyclopedia, from which this passage was taken, goes on to remark that there may be vagueness and uncertainty concerning any case of war being considered, and of course there is a great deal of vagueness and ambiguity in the passage itself. It does, however, provide some guidelines that have a moral basis: That the reason for war must be serious enough to outweigh its evils; that it cannot be carried on for prestige, for territory, or to increase the influence of the nation waging it; the part about a war not being waged to convert heathens to Christianity should be expanded to include converting or punishing other religions, races, or nations for not believing in the aggressors' policies or religions; that all peaceful means of settlement must have been exhausted; and that a nation's methods, once war is declared, must be legitimate. Even such justifications, however, would seem to apply only to limited nonnuclear wars, because there is probably no political situation important enough to justify the possibility of setting off World War III and risking the total destruction of the human race and the world.

The Indefensibility of Nuclear War. Even the arguments in support of a just war pale when one stops to consider the total devastation that could result from a nuclear war. This carries over to any defense of even limited wars because there is always a possibility that one of these could set off a large-scale nuclear holocaust. Given the tendency toward violence of the human species in general (*Homo sapiens* is the only species that destroys itself), it is probably too much to hope for that wars of all kinds can ever be totally eliminated, although every effort should be made to do so now and in the future. Barring the success of such an effort, however, any small wars should be contained and not allowed to mushroom into the use of nuclear weapons, especially by those countries that have large arsenals of such weapons. None of the arguments in support of war, including the just-war argument, can morally justify a nuclear holocaust.

Terrorism

"Terrorism" is defined by Caleb Carr in his book *The Lessons of Terror* as

> . . . the contemporary name given to, and the modern permutation of, warfare deliberately waged against civilians with the purpose of destroying their will

to support either leaders or policies that the agents of such violence find objectionable.[4]

Many people may think that terrorism is an activity that has been invented and practiced in the twentieth and twenty-first centuries, but the purposeful targeting of civilians is as old as warfare itself, and terrorism is a type of military warfare practiced by every nation including the United States. Carr also refers to it as total, destructive, or punitive type of war. Terrorism can be traced back to Roman times; the Crusades in which Christians and Muslims employed it on each other; during the Indian and Civil Wars in the United States; the French Revolution; World Wars I and II; the Korean conflict; Vietnam, and the terrorist wars of Afghanistan and Iraq. Other modern day terrorist attacks have occurred in Ireland and England, Israel and Palestine, the Oklahoma City Federal Building, the first bombing of the World Trade Center in New York, and, of course, the total destruction of the World Trade Center on September 11, 2001, in which over 3,000 people, mostly civilians, were killed and many injured.

The main purpose of terrorism is to protest violently against some serious differences of opinion, ideologies, world events, or culture. Terrorists seem to think that the only protest that has any significance is to destroy small or large segments of civilians with the idea that they will not support the policies or ideologies of the country where the attacks take place. Carr, however, argues successfully that even though terrorism has been practiced throughout history, it has continually been a failure because the civilians attacked in such a fashion have turned against and rejected their attackers. For example, in the case of the September 11, 2001, attack, it, if anything, has hardened the resolve of the U. S. government and its civilians against the terrorists.[5] It is important to note that terrorists are indeed soldiers who wage war, albeit a different kind of war, who have a financial base, excellent communications and intelligence, and, in the case of the September 11 attacks, several sovereign countries to sponsor and support them in every way they need. One has to recognize, no matter how terrible the attack on September 11 was, the ingenuity of the attackers. They needed no missiles. They commandeered civilian planes filled with fuel and used them as missiles requiring the terrorist crews to act as suicidal soldiers. Their intelligence was so far superior to ours that no one even suspected the attacks were to take place until they actually occurred.

Argument in Support of Terrorism

Despite the fact that nonviolent protest was put forth by Mohatma Ghandi in India and Martin Luther King, Jr., in America, many organizations formed out of cultures and nations of angry people, many of these in the so-called Third World countries, have come to feel that nonviolent protests are ignored and ineffective at best and only get them killed by their oppressors at worst; therefore, violent actions, such as bombing, the taking of hostages, and guerilla attacks are seen as being the only surefire ways of getting the powers-that-be to recognize them.

Because these organizations feel that they will continue to be ignored, they have resorted to violence in order to bring attention to their causes. It's true that innocent people will die, but terrorists reason that no one not on the side of their cause is innocent, so they don't care. They feel they are in a war for their rights, freedom, culture, religion, or territory, and war means that people will die.

Argument Against Terrorism

The main argument against terrorism is that excessive violence, especially where it involves the lives of innocent people, cannot be condoned. Terrorism, as its advocates state, *is* war, but undeclared war and certainly not war in defense of the innocent. As stated earlier, one can argue for just wars, dutifully declared and fought only for the defense of the innocent by the military of both sides. But the wide-ranging approach to violence that terrorism uses, in which innocent bystanders are murdered, is morally unjustifiable. People who are against terrorism argue that wrongs must be righted by reason, negotiation, and in other peaceful ways. This may take longer, but it is safer for everyone concerned. Furthermore, terrorism usually does not aid the causes of its advocates because it prompts greater terrorism from the other side. Also, it tends to turn against its adherents all those who believe terrorism to be immoral. Therefore, according to those opposed to terrorism, it can never be justified.

The Semantics of Terrorism and Double Standards

Terrorism is a type of violence and, since it is violence that intentionally targets the innocent, it is generally considered to be wrong and is universally condemned. As seen above, consequentialist arguments can be made in support of terrorism. But, because such arguments are essentially attempts to justify violence against the innocent, they are not rationally persuasive. In contrast, non-consequentialist theories, such as Kant's, would hold that terrorism denies the intrinsic worth of persons in that it treats persons solely as means and not as ends.

Igor Primoratz notes the following curious fact about the concept of terrorism: "Nobody applies the word to oneself and one's own actions, nor to those one has sympathy with or whose activities one supports. As the hackneyed cliché has it, one person's terrorist is another person's freedom fighter."[6] In other words, self-interest and partiality foster a double standard relative to the application of the term in the public debate about terrorism by creating an "us versus them" framework for discourse.

The second double standard involves nonstate actors, for example, "insurgents," versus actors engaged in similar violence sanctioned by the political state. The term terrorism, almost as a matter of definition, is applied to insurgents and not to agents of the state—especially when it is one's own political state that is in question.

It is important therefore, as good critical thinkers and individuals trained in ethical reasoning, to be alert to the nuances of political rhetoric and to clarify our meaning of the word terrorism in order to develop well-reasoned arguments about whether it is morally acceptable. Furthermore, one would do well to understand the social, economic, political, and cultural conditions that give rise to and support terrorism—not to rationalize or legitimize terrorist acts—but to eliminate, so far as possible, such conditions. Although certain conditions may help explain terrorism, such conditions cannot justify it.

Cases for Study and Discussion

CASE 1 Invasion of Smaller Nation by Larger Nation

A small nation located on a seacoast has both the commercial ports and the natural resources that a larger neighboring inland nation needs. The larger nation negotiates for use of the ports and purchase of the resources, and an agreement is reached between the two nations that lasts for several years. Eventually, however, a new government that has come to power in the larger nation decides that it should not have to pay for natural resources so close to its own borders and that it should have complete control of the seaports it now uses. After a breakdown of new negotiations, the larger nation invades its smaller neighbor, and the smaller nation aggressively defends itself. Is the larger nation justified in starting a war, and is the smaller nation justified in defending itself?

CASE 2 Iraq War

To what extent does the U.S. invasion of Iraq fit with the Catholic description of a just war? To what extent do you think this invasion was justified at all under any circumstances. To what extent do you think this is a war of terrorism on both sides? Be specific.

CASE 3 Civil War in a Small Country with Large Country's Support

A small Far Eastern country that is rich in natural resources has suffered an ideological split. One-half of the populace advocates communism as a form of government, whereas the other half advocates a democratic form. Two larger powers outside the country develop an interest in the struggle: Country A supports the communist faction, whereas country B supports the democratic faction. Both of the larger countries have vested interests in the Far Eastern country in the form of mines, factories, land, and financial investments. When the two factions in the small country declare war on each other over their differing ideologies in a struggle for control of the entire land, the two larger countries begin to support their respective sides by sending money, arms, supplies, and military advisers. As the democratic faction weakens and begins to lose the war, country B steps up its support by sending in elements of its own army, navy, and air force, committing itself to helping the democratic side by any means other than nuclear warfare. To what extent are the two factions in the Far Eastern country justified in entering into warfare against each other, and to what extent are the larger powers justified in supporting their respective sides.

Capital Punishment

A Definition

As most dictionaries define it, *capital punishment* means "the infliction of death for certain crimes." These crimes often are called "capital crimes," and depending upon the society in question, they have varied from stealing to murder. For the most part, especially in the United States, capital punishment is usually applied for murder—especially premeditated murder—or kidnapping with intent to do bodily harm or kill, and sometimes for instances of treason that endanger the lives of those living in a country.

Theories of Punishment

It would behoove readers to review Chapter 7 on reward and punishment, particularly its treatment of the three major theories as to when and why punishment should be meted out. As a quick reiteration, however, the theories are as follows.

Retributive (Deserts Theory). Punishment should be given only when it is *deserved* and only to the extent it is deserved. It should have no other goal than punishing people who deserve the punishment *because of* some immoral act that they have committed, and the punishment should fit the crime.

Utilitarian (Results Theory). Punishment always should have as its aim the good of society. If punishment will bring about good consequences for people, then it should be given; if it won't, then it shouldn't. It always should be given *in order that* some good can be done; for example, to deter future crime, to protect society, or to rehabilitate a criminal.

Restitution (Compensation Theory). Justice is served only if the victims of a crime or offense are provided with restitution or compensation for the harm done to them. Capital punishment could conceivably be acceptable in all of the preceding theories, at least in some cases but not in others. For example, it certainly would fit the retributive theory, but only if the person to be punished truly deserved the punishment. Utilitarians also might approve of such punishment, but only if the greatest number of good consequences were to come about because of it. If the only compensation for murder, for example, was considered by restitutionists to be the execution of the murderer so as to satisfy and compensate the victim, then capital punishment might be deemed acceptable by them too. However, most restitutionists probably would consider that such punishment actually would thwart proper compensation of the victim because the criminal or offender no longer would be alive to work for the victim's benefit, for example.

Arguments Against the Morality of Capital Punishment

Violation of the Value of Life Principle. Many argue against capital punishment on the grounds that it is a direct violation of the Value of Life principle. They maintain that capital punishment amounts to murder—social murder—directed by society against one of its members. The argument further says that if taking human life is wrong in other instances, then it also is wrong in this instance. True, the argument continues, capital punishment can function as a form of societal retribution or revenge, but in a civilized society, this should not be deemed a sufficient motive for taking a human life.

Effect on the Criminal's Victims or on Society. Because killing a criminal will not bring back his or her victims, or in any way compensate the survivors of the victims, there is really no purpose in taking the criminal's life other than to satisfy the society's need for revenge or the victims' need for retribution. This, according to the opponents of capital punishment, is not a civilized emotion. They feel that capital punishment encourages violence, acts of revenge or retribution, and murder in society at large because it leads to the rationale that if society can kill its members, then individuals also can take revenge into their own hands.

Ineffectiveness as a Deterrent. One of the most common arguments for capital punishment, as we shall see, is that it deters crimes throughout the society; its opponents, however, argue that there is no conclusive evidence to support this claim. They point to history in support of their argument, stating that when capital punishment was used against thieves in England, pickpockets were operating throughout the crowds of watchers who gathered to see a thief hanged. They also question why, if this punishment works so well as a deterrent, executions by hangings, firing squads, in gas chambers, and by lethal injection, are not shown on television or performed in the streets, rather than being carried out in the relative privacy of our prisons. They argue further that killings occur even in prison, right outside the execution chamber. Therefore, they state, capital punishment does not serve as an effective deterrent.

Executing an Innocent Person. Sometimes people accused of capital crimes are convicted on mainly circumstantial evidence, and therefore it is quite possible to execute an innocent person. If even one innocent person is executed, this argument continues, then capital punishment is a moral wrong. Furthermore, because rich people who are charged with capital crimes can afford better attorneys, the people most often convicted of capital crimes are poor people, often members of minority races—for example, African Americans, Hispanics, Native Americans. This means that punishment by killing may be applied unequally to people who commit similar crimes. This is even a more prevalent problem with the introduction of DNA (deoxyribonucleic acid) testing or fingerprinting as it is often known. This testing, developed in the twentieth century, has enabled forensic specialists to acquire a specimen from a person (e.g., saliva, blood, semen) and match it with materials found at the scene of a crime or on a victim's body or clothes. This testing not only has helped to convict guilty people of crimes but also has helped find allegedly guilty people, who are often waiting on death row, innocent of crimes. In addition, other circumstances, such as the unreliability of so-called jailhouse informants, unqualified defense attorneys, and racism as described above, have resulted in the reversal of many capital crimes. The governor of Illinois recently halted executions in his state and declared a moratorium for all of the above reasons, saying, "Until I can be sure that everyone sentenced to death in Illinois is truly guilty—until I can be sure with moral certainty that no innocent man or woman is facing a lethal injection—no one will meet that fate."[7] When his term was up, he pardoned all the prisoners on death row and gave them life imprisonment without parole.

Denial of the Chance for Rehabilitation. The denial of the chance for rehabilitation argument states that nothing is accomplished by capital punishment other than the compounding of the badness already caused by the original crime: Instead of one human life being taken, capital punishment causes two to be taken. Wouldn't it be more valuable, opponents of capital punishment ask, for society to eliminate killing by reforming killers through education and other methods of rehabilitation? They argue further that most killers have been shaped by a corrupt society or a poor early environment (child-abusing parents, for example), and that if we could only reeducate them they could become useful members of society.

Arguments for Capital Punishment

The Effective Deterrent Argument. People who argue for capital punishment strongly disagree with those who state that it is not an effective deterrent. They argue, with irrefutable logic, that capital punishment deters the killer from killing again by terminating his life. They admit that the evidence for general deterrence may not be conclusive, but they strongly believe that many people are prevented from killing, or at least think twice about it, when they know that they may have to face the death penalty for their crime. According to capital punishment's supporters, the reason it isn't always an effective deterrent is that it isn't used enough. Many of its supporters are also in favor of making everyone watch the execution of legally convicted killers so that deterrence would be more effectively reinforced.

The Economic Argument. There is no proof that murderers can be successfully rehabilitated, and sentences of "life imprisonment" seldom really mean life because many murderers are released from prison after seven or ten years. Some have been released and have killed again. With these facts in mind, supporters of capital punishment think that it is much too costly for innocent taxpayers to support killers in prison for long sentences or for life. Why, they ask, should innocent people pay for the continued support of criminals who have proved themselves unfit to live in society? The crimes they have committed are so terrible that there is no reason they should be allowed to live while innocent people pay for their upkeep.

One criticism of this argument is that it costs more to give a criminal capital punishment than it does to give him or her life imprisonment without parole, given all of the appeals and court actions often gone through in the case of a criminal who has been sentenced to death. The main criticism of this argument, however, holds that when human life, even reprehensible human life, is at stake, a civilized society and humanity should not be concerned with monetary costs. Even though it costs a great deal of money to keep criminals in prison, and even more of it when rehabilitation programs are implemented, critics of the economic argument believe that it is more moral to try to make a human life useful than to terminate it even though it is cheaper to execute prisoners than to rehabilitate them. Isn't it extremely dehumanizing, they ask, to argue that the maintenance and possible rehabilitation of human life is less important than mere financial cost? This issue will surface again when we discuss the cost of maintaining the lives of innocent people who are in terminal stages of illness.

The Effect upon Society's Laws. By having the option of applying the death penalty, some argue, we give strong sanction to the entire criminal law enforcement system—we "put teeth" into that system. For example, suppose a criminal is convicted of armed robbery, serves a term in prison, and then is released. The very existence of capital punishment reminds this person that if he or she returns to armed robbery and later kills someone while committing this second crime, the death penalty may be applied.

The sanction argument suggests that criminals will be deterred from escalating the nature of their crimes because of the death penalty threat, and that this in turn gives the entire criminal justice system strength. The threat of the death penalty may even encourage criminals to leave the "armed" out of armed robbery, thus minimizing the chance that an innocent person will be killed.

The main criticism of this argument is that there are other, more humane ways of giving a system of law enforcement sanction. Highly effective legal systems have existed without capital punishment (England's, for example), and there is no conclusive evidence that the existence of capital punishment has any deterrent effect on the thieves, embezzlers, rapists, and other criminals to whom the death penalty cannot usually be applied. Effective prosecution and just punishment would seem to be as, or more, effective in preventing crime as is maintaining the death penalty as a part of the system.

The Forfeiture of Killers' Rights. Another argument for capital punishment, in answer to the violation of the value of life argument, is that killers, having violated both morality and the law, have forfeited their right to be treated ethically. Just as you would kill a rabid dog or a wild animal who threatened the lives of innocent members of society, so too you should punish these killers. Some argue further that capital punishment is merely another form of self-defense, one that applies to the entire society. Just as individual people have the right to protect themselves against killers who threaten their lives, so society has the right to protect itself against anyone who has killed once by ensuring that he or she does not kill again. Prison, they argue, is not an adequate means of ensuring this, because killers can be paroled or can escape as some did in a Texas prison recently and others were murdered; therefore, the argument continues, capital punishment is moral.

It certainly would seem to be the case that people who have killed should forfeit some of their rights. The question is whether this forfeiture should include their very lives. Certain killers have proved themselves to be so dangerous as to forfeit their right to live freely among other innocent people, but does this mean that they must be killed? Furthermore, there are some cases in which killers have been paroled and have lived normal lives from that time on, even contributing something positive to society in the process. There are even cases in which criminals contribute something good to society while in prison.

The Uselessness of Rehabilitation Argument. In answer to the argument against capital punishment based on the inability to rehabilitate those who have been executed is the argument that rehabilitation, especially in the case of murderers, is useless and often impossible. How can serial or mutilating killers be rehabilitated? In the first place, no one can know for sure whether someone has been rehabilitated. Psychology and sociology are inexact sciences when it comes to this issue. Second, how is it possible to rehabilitate a Charles Manson, Ted Bundy, or Jeffrey Dahmer? These heinous killers are no better than societal "mad dogs" and should be "put down," according to proponents of capital punishment. Also, the rate of recidivism (criminals returning to crime) is extremely high.

Revenge. A final, classic argument for capital punishment is based upon the idea of revenge, or the "eye-for-an-eye" concept of justice. This argument says that if people kill, they must forfeit their lives in order to "balance the scales." This is an ancient concept, dating back to at least Old Testament times, and it often has been the basis for long-lasting feuds and vendettas between families, gangs, tribes, or other groups. For example, if the son of a chief of tribe A is killed by a member of tribe B, then the son of the chief of tribe B must be killed, and so on.

This concept has been pretty much (although not entirely) discarded in more civilized societies because it leads to continuing killing and bloodshed—an unnecessary loss of many lives. Another criticism is that this concept conflicts with the moral and legal view that two wrongs don't make a right. Most societies now feel that people who kill can be justly punished without being executed. Besides, as stated earlier, some convicted killers have in fact made positive contributions to society, either while in prison or on parole.

Cases for Study and Discussion

CASE 1 Murder by Two College Students

As an intellectual game, two male college students, ages 18 and 19, attempt to commit the "perfect crime" by kidnapping a young boy and demanding ransom from his parents. They receive the ransom money but kill the boy anyway. Later, they are caught, tried, and convicted of murder and kidnapping with intent to do bodily harm. Their defense attorney, a brilliant lawyer, successfully argues against the death penalty and both men are sent to prison for life. After about five years one of the men is killed in a fight, but the other completes his college education while still in prison and teaches other convicts English. He also volunteers for medical experiments, allowing himself to be injected with malaria germs in order to test new drugs. A model prisoner, he causes no trouble throughout his entire prison term. After about 30 years, he is paroled, whereupon he goes to a different country and continues to teach English. Two years later he dies of natural causes. Should this man have been subjected to capital punishment? Why or why not?

CASE 2 Man Who Kills is Released from a Mental Institution Kills Again

A young man of 20 is guilty of killing both his grandparents and his mother. He is judged to be legally insane and is sent to a mental hospital for the criminally insane. After three years, he is judged to be cured of his mental illness and he is released as sane. Six months later, however, he goes berserk and kills six young people in the mountain area where he now lives. What treatment or punishment should he receive?

CASE 3 Rapist Kidnapper

A 27-year-old man who has been a criminal most of his life is charged with attacking several young couples in a deserted area. Specifically, he is charged with beating the men and then raping the women after having transported them to a different area (thus technically kidnapping them). The man is convicted mainly on circumstantial evidence, and he continually denies that he is guilty. Although he is given the death penalty, he manages to stave off execution for 10 years. While in prison he studies psychology and law and learns a great deal about both. He analyzes how and why he turned to crime, and he writes and publishes several books about his life. He does not express remorse for his criminal activity, and he continues to deny that he is guilty of the last crime with which he was charged. After 10 years, he has exhausted all of his appeals and again is up for execution in the gas chamber. Should he be given the death penalty?

CASE 4 Killer/Cannibalist

A man of 30 is discovered to have enticed boys and men to his apartment to have sex with them. In 15 of these encounters he killed them, had sex with their corpses, ate their flesh, and dismembered their bodies, keeping some body parts in the freezer and disposing of others in a vat of acid. When caught, he admitted to all of these actions. Though obviously bizarre and perverted, he was nevertheless considered to be legally sane—that is, as being able to distinguish right from wrong. What should be done with such a person? Explain in detail, providing reasons for your answer. Should he be executed? Why or why not?

Chapter Summary

   I. Applying the five basic moral principles to the taking of human life
     A. It is questionable whether suicide, which is defined as "an intentional taking of one's life," is moral or immoral.
       1. There are several arguments against the morality of suicide.
         (a) Some argue that suicide is always irrational; there is evidence, however, that although it is an irrational act in some cases, in others it is not.
         (b) The religious argument states that only God can create or end life.
           (1) This applies only to members of a specific religion that states this as its belief.
           (2) It is theologically questionable.
           (3) It removes human responsibility with regard to protecting, preserving, or ending life.

    (c) The domino argument states that if suicide is allowed, then other forms of murder will follow.

        (1) This argument is worthy of consideration.

        (2) There is, however, no conclusive evidence to support it.

    (d) The justice argument questions whether suicide is fair to survivors of the victim.

  2. There are also arguments for the morality of suicide.

    (a) A person has rights over his or her own body and life.

    (b) A person should have the freedom to make decisions concerning his or her own body and life.

    (c) It is entirely up to individual human beings to decide whether their own lives are worth living.

    (d) The main criticism of this argument is that no one has absolute rights over his or her own body or life.

B. It is questionable whether killing someone in defense of the innocent (one's self included) is moral or immoral.

  1. There is one main argument against the morality of such an act:

    (a) The taking of human life is always wrong.

    (b) The main criticism of this argument is that it doesn't recognize the complexities of human existence or that some humans are capable of violating all five basic principles.

  2. There are arguments for the morality of killing in defense of the innocent.

    (a) People have rights and obligations to protect innocent lives (their own included).

    (b) The good of defending the innocent far outweighs the bad of killing a murderer of innocent people.

    (c) The main criticism of these arguments is that violence breeds violence (the domino argument again).

C. It is questionable if war is moral or immoral.

  1. There are arguments against the morality of war.

    (a) It is a direct and massive violation of Value of Life principle, especially when nuclear weapons are used.

    (b) It causes a great deal of useless killing, especially of innocent noncombatants.

    (c) The destruction caused by war far outweighs the gain.

    (d) The solution is to deal with aggression and violence through peaceful means—to pacify one's enemy through nonviolence.

  2. There are arguments for the morality of war.

    (a) War is the best controller of overpopulation.

    (b) It is the "mother of invention."

    (c) It is a great unifying factor and economic boon for individual nations.

    (d) War sometimes is a "necessary evil"—the morally just war does exist.

        (1) Early Catholic doctrine describes the possibility of just wars.

        (2) War is a more encompassing form of defense of the innocent.

  3. Given the devastation possible in a nuclear war, most arguments, including the just-war argument, cannot support a nuclear holocaust: Such a war is indefensible.

  4. There is an old and very destructive method of making war, and that is terrorism.

    (a) Terrorism is defined as war deliberately waged against civilians.

    (b) One of the most difficult aspects of terrorism is the injury and death of hundreds of innocent people and the destruction of property.

(c) Argument in support of terrorism: When people are oppressed or angry about their lot in life, and nonviolent means haven't worked for them, then they feel they must resort to violence. Innocents may be killed, but the terrorists' cause is more important.

(d) Argument against terrorism: Excessive violence, especially when it involves the loss or mutilation of the lives of innocent people, cannot be condoned. Terrorism does not fall under any definition of a "morally just war."

(e) The semantics of terrorism in public discourse reveals two double standards: an "us verses them" mentality and a framework that condemns the actions of nonstate actors and, at the same time, condones similar acts committed by agents of the state—especially one's own state.

D. It is questionable whether capital punishment is moral or immoral.

1. Capital punishment is defined as punishment, usually by death, that is imposed in response to certain "capital crimes" such as murder, kidnapping, rape, and torture.

2. Theories of punishment are as follows:

(a) Retributive or deserts theory: Punishment should be given only when it is deserved and to the extent it is deserved.

(b) Utilitarian or results theory: Punishment is justified only if it will bring about good consequences for everyone.

(c) Restitution or compensation theory: Justice is served only if the victim of a crime or offense is provided with restitution or compensation for the harm done to him or her.

(d) Capital punishment could conceivably be acceptable in all of the preceding theories in some cases but not in others.

3. There are arguments against the morality of capital punishment.

(a) It is a direct violation of the Value of Life principle—a "murder" planned and executed by society.

(b) It doesn't bring back the killer's dead victims or in any way, other than by expressing vengeance, recompense the survivors of the victim.

(c) There is no conclusive proof that it really acts as a deterrent, especially since most executions are performed in relative privacy.

(d) It is possible to wrongly execute an innocent person; and rich people who can afford good lawyers are less frequently subject to capital punishment than are the poor and members of minority races.

(e) Capital punishment eliminates any possibility of rehabilitation and adds the cost of the killer's life to that of his or her victim.

4. There are arguments for the morality of capital punishment.

(a) It is clearly a deterrent for the killer, who is put to death, but it also deters others who are contemplating murder.

(b) It is less costly than imprisonment (critics question this), and there is no reason to make innocent, hardworking taxpayers pay for the upkeep of a guilty killer.

(c) It puts real teeth into laws, giving them force and sanction and strongly encouraging everyone to obey them.

(d) A person who has killed has forfeited his or her right to be treated ethically; therefore, taking such a person's life is not immoral.

(e) Rehabilitation often is infeasible if not impossible, especially when one is dealing with serial and mutilating killers.

(f) It is only fair that killers should pay with their own lives for having taken the lives of others.

Exercises for Review

1. What does it mean for something to be "logically and empirically prior" to something else?
2. Describe the type of approach to moral problems taken in Humanitarian Ethics.
3. What are your general views on suicide, and why? Do you agree or disagree with the conclusions of the author in Appendix 1? Why?
4. What are your general views on taking a human life in defense of the innocent (self included)? Be specific in explaining how and why your views agree or disagree with the author's as expressed in Appendix 1.
5. Do you consider war to be moral or immoral? Why? (If you think it is always immoral, state your reasons; if you think it may be moral sometimes or under certain conditions, describe the conditions and provide reasons that could morally justify war.)
6. Is a nuclear war ever justifiable?
7. Do you think that capital punishment is morally justified? Why or why not? If you believe it is *sometimes* justified, when and when not?
8. Analyze and critically evaluate the author's alternative methods, cited in Appendix 1, of dealing with people who have killed other people. Be specific in your criticisms and/or support of these alternatives.
9. What possible alternatives to capital punishment would you put forth as a ways of dealing with convicted killers?
10. What is terrorism and how does it differ from other kinds of war?
11. Do you think the Iraq is a just war? Why or why not?

Views of Major Ethical Theories on the Taking of Human Life

In this edition of *Ethics: Theory and Practice*, I have decided to add a section in each of the chapters in reference to how the major ethical issues—egoism, utilitarianism, Divine Command Theory, Kant's Duty Ethics, Ross' *Prima Facie* Duties, and Virtue Ethics—might deal with each of the moral issues presented in the chapter. My objective is to have students and instructors try to logically work out how they think each of the major theories would attempt to solve the problems associated with each moral issue. Instructors could assign this section of the chapter to students, and students could write papers, present speeches, and/or debate the questions in panel discussion; or instructors and students could simply enter into class discussion about any or all of the theories.

Because this is the first chapter dealing with a moral issue—the taking of human life—I will suggest how each of the theories might deal with this issue in all of its aspects discussed in this chapter. Then in the remaining chapters, instructors and students may do this on their own. The reason I am adding this section is that because the theories have been discussed in detail in chapters 2 and 3, students and instructors, if they wish, should try to test them out by applying them to moral issues in Chapters 9 through 16.

Suicide

Ethical Egoism

Ethical Egoists undoubtedly would not be against suicide provided that the person has rationally decided that such an act is truly in his or her own self-interest. Egoists certainly would not accept the idea, however, that others should interfere with a suicide attempt. However, they probably would not be against trying to dissuade the person from committing suicide, if they knew the attempt was going to be made, in order to make sure the person really believed the act to be in his or her own self-interest. The egoist would have no problem condoning the suicides in Cases 1 and 2.

Utilitarianism

Because Utilitarianism believes that one ought to do that act or follow a rule that would bring about the best good consequences for everyone affected by the act or rule, one would have to try to determine whether or not a particular suicide would satisfy the requirements of utilitarianism. It is interesting to speculate if rule utilitarians were to establish a rule for or against suicide. I believe they would not establish a rule for it without some qualifications; those having to do with the effect of the suicide on surviving family and friends, for example. Suicide could prove to be a real problem for the utilitarian because the consequences might not be good for the survivors, and this would have to be taken into consideration because utilitarianism is concerned with *everyone's* interest.

Utilitarianism probably would condone the action in Case 1 because William is dying anyway, and his family seems to be in agreement with his action. It probably would condone Joan's suicide in Case 2 because she seems to have no family or friends and considers herself a burden both to herself and others; still, one would have to know to what extent anyone else would be affected by her action.

Divine Command Theory

What would be moral under this theory would, of course, depend upon which set of divine commands would apply here. Some religions might consider suicide an honorable act; others would not. Christianity, for example, considers suicide to be a moral wrong even though it may or may not condemn a person for committing it. Generally speaking, most forms of Christianity would be against the suicides in Cases 1 and 2.

Kant's Duty Ethics

As described in Chapter 3, Kant would not be in favor of suicide because it would violate the Categorical Imperative against killing, including the practical imperative of never using a human being, including oneself, merely as a means to an end. He probably would not accept the suicides in Cases 1 and 2, which he undoubtedly would reject.

Ross's Prima Facie Duties

Ross probably would agree with Kant in general but be somewhat more lenient in the application of his *Prima Facie* Duties. However, suicide would to some extent violate several of the duties—beneficence, nonmaleficence, and self-improvement—mainly because of the effect of the suicide upon survivors; the destruction of human life negating self-improvement; and the possibility of doing harm rather than good to others. Ross, might differ with Kant on Case 1. He probably would not condone the act in Case 2.

Virtue Ethics

In general, Virtue Ethics probably would oppose suicide because it stops a person from creating a virtuous character and cannot be considered a moderate act, but rather an extreme one. Virtue Ethics would probably accept Case 1 as being moral, but probably not Case 2, because it would hold that Joan still has the opportunity to create a more fully developed virtuous character.

Defense of the Innocent

Ethical Egoism

Ethical Egoists probably would condone this, but only if it were in their best interest. For example, if they had to risk their lives in order to defend the innocent, then they might not be in favor of this. But if in defending the innocent they also were acting in their best interest—for example, if "the innocent" were themselves, their wives, children, other family, or friends—they probably would be in favor of it. But again, only if it were seen by them to be in their own self-interest would they take action. They probably would condone killing the runaway thief because he has invaded their privacy and attempted to steal their property, which certainly is not in their best interest. They also would condone Mary's action in that she is acting in her own self-interest and self-defense, and the rapist is not. They also probably would condone shooting the sniper because it would be in their self-interest to eliminate such a destructive person who could be threatening their lives and not acting in anyone's self-interest but his own.

Utilitarianism

This theory would very likely be in favor of defense of the innocent because this generally is an act in the interest of everyone, and the best good consequences would accrue for everyone from an act or a rule that would encourage such action. They probably would not condone Ed's action in Case 1 because everyone's interest is not affected by the boy's action and certainly not the boy's interest. They definitely would go along with the actions in Cases 2 and 3, because it would be in everyone's interest to prevent a rapist from committing crimes, and because the rapist certainly is not acting in Mary's interest and because she has a right to protect herself. Utilitarians definitely would see the sniper's death as being in the best interest of everyone affected by his actions because he is jeopardizing the lives of everyone in that area by his actions. The utilitarian might hope that Cases 2 and 3 could be resolved without killing, but I believe he would see the killing as justified in both of them.

Divine Command Theory

Here again, a great deal would depend upon which religion is involved. For example, Jainists or Quakers, who do not believe in the taking of life altogether, probably would not be in favor of killing under any circumstances. Other religions, however, undoubtedly would believe that killing was justified in defense of the innocent—regrettable, but at times necessary. Most probably would not condone the killing in Case 1, except those religions based heavily upon retribution. However, in Cases 2 and 3, most religions undoubtedly would think the killing was justified, believing that Mary has a right to defend herself against rape and possible murder, and that the sniper was endangering everyone's lives and needed to be stopped before his immoral actions could continue to destroy innocent lives.

Kant's Duty Ethics

Kant, of course, would be against the taking of human life, and certainly would not have justified the actions in Case 1, because the thief was unarmed and not threatening Ed's life. I believe he would relent in Cases 2 and 3, even though killing was involved. He probably would hope that the situations could be resolved without killing, but if they couldn't be, then he would understand the actions of Mary and the policeman. He might consider the actions to be not fully moral, but I believe he would at least understand why they had to occur and at least partially accept them.

Ross's Prima Facie Duties

Ross also would not condone the killing in Case 1, but I believe he would find the actions of Mary and the officer to be in accord with the stronger *Prima Facie* Duties of justice, beneficence, and non-maleficence. Ross would see their actions as being moral.

Virtue Ethics

The proponents of this view probably would not accept Ed's action in Case 1 as being morally justified because it did not seem to indicate a balance between reason and emotion; prevented the thief from being taught virtue and developing a virtuous character; and exceeded moderation. They would regret the actions in Cases 2 and 3 but would probably see Mary and the officer as acting in a virtuous way, as they knew how, under very trying circumstances. On the other hand, they would see the rapist and the sniper as not acting in virtuous ways at all, thus making justifiable whatever actions it might take to stop them from committing their morally wrong acts.

War and Terrorism

In general, probably all of the ethical theories would be against war and terrorism, except under certain circumstances, because they go against almost all of their principles.

Ethical Egoism

In Case 1, this theory probably would condone war in self-defense of the smaller nation. It also might consider the larger nation's actions as being valid in trying to improve its situation by operating in its own self-interest. However, in the long run, ethical egoists might find either nation's actions not to be in its self-interest because of the mass killing and destruction that abounds in war.

In Case 2, they probably would see the actions of the allies as operating in their own self-interest because the larger nation is trying to destroy all the nations and peoples involved in its aggression. As for the larger nation, this theory might consider that, in the short run, its actions would be in its self-interest, but in the long run might not be, especially if it lost the war it started.

Ethical egoists probably would not condone the actions of the two larger nations in Case 3 because of their interference in the country's affairs. It is possible that some egoists might say the two larger countries have a right to protect their own self-interests, but their interference in the small nation's affairs seems more immoral. Ethical egoists probably would not condone acts of terrorism because such acts interfere with the self-interest of the victims who have no warning or chance to act in their own self-interest and save themselves. Only the strongest egoists would support the right of the terrorists to act in their own self-interest.

Utilitarianism

This theory probably would not condone war because it would not be in the interest of everyone affected. It might condone national self-defense when the war has been started by another nation as in Case 1's smaller nation and the allies in Case 2. It would not condone the larger nations' actions in either Case 1 or 2. Utilitarianism probably would be against interfering in the affairs of the small Far Eastern nation by the two larger powers as not being in the interest of everyone concerned by the actions. Rule Utilitarianism probably would have a rule against war except in clear cases of national self-defense, and either form of utilitarianism would be against terrorism as not being in the interest of everyone.

Divine Command Theory

Except for those pacifist religions mentioned above or for those condoning holy wars, most religions are against war because of the violence and destruction involved except in defense of an innocent nation being attacked by an aggressor nation. Most probably would go along with the requirements expressed in the Roman Catholic description of a just war except when it comes to nuclear war. Most religions would not condone the larger nations' aggression in Cases 1 and 2 but probably would accept the right of self-defense of the smaller nation and the allies. Most religions, except for a few extremist factions within particular religions, are opposed to war except in cases of self-defense. Except for these same extremists, most religions undoubtedly would be against any form of terrorism. Case 3 is hard to describe under this ethical theory because many religions might endorse a war against a godless form of government such as communism, but I believe most religions still would not condone the war in Case 3.

Kant's Duty Ethics

Kant, of course, would be against wars and terrorism in general because they violate the Categorical and Practical Imperatives he set forth in his theory because war involves killing and using people merely as means to an end. He might sympathize with the self-defense theory but still would be against taking lives in general. He might accept the extreme situations of the need for national self-defense in Cases 1 and 2 but would feel that such actions are not fully moral. In no way would he condone the actions of the two major powers in Case 3 or even the civil war in the Far Eastern country.

Ross's Prima Facie Duties

Ross probably would be against war and terrorism because these violate at least four of his *Prima Facie* Duties: justice, beneficence, self-improvement (hard to achieve when one is injured or killed or trying to defend himself or herself all the time), and nonmaleficence. He probably would accept defense of the innocent as being justified, but not much else, such as gaining territory. Therefore he probably would accept the self-defense of the smaller nation in Case 1 and the allies in Case 2, but not the actions of the major powers in Case 3 or terrorism in any form or for any reason.

Virtue Ethics

Just as this theory would accept defense of the innocent, it probably would accept the self-defense of the smaller nation and the allies in Cases 1 and 2. It would, however, most likely be against the actions in Case 3 and war and terrorism in general as not being moderate and not being conducive to the development of a virtuous character even though it might see some actions of bravery and heroism as being virtuous in themselves. This theory undoubtedly would be against terrorism in any form as not being moderate or virtuous in any respect.

Capital Punishment

With regard to this issue, the particular cases don't necessarily matter because an ethical theory usually will take a stand for or against capital punishment in general based upon its principles. Therefore, if a person is guilty of a capital crime, the theory will either be for or against execution regardless of particular circumstances.

Ethical Egoism

Given that there is the alternative of life imprisonment without parole, many egoists would probably not demand capital punishment; yet some might, unless they themselves were the perpetrators of capital crimes, in which case they probably would deem it to be in their self-interest not to be executed.

Some egoists might be for capital punishment in their own self-interest so as to protect themselves against the possibility of such criminals ever escaping to kill again. If they or their families are victims of the killer, they may wish to seek retributive justice, it being in their self-interest to see that he is punished so fully he can never kill again.

On the other hand, some also might feel that it would not be in their self-interest to permit social violence that might breed more violence by individuals. Therefore, it is difficult to say exactly what an egoist might accept here. A great deal would depend upon how he has rationalized his self-interest, as we see from the above possibilities. As long as life imprisonment without parole is an alternative, egoists may be against capital punishment, but if they feel it is not in their self-interest to pay taxes to keep a criminal in jail for his lifetime, then they may be for capital punishment.

Utilitarianism

As pointed out earlier in the discussion of the theories of capital punishment, the utilitarian or results theory states that capital punishment should be employed only if it can be shown that the best good consequences will accrue to everyone involved. In other words, if good consequences for everyone cannot be shown to come out of capitally punishing someone, and if there are viable alternatives such as life imprisonment without parole, then capital punishment would not be justified by utilitarians.

For example, because studies of the deterrent argument for capital punishment have been shown to be suspect in that there is no conclusive evidence that capital punishment deters crime, the utilitarian probably would be against it. The only aspect of the crime that utilitarians might be concerned about is whether or not the criminal would be let loose in society again, which would not be in the interest of everyone. If it could be guaranteed that he would not be set free (by means of life imprisonment without parole), then they would be against capital punishment.

Divine Command Theory

Depending upon the tenets of a particular religion, capital punishment might or might not be deemed acceptable. If the religion believes in retributive punishment, then it probably would be for it, believing that humans have a right to judge violators of its commandments and to exact punishment in the name of their god or gods. The more pacifistic religions, of course, would not. Religions that tend to have a stronger theory of mercy and forgiveness also would probably be against capital punishment.

Kant's Duty Ethics

According to Kant: "The Penal Law is a Categorical Imperative; and woe to him who creeps through the serpent-windings of Utilitarianism to discover some advantage that may discharge him from the Justice of Punishment, or even from the due measure of it. . . . For if Justice and right-eousness perish, human life would no longer have any value in the world. . . . Whoever has committed murder must *die* . . . "[8] Kant uncharacteristically approved captital punishment.

Ross's Prima Facie Duties

Ross would be in favor of punishment for criminals under his notion of duty of reparation (criminals making up for wrongs they have done), but would probably be against *capital* punishment because it would violate his duties of beneficence (it would not improve the condition of the criminal as rehabilitation might); self-improvement (how can the criminal improve himself if he is executed); nonmaleficence (not injuring others—preventing injury to others could just as well be accomplished by life imprisonment without parole).

Virtue Ethics

Capital punishment certainly would not be a moderate solution for dealing with criminals under Virtue Ethics, nor would it allow criminals the opportunity to develop a more virtuous character; therefore, I do not believe that in general Virtue Ethics would accept capital punishment. Rather the virtue ethicist would advocate that we try our best to inculcate virtue into such criminals through education and example. No one who cannot or has not developed such a character, by means of education and train-ing, should be set free from prison. I believe the virtue ethicist would prefer life imprisonment without parole for those unable to profit from Virtue Ethics training to capital punishment.

Reader Reactions

Do you agree or disagree with the author's analyses of what the major ethical views would be? Which and why? Support your answers in detail and be sure to include your own analysis of the major ethical theories' views.

Notes

1. William Morris, ed., *The American Heritage Dictionary of the English Language* (Boston: Houghton Mifflin, 1978), 1287.
2. Daniel Callahan, *Abortion: Law, Choice and Morality* (New York: Macmillan, 1970), 417–18. See also Chapter 9.
3. John P. O'Connell, ed., *The Catholic Encyclopedia*, Holy Bible (Chicago: Catholic Press, 1954), 278–79.
4. Caleb Carr, *The Lessons of Terror* (New York: Random House, 2002), 6.
5. Ibid., 12.
6. Igor Primoratz, ed., *Terrorism: The Philosophical Issues:* (New York: Palgrave Macmillan, 2004), xi.
7. *The Bakersfield Californian* (February: 2000), p. 45.
8. Immanuel Kant, "The Science of Right," in *The Philosophy of Law* (Edinburgh: T. and T. Clark, 1887).

Research Navigator™
(http://www.researchnavigator.com)

This web site offers three research databases: EBSCO's *ContentSelect Academic Journal and Abstract Database, New York Times* Search by Subject Archive, and *Best of the Web* Link Library. In addition, this site provides helpful advice on how to conduct efficient and productive research from choosing a topic to polishing the final draft. Beginning philosophy students probably will find the *Best of the Web* Link Library the most appropriate place to start their research.

The free access code necessary to employ Research Navigator™ can be found in the Prentice Hall Guide to Evaluating Online Resources. If your text did not come with this guide, please go to *www.prenhall.com/contentselect* for information on how you can purchase an access code.

Allowing Someone to Die, Mercy Death, and Mercy Killing

Objectives

After you have read this chapter, you should be able to

1. Define and make distinctions among the following terms: *euthanasia, allowing someone to die, mercy death, mercy killing, ordinary* and *extraordinary means* for keeping people alive, *persistent vegetative state* (PVS), and *brain death.*

2. Explain why allowing someone to die has become an issue in the light of advanced medical technology, and discuss a dying person's right to refuse treatment, "living wills," natural death declarations, and durable powers of attorney for health care.

3. Critically analyze and evaluate the moral aspects of allowing someone to die, mercy death, physician-assisted suicide, and mercy killing in light of the hospice approach to care for the dying.

4. Evaluate the question "Is allowing someone to die morally justified?"

5. Evaluate the question "Is mercy death morally justified?"

6. Evaluate the question "Is mercy killing morally justified?"

Definition of Terms

The word *euthanasia* comes from the Greek and originally meant "a good death." However, it also has been interpreted, especially in the twentieth century, to mean "mercy killing," legally a form of murder in most countries of the world. Dr. Richard Lamerton, former director of St. Joseph's Hospice Home Care Service in London, has stated that in using the term *euthanasia* to stand for both mercy killing and allowing someone to die, we seriously blur a very necessary and important distinction between an act of murder and what is merely good medical practice (allowing people to die of natural causes, without using any extraordinary or heroic measures to keep them alive).

Dr. Lamerton states further that even though *euthanasia* once meant "a good death," it no longer has that meaning but rather means mercy killing or murder.[1] Therefore, because of this and the confusion and ambiguity of the meaning of *euthanasia*, I will not use this term but will substitute three other phrases: allowing someone to die, mercy death, and mercy killing. Each of these phrases has a different meaning, and they must be clearly defined and distinguished before one can deal with the important moral issues surrounding them.

Allowing Someone to Die

The phrase "allowing someone to die" implies an essential recognition that there is some point in any terminal illness when further curative treatment has no purpose and that a patient in this situation should be allowed to die a natural death in comfort, peace, and dignity. In no way does this involve an active termination of someone's life. Rather, it involves a refusal to start curative treatment when no cure is possible and the willingness to halt curative treatment when it can no longer help a dying patient.

What it means, in short, is allowing a terminally ill patient to die his or her own natural death without interference or intrusion from medical science and technology. It does not mean that there is nothing that can be done for the patient or that the patient should be abandoned to die in pain and misery. It does mean, however, that medical science will not initiate heroic efforts to save a dying patient and that it will stop any such efforts that have already been started when it becomes clear that they cannot serve any useful purpose for the patient and his or her family.

Mercy Death (Including Physician-Assisted Suicide)

I have coined the phrase "mercy death" to mean taking a direct action to terminate a patient's life because the patient has requested it; in short, mercy death is really an assisted suicide. Chronically or terminally ill patients often are unable to commit suicide and therefore ask someone (often a physician) to "put them out of their misery." These patients not only give their permission to end their lives but also, in most cases, request or even demand that their lives be terminated.

Mercy Killing

The phrase "mercy killing" refers to someone's taking a direct action to terminate a patient's life without the patient's permission. The decision to take such an action is often made on the assumption that the patient's life is no longer "meaningful" or that if the patient were able to say so, he or she would express a desire to die. The important distinction between mercy killing and mercy death is that mercy killing is involuntary, or does not involve the patient's permission or request, whereas mercy death is voluntary and done with the permission of the patient and usually at his or her request.

Current Legal Status of Mercy Death and Mercy Killing

At present, 32 states specifically prohibit mercy death (or assisted suicide), and almost all of the remainder, and most countries of the world, make it illegal under general homicide statutes. However, in Michigan, Dr. Jack Kevorkian has assisted in many suicides of both chronically and terminally ill patients. Dr. Kevorkian and his activities will be discussed later in the chapter. Mercy killing is presently outlawed in all of the U.S. states and most of the countries of the world. However, two legal actions by two U.S. courts of appeal, one in New York and the other in the state of Washington, have muddied the legal questions surrounding assisted suicide and this has led to further appeals and upcoming decisions by the U.S. Supreme Court.

In April 1996, the U.S. Circuit Court of Appeals in Manhattan ruled that New York's manslaughter statute could not be used to prosecute doctors who prescribe lethal drugs to terminally ill patients who ask for them and then use them to commit suicide. The judges wrote: "What interest can the state possibly have in requiring the prolongation of a life that is all but ended? . . . And what business is it of the state . . . to interfere with a mentally competent patient's right to define [his] own concept of existence, of meaning, of the universe, and of the mystery of human life?"[2]

On March 6, 1996, in San Francisco, California, the Ninth Circuit Court of Appeals ". . . declared physician assisted suicide to be a fundamental constitutional right protected by the 14th Amendment's guarantee of 'liberty.' " "The decision how and when to die . . . is one of the most intimate and personal choices a person may make in a lifetime, a choice central to personal dignity and autonomy."[3] We will discuss the impact of these two rulings on mercy death later in the chapter. Suffice it to say that many ethicists find them both controversial and difficult to deal with. Of course, legality is not our main concern in dealing with these problems; we are concerned with whether any of these three options is moral and, if so, under what conditions. Therefore, we will now discuss each of these options in more depth, examining the arguments for and against each of them and exploring the full implications of each. Before doing this, however, it is important that we define one more phrase.

Brain Death

The advanced medical technology and sophisticated procedures available in the twentieth and twenty-first centuries have created new moral dilemmas, one of which involves irreversible brain damage, popularly known as "brain death." Before medical technology became so sophisticated, when patients' hearts or lungs failed, their brains also soon failed, and when their brains failed, heart or lung failure soon followed. In our time, however, we have discovered ways (for example, by using respirators and heart machines) to bypass the brain, thus avoiding heart or lung failure.

If a patient is brought in with a head injury from a motorcycle accident, for example, the emergency crew may get the person's heart and lungs restarted and manage to stabilize these two organ systems. Later, doctors may discover that the head injury was so serious that the patient's brain has been *irreversibly* damaged; in other words, the brain is permanently dead, not just temporarily injured or even partly injured. Without brain activity, the patient is reduced to a body with a beating heart and breathing lungs. After a number of such instances had occurred, the medical community began to recognize the possibility that a person could be pronounced dead in a medical sense if his brain were irreversibly damaged—even if the patient's body could be considered to be alive in all other respects.

In 1968 an *ad hoc* committee was formed at Harvard Medical School to decide upon criteria for determining brain death. The *ad hoc* committee's final report cited four criteria: (1) unreceptivity and unresponsiveness, (2) no spontaneous movements or breathing, (3) no reflexes, and (4) a flat electroencephalogram (EEG).[4] What this means, then, is that people can be declared medically dead even though their hearts and lungs are still functioning. Many people have confused the problem of brain death with allowing someone to die and mercy killing; they maintain that if a doctor or nurse disconnects the respirator or heart machine or feeding tube that is aiding a patient who has suffered brain death, then this person is guilty of allowing the patient to die or of mercy killing. This, however, is not the case; if patients are declared dead in an official medical sense, then any equipment can be disconnected and any procedure can be stopped without there being any implication of wrongdoing. After all, how can a patient who is already medically dead be allowed to die or undergo a mercy killing?

I believe that the confusion that arises in such cases comes from our distaste for disconnecting patients with breathing lungs and beating hearts from machines that would keep these organs functioning. Suffice it to say that brain death has nothing to do with allowing someone to die, mercy death, or mercy killing. Some states (California, for example) have even included brain death in their legal definition of death. There is still a problem, however, in dealing with people who have not suffered brain death, but who are severely brain damaged. Some injuries do not kill the brain; rather, they leave it so badly damaged that when and if patients awake from a coma, their lives are likely to be radically altered. Furthermore, such patients may remain in a coma for an indefinite period yet not meet the criteria cited above for brain death. The issues of allowing someone to die and mercy killing may definitely arise in relation to this last type of case, but they should not be considered as being in any way related to a clear-cut case of total brain death.

Persistent Vegetative State (PVS) or Irreversible Coma

Brain death should be carefully distinguished from persistent vegetative state (PVS). PVS results from damage to the cerebral cortex, or neocortex, which controls the cognitive functions. For this reason, it might be called cortical or cerebral death. The body, however, is not dead because the functions of the brain stem continue in whole or in part. In PVS there may still be, and usually is, spontaneous breathing and heartbeat. Persons in this state often are awake, but they are not aware of what is going on around them. There is no conscious interaction with the environment and no awareness of self or the environment. A person in this state lacks and will permanently lack even that minimal level of functioning that makes life human. They are, in short, incapable of any human interaction. The very famous cases of Karen Ann Quinlan, Nancy Cruzan, and Terrie Schiavo are examples of PVS, as you will see later.

Allowing Someone to Die

As we have already defined it, "allowing someone to die" means allowing a terminally ill patient to die a natural death without any interference on the part of medical science. The problems surrounding this issue, along with those surrounding mercy death and mercy killing, have arisen much more frequently in the twentieth and twenty-first centuries than at any other period. The reason for this, as we have already mentioned, is that advancing medical technology has made it possible for more people to live longer than ever before. As recently as a few years ago, when the heart or lungs failed, a person was sure to die within a short period of time. Nowadays, however, a person can be kept alive almost indefinitely by respirators, heart machines feeding tubes, and pacemakers, miracle drugs, organ transplants, kidney dialysis machines, and so on.

With these advances, which certainly are a blessing for many, we also have incurred problems as to the quality of the lives we are extending. For example, people with kidney failure, who would have died prior to 1960, now can be saved. Many of them adjust beautifully to their situations, but others feel that if the only way they can remain alive is to be hooked up to a kidney machine for the rest of their lives, they would rather be dead.

Medical science also is working very hard on a cure for cancer, frequently a long, drawn-out disease that causes patients to slowly deteriorate and eventually lose their sense of dignity. It is ironic that as these patients' lives are extended by means of advanced medical technology, so too are their pain, suffering, and misery—sometimes in the hope that a cure will be found and sometimes simply because the doctors don't want to give up on any of their patients.

Similarly, because most people live longer than ever before, they sometimes become senile and infirm. We tend to relegate such people to hospitals or nursing homes, where, in many instances, they live out a tiresome, dreary, and despairing existence, often in pain and suffering. Therefore, literally thousands upon thousands of people, of various ages and in various stages of dying, face what many would describe as lives of low quality. If we add to this the extremely well-documented fact that people of the Western world, and especially those living in the United States, generally do not have the ability to face aging or death well, we have a serious problem that we must try to solve in the most ethical way possible.

Very few of us want to see other human beings suffer or live lives from which they are begging to be released. For this reason, it seems to many people that what we need to do is to accept as moral, and then legalize, some methods of allowing patients to die, mercy death, or mercy killing, preferably in some painless form to be administered by doctors, or by patients with the help of doctors so that "miserable, meaningless" lives can be ended with dignity.

It is difficult to question the validity of the motives behind the desire to end the misery and pain of others. Furthermore, we can justify these motives within the five basic principles. Because we revere life and yet *accept death*; because we can bring happiness and eliminate pain, both for patients and their families, creating harmony where there was disharmony, and ending lives lacking excellence whereas enhancing other lives with excellence; because we can be just and fair, not only to patients and their families but also to the rest of society on whom sick and dying patients often are a burden; and because we can grant individual freedom to terminally ill patients to die and be allowed to die, as well as the freedom to decide how and when to die, it seems obvious to many that allowing someone to die, mercy death, and mercy killing can be morally justified.

Let us now examine the arguments for and against allowing someone to die.

Arguments Against Allowing Someone to Die

It is a common assumption that human life always is to be protected and preserved, regardless of its quality, by every means we have at our disposal. This assumption has given rise to a number of arguments against allowing someone to die.

Abandonment of Patients. Some people argue that not using or discontinuing any means that might keep dying people alive even a little longer is tantamount to refusing them proper medical care. They feel that if health care professionals (doctors, nurses, etc.) refuse to apply curative treatments, they are abandoning patients and their families to suffering and misery.

It certainly is true that health care professionals could conceivably abandon patients for whom "nothing more can be done." This probably has happened in the past, and indeed, it may be happening in some cases today. However, there is no reason why this need occur. Abandonment arises from an overemphasis on that aspect of medicine involving curing and healing patients and a deemphasis of the aspect involving comforting and caring for them which is every bit as important. As we shall see a little later, the hospice approach to care for the dying makes this distinction clear and completely eliminates the abandonment problem.

The Possibility of Finding Cures. Another argument frequently offered is that if we are too quick to let people die, we may be denying them the opportunity to be cured of their illness. New cures for disease are constantly being discovered, and there are also so-called "miracle cures," that is, cures that occur in seeming defiance of all medical knowledge. Therefore, it is argued, if we continue every effort to keep dying patients alive, a miracle cure may occur, or a scientific cure (new drug or surgical procedure) may be discovered that will lengthen patients' lives or even cure them completely.

Not all doctors are willing to accept the existence of miracle cures, however, and many of them also argue that the time to be concerned with cures is when the disease is first diagnosed, not when the patient has been completely debilitated by it. They would argue, for example, that the time to perform radical surgery, radiation therapy, and chemotherapy on cancer patients is not when the cancer has completely *metastasized* (spread) throughout the patients' bodies, but when such treatment can do some good, either in slowing cancer growth or in stopping it completely. Using "aggressive medicine" to treat completely metastasized cancer patients, they would argue, is closer to torturing patients than to healing them.

The Impossibility of Opting for Death. Many doctors, as well as others not in the medical profession, argue that by virtue of the nature of medicine, we can never opt for death; we must always choose life. After all, the reason medicine exists is to save lives, not end them, and the minute we start to make those choices that lead to death rather than life the very basis for medicine is nullified. This results not only in the discouragement of doctors, but also in an elimination of patients' trust in doctors, often a necessary adjunct to the healing process.

One of the arguments brought against this view is that there is a great deal of difference between "choosing" death and "accepting" death when it is inevitable. A second argument is that many dying patients do not agree with "everything must be done" to save them, and they strongly object to doctors' overriding their decisions about their own bodies and lives. The doctors, of course, argue that they know best and that they must be the ones to make all the decisions about a patient's treatment. The patients, however, feel that they ought to have the right to refuse treatment as well as to accept it.

Interference with God's Divine Plan. The final argument against allowing someone to die states that only God can create and take away life, and that mere human beings should not be permitted to allow people to die, much less take their lives in an active way. According to this argument, we must use all of our abilities and every method at our command to save, protect, preserve, and extend human life until the Creator has decided that it is time for a terminally ill patient to die. We have, of course, heard this argument before in the last chapter, and we have already discussed some of the problems surrounding it.

In this situation, however, it becomes a two-edged sword; that is, the concept of God's divine plan can be used to argue for or against allowing someone to die. The argument against such an action has already been stated. The argument for allowing someone to die begins with the assumption that God meant for all humans to die and that the development of medicine has interfered to a great extent with God's original plan. That is, God did not mean for human beings to live forever, and when medicine prolongs life it interferes with His plan.

The problem with both sides of the argument, of course, is that it is not at all clear what God's specific plan *is* in relation to allowing someone to die. Furthermore, deciding when to start or stop medical treatment is not a decision made by God. Rather, people—doctors or patients—make these decisions. People who believe in God can certainly say that God has given them a choice with regard to this issue, but they cannot abdicate their responsibility by saying that God is doing the deciding.

Arguments for Allowing Someone to Die

Most arguments for allowing someone to die are based upon the Principle of Individual Freedom—specifically, upon the rights of individual dying patients to make decisions about their own bodies and lives.

Individual Rights over Bodies and Lives. In much the same way as it applied to the arguments for suicide, the idea that people have the right to decide about their own lives or deaths applies to allowing someone to die, and also—as we shall see later—to requesting mercy death. This right also includes the right of rational patients to refuse treatment when they so desire.

There is, of course, a difference between taking a direct action to end one's own life and merely allowing a disease, deemed to be a part of the natural process, to follow its course without interference. And the process of allowing someone to die does not involve suicide or killing of any kind. In "A Patient's Bill of Rights," which was drawn up by the American Hospital Association, patients are accorded, among other rights, "the right to refuse treatment to the extent permitted by law and to be informed of the medical consequences" of their actions.[5]

The main criticism of the individual rights argument was discussed in Chapter 8; to recapitulate, no one has absolute rights over his or her own life and death. This belief is reflected in the phrase "to the extent permitted by law" in the Patient's Bill of Rights—a phrase that obviously limits people's rights over their own bodies and lives. The general view, however, is that mentally competent people (and mental incompetence is very difficult to prove legally) should have the right to refuse treatment in most cases. This point of view is most strongly held when the treatment is as bad if not worse than the disease—which often is the case. For example, many treatments for cancer result in constant nausea, loss of hair, destruction of healthy as well as diseased tissue, and disfigurement. The individual rights argument offers patients the option of simply letting the disease follow its course rather than being subjected to the sometimes horrible effects of the various treatments offered to them.

Shortening of the Period of Suffering. Another argument for allowing someone to die is that it shortens the time during which a dying patient must endure suffering, pain, and misery. Often our highly advanced medical technology is used to prolong the death— rather than the life—of patients so that they can "enjoy" a few more hours, days, weeks, or months of pain. For example, if a cancer patient has about eight hours left to live and goes into kidney failure, then prolonging his or her dying by starting dialysis would be considered to be an extension of pain and suffering, but not of meaningful life. It is much more humane, according to this argument, to alleviate the person's misery by allowing him or her to die of uremic poisoning.

The main criticism of this argument attacks its very basis. Yes, critics may say, allowing someone to die will shorten a patient's suffering, but it also will shorten his or her life, and shortening a person's life is immoral. Furthermore, if the policy of allowing people to die were to become general practice, it might be applied to those whose pain could be controlled and who therefore might have led relatively happy, significant lives.

The Right to Die with Dignity. Another argument for allowing someone to die is that people have the right to die with dignity rather than waste away and suffer until there is little left of their original character. This argument is especially forceful in relation to long-term debilitating and degenerative diseases, such as cancer. The idea at the basis of this argument is that if nothing is done in the way of extensive medical treatment, then patients will die without enduring the indignities of being operated on, fed intravenously, or hooked up to machines. The argument states further that "dignity" also is achieved when patients are given choices concerning the kind of living and dying they will do.

The main criticism of this argument is that the phrase "death with dignity" can mask everything from medical abandonment to mercy death and mercy killing and, furthermore, that no dignity will be lost as the result of a heroic attempt to save people's lives or to keep them alive as long as we possibly can.

Ordinary and Extraordinary Means

There is an important distinction to be made when one is dealing with the problem of allowing someone to die, and it has to do with exactly what means doctors are justified in using to keep people alive. In a speech to anesthesiologists in 1957, Pope Pius XII described two types of means that may be applied in medicine to keep people alive, calling them "ordinary means" and "extraordinary means." What he said, essentially, was that doctors are justified in using extraordinary means up to a point to keep people from dying, but that they are not obligated to use such means indefinitely. In hopeless cases, doctors are obligated only to use ordinary means, and they are given the option either to not start or to discontinue extraordinary means. The distinction inherent in these two phrases sounds promising, but unfortunately the terms often are quite difficult to define clearly. Let us examine more closely what Pius XII said and then see if we can make some clear distinctions ourselves.

Extraordinary, or Heroic, Means. The pope defined *extraordinary means* as those that, "according to circumstances of persons, places, times, and cultures . . . involve a grave burden for oneself or another."[6] This is, of course, a rather vague definition, and because persons, places, times, and cultures vary a great deal, it is not easy to come up with a stock list of extraordinary means. I believe that the situation I described earlier in this chapter of the completely metastasized cancer patient who went into kidney failure is a clear example of this. To apply dialysis in this case would be to employ extraordinary means to save this person's life; on the other hand, to merely try to control pain and keep the patient comfortable would be to use ordinary means of treatment.

If a patient is in a coma as a result of a drug overdose, then perhaps using dialysis to purify his or her blood of the toxic substances would be more justified than it would be in the cancer case; nonetheless, one still might question whether kidney dialysis is not always to some extent extraordinary treatment. Still, there certainly is a difference between keeping a patient comfortable and well cared for and doing radical surgery or giving radiation therapy.

Ordinary Means. The phrase "ordinary means" is almost as hard to define as "extraordinary means," again because of the wide variation in people, places, times, and cultures. We could make the distinction that once a patient's disease has been diagnosed as terminal, then continuing with chemical and radiation therapy or doing radical surgery would be extraordinary means, whereas controlling pain and other symptoms would be ordinary. This example may offer a fairly clear distinction, but there are other cases that are far more problematic.

For example, when kidney dialysis machines were in scarce supply and when individual patients had to pay the expenses (about $30,000 per year at that time), the use of these machines would have been considered "extraordinary" even though they were necessary to keep people with kidney failure alive. Now, however, when there seem to be enough machines to dialyze all kidney failure patients and when about 85 percent of the cost is paid by the government, perhaps dialysis can be considered to be ordinary means. It is interesting, however, that this treatment has placed heavy enough financial, physical, and emotional burdens on a few kidney failure patients and their families that they really did seem to consider it "extraordinary" means to the extent that they discontinued it.

At any rate, whenever there is discussion as to the problems inherent in allowing someone to die, the distinction between these two types of means usually comes into play. Generally speaking, when we are considering allowing someone to die, we are talking about not starting, or about discontinuing, extraordinary means (for example, respirators, heart machines, radical surgery, organ transplants). However, we also may be considering the not starting or discontinuing of ordinary means. For example, feeding patients is often considered to be ordinary means in most circumstances, but doctors can switch from high-nutrient feedings to minimal or no nutrient feedings that will not effectively prolong patients' lives.

There was a case several years ago concerning a man in his eighties who told his family he didn't want to live any longer. From that moment on he refused to eat anything, and he begged his two grandsons not to let anyone force-feed him in any way. They honored his request, and he was allowed to die the death he had chosen.

Similarly, a woman in the advanced stages of metastasized cancer had a large growth blocking the tube that passes food to the stomach. The doctor and her family did not use any extraordinary means, such as surgery, to remove the growth, nor did they try to force-feed her in any way. They merely kept her comfortable, letting her taste homemade food even though she couldn't swallow it and letting her suck on ice chips to quench her thirst. Literally, they were allowing her to die of starvation. As these two cases illustrate, there are times when even the refusal to use ordinary means may also be involved in allowing someone to die.

Appropriate or Inappropriate Care.   Perhaps, given the confusion that abounds in reference to the terms *ordinary* and *extraordinary*, more suitable terms would be *appropriate* and *inappropriate* care. Although initially these terms may seem as vague as the others, they allow doctors, nurses, patients, families, and other caregivers to decide how to treat a patient based upon what is *appropriate* to the particular patient. Rather than trying to decide what would constitute ordinary or extraordinary means, caregivers and patients could then base their decisions on what seemed to suit the particular situation of the patient.

Under this criterion, all means of care would have to be decided upon by the patient, family, doctors, and nurses as to whether or not it would be appropriate for a particular patient in a particular situation. This means that *all* forms of care are subject to the determination of being appropriate for a particular patient so that even food and hydration could be considered inappropriate at certain times as long as the patient was still comfortable and pain-free. The guiding force here would primarily be the clearly stated desires of the patient or the person he has designated to act for him (see advance directives later in the chapter, especially the DPAHC).

Patient Self-Determination Act (PSDA)

In 1990 the U.S. Congress passed the Patient Self-Determination Act (PSDA) as a part of the Omnibus Reconciliation Act (OBRA 1990). The PSDA requires that health care providers inform patients of their rights to make health care decisions and to execute advance directives. It also requires health care providers to educate their staff and community regarding these rights. The following are some of these rights:

1. The right of patients to considerate and respectful care.
2. The right of patients, in collaboration with their physicians, to make decisions involving their health care, including the following:
   (a) The right of patients to accept medical care or refuse treatment to the extent permitted by law and to be informed of the medical consequences of such refusal.
   (b) The right of patients to formulate advance directives and appoint a surrogate to make health care decisions on their behalf to the extent permitted by law.
3. The right of patients to acquire the information necessary to enable them to make treatment decisions that reflect their wishes.

In connection with item 2b, even though advance directives had existed long before, until the effective date of the PSDA (December 1991), there was no requirement that patients be informed that they could execute an advance directive. This directive would eliminate the confusion surrounding persistent vegetative state patients, especially when family and caregivers are trying to decide on appropriate treatment.

Three extremely famous cases concerning patients in a persistent vegetative state have focused the attention of millions of people in the United States on the importance of executing advance directives. They are the cases of Karen Ann Quinlan of New Jersey, Nancy Cruzan of Missouri, and Terri Sciavo of Florida. Interestlingly, despite these real life events, people are not executing advance directives to the extent they should be probably because they don't want to deal with their deaths and dying.

Karen Ann Quinlan. Karen Ann Quinlan was 20 years old when she stopped breathing long enough for a part of her brain to be destroyed; she then lapsed into a persistent vegetative state. She was put on a respirator, but her parents wanted her to be in a natural state without any artificial means of life support; therefore, they petitioned the hospital and doctors to remove the respirator, which they refused to do. After a lengthy court trial that eventually went to the New Jersey State Supreme Court, Quinlan was taken off the respirator and allowed to exist with just simple bed and body care and food and water.

She continued in this persistent vegetative state for another 10 years, finally succumbing to pneumonia while residing in a skilled nursing facility. It should be made clear that at no time was Karen ever brain dead. She would sit up, thrash about in her bed, react to sound, light, and touch, but at no time was she conscious or aware of her surroundings or the people in them.

Nancy Cruzan. Another woman, Nancy Cruzan, 25, lay in a persistent vegetative state for seven years following a serious automobile accident. She was fed through an abdominal tube, and her parents asked that the tube be removed and that Nancy be allowed to die her own natural death. This case was litigated up to the Missouri State Supreme Court and finally to the U.S. Supreme Court. Because Nancy had not executed any sort of advance directive, the U.S. Supreme Court ruled that "clear and convincing evidence" that Nancy desired to refuse treatment was lacking, and therefore that it could not and would not rule that her parents had the right to act as her proxies in such a decision.

When her case was returned to Missouri, after hearing further testimony from several of her friends and acquaintances that Nancy had made clear that she did not want to continue in such a state, a Superior Court judge ruled that this additional testimony provided "clear and convincing evidence" of her desire to refuse treatment and ruled that the feeding tube could be removed. It was, and she died several weeks later.

Incidentally, to indicate the great strain and sorrow caused by dealing with the allowing to die of a loved one, on August 17, 1996, her father, Lester "Joe" Cruzan, at age 62, committed suicide by hanging himself in his carport. He had fought depression all his life, and Nancy's accident, her coma, her lack of recovery, and the strain of fighting for seven years to get the law to allow her to die, finally took their toll. According to family and close friends, he did not commit suicide because he felt guilty about fighting for Nancy's right to die, nor did his suicide note indicate this in any way.[7]

Terri Schiavo. Probably the most notorious PVS patient of extensive media hype was Terri Schiavo because Michael Schiavo, her husband, wanted her feeding tube removed whereas her parents, Mary and Bob Schindler, wanted the feeding tube left in. The Schindlers claimed that Terri smiled and looked at them with love in her eyes. However, a distinguished neurologist, Ronald Cranford, examined her with the following results: The CAT scan showed a massive atrophy of the brain. What Terri Schiavo manifested was a classic vegetative state. It looked as if she was looking at you, but really she was not. It looked as if she was grinning at you, but really she was not. The key test is whether someone can track movement which Terri did not. If you look at the video tape, she was really not looking at her mother. She was really not tracking. Despite this information, many people still argued that her brain was alive. After spending many years trying to improve her condition, Michael stated that he wanted her feeding tube removed. The Schindlers said she was alive despite Dr. Cranford's expert opinion and that they wanted the feeding tube left in. There then followed the strangest series of events involving various arms of government. First, the governor of Florida, Jeb Bush, the president's brother, asked the Florida legislature to give him the power to keep Terri alive which they did. The courts still insisted that her feeding tube be removed. Then Republicans in

Washington passed similar legislation, and President, Bush flew to Washington, D.C., to sign such a bill into law. Never before had politics played such a part in what was a personal matter, and many descried such interference. Despite the interference, the feeding tube was removed per her husband's request. Why do you think the confusion existed between Dr. Cranford's expert opinion and how Terri appeared to nonmedical people? To what extent do you feel government should interfere in such issues? Why is PVS so difficult to deal with compared to brain death? What's the difference between the two?[8] The Quinlan and Cruzan cases, and others like them, have fostered a sense of urgency concerning the rights of people to determine their own treatments and deaths and have led to the creation of the previously mentioned PSDA and to encouraging people to execute advance directives, three of which I will describe now.

Advance Directives

Because being allowed to die seems to have become a significant moral issue of our time, and because this issue involves individual freedom and patients' rights over their own bodies, treatments, and lives, certain documents or directives have been created to allow people to inform others of the kind of treatment they wish to receive if and when they become seriously ill. Through such documents, people hope to ensure that they will receive the kind of treatment they want even if they become too ill later on to communicate effectively to others how they wish to be treated. Further, by means of such documents these people hope to relieve their families, doctors, nurses, and hospitals of the burdens (economic, emotional, moral) of making decisions that would allow them, as patients, to die their own natural deaths "with peace and dignity." There have been various documents or directives: the Living Will and Health Care Proxy, the California Natural Death Act Declaration, and, probably the most well known, the Durable Power Attorney for Health Care (DPAHC). It may depend in what state one resides as to what document is accepted. The most recent in California was passed by the State Legislature on July 1, 2000. Called the Advance Health Care Directive (AHCD) (see Figure 10–1), it is an updated version of the DPAHC. It is more significant than the latter because the legislature had the input of California physicians as to its design.

Regardless of how one feels about such documents, they are evidence of a growing concern on the part of human beings about the encroachment of medicine and medical technology on their freedom, lives, and dignity. These documents also provide further evidence that people wish to have a strong voice in determining the nature of the medical treatment they receive and to exert their own control over their own living and dying. Finally, it is important to note that none of these documents in any way authorizes either mercy death or mercy killing; they pertain only to allowing someone to die.

The Hospice Approach to Care for the Dying

Before we begin to discuss mercy death and mercy killing, it is important that we look closely at a different approach to care for the dying than that generally practiced in this country: I call this "the hospice approach to care for the dying." The word *hospice* formerly meant a refuge for wayfaring strangers. Now, however, it refers to a place where tired,

CALIFORNIA
Advance Directive Planning for Important Healthcare Decisions

Caring Connections, 1700 Diagonal Road, Suite 625, Alexandria, VA 22314
www.caringinfo.org, 800/658-8898

Caring Connections, a program of the National Hospice and Palliative Care Organization (NHPCO), is a national consumer engagement initiative to improve care at the end of life, supported by a grant from The Robert Wood Johnson Foundation.

The goal of Caring Connections is for consumers to hear a unified message promoting awareness and action for improved end-of-life care. Through these efforts, NHPCO seeks to support those working across the country to improve end-of-life care and conditions for all Americans.

Caring Connections tracks and monitors all state and federal legislation and significant court cases related to end-of-life care to ensure that our advance directives are always up to date.

CARING CONNECTIONS

HelpLine
You can call our toll-free HelpLine, 800/658-8898, if you have any difficulty understanding your state-specific advance directive, or if you are dealing with a difficult end-of-life situation and need immediate information. We can help provide resources and information on questions like these:

- How do I communicate my end-of-life wishes to my family?
- What type of end-of-life care is available to me?
- What questions should I ask my mother's doctors about her end-of-life care?

It's About How You LIVE
It's About How You LIVE is a national community engagement campaign encouraging individuals to make informed decisions about end-of-life care and services. The campaign encourages people to:

Learn about options for end-of-life services and care

Implement plans to ensure wishes are honored

Voice decisions to family, friends and health care providers

Engage in personal or community efforts to improve end-of-life care

Please call the HelpLine at 800/658-8898 to learn more about the LIVE campaign, obtain free resources, or to join the effort to improve community, state and national end-of-life care.

HOW TO USE THESE MATERIALS

1. Check to be sure that you have the materials for your state. You should complete a form for the state in which you expect to receive health care.
2. These materials include:
   - Instructions for preparing your advance directive.
   - Your state-specific advance directive forms, which are the pages with the gray instruction bar on the left side.
3. Read the instructions in their entirety. They give you specific information about the requirements in your state.
4. You may want to photocopy these forms before you start so you will have a clean copy if you need to start over.

5. When you begin to complete the form, refer to the gray instruction bars – they indicate where you need to mark, insert your personal instructions, or sign the form.
6. Talk with your family, friends, and physicians about your decision to complete an advance directive. Be sure the person you appoint to make decision on your behalf understands your wishes.

If you have questions or need guidance in preparing your advance directive or about what you should do with it after you have completed it, you may call our toll free number 800/658-8898 and a staff member will be glad to assist you.

Figure 10–1

For more information contact:

The National Hospice and Palliative Care Organization
1700 Diagonal Road, Suite 625
Alexandria, VA 22314

Call our HelpLine: 800/658-8898
Visit our Web site: www.caringinfo.org

Formerly a publication of Last Acts Partnership.

Support for this program is provided by a grant from
The Robert Wood Johnson Foundation, Princeton,
New Jersey.

INTRODUCTION TO YOUR CALIFORNIA ADVANCE HEALTH CARE DIRECTIVE

This packet contains a legal document, the California Advance Health Care Directive, that protects your right to refuse medical treatment you do not want, or to request treatment you do want, in the event you lose the ability to make decisions yourself.

1. Part 1, **Power of Attorney for Health Care,** lets you name someone to make decisions about your medical care—including decisions about life support—if you can no longer speak for yourself or immediately if you designate this on the document. The Power of Attorney for Health Care is especially useful because it appoints someone to speak for you any time can not or do not choose to make your own medical decisions, not only at the end of life.
2. Part 2, **Instructions for Health Care,** functions as your state's living will. It lets you state your wishes about medical care in the event that you can no longer speak for yourself and:
   a) you have an incurable and irreversible condition that will result in death within a relatively short time, or

b) you become unconscious and, to a reasonable degree of medical certainty, will not regain consciousness, or
c) the likely risks and burdens of treatment would outweigh the expected benefits.

Although you have the option to complete only one part of this document, Caring Connections suggests that you complete Part 1 and Part 2 to best ensure that you receive the medical care you want when you can no longer speak for yourself.

3. Part 3, **Donation of Organs at Death** this is an optional section that allows you to record your wishes regarding organ donation.
4. Part 4, **Primary Physician,** this is an optional section that allows you to designate your primary physician.

Note: This document will be legally binding only if the person completing it is a competent adult who is 18 years of age or older.

Figure 10–1   (continued)

INTRODUCTION TO YOUR CALIFORNIA ADVANCE HEALTH CARE DIRECTIVE (CONTINUED)

How do I make my advance health care directive legal?
In order to make your Advance Health Care Directive legally binding you have two options:

1. Sign your document in the presence of two witnesses, who must also sign the document to show that they personally know you (or you provided convincing evidence of identity) and believe you to be of sound mind and under no duress, fraud or undue influence.

Both of your witnesses cannot:

- be the person you appointed as your agent,
- be your health care provider, or an employee of your health care provider.
- be the operator or employee of a community facility,
- be the operator or employee of a residential care facility for the elderly.

In addition, one of your witnesses cannot be:

- related to your by blood or marriage or adoption,
- entitled to any part of your estate either under your last will and testament or by operation of law.

OR

2. Sign your document in the presence of a notary public.

If you are a resident in a skilled nursing facility, one of the witnesses must be a patient advocate or ombudsman designated by the State Department of Aging.

Are there any important facts that I should know?
A copy of your California Advance Health Care Directive has the same effect as the original.

COMPLETING PART 1: POWER OF ATTORNEY FOR HEALTH CARE

Whom should I appoint as my agent?
A health care agent is the person you appoint to make decisions about your medical care if you become unable to make these decisions yourself. Your agent can be a family member or a close friend whom you trust to make serious decisions. The person you name as your agent should clearly understand your wishes and be willing to accept the responsibility of making medical decisions for you. The person you appoint as your agent **cannot be:**

1. the supervising health care provider or employee of the health care institution where you are receiving care; or
2. an operator or employee of a community care facility or residential care facility at which you are receiving care.

Unless:

1. he or she (other than the supervising health care provider) is related to you by blood, marriage, adoption or is your registered domestic partner; or
2. he or she is your co-worker (other than the supervising health care provider) employed by the same health care institution, community care facility, or residential care facility for the elderly where you are a patient.

You can appoint a second and third person as your alternative agents. An alternative agent will step

in if the person you name as agent is unable, unwilling or unavailable to act for you.

Should I add personal instructions to my Power of Attorney?
You can use the space provided under paragraph (2) to limit your agent's authority. Unless the form you sign limits the authority of your agent, your agent may make all health care decisions for you including:

a) consenting or refusing consent to any care, treatment, service or procedure to maintain, diagnose or otherwise affect a physical or mental condition;
b) selecting or discharging healthcare providers and institutions;
c) approving or disapproving diagnostic tests, surgical procedures, programs of medications and orders not to resuscitate; and
d) directing the provision, withholding and withdrawal of artificial nutrition and hydration and all other forms of health care.

One of the strongest reasons for naming a health care agent is to have someone who can respond flexibly as your medical condition changes and can deal with situations that you did not foresee.
    We urge you to talk with your health care agent about your future medical care and describe what you consider to be an acceptable "quality of life". If you want to record your wishes about specific

Figure 10–1   (continued)

treatments or conditions, you can use Part 2 of this document, Instructions for Health Care.

What if I change my mind?
If you wish to cancel your Durable Power of Attorney for Health-Care Decisions you may do so by a signed writing or by personally notifying your supervising health care provider, of your intent to revoke.

Are there any important facts I should know?
Paragraph (4) contains various statements about your agent's authority. Cross out and initial any

portion of these statements that do not reflect your wishes. Paragraph (5) gives your agent the authority to make anatomical gifts, authorize an autopsy, and direct the disposition of your remains after your death.

Cross out and initial any portion of these statements that do not reflect your wishes. Paragraph (6) nominates your agent or alternate agents to be your court appointed guardian should one become necessary. If this is not your intention, cross out initial this section.

COMPLETING PART 2: INSTRUCTIONS FOR HEALTH CARE

Can I add personal instructions to my Instructions for Health Care?
Yes. Paragraphs (7) and (8) allow you to include instructions about certain care and treatment. If there are any specific instructions that you would like to include that are not already listed on the document you may list them in paragraph (9). For example, you may want to include a sentence such as, "I especially do not want cardiopulmonary resuscitation, a respirator or antibiotics." If you have appointed an agent, it is a good idea to write a statement such as, "Any questions

about how to interpret or when to apply my Instructions for Health Care are to be decided by my agent."

What if I change my mind?
You may cancel your Instructions for Health Care at any time and in any manner that communicates your intent to do so.

It is important to learn about the kinds of life-sustaining treatment you might receive. Consult your doctor or order the Caring Connections booklet, "Advance Directives and End-of-Life Decisions."

AFTER YOU HAVE COMPLETED YOUR DOCUMENT

1. Your California Advance Health Care Directive is an important legal document. Keep the original signed document in a secure but accessible place. Do not put the original document in a safe deposit box or any other security box that would keep others from having access to it.
2. Give photocopies of the signed original to your agent and alternate agent(s), doctor(s), family, close friends, clergy and anyone else who might become involved in your health care. If you enter a nursing home or hospital, have photocopies of your document placed in your medical records.
3. Be sure to talk to your agent and alternate agent(s), doctor(s), clergy, family and friends about your wishes concerning medical treatment. Discuss your wishes with them often, particularly if your medical condition changes.
4. If you want to make changes to your document after it has been signed and witnessed, you should complete a new document.
5. Remember, you can always revoke one or both sections of your California Advance Health Care Directive.

6. Be aware that your California document will not be effective in the event of a medical emergency. Ambulance personnel are required to provide cardiopulmonary resuscitation(CPR) unless they are given a separate order that states otherwise. These orders, commonly called "non-hospital do-not-resuscitate orders," are designed for people whose poor health gives them little chance of benefiting from CPR. These orders must be signed by your physician and instruct ambulance personnel not to attempt CPR if your heart or breathing should stop. Currently not all states have laws authorizing non-hospital do-not-resuscitate orders. Caring Connections does not distribute these forms. We suggest you speak to your physician.

If you would like more information about this topic contact Caring Connections or consult the Caring Connections booklet "Cardiopulmonary Resuscitation, Do-Not-Resuscitate Orders and End-Of-Life Decisions."

Figure 10–1 (continued)

CALIFORNIA ADVANCE HEALTH CARE DIRECTIVE
Explanation

You have the right to give instructions about your own health care. You also have the right to name someone else to make health care decisions for you. This form lets you do either or both of these things. It also lets you express your wishes regarding donation of organs and the designation of your primary physician. If you use this form, you may complete or modify all or any part of it. You are free to use a different form.

Part I of this form is a power of attorney for health care. Part 1 lets you name another individual as agent to make health care decisions for you if you become incapable of making your own decisions or if you want someone else to make those decisions for you now even though you are still capable. You may name an alternate agent to act for you if your first choice is not willing, able, or reasonably available to make decisions for you. (Your agent may not be an operator or employee of a community care facility or a residential care facility where you are receiving care, or an employee of the health care institution where you are receiving care, unless your agent is related to you, is your registered domestic partner, or is a co-worker. Your supervising health care provider can never act as your agent.)

Unless the form you sign limits the authority of your agent, your agent may make all health care decisions for you. This form has a place for you to limit the authority of your agent. You need not limit the authority of your agent if you wish to rely on your agent for all health care decisions that may have to be made. If you choose not to limit the authority of your agent, your agent will have the right to:

    (a) Consent or refuse consent to any care, treatment, service, or procedure to maintain, diagnose, or otherwise affect a physical or mental condition;

    (b) Select or discharge health care providers and institutions;

    (c) Approve or disapprove diagnostic tests, surgical procedures and programs of medication; and

    (d) Direct the provision, withholding, or withdrawal of artificial nutrition and hydration and all other forms of health care, including cardiopulmonary resuscitation;

    (e) Make anatomical gifts, authorize an autopsy, and direct the disposition of your remains.

Part 2 of this form lets you give specific instructions about any aspect of your health care, whether or not you appoint an agent. Choices are provided for you to express your wishes regarding the provision, withholding, or withdrawal of treatment to keep you alive, as well as the provision of pain relief. Space is provided for you to add to the choices you have made or for you to write out any additional wishes. If you are satisfied to allow your agent to determine what is best for you in making end-of-life decisions, you need not fill out part 2 of this form.

Part 3 of this form lets you express an intention to donate your bodily organs and tissues following your death.

Part 4 of this form lets you designate a physician to have primary responsibility for your health care. After completing this form, sign and date the form at the end. The form must be signed by two qualified witnesses or acknowledged before a notary public. Give a copy of the signed and completed form to your physician, to any other health care providers you may have, to any health care institution at which you are receiving care, and to any health-care agents you have named. You should talk to the person you have named as agent to make sure that he or she understands your wishes and is willing to take the responsibility.

You have the right to revoke this advance health care directive or replace this form at any time.

Figure 10–1   (continued)

PART 1: POWER OF ATTORNEY FOR HEALTH CARE

(1) DESIGNATION OF AGENT: I designate the following individual as my agent to make health care decisions for me:

_____

(Name of individual you choose as agent)

_____

(address) (city) (state) (zip code)

_____

(home phone) (work phone)

OPTIONAL: If I revoke my agent's authority or if my agent is not willing, able, or reasonably available to make a health-care decision for me, I designate as my first alternate agent:

_____

(Name of individual you choose as first alternate agent)

_____

(address) (city) (state) (zip code)

_____

(home phone) (work phone)

OPTIONAL: If I revoke the authority of my agent and first alternate agent or if neither is willing, able, or reasonably available to make a health care decision for me, I designate as my second alternate agent:

_____

(Name of individual you choose as second alternate agent)

_____

(address) (city) (state) (zip code)

_____

(home phone) (work phone)

(2) AGENT'S AUTHORITY: My agent is authorized to make all health care decisions for me, including decisions to provide, withhold, or withdraw artificial nutrition and hydration, and all other forms of health care to keep me alive, except as I state here:

_____

_____

_____

_____

(Add additional sheets if needed.)

Figure 10–1   (continued)

(3) WHEN AGENT'S AUTHORITY BECOMES EFFECTIVE: My agent's authority becomes effective when my primary physician determines that I am unable to make my own health care decisions unless I mark the following box. If I mark this box [ ], my agent's authority to make health care decisions for me takes effect immediately.

(4) AGENT'S OBLIGATION: My agent shall make health care decisions for me in accordance with this power of attorney for health care, any instructions I give in Part 2 of this form, and my other wishes to the extent known to my agent. To the extent my wishes are unknown, my agent shall make health care decisions for me in accordance with what my agent determines to be in my best interest. In determining my best interest, my agent shall consider my personal values to the extent known to my agent.

(5) AGENT'S POSTDEATH AUTHORITY: My agent is authorized to make anatomical gifts, authorize an autopsy, and direct disposition of my remains, except as I state here or in Part 3 of this form:

_____

_____

_____

_____

_____

(6) NOMINATION OF CONSERVATOR: If a conservator of my person needs to be appointed for me by a court, I nominate the agent designated in this form. If that agent is not willing, able, or reasonably available to act as conservator, I nominate the alternate agents whom I have named, in the order designated.

PART 2: INSTRUCTIONS FOR HEALTH CARE

If you fill out this part of the form, you may strike any wording you do not want.

(7) END-OF-LIFE DECISIONS: I direct that my health care providers and others involved in my care provide, withhold, or withdraw treatment in accordance with the choice I have marked below: (Initial only one box)
    [   ] (a) **Choice NOT To Prolong Life**
    I do not want my life to be prolonged if (1) I have an incurable and irreversible condition that will result in my death within a relatively short time, (2) I become unconscious and, to a reasonable degree of medical certainty, I will not regain consciousness, or (3) the likely risks and burdens of treatment would outweigh the expected benefits, OR
    [   ] (b) **Choice To Prolong Life**
    I want my life to be prolonged as long as possible within the limits of generally accepted health care standards.

(8) RELIEF FROM PAIN: Except as I state in the following space, I direct that treatment for alleviation of pain or discomfort should be provided at all times even if it hastens my death:

_____

_____

_____

_____

_____

Figure 10–1   (continued)

(9)   OTHER WISHES: (If you do not agree with any of the optional choices above and wish to write your own, or if you wish to add to the instructions you have given above, you may do so here.) I direct that:

_____

_____

_____

_____

_____

(Add additional sheets if needed.)

PART 3: DONATION OF ORGANS AT DEATH (OPTIONAL)

(10) Upon my death: (mark applicable box)

[   ] (a) I give any needed organs, tissues, or parts,

OR

[   ] (b) I give the following organs, tissues, or parts only

[   ] (c) My gift is for the following purposes: (strike any of the following you do not want)
   (1) Transplant
   (2) Therapy
   (3) Research
   (4) Education

PART 4: PRIMARY PHYSICIAN (OPTIONAL)

(11) I designate the following physician as my primary physician:

_____

(name of physician)

_____

(address) (city) (state) (zip code)

_____

(phone)

OPTIONAL: If the physician I have designated above is not willing, able, or reasonably available to act as my primary physician, I designate the following physician as my primary physician:

_____

(name of physician)

_____

(address) (city) (state) (zip code)

_____

(phone)

Figure 10–1   (continued)

(12) EFFECT OF COPY: A copy of this form has the same effect as the original.

(13) SIGNATURE: Sign and date the form here:

_____	_____
(date)	(sign your name)
_____	_____
(address)	(print your name)
_____	
(city) (state)	

(14) WITNESSES: This advance health care directive will not be valid for making health care decisions unless it is either:

    (1) signed by two (2) qualified adult witnesses who are personally known to you and who are present when you sign or acknowledge your signature; or

    (2) acknowledged before a notary public.

ALTERNATIVE NO. 1: STATEMENT OF WITNESSES

I declare under penalty of perjury under the laws of California (1) that the individual who signed or acknowledged this advance health care directive is personally known to me, or that the individual's identity was proven to me by convincing evidence, (2) that the individual signed or acknowledged this advance directive in my presence, (3) that the individual appears to be of sound mind and under no duress, fraud or undue influence, (4) that I am not a person appointed as an agent by this advance directive, and (5) that I am not the individual's health care provider, an employee of the individual's health care provider, the operator of a community care facility, an employee of an operator of a community care facility, the operator of a residential care facility for the elderly, nor an employee of an operator of a residential care facility for the elderly.

First Witness:

_____	_____
(date)	(signature of witness)
_____	_____
(address)	(printed name of witness)
_____	
(city) (state)	

Second Witness:

_____	_____
(date)	(signature of witness)
_____	_____
(address)	(printed name of witness)
_____	
(city) (state)	

Figure 10–1   (continued)

ADDITIONAL WITNESS STATEMENT

I further declare under penalty of perjury under the laws of California that I am not related to the individual executing this advance health care directive by blood, marriage, or adoption, and, to the best of my knowledge, I am not entitled to any part of the individual's estate upon his or her death under a will now existing or by operation of law.

_____   _____
(date)   (signature of witness)

_____   _____
(address)   (printed name of witness)

_____
(city) (state)

ALTERNATIVE NO. 2: NOTARY PUBLIC

State of California   )
)SS.
County of _____)

On _____ before me, _____
                                               (insert name of notary public)

personally appeared _____,
                                               (insert the name of principal)

personally known to me (or proved to me on the basis of satisfactory evidence) to be the person whose name is subscribed to the within instrument and acknowledged that he/she executed the same in his/her authorized capacity and that by his/her signature on the instrument the person upon behalf of which the person acted, executed the instrument.

WITNESS my hand and official seal.

NOTARY SEAL _____
                                                 (signature of notary)

STATEMENT OF PATIENT ADVOCATE OR OMBUDSMAN

I declare under penalty of perjury under the laws of California that I am a patient advocate or ombudsman as designated by the State Department of Aging and that I am serving as witness as required by section 4675 of the Probate Code.

_____   _____
(date)   (signature)

_____   _____
(address)   (printed name)

_____
(city) (state)

Courtesy of Caring Connections
1700 Diagonal Road, Suite 625, Alexandria, VA 22314
www.caringinfo.org, 800/658-8898

sick, and dying people can be cared for and comforted. The modern hospice does not deal with acute cases or with emergency medical care; rather, it seeks to help terminally ill patients live as comfortably and meaningfully as they can until they die. The hospice approach involves seven different aspects of patient care. A close examination of these will help to clarify how hospices differ from hospitals and other medical facilities.

Comforting and Caring for Patients. First of all, the hospice approach emphasizes "comforting and caring" for patients rather than "curing and healing" them. As I mentioned earlier, there comes a time in every terminal illness when the possibility of curing patients of their diseases no longer exists. At this point, medical care should not be discontinued, nor should patients and their families be abandoned; rather, the medical care should shift from curing and healing to comforting and caring for the patients. The emphasis here is on *appropriate* medical treatment, which involves pain and symptom control and assistance at all levels to patients and their families until the patients die; it also means continued assistance, when needed, to the patients' families after they have died.

A Team Approach. Recognizing that human beings have dimensions beyond the physical, which is the basic focus of medicine, the hospice approach utilizes a team concept in its care for the dying. The team includes patients, their family and friends, other patients, doctors, nurses, clergy, social workers, physical and occupational therapists, psychologists or psychiatrists, and volunteers. Because sickness, dying, and death involve all dimensions of people, their mental, emotional, social, and religious needs must be met along with the physical needs. The assumption is that dying patients and their families must have total care to get through what often is a difficult time.

Pain and Symptom Control. The hospice approach recognizes that there is a difference between "acute pain" and "chronic pain." Acute pain is that which will eventually disappear—for example, the pain one feels after surgery. Chronic pain, on the other hand, is pain that not only will remain but also is likely to get worse. Obviously, a completely different approach to controlling pain must be used when dealing with the chronic type. Second, the hospice approach recognizes that pain, especially chronic pain, is a complex phenomenon that involves the mental or emotional, the social or sociological, and the spiritual or religious aspects of patients as well as the physical. This is another reason why the hospice approach utilizes a team; there is a basic recognition that social pain can be helped by social workers, mental and emotional pain can be alleviated by psychologists or psychiatrists, and spiritual pain can be eased by clergy.

Once chronic pain has been seen for what it is, a "preventive" rather than a "reactive" approach to pain control should be used. For example, once a terminal cancer patient begins to suffer pain, the method of pain control should not be to wait until the moment the pain returns, thus "reacting" to the pain symptoms; rather, the patient's pain should be prevented from occurring. Pain medication should be given to patients orally wherever possible so as not to further aggravate already existing pain with hypodermic needles, and the method of pain control must be examined daily to ensure that it fits each patient's individual needs. A more detailed description of the hospice approach to pain control may be found in Sandol Stoddard's *The Hospice Movement.*[9]

Outpatient and Home Care. Because dying patients do not as a rule need extraordinary medical care, they often can be treated at home. Whenever possible, the hospice approach encourages dying patients to remain at home, offering both patients and their families total care and support from the entire team whenever it is needed. This brings greater "comfort" to the patients by allowing them to stay in familiar surroundings with their families and their own favorite belongings around them. The key to this type of care, of course, is that complete support and care must be made available by the team. One of the reasons more people have not chosen to die at home, especially in our country, is that there has not been support available to patients and their families, and families aren't always able to cope alone with all of the problems that surround the dying of a loved one. If the support is there, however, then the home often is the place where patients receive the best care and are the most comfortable.

Humanized Inpatient Care. When home care coupled with outpatient care is not feasible—and many times it is not—humanized, homelike, comfortable inpatient facilities should be available. Patients should be placed in wards so that they can relate to others in similar situations. The rooms should be warmly decorated and should have large floor-to-ceiling curtained windows and at least partial carpeting. Patients should be allowed to have their own familiar belongings around them (easy chairs, plants—even pets, where feasible), and visiting hours should be liberal, with no restrictions on age so that children can visit their parents and grandparents. Food and drink of the patients' choice (including alcoholic beverages if desired) ought to be available. And, finally, patients should be kept pain- and symptom-free and be given loving care, but they should be spared the intrusion of extraordinary or inappropriate medical technology, such as intravenous lines, respirators, and so on.

Freedom from Financial Worry. All hospice care, in- or outpatient, should be performed on a nonprofit basis. Where available, existing medical insurance, private or government, should pay for as much as possible, but no hospice patient should be refused treatment because of lack of finances. Nor should patients be dunned for money. Many hospices will tell patients and their families how much their care costs and ask them if they can contribute anything toward their care, but usually they are asked only once and never refused treatment because they have no money. Hospices derive their financial support mainly from fund-raising activities, grants, and donations or memorial gifts. Also, it has been proved that keeping dying patients at home on an outpatient basis or even in hospice facilities is far less expensive than keeping them in convalescent homes or acute care hospitals. This is not the main reason that one should consider the hospice approach, however; rather, what is impressive is the humane and compassionate care it provides for dying patients and their families.

Bereavement Counseling and Assistance. Helping dying patients and their families to adjust to the fact of death before, during, and after its occurrence is an important part of the hospice approach. This is yet another reason that the team approach is used—so that social workers, clergy, trained volunteers, and other nonmedical members of the team can aid medical personnel in caring for the entire family unit. Too often in our society the patient is cared for and the family is forgotten. When the patient dies, however, the grieving family remains, and often its members experience tremendous difficulty when dealing with the death of their loved one. If the family *and* the patient can be treated as a unit during the dying period, then much of the difficulty that might occur after the patient dies can be averted—that is, family members can go through at least some of their mourning while the patient is still with them.

Some Concluding Comments. The hospice approach allows patients to die their own natural deaths in peace and dignity and with the full support of their families, friends, the medical community, and society in general. Because two of the main reasons for mercy death and mercy killing are to "put people out of their pain, suffering, misery" and to end lives that allegedly have no meaning, the hospice approach obviates the need for such measures in most instances. If patients can die in peace and dignity, free from pain and suffering, they will have no need to commit suicide, assisted or otherwise, or have their "lives of despair" terminated for them. The reasons for mercy death and mercy killing have not been completely eliminated, but a humane alternative does exist in many of those cases that might call for such drastic measures.

Cases for Study and Discussion

The followingc cases should be studied together because they have a number of elements in common. Some discussion questions related to the two cases are presented after the second case description.

CASE 1 Down Syndrome Child with Intestinal Blockage

A 38-year-old nurse gave birth to a baby girl who had both Down syndrome (a disease that involves mental retardation) and an intestinal blockage. This type of birth often occurs in women over age 35. The nurse and her husband agreed that the child's existence would be poor in quality because of her mental retardation, and, knowing that she would die if the intestinal blockage weren't removed, they refused to sign a permit for surgery to remove the blockage and told the doctors to do nothing to save their daughter. The doctors and the hospital agreed that the parents had the right to make this decision, so the child was left in the nursery to die. After 11 days, she died of starvation.

CASE 2 Down Syndrome Child with Heart Defect

Another woman, age 42, was rushed to the hospital to have her baby, but the little girl was born in the car on the way to the hospital. The child was born with Down syndrome, intestinal blockage, and a hole in her heart that made it very difficult for her to breathe. The woman and her husband already had three children and had not planned for this one. Because of these problems, they also had both financial and marital difficulties. They refused to sign the permission form the doctors needed in order to remove the intestinal blockage, saying that even if the little girl survived this surgery, she still would have to have heart surgery later on. Furthermore, they said that if she managed to survive the heart surgery, she would still be severely mentally retarded. The doctors disagreed with the parents, and after obtaining a court injunction allowing them to operate, they removed the blockage. The parents did not even name their daughter, and they refused to take her home until the pressure put upon their other children by their peers forced them to do so. A year later the little girl was still alive, but because of her heart defect she often had to gasp for breath. The parents were so unhappy with the situation that the mother even contemplated smothering the infant with a pillow, but she could not bring herself to do it. The family's financial situation was deteriorating, and the mother was concerned because the longer they kept the baby, the more everyone in the family was becoming attached to her and the harder it would be for them all if the baby were to die. The parents blamed the doctors and the judge who handed down the injunction for creating this nearly unbearable situation.

Some questions for study and discussion

1. Both of these cases are quite similar except that the second baby has an additional serious defect, the hole in her heart. Should this make a difference?
2. Which set of medical personnel do you feel did the "right thing"? Explain your answer, giving specific reasons.
3. How would you resolve the conflicts among the following rights involved in these two cases?
   (a) The right of the babies, regardless of their problems, to medical care that could save their lives.
   (b) The right of parents to decide whether their defective or deformed babies should be allowed to live, when, in the past, they would not have lived because our medical technology was less advanced.
   (c) The doctors' and hospitals' right to save lives when they know they can.
   (d) The conflicting rights of society to (1) protect its members (in this case, the babies) and allow them to live and (2) not be burdened with defective and deformed children when the omission of extraordinary care would allow the children to die of natural causes.
4. In The first case, how do you feel about the fact that the baby was left for 11 days to die of starvation? Do you feel she should have been immediately and painlessly killed instead, or do you feel she should have been operated on regardless of the parents' wishes?
5. If parents do not wish to take the responsibility of raising children who have defects and deformities, do you feel society as a whole has an obligation to give such

parents extensive financial and social aid in raising the children, or to assume the responsibility for raising such children itself?

6. If society or the parents have to institutionalize such children in places where bare maintenance is all the children receive, do you think it would be better to allow the children to die, as in the first case?

7. To what extent do you think that not performing what is a relatively simple and safe surgery on a deformed or defective child amounts to unfair discrimination against handicapped children?

CASE 3 A Man Who Beat His 11-Year-Old Stepdaughter Wants Say in Keeping Her on Life Support

A man accused of beating his 11-year-old stepdaughter to the point where she is in a persistent vegetative state asked judges on the case to allow him to have a say in continuing or discontinuing life support. She is currently on a respirator and a stomach feeding tube. The judges were sceptical about his request. If the judges have the respirator and the feeding tube removed, one interesting consequence is that if the girl dies, then the stepfa-ther could be tried for murder. If you were a judge on this case, how would you rule? Are there any circumstances where you might rule in the man's favour? What would they be?[10]

Mercy Death

As stated at the beginning of this chapter, the phrase "mercy death" means a *direct* action taken to terminate someone's life at his or her request—it amounts to an assisted suicide. Patients, often because they are in pain or because they just do not want to live longer, ask to have their lives ended immediately, usually by some painless means. The motives for such a request vary. Often such patients do not feel they will have the courage to commit suicide and want someone to help them, whereas at other times patients are not able to end their own lives because they either are paralyzed or are too weak to do it themselves. In any case, however, these patients want to be mercifully put to death, not just allowed to die.

I have made a distinction between allowing to die and mercy death, but in the New York U.S. Circuit Court of Appeals ruling, cited earlier in this chapter, the court did not find that suicide was a constitutional right but that New York failed to honor the constitutional guarantee of equal protection under the law. According to the court's ruling, patients on life-support equipment are allowed to hasten their deaths by instructing doctors to turn equipment off, but patients wanting lethal medication are denied it; therefore, the court ruled that any distinction as to the way in which a person chooses to end his own life constitutes irrational and unjustifiably unequal treatment under the law. This raises serious questions about mercy death to be discussed later.[11]

Arguments Against Mercy Death

Many of the same arguments used against suicide are applicable to mercy death, at least to some extent, but the issues surrounding mercy death are further complicated by the fact that someone else has to do the killing. Let us examine the arguments used against suicide as they apply to mercy death.

The Irrationality of Mercy Death. This argument may have less force here than when it is applied to suicide for people are more likely to accept as rational a decision to die when the person making the decision is to die soon anyway and/or when his or her life at the time of the decision is full of pain, suffering, and misery. Furthermore, even when people who request mercy death are not in imminent danger of dying, their lives may now be so radically altered that they would rather not live anymore (for example, a physically active person who will be permanently paralyzed from the neck down because of a serious accident). Despite these mitigating factors, however, the argument against mercy death goes on to say that people who are suffering and in pain are in such a state of fear and depression that they simply cannot make rational decisions. If these people will patiently wait to see what therapy and medical science can do for them, the argument continues, perhaps they will adjust to their situation and change their minds about dying.

The criticism of this argument is that many requests for mercy death have come from people who have tried for some time to live with their tragic situation and have still decided that death is preferable to a limited life. Also, it is difficult to argue that because a person is suffering he or she cannot make a rational decision in favor of death.

The Religious Argument. The religious argument applies to mercy death in much the same way as it does to suicide. Indeed, it gains force in this case from the fact that a second person must do the killing, which, in religious terms, is even worse than suicide. The religious argument maintains that killing is killing, regardless of the motive, and states that no one has the right to take innocent people's lives, even at their request.

This argument is further supported by many of our laws. It is true that most states and countries have repealed those laws designating suicide as illegal, but many of them still have laws against helping others to commit suicide. People who do this can, in fact, be charged as accessories to murder. Mercy death does fit our earlier definition of "murder" except that the phrase "especially with malice aforethought" does not apply. Furthermore, it differs from murder in that it is not done against the will of the "victim."

In addition to the criticisms already presented in rebuttal to the religious argument against suicide, there is another criticism we can consider: It is precisely the difference in motive that makes mercy death morally acceptable, especially because the person to be put to death agrees to his or her own death and requests it. Most killings are committed from motives of greed, revenge, anger, hate, or viciousness; mercy death, on the other hand, is done out of love and mercy for a person who is suffering.

The Domino Argument. Both the domino argument and the criticisms of it apply here in much the same way as they do to suicide, war, and capital punishment. Those who argue against mercy death, however, believe that the domino effect that results from permitting mercy death can be much more pernicious than in those other cases. It is obvious, they say, that if mercy death, which is performed at a person's request, is authorized or given moral sanction, the next step will be mercy killing; that is, decisions for death will be made by others for those unable to request death for themselves. Once we open the door for the one, they say, it is open for the other. As I have mentioned before, this is a possibility that should concern us. It is also possible, however, to legally allow mercy deaths and not mercy killings, just as it is legally possible to permit the allowing of someone to die (as does the California Natural Death Act described earlier) without condoning either mercy death or mercy killing.

The Justice Argument. Here again, many of the same arguments that apply to suicide apply also to mercy death. There are some additional problems, however. For example, is it just for people to ask others to kill them? Doesn't this place a terrific burden of guilt and depression on the person who has to perform the act? And what about the feelings of guilt and loss on the part of the family members? Won't they always wonder whether something more should have been done, perhaps on their part, to help the person live? There is no doubt that mercy death places a greater burden on others than suicide does.

The Possibility of Finding Cures. The arguments here are much like those presented in the discussion of allowing someone to die, and they are best characterized by the cliché, "Where there's life, there's hope." The counterarguments also are the same, with the additional criticism that many patients who request mercy death either feel they have no chance of being cured or find the wait for a cure too painful to bear.

The Hospice Alternative. In his article "Euthanasia," Dr. Richard Lamerton has said, "If anyone really wants euthanasia, he must have pretty poor doctors and nurses."[12] He might just as easily have said that the patient must be receiving pretty poor medical care from the entire society. According to the hospice argument, because we already know that the hospice approach will work, we should exert our efforts in that direction rather than in trying to discover how we can morally and legally justify mercy death or mercy killing. Under the five principles, the hospice approach reveres, preserves, and protects human life; it promotes goodness by giving pleasure and avoiding pain, by creating harmony, by making lives as excellent as they can be, and by allowing and encouraging creativity at whatever level is possible; it provides for honesty and truth telling by dealing with the patients where and as they are and relating to them as real and whole human beings, not merely as diseased bodies; and it gives patients and their families the freedom to enjoy life and each other for whatever time is left, while at the same time allowing them the freedom of a truly dignified death, not by killing but by compassionate treatment.

It seems obvious, then, that if all of these things can be done to alleviate pain and misery and meaninglessness in people's lives, and if the hospice approach can be made the rule rather than the exception, then the need for mercy death or mercy killing should be decreased a great deal, if not eliminated entirely.

The criticism of this argument is that there may be some patients who do not want any further treatment of any kind, in a hospice or elsewhere, and who choose death rather than a limited life. Furthermore, there are those to whom the hospice approach doesn't really apply—for example, paraplegics, quadriplegics, victims of paralysis, and other patients who suffer from extremely debilitating chronic, but not necessarily terminal, diseases. In the opinion of such patients, the alternative of mercy death is still viable.

Arguments for Mercy Death

Individual Freedom and Rights. The main argument for individual freedom and rights, as in the suicide issue, is the argument that people ought to have the right to decide when their lives should end. If they choose not to live any longer and request to die, we should oblige them, recognizing that they have made a free, rational choice. All we are doing is carrying out their decisions in a spirit of love, compassion, and mercy.

The difference between mercy death and suicide, however, is that in the case of mercy death we are asked to end their lives for them, and this can certainly be seen as an infringement upon our rights and freedom. I remember hearing a doctor expressing this point of view on a television documentary called *Right to Die.* The doctor said, "You have the right to choose death for yourself, but you do not have the right to involve *me* in your choice."

Human Rights versus Animal Rights. Another argument states that just as we are generally willing to put animals out of their misery when they suffer, so we should accord our fellow humans, who certainly are of higher worth to us, the same consideration. Furthermore, because they have asked us for death, we should have no compunction about ending their lives mercifully.

The main criticism of this argument is that the rights of human beings to live or die are not in any way the same as those of animals. Western religions, of course, maintain that human beings have immortal souls, but even nonreligious humanists talk about the "human spirit," or personality, stating that it should be accorded a greater respect than the mere physical self.

A counterargument to this is, "Yes, humans and animals are different, but above all this should mean that humans have free will and therefore should be able to decide for themselves whether or not they should end their own lives with or without assistance."

Changes in Attitudes Toward Mercy Death

Several events reflect a change in attitude toward mercy death.

Active Advocates for Mercy Death. As has been stated earlier, presently mercy death is illegal in many of the 50 states and in most countries of the world, but there is strong advocacy not only for allowing people to die their own natural deaths, but also for allowing people to be assisted by doctors in committing suicide when they no longer feel that their lives are worth living (mostly, but not always, when their illnesses are terminal). Two men—Derek Humphry and Dr. Jack Kevorkian—have been active in furthering the cause of mercy death, or assisted suicide.

Derek Humphry is an Englishman, now residing in the United States. In 1975 Humphry, while still living in England, assisted his first wife, Jean, in committing suicide when she was dying of cancer. This was perhaps a somewhat strange action because both of them resided in the country where the modern day hospice was brought to life. Humphry wrote a book about it called *Jean's Way.* In 1980 in California, Humphry founded the Hemlock Society, which is famous for two things: (1) working to change laws so that doctors can legally help terminally ill patients to commit suicide and (2) giving advice to people who have decided to die on their own when doctors cannot or will not help.

The Hemlock Society attempted to introduce legislation in both California and Washington that would legalize assisted suicide, but both measures failed. After these failures, Humphry and his second wife wrote *The Right to Die: Understanding Euthanasia* in 1986. He then wrote his most famous and best-selling book, *Final Exit*, in 1991, which, as *Playboy* described it in its interview with Humphry, "is nothing short of the last self-help book you'll ever need."[13] He has published a fourth book, *Dying with Dignity: Understanding Euthanasia*. Humphry is currently assisting a group called Californians Against Human Suffering with their initiative, which was on the ballot in California in November 1992 and did not pass.

Dr. Jack Kevorkian from Detroit, Michigan, is much more famous and controversial than is Humphry. A retired pathologist, Kevorkian has helped over 130 people to commit suicide, few of whom, interestingly enough, could have been classified as terminally ill. He has been brought to trial several times and acquitted of assisting suicide. It should be noted that in all of these cases, Dr. Kevorkian provided the means, but the people themselves administered their own suicides. However, on September 17, 1998, Dr. Kevorkian helped Thomas Youk, suffering with Lou Gehrig's Disease (ALS), to die and videotaped the whole event. He then went on television during *60 Minutes* and showed the whole event and answered questions as well. He was found guilty and sentenced to jail for taking Mr. Youk's life and is currently serving out his sentence in prison. He will probably not live out his sentence.

Court Decisions. There is only one physician-assisted suicide law in effect in the United States. It is the "Death with Dignity" law in Oregon, first passed in 1994, prevented from going into effect by a court injunction, reaffirmed by voters in November 1997, after which it finally went into effect. Interestingly, a study was done in its first year of 1998, and the fears surrounding the passing of the law were discovered to be unfounded. Only 15 terminally ill people used it to end their lives without suffering any painful, lingering deaths that opponents had warned about.[14]

Pending Legislation. Even though the Oregon law seems to be working to its people's satisfaction, the House of Representatives recently passed a bill that would make it a federal crime to prescribe drugs to help terminally ill patients end their lives. A similar bill is now in the Senate, but has not yet reached the floor. In addition, the American Medical Association (AMA) recently voted to back such legislation. Needless to say, Oregon lawmakers have expressed outrage at the federal government's attempt to usurp Oregon's right as a state to keep such a hard-won law, which seems to be working. There is a definite controversy between what many people desire and the government and doctors who are against it. Interestingly, it is the Republican party, currently in office that is fighting to kill the Oregon bill. This party has always supported states' rights but attacks them in its attempts to kill the bill.

Lack of Autonomy of Patients in Medical Care. Dr. Christopher Meyers, director of the Kegley Institute of Ethics at California State University, Bakersfield, California and an expert in medical ethics who consults with Bakersfield area hospitals, stated in an article in the *Bakersfield Californian* newspaper ". . . who other than a truly desperate person would choose to spend his or her final moments in the back of a Volkswagen van sucking on carbon monoxide, as many of his [Dr. Kevorkian's] clients have done? What could create such desperation? A realization that soon one will be facing pain and loss of identity and dignity, with little or no control over either the disease process or how one's final days are to be lived." He goes on to say that physicians and pharmacists have a monopolistic control over pain medication, and physicians also have the same kind of control over drugs that might hasten death and medical technologies that can vastly improve a dying person's quality of life: "The point is, when one is gravely ill and/or in need of hospitalization, nearly all aspects of personal control are lost."[15]

Dr. Meyers abhors the fact that patients in need of autonomous relief have to turn to a man of such questionable taste and judgment as Dr. Kevorkian, but he also sees no future remedy of the medical establishment granting autonomy to its patients. He therefore believes that physician-assisted suicide should be made a legal option. He enumerates several safeguards that will be discussed later.

Health Care Personnel Have Practiced Forms of Assisted Suicide. It is certainly not unknown that some doctors in the United States and other countries of the world (e.g., Holland, Sweden) have at times practiced some form of assisted suicide. A recent controversial study of 850 nurses revealed that 141 of them had received requests from patients or family members to engage in assisted suicide. One hundred and twenty-nine of these said they had carried out these practices at least once, and 35 said they had hastened a patient's death by only pretending to carry out life-sustaining treatment that had been ordered.[16] Despite the inconclusiveness of the study and the small sampling of nurses surveyed, the answers of the nurses are indicative of their need to help patients when they are in pain, deteriorating, and dying. Some nurses have said that, if the real facts were known, the figures would be much higher than reported.

Strong Desire for Greater Autonomy and Control over Life and Death. There is and has been over the last 10 years a greater desire on the part of people who are suffering painful, deteriorating or terminal illnesses to have autonomous control over their bodies and lives. For instance, one of the people who was assisted in suicide by Dr. Kevorkian was a woman, 43 years old, who had discovered that she had Alzheimer's disease. She wanted to die before she had to suffer as her mental condition deteriorated. Several of Kevorkian's "patients" had muscular dystrophy and were tired of trying to live such a limited handicapped existence. None of these people was a terminal case, but many patients who are terminal, due to cancer and other fatal diseases, also have requested the right to choose not to suffer any further and want to be able to have physicians help them die.

Suggested Safeguards for Mercy Death

Whether or not any of us believes that mercy death is morally justified, it seems inevitable that in the future, near or distant, it will become partially or completely legal. It is important, therefore, that some careful legal safeguards be proposed before this happens; otherwise, ethics and the law may be caught by surprise, as they have been already by the actions of Dr. Kevorkian and the two circuit courts of appeals' decisions. Besides, as columnist Ellen Goodman has said: "Most Americans support legal, assisted suicide—as I do—for the most personal of reasons. We just might want it someday."[17]

Safeguards in the Oregon Law. The Oregon law allows doctors to write prescriptions for aware adult, terminally ill patients who have asked for them both orally and in writing. There is a 15-day waiting period, two witnesses and a second doctor are required; patients must be informed about other options, and they must take the drugs themselves. On January 17, 2006, the Supreme Court voted to uphold Oregon's physician-assisted suicide law.

Safeguards Proposed by Dr. Meyers. In Dr. Christopher Meyers's discussion of the lack of autonomy problem and physician-assisted suicide, he has presented several safeguards:

> (1) The first request for death assistance must occur at least two months prior to the provision of such assistance; (2) the request must be repeated twice more in two-day and one-week intervals; (3) all requests must be initiated by the patient and cannot come as the result of a question from any other party; (4) all requests must be witnessed in writing by someone who has no economic interest in the patient's life or death and who can attest that the request appears to be made by a competent person who is not under undue influence from medications or from pressure from family or loved ones; and (5) the request for death assistance must be reversible at anytime. The patient must be informed that such a reversal, if it were requested during the death-assisting procedure, could worsen his or her medical condition.[18]

Russell's Safeguards. O. Ruth Russell, in her article "Moral and Legal Aspects of Euthanasia," published in 1974 in the *Humanist* magazine, states her belief that (1) any law legalizing physician-assisted suicide should be permissive rather than mandatory or compulsory; (2) there can be no secrecy; (3) there has to be a written, notarized request; (4) an advisory panel is to be used; (5) several doctors must be involved; (6) a waiting period will be required; and (7) it will be a criminal offense to falsify any documents, coerce patients or next of kin, or perform any malpractice involving any act of euthanasia.[19]

Evaluation of Safeguards

Most of the above safeguards are significant, but some are more necessary than others, and there may be additional ones that should be included. I believe that the following safeguards should be a part of any law that permits physician-assisted suicide.

Permissive Rather than Compulsory or Mandatory. Any law that authorizes physician-assisted suicide should, of course, be permissive rather than mandatory. No one but the person desiring assistance or his or her designated agent should request it. Further, no one should be forced or coerced in any way to request such assistance, and physicians or other health care personnel should not be required to carry out any such request against the dictates of their moral conscience.

A Written Request. There must be no secrecy involved. Everything must be done in the open and aboveboard. Any such request should be made in writing by the person requesting assisted suicide, and this request should be witnessed by disinterested persons and notarized. An advanced directive could be used for this purpose, or additional pages or sections could be added to them, although I do believe that such requests must be notarized. Any such request can be revoked by the patients or their designated agents at any time, either orally or in writing, but patients should be warned, as Dr. Meyers suggests, that revocations after the process has begun may result in the worsening of the patients' condition.

A Waiting Period. There should be a waiting period, and I believe that Dr. Meyers's suggestion of two months, from the time of request to actually providing assisted suicide, is a fair one. I also agree with the necessity of repeating the request two days later and one week later, and I would add, one month later as well. There could be places provided on any form used where patients or their agents could repeat or verify the initial request. Before and during this waiting period, other options, such as hospice care, appropriate pain control, and whatever other appropriate care is available should be carefully explained.

Counseling. Also, before and during the waiting period, a trained counselor should be made available to aid patients in making their decisions and to ensure that they are rationally competent to request assisted suicide and are not being forced or coerced in any way by families, friends, or health care personnel. If there is a serious question of mental competency, psychiatrists or psychologists could be called in to present their findings.

More Than One Doctor. More than one doctor should be involved in the diagnosis and prognosis of patients' illnesses and lives, and patients will have to be fully informed concerning their condition.

Any Abuse of Safeguards Punishable as a Criminal Offense. Any coercion of patients or next of kin, falsification of documents, or performance of any malpractice involving any act of mercy death should be deemed criminal offenses punishable by law.

Assisted Suicide Should Be Painless. It should go without saying that any mercy death or assisted suicide should be painless (which is why physicians should administer it) and performed in a comfortable, pleasant place of the patient's choice.

Other Possible Safeguards. Additional safeguards could involve having a judge or court commissioner approve the mercy death after hearing and seeing all of the evidence including the patient's own words if that is feasible. If not, then the words of patients' families and designated agents should be heard. Also, there could be, as Ms. Russell has suggested, a panel or committee, such as a bioethics committee, of disinterested persons, that could hear and see all of the evidence and advise all those involved. Either of these, especially the court situation, could prove to be restrictive of patients' autonomy, but either certainly would make it harder for a questionable mercy death to be carried out.

Concluding Remarks on Mercy Death

I want to reiterate that I am not advocating mercy death or physician-assisted suicide but merely making suggestions for safeguards in the event it is legalized. What would pretty much eliminate the need for these actions is an expansion of the hospice approach, especially as it involves pain and symptom control. It is my belief that if suffering people, terminal or otherwise, were rendered as free as possible of pain and discomfort, there would be less need for mercy death, physician-assisted or otherwise. Yet to establish a more sensible approach to pain and symptom control would require radical changes in the training of physicians and to a lesser extent pharmacists. These professionals would then have to give autonomy to those patients and their families who are now in real need of such control. Dr. Meyers and I think it unlikely that such changes will take place in the near future, and as long as they don't, people will continue to request assisted suicide and to seek out people such as Dr. Kevorkian. If mercy death is to be allowed and legalized, then there needs to be a guarantee that it will be conducted as morally and legally as possible.

Cases for Study and Discussion

CASE 1 Man Trapped by Fire in His Car

A truck overturns on one of our major highways, and the engine catches on fire, engulfing the cab, where the driver is trapped. A highway patrol officer arrives on the scene and realizes that no one can get near enough to the cab to get the driver out. The driver sees the patrolman and begs the officer to shoot him so that he won't have to suffer the horror of burning to death. The officer is close enough to kill him instantly. What should he or she do?

CASE 2 Paralysed Brother Wanting to Die

A 24-year-old man named Robert who has a wife and child is paralyzed from the neck down in a motorcycle accident. He has always been very active and hates the idea of being paralyzed. He also is in a great deal of pain, and he has asked his doctors and other members of his family to "put him out of his misery." After several days of such pleading, his brother comes into Robert's hospital ward and asks him if he is sure he still wants to be put out of his misery. Robert says yes and pleads with his brother to kill him. The brother kisses and blesses Robert and then takes out a gun and shoots him, killing him instantly. The brother later is tried for murder and acquitted by reason of temporary insanity. Was what Robert's brother did moral? Do you think he should have been brought to trial at all? Do you think he should have been acquitted? Would you do the same for a loved one if you were asked?

CASE 3 67-year-old Woman Wanting to Die

A 67-year-old woman has been sick for the last 10 years with heart, lung, and kidney problems that have given her a great deal of pain and discomfort. In her own words, her life is "a misery" and "not worth living." Her children all are grown, and she lives alone with her husband, who is 68. She has talked with him on several occasions during the past two years, begging him to help her to die. She has told him that she is tired of living and that she gets no pleasure from her life anymore. On this particular morning, they discuss her life and death for four hours, and again and again she begs him to help her to die. Finally he gives in to her wishes and takes her out to the garage, puts her in their car, turns on the engine with the garage door closed, and goes back into the house for about an hour. At the end of the hour, he takes her out of the car, calls the police, and tells them what he has done. They arrive on the scene and arrest him for murder. Did the husband do the right thing? Did the wife have the right to request this action of her husband? Did he have an obligation to satisfy her request? Should he have been arrested?

CASE 4 Dr. Kevorkian

As previously discussed, Dr. Kevorkian originally invented a suicide machine that he could hook up to an intravenous line that is inserted into a person's arm, so that the person can push a button or release a clamp and administer a fatal but painless dose of chemicals. More recently, he used carbon dioxide that the people can inhale until they die. Few of the people who used his machine or the carbon dioxide were terminally ill people. For example, one 43-year-old woman had just been diagnosed as having Alzheimer's disease, one had severe pelvic pain, and another had multiple sclerosis. Do you think that what he was doing was moral or immoral? Why? Would it make any difference to your decision if the people had been terminally ill? Do you agree with what was done to the doctor legally? Why or why not? If you were asked by someone you loved to help him or her die, and you had the means, like Dr. Kevorkian, to do so, what would you do? Why? Would you like doctors to have the right to assist people in committing suicide? Why or why not? Would the people have to be terminally ill, in your opinion, or not? Why?

Mercy Killing

Mercy killing is similar to mercy death in the sense that it involves a direct action taken in order to end someone's life; the difference is that mercy killing is not done at the person's request. People who perform mercy killing may assume that the person they are going to kill wants this act to be done, but they don't know for sure, nor do they have the person's explicit request or permission to perform the act. Very often the decision to go ahead with a mercy killing is based upon a belief that the "victim's" life is no longer worth living because he or she is existing as a mere mindless organism, not as a full human being.

Therefore, mercy killing can be defined as the termination of someone's life, without that person's explicit consent, by a direct means, from a motive of mercy; that is, in an attempt to end suffering and/or "a meaningless existence." Obviously, the greatest moral problem associated with mercy killing is that, as opposed to allowing someone to die mercy death, in this case the patient's consent cannot be obtained, nor can his or her desires be known for sure. "Mercy killers" must come to a decision about someone else's life without the person's permission or acquiescence.

Arguments Against Mercy Killing

Many of the arguments that have been used in relation to mercy death and allowing someone to die apply also to mercy killing. I will not repeat all of these arguments here but will try to emphasize the main aspect that distinguishes mercy killing from the other two categories; that is, the lack of consent on the part of the "victim."

Direct Violation of the Value of Life Principle. Mercy killing is a direct violation of the Value of Life principle, especially because, unlike defense of the innocent, war, and capital punishment, it usually involves taking the life of an innocent person. As in the mercy death situation, the argument here is that murder is murder regardless of motive; therefore, mercy killing is nothing less than premeditated murder. This argument is even more convincing here than in the case of mercy death because in this case people either haven't given or can't give their consent to having their lives terminated.

The Domino Argument. Because the consent of patients cannot be obtained, an outside decision about the worth, value, or meaning of their lives has to be made, and according to this argument against mercy killing, this sets a dangerous precedent. In the first place, who has the right to decide whether any person's life is worthy, has value, or is meaningful? What standards are to be used when making such a decision? Won't the sanctioning of such an action set a dangerous precedent for the elimination of old, senile people, for example, because they may be considered "useless" by a youth-oriented society? Can we allow such decisions to be made? If so, by whom should they be made? This is certainly one of the more serious problems related to mercy killing, and it is one that does not affect either allowing someone to die or mercy death to so great an extent. In both of the latter cases, the individual decides what the worth of his own life is, whereas in mercy killing one person decides for another.

The Possibility of Finding Cures. Both this argument, which states that mercy killing should not be authorized because cures may be found, and the criticism of this argument, are the same as those for allowing someone to die and mercy death.

Arguments for Mercy Killing

Mercy for the "Living Dead." The main argument for mercy killing is that it is not a violation of the Life principle because in most cases the people killed are not fully alive as human beings; rather, they are existing as mere organisms, a network of organs and cells. It is an act of mercy, a proponent of mercy killing might argue, to end the life of those people, who, although not "brain dead," have suffered 80 percent brain damage. Even if such people recover from their comas, the damage to their brains is so extensive that their lives will never again be normal. They will have a plantlike existence, exhibiting no personality or real human consciousness whatsoever; therefore, it is an act of mercy to end their existence.

The main criticism of this argument is that one actually is murdering such people. Because they cannot be declared dead under any acceptable medical or legal criteria, a dangerous precedent is set when someone is sanctioned to directly end their lives. It is one thing to allow them to die by refusing to use any extraordinary means to save them if they are attacked by pneumonia or kidney or heart failure; it is quite another, however, to directly murder them, even out of a motive of mercy.

Financial and Emotional Burdens. People with extensive brain damage, along with many other sick and injured people, are financial and emotional burdens upon their families and on society. Such burdens often are tremendous, and, some argue, they serve no significant purpose because patients in such situations gain absolutely nothing from their maintenance except the continuation of what is assumed to be a minimal and worthless existence.

The main criticism of this argument is that finances should not be a determining factor where human life is concerned. It is true that the emotional burden often is difficult to bear, but here again we should not sanction the sacrifice of one human life simply in order to ease the emotional burden upon another.

The Patient's Desire to Die. Another argument for mercy killing is that if patients with brain damage could communicate with us, they would say that they would rather be killed than linger on as burdens to their families and society or to exist as organisms without consciousness.

The main criticism here, however, is that we cannot *know* any of this for certain because the patients cannot communicate. It is possible that advance directives could be revised so as to include mercy killing as well as allowing someone to die, but it might be very difficult to get such documents legalized. Faced with such a directive, the state probably would feel that it had the obligation to preserve and protect human life rather than authorize the execution of innocent people, regardless of the status of their existence.

The Possibility of Establishing Legal Safeguards. One of the strongest arguments against both mercy death and mercy killing is that if such actions were sanctioned they undoubtedly would be abused. For example, if it were legal to perform mercy killing on people who had reached a certain point in their illness or a certain age, wouldn't such a law invite abuse by people who wanted such things as organs to transplant, inheritances, or the elimination of personal financial burdens, and couldn't it become an instrument of revenge or of other motives usually connected with killing that is not "mercy" oriented? As we have seen, it is possible to establish safeguards similar to those that have been suggested for mercy death or assisted suicide.

The main criticism of this argument is that although most of these safeguards provide for mercy death, few of them would be of any use in protecting people against mercy killing against their wills. Any legislation that would give power to the state or to certain individuals to take the lives of those who were too "unworthy" or too "useless" to live would be extremely hard to enforce, and there would be little protection for helpless, innocent human lives.

Cases for Study and Discussion

CASE 1 Abortion Baby Born Alive

A doctor who was performing a legal abortion on a woman five months pregnant noticed that the "aborted fetus" actually was alive, so he held the fetus's head inside the woman's vaginal canal until the fetus suffocated. The doctor's thinking was that the fetus was intended to be killed or born dead during the abortion, and that its being born alive was an error that could result in an unwanted or deformed child. Therefore, he felt that he had performed an act of mercy. What do you think about the doctor's action?

CASE 2 Sister Pulls the Plug on Her sister

Laura, a 19-year-old woman, fell into a coma because of an overdose of drugs and alcohol. She was given emergency treatment at a hospital and was placed on a respirator, which stabilized her breathing. She remained in a deep coma, and when she was tested by neurologists and neurosurgeons it was discovered that about 70 percent of her brain was irretrievably damaged. She was not brain dead, however: She reacted to pain, her eyes sometimes would open and her pupils contract, she would at times thrash about, and her EEG showed some brain activity. She was in a persistent vegetative state. Because she could not be pronounced dead in any medical or legal sense, the hospital and doctors refused to take her off the respirator or to stop any other treatments they were giving her. At one point Laura's sister was alone in the room with her and, thinking that Laura wouldn't want to live on in this way, she disconnected the respirator and caused her sister's death. Discuss in detail your reactions to the sister's decision.

CASE 3 Tay-Sachs Diseased Child

Before much was known about Tay-Sachs disease, Betty and Irv, a young Jewish couple, gave birth to a son who had this disease. They were told by their doctor that the boy would become very sick and slowly degenerate over a period of about a year, and then he would become blind and suffer convulsions. They were also told that there is absolutely no cure for the disease and that their son was sure to die. After watching the child for about six months Irv was not able to stand it any longer. He put a pillow over his son's face and suffocated him. Under these circumstances, do you feel that Irv was justified in performing a mercy killing? The couple wanted another child. Given that they have a one in four chance to produce another Tay-Sachs child, what should they do?

CASE 4 A 75-Year-Old Man Shoots His Wife Who Has Alzheimer's Disease

A 75-year-old man in Florida, a state containing many retired and sick senior citizens, shot his wife twice in a mercy killing. The wife was suffering from Alzheimer's disease and osteoporosis (a degenerative bone disease). The couple was well off because the husband was a retired engineer. He had hired several women to care for his wife, who often was disoriented, irritable, and confused. The wife did not deal well with these women and was constantly embarrassing her husband by showing up in public, sometimes half-dressed and confused. One day she sought him out at a condominium owners' meeting and was particularly confused and troublesome. He took her back to their condominium and sat her down on a couch. He then picked up a pistol he owned and shot her in the back of the head once and then a second time because he thought she might still be alive. The man was arrested for murder in the first degree, tried, convicted, and sentenced to a minimum of 25 years in prison (Florida law for a first-degree murder conviction).

Several points about this case should be noted: (1) There was no evidence that his wife had asked for death, nor that he had asked her if that was what she had wanted. (2) He showed very little remorse in court, stating that he believed he had acted morally. (3) The prosecuting attorney stated that the husband's sentencing was correct because allowing him to go unpunished would set a dangerous precedent in Florida: Any time confused or sick old people became hard to care for or deal with, someone could mercy kill them with impunity. (4) Despite being well off, at no time did the husband look into or attempt to place his wife in one of the many facilities established to care for Alzheimer's patients.

Because the husband was 75 and not well, many people, including his daughter, thought that his sentence should be commuted or that he should be pardoned because he would probably die in prison. His case was referred to a commission appointed by the governor to make recommendations concerning the husband's situation, but the commission ruled that he should remain in prison. Several years later the governor commuted his sentence, and he is now out of prison. Do you think that what the husband did was moral or immoral? Why? Do you think this case was handled correctly? Why or why not? Do you feel that the husband should have been prosecuted at all? Why or why not? Do you feel that he tried all available alternatives before killing his wife? If not, what should he have done? Do you think his sentence should have been commuted or not? Why? How is this case different from the preceding cases we looked at in the mercy death section of this chapter? Are the other cases more justifiable than this one? Why or why not?

Chapter Summary

I. Definition of terms
   A. *Euthanasia* is a confusing and ambiguous term because it is subject to emotionalism. The word originally meant "a good death." More recently it has come to mean mercy killing.
   B. Because this term is so confusing, it has been replaced in this book by three phrases: "allowing someone to die," "mercy death," and "mercy killing."
   C. Allowing someone to die involves both not starting curative treatment when no cure is possible and stopping treatment when it is no longer able to cure a dying patient. It means allowing a dying patient to die a natural death without any interference from medical science and technology.
   D. Mercy death is the taking of a direct action in order to terminate a patient's life because the patient has voluntarily requested it—essentially an assisted suicide.

E. Mercy killing is the taking of a direct action to terminate a patient's life without his or her permission.

F. It should be noted that neither mercy death nor mercy killing is legal in the United States or in most countries throughout the world.

G. Brain death occurs when a patient has a normal heartbeat and normal respiration but has suffered irreversible and total brain damage.

   1. The criteria for "brain death" are unreceptivity and unresponsiveness, no spontaneous movements or breathing, no reflexes, and a flat EEG.

   2. When patients are declared "brain dead," removing life-support equipment or stopping treatment obviously cannot be the cause of their death, so this does not constitute allowing someone to die, mercy death, or mercy killing.

H. Persistent Vegetative State (PVS) results from damage to the cerebral cortex, or neocortex, which controls the cognitive functions. A PVS patient is not brain dead but lacks, and will permanently lack, even those minimal functions that make a life human.

II. Allowing someone to die

   A. This problem has become more crucial in the twentieth and twenty-first centuries because of the availability of advanced lifesaving and life-supporting technology and procedures.

   B. There are a number of arguments against allowing someone to die.

      1. Some say it is tantamount to abandoning a dying person, though this need not be the case if we distinguish carefully between the "curing and healing" and "comforting and caring for" aspects of medicine.

      2. Cures may be found or miracle cures may occur.

      3. We can never choose death over life—we can never opt for death. Medicine must save lives, not end them. There is a difference, however, between accepting death as inevitable and choosing it.

      4. Some argue that allowing someone to die interferes with God's divine plan. One also can ask, however, which constitutes interference with God's plan: allowing someone to die when his or her time has come or prolonging the person's death? The argument can be used to support either side.

   C. There are a number of arguments for allowing someone to die.

      1. Individuals have rights over their own bodies, lives, and deaths. One also can argue, however, that their freedom is not unlimited.

      2. Patients have the right to refuse treatment, and we should not overrule this right—treatment often will not cure a particular patient, and sometimes it is worse than the disease.

      3. Allowing someone to die will shorten suffering; however, it also will shorten the person's life.

      4. Patients have the right to die with dignity. The phrase "dying with dignity," however, can cover up abandonment, mercy death, and mercy killing.

   D. Extraordinary means to keep people alive are those that involve a grave burden for oneself or another, and they vary according to circumstances involving persons, places, times, and cultures. Such measures as radical surgery, radiation therapy, respirators, and heart machines probably fall into this category when they are used merely to prolong dying.

   E. Ordinary means also are difficult to define, but for terminally ill patients they would include controlling pain and other symptoms as opposed to performing radical surgery or using respirators or heart machines.

   F. *Appropriate* or *inappropriate* care are perhaps more suitable terms than *ordinary* and *extraordinary* due to the confusion surrounding the latter terms. Thus, people could decide what would be appropriate or inappropriate care depending upon the particular situation of a patient.

    G. The Patient Self-Determination Act (PSDA), effective December 1991, was passed with a view to giving patients a number of rights:
        1. The right to considerate and respectful care.
        2. The right to make decisions involving their health care, including the following:
            (a) The right to accept or refuse treatment.
            (b) The right to formulate advance directives and appoint a surrogate to make health care decisions on their behalf.
        3. The right to the information they require in order to make treatment decisions.
    H. Advance directives.
        1. Three cases, the Quinlan, Cruzan, and Schiavo cases, were instrumental in raising the consciousness of many people concerning the need for advance directives.
        2. Various directives have been the living will and health care proxy, the California Natural Death Act Declaration, and the Durable Power of Attorney for Health Care (DPAHC).
        3. The Advance Health Care Directive (AHCD) passed by the California Legislature on July 1, 2000, which is the best advance directive I've seen so far.
    I. The hospice approach to care for the dying can solve most of the problems surrounding allowing someone to die, and often it can eliminate the necessity for mercy death and mercy killing.
        1. There is an emphasis upon comforting and caring for patients rather than upon curing and healing them.
        2. The team approach is utilized so as to provide support for patients and their families.
        3. Hospices take a unique approach to pain and symptom control.
            (a) They recognize the difference between acute and chronic pain.
            (b) They recognize that pain has four levels—physical, mental or emotional, sociological, and spiritual—and they attempt to treat all four levels.
            (c) They utilize the preventive rather than the reactive approach to pain control.
        4. They utilize outpatient and home care wherever possible, using the team approach to provide all levels of support.
        5. Where this is not possible, hospices provide homelike, humanized inpatient care in comfortable surroundings.
        6. They attempt to provide freedom from financial worry for patients and their families.
        7. They provide bereavement counseling before, during, and after a patient's death.
        8. This approach allows patients to experience a natural death in peace and dignity while receiving support from their families, friends, the medical community, and society in general.
        9. This approach also obviates most of the need for mercy death and mercy killing, at least so far as it concerns suffering, terminally ill patients.
III. Mercy death (voluntary dying or assisted suicide)
    A. The arguments against mercy death are much like those used against suicide except that in the case of mercy death the issue is further complicated by the fact that someone else has to do the killing.
        1. The argument of irrationality has less force here than in the case of suicide because of the patients' pain and suffering and because they are going to die soon anyway. However, one can legitimately ask whether patients in extreme pain and suffering can ever be rational in choosing death.
        2. The religious argument remains the same except that the situation is further complicated by the fact that someone else has to do the killing; the mercy motive, it is argued, does not justify murder.

3. The domino argument has additional force in that if mercy death is allowed, mercy killing may soon follow.
4. The justice argument in this case involves the guilt and other negative feelings of the person who has to do the killing, and it also involves the burden of guilt placed on family members because they couldn't do anything to prevent their loved one from wanting to die.
5. That a cure may be found is another argument presented here.
6. One can argue that the hospice alternative has eliminated the need for mercy death; however, some patients may not want any treatment, hospice treatment included, and therefore it can be argued that they should be allowed to choose death.

B. The arguments for mercy death are much like those for suicide.
   1. Patients should have the freedom to decide about their own deaths, and the person who performs the act merely carries out the patient's wishes.
   2. We do the same for dumb animals, and we owe our fellow humans at least as much consideration and mercy.

C. Changes in attitude toward mercy death.
   1. Events reflecting a change in attitude:
      (a) Active advocates for mercy death, such as Derek Humphry and Dr. Jack Kevorkian.
      (b) Court decisions of two circuit courts of appeals and the Oregon law.
      (c) Lack of autonomy of patients in medical care.
      (d) Health care personnel have practiced forms of assisted suicide.
      (e) Strong desire for greater autonomy and control over one's life and death.
   2. Suggested safeguards for mercy death.
      (a) Those in the Oregon law.
      (b) Those proposed by Dr. Christopher Meyers.
      (c) O. Ruth Russell's safeguards.
   3. Evaluation of safeguards:
      (a) Law should be permissive, not mandatory.
      (b) There should be a written request.
      (c) There should be a waiting period.
      (d) There should be counseling.
      (e) More than one doctor should be involved.
      (f) Abuse of safeguards should be a criminal offense.
      (g) Assisted suicide should be painless.
      (h) Other possible safeguards include having a courtroom judge or commissioner or a panel hear the request and its evidence.

IV. Mercy killing
   A. Mercy killing is the termination of someone's life without that person's explicit consent by a direct means out of a motive of mercy.
   B. There are several arguments against mercy killing.
      1. It is a direct violation of the Value of Life principle—murder is murder, regardless of motive.
      2. Because the consent of patients cannot be obtained, mercy killing involves an outside decision about the worth of their lives and sets a dangerous precedent for eliminating others who may be considered "useless" to society. Who should be entrusted with decisions concerning the worth of people's lives?
      3. Cures may be found, or patients may come out of deep comas; if we kill them, we eliminate these possibilities.

C. There are several arguments for mercy killing.
1. We are not violating the Value of Life principle because most of those who undergo mercy killing are not fully alive human beings; rather, they are mindless organisms.
2. The longer people continue to "merely exist," the greater the financial and emotional burdens on the family and on society.
3. If patients in such situations could make their wishes known, they would say that they wanted to die. The only trouble with this argument is that we cannot know this for sure because the patients cannot communicate with us.
4. Legal safeguards can be clearly established so as to prevent abuses of legalized mercy killing.

Exercises for Review

1. Define the following terms, showing the distinctions among them: *allowing someone to die, mercy death, mercy killing, brain death, persistent vegetative state, ordinary* and *extraordinary means* and *appropriate* and *inappropriate care.*
2. How do mercy death and mercy killing, in general, differ from other types of killing? Do you agree that there is a real difference here? Why or why not?
3. Why have dramatic advances in medicine forced us to take an increasingly harder look at allowing someone to die, mercy death, and mercy killing?
4. Explain the hospice approach to care for the dying. Do you think this eliminates the necessity for mercy killing and mercy death? Why or why not?
5. What are the living will, California Natural Death Act Declaration, and the Durable Power of Attorney for Health Care (DPAHC), and how do they differ? Do you think such advance directives are important? Why or why not? Which do you think is or are more useful, and why?
6. Select the advance directive you like the best, and complete it for yourself (if you strongly object to doing this, carefully explain why).
7. What kinds of safeguards, if any, are necessary in any consideration of allowing someone to die, mercy death, and mercy killing?
8. To what extent do you think the following are moral or immoral: allowing someone to die, mercy death, and mercy killing? Be specific, and support your answer with evidence whenever possible.
9. Assuming that such acts were legal, could you yourself ever allow someone to die or perform the acts of mercy death or mercy killing? If not, why not? If so, under what circumstances? Describe the circumstances fully, and explain the reasoning behind your answers.
10. If mercy death and/or mercy killing *were* legalized, should doctors terminate patients' lives? Why or why not? If not, who should terminate them? Why? Could you do this for members of your family or friends? Why or why not?

Views of the Major Ethical Theories on Allowing Someone to Die, Mercy Death, and Mercy Killing

Describe as fully as you can how each of the major ethical theories—Ethical Egoism, Utilitarianism, Divine Command, Kant's Duty Ethics, Ross' *Prima Facie* Duties, and Virtue Ethics—probably would deal with the moral issues of allowing someone to die, mercy death (assisted suicide), and mercy killing. Refer to Chapter 9, "The Taking of Human Life," for an example of how you might go about completing this assignment.

Notes

1. From a presentation given by Dr. Lamerton, M.D., at Bakersfield College, April 10, 1975.
2. David Kaplan, "Is It a Wonderful Life?" *Newsweek* (April 15, 1996), 62.
3. Ibid.
4. Henry K. Beecher et al., "A Definition of Irreversible Coma," *Journal of the American Medical Association* 205 (August 1968), 85–88.
5. John Behnke and Sissela Bok, *The Dilemmas of Euthanasia* (Garden City, NY: Anchor Books, 1975), 157–59.
6. Pope Pius XII, "The Prolongation of Life," *Pope Speaks* 4 (1958), 393–98.
7. Peter Annin and Marc Peyser, "A Father's Sorrow," *Newsweek* (September 2, 1996), 54.
8. *The Bakersfield Californian* (October 2003), A5.
9. Sandol Stoddard, *The Hospice Movement: A Better Way of Caring for the Dying* (Briarcliff Manor, NY: Stein and Day, 1978), 221–29.
10. *The Bakersfield Californian* (December 7, 2005), A13.
11. Ibid.; Kaplan, "Is It a Wonderful Life?"
12. Richard Lamerton, "Euthanasia," *Nursing Times* (London), February 21, 1974.
13. David Scheff, "Playboy Interview with Derek Humphry," *Playboy* (August 1992), 49–144.
15. *The Bakersfield Californian* (February 18, 1999), A3.
16. Christopher Meyers, *The Bakersfield Californian* (April 28, 1996), B7.
17. Ellen Goodman, *The Bakersfield Californian* (April 12, 1996), B4.
18. Meyers, *The Bakersfield Californian*, B7.
19. O. Ruth Russell, "Moral and Legal Aspects of Euthanasia," *The Humanist* 34 (July–August 1974), 22–27. See also Russell's *Freedom to Die: Moral and Legal Aspects of Euthanasia* (New York: Human Sciences Press, 1975).

Research Navigator™
(*http://www.researchnavigator.com*)

This web site offers three research databases: EBSCO's *ContentSelect Academic Journal and Abstract Database*, *New York Times* Search by Subject Archive, and *Best of the Web* Link Library. In addition, this site provides helpful advice on how to conduct efficient and productive research from choosing a topic to polishing the final draft. Beginning philosophy students probably will find the *Best of the Web* Link Library the most appropriate place to start their research.

The free access code necessary to employ Research Navigator™ can be found in the Prentice Hall Guide to Evaluating Online Resources. If your text did not come with this guide, please go to *www.prenhall.com/contentselect* for information on how you can purchase an access code.

Abortion

Objectives

After you have read this chapter, you should be able to

1. Define the following terms: *conceptus, zygote, embryo, fetus, child, viability, amniocentesis,* and *Chorionic Villus Sampling (CVS).*

2. Understand the present legal status of abortion in the United States.

3. Understand that abortion involves the conflict of two basic principles: the Value of Life principle and the Principle of Individual Freedom.

4. Understand that, along with a moderate position, it involves a conflict of two "absolute right" positions: the strong antiabortion (prolife) position and the strong abortion-on-request (prochoice) position.

5. Discuss when human life begins, and present the stages in the development of the conceptus.

6. Distinguish between potential and actual human life and define and differentiate among life, human life, and human person.

7. Discuss who should make abortion or no-abortion decisions, and why.

8. Present and discuss alternatives to abortion.

Introduction to the Abortion Issue

Definition of Terms

Many moral issues involve special terms or phrases that need defining, and the abortion issue is one of these. Before going on to discuss abortion, therefore, we shall briefly examine a few terms that relate to this issue.

Abortion. An *abortion* is the premature termination of a pregnancy—that is, termination prior to birth. A *spontaneous abortion* is the same thing as a miscarriage, whereas an *induced abortion* is caused by the woman herself or by another, usually a medical doctor.

Zygote. A *zygote* is the cell or group of cells that results from the union of the sperm and egg cells.

Embryo. The term *embryo* refers to the developing human individual from the second through the seventh weeks of gestation, or pregnancy.

Fetus. The term *fetus* refers to the developing human individual from the eighth week until birth.

Child. The term *child* is normally used after the fetus is born. However, as you shall see, it is also often used by strong prolife advocates to refer to the developing human individual from shortly after conception onward.

Conceptus. The very useful term *conceptus*, coined by Daniel Callahan, means "that which has been conceived."[1] It is useful because it is a neutral term that can be used to refer to the developing human individual from conception until birth, thus avoiding the many emotional overtones given to the other terms by both sides of the abortion issue.

Viability. Viability occurs somewhere between the twenty-sixth and twenty-eighth weeks of gestation when the conceptus is considered *viable*, that is, able to survive outside of the mother's womb. Birth usually occurs between the thirty-ninth and fortieth weeks of pregnancy.

Ultrasonic Testing. Early in a pregnancy, at least by 12 weeks, an ultrasonic test can be performed on the woman's abdomen to determine various information about the embryo or fetus (depending on when it is performed). It is done by a sound/echo system from which pictures can be seen. Since this is a test that is basically noninvasive, it may be performed at various stages of pregnancy to acquire information about the embryo or fetus, including gender, heartbeat, and even to some extent possible birth defects. In the latter case, it is not as accurate or conclusive as amniocentesis.

Amniocentesis. In *amniocentesis*, which can be performed after the sixteenth week of pregnancy, a needle is inserted into the amniotic sac, where the conceptus is gestating, and some of the amniotic fluid is withdrawn. When this fluid is tested, a great deal of information about the conceptus—its sex and the presence or absence of certain abnormalities—can be determined.

Chorionic Villus Sampling (CVS). CVS is another tool that can be used to diagnose genetic defects in the fetus as early as the ninth week of pregnancy. In CVS, a flexible catheter, inserted vaginally, is guided by ultrasound along uterine walls. Suction allows the catheter to extract fetal cells from the threadlike projections (villi) on the chorion, the outermost embryonic layer. The advantage of this procedure over amniocentesis is obviously the fact that results and diagnoses can be acquired much earlier, allowing for early abortion if the woman desires it. The disadvantages are that some studies have revealed the CVS may be the cause of limb deformities in children born to mothers who had the CVS procedure.[2]

General Statement of the Abortion Problem

Two basic principles come into conflict in the abortion issue: the Value of Life principle (basically in relation to unborn life, but also in relation to the life of the mother) and the Principle of Individual Freedom, that is, the mother's right over her own body, procreativity, and life.

Another basic question that comes into play in this issue is when human life begins and, perhaps more importantly, at what point it is to be valued and protected to the same extent as the lives of human beings who already have been born.

Yet another conflict between the positions for and against abortion centers on so-called *absolute rights.* According to the strong antiabortion (prolife) position, the conceptus has an absolute right to life from the moment of conception onward. According to the strong abortion-on-request (prochoice) position, however, women have absolute rights over their own bodies and lives. Both of these positions, and the arguments used to support them, will be discussed in detail later in the chapter.

Abortion in American History. From colonial times to the nineteenth century, the choice of continuing pregnancy or having an abortion was the woman's until "quickening" (the time when she is first able to feel the fetus move). An abortion in the first or even second trimester was at worst a misdemeanor. In 1800, there was not a single statute in the United States concerning abortion, but by 1900, it had been banned at any time in pregnancy by every state. According to Carl Sagan, this was due mostly to the change from an agrarian to an urban-industrial society and to the lowering of birthrates in the United States. Sagan also states that the newly formed American Medical Association (AMA), in trying to enhance its status and the status and influence of physicians, put a great deal of force behind the laws so that the choice concerning abortion was taken totally out of the hands of women. Finally, in the 1960s, a coalition of individuals and organizations, including the AMA, sought to overturn laws against abortion and reinstate the previous values, which were later embodied in *Roe* v. *Wade* in 1973.[3]

The Legal Status of Abortion in the United States. At the present time, abortion is legal in the United States and in many other countries. In the famous *Roe* v. *Wade* decision of the U.S. Supreme Court in 1973, which continues to be upheld, most individual state laws making abortion illegal were ruled unconstitutional. The Supreme Court stated that an abortion is permitted at the request of the woman without restriction in the first trimester (12 weeks) and, with some restrictions to protect a woman's health, in the second trimester. It allows states to forbid abortion in the third trimester except when there is a serious threat to the life or health of the woman.

On July 3, 1989, however, the Supreme Court heard another case, *Webster* v. *Reproductive Health Services*, in which it ruled that states had the constitutional right to legislate against using public funds, lands, institutions, and employees to perform abortions except when the mother's life is in danger. Further, in essence, the Court did away with the trimester decision-making process, accepting the importance of protecting potential human life from conception onward, and stating that the provision of the *Webster* v. *Reproductive Health Services* case that required the doctor to run several tests to determine the viability of 20-week fetuses was also constitutional. If such fetuses are determined to be viable, then an abortion cannot be performed. What the Court did, in effect, was to dilute *Roe* v. *Wade* to the extent that allowed at least some abortion decisions to be restricted by state law. The Court also agreed to hear three more cases in October 1989, the beginning of its next session, which could further change the original *Roe* v. *Wade* decision.

In July 1992, the Supreme Court heard another case, from Pennsylvania, *Planned Parenthood* v. *Casey*, in which it upheld a woman's right to choice (for example, it ruled against a woman's having to get her husband's permission). However, the Court also allowed Pennsylvania to institute a "gag rule" in any clinic receiving state or federal funds, meaning that no staff member of a clinic, except physicians, could counsel a woman on abortion. Also, there was a waiting period before any woman could have an abortion. Even though the Supreme Court did not throw *Roe* v. *Wade* out, it did allow states to restrict abortion counseling and the availability of abortion.

These changes, if enacted by states into laws, could strongly affect the rights of women from lower economic classes to secure abortions because most of them depend on public funding and assistance. The viability requirement, if enacted by states into laws, could vitally affect late abortions for fetal reasons—that is, when the woman has discovered through amniocentesis or CVS that her fetus will, if carried to term, be born with deformities of some kind. Presumably, if the fetus were determined to be viable by a doctor, then a late abortion for fetal reasons could not be performed. To what extent such laws will be enacted by other states remains to be seen, but restrictions on abortion rights are likely to come in the future. Essentially, then, abortion is legal in the United States. Of course, that abortion is legal does not necessarily make it moral, and it is the moral question that we will be most concerned with in relation to this issue. In fact, the major questions we will deal with in this chapter are "Is abortion moral? If so, under what conditions? If not, why not?"

When Does Human Life Begin?

The first question to be examined in any discussion of the morality of abortion must be "Is abortion the taking of a human life?" In Chapters 10 and 11 of his book *Abortion: Law, Choice and Morality* (a book I urge those on both sides of the abortion issue to read because of the extensive evidence, rational arguments, objectivity, and compassion it offers), Daniel Callahan outlines several arguments for determining when life exists. He finally settles on the developmental view as the best approach to understanding the "conceptus." According to this view, one recognizes that *life* is present from conception but allows for the possibility that there may be a later different point at which such a life can be considered to be *human*.

It would seem to be obvious that human life *in potentiality* is existent in various stages of development during the nine months of gestation. I want to clarify here that when I use the word *potentiality* I am referring to the stage of zygote and to nothing previous; although some potentiality exists in both the sperm of the male and unfertilized ova of the female, they must be brought together under the appropriate conditions for there to be the beginnings of a new life. Once an ovum has been fertilized, a process is begun that, barring accidents (miscarriage, or spontaneous abortion) or intentional actions (induced abortion), will eventually result in the birth of a human being.

Therefore, if we wish to make decisions consistent with the Value of Life principle, revering life and accepting death, we must recognize that human life *in potentiality* exists from conception. The conceptus passes through various key stages of development:

1. All human life starts from a fertilized egg the size of a period at the end of a sentence; one cell then becomes two and then four, and by the sixth day the egg has implanted itself on the walls of the uterus.
2. By the third week, the forming embryo is about two millimeters long and is developing various parts, but it looks a little like a segmented worm.
3. By the end of the fourth week it has grown to five millimeters (about one-fifth of an inch). Its tube-shaped heart is beginning to beat; it has gill-like arches and a pronounced tail; and it looks something like a newt or a tadpole.
4. By the fifth week, gross divisions of the brain can be distinguished, and developing eyes and limb buds appear.
5. By the sixth week, it is 13 millimeters (about half an inch long); its eyes are still on the side of the head, as in most animals, and its reptilian face has connected slits where the mouth and nose eventually will be.
6. By the end of the seventh week, the tail is almost gone, sexual characteristics can be discerned, and the face is mammalian but somewhat piglike.
7. By the end of the eighth week, the face resembles a primate's but is still not quite human; some lower brain anatomy is welldeveloped, and the fetus shows some reflex response to delicate stimulation.
8. By the tenth week, the face has an unmistakable human look, and it begins to be possible to distinguish male from female fetuses.

9. By the fourth month (16 weeks), one can distinguish faces of fetuses from one another; the mother can feel the fetus move by the fifth month; the lungs don't begin to develop until the sixth month; and recognizably human brain activity begins intermittently around the middle of the seventh month.

10. Brain waves with regular patterns typical of adult human brains do not appear in the fetus until about the thirtieth week of pregnancy—near the beginning of the third trimester. Fetuses younger than this, however alive and active they may be, lack the necessary brain architecture—they cannot yet think.[4]

At which of these stages can we say that the conceptus is a human life? Every stage is vital, but the closer the conceptus gets to viability, the more human qualities are present (at least biologically and genetically). This is why most people who advocate or even "suffer" an abortion to be performed argue that it should be done as soon as possible after pregnancy is discovered. There is, of course, some validity to this argument. Obviously, less human potential has been realized at earlier stages of development, but at any of these stages potential human life does exist.

Many antiabortionists argue that human life is an actuality at any stage after conception. Although it is certainly true that by an abortion actual life is being taken or prevented from continuing, it is very difficult to positively state, in some of the earlier stages at least, that the life is fully human. On the other hand, it is equally difficult to argue that the fetus is not an actual human life *in the womb* after the twelfth week, when "the brain structure is essentially complete and a fetal electrocardiograph through the pregnant woman can pick up heart activity."[5] The arguments that viability or actual birth, when the child can breathe on its own, are the only points at which human life begins, rely too heavily on humans' being able to survive without life support of some kind. Many human beings are dependent on some person or some machine in order to stay alive, and it is difficult to argue that if they cannot breathe for themselves or eat and drink on their own, they are not actual human beings. The length of time that a child, once born, is heavily dependent on both of his or her parents is in itself almost a refutation of the viability argument, or the argument "once born, now human."

What the available data essentially illustrate is that there is human life either in potentiality or in actuality from the moment of conception. This means that the Value of Life principle is definitely involved in any consideration of abortion. We cannot say with any validity that the conceptus is nothing more than—as I heard one woman phrase it—"an intrusion upon the woman's body," like some unnecessary tumor or invading virus. It is not even like any of her organs, which of course may be removed for various reasons. It is, rather, a very special organism, one that develops slowly but surely into a human life, and one must recognize this fact when discussing what is to be done with or to it, either for its own good or for the good of someone else (usually the woman who is carrying it).

The biological, genetic, and physical data remain the same regardless of the position we take concerning when human life begins, and they do not in themselves answer the important question "At what point in development is the conceptus to be valued to the extent that terminating its life would be equivalent to terminating the life of someone already born?" This determination, as we shall see, is not made solely on a basis of biological or genetic data; rather, it is made on some sort of moral bias or assumption.

The strong prolife position takes the genetic view that human life is to be valued from conception onward. The strong prochoice position, on the other hand, takes the view that human life does not have value until birth. There are, of course, various positions between these two extremes, such as, for example, the view that human life is to be valued only from the moment of viability onward.

Arguments Against Abortion

The Genetic View of the Beginning of Human Life

The strong prolife position, as I have mentioned, accepts the genetic view as to when human life begins and when it is to be valued as such. According to this view, human life starts at conception; that is, as soon as the chromosomes from the sperm of the father and the ovum of the mother are united, then a human being exists that must be valued in the same way as if "he or she" were already born. The basis for this argument is that because a person's genetic makeup is established at conception, and because, once established it "programs" the creation of a unique individual, then the human being exists from the point of conception onward and must be valued as a human life. If we are truly concerned about protecting and preserving human life, the argument continues, then the safest position for us to hold is this one. Because people cannot agree on when human life actually begins—or, in a religious sense, when the human "soul" is present—then by valuing a conceptus as human from conception onward we are ensuring that we do not act immorally or irreverently toward human life, and especially toward innocent, unborn human life.

The Sanctity or Value of Life Argument

We already have discussed the arguments concerning the sanctity or value of life in the two previous chapters, but this factor becomes even more crucial in relation to the issue of abortion precisely because the conceptus is innocent and cannot defend itself from being killed. The sanctity or value of life argument states that every unborn, innocent *child* (and this term, or the term *person*, is used by the strong prolife advocates instead of the terms *embryo, fetus,* and *conceptus*) must be regarded as a human person with all the rights of a human person from the moment of conception onward. The word *innocent* is a key one here: Some strong prolife advocates may accept killing in self-defense, capital punishment, or war as moral because the lives involved are often not "innocent." This argument holds that the conceptus not only has a right to life, but also that his or her right is absolute. This means that it overrides all other rights that might come into conflict with it, such as a woman's right to determine the course of her own procreative life or even her right to decide between her own life and the life of her conceptus if her pregnancy is complicated in some way.

The Domino Argument

This argument has been discussed in detail in the two previous chapters, but according to prolife proponents it is most forceful when applied to the abortion issue. They argue that recent history offers proof of the validity of the domino argument, stating that the individual killings, mass tortures, and genocide committed by the Nazis under Adolf Hitler began with the legalization of abortion. They feel that abortion is more likely to set in motion the domino effect than any other type of act because it is not as visible or blatant as the murdering of already born children or adults. Because women never see their conceptuses, it is easier for them to disregard the human life involved; however, the argument continues, the minute we display a disregard for any form of innocent human life, born or unborn, we will start the domino effect, which can end only in a complete disregard for human life in all of its aspects.

The Dangers of Abortion to the Mother's Life

Another argument against abortion states that abortion procedures are dangerous to the mother's well-being, life, and future procreativity. These dangers have two aspects: the medical and the psychological.

Medical Dangers. The medical dangers argument is that abortion involves an intrusion into the woman's vagina and womb that poses some danger to her body, especially these two parts of it. In order to understand specifically what these dangers are, we will briefly examine the abortion methods used at various stages of pregnancy.

1. *Uterine aspiration.* In this method a suction machine (aspirator), which consists of a plastic instrument at the end of a hose, is used to "aspirate," or suction off, the conceptus and related material. This method generally is used prior to the twelfth week of pregnancy, but it is an improvement on dilatation and curettage (D & C) in that it does not require the use of a sharp curette. There are still possibilities of infection, however, but there's much less chance of uterine perforation. This method has come to replace the D & C in most early abortion situations.

2. *Saline abortion.* This procedure, like the hysterotomy, usually is performed during later pregnancies (after the twelfth week), and generally is preferred to the hysterotomy (see item 3). In this procedure, a needle is inserted through the abdominal wall into the amniotic sac, where the conceptus is floating. Some of the amniotic fluid is drawn off and replaced by a glucose, saline, or prostaglandin solution. In about 20 hours, the woman goes into labor and usually delivers a dead fetus. There is some danger inherent in the injection of such substances into the amniotic sac. Also, even though the doctor performs the abortion procedure, he or she doesn't need to be present during delivery, which may cause problems when complications arise. This method also can cause some psychological problems because the woman involved has to go through labor just as if she were having a baby, yet the result is a dead fetus.

3. *Hysterotomy.* After the twelfth week of pregnancy, a miniature caesarean section can be performed. An incision is made in the abdominal wall and the conceptus and related material are removed, after which the incision is closed. There is always danger involved in major surgery, and once a caesarean operation has been performed on a woman, any babies she may have in the future may also have to be delivered by caesarean section.

4. *Partial Birth Abortion.* Also referred to as "dilate and extract" or "intrauterine inter-cranial abortions." This type of abortion most often is done during the fifth month of gestation but sometimes during the end of the second trimester (around the 26th week), and usually only for very serious situations, such as the health, including mental health, of the woman, or if the fetus has been found to be dead, badly mal-formed, or suffering from a serious defect. The procedure involves the dilation of the woman's cervix, after which the fetus is partially removed from the womb, feet first. The surgeon then inserts a sharp object into the back of the fetus's head, removes it and inserts a vacuum tube through which the brains are extracted. The head of the fetus contracts at this point allowing the fetus to be more easily removed from the womb.

5. *Self-induced abortion.* Almost all of the experts agree that self-induced abortions are probably the most dangerous of all abortions because they are not done under proper medical supervision. They easily can result in infections and hemorrhaging, complications that can kill both the fetus and the woman. No one that I know of supports or promotes such abortions; in fact, one of the strongest arguments for allowing abortions to be legalized has been to discourage women from performing self-induced abortions.

Aside from the potential dangers of abortion methods in general, abortion increases a woman's chances of having miscarriages in later pregnancies; this is especially true for young girls who have had an abortion. Also, repeated abortions increase the level of danger. All of this leads prolife proponents to conclude that pregnancy and childbirth are normal functions of a woman's body and that artificial interruption of these functions can cause medical problems that make such procedures hazardous to women.[6]

Psychological Dangers. The psychological dangers argument is that it is psycholog-ically very destructive to a woman to authorize the "killing of her baby." A woman who has committed such a terrible act, prolife supporters argue, has to live with a great deal of guilt. In fact, the emotional scars will never be eradicated from her psyche, whereas if she had gone through with her pregnancy, even though it might have required a psychological adjustment, it would never compare with having to adjust to the guilt resulting from an abortion.

The Relative Safety of Pregnancy

One of the strongest arguments put forth for abortion is that pregnancy can endanger a woman's health and even her life. The prolife people, however, maintain that these dangers have been virtually eradicated by advances in medicine. We are at the point now, they argue, where with only a very few exceptions a woman can be brought safely through a pregnancy. In the case of those few exceptions, as Father Josef Fuch, a Jesuit theologian, puts it, "There is in fact no commandment to save the mother at all costs. There is only an obligation to save her in a morally permissible way. . . . Consequently only one obligation remains: to save the mother without attempting to kill the child."[7] Father Fuch seems to be suggesting here that if the mother cannot be saved, then her life may have to be sacrificed in order to allow her child to be born, an action not morally acceptable to many, if not most, people.

The Existence of Viable Alternatives to Abortion

If a child is unwanted or if it is to be born deformed in some serious way, viable alternatives to abortion do exist. There are literally millions of childless couples who would love to adopt a child and raise it as their own. As a matter of fact, the number of babies now available for adoption (especially Caucasian babies) has dropped tremendously ever since abortions became legal in the United States. There are many fine, reputable agencies that can place children unwanted by their natural parents in homes where they will be cared for and loved. And even if such homes cannot be found, there are governmental institutions in which unwanted or deformed children can be placed and cared for by trained personnel. Certainly the fact that a conceptus is unwanted or handicapped cannot be a moral justification for "murdering" it, according to the prolife people.

The Irrelevance of Economic Considerations

Many women desire an abortion because they feel they cannot financially afford to go through a pregnancy or raise a child. The prolife proponents argue, however, that where innocent, unborn human life is involved, economic considerations cannot come first. If a woman becomes pregnant, she, along with the conceptus's father, must accept the financial responsibility for the birth and raising of their child. There are agencies in society—welfare, Medicaid, and private charitable organizations—that can give financial assistance to pregnant women whether they are married or not. According to this argument, families that are financially overburdened should be judicious about having more children, but if the woman does become pregnant, she cannot use financial problems as a reason to "take the lives of unborn children."

Responsibility for Sexual Activities

The responsibility for sexual activities argument states that whenever women engage in sexual acts with men, whether contraceptives are used or not, they must realize that pregnancy may ensue. Furthermore, they must accept the responsibility for their actions, whether or not the men shoulder the responsibility with them, and they cannot sacrifice an innocent human life because of their carelessness or indiscretion or because of the failure of a contraceptive device. A woman is responsible for not getting pregnant in the first place, according to the argument, and there are many methods she can use to avoid pregnancy. However, if it does occur, it is her responsibility to go through with it and give birth to her child.

Rape and Incest

Pregnancies resulting from rape are fairly rare, and those resulting from incest are rarer still. If rapes are reported in time, contraceptive procedures can be used effectively. If, however, women do become pregnant after rape or incest, this argument maintains that the destruction of innocent unborn human life is still not justified. Women must go through with the pregnancies and, if they do not want the children because of the circumstances of their conception, they should put them up for adoption or place them in government-run institutions. In any case, according to this argument, innocent, unborn conceptuses should not have to pay with their lives for the sins or crimes of others.

Arguments for Abortion

The argument for abortion essentially states that a woman ought to be allowed to have an abortion, regardless of the reason, if she requests it. Furthermore, she ought to be able to have her abortion without suffering recrimination, guilt, or restrictions, legal or otherwise. This position is based upon several arguments.

Absolute Rights of Women over Their Own Bodies

The central argument for absolute rights of women over their own bodies is that women, like men, should have absolute rights over their own bodies, including procreative rights. In the past, women, because of an "accident of nature"—the fact that they are the ones who get pregnant—have not shared in these equal rights, but now that birth control is possible, they can. These rights also must include abortion, which is, according to this argument, just another method of birth control that is used when other methods fail or have not been used. To carry this argument one step further, any conceptus is a part of a woman's body until it is born; therefore, she has absolute say over whether it should continue to live in that body or whether it will be allowed to be born.

There are several corollaries to this major argument. First, there is the assumption that enforced maternities should not take place. No woman should be forced or even urged to go through her pregnancy against her will; she, and she alone, must decide her future. Second, it is male domination that is responsible for strict abortion laws. Because men do not know what it is like to be pregnant they can afford to be "highly moral" about the lives of conceptuses. Third, female freedom is ultimately dependent on full and free control of procreative life, and this includes abortion as well as other methods of birth control.

For example, let us say that a woman wants to pursue a career in medicine, which requires a long and arduous period of study. If she gets pregnant for one reason or another, unless she has complete control over her procreativity, her life's desires may never in fact be realized. The implication is that a woman shouldn't have to go through pregnancy, giving birth, and raising a child if this could completely destroy her life plans. How many men are required to make such a sacrifice? The answer is virtually none, and according to the absolute rights argument, this is unfair to women. A man always has complete control over his sex life, except in cases of forced sexuality such as rape or child molestation, and a woman is entitled to the same freedom and rights. True, both she and the man can share the responsibility for contraception, but abortion must also be available when these methods fail or are not used for one reason or another.

Birth as the Beginning of Human Life

The prochoice point of view assumes that until a child actually is born, human life does not exist, at least not to the extent that the conceptus should have the same rights as people who already have been born. As mentioned earlier, as long as the conceptus is within the woman's body it is a part of her body and is subject to her decision as to whether it is to be carried to term or not. Most prochoice women probably would argue that abortions should be performed as early as possible, both because the conceptus is less developed and because this is safer for the woman. However, abortions also should be allowed later in pregnancy if, for example, a woman discovers that the conceptus will be born seriously deformed, which can't be determined until around four months after conception. In any case, because, according to this argument, an unborn conceptus at any stage of development cannot be considered to be a full human being, then its right to life is not absolute; rather, this must be subordinated to the woman's right over her own body and life, which is absolute, just as men's rights are.

The Problem of Unwanted or Deformed Children

Since the arrival of significant birth control methods, including abortion, it has been possible to ensure that every child born into the world is thoroughly wanted. And now that people can limit the size of their families, they can better control the quality of their lives and the lives of their children. This argument states that given present-day conditions—overpopulation, pollution problems, economic difficulties—only children who are planned for and really wanted should be brought into the world, and abortion makes this possible. If a woman becomes pregnant, she must bear the responsibility for her pregnancy and should not pass this burden onto society. If she is willing to bear the child and raise it, she should be allowed to do so, but if she does not intend to take responsibility for it, she should have it aborted rather than put it up for adoption or have it institutionalized and allow it to become a burden upon others.

There are two additional assumptions that contribute to the prochoice position on unwanted or deformed children.

Adoption as a Poor Solution.   According to prochoice advocates, adoption is not as viable an alternative as the prolife forces would have us believe. First, even if a woman agrees to put her child up for adoption after it is born, she still has to go through nine months of pregnancy, which will hamper her freedom and life a great deal. Second, it is much more difficult, both physically and psychologically, to go through pregnancy and give a child up for adoption than it is to have a conceptus aborted before it is born. Third, adoptive children don't always have as pleasant an existence as prolifers would have us think. Adoptive children often feel rejected when they discover that their natural mothers gave them up. Often they go in search of their natural parents regardless of the love and quality of their adoptive parents and homes. Also, some of these children end up moving from foster home to foster home, enduring a poor qualify of life.

    Lack of Humane Institutions. One of the arguments of the prolife people is that orphaned and handicapped children can be maintained in institutions established by society for this purpose. The prochoice people answer, however, that life these days is difficult enough for children who are wanted or "normal," and they question why women would want to give birth to children who are not wanted or who will be handicapped, especially those with serious handicaps. Furthermore, the quality of the institutional or even private care available for deformed children is below minimum and sometimes inhumane; therefore, bringing children into such situations is much worse than terminating their lives before they are born. It goes without saying, according to prochoice people, that no woman, with or without a family, should be required to give birth to or raise a deformed child unless she wants to. With the availability of the amniocentesis and CVS procedures that I described earlier, women can, in many cases, know between the fourth and fifth month of pregnancy whether or not their child will be deformed, and they can choose whether to abort the deformed conceptus or to give birth to it.

The Relative Safety of Abortion

The argument of the prolife people, the one that states that abortion is dangerous to women's medical and psychological well-being, is flatly rejected by the prochoice people.

    The Medical Aspect. First, according to the prochoice position, the only dangerous abortions are either self-induced abortions or those that were performed by unqualified personnel in unsanitary conditions at the time when abortions were not legal. Many more women lost their lives from these procedures than have done so since abortion has been legalized. As long as abortions are performed by qualified medical personnel in qualified medical settings, the risk for all of the procedures, according to the prochoice argument, is minimum. Essentially, abortion in the first 12 weeks is a minor procedure that carries with it almost no risk. Later abortions are, of course, more complicated, but even in such cases, given the appropriate medical care and facilities, women can be brought through abortions quite safely.

    As a matter of fact, prochoice people would argue, abortions are much safer—especially in the early stages of pregnancy, when they are most often performed—than going through nine months of pregnancy. This is particularly the case when the woman has some sort of debilitating illness (for example, diabetes, hypertension, or a diseased heart). They maintain that the drain on a woman's strength, health, and body caused by going through pregnancy leaves marks that can far outlast the short-term effects of an abortion procedure, especially when abortion is performed early in the pregnancy.

    The Psychological Aspect. Some women who decide to have an abortion may, of course, feel guilt, but many women do not experience any such feelings because they do not consider the conceptus to be a human being in any respect. Furthermore, if guilt feelings do exist, they can be overcome either by the women themselves or with counseling. The prochoice people go on to say that most of these guilt feelings, if they do exist, will be temporary, and that they are nothing compared to the psychological damage of going through nine months of pregnancy and then bearing an unwanted and/or deformed child.

Also, if a woman has to spend 18 or more years raising a child when she really doesn't want to, the psychological damage she suffers may be longer lasting and much more detrimental than a few hours, days, weeks, or even months of guilt over having to abort an unwanted conceptus. Moreover, going through a pregnancy and having to give a child up for adoption will cause greater psychological damage than having an early or even a late abortion. The prochoice people also believe that this psychological damage extends to the child itself once it is born. What psychological damage will be wreaked upon children who grow up unwanted and unloved by mothers who were forced to have them against their will? Physical and emotional deprivation extending to child abuse and even death is far worse, the argument states, than not letting the child be born at all.

Refutation of the Domino Argument

As far as the domino argument is concerned, prochoice people argue that there is no hard evidence showing that legalizing abortion is likely to result in a loss of reverence for human life in any other area. They point to the many laws against capital punishment in existence around the world; the laws against mercy death and mercy killing; and to other laws against murder in all forms. They also argue that the Hitler example does not provide support for the prolife position. They maintain that Hitler's motives were *never* beneficent in any sense of the word—that he was out to destroy any enemies of the Third Reich, innocent or not.

The prochoice people argue further that they are not favoring mandatory abortion in any way, shape, or form; rather, all they want is free choice for women who do not want to go through with pregnancies. Making abortion legal does not mean that eventually all Jewish women, for example, would be forced to abort because they and their offspring would be considered unfit or subhuman as was the case in the Third Reich; it only means that women of all races and religions would have a choice in terms of abortion. They argue further that the availability of abortion has not made women more callous toward human life, but that it has, in fact, made them more loving of the children that they really wanted and planned for.

The Danger of Pregnancy to the Mother's Life

Another argument of the prochoice advocates is that pregnancy does pose dangers to the health and life of women. Furthermore, they believe that if human lives have to be traded off, the life of someone already born, in this case the pregnant woman, should obviously take precedence over the life of an unborn conceptus. They would disagree strongly with Josef Fuch, maintaining that abortion is a permissible way to save a woman's life when it is threatened by a complicated pregnancy. In fact, they believe that even if there is only *some* risk to the woman, she still has the right to choose to save her own life over that of the unborn conceptus.

Rape and Incest

The prochoice people would argue that rape and incest are two of the most serious crimes committed against a woman and that under no circumstances should she be forced to endure an unwanted pregnancy resulting from either of these actions. There is no argument, they feel, other than the woman's own desire to go through with the pregnancy, that would justify putting her through the torment of pregnancy and childbirth under these circumstances.

Responsibility for Sexual Activities

The prochoice advocates would agree with their prolife opponents that women must accept responsibility for their sexual activities, but, as I stated earlier, they believe that this responsibility definitely includes the right to terminate a pregnancy. They are particularly disturbed by the notion that "if a woman is stupid enough to get pregnant despite the availability of contraceptive devices and the ability to abstain from sex, then it's her fault, and she must go through with the pregnancy." To them, this attitude reflects society's desire to punish women for their carelessness or indiscretions. They feel that no matter how pregnancy occurred, the woman does not deserve punishment any more than does the man who also is responsible for the pregnancy; in no way should a woman be abused or discriminated against for exercising her free choice in dealing with her problem.

Abortion as the Woman's Choice

The final argument for the prochoice position is that abortion is purely a medical problem and, therefore, women should be legally free to make a private decision about their bodies and their lives that should not be intruded upon by others. No one else has to go through the pregnancy; no one else has to go through the childbirth; and no one else has to then devote 18 or more years to raising the child; therefore, the final decision to abort or to go through with pregnancy must be the woman's and hers alone with no interference from anyone else or any part of society.

The More Moderate Positions on Abortion

As I have mentioned before, the strong prolife and the strong prochoice positions embody the extreme approaches to the abortion issue. As I have also mentioned, there are more moderate positions that can be found all along the spectrum between these extremes. It is difficult to characterize all the moderate positions on abortion, for some may allow abortion in cases of rape or incest or when the mother's life is in danger, but not for other reasons. Some may allow abortion up to viability but not after, whereas others may allow it up to 12 weeks, but not after. Some may allow abortion for psychological reasons or in cases of fetal deformity, whereas others may not. Because of this diversity, what I will present in this section is a set of basic assumptions that the more moderate positions might hold and that also will embody criticisms of the two extreme positions.

An Unresolvable Conflict of Absolutes

One aspect of the abortion issue that most moderates would agree upon is that neither of the extreme positions is workable: They are both based on unresolvable and conflicting "absolutes" that, in turn, are based on questionable premises. The first approach to this problem generally taken by moderates is that there are no absolute rights—there are strong rights, but there are no rights that supersede all other human rights. In Chapter 5, I showed that there are such things as absolute *truths*; I never said, however, that there were absolute *rights*.

No Absolute Right to Life. The Value of Life principle is important, but it is not the only value there is—that's why there are other principles. As I have mentioned before, many people have sacrificed their lives for ideals that the other principles embody: goodness, justice, freedom, and honesty. It also is true that the Value of Life principle involves other aspects besides the mere right to existence—even the right to existence of innocent, unborn life.

One of these other aspects of the life principle is the survival and integrity of the human species. This aspect includes the problem of overpopulation and the burden placed upon society when children are born with deformities. A second aspect is the right of families to procreate and reproduce their own kind without hindrance. Obviously, this aspect comes into conflict with the first aspect in cases where families exhibit a high risk of passing on genetic deficiencies that may cause burdens upon society as a whole. A third aspect is the integrity of bodily life, which involves the protection of human beings from life-threatening situations such as war, capital punishment, poverty, mercy death and mercy killing, suicide, and abortion. Finally, a fourth aspect is the freedom to live life in the way that we want to —an aspect that affects both the pregnant woman and the conceptus.[8]

As we can readily see, then, the Value of Life principle involves a great deal more than just the right to life of the unborn (although this is definitely included), and that is why we cannot say that anyone has an *absolute* right to life.

No Absolute Rights over One's Body. I have already described in several chapters situations in which people do not have absolute rights over their bodies. Generally we view the rights of individual people over their bodies as being strong, but we do not, for example, allow people ridden with plague or other contagious diseases to refuse treatment or quarantine, because if we did so, they could harm or even cause the death of others. We also feel that people should be prevented from mutilating or killing themselves whenever this can be done without employing destructive or excessive force.

However, in earlier chapters on suicide and mercy death, I described the position that individual human beings should have the basic freedom to decide about their own living or dying, and this, of course, includes a complete decision over what is done to their bodies. That is, all individuals can refuse treatment for themselves and die rather than live because it is their bodies and lives that are at stake. Our courts generally have upheld individuals' refusals of treatments as long as these refusals were for themselves and not someone else. Patients with kidney failure have refused dialysis because they did not want to live what they felt was the undignified life of a dialysis patient, preferring to die instead; other patients have refused surgery and radiation and chemical therapy because of what it would do to their bodies and lives. All of these situations come under the heading of individual rights, and no one has the right to interfere with these decisions so long as severe harm is not being done to anyone else.

This argument, however, falters somewhat when we begin to talk about a pregnant woman's rights over her own body. The problem here, of course, is that her body and her life now contain another body and life in some stage of development. For this reason, the argument of individual rights over one's body does not hold in an absolute sense, because now what affects this woman's body and life will also affect the body and life of another potential human being. In her moral considerations, which involve her life and the life of the conceptus, the woman should observe the Value of Life principle.

Much less moral justification can be given for the taking of a human life if that life could be a normal one, with the possibility of its also being good and meaningful. This does not mean that the woman's individual rights over her life and her body should not be considered—they definitely should, and the final decision to abort or not abort still must rest with her—but it does mean that there is also another potential or actual human life and body at stake in her decision. Therefore, the pregnant woman does not have *absolute* rights over her body, but neither does the conceptus have an absolute right to life.[9]

The Problem of When Life Begins—A Synthesis

Generally, those who hold a moderate position feel that the genetic or strong prolife view of when human life begins draws the line too early, even though this provides for the safest and most consistent means of protecting human life from its earliest stages onward. It is difficult for moderates to accept the idea that a group of cells—regardless of their potentiality—can be considered a human being with full personhood and all the rights accorded to human beings who are already born.

On the other hand, waiting until birth to assign value to developing human life seems wrong because it disregards the significance of the increasing potentiality toward human life that occurs throughout the entire gestation period. The attempt to determine when a conceptus becomes human has caused people to draw some rather ridiculously fine lines. For example, what essentially is the difference between a fetus in the thirty-eighth week and one that is newly born? Is this difference significant enough to allow one fetus to be valued as human, whereas the other is not?

The moderate position essentially takes what Daniel Callahan calls "the developmental view of when human life begins." What this view essentially maintains is that although conception does establish the genetic basis for an individual human being, some degree of development is required before one can legitimately speak of the conceptus as an "individual human being."

Furthermore, this view suggests that because the human individual develops biologically in a continuous fashion, it might be worthwhile to consider the possibility that human rights develop in the same way. Callahan goes on to say that the simplest and most satisfactory position on abortion is to avoid ascribing any legal or theological status to the embryo during the first two weeks of development. Beyond this time, however, the embryo becomes increasingly important, and at viability the fetus should have almost the same rights as a newborn child.[10]

In her brilliant essay "Ethical Problems of Abortion," Sissela Bok essentially holds, like Callahan, to the developmental viewpoint. She also argues well for the difficulty of defining the term *human being* and lists instead some cogent reasons for protecting life:

1. Killing is seen as the greatest danger for victims because the knowledge of it causes "intense anguish and apprehension" and the actual taking of life can cause great suffering. Furthermore, once life has begun, its continued experience is so unique and valuable that no one should be deprived of it.
2. "Killing is brutalizing and criminalizing *for the killer.*"
3. Killing affects the family and friends of the victim, causing them great grief and loss.
4. Therefore all of society "has a stake in the protection of life" because killing "sets patterns for victims, killers, and survivors that are threatening and ultimately harmful to all."[11]

Bok goes on to say that these criteria do not lead her to the conclusion that early human life is unimportant; on the contrary, she believes that the conceptus definitely should be considered, along with the mother, as having value. However, she is led by these criteria to suggest that abortion on request should be allowed up to the end of the first trimester (the first 12 weeks, or three months). Between the thirteenth week and the twenty-sixth to twenty-eighth weeks (when viability occurs), special reasons, such as severe malformation of the conceptus, should be required to justify an abortion; and from viability onward, abortions should not be allowed except when the fetus is dead; the fetus is alive, but continued pregnancy would place the woman's life in severe danger; the fetus is alive, but continued pregnancy would grievously damage the woman's health and/or disable her; the fetus is so malformed that it can never gain consciousness and will die shortly after birth.

These guidelines, Bok adds, do not in any way suggest that abortion can be morally justified for everyone. Doctors, nurses, and prospective parents who feel that participation in an abortion would adversely affect their lives and their feelings are perfectly justified in refusing to have or perform an abortion at any stage in pregnancy.[12] Generally, then, Bok's position (which, as I have said, coincides with Callahan's) could accurately be described as the "moderate" position as to when human life begins and, more importantly, when it has sufficient value to cause it to receive the same protection as already born life.

Cases for Study and Discussion

CASE 1 Dilemma of Teenage Abortion

Janice, 15, and Bob, 16, have had sexual intercourse several times, and now Janice has discovered that she is two months' pregnant. Janice's mother was raised a Roman Catholic, and she does not want her daughter to have an abortion. Neither, however, does she wish to raise or help Janice raise the child. Instead, she wants Janice to go through with the pregnancy and give the child up for adoption. Janice's father is an agnostic, and he wants her to have an abortion because he knows that Janice is a good student and is interested in a law career—he is a practicing lawyer himself. Bob, who wants to be an engineer, also wishes Janice to have an abortion, and he is willing to see that all of her expenses are paid. Janice herself is quite confused about what she wants. She has been raised a Roman Catholic and shares some of her mother's misgivings about abortion, although she is not as committed to her faith as her mother is. She has talked to a young, sympathetic priest at her church, but he has told her she must not have an abortion as this would be a mortal sin. She also has gone to an abortion clinic to discuss the abortion procedure and its cost. What should Janice do, and why? Support your statements.

CASE 2 Middle-aged Couple Deciding on Abortion or Not

Mary, 38, is married and has three children, ages 10, 15, and 18. Her husband manages a service station, and Mary has been working part-time as a bank teller. They are having a difficult time financially because their 18-year-old has just started college and they bought a new house a year ago. Although Mary was using a contraceptive, she now discovers that she is one month pregnant. She and her husband do not want any more children—indeed, they had thought they were finished bearing and raising them. Adding to their other reasons for not wanting any more children, they also are worried by the knowledge that women who have pregnancies late in life have a greater chance of bearing a child with Down's syndrome. They finally decide that Mary should have an abortion. Were they right in making this decision? Should Mary wait until the fourth month and have an amniocentesis performed to see if the baby has Down's syndrome? If the baby does, then what should they do, and why?

CASE 3 Tay-Sachs Couple

Leonard, 25, and Rachel, 23, discover that they are Tay-Sachs carriers after Rachel has become pregnant, and the doctor informs them that they have a one-in-four chance of bearing a Tay-Sachs child. Tay-Sachs is a fatal disease that is both degenerative and particularly horrible. They decide to wait until the fourth month of Rachel's pregnancy to have an amniocentesis performed. The results, which they receive in Rachel's fifth month of pregnancy, show that she will indeed give birth to a child with Tay-Sachs. What should they do?

CASE 4 Young Couple Whose Fetus has Down Syndrome

Lupe and Robert, both in their early twenties, are having their first child. Because Lupe had some problems early in her pregnancy, her doctor recommends that an amniocentesis be performed. At four months of pregnancy she undergoes the procedure, and the results six weeks later show that Lupe will give birth to a child with Down Syndrome. The results do not indicate how severe the mental retardation will be or if there are any other deformities. Lupe and Robert want children very badly, but they would rather not have to raise a mentally retarded child, especially because they are young enough to try again for a normal child. What should they do?

CASE 5 Middle-aged Couple Have An Abortion Because of Sex of Fetus

Bill, 37, and Isabel, 35, are married and have three daughters. One night when they had sexual intercourse Isabel forgot to wear her diaphragm, and she became pregnant as a result. After adjusting to the idea, Bill and Isabel decided it would be nice if they could have a son, because they already have three daughters. However, because Isabel is 35, she decides to have an amniocentesis performed to see if her fetus has Down Syndrome. After the procedure has been done, the genetic counselor informs Bill and Isabel that the child will be normal as far as the test can determine and also that the child will be a girl. Because Bill and Isabel do not want another girl, Isabel has an abortion, after which she has herself sterilized so that she can have no more children. Do you feel that she did the right thing?

CASE 6 Multiple Births

Because of the increase of treatments for infertility, many multiple births have resulted after such treatments are completed. Two recent cases occurred, one in which a pregnant woman who discovered she was going to have twins decided she could only afford one child and had an abortion, which set off heavy protests in England. A second woman on finding out that she had four to six fetuses, wished to abort about half of them because she said she didn't want and couldn't afford that many children. To what extent do you think such requests for abortion are moral or immoral? Explain in detail. Do you feel at all differently about this type of abortion than you do about single fetus abortions? Why or why not?

Chapter Summary

I. Introduction to the abortion issue
   A. A number of terms related to the abortion issue must be defined.
      1. *Abortion* is the premature termination of a pregnancy.
         (a) A *spontaneous abortion* is a miscarriage.
         (b) An *induced abortion* is caused by the woman herself or by another, usually a doctor.
      2. *Zygote* is a cell or group of cells that results from the union of the sperm and egg cells.
      3. *Embryo* is a term to describe the conceptus between the second and eighth weeks of gestation.
      4. *Fetus* is the term used to describe the conceptus from the eighth week onward until birth.
      5. *Child* is the term normally used after the conceptus is born.
      6. *Conceptus* is a neutral term, coined by Daniel Callahan, that means "that which has been conceived."
      7. *Viability* is that period of pregnancy somewhere between the twenty-sixth and twenty-eighth weeks when the conceptus is considered *viable*—that is, able to survive outside of the mother's womb.

8. *Amniocentesis* is a procedure that can be performed after the sixteenth week of pregnancy and that reveals a great deal of information about the conceptus, including its sex and possible deformities.

9. *Chorionic Villus Sampling (CVS)* is another tool that can be used to diagnose genetic defects in the fetus as early as the ninth week of pregnancy.

B. The abortion issue is highly complex, involving a great number of factors.

1. Two basic principles come into conflict in relation to abortion: the Value of Life principle and the Principle of Individual Freedom.

2. Another basic question is, When does human life begin, and at what point is it to be valued and protected?

3. Abortion also involves two conflicting "absolutes."

    (a) According to the prolife position, the conceptus has an absolute right to life.

    (b) According to the prochoice position, a woman has absolute rights over her body and life.

4. Abortion has gone through various stages of acceptance and rejection in American history:

    (a) From colonial times to the nineteenth century, the choice was the woman's until "quickening."

    (b) By 1900, it had been banned at any time in pregnancy by every state.

    (c) In 1973, *Roe* v. *Wade*, in effect, made abortion legal in all of the 50 states.

5. The legal status of abortion in the United States has also seen changes.

    (a) In 1973, the Supreme Court essentially made abortion legal in the first two trimesters of a woman's pregnancy, but allowed states to forbid abortion in the third trimester except in the case of a serious threat to the life of the mother.

    (b) In July 1989, in *Webster* v. *Reproductive Health Services*, the Court allowed states to put some restriction on abortions when federal and state funds were used and did away with the trimester system.

    (c) In July 1992, in *Planned Parenthood* v. *Casey*, the Court allowed further restrictions while at the same time upholding a woman's right to choice.

II. When human life begins

A. *Life* is present from conception, and from this point on it develops.

B. There are certain key stages in the conceptus's development.

1. All human life starts from an egg the size of a period at the end of a sentence.

2. By the third week the embryo is developing various parts.

3. By the end of the fourth week, its heart begins to beat.

4. By the fifth week divisions of the brain occur, and developing eyes and limb buds appear.

5. By the sixth week it is about half an inch long, its eyes are still on the sides of the head, and it is developing slits where its mouth and nose will be.

6. By the end of the seventh week, sexual characteristics can be discerned, and the face is mammalian but somewhat piglike.

7. By the end of the eighth week, the face resembles a primate's, there is some lower brain anatomy, and the fetus has reflex reactions.

8. By the fifth month, the mother can feel the fetus move. Lungs begin to develop during the sixth month, and human brain activity begins at about the seventh month.

9. Brain waves with regular patterns typical of adult humans begin only at about the thirtieth week of pregnancy.

C. There is *human life* either in potentiality or in actuality from the moment of conception. (Many consider that actual human life begins after the third month of life in the womb.)

III. Antiabortion (prolife) arguments
  A. The prolife group believes in the genetic view of the beginning of human life—that human life begins at conception.
  B. One prolife argument is based on the sanctity or value of life.
    1. The right to life is absolute, especially the right of innocent, unborn life.
    2. Every unborn "child" must be regarded as a human person with all the rights of a person from the moment of conception onward.
  C. The domino argument applies to this issue much as it does to others. One proof of its validity cited by the prolife group is that Hitler started his history of atrocities by legalizing abortion.
  D. Abortion is both medically and psychologically harmful to women.
  E. The danger of pregnancy to a mother's life is almost nonexistent because of medical and technological advances.
  F. There are viable alternatives to abortion.
    1. Unwanted babies can be put up for adoption.
    2. There are institutions and agencies to care for unwanted and/or deformed children.
  G. Economics cannot be a consideration when human life is concerned.
  H. Women must accept full responsibility for their sexual activities, and when these activities result in pregnancy, innocent life cannot be sacrificed because of women's carelessness or indiscretion.
  I. Rape or incest usually don't present problems because contraceptives often can be used in time; when they can't, however, even such means of conception do not justify the taking of innocent lives.

IV. Abortion-on-request (prochoice) arguments
  A. Women have absolute rights over their bodies, and the conceptus is part of a woman's body until birth.
  B. A conceptus cannot be considered a human life until birth.
  C. Unwanted or deformed children should not be brought into the world.
    1. It is more responsible to have an abortion than to burden society with an unwanted or deformed child.
    2. Adoption is not always a solution.
  D. Abortion is a no-risk medical procedure. Medical and psychological problems are much greater for women who go through pregnancies than for those who have abortions.
  E. The domino argument used by prolife groups is not supported by hard evidence. Hitler's overall motives for permitting abortions were not at all the same as the motives of today's women.
  F. Pregnancies resulting from rape and incest should never have to be gone through by any woman because of the horror of the circumstances of the conception.
  G. Women do have responsibilities for their sexual activities, and having abortions when necessary is a part of these responsibilities.
  H. Abortion is and must be totally a matter of the woman's choice—no one else should be able to interfere.

V. The more moderate positions on abortion
  A. The strong prolife and prochoice positions present an unresolvable conflict of absolutes.
    1. There is no absolute right to life, even though the Value of Life principle is important.
    2. There is also no absolute right over one's body and life, even though it is a strong right.
  B. The problem of when life begins may be considered through a synthesis.
    1. The prolife position draws the line (for when life begins) too early.
    2. The prochoice position draws it too late.

C. The moderate favors the developmental view of when life begins, which states that life does indeed begin at conception but gains value as it develops through the gestation period.

Exercises for Review

1. When, in your opinion, does human life begin? Substantiate your answer with as much evidence and reasoned argument as you can.
2. How would you distinguish among the following: life, human life, human person, potential life, actual life?
3. Briefly describe the five major stages of the development of the conceptus.
4. Do you agree or disagree with the position that the mother must be the one to make the final decision on whether to have an abortion? Why? Should anyone else be involved in the decision? If so, who, and if not, why not?
5. What workable alternatives to abortion would you recommend, and why?
6. Under what conditions do you feel it is moral to have an abortion? Under what conditions do you feel it is immoral? Be specific in giving reasons for your answers.
7. Would you classify abortion as murder, mercy killing, self-defense, or merely as the elimination of an organism? Explain.
8. What are the problems with the concepts that a woman has absolute rights over her own body and that a conceptus has an absolute right to life? Be specific.
9. Do you agree that if we are going to take a strong stand against abortion, we must do much more in the way of counseling and giving other kinds of assistance to the prospective mother? Why or why not? What kinds of assistance and counseling do you feel are necessary? (See Appendix 3, p. 458.)
10. What do you think of the moderate position on abortion? Do you feel that it successfully resolves the conflict between the two extreme positions or not? Why?

Views of the Major Ethical Theories on Abortion

Describe as fully as you can how each of the major ethical theories—Ethical Egoism, Utilitarianism, Divine Command Theory, Kant's Duty Ethics, Ross' *Prima Facie* Duties, and Virtue Ethics—probably would deal with the moral issue of abortion. Refer to Chapter 9, "The Taking of Human Life," for an example of how you might go about completing this assignment, and Chapters 2, 3, and 4 for a discussion of the major ethical theories.

Notes

1. Daniel Callahan, *Abortion: Law, Choice and Morality* (New York: Macmillan, 1970), 44.
2. Jean Seligman et al., "Is My Baby All Right?" *Newsweek* (June 22, 1992), 62–63.
3. Carl Sagan and Ann Druyan, "Is It Possible to Be Pro-Life and Pro-Choice?" *Parade Magazine* (April 22, 1990), 2.
4. Ibid., 6.

5. Callahan, *Abortion*, 373.

6. See Ibid., 31–43, for a fuller discussion of abortion hazards.

7. Ibid., 425.

8. Ibid., 328–33.

9. Callahan argues that either of these extremes—absolute right over one's body and absolute right to life—are one-dimensional and too simplistic for such a complex moral issue. See Chapters 12, 13, and 14 for a discussion of both extremes and synthesis of their conflicting views.

10. See Chapter 11 in Callahan for a full discussion of the various views concerning when human life begins, and especially pp. 384–90 for a description of the developmental viewpoint.

11. Sissela Bok, "Ethical Problems of Abortion," *The Hastings Center Studies* 2, no. 1 (January 1974), 42.

12. Ibid., 42–52.

Research Navigator™
(http://www.researchnavigator.com)

This web site offers three research databases: EBSCO's *Content Select Academic Journal and Abstract Database, New York Times* Search by Subject Archive, and *Best of the Web* Link Library. In addition, this site provides helpful advice on how to conduct efficient and productive research from choosing a topic to polishing the final draft. Beginning philosophy students probably will find the *Best of the Web* Link Library the most appropriate place to start their research.

The free access code necessary to employ Research Navigator™ can be found in the Prentice Hall Guide to Evaluating Online Resources. If your text did not come with this guide, please go to *www.prenhall.com/contentselect* for information on how you can purchase an access code.

Lying, Cheating, Breaking Promises, and Stealing

Objectives

After you have read this chapter, you should be able to

1. Define *lying, cheating, breaking promises,* and *stealing.*

2. Understand why these moral issues are significant.

3. Explain the arguments for and against lying, cheating, breaking promises, and stealing.

4. Analyze and critically evaluate specific cases involving all of the above moral issues.

Introduction

Other than the taking of human life, the moral issues of lying, cheating, breaking promises, and stealing are usually considered the most important and the least acceptable moral violations humans can perform. These actions usually are not in direct violation of the Value of Life principle, as are the moral issues in Chapters 9, 10, and 11, but definitely constitute violations of the Principles of Truth Telling and Honesty, Justice and Fairness, and Goodness or Rightness. They also can be considered to be violations of the Principle of Individual Freedom in that they tend to give unjustified freedom to the perpetrators but deny freedom to the victims of such violations.

I have chosen to place this chapter right after the chapters on taking human life and before the chapters on human sexuality, bioethics, business ethics, and environmental ethics because many of the issues in the following four chapters are in fact specific or applied instances of violations of telling the truth, being honest, keeping promises and agreements, and respecting the belongings of others. For example, adultery in the moral area of human sexuality usually involves telling lies by the adulterers to their spouses. It certainly involves breaking promises usually stated in the marriage vows concerning fidelity. *Adultery* is also sometimes referred to as "cheating on your wife (or husband)." And finally, some adulterers often are considered to have stolen another person's spouse.

In the area of medical ethics or bioethics, lying can be involved in the decision as to whether to tell patients about the seriousness of their illnesses. Cheating takes place when patients are given treatment they don't need and are charged for it. A promise may be broken when doctors assure their patients that they will not abandon them, but then do. And stealing is seen in the overcharging or in the robbing of a patient's dignity or right to make choices about his or her own treatment.

In business ethics, false or misleading advertising is lying. Cheating is involved when a product is made with inferior materials. Breaking promises is the issue when employers or employees don't keep agreements that have been negotiated. And stealing is the proper term to describe what happens when employers or employees pilfer or embezzle from their companies or when companies steal from their employees or steal ideas from each other.

The significance of the moral issues in this chapter cannot be overemphasized because violations and nonviolations affect every level and activity of our daily lives. I have pointed out how they generally affect certain areas of our lives, but they come into play in all human relationships and therefore require careful scrutiny. In this chapter, I will state the issues as fully as I can, giving arguments for and against lying, for example, and citing cases for the application of these arguments. Further, I hope that both instructors and students will apply the arguments in these issues to their own experiences, bringing in their own applicable cases for discussion and striving to reach some kind of resolution whenever possible.

Definitions of Key Terms

Lying.   Lying, according to Sissela Bok in her book *Lying*, is "an intentionally deceptive message in the form of a statement."[1] The dictionary defines a *lie* as "anything meant to deceive or give a wrong impression."[2]

White Lie.   According to Bok, a white lie is "a falsehood not meant to injure anyone, and of little moral import."[3] Bok presents this definition as how she understands most people to define a "white lie" but does not herself feel that white lies have little or no moral import.

Lies of Commission and Omission.   I would like to add a further distinction to the definition of lying, which is that some lies are lies *of commission* or are direct statements that are outright lies. Other lies are lies *of omission*, which involve the not stating of certain information that is vital to a decision, relationship, or other important human activity. For example, to tell someone you are no longer taking drugs or drinking when you actually are, would be a lie of commission; on the other hand, to allow them to go on believing you have quit when you haven't, especially when the issue is vitally important to your relationship, would be a lie of omission.

Cheating. To cheat is "to deceive by trickery; swindle; to mislead; to act dishonestly or practice fraud."[4] As you can see by this definition, cheating and lying both fall under the general heading of deception.

Promise. According to the dictionary, a promise is "a declaration assuring that one will or will not do something; a vow." To break a promise, then, is to fail to conform to or to act contrary to or to violate the promise.[5]

Stealing. Again according to the dictionary, stealing is taking something without right or permission, generally in a surreptitious way.[6] In a legal sense, larceny is the felonious taking and removing of another's personal property with the intent of permanently depriving the owner.[7] This is further broken down into degrees such as "grand larceny" and "petit (or petty) larceny," which are based on some arbitrary standard.[8] For example, stealing apples from a grocery store is usually considered petty larceny, but stealing a car is grand larceny.

Nonconsequentialist and Consequentialist Views

It will prove to be of some value to return to the basic approaches to morality described in Chapters 2 and 3 because their basic positions on these issues are almost diametrically opposed, with the exception that the act nonconsequentialist in these issues would probably be closer to consequentialist theories than to the nonconsequentialist.

Rule Nonconsequentialist Views

As we might expect, the rule nonconsequentialist views, most typified by Kantian Duty Ethics, would be opposed to any of the four acts. Kant would argue that we cannot universalize lying, cheating, breaking promises, or stealing because they all would be contradictory if we did. For example, if we said that everyone should always lie, then we would contradict the meaning of truth telling; if we said that everyone should break promises, then promises would no longer have any meaning. He also would state that we would be treating human beings as means rather than ends if we lied to them, cheated them, broke our promises to them, and stole from them. Although Sir William David Ross might allow any of these if serious matters warranted it, his basic position, like Kant's, is that generally we should not lie, and so forth. This same position is held by St. Augustine (A.D. 354–430) and by John Wesley (1703–1791), the British founder of Methodism.

This traditional view that lying, cheating, breaking promises, and stealing are always wrong, then, is fairly strong in our history. Sometimes these actions are viewed as the next worst immoralities to taking human life, and in some cultures and their moral codes they *are* worse than killing and death. Very often, for example, a culture will punish such immoral acts by death, whereas in others, the violation of these important moral codes will bring such disgrace upon the perpetrator and even his family that he will be seriously ostracized from the group and may even commit suicide, seeing death as more honorable than living under such circumstances.

Consequentialist and Act Nonconsequentialist Views

Act Nonconsequentialism. The reason I have not included act nonconsequentialism with rule nonconsequentialism is that even though act nonconsequentialists do not use consequences in their decision making or consider them important, in their approach to morality, which is based upon feelings or intuition alone, they would not necessarily take a stand for or against these issues unless they *felt* like it. It seems quite possible that they might feel like lying or breaking promises at one time and not feel like it at others; therefore, although they might establish a permanent position against doing these acts on the basis of their feelings in general, they would not have to opt either for or against and could change their positions on these matters from situation to situation based upon how they felt at any particular time.

Consequentialism. Consequentialist theories would bring ends, results, or consequences into the picture whenever lying, cheating, breaking promises, or stealing is contemplated. Obviously, if consequences would warrant it, then any of the preceding could be acceptable. Consequentialists, even rule utilitarians, could not, based on this theory, say that we should *never* lie, cheat, break promises, or steal. They would state instead that these should or should not be done based upon whether or not what you did brought about the best consequences.

Ethical egoists would allow for doing any of these, provided that they could be reasonably sure it would be in their best interests to do them. They could, of course, not ever do any of them or do some of them only sometimes, but there certainly would be no absolute prohibition against doing any of them because it might be in their self-interest to do them.

Act utilitarians might do or not do any of them if they thought the action would bring about the best consequences for everyone affected by the act. If they thought lying would bring about the best consequences for everyone, for example, they certainly would lie.

Rule utilitarians might have rules against all four actions if they thought that bad consequences generally would ensue if people didn't basically adhere to rules prohibiting the four actions. They would have to make exceptions, of course, to those rules or qualify those rules in circumstances where violating the rules would definitely bring about the best consequences for everyone.

Although people may fall into any of these different categories—given that there are ethical egoists, Kantians, and act and rule utilitarians—I believe that most of us feel such acts are wrong in general because they tend to destroy the trust that is so essential to vital human relationships. People like to think, for example, that others will not lie to them, cheat them, break promises they make to them, or steal from them. Yet many are realistic enough to realize that someone may do these things, and they therefore must be on their guard.

The recipients of lies, cheating, broken promises, and theft often feel disappointed, resentful, angry, and upset, reactions that do not engender contentment or happiness. In addition, their ability to trust the offenders is diminished and may lead to a general distrust of all human relationships. In my estimation, most people will not hold to principles of "never" or "always" where lying, cheating, breaking promises, or stealing are involved; though generally against them, they will permit them in certain circumstances. Of course, as we learned in Chapter 1, what the majority does has nothing to do with what it ought to do, but in a practical sense we should be aware of the impact of these actions on our daily lives. I intend to present for each action what I feel are the major arguments pro and con, and each of you can decide for yourselves which arguments are the most compelling.

Lying

Arguments Against Lying

Dupes and Deprives Others. A major argument against lying is that it misinforms the people lied to and thus may frustrate them from reaching their own objectives. For example, suppose a wife and mother of two children wants to stay home with her children, but her husband says he is going to school and wants her to take a job so that he can continue. After a month, he decides not to stay in school and drops out but tells his wife he is still attending. By so lying, he has thwarted her wish to stay home and raise their children. His lying has not only blocked his wife's objective but has also deprived his children of their mother's care.

In another example, Jane thinks she has a chance for a promotion at the company where she works because the present manager tells her so, although he has actually selected David for the job. Thus Jane may decide not to seek a better job elsewhere or may turn one down, hoping she will be promoted where she is. The manager, first of all, has led Jane to believe she has more alternatives than she really has, which is a violation of the Justice principle—it's unfair to her. Second, although she would much rather stay with her present firm if she could move up, the manager's duplicity has caused her to lose confidence in what, for her, may have been the best alternative.

Causes Distrust in Human Relationships. Another major argument against lying is that it causes a breakdown in human relationships. If you think about it, human relationships are at their best when people can trust each other. Was Jane mistaken in trusting her boss? Most ethicists who do not support lying feel that we should be able to proceed on the positive assumption that we can trust, not on the negative one that we cannot. An entirely different atmosphere exists when human relationships are approached negatively rather than positively.

Lying not only causes distrust but also resentment, disappointment, and suspicion in the deceived. For example, if a woman has been continuously lied to by her husband and the marriage relationship therefore collapses, she may continue to distrust all future relationships with others, especially men. Thus, lying not only has ruined this relationship for her, it has also affected all future relationships as well. This may explain why some people who have been lied to say, "It's not so much what you did [for example, had an adulterous affair], but that you lied to me about it."

Human relationships generally depend on the communication of thoughts, feelings, and information. Because lying essentially amounts to a failure to communicate honestly, human relationships are very hard to establish or maintain when their main foundation—honesty—is undermined or destroyed.

The Domino Argument.   The domino argument has been discussed in previous chapters, but it bears looking at again in connection with lying. I have said that the domino argument in itself, without further evidence, will not influence people to refrain from performing certain acts. Nevertheless, we always should be aware that what we do may affect us and others by causing additional problems or reverberations beyond the initial action.

Those who are against lying feel that one lie tends to beget others in order to maintain the first one. As Sissela Bok states,

> It is easy, a wit observed, to tell a lie, but hard to tell only one. The first lie "must be thatched with another or it will rain through." More and more lies may come to be needed; the liar always has more mending to do. And the strains on him become greater each time—many have noted that it takes an excellent memory to keep one's untruths in good repair and disentangled. The sheer energy the liar has to devote to shoring them up is energy the honest man can dispose of freely.[9]

For example, in refusing to tell dying patients the truth about their condition, a situation is set up in which many other lies must follow so as to back up the first. It might be argued that lying will make the patients try harder to recover (even though recovery may not be possible), and that knowing their true condition will only depress them and make communication with them harder and their last days terrible. The initial lie will seem reasonable in this setting. However, if patients ask any serious questions about their condition, then more lies may have to be told. Precautions must be taken to prevent any information or even hints from leaking through to disrupt the growing web of lies that began innocently enough as a way of providing "protection" for the dying patient.

Added to the difficulties of maintaining the initial lie (which was one of omission, not commission) is the fact that many people are involved in the care of such a patient. Thus, as the patient's situation worsens and more procedures (or fewer, when a doctor deems there is nothing more to be done) have to be done, the patient may ask questions of all these people, causing more lies to be told: "I don't know; you must ask your doctor. You're going to get better. There's no need to worry." The irony of all this, according to Dr. Elisabeth Kübler-Ross, who has worked with dying patients for many years, is that all those she dealt with knew the seriousness of their illnesses whether or not they had been told, and many even knew when they were going to die.[10] This means that the deception was not only painful and blocked communication, but it also was not really necessary because the truth was generally known to everyone involved—even those whom the lies were supposed to protect.

Additionally, once a lie has been told, further lying in other situations becomes easier, often to the point where liars no longer can distinguish between what is or is not the truth as they know it. And if a liar gets away with one lie that he has told in order to "save his neck," in no matter how trivial a situation, then future lying becomes easier and sometimes almost a way of life. Habitual lying, of course, increases the chance of discovery, leading to the breakdown of trust and the dilution, if not destruction, of vital human relationships. Therefore, although the domino argument may not in itself prohibit one from doing an act, in the case of lying it is especially pertinent and should be carefully considered.

Unfair Advantage or Power for Liars. Another argument against lying is that because most liars do not themselves wish to be deceived, then to deceive others gives liars an unfair advantage. This is, of course, a violation of the Principle of Justice. A perfect example of the power one person can have over another may be found in Shakespeare's play *Othello.* Iago, Othello's aide, weaves one of the most insidious webs of lies ever seen in drama and literature. By the end of the play, Iago has not only controlled Othello's every move but also caused the death of Othello's wife, Desdemona, about whom most of the lies were concocted, and the injury and death of several others, including Othello himself. The power Iago has over most of the people in the play is almost unbelievable, and all of it is attained through the diabolical cleverness of his many deceptions.

Self-destructiveness of Lying. A major disadvantage in lying is that once liars are found out, their word is no longer trusted, their deceptions fall apart, and their power is decreased or lost. The Watergate affair during President Nixon's administration exemplifies this loss of power. Few people are as powerful as the president of the United States, and Nixon evidently maintained some of that power through various deceptions. As long as the public generally did not know this, he retained and even increased his power, but once his lying and dishonesty had been discovered, he definitely lost prestige and was forced to resign rather than be impeached. On the other hand, President Bill Clinton also lied to the public about his sexual affair with an intern, Monica Lewinsky, which certainly increased distrust of him and also caused many people to lose respect for him. However, he did not seem to lose a lot of power as president, probably because he was not lying about his presidential or political actions, but rather his personal life. Although most people were disgusted by the affair and his lying about it, they felt it did not relate directly to his duties and actions as president.

Another effect on the liars themselves, according to proponents of this argument, is that lying undermines one's own self-image. In other words, liars lose self-esteem because of their deceptions, and the more often these occur, the greater the loss.

Effect of Lying on Society. Bok assesses the general overall effect of lying on society as follows: "The veneer of social trust is often thin. As lies spread . . . trust is damaged . . . .

When it is damaged, the community as a whole suffers; and when it is destroyed, societies falter and collapse."[11] Many people in the United States and the world were shocked by President Nixon's lying in the Watergate affair. Trust in politicians and lawyers, shaky to begin with, fell to a new low. Some faith was renewed through the efforts of Archibald Cox and Leon Jaworski, chief prosecutors, and Senator Sam Ervin, who was in charge of the investigative committee, but the American public certainly experienced a loss of morale and faith in its leaders that hadn't occurred before to such an extent in the nation's history. Most people feel that a person's word is his or her bond and that it should be possible to trust everyone. Therefore, every breach of honesty destroys that belief, causes cynicism, condones lying, and destroys the thin "veneer of social trust." If the holder of the highest office in the land can and does lie, then why should not anyone else at any level of human relationships? Let's hope that most people won't let a bad example influence them in this way, but the temptation is certainly always there.

Arguments for Lying

Most ethicists and others would not argue in favor of lying all the time, although some people might. Inveterate liars usually will *not* lie all the time because they can then be more strategically effective when they do. If one lies all of the time, one has a greater chance of being found out and of losing at least the semblance of trustworthiness, something a "good" liar needs to maintain.

Most arguments for lying suggest that sometimes there are good reasons for telling lies. Therefore, to state unequivocally, as do Kant and others, that lying is never moral and should never be allowed, would be impractical and in some situations perhaps immoral. In some cases, they say, lying should be encouraged. For example, people ought to be able to lie when they need to or when lying could prevent the occurrence of a more serious moral infraction, such as killing.

Defense of the Innocent, Including Self-defense. According to Bok, "Deceit and violence . . . are the two forms of deliberate assault on human beings. Both can coerce people into acting against their will."[12] In most instances, however, ethicists deem lying to be less harmful to human life than violence, especially when the latter terminates human life. With some exceptions, if killing or allowing innocent lives to be lost is wrong, and if one can save such lives by lying, most ethicists allow for lying in such instances. For example, if an extremely angry man is looking for his gun to kill someone, and if you know where it is, these ethicists will state that you are justified in lying and not telling him where it is in order to save the lives of his intended victims. He may indeed find a gun somewhere else, but you at least have done all you can, by lying, to protect the potential victims.

Another example would be a wartime situation in which a member of the underground knows where other members are hiding. He would be justified in lying about their whereabouts rather than risking their capture and death.

One question arising in such a case is this: What constitutes defense of the innocent or self-defense? In the preceding two examples, the situation is clear, and in either case one can see that lives would be protected by lying. However, what about the president of a major corporation vital to national defense who is accused of embezzling funds and lies about it? When found out, she might argue that even though she was not protecting herself by her lie, as president of the company she felt a responsibility to lie to protect shareholders, workers, and also the "innocent public" for whom her corporation manufactures defense products. Are her contentions justified? First, it might be seriously argued that for her crime to be covered up, only to surface at a later date, would cause even more problems in the future. Second, it's unlikely that her being found out and removed from the presidency would seriously affect the lives she is presumed to be "protecting" by lying, because someone else could function as president.

National Security. Many ethicists argue for lying in order to maintain national security, an act that certainly may protect many innocent people. For example, if a woman spying for her country is caught, she may then lie about information she has in order to protect her country's security. Presidents and other members of the government sometimes state that they cannot reveal certain important information to the press or public because "it would endanger national security." Such people certainly should have some discretion in revealing information that would seriously affect national security, but they must be very careful not to abuse this right in order to protect their own self-interest.

For example, President Nixon often claimed that the reason he lied about the Watergate affair, the tapes, and everything else, was that telling the truth would have endangered national security. Obviously, national security was affected very little, although morale may have been. One could argue for national security in this instance only on the broadest basis, as, for example, that other world powers might condemn the United States because of its president's actions. It would be Nixon who would lose prestige, however, not the nation as a whole, which cannot take the responsibility for its president's actions. National security could be used as a valid reason for lying in certain circumstances only as long as it was not abused by members of the government or the military. President Clinton never used national security as an excuse, and indeed his actions did not seem to affect his or the United States' status worldwide. What he did certainly affected people's opinions of his character, but many foreign countries that have a more liberal view of sexual activity than the United States, while not necessarily supporting his actions, did not see them as detrimental to our country's relations with them.

Trade Secrets in Business. Ethicists favoring lying might argue that businesspeople may lie justifiably, either by omission or commission, rather than reveal vital trade secrets to their competitors. They aver that no businessperson has an obligation to tell competitors of his or her inventions or patents, which would give competitors unfair advantage. This permission to lie can also be extended to anything that would be in the business's self-interest, such as false and misleading advertising and lying for unfair advantage over other people or companies. Very often arguments sanctioning lying in business try to separate actions in the business world from those in life outside it, on the principle that in business anything goes, whereas one should never lie to loved ones or friends.

"Little White Lies." Many people, including some ethicists, allow for unimportant or harmless "little white lies," which are told to avoid hurting people's feelings or to protect those lying from embarrassment. The arguments for these lies are that people need to have leeway in social intercourse and daily activities in order to keep things running smoothly. For example, if one woman asks another how an expensive new dress looks on her, the other woman might answer that the dress looks fine even if she doesn't think so because she doesn't want to hurt the asker's feelings. In another case, a young man might ask a young woman for a date, but she doesn't want to go out with him because she dislikes his looks and personality. Rather than hurt his feelings and to save herself from the embarrassment of telling him her real reasons for not wanting to go out with him, she will lie and state that she already has a date when she really doesn't.

In all of these instances the liars usually feel that what they are lying about is unimportant, and that lying is a tactful way to avoid hurting people's feelings and save the liars some embarrassment. Further, they argue, in getting along in the world, lying sometimes can maintain the "social veneer" rather than crack it, as is advocated by the people who argue against lying. In other words, rather than hurting someone or suffering embarrassment, and as long as no serious harm is done, it's all right to lie to prevent either from happening.

Moderate Position

As with other topics in this book, a moderate rather than a strict pro or con attitude toward lying is the one most people probably favor. It advocates that, generally, one should avoid lying if possible and lie only as a last resort or clearly to save a life. This viewpoint is well expressed by the old saying "Honesty is the best policy." Moderates feel that lying is a serious matter, however little or white the lie. Moderates agree with those opposed to lying that the domino argument makes sense—that the more you lie, the easier it is to do so, and that one lie leads to another and another and another. They also agree that lying tends to break down the "social veneer," brings harm to those deceived, and destroys the integrity and human dignity of the liar whether or not he or she is caught.

Further, they believe that it's important to consider the consequences of *any* lie, however trivial. For instance, the woman who has lied to her friend about her dress may lose that friend if her lie is found out. Moreover, if by lying she encourages her friend to wear an unbecoming dress, then her lie has hurt, not helped, her friend. In the example about the man rejected for a date, if he happens to learn that the woman didn't have another date, then his feelings will be hurt much more than if she had told him the truth. Thus, moderates argue, the consequences of even white lies may be worse than if one had told the truth.

One point moderates stress is that lying is not the only other alternative to giving someone truthful information that might hurt. As Elisabeth Kübler-Ross has stated, the important question is not whether I should tell the truth, but *how* I should tell the truth, or how I should share information, important or not, with others who are asking me questions or who need to know what the truth is.[13] In other words, one does not have to be brutally frank. One can tell the truth, however terrible, but gently and with an intent to support and to give hope wherever possible. In the case of the women and the dress, for example, the friend could tell the one who asked, "Actually, I don't think that dress especially suits you, and I suggest you take it back and buy another. Because you thought enough of me to ask my opinion, may I help you return the dress and look for one that would be more flattering to you?" By replying in this way, the woman would not be lying, and she would be giving her friend some hope and encouragement about purchasing another dress that would be more becoming.

Even in situations where the truth is frightening to both hearer and deliverer, it can still be stated without materially harming another. Take a situation in which a family has been in a serious car accident and a wife/mother was killed, the husband/father is very critical, and the son is basically all right. What do you tell the father who asks about the others in his family? Do you lie and say that they are all right, or do you tell the truth? First you should stress that his son is doing well. Because of his critical condition, you would merely say that his wife was also injured in the accident (the truth) without saying anything further until he becomes stronger. However, if he asks you point-blank "Is she dead?" or states, "She's dead, isn't she?" Dr. Kübler-Ross says that you should be truthful but try to stress that his son is alive to give him a reason to try to recover.[14]

The basic thrust of the moderate position, then, is that one should generally try to tell the truth because telling lies often causes more problems than not doing so. Moderates also feel that

1. If people do choose to lie, they must try to make the consequences of their lying as harmless as possible.
2. People should try to avoid habitual lying and be aware of the risks of telling even one lie or a white lie.
3. People also should be aware that lying may have a deleterious effect not only upon the deceived, but also upon the deceiver.
4. People should never lie about important matters that may affect the recipient of the lie significantly.
5. Lying is allowed when there is no other recourse and when innocent life is really at stake, such as in the cases cited earlier concerning the enraged killer in search of his gun, the member of the underground during wartime, and the captured spy. Every other type of situation must be fully justified and the consequences carefully weighed. People should favor telling the truth, however, remembering that *how* they tell it is as important as the telling.

Cases for Study and Discussion

CASE 1 80-Year-Old Woman Whose Son Dies from a Heart Attack

Jesusita, 80 years old and with a bad heart, is living in a convalescent hospital where she is visited regularly by her 50-year-old son, along with other members of the family. Her son dies suddenly one night of a heart attack. The remaining members of the family feel that she shouldn't be told of this because of her own weak heart, and in collusion with the hospital staff, no one tells her. After a week, Jesusita asks why her son hasn't visited her, and the family tells her he is on a business trip, hoping she will forget about him. But the next week she asks where he is and when he will return. She also wants to know why he hasn't called her or written a letter or postcard from where he is. The family tells her he is very busy but should be back soon. Another week passes and Jesusita becomes very restless and upset about her son not visiting her; she becomes harder and harder to care for, and she cries a lot. The staff and family gather to discuss what to do about the situation. They wonder whether they should tell her the truth now or think up some more excuses.

1. Did they do the right thing in the beginning by lying to Jesusita?
2. If she were your mother or grandmother, and your brother or uncle had died, what do you think she should be told? Why or why not?
3. If you had done what they did or if you were staff dealing with this situation, what would you advise? Do you feel she should be told the truth now? If so, how would you do the telling? If not, how would you suggest this situation be handled?
4. Do you think it would have been better to tell her the truth in the beginning? Why or why not? Do you think not telling her in the beginning has made the situation better or worse? Why or why not? If so, in what ways?

CASE 2 Wife and Child Abuse

Mike and Barbara Barnes live next door to you with their two children—Casey, a boy, and Shelley, a girl. Mike often comes home drunk and usually acts violently toward Barbara and the children, giving them black eyes, bruises, and even broken bones. One night, after a particularly severe beating of all of them, Barbara visits you after Mike has passed out. She tells you she is going to a shelter for battered wives and children and asks you not to reveal to Mike where they have gone. Having always prided yourself on your truth telling, what do you tell Mike the next morning when he asks you to tell him where Barbara and the children have gone, expressing remorse for what he has done? Do you adhere to your past principles and tell him the truth, or do you lie to him? Why or why not? What exactly would you tell or not tell him, and why?

CASE 3 Adulterous Affair

Tom has been having an affair with his secretary, Francine, for about a year now, but both decide to end it. Francine leaves the company and gets a job in another state. Tom doesn't think that his wife, Carol, knows about the affair, but he feels very guilty and wonders whether he ought to be honest about it and tell her. He doesn't intend to have another affair and feels that he does love his wife and their three children. Yet he has strong guilt feelings and an urge to confess his adultery to Carol. He asks one of his friends, Doug, who knows of the affair, what he should do, and Doug tells him to leave well enough alone: "What she doesn't know won't hurt her," Doug says. Tom goes to confession and tells the priest what he has done. This particular priest (some might *not* say this) advises him to tell Carol, express his remorse, and promise never to do it again. Carol notices how preoccupied Tom is and asks him if there is anything wrong. What should Tom do? Should he tell Carol the truth or not? Why? Suppose, if he tells Carol about the affair, she asks for a separation and maybe even a divorce? And if he chooses not to tell her the truth, can he alleviate his strong guilt feelings? Would it be better or not in this case to tell the truth? Why?

CASE 4 Bill Clinton's Affair

President Bill Clinton had a sexual affair with a 21-year-old White House intern and then lied about it in court and in the media. He was then brought up for impeachment but was not impeached. To what extent do you think he should have been impeached? Why do you think he wasn't? Is what he did morally wrong? Why and in what sense? To what extent do you think what he did affected his position as president? Do you think his lies were worse, less worse, or about the same as President Nixon's? Why? To what extent do you think a president's personal life should be beyond reproach? Is it possible for a president to have a questionable personal life and still be an effective leader? Why or why not?

Cheating

Cheating, like lying, involves deception and dishonesty, except that lying is basically verbal, whereas cheating generally is nonverbal. Lying, as Bok defines it, is a statement of deception. Cheating, on the other hand, is an action meant to deceive. For example, if students copy the answers from your test, for which you have studied hard, that's cheating. If you tell them to stop cheating, and they deny that they have cheated, then that's lying.

Cheating can take many forms. As stated earlier, adultery usually encompasses both "cheating on one's spouse" and lying to cover up the action. People can cheat on their income tax, on forms used in their businesses (for example, deductions for expenses), in games played with others (whether simple games or serious gambling, such as poker), on insurance claims, on tests in school as already mentioned, on applications for employment or unemployment, and in sports.

Cheating, like lying, is a serious infraction of most moral systems because, like lying, it shatters the trust needed for the continuance and survival of human relationships. For example, if you buy a used car that is supposed to have 40,000 miles on it, but the dealer has turned the odometer back and it really has 140,000, then you have been cheated. You probably will never buy a car from that dealer again and may be wary even of honest businesspeople. If you are playing poker with presumed friends whom you think you can trust and you discover that one of them has been playing with marked cards, you probably will never trust that person again—certainly not in a card game where you stand to lose a good deal of money.

Arguments Against Cheating

Unfair and Unjust to Others. Obviously, cheating is unfair and unjust to those who are dedicated to "fair play." It's as if everyone, including the cheater, is playing by rules understood by all, but the cheater then abrogates the rules and deceives everyone else. For example, if other students are trying to get good grades and you cheat and get them, then your getting grades unfairly may deny the other students what they have earned and truly deserve. In addition to demeaning the importance of their careful studying, you also may skew the grading scale so that some students who might have gotten better grades through honest studying get worse ones.

In the same way, people playing in a game with a cheater may lose the game unfairly. This of course is a violation of the Principle of Justice and Fairness and also of a general code that most people observe when playing games or gambling. Game players generally agree to abide by the rules. If it's a trivial game and someone cheats, we won't want to play any further, because the game has lost its value. In a gambling game like poker, some deception is accepted, as when you fool your opponents into thinking you have a good hand when you don't. But one does not mark cards, deal from the bottom of the deck, or bring high cards into the game in a dishonest manner. In casino gambling, cheaters when caught are often ostracized, and in illegal gambling they sometimes have been beaten or even killed. Players in such games are expected to follow the basic rules and to take them very seriously.

Falsified Qualifications. Another argument against cheating pertains to the serious effect it has upon others with regard to professional qualifications or licensing. If, for example, medical or law students cheat when acquiring the crucial facts they must know in their intended professions, then their not learning them could cause loss of life or other kinds of harm to others. The cheating is even worse when it results in obtaining a license on the basis of presumed qualifications falsely attained. To some people, cheating on an exam or two doesn't seem very serious. "After all," the student may say, "when am I ever going to use this dull and ancient anatomy information?" If such a student, however, becomes a surgeon and neglects to perform an important procedure because he or she missed really learning something about anatomy in medical school, then someone's life could be in danger.

Effects on the Cheater. I have mentioned the harm that can be done to others by not being properly qualified or being falsely licensed because of cheating, but the effect on the cheater is also significant. People who cheat hurt themselves in the long run, which is another argument against cheating. If something bad occurs as a result of people's cheating, then they can be held responsible and subject to the law, both criminal and civil, and perhaps even lose their license to practice their profession.

And cheating, like lying, can become a habit. It's easier to cheat than to study or do other hard or necessary work. Successful cheaters may become lazy and generally will cheat again at an opportune time. This weakens their moral fiber and can affect their whole lives adversely, especially if they get caught. If people know that you cheat, the needed trust for vital human relationships, as in lying, will be broken, and you won't be able to maintain strong relationships. As in the gambling example, no one wants to play poker with a known cheater because the basic code and rules of the game are then destroyed. Further, if businesspeople become known as cheaters in their dealings with others—for example, in the manufacture of their products—their credibility is weakened as much and maybe more so than if they had lied.

Arguments for Cheating

Surviving and Winning. Many people who condone cheating regard the world and society as a "dog-eat-dog" jungle of corruption where one can survive only by using corrupt means such as cheating. They believe that "all's fair in love and war" and anything else and that people should cheat if necessary to get what they want and need. Such people see the world as so competitive and ruthless that in order to survive, one may have to break all the moral dos and don'ts and lie, cheat, break promises, and even steal if it will get them ahead.

Also found, along with this viewpoint, is the idea that winning is the most important thing in life, so if you can't win fairly, then win any way you can. In our moral teachings, good sportsmanship and fair play are supposedly held in high esteem, but in specific cases and instances, winning sometimes takes precedence over moral teachings. Often we see this in sports involving children. In many of children's competitive sports, such as baseball, the main goal in teaching is to have the children enjoy playing a game. To fulfill this goal, good mediocre, and poor players are distributed evenly among the competing teams, and the rules decree that everyone must play at least one inning. Often, however, if it's a close game, the manager will not use the lesser players, or play them so little that they learn nothing. This may win games, but it does not fulfill the stated goal, nor is it fair to the lesser players on the winning manager's team or to the other managers and their team members.

Everybody Does It. Right along with the "dog-eat-dog" theory is the "everybody does it" argument. This assumes that because most people probably cheat at some time in their lives, everyone is justified in also doing so if necessary. The argument further says that it's commonly known that all people cheat on their income taxes, on insurance claims by including other earlier damages, on expense vouchers, in golf games, and on their wives or husbands. One problem with this attitude is that it is questionable whether *most* people do these things. Another problem is that even if some or most people do these things, this does not mean that people *ought* to do them, as discussed in Chapter 1 in the difference between descriptive and prescriptive approaches to morality. History reveals that even the majority can be morally wrong, so "everybody does it" is not a very supportable or justifiable argument for doing something.

As Long as You Don't Get Caught. Many argue that cheating is all right if you can get away with it. Being caught is what's bad, not cheating. And the less chance you have of being caught, the more justified your cheating will be. This attitude could work with consequentialist, but never with nonconsequentialist theories. And even with consequentialist theories, being caught or not has nothing to do with whether an action is right or wrong. Only if you can show that greater good consequences can come from cheating could you justify it in any way.

Cases for Study and Discussion

CASE 1 Cheating on a History Test

Mike has an average of between a C+ and a B– in his history class, and the last exam he is taking could make all the difference. He has studied, but he didn't finish one section on World War II. When he starts the test, he discovers many more questions than he expected on that section. He needs a B in this class to get into graduate school. He notices that Renee, sitting next to him, seems to know the answers to the questions he needs. She likes him a lot and has not minded his looking at her tests before. A student stops to talk to the teacher on his way out of the testing room, and Mike sees that the teacher's vision will be blocked long enough for him to get the correct answers from Renee. Should Mike cheat or not? Consider the following questions in your deliberations:

1. Would it make any difference to your answer if the test grade were not as crucial to Mike's career? Why?
2. Considering that Mike has a good chance of not being caught, why shouldn't he cheat?
3. What arguments would you give to justify Mike's cheating or not cheating? Be specific.

CASE 2 Damaged Fender Included in Claim

Dick and Lorraine have been insured with Farmer's Mutual for their automobiles and house for 10 years. During this time they have filed one claim for only $500, and the costs of premiums have risen 100 percent. One day, while backing out of the garage, Lorraine badly damages the right fender, but she and Dick delay having it fixed. After several weeks, someone hits the right side of the car, while parked, damaging everything but the right front fender. In attempting to get the car repaired, they try to decide whether or not to include the fender, which is much more than their deductible allowance, in their estimate of the damage. Should they? They feel that the insurance company has made literally thousands of dollars from their premiums alone, not to mention those of other clients. They argue that the big corporations have made millions from their subscribers; they won't miss a few hundred or even a thousand dollars. Many of their friends have done the same thing on occasion, saving themselves hundreds of dollars. Because the fender could easily have been damaged in the same accident, it's unlikely their cheating would be discovered. What do you think they should do, and why? How would you answer all of their arguments for including the fender in the claim if you believe they shouldn't? If you believe they should include it, explain why, and provide arguments you would add to justify their action.

CASE 3 Ethics Professor Forging Letter of Recommendation

Mark, an ethics professor, has completed a manuscript for a new book entitled *Being Moral*. Before submitting it to a publisher, he writes a phony letter of recommendation from a well-known ethicist and sends it with his manuscript, reasoning that because there are so many ethics books on the market, his manuscript won't have a chance without something special to recommend it. The publisher accepts the book for publication. Just as he begins to distribute it, he discovers that the letter is a fake. At first the publisher thinks he might publish the book anyway, but then he decides not to, given the fact that the author is an ethicist and the book is about ethics. Was what Mark did wrong? Why or why not? Do you think the publisher was wrong to pull the book off the market for the reasons given? Why or why not? Does what Mark did seem worse to you because he is a teacher of ethics? Why or why not? How would you feel about using such a text knowing what the author had done? Be specific.

Breaking Promises

As stated earlier, a promise is a declaration, a vow, or an agreement into which a person enters freely. To the extent that a person is forcefully or subtly coerced into making a promise, he or she should not be expected to keep it as if it were made freely.

Implied Agreements

There are many *implied* agreements that allow us to live safely and meaningfully with each other in various groups in our societies. Some of these are

1. Not to do harm to one another.
2. Not to lie or cheat.
3. To obey laws for the general good.
4. To stop at red lights and stop signs.
5. To treat each other with respect and dignity.
6. To keep promises we make.

This chapter, however, will deal only with direct promises such as "I promise not to tell anyone what you have just told me because you have asked me not to."

A Form of Dishonesty

Breaking promises, like cheating, is a form of dishonesty and it also constitutes outright lying when the person making the promise has no intention of keeping it. An example is if you say to someone, "I promise I won't tell anyone what you told me," but then think to yourself, "Wait until Maureen hears this!" Not intending to keep the promise you just made violates the same bases of trust abused by lying and cheating and therefore is considered by most people to be an important moral issue.

A Person's Word

In earlier times, a person's promise or "word" was an integral part of his or her reputation, and many promises and agreements were made verbally or by just shaking hands. Some promises—usually personal ones—are still made in this fashion, but many are now written down, witnessed, notarized, and otherwise elaborately executed. One reason for this is the complexity of many contracts and agreements (sets of formal promises). But also, such written and carefully executed agreements are necessary because in modern society fewer people actually honor their agreements or promises.

For example, when my wife and I moved two houses into one, we sold some appliances, furniture, and clothes to three individuals. They made small down payments and agreed to pay the rest later. Not *one* of the three kept his promise! We haven't been able to locate them, and we've just written off the losses. On the other hand, some people I know, including myself, *would* keep such promises. All things considered, it's important to get a written agreement on such matters so that people can be sued if necessary.

However, even written agreements and promises (contracts or policies) do not guarantee that promises will be kept. Some people who violate them think they won't be caught or that no one will take the time or trouble to sue them. There are many aspects involved in keeping or breaking promises, and therefore this is an important issue that arises in all types of human relationships and activities.

Arguments Against Breaking Promises

Destruction of Personal Relationships. Next to lying, no action has a greater effect on relationships than breaking promises. One of the most emotional statements a person can make to another is, "But you *promised*!" When we are asked to promise something, or when we promise on our own to do something, most people tend to believe our word. If we break our word, it weakens our relationship with that person. For example, a superintendent of a school district urged many of the older faculty in the district who were close to retirement to leave by July 1. One of the incentives promised was that they could keep their almost full-coverage health plan although the active faculty was having to change to a health plan with less coverage because of financial difficulties within the district. However, on July 1, the superintendent moved everyone—retirees and active faculty—into the new plan with lesser coverage. Breaking his promise aroused tremendous protest in the district among both retirees and active faculty. After much discussion and concern on the part of both faculty and retirees, the situation finally was rectified, and the superintendent had to make good on his promise. However, the lack of trust that existed between him and the active faculty and retirees made it difficult to form agreements on other matters.

Domino Theory. As in lying and cheating, the domino theory is relevant here. Once a person breaks a promise and gets away with it, it's easier to break other promises, especially when convenient. For example, if a spouse commits adultery, it's easier to continue doing it with the same person or with others. In other words, it can become a way of life, as with lying or cheating. Of course, a person may break a promise for a serious reason, but one must be on one's guard against breaking one's promises, so that it doesn't become a habit.

Effects on People's Life Choices. Because people depend upon the promises made to them and the implied and direct agreements they have with others, breaking them can seriously affect their lives. For example, in the health-plan situation described earlier, most, if not all, of the older faculty retired earlier than they wished to, mainly because of the health plan. Many would have worked another year or two to gain more retirement benefits if they were not to benefit from their previous good health plan. So the superintendent's keeping or breaking his promise had a most important effect on their lives. In another example, if a woman promises to marry a man within a year, and he works hard toward that goal and sacrifices to build a nest egg, if she breaks her promise because she has found someone else whom she has been seeing for six months, she will significantly hurt the man to whom she made the promise.

Destruction of General Social Trust. There is no doubt that breaking promises also affects society in general. Kant's position is that if we were to establish a rule that promises should always be broken, then the word *promise* would be totally contradicted and lose its meaning. It amounts to saying, "I promise . . . but I have absolutely no intention of keeping my promise." Promises sometimes must be broken for good and serious reasons, but the intentional breaking of promises must seriously concern society in general. As I stated earlier, much of what we do is based upon promises or agreements, so when these start to break down, the "thin veneer" of social trust begins to warp and crack. This loss of trust is very evident with regard to promises in political campaigns. Voters generally are somewhat cynical about politicians, many of whom seem to promise the moon but when elected show more concern for helping special-interest groups or for gaining money or power for themselves. Indeed, some politicians who do try to keep their promises, especially with regard to controversial issues (abortion, for example), sometimes fail to achieve reelection. As a result, many candidates for office tend to dodge important issues, and promise nothing really significant during their campaigns. This further weakens the trust people have in their elected representatives.

Loss of Personal Integrity. A final argument against promise breaking centers upon the loss of personal integrity for the person who fails to keep promises. As with lying and cheating, promise breaking involves not only loss of reputation for honesty with other people but also loss of one's self-esteem. We may have a difficult time living with ourselves once we have "gone back on our word" and let someone down. Even those who behave as if they don't feel any guilt may actually feel it within. For example, many spouses who break their marriage vows (promises) experience tremendous guilt feelings, regardless of whether they are found out. When they are, the guilt feelings are multiplied not only because of the injury to their spouses, but also because of the adverse effects upon their children and the entire family unit. Most people have some moral sense and therefore cannot escape from their promise breaking totally unscathed.

Arguments for Breaking Promises

Changed Circumstances. One argument favoring promise breaking is that an individual who has made a promise should have the right to break it when the circumstances under which it was made change. An example would be that of marriage vows made when the spouses were in love. If they "fall out of love," then the situation has changed and the vows should no longer apply. Suppose, for instance, that the sexual relationship of a married couple is no longer vital, because one spouse has become indifferent to that aspect of their relationship. Proponents for breaking promises might feel therefore that the other spouse has no obligation to remain faithful.

Another example might be if a person borrows some money from a friend and promises to pay it back at a certain time. Later, however, he loses his job and decides to forget his promise and not repay the loan because the situation has changed so drastically. It could be argued that despite this the borrower still has an obligation to pay *sometime* and ought to make arrangements to do so. But defenders of his action would dispute this on the basis that individuals must have the right to break such a promise when it interferes with their own interests and welfare.

When There Are Moral Conflicts. Those who defend promise breaking also believe that promises can be broken when important moral conflicts are involved. For example, suppose Bruce tells his good friend Louise that he is secretly going to a cabin in the mountains they both know about because he is having financial difficulties and although he wants her to be able to contact him, he doesn't want anyone else to know where he is. He asks her to promise to tell no one of his whereabouts, and she agrees. Later she is visited by police, who reveal that Bruce's partner has been violently murdered and that Bruce is their prime suspect. Is she still obligated to keep her promise to Bruce, or should she break it to aid the police? Proponents of promise breaking would argue for the latter, in that protecting human life takes precedence over keeping one's word.

When It's a Trivial Issue. Promise breaking proponents also feel that promises may be broken when doing so will do no harm or when they seem trivial. Suppose, for example, that a family has a rule that their children have only one piece of candy a day, but Freddie takes three pieces and makes his sister Marie promise not to tell on him. She agrees, but when their mother arrives home, Marie immediately tells what Freddie has done, and he is punished for breaking the rule. When he asks Marie why she broke her promise, she explains that she had her fingers crossed, so the promise didn't count. To defenders of promise breaking, the situation is trivial and has caused no real harm. Of course Freddie *was* punished, but the counterarguers would point out that Freddie *did* indeed break the rule, and in any case it is still a minor issue.

Another example is when someone makes a small bet, let's say a dime, and then when he loses refuses to pay (a form of promise breaking) because he thinks the bet is too trivial to honor. Is there any serious harm done here? Some would argue that breaking promises, even in such small matters, still tends to destroy the social trust that exists in all human relationships and therefore is never minor. As was pointed out in Sissela Bok's discussion of "little white lies," the whole social fabric is injured when even the smallest promises are broken. Could Freddie ever trust Marie again to keep her promises? Did the person who won the dime but was not paid learn something about this so-called friend that would lead that person never to trust him again in either small or large issues? This argument should be scrutinized closely, not for the triviality of a situation or the little harm done within it, but for what it can mean in a larger sense.

Where Unusual Situations Justify It. Another argument for promise breaking centers on situations in which promises are made that later may and perhaps should (in the view of the promise maker) be broken. Suppose, for example, a friend on his deathbed reveals that he has made you an heir to his estate because he wants you to use the money to care for his cats and dogs, leaving out of his will his two devoted children. He begs you to promise to execute his wishes so that he can die in peace. You do so, but after his death, feeling that his children should inherit most of the estate rather than the animals and that what he has done is morally wrong, you break your promise so that his estate will go to his rightful heirs. Your action in this unusual situation would be defended by proponents of promise breaking in that what you do after your friend's death will not be known by him, and also the children deserve the inheritance more than the animals.

No Promise Is Sacred. The Latin phrase *caveat emptor*—"let the buyer beware"—is used by some to sanction promise breaking. The implication is that it is foolish and naive to believe that a promise will be kept simply because it was made, and that it is more realistic to accept that it probably will be broken. In a way this shifts the responsibility onto the recipient rather than the promise maker and entirely reverses the concept of social trust under which we live. It certainly promotes an atmosphere of wariness and distrust in human relationships.

Cases for Study and Discussion

CASE 1 Promise Not to Smoke

Bernard and Janice are considering marriage, but Bernard smokes and Janice can't stand smoking. She will marry Bernie only if he quits. Before they are married, he promises to do so and presumably does. He is a psychiatric nurse and works in an atmosphere where almost all patients and staff members smoke. After several years of marriage, Janice discovers that Bernie never gave it up but just hasn't smoked at home. He evidently brushed his teeth and used breath mints before he came home, and the smell of smoke on his clothes was attributed to the atmosphere in which he worked. Very upset, she feels that he has broken an important promise to her. Do you feel that this promise was a trivial one and that Janice is being unreasonable? Why, or why not? Does the fact that this promise was made in connection with their marriage have more significance than it otherwise might? Why? Their marriage later ended after a series of other broken promises, not the least of which was an affair of Bernie's that constituted a negation of his marriage promises or vows. In your experience, to what extent do people who break a promise on one occasion continue to do so on other occasions? Give examples.

CASE 2 Promise to a Dying Friend

Harold and David, in their mid-twenties, are avid mountain climbers. David has been dating Harold's sister, Doris. During a mountain-climbing expedition by just the two men Harold is seriously injured and is dying. He begs David to promise to marry Doris, who, as Harold knows, is very much in love with David. Moreover, Harold is worried about what will happen to her when he dies. Because Harold is David's best friend, David promises he will marry Doris. After Harold dies, David tells no one about the promise. He enjoys Doris's company, but he doesn't love her and breaks his promise to marry her. Did David do the right thing? If no one knows about a promise, does it have to be kept? Why or why not? Under what conditions, if any?

CASE 3 Mother Lying to Teenage Daughter

Wanda is divorced from her husband and lives alone with her 10-year-old daughter, Sandy. She has told Sandy that she will always tell her the truth about anything she asks, and if she doesn't know what the truth is, she will find it out for her. After about a year without dating, Wanda meets Howard and they begin seeing each other. After a while, they discreetly engage in sex, usually when Sandy is with her father on weekends. Sandy suspects this and finally gets up enough courage to ask her mother about their relationship. Embarrassed and concerned about her image with Sandy and feeling that Sandy is too young to understand, Wanda tells her they are not having sex. One weekend Sandy comes home unexpectedly and finds Wanda and Howard in bed together. Sandy is very angry with her mother and asks how long this has been going on. Not wanting to lie to her anymore, Wanda tells Sandy, "For a couple of months." Sandy yells, "You lied to me!" and "You promised you would always tell me the truth!" Wanda also becomes angry and tells Sandy she is too young to understand what's going on, and when she gets older she *will*. She also tells her that what she does when Sandy is not around is none of Sandy's business. Should more leeway be allowed in keeping or breaking promises where children are involved because they may be too young to understand? Why, or why not? Does Sandy have a right to know the truth about her mother's life outside of their immediate relationship? Why, or why not? Are Wanda's reasons for not telling Sandy and her reactions to Sandy's anger justified? Why, or why not? How do you think Wanda should have dealt with this whole situation if you don't like the way she did deal with it? Why? Be specific.

Stealing

A basic assumption in most societies and cultures is that stealing is an immoral act. If the victim of theft needs what is stolen from him to survive, then the theft is even more reprehensible. Stealing applies not only to the taking of material things, but also to the stealing of ideas (for example, plagiarizing), inventions, and other creations by an individual.

Arguments Against Stealing

Property Rights. Stealing involves taking someone else's property without that person's permission. This is a violation of property rights, which often are considered to be as important or even more important than life itself. Many people feel strongly, for example, about governments taking private property or forcing people to sell their property for the "public good." Often when people won't willingly sell their property, they can be forced by the state to do so. In one way or another, it will condemn the property so that a freeway, public building, or even a private building can be constructed on it. Property rights, especially in a democracy, are considered important, and stealing therefore is strongly condemned. Even in societies where property is owned by the state rather than private individuals, stealing is forbidden because it is stealing from the state, which actually means stealing from all the people of the state.

Breakdown of Trust. Like lying, cheating, and breaking promises, stealing severely breaks down trust among people. People who have earned their possessions feel that they have an inalienable right to them. When a theft occurs and the thief is known, any relationship with that person will be difficult to maintain because of the loss of trust. If you've ever been the victim of theft, and you suspect someone you know such as a friend or even a relative, you can never truly trust that person again. Moreover, if you were actually to catch that person stealing, then your relationship with him or her will usually be destroyed.

For example, most of us feel we can leave money or jewelry around our homes without locking them up, but once such things are stolen, we will probably take more precautions against everyone, including family and friends. Once stealing has taken place, trust is abrogated.

Invasion of Privacy. Another argument against stealing is that it is an invasion of privacy. The thief violates the privacy of the victim's person, home, car, or office. A further assault on privacy takes place when a thief steals a wallet or a purse and then has access to the person's identity and credit cards. This can interfere with the victim's daily life until matters can be straightened out and new cards obtained.

The Domino Argument. Some people, of course, are habitual thieves and steal for a living. They had to start somewhere, which recalls the domino theory. Once people steal and get away with it, they may tend to steal again, especially if they discover that they can get what they want easier and faster than if they have to work at a steady job. Stealing becomes a pattern, a way of attaining what the thief aspires to—"if you want or need something, just steal it" can become the motto by which they live. Consider the number of thieves who spend time in prison and return to stealing after their terms are up and they are back in society.

Material Losses to Victims. In addition to the invasion of privacy, victims of theft also suffer the loss of hard-earned or cherished items. When people's cars are stolen, for example, they may get them back and the insurance may pay for damages, but the loss has been a terrible inconvenience, and their cars are not the same after thieves have used and abused them. When ideas, inventions, or other aspects of creativity are stolen, the victims suffer even greater loss, for it involves the products of their own thinking. An example would be if someone discovers or invents something that revolutionizes an industry or our lives, and a big corporation steals it from the inventor so that she gets no recognition, reimbursement, or reward for her own ideas.

Effect on the Thief. In addition to the punishments of fines and imprisonment, proponents of arguments against stealing point out that stealing also affects a thief's self-image. When thieves are caught, they generally lose the trust and respect of others. But even if they are not caught, and if they continue to steal, it's likely that their precarious existence and the guilt they feel will seriously affect their self-respect. Of course, some thieves enjoy stealing (see the Thrills and Adventure section later in this chapter) and find it exciting and more interesting than working at a steady job.

Overall Effect on Society. Opponents of stealing see it as a threat beyond the loss of personal possessions. In a neighborhood where many thefts have occurred, for example, people may be constantly worried that they and their homes will be victimized at any time. Additionally, because many thieves are armed with dangerous weapons, injury or possible death can occur. But even if they don't, the victims will suffer in that their trust in their fellow human beings can't help but be lessened.

Like the other moral issues discussed in this chapter, stealing and the fear that it engenders cause a breakdown in human relationships that are based upon mutual trust. If theft has not occurred and is not threatened, people tend not to be afraid or generally concerned about the possible loss of their possessions; but when it is definitely indicated that it may occur because it has happened to someone else nearby, then people's attitudes are changed from trust and security to distrust, fear, and insecurity. Therefore, stealing has enormous effects upon the entire social fabric.

Arguments for Stealing

Corrupt Economic System. One argument for stealing rests on the assumption that we live in a corrupt social and economic system in which the rich get richer and the poor get poorer. The only way to balance these inequities is by sometimes stealing what you need and want. Everyone needs to have basic necessities and even some luxuries, and if the entire system prevents this, then people are entitled to steal when they get the chance.

Sometimes people attempt to balance what they deem to be inequities by stealing, in small ways or large, from the companies where they work, on insurance claims, in taxes to the government, and from other human beings, especially those who are better off than they are. A good example of this attitude is given in Case 2 of Chapter 15 on business ethics, where Steve's union can get him an 8 percent raise when he had hoped for 15 percent. To make up the difference, Steve steals tools and materials from the plant where he works to remodel his house, which is what he had intended to do with the expected raise.

Many people justify padding their expense accounts because they consider themselves underpaid by their companies. They cheat on their income taxes because they feel the government wastes tax money anyway and they ought to get some good out of what they give to the government. Or they misrepresent their losses to insurance companies because of large sums they have paid in premiums over the years and because they feel that the insurance companies won't miss it while they themselves never have enough money to live on.

Crucial Emergency Situations. Many people who do not condone stealing in general would allow it in crucial emergency situations, such as if a family is poor, the parents cannot get work, and there is no food for the family to eat. If the husband steals food so that his wife and children won't starve, then stealing is justified in this case. Another example is that if a man is chased by killers and finds a car with keys in it, to save his life, he may steal the car. Human life is more important, according to this argument, than property rights, and stealing, when more important issues such as preserving human life are at stake, is morally justified.

Thrills and Adventure. To some, stealing provides a life of excitement, thrills, and adventure not obtainable in ordinary life and is therefore worth the risks involved. The notorious bank robber Willie Sutton, who spent most of his life in prison for theft, felt that his life out of prison was more exciting when he could steal than it was when leading a mundane existence in a nine-to-five job. How many thieves would take this position is uncertain, but whether such an exciting regimen is worth all the time spent in prison or suffering other hardships can be decided only by the thieves themselves.

From Institutions and Organizations. Many people think that stealing from fellow humans is not justified but that stealing from big institutions and organizations is. Because most large organizations and institutions make huge profits at the expense of us "little guys," they argue, then we have a right to recoup some of what they get from us by stealing from them in various ways. I mentioned earlier that stealing small or large items from the companies where we work, padding our expense accounts, cheating on income taxes, and making false claims against insurance companies are all ways of "getting even" with big business and big government for acquiring more than they deserve. Stealing from large organizations and institutions is morally justified, according to this argument, in that it helps to rectify the imbalance in goods and services received.

As Long as You Don't Get Caught. As with cheating, some argue that it isn't stealing that is wrong but rather getting caught. Therefore, they probably would argue, you shouldn't steal if there's a good chance you will be caught and therefore punished. They sanction stealing if it can be done safely. This argument is not concerned with a moral issue in stealing, but rather with the consequences of it if one is caught. It would be rejected by nonconsequentialists and at least some consequentialists (unless more good consequences came from stealing than not) as in the matter of cheating and not getting caught.

Military and Government Secrets. Many feel that stealing military or government secrets in wartime and also peacetime is justified in the interest of national security. Therefore, if the United States knew that one of its enemies had a secret weapon that it had recently developed, our undercover agents would be perfectly justified in stealing the plans for it if it would enable our nation to keep ahead of its enemy in military preparedness.

An interesting reversal of this argument is the justification of stealing one's own country's secret documents so as to expose injustice. The Pentagon Papers, for example, were stolen and given to the press in order to reveal improper practices by the government and the military in conducting the Vietnam War. The justification for this theft and the revelation of the contents of the stolen documents was that the immorality should be exposed and not allowed to continue. It's interesting to speculate whether the same people who would justify stealing secrets from foreign powers for national security would also justify stealing from our own government to reveal immorality and corruption.

Similar to these two instances is the stealing of trade secrets in business activities. To exceed or stay abreast of one's competitors, one needs to know what plans they have that might give them control over the entire market, including oneself. Some support such theft (it's called "industrial espionage") as being a necessity in the competitive business world we live in. Others see and abhor it as simply stealing.

Cases for Study and Discussion

CASE 1 Theft of a Title for an Ethics Text

Seven years ago, Victor published what has become a popular ethics textbook called *Ethics with Applications*. The book is now in its third edition. Looking through flyers for new ethics texts, he sees one with exactly the same title as his. Dismayed, he immediately contacts his editor, who tells him that titles, unfortunately, cannot be copyrighted but are fair game for anyone who wants to use them. Victor angrily writes both the publisher and the authors of the other text, complaining that they have stolen his title. They never answer him, and he remains extremely upset. He would never knowingly steal someone's title and can't understand their action. Even though what they did is legal, are they morally obligated not to use Victor's title? Why, or why not? Should they at least apologize for doing so? Is there anything else they could do to make things right, or do they need to? Why, or why not? If titles cannot be copyrighted, then can this be considered stealing? Why, or why not? Is this an important or trivial issue, to your way of thinking? Why, or why not?

CASE 2 Stealing Food

During wartime, Katia and her family have been starving because their town has been bombed and is under siege. She breaks into someone's house, finds food in the kitchen, and steals it for her family. Is she justified in stealing in this instance? Why, or why not? Be specific. Would it make any difference if it were during peacetime but times were hard, and Katia couldn't get a job and earn money to buy food? Why, or why not?

CASE 3 Looting

During riots in various cities throughout the United States, many poor people looted TV and appliance stores for items they said they were denied by a corrupt society that segregated and oppressed them. Some of them said that such items were not really luxuries because most Americans had them. Do you believe that this stealing was justified or not? Why? If not, how does it differ from stealing food? Is there anything to the poor people's arguments? Why, or why not? Are there any times when you would justify stealing? If not, why not? If so, when? Be specific.

CASE 4 Changing of a Will

Leroy died suddenly, leaving behind him Margaret, his wife, who was suffering from atherosclerosis (hardening of the arteries) of the brain, for whom he had cared devotedly because she was practically an invalid. In his will he left his substantial estate to her, to go upon her death to his side of the family. He had actually earned all the money because Margaret had never gone to work. Margaret's sister, Anne, and her husband, Eric, an attorney, agreed to take care of her, putting her into a skilled nursing facility near their home for which all expenses were paid from Leroy's estate. While she was still alive, they changed Margaret's will, splitting the estate 40/60 in favor of her side of the family. They had a doctor certify that she was mentally competent to make such a change, but Leroy's family, who had visited her, noticed that she was capable of very little in the way of decision making. As longtime friends of Anne and Eric, they had trusted them not to do anything improper. When they learned that Anne and Eric had changed Leroy's will under what they felt to be very shady circumstances, they accused them of stealing. Do you believe that what Anne and Eric did was theft? Why, or why not? Do you feel they had a right to change Leroy's will? Why, or why not? If they felt their side of the family had been wronged, was there anything that Anne and Eric could have done differently to rectify the problem? What, and why? This action ended a friendship of many years' standing and caused hard feelings on both sides. Are such effects worth considering in such a situation? Why, or why not?

Chapter Summary

I. Definition of key terms
   A. Lying is an intentionally deceptive message in the form of a statement or piece of information deliberately presented as being true—anything meant to deceive or give a wrong impression.
      1. A white lie is a falsehood not meant to injure anyone and is often considered as having little moral import.
      2. Lies of commission are direct statements that are outright lies. Lies of omission involve not stating certain information that is vital to an important human activity.
   B. Cheating is deceiving by trickery, swindling, misleading, and acting dishonestly or practicing fraud.
   C. A promise is a declaration or vow that one will or will not do something, and to break a promise is to fail to conform to or to act contrary to or to violate the promise.
   D. Stealing is taking something without right or permission, generally in a surreptitious way.

II. Nonconsequentialist and consequentialist views
   A. Rule nonconsequentialist views are opposed to any of the four acts at any time.
   B. Consequentialist and act nonconsequentialist views.
      1. Act nonconsequentialists would not necessarily take a stand for or against these issues unless they felt like doing so.
      2. Consequentialist theories would accept any of the four actions if the greatest good consequences would result.

III. Lying
   A. Arguments against lying are as follows:
      1. Lying may obscure objectives of those lied to.
      2. It may hide relevant alternatives.
      3. It causes distrust in human relationships.
      4. The domino argument seems to have more relevance here than it does with other moral issues because very often one lie of necessity leads to another to protect the first, and so on.
      5. Lying gives an unfair advantage or power to the liar.
      6. Lying has a deleterious effect upon society in general.
   B. Arguments for lying also exist.
      1. Lying is justified in defense of the innocent, including self-defense.
      2. Lying is justified for reasons of national security provided this reason is not abused.
      3. Lying is moral when it is done in order to protect trade secrets in business.
      4. Little white lies should be allowed as a way of getting along with others in our daily lives.
   C. The moderate position has the following aspects.
      1. This position would generally accept the attitude that "honesty is the best policy."
      2. One must be very careful of the consequences of any lie, even white lies.
      3. Lying is not the only alternative to telling hurtful truths—one may tell this truth gently, compassionately, and with hope wherever possible.
      4. If people have to lie, then they must try to make the consequences of the lying as harmless as possible.
      5. One should try to avoid habitual lying.
      6. One should be aware that lying also can have a bad effect upon the liar as well as the person lied to.
      7. One should never lie about important matters that may affect the recipient of the lie adversely.
      8. Lying can be allowed when there is no other recourse and when innocent life really is at stake.

IV. Cheating
   A. Cheating is related to lying, in that deception and dishonesty are both being practiced, but lying generally is verbal whereas cheating is basically nonverbal.
   B. There are arguments against cheating.
      1. It is unfair and unjust to others.
      2. Falsified qualifications for professions, for example, will have a serious effect upon everyone.
      3. Effects on cheaters may also be destructive if they are caught in a lack-of-qualifications situation and also because it can become a habit affecting the cheater's relationship with others.
   C. Arguments for cheating are as follows.
      1. The world is a dog-eat-dog jungle, one in which you often must cheat to survive and get ahead. Also, winning is everything, no matter how you do it.
      2. Everybody does it; therefore, why not cheat?
      3. It's all right to cheat, so long as you don't get caught.

V. Breaking promises
   A. Implied agreements such as the following allow us to live safely and meaningfully with each other in society:
      1. Not to do harm to one another.
      2. Not to lie or cheat.
      3. To obey laws imposed for the general good.

      4. To stop at red lights and stop signs.

      5. To treat each other with respect and dignity.

      6. To keep promises we make.

  B. Breaking promises is a form of dishonesty, as is cheating.

  C. In earlier days, a person's promise or word was an integral part of his or her reputation, but now many promises or agreements have to be written down for two reasons:

      1. Because they are much more complex than they used to be.

      2. Because fewer people actually honor their agreements these days.

  D. Arguments against breaking promises.

      1. Breaking promises destroys human relationships.

      2. Again, the domino argument applies here.

      3. Breaking promises seriously affects people's life choices.

      4. Breaking promises destroys general social trust.

      5. Loss of personal integrity may result if people continually break their promises.

  E. Arguments for breaking promises.

      1. One should have the individual freedom to decide which promises to keep and which to break. Any rules against breaking promises are a denial of such freedom.

      2. Breaking promises should be allowed when more important moral issues are involved, such as protecting and saving human life.

      3. It also should be allowed when no harm is done to anyone by breaking the promise.

      4. Promises made in unusual situations, as for example to satisfy someone on his or her deathbed, can justifiably be broken later on, especially for good reasons.

      5. Just as we often say, "buyer beware," recipients of promises also should beware—they shouldn't count on promises being kept.

VI. Stealing

  A. A basic assumption in most societies is that people are entitled to what they have inherited, invented, created, and earned; therefore, stealing generally is considered to be immoral.

  B. There are many arguments against stealing.

      1. People have property rights, which often are considered as important or even more important than life itself.

      2. Like the other three moral issues discussed in this chapter, stealing breaks down the trust people have in one another.

      3. Stealing constitutes a serious invasion of privacy.

      4. The domino argument applies here, as well as in the other three issues.

      5. Stealing has destructive effects, both physical and psychological, upon victims.

      6. Thieves themselves can be seriously affected through loss of integrity and through punishment if they are caught.

      7. As with the other three issues, stealing also has a bad effect on society in general.

  C. Arguments for stealing are as follows.

      1. We live in a corrupt economic system in which the rich get richer and the poor get poorer, and sometimes the only way to achieve some sort of balance between these inequities is to steal.

      2. Stealing should be allowed in crucial emergency situations, such as to prevent the starvation of children.

      3. Stealing is a way out for those who crave a life of thrills, adventure, and excitement.

      4. It is allowable to steal from institutions and organizations because they can afford it and end up with most of our money anyway.

5. As with cheating, one ought to be allowed to steal as long as one doesn't get caught.
6. It can be condoned when it involves stealing government and military secrets from potential or real enemies so as to protect one's own national security.

Exercises for Review

1. In your own words, define *lying, cheating, breaking promises, stealing, white lies,* and *acts of commission and omission.* Give a clear example of each.
2. What is the "domino argument," and how does it apply to the four moral issues described in this chapter? Do you think it's an important consideration or not? Why?
3. What are the arguments *against* lying, cheating, breaking promises, and stealing, and to what extent do you agree or disagree with them? Be specific. Present any other arguments you can think of and justify them as fully as you can.
4. What are the arguments *for* lying, cheating, breaking promises, and stealing, and to what extent do you agree or disagree with *them*? Again be specific, and present any others you can think of.
5. To what extent do you feel that lying, cheating, breaking promises, and stealing really have an effect upon society in general? Give specific examples or illustrations.
6. To what extent do you feel that doing these things really has an effect upon the one who does them? Again, give examples and illustrations to show how they do or do not have an effect.
7. Defend or attack the position that "little white lies" are not important or serious in any way and are in fact needed in our everyday human relationships.
8. Discuss fully the idea that it's all right to lie, cheat, break promises, or steal, "as long as you don't get caught." To what extent do you support this contention, and why? Be specific.
9. To what extent do you agree or disagree with the statement that "promises and agreements need to be written down more today than in the past because fewer people actually honor their promises and agreements"? Why? Give examples to support your position.
10. To what extent and in what instances do you lie, cheat, break promises, and/or steal? Why or why not? Be specific, and give examples.

Views of the Major Ethical Theories on Lying, Cheating, Breaking Promises, and Stealing

Because I have already given a brief overview of all the theories except Virtue Ethics, state whether you agree or disagree with this overview, expand upon it, and include Virtue Ethics in describing how these theories—Ethical Egoism, Utilitarianism, Divine Command Theory, Kant's Duty Ethics, Ross' *Prima Facie* Duties, and Virtue Ethics—would deal with the moral issues of lying, cheating, breaking promises, and stealing. Refer to Chapters 2, 3, and 4 to refresh your memory on the theories, and to Chapter 9, "The Taking of Human Life," for an example of how you might go about completing this assignment.

Notes

1. Sissela Bok, *Lying: Moral Choice in Public and Private Life* (New York: Vintage, 1979), 16.
2. William Morris, ed., *The American Heritage Dictionary of the English Language* (Boston: Houghton Mifflin, 1978), 754.

3. *Bok, Lying*, 61.

4. Morris, *American Heritage Dictionary*, 229.

5. Ibid., 1047, 162.

6. Ibid., 1261.

7. Ibid., 738.

8. Ibid., 573, 981, respectively.

9. Bok, *Lying*, 26–27.

10. Elisabeth Kübler-Ross, *On Death and Dying* (New York: Macmillan, 1969), 262.

11. Bok, *Lying*, 28.

12. Ibid., 19.

13. Kübler-Ross, *On Death and Dying*, 28.

14. Elisabeth Kübler-Ross, *Coping with Death and Dying*, a set of audiotapes; date and publisher unknown.

Research Navigator™
(http://www.researchnavigator.com)

This web site offers three research databases: EBSCO's *ContentSelect Academic Journal and Abstract Database, New York Times* Search by Subject Archive, and *Best of the Web* Link Library. In addition, this site provides helpful advice on how to conduct efficient and productive research from choosing a topic to polishing the final draft. Beginning philosophy students probably will find the *Best of the Web* Link Library the most appropriate place to start their research.

The free access code necessary to employ Research Navigator™ can be found in the Prentice Hall Guide to Evaluating Online Resources. If your text did not come with this guide, please go to *www.prenhall.com/contentselect* for information on how you can purchase an access code.

Chapter

13

Morality, Marriage, and Human Sexuality

Objectives

After you have read this chapter, you should be able to

1. Distinguish between the public, or societal, and private aspects of human sexuality.

2. Discuss the purposes of human sexual activity.

3. Discuss the following moral issues in sexuality: premarital sex; sex in marriage-type relationships (including the issues of homosexuality and adultery); prostitution; masturbation; pornography; and perversion, or unnatural sexual relations.

Major Aspects of Human Sexuality

The first distinction we must make when discussing morality and human sexuality is that which exists between its public, or societal, aspect and its private aspect. First of all, the public aspect is concerned with the way in which matters of sex *overtly* affect others, and the basic governing principles of morality here are life, goodness, and justice. The private aspect, on the other hand, is concerned with sexual relations between or among consenting adults, and the basic governing principles in this case are those of goodness, justice, freedom, and honesty.

In other words, it is important to distinguish between two kinds of actions involving human sexuality: those that have such an adverse effect on people other than the participants that they should be forbidden by moral commandment or by law, and those that affect only the participants and should therefore be left up to the private moral deliberations of the people concerned. Needless to say, one of the main issues surrounding human sexual activity is whether we should greatly restrict such activities on the one hand or allow a great deal of sexual freedom on the other. Before dealing with arguments concerning restriction or liberalization of sexual activity, it probably would be of value to examine what the meaning and purposes of human sexuality are deemed to be.

The Meaning and Purposes of Human Sexuality

The meaning and purposes of human sexual activity appear to be four-dimensional, involving (not necessarily in order of importance) procreation; pleasure; an expression of love for other people; and an expression of friendship and liking. These, of course, need not be mutually exclusive, and often they are not; however, sexual activity also may be limited to only one of these purposes. Although procreation is a rather obvious purpose of sexuality, sexuality is also—in the opinion of many—the deepest and most intimate expression of the love of human beings for one another. This does not mean that one cannot love others without sexual activity—if that were true, one could never love his or her children, brothers, sisters, parents, or grandparents without being incestuous. What it does mean is that when a love involving meaningful sex occurs, it is deeper than any other kind of love. For instance, two people need not have sex in order to love each other, but deep and loving sex between two persons can add a rich new dimension to any love.

It is, many feel, a terrible oversight on the part of society in general that the loving aspect of sex has been considered relatively unimportant when compared to its procreative aspect or to other areas of human relationships. Our society has, at least until recently, often emphasized that sex is somehow a necessary evil. This approach to human sexuality implies either that its primary purpose is to produce children or that sexuality is not a very important aspect of human relationships and human life. This is an attitude reflected in many of our laws, which are throwbacks to nineteenth-century Victorianism. In the Victorian era, all kinds of private sex acts between or among consenting adults were forbidden, to the extent that if a husband and wife wished to practice oral sex, for example, they would, under the law, be guilty of a felony.

Many of these archaic and unfair laws (unfair, that is, when applied to all human beings) have been repealed in many states and revised in accordance with the American Bar Association's suggestions. The reason for this change in attitude is that these laws reflected a view of human sexual activity that does not square with studies made in the nineteenth and twentieth centuries, including those of Freud, Kinsey, and Masters and Johnson.[1]

Almost all the research conducted by twentieth-century psychologists (see the bibliography at the end of this book) reveals, first of all, that sexuality as it is practiced did not and does not adhere to the general societal moral pronouncements and laws. Second, it reveals that human sexuality for many people is very limited and that sexual relations often are unsatisfying because of these people's upbringing, which has been strongly influenced by the taboos against meaningful sexual relations set up and generally sanctioned by their society. Third, this research reveals that psychologically, sexuality is extremely important to human living and especially to human relationships. In view of such strong evidence, it seems that the expression-of-love, friendship-and-liking aspects of human sexual activity should be emphasized more than they have been—in fact, that they should be emphasized at least as much as procreation and pleasure.

The conservative, or restrictive, view of sexual activity often emphasizes either the procreation aspect of sex or the view that sex is a "necessary evil"—that is, a biological urge felt by men (but not, it is implied, by women) that must be satisfied. Advocates of complete freedom in sexual matters, on the other hand, usually emphasize the pleasure aspect and the rights of individuals to enjoy such pleasure. There is also a more moderate position, of which proponents tend to accept both the procreative and pleasure aspects while also including—and often emphasizing more strongly—the expression-of-love, friendship-and-liking aspects. I do not want to suggest that the lines are always drawn this clearly; a proponent of sexual freedom may, for example, strongly emphasize the expression-of-love aspect—as may a supporter of the conservative view. However, the general tendency is for each group to emphasize the aspects in the way in which I have described.

Moral Issues and the Public Aspect of Human Sexuality

Those sexual acts that immediately affect the public or individuals in such a way so as to bring them possible harm, that are generally considered immoral, and that usually are controlled by laws are rape, child molestation, and sadism performed on unwilling victims. The possible harmful effects that can ensue from these three types of acts are bodily harm and/or death and the general perniciousness of forced sexual activity. No matter what set of ethical principles they endorse, most people generally agree that these acts are immoral and that there should be laws and/or moral taboos forbidding them.

Other activities considered by many to be against the public interest are pornography; homosexuality; sex outside of marriage (including premarital and extramarital sex and adultery); prostitution; masturbation; nonmonogamous marriages; and "unnatural," or "perverted," sexual activity. Agreement about the immorality of these activities is not, however, as general or as clear as is agreement about the first three activities. I will present specific arguments for and against these issues later in the chapter, but first it is worthwhile to examine some arguments for and against sexual freedom in general.

Arguments Against Sexual Freedom

Violation of Tradition and Family Values. The first argument against sexual freedom is that such freedom is a violation of the traditional moral "absolutes" embodied in our Judeo-Christian heritage. According to this tradition, heterosexual sex is the only morally permissible sexuality. Furthermore, sexual acts should be performed as "God and nature intended" (that is, generally in the "missionary position," with the man on top and the woman on the bottom). Finally, sexual activity must take place only within a legally and, preferably, a religiously sanctioned marriage between one man and one woman who are joined together mainly for the purpose of bringing children into the world. Outside of marriage the only acceptable approach to sexuality is abstinence. Of course, pornography, homosexuality, sex outside of marriage, prostitution, masturbation, nonmonogamous marriages, and "unnatural," "perverted," sexual activity are considered to be violations of these traditional moral teachings, either because they tend to undermine our family and societal structure, or because they eventually will lead to the destruction of these institutions.

The Domino Argument. The domino argument applies here, as it does to so many moral issues and this time in two ways. First, allowing sexual freedom in any of the areas named previously will eventually lead to violations in more dangerous areas. It is argued that if, for example, we allow people the freedom to read, view, and acquire pornography openly, eventually there will be an increase in rapes, child molestation, and sadism performed on unwilling victims, all of which may lead to sexual murders. According to this argument, pornography so inflames the sexual appetites and desires of people that they will have to find outlets for these appetites and will resort to these unacceptable means. Second, it is argued that allowing more sexual freedom in these areas will undermine our society and all the good and decent things it stands for, such as the family, respect for marriage, love rather than lust, respect for the human body, respect for women and men, and respect for children.

Offensiveness to Public Taste. This argument presumes a certain general agreement concerning what is acceptable and what is offensive to the public taste. Heterosexual relationships are acceptable, whereas homosexual ones are not. Monogamous marriages are acceptable, whereas polygamous (more than one wife) or polyandrous (more than one husband) ones are not. Sexual activity within a marriage is acceptable, whereas outside of marriage it is not, and so on.

Social Diseases and AIDS. The social-diseases argument cites the probability of getting certain social diseases, such as syphilis, gonorrhea, herpes, chlamydia and the dreaded and fatal acquired immune deficiency syndrome (AIDS), through sexual promiscuity and sexual freedom. The proponents of this argument state that all of the so-called sexual freedom of the 1960s, 1970s, and 1980s has led to an increase in such diseases, which are not only painful, destructive, and contagious, but also in many cases (especially with AIDS) fatal. A return to and reemphasis of traditional sexual morality would be the best way to eliminate such terrible diseases, according to proponents of this argument.

Arguments for Sexual Freedom

Individual Freedom. The main argument presented by the proponents of this position is that people ought to have the freedom to do what they want to do, as long as they are consenting adults and are not materially or directly harming other members of society by their actions. Obviously, people should not be free to rape, to molest children, or to perform sadistic acts on unwilling victims; however, they ought to be completely free to have any kind of sex they wish with other consenting adults or by themselves, in or outside of marriage, as long as they do not harm others.

Traditions Seen as Irrelevant. Even though the prosexual freedom advocates recognize that there are Judeo-Christian or other traditions that have, in the past, served as guides for sexual morality, they do not consider such traditions to be "absolute." In fact, they argue that such traditions are based upon archaic views of the biological and psychological makeup of human beings—views that twentieth-century advances in the sciences and social sciences have revealed to be inaccurate. Now that we know more about human sexuality, the prosexual freedom forces argue, we should allow a wider and more open expression of one of the most important human drives in existence.

They also argue that there is no clear-cut indication of what "God and nature intended" in sexuality except what is condoned or prohibited in certain religious teachings, which one may or may not believe. They state that the marriage contract is merely a piece of paper, and that there is evidence that sex that takes place outside of marriage can be just as meaningful as that which takes place within it. Furthermore, sex between homosexuals and in polygamous or polyandrous relationships or marriages can be as meaningful as sex between heterosexuals in monogamous marriages. Because human beings are so varied and unique in their feelings and desires, sexual-freedom proponents argue, they ought to be allowed the greatest freedom of sexual expression possible as long as they do not harm others.

Refutation of the Domino Argument. The sexual-freedom proponents would argue that there is no hard evidence to suggest that allowing greater sexual freedom in the seven "questionable" areas will lead to violations in the areas of rape, incest, and forced sadism. They argue further that some evidence exists that in countries such as Denmark, where pornography has been made totally legal and freely available, the rate of sexual crimes, such as child molestation, has dropped. Sexual-freedom supporters see pornography as a force that relieves sexual repressions and eliminates the need for these more harmful types of sexual activities.

Even if, however, there are abuses of freedom in relation to pornography—for example, sexual murder or so-called kiddie porn—laws can be passed restricting and punishing people involved in those activities without restricting people's general freedom of access to pornography. Second, this argument states that rather than undermining our society, greater sexual freedom will enhance it by allowing for fuller sexual expression. This in turn will deepen the love, respect, and intensity of human relationships, which can only improve marriage, family life, and society in general.

Offensiveness to Public Taste. According to the sexual-freedom proponents, offensiveness to public taste is not in itself a reason to halt the activities of others, and therefore it should be considered more of a violation of customs and manners than a violation of morality. Bodily harm and/or death are immoral under most ethical principles, but offensiveness to public taste is not unless it can be shown that the Principle of Justice has been seriously violated. This does not mean that the rights and feelings of others in matters of taste should not be considered; what it does mean is that the excuse that something is offensive to others, even though they are not required to participate in any way, is not sufficient to bar someone, either by moral censure or by law, from engaging in certain activities.

Discretion certainly should be employed in the public display of pornography and other sexual activities offered for those who wish to participate (topless or nude shows, films, and so on), and there should be control of indecent exposure, overt solicitation, or coercion to participate in any sexual activities. However, this is not to say that an open display of affection that does not involve indecent exposure or overt solicitation or coercion is immoral even though—especially between or among homosexuals—it may offend some people's tastes. Therefore, if sexual activity does not violate any of the preceding criteria, and it often does not, it then becomes, according to the sexual-freedom proponents, largely a private matter to be dealt with between or among consenting adults.

There are many ways in which the problem of offensiveness to public taste can be handled. For example, if people want to sunbathe or swim in the nude, then special locations can be purchased or set aside for them to do so. Those who do not wish to do so need never go near these locations. If some adults want to view pornographic films, buy books, or see live nude people, then as long as those who do not want to do such things are not forced to do so, and as long as these theaters, bookstores, and nude shows are obviously marked and advertised to show what they are, then how can there be an overt offense to taste?

Furthermore, there is no conclusive evidence that participation in any of these activities has caused harm to society in general; that is, that people who read pornographic books, for example, go out and molest children or rape others. In fact, as mentioned earlier, some studies have shown that in countries where laws against pornographic shows, films, and books have been relaxed, overt sexual crimes have tended to decrease. The proof for this is not conclusive either, but if there is no conclusive proof either way, then such activities should not be considered immoral or illegal merely for the above reasons.

Social Diseases and AIDS. Proponents of sexual freedom certainly recognize the dangers of social diseases and especially AIDS; however, proper precautions can certainly be taken to avoid or minimize the contracting of such diseases, such as abstinence (if a person desires), the use of condoms and other devices and chemicals, and the careful choosing of one's sexual partners. Such choices, however, should be free ones, and no one's freedom should be curtailed just because such diseases might be contracted. After all, smokers may get cancer and drinkers may get cirrhosis of the liver, but this does not mean we have the right to restrict their freedom to indulge in these activities.

Premarital Sex

Premarital sex refers to those sexual relations that occur prior to marriage; it is referred to in the Bible as "fornication."

Arguments Against Premarital Sex

The Undermining of Traditional Morality and Family Values. As I have mentioned, the conservative position toward liberalizing sexuality states that one of the greatest problems created by encouraging or even allowing premarital sex is that it tends to undermine traditional Western morality and family values. According to this view, as we have said, sexuality should be something reserved for a heterosexual, monogamous marriage and used mainly, but not necessarily exclusively, for purposes of procreation. Allowing premarital sex discourages the special and unique relationship that exists between one man and one woman in a lifetime of marriage, it undermines both marriage itself as an institution and family values, and it encourages sexual activity that is separate from "true" love and from having children. According to this argument, the only acceptable form of sexuality for boys and girls and men and women is no sexuality, or abstinence until marriage.

The argument continues that if marriage breaks down, then the traditional family unit breaks down, and the family unit is the basic building block of traditional Western society. Premarital sex also encourages an inflated view of sex as the most important aspect of marriage, thereby further eroding one of our most important social institutions. According to this view, sexuality is considered to be such an intimate part of the relationship between a man and a woman that it must have the stability and security of the marriage relationship to foster and support it.

The Encouragement of Promiscuity. Another argument that supports the conservative point of view is that premarital sex fosters promiscuity and encourages transitory rather than lasting human relationships. If sex is allowed outside of marriage, it becomes separated from its "true" purposes, which are to enhance marriage relationships and family values and produce children. Instead, according to this argument, the only purpose of premarital sex is to achieve selfish individual pleasures without accepting the responsibility for one's own actions or the lives of others involved. Premarital sex also encourages promiscuity, in that without marriage the societal restrictions are loosened, and one can virtually have sex with anyone at any time. Therefore, the lasting, meaningful relationships between men and women that are established and developed through marriage are replaced by "one-night stands," which reduce human relationships to the animal level.

Social Diseases and AIDS. One of the most powerful arguments against premarital sex is the possibility of spreading social diseases and especially AIDS. People who argue against premarital sex state that abstinence is the best way to avoid contracting these diseases. Therefore, as traditional family values have always taught, one should abstain from sexual intercourse or other sexual activity until one gets married. Before men and women get married they should voluntarily be tested for the AIDS virus to ensure that neither partner will infect the other. Obviously, however, premarital sex puts one in danger of contracting such diseases and passing them on to other sexual partners or future wives or husbands.

The Fostering of Guilt and Ostracism. Because premarital sex is frowned upon by our culture and our society, it can result in various degrees of guilt and ostracism for those who engage in it. Whatever is initially felt by individuals who want to engage in premarital sex, most of the people around them—especially their parents, other relatives, and sometimes their friends—generally are opposed to their actions, and because of this they may experience guilt and be ostracized from accepted society.

Having Children. Within the accepted marital relationship, children who are brought into the world can be protected and raised with some security. They will also legally have a family name. There is always the possibility within the premarital relationship that children will be born, and if they are, they may be raised out of wedlock. If a couple decides on an abortion, then the premarital relationship has fostered yet another moral wrong: the murder of an innocent fetus. If children are raised in such a relationship, what will they think once they discover that their parents are not married, while everyone else's parents are?

The Compatibility and Experience Fallacy. One argument often given for premarital sex is that it allows people to gain sexual experience so that when they enter into marriage they will know what they are doing. Another aspect of this argument is that people who have sex or live together are able to find out whether they are really sexually compatible, thus avoiding the misfortune of finding out after they are married that they aren't and perhaps never will be.

According to the conservative view, this argument provides no excuse for premarital sex. After all, classes in marriage and the family and in sex hygiene are now offered in school, and there are many good scientific books available on the subject. The compatibility argument, furthermore, places the sole emphasis for a relationship upon sexual attraction, and a marriage is much more than that. Besides, any advantages gained in the way of experience or knowledge about compatibility are far outweighed by the violation of the sacredness of marriage and family values, the inevitable loss of respect that occurs when two people become mere sex objects in each other's eyes, and the instability of the relationship. For if there is no marriage, people who live together can leave at any time they want to, experiencing no sense of concern for the other person or for any children who may have resulted from their relationship. Also, it is argued, there is something unique in the marriage of two people who come to each other as virgins because sex then becomes a very special offering of love from one person to the other. For this reason, as well as the others cited, premarital sex, therefore, should not be encouraged or allowed.

Arguments for Premarital Sex

The Obsolescence of the Old Traditions. Certainly the prevalence of premarital sex may change the society's lifestyle, but, according to the liberal viewpoint, the old traditions already have been undermined because they simply are no longer applicable in an advanced, technological, and rapidly changing world such as ours. The family unit already has become more mobile and flexible in reaction to the complexity of our modern culture. Some of the changes that have taken place in society are for the better and some are not, but, according to the liberal view, what we need is a number of alternative lifestyles that will allow us to enjoy the freedom and individuality that are encouraged these days.

Besides, the sexual-freedom proponents argue, what is so great about the old style of marriage and family values in which the father is a dictator and the mother a slave to her housework and her children? Furthermore, what is good about hypocritical marriages in which unhappy couples stay together just because they are married or "because of the children"? Many adulterous relationships are spawned by these "sacred" but unsatisfying marriages, and how is that any better than premarital sex? At least the two people involved in a premarital relationship can have some prior agreement that if it doesn't work, they will try something else.

Social Diseases and AIDS. It is unreasonable in our modern day and age to advocate abstinence from sexuality. The proponents of premarital sex state that abstinence is unnatural and an elimination of one of humanity's greatest pleasures. All one needs to do is take the proper precautions, such as using a condom and eliminating certain sexual acts that perpetuate the spread of AIDS, for example. Further, one can enter into a relatively monogamous premarital sexual relationship or limit one's partners to those who are known to be free from these diseases. Social diseases in themselves, then, are not a sufficient reason for not engaging in premarital sex.

The Promiscuity Fallacy. First of all, many premarital sex arrangements do not condone promiscuity. Many of these affairs are long-lasting—sometimes as long-lasting as a marriage—and such relationships may even develop into marriages. Second, sexual-freedom proponents ask, is the level of promiscuity in premarital relationships any greater than that in marriages? Does being married preclude the fact that one or both spouses will be promiscuous? Third, even if unmarried people are promiscuous, as long as they are freely consenting adults, whose business is it but theirs?

The Guilt and Ostracism Fallacy. People's views of premarital sex have changed a great deal, and few people who engage in premarital sex nowadays are ostracized from society; this also applies to children born out of wedlock. People simply are not as concerned about these matters as they used to be. Guilt, furthermore, is a matter of private conscience, and as long as the consciences of the people who enjoy premarital sex are not disturbed, then why should anyone else's be? People who do not approve don't have to condone or engage in premarital sex themselves, and they shouldn't concern themselves with other people's behavior as long as it doesn't intrude into their lives. Parents of people involved in premarital sex certainly don't have to condone these activities in their own homes, but what their children do on their own is their business as long as they are consenting adults.

Contraception and Responsibility. People who engage in premarital sex can, of course, use contraceptive devices, and they probably do use them more often than not. Often, proponents would state, the children resulting from such relationships are cared for as well as or even better than they would be if they were born into a marriage. Furthermore, when such couples plan for or discover they are going to have a child, they often will get married out of respect for the child's position in their relationship and in society in general. And, if an accidental or unplanned pregnancy occurs, then abortion exists as a viable alternative. This alternative often is used even within those marriages where children are not wanted, so why can't it be used here also?

Sexual Experience and Compatibility. Sexual experience and compatibility, according to those who would allow premarital sex, is one of its greatest advantages. They feel that learning through experience what sexuality is all about and relating to different people sexually will enable people to discover what type of relationship they want and what type of person they want to share it with.

One of the myths of our culture is that sexual activity is a natural ability that one can easily draw upon after one is married. As a matter of fact, a sexual relationship, not mere biological coupling, is terribly complex and requires a great deal of knowledge and ability. Sexuality does not "come naturally," and is particularly hard to acquire in a culture that has repressed it for so long. A good sexual relationship also requires a level of awareness of and comfort with one's body and the bodies of others so that greater freedom can be attained. Premarital sex is the best means of achieving sexual experience and knowledge, especially if two people are considering a long-lasting relationship. If they live together from day to day, they will find out over a period of time whether they will be compatible in a marriage. Even if they discover that they are not compatible, they probably will have learned something about themselves that will not only help them to avoid making the serious mistake of entering into marriage but also will help them to discover what kind of partner they really do want.

Sexual Pleasure. Another advantage of premarital sex is that sexual activity is pleasurable in itself, whether or not it leads to marriage or even a lasting relationship. When premarital sex is allowed, sexual pleasure can be enjoyed freely to the extent any individual wishes without the need for permanent commitment. This kind of relationship may not be suitable for some people, but those who find it morally acceptable ought to be free to indulge in it without regard to society's standards or the wishes of others who are not involved in their relationship or relationships.

A Private, Not a Public, Matter. Despite what the critics of premarital sex say about the undermining of Western traditions and family values, premarital sex is one of those private sexual matters that should be left to the discretion of free, consenting adults. As the liberal arguments presented at the beginning of this chapter illustrate, this is a matter for individuals to decide, and just because some or even the majority of people living in our society do not approve of premarital sex, as long as it is not forced on them or their children it should both be allowed and be considered moral.

Sex in Marriage-Type Relationships (Including Nonlegal)

A marriage-type relationship is one that is continuous and lasting (or intended to be) rather than temporary or transitory. There is, of course, some overlap between this type of relationship and a premarital one. For example, some premarital sex relationships that begin as transitory or temporary may become permanent or lasting. Also, many people classify any sexual relationship occurring between two never-married people as premarital or *extramarital* (occurring *outside* of marriage). The latter term also is often used to mean adultery, which will be dealt with later. However, I am using the phrase "marriage-type" to refer to any relationship that is intended by the two or more people involved to be permanent or lasting and in which sex is a deeper part of a more involved human relationship than is the case in many premarital relationships.

The purpose of sex in a marriage-type relationship appears to be twofold. First, it provides a deep and intimate expression of love between or among persons, including the giving and receiving of pleasure. Second, it provides the means for procreating, or having children. These purposes are not *necessarily* compatible *or* incompatible. That is, people may have a permanent or lasting sexual relationship without ever having children; or, in expressing their love for each other, a man and a woman may end up having children as a part of that expression.

Obviously, this description of "a deep expression of love" as the main purpose of sex does not square with some societal and religious views. Nevertheless, I do not believe that merely because the main way children can be created is through sexual intercourse between a man and woman (at least at the present time, with the exception of artificial insemination, although life created in the laboratory is a distinct future possibility, especially given the recent successes in producing test-tube babies) that procreation must *necessarily* be the only valid reason or purpose for the sex act. To take this stand reduces human beings to the level of animals who mate instinctively and infrequently for purposes of procreating their species and relegates sex to a merely biological function.

The overwhelming evidence amassed by psychology in the nineteenth and twentieth centuries strongly suggests that human beings are not merely instinctive animals, mating only at certain times of the year for procreative purposes, nor is human sexual intercourse merely a biological function; rather, it is a deep and personal expression and communication of oneself to others that brings forth one of the greatest human pleasures and in which a great deal of oneself is involved.

This also may include the desire to join together in the creation of a child, but it need not—the expressing of love and the giving and receiving of pleasure are both valid reasons for engaging in sexual activity. That even animals express some love and affection before, during, and after sexual intercourse would seem to be supported by observation, but the type of expression they indulge in pales alongside that which human beings are capable of. Furthermore, because the need and desire for sexual love among human beings does not diminish after children are created and because even childless couples have such desires and needs, then it becomes more questionable to classify human sexuality as being solely a means of procreation.

Various Types of Marriage Relationships

In using the phrase "types of marriage relationships," I am referring to nonlegal marriages as well as those that have been legalized by certificate or sanctioned by a particular religion. What I mean by "marriage" is an agreement, legal or nonlegal, between people to live together and share each other's lives in a deep, meaningful, and (intentionally) lasting way. Such a relationship usually includes sexual expression, but it need not (even some legal marriages—the so-called brother and sister marriages—are entered into for mutual convenience, and the people involved have agreed not to have sex as a part of their relationship). Given this definition, then, many different types of "marriage" relationships are possible.

Monogamy. The most common type of marriage relationship in the Western world is monogamy, which involves one man and one woman. There are advantages, both legal and otherwise, to having a monogamous marriage relationship:

1. The love relationship can be so intimate and involved that most people would find it very difficult to have more than one such relationship.
2. Financially, it usually is much easier for two people to support each other.
3. Legally, in our present societal structure, it is nearly impossible for a husband to have more than one wife or for a wife to have more than one husband.
4. As has been argued earlier, such a relationship, if kept monogamous, will avoid the contracting of social diseases and AIDS.

Despite these advantages, there are no evident *rational* moral reasons why monogamy need be the only valid marriage-type relationship. The Bible decrees that monogamy is the most accepted form of marriage, but unless one feels morally obligated to follow that particular set of teachings, there seems to be no reason why other forms of marriage should be deemed either illegal or immoral as long as ethical principles are adhered to. (It would be terribly unfair, for example, for a person to have more than one spouse if the two spouses did not know about it and had not agreed to such an arrangement.) From experience, then, it appears that monogamy relates best to Western culture, but that does not mean that other forms cannot coexist.

Polygamy (Including Polyandry and Bigamy). Strictly speaking, *polygamy* means having more than one husband or wife, *polyandry* means having more than one husband, and *bigamy* means having two wives or two husbands. However, I shall refer to all of these types of situations as polygamy. As long as all of the people involved are informed about the situation and agree to be involved in it, no form of polygamy need be considered immoral in and of itself.

Many cultures (including the ancient Hebrew culture depicted in the Bible) have accepted various forms of polygamy, and they have worked with varying degrees of success. Quite often men have had more than one wife and kept them subordinate and submissive; *this* is considered by many to be immoral—unless the wife knowingly prefers it this way—under principles involving justice and freedom. However, especially where there has been a shortage of men or women, some form of polygamy often has saved from extinction the culture in which it was practiced, protecting it by ensuring procreation and also by making it possible for men or women who did not want to live without a mate of the opposite sex not to have to live alone. The Islamic and early Mormon cultures are good examples of polygamy's success. There may have been violations of ethical principles in these cultures, but one would be hard put to blame them *necessarily* on the fact that polygamy rather than monogamy was being practiced.

Group Marriage (With and Without "Free Love"). A great deal of experimentation with marriage-type relationships has occurred during the last half of the twentieth century. One example of this is the "group marriage," with or without "free love." This approach to marriage grew out of the desire in the 1960s to return to a communal and cooperative kind of living in which various people, sometimes already married (legally or nonlegally) and sometimes not, chose to live together in a community—sometimes small (as in one house), sometimes large—usually partially or completely outside of the larger society from which they originally came. In most of these types of marriages, the children are raised in common and all of the adult members are parents; however, some of these groups retain the small family unit.

Some groups indulge in "free love"; that is, any two or more people in the group may have sexual relations as they so desire on a "free" basis as long as no force or coercion is used and without regard to any previous monogamous arrangements. Other groups keep a monogamous autonomy, merely choosing to live more closely together with other couples or single people than our society generally encourages or makes possible. Again, the children may either be raised in common by all of the people or be kept within the usual monogamous relationships while at the same time having a closer relationship with other children and adults than our society usually makes possible.

It is very difficult to assess the results or effects on the human beings concerned in such relationships because this kind of experimentation has not been going on for very long; also, few scientific studies are being made of these groups because of the members' desire for privacy. One of the advantages of group marriage cited by members or former members is that the children (when all the adults were considered to be their parents) received a great deal of attention from all kinds of adults and were never without supervision or diversified companionship. A second advantage often cited is that when members of such groups are compatible, very meaningful communities often develop, thus avoiding much of the isolation and alienation often found in our dehumanized technological society.

Most reports indicate that those group marriages in which free love is not accepted tend to have less friction and upheaval than those in which it is accepted. This may indicate sexuality is so intimate, intense, and personal that it is difficult to diffuse it among several adults without engendering strong feelings of jealousy, guilt, and sadness at being separated from a loved one who goes off with someone else. It also may indicate that because our culture has been so steeped in monogamy, it is extremely difficult to adjust to free-love relationships. Another advantage to the non-free-love approach is that any chance of contracting or passing on social diseases or AIDS is minimized.

Arguments Against Nonmonogamous Marriages

The conservative view of family values accepts monogamy as being the exclusive marital relationship for the reasons I have already described. To summarize them: First, marriage is prescribed in the Bible, which is the great moral book of Western tradition and family values.

Second, whether one believes in the Bible or not, marriage is part of our society's tradition. Third, the love relationship is too intimate to involve more than one man and one woman. Fourth, such a relationship will eliminate any problems connected with social diseases or AIDS provided spouses keep their marriage vows. And, finally, children are better off when they are raised in the traditional family structure. This does not mean that groups of families cannot live in some kind of communal situation, but according to this conservative view, the immediate family structure, the nuclear family unit, should remain autonomous.

Arguments for Nonmonogamous Marriages

The liberal view does not prescribe a specific type of marriage; instead, it encourages alternative family lifestyles and family values as ways of adapting to our changing culture. Proponents of liberalization also would remove all laws forbidding nonmonogamous marriages on the grounds that they constitute an interference with private sexual and family matters. The emphasis, if this group had its way, would be on the freedom of consenting adults to experiment with or adopt any type of freely chosen marriage or family lifestyle as long as people were not directly harmed (for example, children were not abused or neglected).

They would not accept offenses to taste or to tradition as valid excuses for legislating against or otherwise forbidding these alternative lifestyles, but they would insist that everyone involved in a relationship fully understand and accept it. For example, if a man wanted to have two separate wives and families, then each wife and family unit should know about the situation and agree to it. This is merely a matter of dealing honestly and truthfully with people.

Homosexual Marriage

Homosexuality means sexual attraction or love for a man by a man, or sexual attraction or love for a woman by a woman; the latter also is called lesbianism. Homosexuality is, for the most part, frowned upon in our culture, although it is accepted in some areas of the world. In some nations and states it is illegal, and often it is considered immoral. The Bible, especially the New Testament, is firmly opposed to it, a fact that concerns people who adhere to the Bible, but it need not be a concern for those who do not. Furthermore, if the main purpose of sexuality is a deep and intimate expression of love, and if procreation is only secondary, as I have argued, then one cannot attack homosexuality as unnatural merely because it can never result in the creation of children as can heterosexual relationships (that is, sex between or among members of the opposite sex). It is an obvious empirical fact that some men prefer to have sex with and can truly love only other men and that some women feel the same way toward other women.

Psychologists are not agreed as to whether homosexuality is "abnormal," or, in some cases, "normal," but it should be noted that the American Psychological Association has taken homosexuality off its list of mental illnesses. Some experimentation has been done to try to determine whether homosexuality in males is caused by a chemical imbalance (mainly of the male hormone testosterone), but the results have not been conclusive. Some have argued that homosexuality is environmentally induced (for example, in young boys who have cruel or indifferent fathers and doting mothers), but there is no conclusive evidence for this, either. Many homosexuals themselves argue that they are not at all abnormal; rather, they feel that they have freely chosen a sexual lifestyle that is just as valid as heterosexual relationships, and they argue that it is society's problem if it is too narrow-minded to accept their chosen lifestyle. Let us now take a look at arguments against and for the morality of homosexuality.

Arguments Against Homosexuality. The basic argument against the morality of homosexuality is that it is unnatural and perverse; that is, it goes against the laws of God, traditional family values, and the moral values of Nature. As I have pointed out, there are sections of both the Old and New Testaments of the Bible that call homosexuality "an abomination" and prohibit it as an unacceptable sexual activity. In fact, many if not most of the world's major religions are opposed to it, branding it as immoral. An argument also used by nonreligious people is that homosexuality is unnatural—that is, one that goes against the moral laws of Nature. The main evidence for this conclusion is that the primary purpose of sexuality is to procreate, and because homosexuals obviously cannot do this, they are perverting the true meaning of sexuality.

Second, it is argued that homosexuality sets a bad example for children and that it attempts to proselytize (that is, gain followers or adherents for its cause), thereby undermining our traditional family and cultural values. In this proselytizing process, the argument continues, young boys and girls often are molested by homosexuals, and this of course is a terrible crime. Furthermore, if their proselytizing is greatly successful, what will become of the human race when procreation is no longer feasible because most, if not all, people have become homosexual? Our tradition under God's law and in accordance with nature is heterosexual, and we owe it to our children to see both that they are informed of this and that they are protected against homosexuals' teaching or preaching their immoral beliefs to them.

Third, those who argue against homosexuality feel that the homosexuals are totally responsible for the AIDS crisis because they are in a high-risk group (along with drug abusers) and because many of the first AIDS victims in the United States were homosexuals. Many, especially religious people, feel that AIDS is a manifestation of God's displeasure with homosexuality; but religious or not, many feel that homosexuality and bisexuality are the major causes of the spread of AIDS and that therefore homosexuality should be banned. They also feel that the AIDS crisis weakens any argument supporting homosexuality as a private type of sexuality that doesn't affect or harm others.

Finally, homosexuals and homosexuality are offensive to our taste and our sense of family values in our basically heterosexual society. Therefore, we have absolutely no obligation to condone or legalize homosexuality in any way; as a matter of fact, we have, instead, the obligation to legislate against and otherwise prohibit it in order to protect our children and family values and the moral future and physical survival of our society.

Recent legislation certainly has presented "loud and clear" this rejection of homosexuality, in that the U.S. Congress, and various state legislative bodies have passed laws freeing the states from condoning legal same-sex marriages and other benefits, such as rights against job discrimination.

Arguments for a Homosexual Alternative. First of all, there is no conclusive evidence that because most people are heterosexual in our society homosexuality is therefore immoral or unnatural. As we saw in Chapter 1, it cannot be proved that natural moral laws do indeed exist. As for religious laws, they have force if one is a member of a particular religion, but they have little effect on those who aren't. Furthermore, many members of various religions interpret religious teachings differently. For example, Christians who favor homosexuality or who are homosexual themselves argue that Jesus' "commandment" to love one another is much more important than minor references to sexuality between members of the same sex.

Second, the main issue involved in homosexuality is the right of freely consenting adults to engage in private sexuality in any way they see fit as long as it does not directly harm others. This is, after all, a private, not a public, sexual matter, and even if it offends some people's tastes and family values, that is no reason for branding it as immoral. As long as no other laws are broken and people are not harmed or killed as a result of homosexuality, then freedom in this sexual matter ought to be allowed. Furthermore, as far as the AIDS crisis is concerned, as soon as it became clear what types of sexual activity caused AIDS, homosexuals as a group lowered the rates of infection and contagion tremendously through more careful behavior—much more so than drug abusers who are now probably the largest group of AIDS victims because they use and share infected needles. Therefore, people who believe that homosexuality is moral argue that we don't discriminate against heterosexuals when they contract the other social diseases or even AIDS, so why should we do so with homosexuals?

Third, the condoning of homosexuality does not mean that child abuse or molestation is also condoned—it isn't, and it should continue to be branded as immoral. Most child molestations, in fact, are probably more heterosexual than homosexual in nature, except for the recent scandals of abuse of young boys by priests in the Roman Catholic Church, usually involving men and young girls. Sadism performed on unwilling victims, child molestations, and forced sexuality of all kinds have no direct connection with homosexuality as a lifestyle, and laws against such activities should remain in force. That some homosexuals, like some heterosexuals, are guilty of such crimes doesn't mean that homosexuality itself is immoral. There already are laws, the argument continues, that forbid proselytizing for any type of overt sexuality in schools, and there also are laws protecting children against pornographic sexual materials (films, books, live shows). Furthermore, it is difficult to prove that homosexuals proselytize any more than heterosexuals do.

The last appeal made by those who believe that homosexuality is morally acceptable is that although homosexuals may have different sexual preferences, they are still human beings; therefore, they should not be discriminated against in any way by society.

As far as family values are concerned, those who argue for acceptance of a homosexual or lesbian lifestyle state that, whether there are children or not, a monogamous homosexual or lesbian couple can establish and maintain a healthy family atmosphere regardless of the fact that they are of the same sex. They would argue further that there are many examples of cases in which lesbians or homosexuals have given birth to or adopted children and have raised or are raising them in a healthy environment, one which they allege has no adverse effects upon the children. In fact, the argument continues, such children are more tolerant of diverse lifestyles because of their experiences and are treated just as lovingly as if they were living with heterosexual parents. The fact that same-sex marriage is becoming somewhat more acceptable is evidenced by laws in California, Massachusetts, England, and Africa which have legalized them. It is possible that other states and countries may follow.

Adultery

Before leaving the topic of marriage-type relationships, it is important to discuss the matter of adultery, sometimes also referred to as *extramarital sexual relations* (sexual relations outside of a marriage contract, agreement, or relationship). Adultery actually means the voluntary engaging in sexual intercourse with someone other than one's marriage partner. It involves infidelity or unfaithfulness in the marriage relationship, especially in its sexual aspects, and generally is considered to be immoral by our society. Our question, however, is not what society in general thinks, but what grounds we can give for describing adultery as being moral or immoral.

It would be foolish, of course, not to recognize that many marriages are not ideal, that one (or both) of the partners may not relate well to the other at any level, including the sexual. This means that dissatisfied partners often look for other human relationships that will fulfill them in ways their own marriage relationship will not, and when their marriage relationship is an unhappy one, people often are tempted to engage in adultery with a person they feel will make them happy or give them pleasure, if only for a brief period of time. (Occasionally, this time lengthens and leads to some form of permanence.)

What usually happens when people are tempted to engage in adultery is that they simply begin the adulterous relationship and worry about the consequences later. The problem with this approach, however, is that the damage is done before any attempt is made to solve the marital problems with any degree of honesty or justice. Once an innocent spouse has been betrayed in this way, it is very difficult to resolve marital problems and to maintain the unity of the marriage relationship.

Arguments Against Adultery. The main argument against the morality of adultery is that adultery is a direct violation of traditional family values and of the most personal and intimate human contract into which two people can enter. When people get married, they usually contract to live together as husband and wife and to be faithful to each other—this especially means sexually faithful. Committing adultery involves lying, cheating, and infidelity on the part of one marriage partner or another, and these actions are viewed as being morally reprehensible by most ethical systems.

Adultery also is destructive of the marriage relationship; it can lead to separation or divorce and to the injuring of innocent children. Even when both spouses agree to adultery (for example, in so-called "wife swapping" or "swinging"), they are making a mockery of marriage, which is our greatest traditional human institution. If they want to have this much freedom, why do they marry at all? The only virtue of such activities as wife swapping and swinging, as opposed to most other forms of adultery, is that at least the spouses know and have agreed to what they are doing, so lying and dishonesty are not issues. There is again the problem of social diseases and AIDS, which an adulterous spouse can contract and then, even worse, pass on to his or her spouse. Hence, this is another important reason not to indulge in adultery.

Arguments for the Morality of Adultery. The basic argument for the morality of adultery is that individuals ought to be free to do what they want to do in terms of their own private sex lives, and whether they lie, cheat, or are unfaithful to their spouses is their business and no one else's—certainly not society's. Some people who condone adultery would say that the basic ethical assumption here is that "what they don't know won't hurt them"; bad results occur only when adultery is discovered. If adulterers are discreet and can avoid breaking up their families, then what's wrong with adultery? One of the problems certainly is the contracting of social diseases or AIDS, but if the adulterer practices safe sex, then whose business is it what he or she does?

Furthermore, some argue that families should not be broken up under any circumstances because of the children involved and for economic and social reasons, and, according to this argument, adultery provides a means by which unsatisfied spouses and their families "can have their cake and eat it, too." That is, wives, husbands, and children continue to have economic security and social status while the adulterous spouse or spouses additionally enjoy a satisfying sex life. As long as these affairs can be conducted smoothly and discreetly, then what's wrong with adultery? Finally, wife swapping and swinging are no more than sexual lifestyles, and as long as adult couples freely consent to such arrangements, no harm is done. These are, after all, private sexual matters, and society should not interfere in any way.

Masturbation

Masturbation is a sex act that people usually perform with and by themselves.

Arguments Against Masturbation

In earlier times, all kinds of superstitious arguments were applied against masturbation—for example, the notion that people who performed this act too often would go insane or deplete their physical strength. However, there are basically only two arguments used against it today. First, there is the religious argument that it is an abuse of one's sexuality, which is a gift given by God. The second argument is that it causes people to become preoccupied with sex and can lead them to other sexual "violations" of morality (fornication, pornography, adultery, and so on). Another argument that serves as a corollary to both of these is that masturbation constitutes a failure in self-control.

Arguments for Masturbation

All the information revealed by modern science indicates that masturbation is a perfectly normal act, both biologically and psychologically, and that it causes no ill effects whatsoever.

As a matter of fact, the argument continues, it is probably one of the earliest and best ways that human beings can become familiar with, knowledgeable about, and at ease with their own bodies and their own sexuality.

For example, until recently women in our culture were taught that it is wrong to masturbate and, further, that it is not even necessary that they attain orgasm. Many women, in fact, are not sure what orgasm is and have never experienced it. Through masturbation, they can learn what about their bodies causes orgasm and gives them the greatest pleasure, and this could aid them in finding more meaningful sexual relations with others. At any rate, sexual liberals can see no disadvantages in masturbation, and because it can harm no one else because it is usually a private act performed by one person alone, they argue that it cannot be considered immoral. It also can be considered the safest sexual act in an age of AIDS and sexually transmitted diseases.

Pornography

Pornography is a vague term, difficult to define. It usually refers to *obscene* literature, art, film, or live display. The word obscene usually means morally offensive according to the general and prevailing standards of morality in any particular culture, society, or group. The Supreme Court of the United States has tried to use the standard definition that pornography is that which appeals to the prurient interest (lust and desire for the impure in thought and deed) and which has no redeeming social, literary, or artistic value. However, within the last 50 years, legal attempts to permit or ban so-called pornographic works or activities have run into problems because it is extremely difficult to decide what is or is not pornographic and to whom.

Pornography seems to involve a definite matter of taste on the part of most people, and tastes differ tremendously. Such things as formalized instruction in sex hygiene are labeled obscene by some, and any kind of nudity (for example, even in a classical Greek sculpture) or any work that contains four-letter words is labeled obscene by others. Some people, on the other hand, can view the most explicit scenes involving bestiality or sadism and find nothing obscene about them. With such differing tastes and opinions about "obscenity" and "pornography," how do we determine whether or not pornography is moral? Let's look at the arguments against and for its morality.

Arguments Against Pornography

First of all, those who would argue against pornography consider it degrading to humans. A preoccupation with pornography, they maintain, will lower the viewer's, listener's, or reader's humanity to the animal level, and as such preoccupation becomes more widespread it will destroy the moral fabric of our civilization.

Second, because some restrictions on pornography have been lifted, it has escalated to an even greater level of criminality, including the filming of actual sadistic sexual murders and the use of children in pornography (child molestation and kiddie porn). This would not have occurred if pornography had continued to be restricted by law.

Third, pornography constitutes a degradation of family values, human sexuality in general, and the sexuality of women in particular. It emphasizes lust rather than love and exploitation and domination rather than tenderness, respect, and reciprocation.

Finally, pornography encourages the trafficking in sex, rape, homosexuality, child molestation, sadism, prostitution, exhibitionism, voyeurism, and all kinds of other sexual "perversions," and for this reason it cannot do anything but lower and destroy human dignity. For all of these reasons, sexual conservatives argue, pornography should not be considered moral in any way and, in fact, should be considered perniciously immoral and be severely restricted or completely banned.

Arguments for Pornography

The basic argument for the morality of pornography is that because tastes and opinions in this area differ so widely, the use of pornographic materials is obviously a matter of individual discretion. As long as people are not coerced into reading, listening to, or viewing it, it should be available to consenting adults.

Second, there is no proof that pornography is degrading (it is, after all, a matter of opinion and taste) or that it will destroy our moral fabric. In fact, as mentioned earlier, there is evidence to indicate that it helps to eliminate sexual repression, relieve sexual tensions, and actually lower sex crime rates rather than raise them. In one study, done after 11 years of having no restrictions on pornography in Denmark, child molestation was down 56 percent, indecent exposure was down 58 percent, and voyeurism was down 80 percent. Rape, however, was on the increase, "but only by a small fraction relative to the rising rates of robbery and vandalism."[2] In fact, the study further maintains that after restrictions have been lifted for a while, the interest in pornography begins to drop off and sales go down as people begin "to take it in stride."[3]

Third, although it is true that pornography can involve actual sexual crimes, our laws against murder and against child abuse and molestation can be enforced to stop this type of criminality.

Finally, that pornography is "degrading and exploitative" is again a matter of personal opinion, taste, and definition. Some might find pornography exciting, pleasurable, and fantasy fulfilling. Furthermore, because the men and women who perform in pornographic movies, for example, generally do so willingly, how can they be considered to be degraded or used? Pornography may not present the loving and tender aspects of sex, but no one can deny that lustful and aggressive aspects of sex also exist, and their depiction therefore has its own validity. For these reasons proponents state that pornography should be considered a moral activity when indulged in by free and consenting adults. It also should be considered a private sexual matter that should not be legally controlled unless it causes harm to others.

Prostitution

Sometimes referred to as the "world's oldest profession," prostitution is, like pornography, a confused issue in morality. Some regard it as a "victimless" crime, whereas others brand it a terribly immoral act. What prostitution essentially means is that people will pay others (prostitutes—male or female) to have sex with them.

Arguments Against Prostitution

Extramarital and Commercialized Sex Is Immoral. The conservative position is, of course, opposed to sex prior to or outside of marriage and doubly opposed to the commercialization of sex when pleasure is the only reason for it. It may be the world's oldest profession, but it is also the world's most immoral one, according to this argument. Prostitution fosters a lack of respect for the prostitute (usually a woman) and for human sexual activity itself, which is supposed to enhance the intimacy of a relationship between partners and also to contribute to the creation of children. Instead, prostitution limits human sexuality to an animalistic act of lust.

Causes Crime. Prostitution is a big business, one usually managed and run by the criminal element in the United States. Prostitutes often are treated like animals by their pimps and customers; many are beaten, and ultimately some are killed. In addition, many prostitutes have been addicted to drugs by their pimps to keep them dependent upon them and always in need of money. According to the critics, because of all of this, prostitution is the most degrading and immoral of activities and should be eliminated from our culture.

Social Diseases and AIDS. There is no faster or more certain way of transmitting social diseases and AIDS than prostitution, for in addition to its being transmitted sexually, prostitutes also may become infected by needles as drug abusers. Because prostitutes and their customers, or "johns," generally don't know each other, there is no clear way of knowing who might or might not have these diseases. Further, because prostitutes and their clients may have many partners, the chances of spreading these diseases are multiplied.

Arguments for Prostitution

Safe Sexual Release. Prostitution is the world's oldest profession because human beings have sexual needs that are not always able to be satisfied by dating and marriage, partially because of all our taboos against sex as pleasure giving and against sex outside of marriage. With prostitution, people can have the pleasure of sex by paying for it and not having to become involved with their partners—sex can be enjoyed for pleasure only, without any commitments and with no strings attached. It also provides a safe sexual release, which may eliminate the desire to rape or molest children (not in all cases, of course, but in general).

A Victimless Crime. Proponents of prostitution as moral argue that it should not be considered either immoral or illegal because there really are no victims. Presumably, prostitutes have chosen at some point to do what they are doing, and so have their clients. It is a crime only because society has legislated against it, but there shouldn't be such laws. People should be free to be prostitutes or to go to them, and such freedom shouldn't be interfered with.

Social Acceptance and Governmental Control. The solution to any problems arising out of prostitution, such as crime, abuse of prostitutes, and social diseases, would be solved by social acceptance or at least social permissiveness and proper government regulation and control. "Houses of ill repute" could then be privately run but regulated by city, county, state, or federal governments so that sanitary conditions could be established and testing for social diseases could be done. In addition, the criminal element could be eliminated by such control and policing. All of these problems, according to the proponents of prostitution as moral, could be eliminated if society would just accept that people have sexual needs and allow them to satisfy them in an acceptable yet regulated manner.

Sexual Perversion or "Unnatural" Sexual Activity

Sexual perversion often is as difficult to define as pornography. Some people think that any sexual activity other than sexual intercourse between a man and a woman in the traditional "missionary" position described earlier is perverted or unnatural. Others feel that any type of regular sexual intercourse between a man and a woman, but nothing else, is all right, and still others allow that "anything goes" as long as pleasure is given and received.

As I mentioned at the beginning of the chapter, many sexual activities, such as oral sex, anal sex, sadism, masochism, homosexuality, group sex, and bestiality (sex acts between human beings and animals) have been listed as "unnatural" or "perverted." The conservative viewpoint is that all of these except for traditional sexual intercourse between a man and a woman are perverted. The liberal viewpoint varies, but essentially it states that as long as a sex act is performed between or among freely consenting adults it is a matter of individual freedom and should not be legislated against or forbidden in any way.

Bestiality presents a special problem. Although it is probably rare (though perhaps less rare in rural areas), it does not fit the description of sexuality "between or among consenting adults." One partner to the sex act, that is, the animal, cannot consent; therefore, one could say that bestiality is immoral because the animal is not a consenting adult human being. However, when we consider that we kill animals for food without their consent, we can ask if it is worse to have sex with them and to let them live than to kill and eat them. Some people also feel that sex between a human being and an animal is even a greater crime against natural laws than are sex acts between human beings of the same sex. The extreme liberal, I suppose, would condone bestiality, whereas the "moderate" liberal might or might not condone it; the conservative, of course, would vehemently condemn it.

Cases for Study and Discussion

CASE 1 Two Teenagers Living Together

Two college students, Tom, 19, and Barbara, 18, have decided to live together both for sexual reasons and because they enjoy each other's company. Barbara intends to take birth control pills, they intend to share expenses, and they have an agreement to be honest with and faithful to each other throughout the entire relationship. They also have agreed that if either one of them wants to break off the relationship, he or she has only to say so and the relationship will end with no recriminations. Is what they are doing moral? Why or why not?

CASE 2 Two Homosexuals Living Together

You have been working with Richard for about a year and have always found him witty, intelligent, compassionate, and friendly. One night he invites you to have dinner with him and his friend Walter at their apartment. You discover that the two men are homosexuals and that they have been living together for about three or four years. You are surprised to find that they are not effeminate in any way; in fact, except that they prefer homosexuality to heterosexuality, they are in no way different from a lot of other nice people you know. They do not molest children, nor do they attempt to impose their values on anyone else; all they want is to live together happily and in peace. Is what Richard and Walter are doing moral? Why, or why not?

CASE 3 Two Unmarried Seniors Living Together

Sarah and Ben, both in their seventies and widowed, have fallen in love and feel a strong need for each other's companionship. Because Sarah would lose her social security pension if she remarried, they have moved into an apartment together without getting married and are enjoying a full sex life. Their grown children for the most part are very upset by this and constantly tell Sarah and Ben how they feel about their domestic arrangement. Some of the children even refuse to call or visit them because they are living together. Despite this situation, Ben and Sarah seem to be happy. Is what they are doing moral? Why or why not?

CASE 4 Adultery

Eric, 45, is married to Joanne, 43, and they have three teenage children. Generally speaking, they have a pretty good marriage, except for their sex life. Although they both know it is poor, they don't discuss it very often. Over a period of several months Joanne notices a change in Eric, and finally she asks him if there's anything wrong. Eric blurts out that he is in love with another woman with whom he's had an affair for several months. Joanne is so angry and hurt that she immediately demands that he leave the house and states that she wants a divorce. They both refuse to seek help from marriage counselors, and eventually the divorce ensues at a great emotional cost to Eric, Joanne, and their three children. Was what Eric did moral? Why, or why not? Do you feel Joanne handled his adultery well or not? Why, or why not? Should Eric have told her? Why, or why not?

CASE 5 Pornography in Theaters and Stores

One street in a small town has several stores that sell pornographic materials and a theater that shows pornographic films. Various parents and religious groups in town want the licenses for these places of business to be revoked because, as they put it, these places are a "blight on the community" and a bad influence on everyone, particularly the young people of the town. The managers of the stores, however, carefully check identification cards in order to make sure that no one who is underage can enter, and there are no pornographic displays in the windows or anywhere outside the buildings. The owners of the stores and the theater feel that those who enter their businesses want to be there and seem to enjoy themselves. Should their licenses be revoked, and should pornography in the town be further restricted because what these proprietors are doing is immoral? Why, or why not? If you think there should be further restrictions, then what should they be?

Chapter Summary

I. Major aspects of human sexuality
   A. The public, or societal, aspect is concerned with how matters of sex overtly affect others, and the governing principles of morality here are life, goodness, and justice.
   B. The private aspect is concerned with sexual relations between or among consenting adults, and the governing principles here are goodness, justice, freedom, and honesty.

II. Moral issues and the private aspect of human sexuality
   A. The meaning and the private aspect of human sexuality is not one-dimensional but includes the following:
      1. Procreation.
      2. Pleasure.
      3. An expression of love for another.
      4. An expression of friendship and liking.
   B. The conservative, or restrictive, position concerning sexual activity often puts the most emphasis on the procreative aspect or the view that sex is "a necessary evil."
   C. The position advocating complete freedom in sexual matters usually emphasizes the pleasure aspect and the right of individuals to enjoy such pleasure.
   D. The more moderate position tends to accept both the procreation and pleasure aspects while also including—and often emphasizing more strongly—the expression-of-love aspect.

III. Moral issues and the public aspect of human sexuality
   A. Sexual activities that affect the public or others in such a way as to bring them possible harm include the following:
      1. Rape.
      2. Child molestation.
      3. Unwilling sadism.
      4. Less clearly, pornography, homosexuality, prostitution, "unnatural" sexual activities, sex outside of marriage, masturbation, and nonmonogamous marriages.
   B. Most ethical systems are agreed that the first three types of activity under point A are immoral, but there is less agreement on the seven activities listed in item 4.

C. There are a number of arguments against allowing people the sexual freedom to engage in the last seven activities:
1. These activities are a violation of traditional morality and family values.
2. According to the domino argument, allowing these seven activities will eventually lead to a general acceptance of the first three immoral activities.
3. These activities are offensive to public taste.
4. Probability of getting social diseases, including AIDS.

D. There are several arguments for allowing people the sexual freedom to perform these activities.
1. Individual rights and individual freedom should take precedence because these activities cause no direct harm to others.
2. Traditional family values, which oppose such activities, are not absolute.
3. There is no hard evidence to support the domino argument; furthermore, laws can be passed to prohibit these activities from escalating toward the first three.
4. Offensiveness to the public taste is not in itself sufficient cause to deny individual rights in these matters, and if discretion is used, the offensiveness to others can be minimized.
5. Proper precautions can be taken to guard against social diseases and AIDS; therefore, this is no reason to deny one freedom in the area of sexuality.

IV. Premarital sex
A. The term *premarital sex* refers to sex relations that occur prior to marriage; it is called *fornication* in the Bible.
B. There are several arguments against premarital sex.
1. It undermines traditional morality and family values.
2. It fosters promiscuity.
3. It fosters social diseases and AIDS.
4. It fosters guilt and ostracism.
5. It can be detrimental to the children born of such a relationship.
6. The opportunities provided by premarital sex to test compatibility and gain sexual experience are no excuse for such activity, and any advantages obtained in these areas are outweighed by the violation of the sacredness of marriage and the loss of respect that inevitably ensues.
C. There are several arguments for premarital sex.
1. Old moral traditions are no longer applicable in our changing society.
2. Abstinence is not acceptable, and proper precautions can eliminate most concerns about social diseases and AIDS.
3. Promiscuity is not a necessary adjunct of premarital sex, but even if promiscuity occurs, as long as the people involved are freely consenting adults, what difference does it make?
4. Not as much guilt or ostracism occurs these days because of our changing mores (for example, the recognition and acceptance of illegitimate children). Furthermore, as long as those involved can handle the guilt or ostracism that may occur, that is their choice.
5. Contraception and sexual responsibility can eliminate any problems concerned with the children that result from such a union. Contraception can prevent pregnancy, and if a child is born, sexual responsibility ensures that the couple will marry or otherwise provide for its care.
6. The opportunity provided by premarital sex to gain sexual experience and to test compatibility is one of its greatest advantages.
7. That sex gives great pleasure is also an advantage.
8. Premarital sex is a private, not a public, matter, and legislation should not enter into it.

V. Sex in marriage-type relationships (including nonlegal)
   A. Marriage-type relationships are continuous and lasting rather than temporary.
   B. Their main purpose is to provide a deep and intimate expression of love between or among persons, including the giving of pleasure.
   C. A secondary but not unimportant purpose is to procreate.
   D. The purposes noted in points B and C are not *necessarily* compatible *or* incompatible.
VI. Various types of marriage relationships
   A. Monogamy, the marriage relationship involving one man and one woman, is the most common type in the Western world.
   B. Polygamy, including polyandry and bigamy, means having more than one husband or wife.
   C. Group marriage, with and without "free love," involves a communal or cooperative kind of living arrangement and may include already married and/or single people.
   D. There are several arguments against nonmonogamous types of marriage.
      1. Only monogamy is prescribed in the Bible.
      2. Monogamy is an essential part of our society's tradition.
      3. Love relationships are too intimate to involve more than one man and one woman, and children are better off raised in the traditional monogamous family structure.
      4. Such a relationship will eliminate any problems connected with social diseases or AIDS, provided spouses keep their vows.
   E. There are several arguments for allowing nonmonogamous marriages.
      1. It is not up to society to prescribe a specific type of marriage, and our changing culture encourages experimentation with alternative types of marriage.
      2. All laws prohibiting nonmonogamous marriages should be removed because they encroach on private sexual matters.
      3. Consenting adults should be free to experiment with alternative types of marriage.
      4. As long as there is honesty in a relationship, any type of marriage that does not directly harm others should be deemed acceptable.
   F. Homosexual marriage is a married relationship between two men or two women.
      1. There are several arguments against the morality of homosexuality.
         (a) It is an unnatural and perverse form of sexuality.
         (b) It is against the laws of God.
         (c) It sets a bad example for children, and it is dangerous because its adherents attempt to proselytize for its cause.
         (d) It is totally responsible for the AIDS crisis, which makes it a public rather than a private act.
         (e) It is offensive to the taste of most people in our society and to our basically heterosexual traditions and family values.
      2. There are several arguments for the morality of homosexuality.
         (a) There is no conclusive evidence suggesting that homosexuality is unnatural or immoral.
         (b) It is the right of freely consenting adults to engage in private sexuality in any way they see fit.
         (c) Homosexuals as a group have lowered rates of infection and contagion tremendously through careful behavior and shouldn't be discriminated against any more than heterosexuals are.
         (d) The acceptance of homosexuality doesn't mean that child abuse or molestation is condoned; in fact, more of these crimes probably are committed by heterosexuals than by homosexuals.
         (e) Homosexuals are human beings, and for this reason they should not be discriminated against in any way by society.

VII. Adultery
   A. Adultery is the voluntary engaging in sexual intercourse with someone other than one's marriage partner.
   B. There are several arguments against the morality of adultery.
      1. It is a violation of traditional family values and the most personal and intimate contract into which two people can enter.
      2. It involves lying, cheating, and infidelity, all of which are morally reprehensible.
      3. It is destructive of the marriage relationship and traditional family values and can lead to separation or divorce and to the emotional injuring of innocent children.
      4. Even when both spouses agree to adultery, it makes a mockery of marriage.
      5. There is again the problem of social diseases, with the additional problem of transmitting such diseases to one's spouse.
   C. There are several arguments for the morality of adultery.
      1. Individuals ought to be free to do what they want with their own private sex lives.
      2. What spouses don't know won't hurt them—getting caught is the only thing that can cause harm.
      3. As far as social diseases and AIDS are concerned, if an adulterer practices safe sex, then whose business is it what he or she does?
      4. Marriages generally should not be broken up if doing so threatens financial security and the security of the children; adultery provides a means whereby adulterers and their families can "have their cake and eat it, too."
      5. "Wife swapping" and "swinging" are just other sexual lifestyles, and if couples agree to such practices there is no reason why they should not be allowed.

VIII. Masturbation
   A. Masturbation is a sex act that people usually perform with and by themselves.
   B. Arguments can be made against the morality of masturbation.
      1. In a religious sense, it is an abuse of one's sexuality, which is a gift from God.
      2. It causes people to become preoccupied with sex and can lead them to other sexual violations of morality (fornication, pornography, adultery, and so on).
   C. Arguments can be made for the morality of masturbation.
      1. It is perfectly normal both biologically and psychologically, and it causes no ill effects.
      2. It is the best way of learning about sex and getting in touch with our own bodies.
      3. It can be considered the safest form of sexual activity.

IX. Pornography
   A. Pornography is difficult to define, but generally it has been defined by the U.S. Supreme Court as that which appeals to the prurient interest and which has no redeeming social, literary, or artistic value.
   B. There are several arguments against the morality of pornography.
      1. It is humanly degrading, and as it becomes more widespread it will destroy the moral fabric of our civilization.
      2. It can involve actual sex crimes such as sexual murders, child molestation, and kiddie porn, which have, in fact, occurred.
      3. It degrades human sexuality in general and women in particular.
      4. It encourages trafficking in sex, rape, child molestation, sadism, prostitution, exhibitionism, voyeurism, and other types of sexual "perversions."
   C. There are several arguments for the morality of pornography.
      1. Consenting adults have the right to view, read, or listen to anything they wish.
      2. There is no proof that pornography is degrading or that it will destroy our moral fabric.

3. It can involve actual crimes, but we have strong enough laws to stop such crimes if they are committed.
4. That it is "degrading and exploitative" is a matter of taste and opinion; to many it is exciting and pleasurable.

X. Prostitution
  A. Prostitution, like pornography, is a confusing issue in morality. It essentially means people paying others (prostitutes) to have sex with them.
  B. There are several arguments against prostitution.
    1. Extramarital and commercialized sex is immoral from the conservative point of view.
    2. Prostitution causes crime and degradation.
    3. There is no faster or surer way of spreading social diseases and AIDS.
  C. Arguments for prostitution also exist.
    1. It is a safe sexual release in a sexually repressive society.
    2. It is a victimless crime in that both prostitutes and their customers enter into sexual activity freely.
    3. If there were social acceptance and governmental control, then the criminal and social disease aspects of prostitution could be eliminated.

XI. Sexual perversion
  A. Sexual perversion, or "unnatural" sexual activity, is as difficult to define as pornography.
  B. The conservative viewpoint is that activities such as oral sex, anal sex, sadism, masochism, homosexuality, group sex, and bestiality are perverted. The only sex activity that isn't perverted is sexual intercourse between a man and a woman, generally in the "missionary" position.
  C. The liberal viewpoint varies, but in general it states that as long as a sex act is performed between or among freely consenting adults it is a matter of private discretion and should be considered to be moral.
  D. Bestiality (sex between human beings and animals) presents a special problem in that it extends beyond the category of "freely consenting adults." For this reason, some would say that this type of sex involves "animal molestation" and is therefore wrong. Yet we kill animals and eat them; is this any more respectable than having sex with them and letting them live?
    1. The extreme liberal would condone such activity.
    2. The moderate liberal might or might not condone it.
    3. The conservative would vehemently condemn it.

Exercises for Review

1. Distinguish between the public and private aspects of human sexuality. Do you think the distinction is a valid one? Why, or why not?
2. Do you agree or disagree with the description given of the meaning and purpose of human sexuality, especially the prime importance given to sexuality as a deep and intimate expression of love for another? Why, or why not?
3. How can the five basic ethical principles be applied to the area of human sexuality?
4. What are some of the advantages and disadvantages of engaging in premarital sex?
5. How does a marriage-type relationship differ from other relationships, and what are two of its purposes?

6. In your own words, briefly define *monogamy, polygamy, group marriage*, and *homosexual marriage*. What positions do you take in reference to the morality of each of these relationships? Why?

7. What are your personal views on the moral issue of adultery? Consider the arguments presented for and against adultery when answering this question.

8. Explain why masturbation is or is not an immoral sexual act.

9. How would you define *pornography*? Give examples of the type of literature and activities you consider pornographic, and explain why you place them in this category. Do you think pornography is moral or immoral? Why?

10. How would you define *unnatural sex*, or *sexual perversion*? When is it moral and when is it immoral, if ever?

11. To what extent do you think prostitution is moral? What effect does the argument that social acceptance and governmental control would eliminate the crime and social-disease problems have on your views of this activity? Answer in detail.

12. Define *family values*.

Views of the Major Ethical Theories on Morality, Human Sexuality, and Marriage

Describe as fully as you can how each of the major ethical theories—Ethical Egoism, Utilitarianism, Divine Command Theory, Kant's Duty Ethics, Ross' *Prima Facie* Duties, and Virtue Ethics—probably would deal with the moral issues of human sexuality and marriage described in this chapter. Refer to Chapters 2, 3 and 4 for a description of the theories and to Chapter 9, "The Taking of Human Life," for an example of how you might go about completing this assignment.

Notes

1. See Sigmund Freud, *Collected Papers of Sigmund Freud*, Volume 8, *Sexuality and the Psychology of Love* (New York: Collier Books, n.d.); and Virginia E. Johnson and William H. Masters, *Human Sexual Response* (Boston: Little, Brown, 1966).

2. Lloyd Shearer, "Porno and Crime," *The Bakersfield Californian* "Parade" (December 10, 1978), 17.

3. Ibid.

Research Navigator™
(http://www.researchnavigator.com)

This web site offers three research databases: EBSCO's *ContentSelect Academic Journal and Abstract Database, New York Times* Search by Subject Archive, and *Best of the Web* Link Library. In addition, this site provides helpful advice on how to conduct efficient and productive research from choosing a topic to polishing the final draft. Beginning philosophy students probably will find the *Best of the Web* Link Library the most appropriate place to start their research.

The free access code necessary to employ Research Navigator™ can be found in the Prentice Hall Guide to Evaluating Online Resources. If your text did not come with this guide, please go to *www.prenhall.com/contentselect* for information on how you can purchase an access code.

Chapter
14

Bioethics—Ethical Issues in Medicine

Objectives

After you have read this chapter, you should be able to

1. Know how ethics can be applied to specific areas of human life, such as bioethics.

2. Know what the term *bioethics* means and describe the areas and issues it covers.

3. Understand the rights and obligations of health care professionals and patients and their families as they are defined according to three different views: paternalism, radical individualism, and reciprocity.

4. Understand the importance of truth telling, confidentiality, and informed consent to significant relationships between professionals and patients.

5. Understand what some of the ethical issues are in the areas of allocation of scarce medical resources, behavior control, human experimentation, and genetics.

Introduction and Definition of Terms

The last chapters in this book—this one, which is concerned with bioethics, Chapter 15, which is concerned with business and media ethics, and Chapter 16 on environmental ethics—are included here in order to show how ethics is applied in specific aspects of society and human life and how ethical problems and issues affect human beings at all levels and in all areas of life. As a matter of fact, ethical problems arising in areas such as medicine and business have fostered a revival of interest in ethics, not only as theory or as an aspect of religion but also as something that must be applied to human affairs in a practical way. I believe that the issues that have arisen in medicine have served as the greatest catalyst in our time for the renewed interest in applied ethics.

Bioethics means "life ethics," or ethics in medicine. It covers a larger area of concern than the phrase "medical ethics," which often is used to refer strictly to the doctor-patient relationship or to such issues as whether doctors should advertise, split fees, or report incompetence within their ranks. Bioethics covers the following areas in medicine: treatment of dying patients, allowing someone to die, mercy death, and mercy killing (see Chapter 10); behavior control; human experimentation and informed consent; genetics, fertilization, and birth; health care delivery and its costs; population and birth control, abortion (see Chapter 11), and sterilization; allotment of scarce medical resources, organ transplantation, and hemodialysis; stem cell research, cloning; and truth telling and confidentiality in medicine.

In short, what bioethics really is concerned with is the establishment and maintenance of vital and moral human relationships between the sick and the dying on the one hand, and the healthy and medical professionals on the other. It is concerned with "treatment" in the broadest sense; that is, it deals not only with how we treat patients in a medical sense, but also with how we relate to, or deal with, our fellow human beings, especially in matters of illness, injury, dying, and death. If you will refer to my working definition of *morality* in Chapter 1, you will find that except for the reference to sickness, injury, and dying, the idea of significant human relationships is the same, only more specifically applied.

Health Care Professionals and Patients and Their Families—Rights and Obligations

Health care professionals are doctors, nurses, attendants or aides, therapists, technicians, and all others involved in medical aid. There are three major views of what the relationship between health care professionals and patients and their families should be.

Paternalism

Paternalism, as the name suggests, is the position that argues that health care professionals should take a parental role toward patients and their families. According to this position, professionals have a superior knowledge of medicine; therefore, they and they alone are privileged, because of their long and specialized training, to decide what is in the best interest of patients and their families. This attitude is characterized by the old cliché "The doctor always knows best."

A number of arguments are put forth to support this viewpoint. First of all, laypeople lack the professional knowledge of medicine to deal with both physical and mental illness and injury; therefore, they have no way of knowing what is best for them. Second, because of their long, hard professional education and because of their experience, professionals (especially doctors) know the characteristics of diseases and injuries; therefore, patients should place themselves totally in the professionals' hands. Finally, any and all decisions about patients' care and treatment, including the information that should be given them and decisions concerning hospitalization, tests, and so on, should be completely in the hands of the doctors and their professional assistants. Patients must trust them and not interfere with the treatment suggested.

Under paternalism, there are two possible models: the engineering model and the priestly model.

The Engineering Model. According to Robert Veatch, a renowned bioethicist, this model is an outgrowth of the biological revolution in which a physician behaves like an applied scientist. As such a scientist, the physician must be value free and purely scientific in his approach to treating patients. Physicians in this model, therefore, supposedly separate themselves from any values that they or their patients might have. These physicians are "engineers," technically and mechanically well qualified to treat their patients as if the latter were biological machines.

The foolishness and dangers of this model have been powerfully revealed in the development of the atomic and hydrogen bombs and in Nazi medical research and experimentation on human beings in World War II. Also, such physicians cannot logically be value free because each choice and decision they make requires a frame of values on which they are based. Practically every decision physicians make on a daily basis requires them to consider values. For example, whether to give a genuine drug or a placebo or whether to start or stop treatment of a patient is as much a value as a medical decision. Further, if physicians could really be value free, that would make them mere engineers or plumbers, making repairs, connecting tubes, and flushing out systems with no questions asked.[1]

Priestly Model. The second model that Veatch describes goes to the opposite extreme, making the physician a new priest. Veatch quotes Robert Wilson, a sociologist of medicine, as saying, "The doctor's office or the hospital . . . have somewhat the aura of a sanctuary. . . . "[2] Therefore, physicians now are acting as priests toward their patients who are their "parishioners," and the emphasis is placed on the ethical principle of "benefit and do no harm to the patient." This certainly is not an insignificant principle, but according to Veatch, there are other principles that may be overlooked because of an emphasis on this one principle, such as protecting individual freedom, preserving individual dignity, truth telling and promise keeping, and maintaining and restoring justice. By emphasizing the first principle described, the other principles may be ignored. The other problem with this theory is that the physician as priest is still making the decisions for the patient and doing, as priest, what he thinks "is best for the patient."[3]

Radical Individualism

Radical individualism is the position that patients have absolute rights over their own bodies and lives and therefore may reject all the recommendations of health care personnel (especially doctors).

There are a number of arguments supporting this position. First, doctors are human like everyone else, and they are capable of making errors in judgment, diagnosis, prognosis, and treatment. They are even at times guilty of malpractice, negligence, or maltreatment. Second, patients (or their families when patients are totally incapacitated) are best qualified to decide if, how, when, and what treatment is to be given; after all, their bodies and lives are at stake, not those of the professionals. Third, many issues having to do with treatment are not strictly medical, and professionals sometimes are not qualified to make appropriate decisions concerning such issues (for example, at what point debilitating, painful treatment should be stopped, because its negative effects outweigh any curative powers it may have). Fourth, with the expansion of media information, such as the internet, these days laypeople are better educated about their bodies and minds and about the illnesses and injuries that affect them. They also are able to understand their medical condition, diagnoses, and prognoses if professionals will only have the kindness and courtesy to explain things to them clearly and in plain language. Because they can understand these things, they are qualified to make decisions about how they should or should not be treated. Finally, paternalism often has led to total patient dependence and sometimes to complete dehumanization, with a patient being regarded merely as a living body to be investigated, analyzed, medicated, or operated on without recognition that a *person* still resides within it.

The problem with this view is that it places *all* decisions in the hands of patients, who may not be as knowledgeable about their medical problems or as well qualified to make such crucial decisions as they need to be. Secondly, many patients do not want to be responsible for making decisions completely on their own without the help of their families or health care personnel, including their doctors.

The Reciprocal View

The reciprocal view involves a team approach to treatment much like that described in the hospice approach to care for the dying (see Chapter 10). In this view, patients and their families are key members of the team, and doctors, nurses, and other health care professionals work together to do what's best for patients and their families. This position is supported by a number of arguments, some of which are similar to those made for radical individualism.

First, professionals, particularly doctors, are neither gods nor valid father figures; rather, they are human beings with specialized education, training, and experience, which makes them an important element in the care of patients and their families.

Second, many of the decisions concerning the treatment of patients and their families are not strictly medical in nature and therefore should not be made solely by medical professionals. Doctors need to rely on other health care personnel, such as nurses; psychiatric, physical, and occupational therapists; and nurses' aides. They also need the support of nonmedical personnel such as clergy, social workers, and trained volunteers if they are to properly treat patients and their families as whole human beings rather than medical specimens.

Third, it is important to recognize the right of individual patients to make free choices concerning their treatment because it is their bodies and lives that are at stake. As

I have already discussed, such a right is not "absolute" but is and should be given high priority. The recognition of this right is exemplified by the creation and dissemination of a list of patients' rights (see the section on Patient Self-Determination Act in Chapter 10). In addition to the right to participate actively in decisions regarding medical care, including the right to refuse treatment, patients also have the right to considerate and respectful care; information about their diagnosis, treatment, and prognosis; the information they require in order to give their informed consent to any procedure; and full knowledge about human experimentation, and the right to refuse it.[4]

All of this means that neither patients nor professionals alone "know best," but that decisions involving care and treatment are to be reciprocal (that is, involving give and take) rather than dictatorial, paternalistic, or anarchistic. Obviously, professionals do "know best" in certain areas, but they should share their information and expertise with patients and their families. In this way, proper recommendations can be made as to alternatives of care and treatment, and proper decision making can be accomplished. Furthermore, patients and their families are entitled to more than one professional opinion.

Patients must realize, however, that no matter how well informed they are, they can't know everything about medicine, and they must defer to professionals in some areas. However, once they have become well informed (and they have a right to be), they certainly are qualified to make decisions about their care and treatment. In some areas, they definitely "know best." In other words, patients and their families are entitled to be apprised of all the expertise that can be brought to bear on their cases so that they can make important decisions. According to this view, in short, all decisions should be arrived at through a free exchange of ideas and a full discussion of alternative methods of care and treatment, with final decisions being made jointly by patients or their families (when patients are incapacitated) and their doctors.

In other words, reciprocal care calls for proper, intelligent, and informed communication between patients and their doctors. Doctors can facilitate such communication, as one family practice doctor in Seattle did, by furnishing their patients with a list of questions to ask:

1. What is wrong with me?
2. What caused it?
3. What should be done about it?
4. What will it cost?
5. How long will it take?
6. What tests should be done and why?
7. What is my prognosis?
8. What will you do next?
9. Is it necessary?
10. Is it dangerous?
11. Do I have any alternatives? If so, what are they?
12. If I must go into the hospital, how long will I be there?
13. How long will I be laid up, and when can I go back to school or work?[5]

Such a list of questions can really help to stimulate communication between doctors and patients and also enhance the doctor-patient relationship.

There are two models under the reciprocal view: the collegial model and the contractual model.

The Collegial Model. In this model, ". . . the physician and the patient should see themselves as colleagues pursuing a common goal of eliminating the illness and preserving the health of the patient. The physician is the patient's 'pal.' "[6]

Veatch sees the problem here as being that of whether doctors and patients can really assume mutual loyalty and goals of common interest. He goes on to say that ethnic, class, economic, and value differences make the collegial model more of an ideal than a reality.[7]

The Contractual Model. Veatch goes on to say that what is needed is ". . . a more provisional model which permits equality in the realm of moral significance between patient and physician without making the utopian assumption of collegiality."[8] This contract should not be merely legalistic but more like a covenant as in the traditional religious or marriage sense. The bases for such a contract are freedom, dignity, truth telling, promise keeping, and justice, and there must be trust and confidence even though there is not a full mutuality of interests because of the value differences described above.

Veatch believes that "Only in the contractual model can there be a true sharing of ethical authority and responsibility . . ." because this model ". . . avoids the moral abdication on the part of the physician in the engineering model and the moral abdication on the part of the patient in the priestly model. It also avoids the uncontrolled and false sense of equality in the collegial model."[9]

The difficulties associated with this model are how to execute the contract (oral or written) and what to include in it. Isn't this all rather vague? The health care field already has several contractual type forms—advance directives and various "Do Not Resuscitate" forms that the patient may sign—but Veatch seems to be talking about an agreement that is something more than these kinds of forms: an overall contract for medical care.

At any rate, it is important in using this model (1) to know the patients and to base the contractual relationship on their needs and personalities; (2) when in doubt, to err on the side of patient autonomy; and (3) to be cognizant of how power asymmetries and the fact of illness affect interactions and communication between physician and patient.

Truth Telling and Informed Consent

The issue involving truth telling is to what extent patients and their families should be told the truth about their illnesses, injuries, and/or dying. The term *informed consent* refers to a formalized procedure whereby patients (or family members, when patients are incapacitated) "consent," usually in writing, to some sort of medical treatment, procedure, or surgery that may have questionable side effects, affect patients' future lives, or even involve the risk of death. Somewhat akin to the discussion of patients' and professionals' rights and obligations, there are two views of truth telling in medicine: the paternalistic view and that of the patients' right to know.

The Paternalistic View of Truth Telling

There are several arguments put forth to support the paternalistic viewpoint. First, because patients are not medically trained, they cannot understand what doctors tell them; therefore, they do not need to know more than the fact that professionals are doing their very best for them. Second, it is best both for patients' morale and for their will to get better or will to live if they are not told the truth—especially if it is bad news, because full knowledge of their situation might cause them to "lose heart" and not fight to survive. Third, it would serve no purpose to give them bad news, because if the prognosis is that they are going to die, for example, they will die anyway; therefore, one should let them live out the time they have left as happily as they can. Fourth, it is all right to tell the families but not the patients—patients should be protected from bad news. Finally, it is important for the doctor, nurses, and other professionals, as well as the family members, to avoid "being morbid" by discussing with patients the seriousness of their illnesses, injuries, or dying. Everyone connected with patients should try to cheer them up and to deny bad news whenever possible.

The Patients' Right to Know

There are a number of arguments made in support of the patients' right to know, many of them criticisms of the paternalistic arguments. First, because it is the patients' bodies and lives that are involved, not those of the health care professionals or even other family members, patients have a right to know everything and should be told all. Second, it is much easier to treat and deal with patients if they are aware of what is going on, and if professionals and family members don't have to constantly pretend that patients' illnesses or injuries are not serious or that patients are not dying.[10] Third, patients often become angry when they didn't know in advance about side effects or other painful or disturbing aspects of treatment. (For example, a woman whose radiation therapy made her arm swell and become very painful became angry because she was never told she might have this problem.)

One negative aspect of the patients' rights position is that some professionals adopt this view so fervently that they are brutally frank with their patients, often leaving them without any hope or frightening them unnecessarily. As I pointed out in Chapter 12, it is a false dilemma to assume that you either must give people terrible news or lie to them.

The Moderate Position

A third view, one that lies somewhere between paternalism and brutal frankness, is a sharing of appropriate information with patients when they do want to know it and to the extent that they want to know it. This view lets patients be the guide in determining the information they will receive. It involves the following aspects:

1. Listening to patients carefully and hearing what they are really asking or trying to ask.
2. Not avoiding persistent, roundabout, or direct questions, but rather answering them truthfully yet not brutally.
3. Not forcing information on patients when they are not ready just because the professional is ready to discuss the matter or is too busy to wait until patients are ready.

4. Not avoiding the truth by using medical and technical language or jargon, but trying instead to explain in lay terms everything that patients need or want to know.

5. Being aware that explanations or answers may have to be given in gradual doses or more than once because human beings often will defend themselves against the shock of bad news by not really "hearing" what is being said.

6. Always telling the truth clearly, gently, and humanely, never brutally, coldly, hopelessly, or cruelly.

7. Never leaving patients and their families without some hope, even if it is only the hope that professionals will keep trying to do the very best they can to cure patients and to keep them comfortable and out of pain.

Informed Consent

As I mentioned earlier, *informed consent* is a more formalized approach to truth telling and to involving patients in decisions concerning their treatment. This approach has become necessary in our time because of the many complex technological tests, procedures, and surgeries required, not only for individual therapeutic reasons but also for experiments that can help science to benefit others (by testing reactions to new drugs, for example). I shall discuss the problems of human experimentation later in this chapter.

In our country, the Department of Health and Welfare, with the agreement of the American Medical Association (AMA) and most hospitals, mandates that patients on whom complex, painful, risky, or dangerous procedures need to be performed, either for their own good or for the good of others, should be fully "informed" of what is to be done, why it is to be done, when it is to be done, and what to expect in the way of pain, discomfort, or risk. For example, except in emergency situations—in which saving a life requires immediate action—patients or their closest next of kin (wife, husband, parents, children) must authorize any procedure of a serious nature such as surgeries and laboratory tests of certain kinds, as well as certain types of therapy, such as chemotherapy or radiation therapy.

The assumption behind the "informed consent" approach is that in order to intelligently "consent" to a procedure, patients must be fully "informed"; furthermore, they must agree in writing to undergo the procedure in order to avoid any later confusions and legal complications that may arise from it. In order to facilitate the informed consent procedure, many hospitals and laboratory groups have printed informed consent forms for patients to read and sign. These forms should do the following: Explain the procedure and its purpose clearly and in ordinary language; explain what kinds of discomfort or pain the procedure may cause patients to feel before, during, and after its completion; explain any and all complications that may arise because of the procedure; state how long the procedure will take; include a statement that the patient's doctors have judged that the procedure should be performed, for the patient's best interests and welfare and despite any discomforts or risks. Figure 14–1 provides an example of an informed consent document.

Four factors may inhibit informed consent (1) the nature of illness of or injury to patients and the various medications they may be taking; (2) physicians' attitudes; for

---

Permit for Percutaneous Trans-Hepatic Cholangiography

The term *percutaneous trans-hepatic cholangiography* means a study of the bile ducts (part of the drainage system of the liver) that is performed by entering a bile duct in the liver with a catheter (tube) that is passed through the skin to reach the proper position. Your doctor has requested that we perform a trans-hepatic cholangiogram on you to help him in his care of you. Because this type of examination is probably new to you, this note is intended to explain what you should expect.

Trans-hepatic cholangiography is performed by introducing a small catheter into a bile duct in the liver. The catheter is introduced in combination with a sharp stylet (special needle). It will be passed through the skin under your right ribs. More than one attempt may be needed to position the catheter. It is unusual to make more than four complete attempts. Once the catheter is positioned, an "x-ray dye" will be injected and films will be taken in several projections to help to identify your problem.

What will you feel? You will be sedated before the procedure, and, if needed, more sedation can be given during the procedure. We will use a local anesthetic where the catheter is introduced. This will sting and burn for about 30 to 40 seconds. Insertion of the catheter is done with a rapid motion and often causes a sharp pain, which is generally short-lived. The major source of discomfort is leakage of bile or blood around the catheter into the abdomen. This is painful but can be treated with pain medication. This leakage is unpredictable, but probably occurs in 10 to 20% of patients.

What are the complications? The two most common complications have already been mentioned—bile leak and bleeding. Bleeding always occurs but is generally minor. Bile leakage into the abdomen often occurs when a dilated bile duct is entered and may be painful. This problem is the reason why the examination is performed only when surgery is planned to follow. There are a series of other complications related to catheter positioning that are unusual, but we will discuss them with you if you wish. The "x-ray dye" occasionally causes an "allergic" type reaction that cannot be predicted in advance. This generally consists of hives or nausea, but rarely is the reaction life-threatening or fatal (less than 0.0025% or 2 in 100,000 cases). This type of reaction is carefully watched for, and treatment can be instituted promptly should this occur. Occasionally infection of bile ducts can be spread into other parts of the body during the procedure.

The study will take 30 to 60 minutes. We should point out that a negative study—failure to enter a bile duct—provides important clinical information and may be the anticipated result of the study. If this occurs you may be returned to your room.

It is the judgment of your doctor that the potential benefits of this procedure as far as diagnosis of your condition far outweigh any of the above possible complications.

I have read and understand the above statements and have discussed them to my satisfaction and I consent to the performance of the above procedure by a qualified physician assigned by the above medical corporation upon

_____ (Name) _____ (Unit No.) _____ (Date)

_____ (Signature) _____ (Witness)

Figure 14–1   An informed consent document.

example, arrogance; (3) patients' attitudes; for example, submissiveness; and (4) power asymmetries.

The best approach to getting informed consent is for the physician who is requiring or performing the procedure to explain it in some detail in addition to having the patient read the form. Patients and their families also should be encouraged to ask any questions they wish, and should be given honest and clear answers. The idea behind such verbal explanations is that when patients sign these forms it is important that they have truly been fully informed; merely reading a paper is often not enough, especially when patients are confused, worried, or even scared about the procedure.

Doctors' Reactions to Truth Telling and Informed Consent

Some doctors are opposed to full disclosure of truth to their patients and also are opposed to informed consent, except as a mere formality. First of all, such doctors feel that patients don't need to be fully informed because doctors know what they are doing and explanations of complicated medical procedures will only confuse patients and break down the relationship of faith and trust that should exist between doctor and patient (engineering or priestly paternalism).

Second, patients often don't want to hear explanations, and forcing them to against their wills constitutes an invasion of their rights; furthermore, making them face facts about their physical or mental status or well-being that they aren't ready to accept is a highly questionable, perhaps even dangerous, course of action.

Third, every procedure has its risks, but there is no reason to frighten patients unnecessarily when the odds are only, for example, two in one hundred thousand that a particular allergy or side effect will occur.

Fourth, such explanations may unnecessarily frighten patients to the extent that they will refuse to undergo a procedure that may be necessary to their health or well-being.

Finally, doctors sometimes feel that by describing certain side effects, such as headaches, for example, they can induce such problems through the power of suggestion; that is, patients may worry so much about getting a headache that the worry actually brings one on. Doctors sometimes feel that if patients don't know that they "are supposed to" have some sort of reaction, they won't get it, at least not psychosomatically.

The other extreme in truth telling is, of course, to go overboard and "tell all." Some doctors feel that it is important that patients know every "sordid" detail of what is going to happen to them, whether they want to or not. For example, a woman in her mid-seventies who had broken her hip and was to undergo orthopedic surgery was told by the anesthetist that he was going to use curare, a paralyzing drug, to anesthetize her. He explained in detail how her heart would stop beating for a short while, but assured her that he would be able to "bring her back from the dead." The woman told the anesthetist—and I believe rightly so—not to give her so many details; to just do his work and not discuss it with her. It would seem that giving information to such an extent really serves no purpose unless the patient insists on knowing *every* last detail, which very few would. Except in such cases, overly detailed explanations merely cause unnecessary anxiety.

Patients' and Families' Reactions to Truth Telling

As we have already mentioned, some doctors base their decisions concerning what information to give, on their own judgment as to what patients and their families do or do not want to know. It certainly is true that many patients and families don't want to know the truth; they prefer to deny that "terrible things" are happening to them. However, most patients want to know what is happening to them because it is their bodies and lives that are at risk. Perhaps they don't want or need to know all the details, but they do want to know the crucial facts.

Furthermore, just because patients and their families sometimes want to deny the existence of serious illness, injury, dying, and death, doesn't necessarily mean they don't really want to know the truth. After all, there is often "unfinished business" that can be accomplished once the truth has been faced: dealing with inheritance and wills, settling family feuds, resolving other relationship problems, and doing things that families have always wanted to do but have put off. If patients and their families are not told the truth, they can miss an important opportunity to put their lives in order.

A great deal of sensitivity is required on the part of the whole health care team, especially doctors, to know what to tell and when to tell it, and to be able to gauge possible reactions of patients and their families to different types of information. The team members must let patients guide them as much as possible in determining what information to give. Needless to say, it is difficult to deal well with the issue of truth telling, and health care professionals—especially doctors—should be given extensive training in patient-professional relationships.

Generally speaking, according to this point of view, patients and their families should be kept as fully informed as possible about their situation, especially when it is clear that they really do want to know. Such openness and honesty helps to prevent the often painful game playing that goes on when people aren't honest with each other. Patients and their families should be dealt with truthfully, honestly, and compassionately but without cruelty, coldness, or brutal frankness. If, however, they consistently indicate that they don't want to be told about a specific situation, and if leaving them in ignorance would do no harm to them or their families, then one can avoid telling them until they indicate that they are ready to know. Finally, if patients want to know the truth about their illness but their families don't want them to, the patients' wishes should come first—family members should be counseled to allow the patients to be given the knowledge that they want and need.

Confidentiality

Confidentiality in patient-doctor relationships would on the surface seem to be fairly clear—that is, whatever a doctor and patient discuss and whatever the patient reveals in this relationship is to be held in strictest confidence, just as in other professional relationships such as lawyer-client, counselor-client, or rabbi/priest/minister-parishioner. And yet as it turns out, confidentiality is by no means so clear-cut an issue in the doctor-patient relationship. For example, what happens when a doctor tests a patient for a sexually transmitted disease (STD), including AIDS? The law is clear—STDs have to be reported—but it also is clear that test results showing that a patient is HIV positive or has AIDS are generally not to be revealed. Other infectious diseases, such as leprosy, tuberculosis, or plagues must be reported by individuals' names, but not HIV positive or AIDS results, which can be reported only anonymously as numbers of such cases.

Positive HIV Tests and AIDS

Spouses and Partners. Because of tremendous misunderstandings concerning the AIDS epidemic, and the stigma connected with people who are HIV positive or who have AIDS, laws have protected such people from being singled out because they could lose their jobs, societal status, and even friends if these results were revealed. However, problems have arisen with regard to matters of justice or fairness, especially those relating to sexual partners or drug-using partners. For example, should this information be revealed to such partners or spouses so that they can protect themselves from infection, especially because AIDS is a fatal disease with no cure as of yet?

For example, if a man goes on a trip, has sexual contact with an HIV-positive man or woman, and then tests HIV positive himself, should his wife or other sexual partners be told about his infection, or should his confidentiality be protected as it would be under most other medical circumstances? One solution, of course, is to urge the man to tell his wife or partner or to get his permission to let the physician do so; but what if he refuses?

The Centers for Disease Control (CDC) recommends that if HIV-infected persons are unwilling to notify partners, then physicians should use confidential procedures so as to ensure that partners are notified. Unfortunately, just what is meant by "confidential procedures" is not clear. A California law now permits disclosure by a physician to a spouse or to a needle-sharing partner if attempts to obtain the patient's voluntary consent have failed. The physician, however, is not required to make or not make such disclosure and is protected from liability no matter which approach he or she takes. Both the American Psychological Association (APA) and the American Medical Association (AMA) agree that it is ethically permissible for physicians to notify an identifiable person in danger of contracting the virus from a partner if they have good reason to believe that the infected person has failed to or is unwilling to do so. Another way of resolving this dilemma is to warn infected persons of the limitations of confidentiality before counseling them.

Health Caregivers with HIV/AIDS. Another problem has arisen with regard to health caregivers who are HIV positive or who have AIDS. If this information were to be revealed, then most such people would be out of a job; and yet, is it fair to their patients not to know that their health caregivers have this problem? A young woman died as a result of having been infected with the AIDS virus from her dentist, who has also since died from AIDS.

Some health caregivers feel that there would be a double standard if caregivers had to reveal their problems, but patients did not because the livelihoods of the former would be at stake. As health caregivers, they should, of course, take the responsibility for their infectiousness and remove themselves from any part of their work that would involve the possibility of passing on their body fluids to patients. For example, a surgeon should stop doing surgery and retrain or go into a different area within the same medical field for which he or she already is trained. But again, what if such doctors choose not to take that responsibility? What should be done? Shouldn't caregivers have the same protection as anyone else who tests HIV positive or has AIDS?

As one can see, the matter of confidentiality is not always so simple and straightforward as it might at first appear to be. It would seem that, as a general rule, confidentiality should be maintained to the utmost degree. At the same time, however, everything also must be done to protect the innocent from any kind of contagion. In these difficult times, every effort must be put into both of these areas of medicine, and people who are capable of infecting others must bear the responsibility of warning others. If they refuse, then confidential action must be taken so as to protect the innocent. Each case or situation must be dealt with on an individual basis.

Guilt and Innocence in Treating Patients

Another general medical ethical issue that sometimes arises relates to the effect on the treatment of patients by health care professionals, who have judged their patients to be either "guilty" or "innocent"; that is, the degree to which a patient is deemed to be the cause of or contributor to the illness for which he or she is being treated. For example, it often is difficult for a health practitioner to be objective when dealing with alcoholics or drug abusers if any members of his or her family have used alcohol or drugs or, worse yet, died as a result of either form of abuse. Similarly, it must be hard for the parent of a small child to treat a child abuser for an injury or a disease.

This inability to suspend personal feelings that can cloud professional judgment has to some extent always been a problem in medicine, especially when medical personnel are obliged to keep treating patients who continuously abuse themselves and thereby give rise to their own injuries or disease. Allowing personal attitudes to compromise patient care has become a more prevalent dilemma since the increase in the number of AIDS patients. Will a doctor or nurse treat an AIDS patient differently if that patient became infected due to receiving tainted blood from a transfusion as opposed to having acquired the disease as a result of sexual activity or drug abuse? Should this difference in treatment or attitude in giving treatment be allowed for, or not? Perhaps this question can be answered only when we have determined what a health professional's purpose in life is. Most will agree that it is not the job of such a professional to try, judge, or convict any patient of crimes, no matter how heinous. It is, rather, the task of such professionals to treat a sick or injured patient to the best of their knowledge and ability regardless of the patient's religion, race, lifestyle, or alleged or known involvement in criminal activity. Of course, this is often easier said than done, but just as a court reporter must report testimony accurately and without judging the guilt or innocence of a defendant, so must health care professionals treat sick and injured patients as well as they can regardless of those patients' backgrounds. Such professionals need not like these patients or in any way condone what they have done or are doing, but neither must they allow their own preconceptions or feelings to enter into the quality of treatment they give to them.

Ethical Issues in Medicine

We have already dealt with two major bioethical issues: the questions surrounding allowing someone to die, mercy death, and mercy killing (in Chapter 10), and those surrounding abortion (in Chapter 11). Because this book can serve as no more than an introduction to bioethics, there is only enough space to present problems in three other areas: behavior control, human experimentation, and genetics. For a more complete discussion of bioethics, you may want to read some of the texts listed in the Supplementary Reading section at the end of this book.

Ethics and Behavior Control

Behavior control is that aspect of bioethics which deals with general questions concerning the extent to which the behavior of human beings should be controlled by the various technologies available to us in our century. In particular, the following specific questions arise:

- How do we determine what constitutes undesirable or socially unacceptable behavior?
- Who defines such behavior, and to what extent should we control or eliminate it?
- Which methods of controlling behavior are considered ethical, and which are not?
- Who should determine how and to whom behavior control is to be applied—the individuals suffering psychological problems, their families, others living around them, the government, their doctors, medicine in general?

These issues are particularly crucial in cases involving mentally ill patients, prisoners, children, or antisocial human beings.

Before going any further, it is important that we understand precisely what *behavior control* is. It has been defined as the modification, or changing, of individuals' behavior, by means of various technologies, with or without their permission and with or without coercion. Some means used in behavior control are drugs, psychotherapy, behavior modification techniques (reward or aversive conditioning), electrical brain stimulation (EBS), hypnotism, biofeedback, surgery, and incarceration.

The major ethical issue that arises in terms of behavior control is that such control involves an encroachment upon or even an elimination of individual freedom: the question then, is to what extent this should be allowed. Our recent past as well as present history are rife with situations that give rise to these issues. For example, it was discovered that about two hundred male sex offenders in California had been given a choice of prison or castration. In another case, which occurred in the South, two mentally retarded young African American girls were told that they were getting birth control medication but instead were sterilized by the government without their knowledge or permission. Mental patients who are subject to episodes of violence have either been kept totally sedated on drugs or subjected to brain surgery, both of which eliminate their violent episodes but also transform them into virtual zombies. In some cities, hyperkinetic children have not been allowed to go to school unless their parents have agreed to give them a drug that slows their level of activity—but which also may have questionable side effects.

Some prisoners and mental patients are kept sedated so that they can be controlled more easily in understaffed institutions. People who are subject to depression sometimes are given electroshock therapy or have electrodes implanted in their brains that, when stimulated, eliminate the depression—again with possible questionable side effects. Many people have sought to eliminate "bad habits" such as drinking alcohol, taking drugs, and overeating by going to clinics where they are aversively conditioned (that is, made to suffer physical or mental discomfort) for continuing the habit and are rewarded for stopping it. These are just a few of the many situations in which ethical issues of behavior control arise. Implied in all of them are various problems and concerns, and it is these that I now will attempt to clarify.

Ethical Issues and Problems with Behavior Control. Because much behavior control is subtle, we must question whether we have the right to change people's behavior whether they know it or not or whether they consent or not. Ardent probehaviorists would say "yes" for several reasons. They would insist that we have a good idea of what "normal behavior" is, and that when people don't conform to it, their behavior should be changed for their own good and the good of others. The farther away from the norm the behavior is, they would argue, the more drastic the control must be (for example, a scolding might be sufficient for a child who swears, but brain surgery would have to be considered for an adult given to episodes of uncontrollable violence).

Strong antibehaviorists, or individualists, however, would disagree. They believe that we *don't* know what the standard for normal behavior is and that setting one arbitrarily would be highly dangerous. Individual freedom, uniqueness, and creativity are to be encouraged and prized, and if these are to exist we must allow for some deviation from the norm. True, they say, some behaviors should be discouraged and some encouraged, but proper ethical procedures must be employed at all times. For example, simply because a person in a mental hospital is in favor of brain surgery to curb his violence does not necessarily mean that the doctors should comply with his wishes. According to the antibehaviorists, we must ask several important questions concerning the protection of such people's rights as individuals. For example, can they really know, if they are so mentally disturbed that they must be institutionalized, what they are consenting to? Are they competent to judge what is best for them in such situations?

Another question that comes up with relation to changing behavior is how far can we carry the use of rewards, bonuses, or punishments. Doesn't it constitute rather strong coercion to give a man a choice between three to six years in prison and castration, or to give an impoverished man in India a bonus for having himself sterilized? Can people be considered to "freely" consent when they are being forcibly or even subtly coerced by financial rewards or promises of freedom?

Yet another problem that arises involves the therapist or controller as well as the patient. First of all, who should such controllers be, and to whom should they be responsible? To the society in which they live? The institutions at which they work? Their government? Their patients? For example, if a homosexual who lives in a militantly heterosexual society comes to a therapist for help, what is the therapist's duty? Should he or she help the homosexual to adjust to this type of sexuality and to the possibility of ostracism by some segments of society, or should the therapist try to steer the homosexual toward heterosexuality? Therapists' decisions about their responsibilities affect their patients and, more indirectly, the rest of society.

Human Experimentation

Human experimentation means the use of human beings for experimental purposes for their own therapy, for the good of humanity in general, or for the purpose of advancing scientific knowledge. Why is the question of human experimentation even raised? First of all, medical knowledge concerning human beings can be advanced only so far by experimenting on animals; sooner or later a drug, procedure, or technology must be used on human beings if medicine is to discover whether it is effective or ineffective. Also, experimentation sometimes is done in areas that apply only to human beings, not to any other animal species; in such cases, experimentation on animals simply will not yield the necessary knowledge.

This problem becomes even more crucial in relation to pediatric medicine (medicine pertaining to children). Children are physically and mentally different from adults, which means that even if adults can be safely and ethically used for experimentation purposes, such data are often not very useful in the treatment of children. Experimentation on children, however, raises even more serious ethical problems because they are rarely thought of as being competent to freely consent to experimentation. One can even raise the issue of whether parents or guardians really can decide for their children, without their consent, whether they will undergo experimentation that may cause pain or discomfort, or even place them in a life-threatening situation. The main questions here, then, are to what extent human beings can be experimented upon and under what conditions, and to what degree must they be informed about and freely consent to such experimentation.

The Proexperimentation Argument.   Those who take a strong proexperiment stance believe that as long as a specific experiment can advance scientific knowledge or aid humanity in some way, human experimentation is justified. People who are to be experimented on should be informed just enough so that they know something about what's being done to them, but not enough to interfere with the outcome of the experiment.

People in prison or in mental institutions who are willing to participate should be allowed to volunteer to aid humanity; in this way, they can make up for their previous crimes or their present uselessness. As an incentive, such people can be offered rewards (for example, parole, release, or a better living situation). It is, further, even justifiable to experiment on institutionalized children or on children whose parents have given consent, in order to cure them when nothing else has worked or to benefit future children with similar problems.

The Antiexperimentation Argument.   According to this point of view, human beings generally should not be used for experimentation. If science can't advance its knowledge by using animals, it simply cannot be advanced. No experimental drug or procedure should be used on any human being unless the following criteria are met: It is a last resort; it is meant to cure the person on whom it is used; the patient has given fully informed consent; and science has gone as far as it can with animal experimentation. Opponents of human experimentation point to the terrible experiments performed by doctors of Nazi Germany during World War II. Never again, these people argue, can science be given carte blanche to perform experiments on humans.

Furthermore, experimentation must never be done on human beings who are not mentally competent to consent, including people in mental institutions and all children, whether or not their parents are willing to consent. Experiments also must never be performed upon people who are not really free to consent, such as those incarcerated in prisons or other institutions. Finally, any human experimentation that is done, after all of these criteria have been satisfied, must also be extremely safe; it must not involve serious risk of illness, injury, or loss of life.

Immanuel Kant's Practical Imperative (see Chapter 3) can be very useful here. Remember that the principle states that each human being must be considered as a unique end in himself or herself and never used merely as a means to someone else's end. In human experimentation this would mean that no human being could be used for experimentation unless it would be therapeutic for that human being and would not be any more harmful or risky than other treatments that generally would be used for such patients. This would mean that no experimentation only for "the good of humanity or others" could be done. If this "good" were an indirect result of the experimentation, then it would be allowed, but the experimental procedure must be for the primary benefit of the patient on whom it is to be performed.

Many medical ethicists will follow this imperative as a guideline, but they may also allow experimentation when the person to be experimented on can give fully free and informed consent, realizing that the experiment may not be therapeutic for him or her, but for the good of humanity or the advancement of science. Where there is any doubt, however, the Practical Imperative forms a useful ethical criterion for human experimentation.

Genetics and Stem-Cell Research

Genetics is that area of medicine and science which is concerned with the manipulation and control of the human genetic makeup. Research in genetics includes everything from discovering the causes of genetic problems and correcting such problems to creating human life in the laboratory. The main problem caused by genetics arises from determining how to use the technology we have to help us acquire genetic information and manipulate genes. It is obvious that this problem is very important, especially when we consider the potentially enormous effect of genetic manipulation upon individuals, families, and the overall gene pool.

There are, first of all, such procedures as amniocentesis and chorionic villus sampling which have been discussed earlier in Chapter 11 on abortion, and other investigative and diagnostic procedures that can bring us important information about genetic defects or abnormalities. This information can, in turn, enable us to correct such deficiencies—if and when we can perfect the corrective procedures—or to avoid them altogether by means of either abortion or birth control, including sterilization. Genetic counseling is, therefore, intimately tied to important ethical questions.

Second, even more crucial ethical problems will arise as we approach the point at which we can correct and avoid genetic defects, cure diseases, or create life in the laboratory. Someday, we may even be in a position to decide what male and female types would best ensure the survival of the race and then reproduce them artificially. We could go even further and decide, as in Aldous Huxley's *Brave New World*, how many intellectuals, laborers, white-collar workers, and other types of people a "balanced, well-functioning society" needs and then create such a society in the laboratory.

At this point in scientific development these are somewhat exotic problems, but there is no reason to think that we will not be able to do these things in the future. Frogs and even mammals (for example, sheep) have been cloned with some success. Also, scientists already have declared a moratorium on various types of experimentation having to do with creating life in the laboratory. As does human experimentation, the issue of genetic experimentation and development arouses strong opinions on both sides.

The Argument for Genetic Experimentation and Development. According to this argument, nothing and no one should stand in the way of advances in scientific knowledge and the chance to cure diseases or perfect the human race. The more we know about genetics, the more we can improve the human race and condition, and the better things will be. This betterment should be our primary goal; we should not worry about such trivial matters as the effects of experimentation upon the gene pool, or whether our information and abilities will result in abortion, sterilization, the elimination of defects, or the ability to create life in the laboratory. Self-imposed moratoriums and laws that prevent scientific advancement cannot be justified.

The Argument Against Genetic Experimentation and Development. According to this argument, in the case of anything that tampers with the natural life process or interferes with God's or Nature's plan, no scientific experimentation in this area, especially the artificial creation of life, should be allowed. Nature or God had a purpose in allowing some imperfections to exist in the human species, and tampering with this purpose could prove disastrous, not only to the natural development and progress of humanity but also to its moral and spiritual development. Nature or God has placed upon this earth human beings with handicaps and genetic problems to help us recognize that human imperfections do exist and also to encourage us to love and care for less fortunate human beings. If we create completely perfect human beings and eliminate all of those with imperfections, we will lose our humanity, both from a biological-physical and a moral-spiritual point of view.

Stem Cell Research

One of the most controversial types of genetic research today is stem cell research. Stem cells, the so-called master cells of the body, have the potential to become many different kinds of cells. They are the means by which cells in the body can be replenished. In the very early embryo, these cells have the power to become any kind of body cell. Adult stem cells, on the other hand, have the capacity to become a variety of cells, but not all kinds. They are difficult to obtain and very hard to coax into developing into other tissues; consequently, their use would involve much more time and money to obtain the desired results. Scientists hope to obtain lines of the embryonic cells, that is, large numbers of them grown from a common source and coax them into becoming specific kinds of cells. The desire of these scientists is to use stem cells to repair damaged tissues in the body, such as heart tissues to repair damaged hearts and nerve tissues to repair damaged spinal columns or reverse the effects of Alzheimer's or Parkinson's diseases.[11]

The Moral Issue of Using Embryonic Stem Cells. Although embryonic stem cells are much easier to use than adult stem cells, the moral issue for many, especially strong antiabortionists such as the Catholic Church, is that the procedure of extracting stem cells from a five- to seven-day-old embryo kills the embryo. Many prolife people argue if we allow this, we do not respect human life (assuming that human life begins at fertilization of the egg by sperm—the strong prolife point of view) and what is done is tantamount to abortion or the murder of human life in the embryonic stage. The moral dilemma occurs because scientists figure they can use such cells to develop tissues which can be used in curing chronic, disabling diseases such as Parkinson's, Alzheimer's, diabetes, and spinal cord injuries.

Government Limits. President George W. Bush, faced with this dilemma and torn between his prolife views against abortion and yet the desire to cure various diseases, said that federal funds will be used only for research on existing stem cell lines that were derived (1) with the consent of the donors; (2) from excess embryos created for reproductive purposes; and (3) without any financial inducement to the donors. No federal funds will be used for (1) stem cell lines derived from newly destroyed embryos; (2) the creation of human embryos for research purposes; or (3) the cloning of human embryos. The irony of his plan is that it satisfies neither the scientists, who want greater freedom and financial support for research, nor the prolife supporters. Bishop Joseph A. Fiorenza, president of the U.S. Conference of Catholic Bishops states the prolife position when he said, "The trade-off he [Bush] has announced is morally unacceptable. It allows our nation's research enterprise to cultivate a disrespect for human life."[12] Scientists are disappointed because there are only a few stem cell lines available under Bush's plan, which, of course, drastically limits their research. Some states, such as New Jersey and California, have passed legislation legalizing stem cell research with fewer limitations than Bush's plan and with financial support coming from private or nongovernmental, sources.

Possible Solution. The latest research has shown that adult stem cells can be isolated and developed. If such research continues to be successful, there may be no reason whatsoever to use embryonic stem cells, which, of course, would resolve the dilemma.[13] It remains to be seen how long such research will take and whether scientists are willing to wait until the research is successful or whether they will deem the adult stem cells as useful as embryonic ones.

The Ethics of Body Trading and Tissue Banking

Rapid progress in biotechnology has outpaced regulation and the public, too, lacks both an awareness of, and understanding about, a highly lucrative global industry of body trading: body part buying, selling, retrading and transplanting. Staggering advances in biotechnology and medical science concerning new uses for human tissue have given rise to a host of ethical, legal, and political issues that accompany the commercial enterprise of body trading. Altruistic donors, through ignorance, are routinely exploited and relatives are stunned, dumbfounded, and outraged to learn that their loved ones have become products in the profitable tissue commerce business.

In addition to organ transplants, approximately 650,000 Americans each year undergo surgery that uses soft-tissues, skin, bones, and tendons taken from cadavers. But, there are serious issues about the clandestine nature of body part procurement and a range of possible risks associated with product lines. Companies that process human tissue purchase body parts from hospitals, universities, and other institutions to which bodies are donated in good faith for research purposes. Procurement of bodies from Third World Nations is even more problematic. A cadaver often generates over $200,000.00 in market value. Tissue companies reap high profits and trade on the global exchanges. Much of this industry is market driven and shareholders place pressure on management to show profits quarter after quarter.

Due to lack of regulation (much of the industry in America is still governed by Blood Shield laws passed in the 1950s and 1960s), there are a number of product risks. Tissue can transmit the following to a transplant host: hepatitis, HIV, mad cow disease, bacteria, and other communicable diseases. There is also a failure to disclose information about the cadaver's lifestyle, sexual habits, prior illness, and whether he or she was a smoker, drinker, or drug user. Furthermore, there is not adequate research concerning the ways a cadaver's former lifestyle might impact the transplant host.

There is a need for better global regulation of, and public disclosure and transparency within, the body trading industry. Ethical, legal, and social issues must be more clearly defined in those cases that determine the status of body parts.

Cases for Study and Discussion

CASE 1 67-Year-Old Cancer Patient

Richard is a 67-year-old man with terminal cancer. He has just had a liver scan and been told to visit his doctor, an oncologist (that is, a cancer specialist whose work focuses on tumors), and get the results. When Richard arrives, the doctor says that there has been no change in his condition, which is, nevertheless, not good. Richard asks the doctor what can be done, and he replies that there is no remedy for this kind of cancer. Becoming somewhat agitated, Richard asks the doctor what he would advise him to do, but the doctor merely repeats his opinion that there is nothing to be done. By this time Richard is both frustrated and upset, and he asks the doctor why he won't care for him and doesn't care about him. In response the doctor gives Richard a prescription, but he makes it clear that the drug is being prescribed only as a psychological crutch—that it will not improve Richard's health. When he finally leaves the doctor's office, Richard feels totally depressed, abandoned, and dehumanized. Do you feel the doctor handled Richard's case well? If so, why; if not, why not? How would you have handled the situation or advised the doctor to handle it? Discuss both the truth telling aspect of what the doctor said and his methods of giving out information and relating to his patient.

CASE 2 Abortion for Reasons of Gender of the Embryo

In Chapter 11, which dealt with abortion, I described a case in which a middle-aged wife became pregnant and underwent amniocentesis testing to see if the baby would have Down syndrome. When the procedure was over, the genetic counselor was happy to inform the prospective parents that their baby would be quite healthy. She also told them, however, that the sex of the child was female. The husband and wife then decided to have an abortion because they already had several daughters, and the genetic counselor was beside herself with shock and concern. She felt that she might have done the wrong thing by revealing the sex of the child to the parents—that if she had merely told them about the Down syndrome results, they would not have decided on an abortion. Should the counselor have withheld the information about the sex of the child? Do the parents have a right to know all of the information disclosed by amniocentesis, only the information that is crucial to the health of the child, or only the information for which they ask? In short, what are counselors' obligations in revealing the results of such tests?

CASE 3 Video Taping Patients

A psychologist wants to videotape some of his patients during their therapy sessions, partly for a study he is doing and partly as a teaching device for advanced psychology students. He feels that if the patients know they are being taped, they won't act naturally, which will both taint his study and diminish the film's value as a teaching device. For this reason, he feels that the patients should not know that they are being taped even though what they do or say on the tape may reveal certain aspects of their private feelings and lives. What should the psychologist do? Should he tell the patients he is taping them, or should he just go ahead and tape without their permission, assuming that he is just going to use the tapes for his own research and as a teaching device? Are there any other alternatives you can think of for the psychologist to follow?

CASE 4 Experimenting on Children

A doctor-researcher in residence at a private institution for mentally retarded children discovers that the children in one of the dormitories have dysentery, whereas those in the other dormitories do not. She decides to experiment with the children, both to see what has caused this particular phenomenon and to study the effects of dysentery and its various cures upon children in general. She sets up a scientific study with control groups (in which some students receive medication and some do not), and part of her experiment involves infecting healthy children with dysentery germs. The institution for which she works has a long waiting list, and the doctor takes advantage of this, admitting only those children whose parents will sign a release allowing her to conduct experiments upon them. What are the ethical implications of what the doctor is doing? Should such experimentation be allowed? Why, or why not?

CASE 5 Homosexual Seeking Help

John, 25, comes to a psychiatrist very depressed about his homosexuality. He has had two heterosexual relationships, neither of which was satisfactory, and numerous homosexual ones, some of which were satisfactory and some of which were not. He also has used his homosexuality as a means of getting jobs, money, and other benefits. John is not quite sure what he wants to do about his homosexuality, but he does know that he is not very happy the way he is. What should the psychiatrist do? Should he try to help John become a heterosexual? Should he try to get him to adjust to his homosexuality? Discuss both of these alternatives, and describe the psychiatrist's responsibilities to himself, to John, and to society in general.

CASE 6 Woman in a Mental Institution

Mary, 45, is in a mental institution, on a ward for violent people. She is given to episodes of extreme violence during which she loses all control and becomes very dangerous. Between such episodes, she remembers at least some of what she has done, but when one of these episodes comes on, she just can't seem to stop or control it. There doesn't seem to be anything physiologically wrong with her brain, but a doctor suggests to her that she have surgery performed that will eliminate her violence.

The doctor explains that this operation may cause extreme loss of memory—to the extent that Mary could read a newspaper and immediately forget everything she has read. Furthermore, the operation will make Mary so passive that she probably will not want to do very much with the rest of her life; however, after undergoing such an operation, she probably could be released from the institution. Mary is so deeply distressed by her violent episodes that she signs a release to have the surgery performed.

Describe the implications of informed consent in this case, and discuss Mary's ability to give it freely as an inmate of a mental institution. Also, discuss the extent to which coercion exists in the doctor's promise that Mary's violent episodes will end and in the suggestion that she may be released from the institution. Can Mary fully understand what she is agreeing to? And even if she does not fully understand, because she hasn't been cured by other methods, should she be allowed the brain surgery as a viable alternative or not?

CASE 7 Prisoner and Heart Transplant

Recently a 31 year old twice convicted robber became the first California state prisoner—and likely the first in the United States to receive a heart transplant, a scarce and expensive resource, He suffered from a viral infection that had damaged his heart valves. He experienced congestive heart failure and was placed higher on the list because of his urgent medical condition. Many people, including some ethicists, thought that taxpayers shouldn't spend $1 million on a convict who was serving a 14-year sentence for a violent felony. Others, again including ethicists, thought that no distinction should be made between a convicted felon and anyone else who needed a heart transplant (refer to Chapter 7 and the committee deciding social worth for kidney dialysis). In 1976, the U.S. Supreme Court ruled that prisoners must receive adequate medical care. One of the biggest problems in heart transplantation is the many medications necessary to prevent the body from rejecting the new heart and biopsies necessary during the first year following the surgery. This difficulty became apparent in this case in that the inmate died within the first year. The comment was made by the prison warden that prisoners generally don't take care of themselves and often don't take their medications. Do you think that major medical care, such as transplants, should be performed on prisoners? Why or why not? Would it make any difference if they were on death row, serving life sentences without parole, or serving determinate sentences, such as this inmate? Support your position with logical argument and proof.

CASE 8 Stem Cell Research

Do you think that stem cell research should be allowed to continue from embryos and/or adults? Why or why not? Support your answer with proof and logical argument. Should the government subsidize such research? Why or why not? If you agree that embryos should be used, which kind? Those from aborted fetuses? Leftover embryos from fertility processes? Should embryos be raised for research purposes? Why or why not?

Chapter Summary

I. Introduction and definition of terms
  A. *Bioethics* literally means "life ethics," or ethics in medicine.
  B. Bioethics covers the areas of caring for the dying; allowing someone to die, mercy death, and mercy killing; human experimentation and informed consent; genetics, fertilization, and birth; health care and its costs; population and birth control, abortion, and sterilization; allocation of scarce medical resources; and truth telling and confidentiality in medicine.
  C. It is essentially concerned with the establishment and maintenance of vital and human relationships between the sick and dying and the well and the professional.
II. Health care personnel and patients and their families—rights and obligations
  A. Paternalism is the position that professionals should take a parental role toward patients and their families.
    1. Laypeople don't know what's best for them; therefore, they should place themselves totally in the hands of professionals because they and they alone have the proper medical background.
    2. Patients and their families are essentially like children when it comes to medical problems, so the professionals should serve as father figures.
    3. There are two possible models under paternalism:
      (a) The engineering model, in which the physician tries to be an applied scientist who is value free. The problem here is that physicians cannot logically be value free.
      (b) The priestly model, which is the opposite extreme—the physician is a new priest. The problem is that he or she is still making decisions for the patient.

B. Radical individualism is the position that patients should have absolute rights over their bodies and lives and may therefore reject doctors' recommendations.
  1. Doctors are nothing more than humans with special training, and therefore are capable of making errors.
  2. Patients and their families are better qualified than anyone else to make decisions concerning their own treatment because their bodies and lives are at stake.
  3. Many issues having to do with treatment are not strictly medical, and professionals are not qualified to make decisions about them.
  4. Many lay people these days are quite knowledgeable about their bodies and about medicine, and even when they are not, they can be made to understand the nature of their medical problems when these are explained clearly and in plain language.
  5. Paternalism often has led to total patient dependence on doctors and sometimes has resulted in dehumanization.
  6. Problems with this model are that patients may not be qualified or knowledgeable enough to make decisions on their own; also, many patients don't want to be entirely responsible for such decisions.
C. The reciprocal model utilizes the team approach, in which patients and their families work with health care personnel to do what is best for patients.
  1. Professionals are not gods or even father figures; they are merely human beings with specialized training.
  2. Many decisions are not strictly medical; therefore, they should not be made strictly by professionals. Doctors need to rely on other support personnel (nurses, therapists, etc.) as well as nonmedical personnel, such as social workers, clergy, and trained volunteers in order to properly care for patients and their families as whole persons.
  3. This view recognizes the importance of individual patients' rights in all medical areas.
  4. It accepts the idea that neither patients nor professionals alone "know best," but that decisions should be reciprocal (involving give and take) rather than dictatorial, paternalistic, or anarchistic.
  5. Patients are entitled to know what is happening to them, and decisions should be arrived at through a free exchange of ideas and be made jointly by everyone on the team.
  6. There are two models under the reciprocal view:
     (a) The collegial model, in which the physician and patient see themselves as colleagues pursuing a common goal. The problem with this model is whether physicians and patients really can assume mutual loyalty and goals of common interest, given all their differences.
     (b) The contractual model is supposed to permit moral equality between physician and patient, without indulging in any utopian assumption of collegiality. The problems associated with this model are how to execute the contract and what to include in it.
III. Truth telling and informed consent
  A. The main issue here is to what extent patients and their families should be told the truth about their medical situations and to what extent they should not.
  B. *Informed consent* is a formalized procedure in which patients or their families consent in writing to medical procedures involving some degree of risk to their health or lives.
  C. The paternalistic view holds that because patients are not medically trained, they cannot understand what doctors tell them; therefore, they do not need to know more than that professionals are doing their very best for them.
    1. It is best for patients' morale and their will to get better or will to live that they aren't told bad news.

2. Keeping patients in the dark allows them to live the remainder of their lives without worry, concern, or depression; telling them bad news will not keep them from dying.
3. It is all right to tell the bad news to the families, but not to the patients.
4. Professionals and patients' families should avoid being morbid and should try to cheer up patients.

D. There are several arguments supporting the position that patients have a right to know about their condition.
1. They have a right to know because it is their bodies and lives that are at stake.
2. It is much easier to deal with patients who are aware of what is going on, as this makes pretense unnecessary.
3. Patients often are angry and feel dehumanized if they don't know what is going on or aren't told what to expect.
4. This approach, however, may lead some professionals to be frank to the point of being brutal or even cruel in telling patients the truth.
5. It is a false dilemma to assume that you have to either give people terrible news or lie to them.
6. A third view, the moderate position, which lies between paternalism and brutal frankness, favors the sharing of appropriate information when patients want and/or need to know it, letting the patients be the guide as to how much information should be revealed. This involves the following:
   (a) Listening to and really hearing patients.
   (b) Answering patients' questions truthfully and compassionately.
   (c) Not forcing information on patients but letting them decide what should be told and when it is to be told.
   (d) Not avoiding questions or issues by means of employing technical medical language or jargon.
   (e) Recognizing that explanations may have to be given in parts or more than once because of the shock of the news and resultant patient denial.
   (f) Always giving information clearly, gently, and humanely, never coldly, brutally, or cruelly.
   (g) Never leaving patients and their families without some hope, even if it is only that the patients will be cared for and kept free of pain.

E. Informed consent is necessitated in our times by the increased use of complex technological tests, procedures, and surgeries, not only for therapeutic reasons but also for experimental purposes.
1. In the United States, patients must be informed of the risks involved in any procedures that are to be performed upon them.
2. The assumption behind this approach is that in order to intelligently consent to any procedure, patients must be fully informed; they also should consent in writing so as to avoid future confusions or legal problems.
3. Most informed consent forms do the following:
   (a) Explain the procedure and its purpose clearly and in ordinary language.
   (b) Explain what the procedure will cause the patient to feel in the way of discomfort or pain before, during, and after the procedure.
   (c) Explain any and all complications that may arise because of the procedure.
   (d) State how long the procedure will take.
   (e) Include a statement that the patient's doctors have judged the procedure to be so important to the patient's well-being that the risks involved are justified.

4. Several factors that could inhibit informed consent are illnesses or injury of the patient; various medications; physicians' and patients' attitudes (arrogance v. submissiveness); and power asymmetries.

5. Often the best approach is for the physician to provide information in person as well as providing a consent form for the patient to read and sign; this will help to ensure full understanding and truly informed consent.

F. Doctors vary greatly in their reactions to truth telling and informed consent.

  1. Doctors who generally are against both full disclosure of the truth and informed consent support their position with a number of arguments.

    (a) Doctors know what they are doing, and having to explain complicated medical procedures to patients will only confuse the patients and break down the relationship of faith and trust between doctor and patient.

    (b) Patients often really don't want to know the truth, and forcing it upon them against their wills both invades their privacy and is bad for their morale.

    (c) Every procedure has its risks, but there is no reason to frighten patients unnecessarily, especially when the risks are very slight.

    (d) Patients may be unnecessarily frightened to the point where they will refuse to have the necessary procedures performed.

    (e) Unnecessary side effects also may be brought on by the power of suggestion.

  2. Some doctors, on the other hand, have gone overboard in giving information whether or not the patients want to hear it, thus causing unnecessary anxiety.

G. The reactions of patients and their families to truth telling and informed consent also vary.

  1. Some patients, and their families, don't want to know the truth because they wish to continue denying their problems. However, most patients do want to know what is happening to them; perhaps they don't need to know everything, but they certainly want to know the crucial facts.

  2. That patients and their families want to deny their problems doesn't necessarily mean they don't want to know the truth. After all, there may be unfinished business to take care of, and knowing the truth may help all of them take care of it.

  3. A great deal of sensitivity is necessary on the part of the whole health care team to know how, what, when, and where to tell the truth.

H. There are a number of guides to truth telling and informed consent.

  1. Generally, patients and their families should be kept as fully informed as possible, especially when they clearly want to know the truth.

  2. They should be dealt with truthfully, honestly, and compassionately and without cruelty, coldness, or brutal frankness.

  3. If they consistently indicate that they don't want to know the truth, and if ignorance will do no harm to them or their families, then one can avoid telling them until they do want to know.

  4. If patients want to know the truth but their families don't want them to, then the patient's desire should come first.

IV. Confidentiality

A. Generally the matter of confidentiality seems fairly clear in that what goes on between doctors and patients should always be confidential. Usually, this is the case.

B. The problems with HIV testing and AIDS have, however, made the matter of confidentiality a difficult issue in the following cases:

  1. Spouses and partners deserve to be protected.

  2. Patients deserve to be protected from health caregivers infected with HIV or AIDS.

C. As a general rule, confidentiality should be maintained, but at the same time everything must be done to protect the innocent from any kind of contagion.

1. People who are capable of infecting others must take the responsibility for warning them.
2. Where they won't or can't, confidential action must be taken in order to protect the innocent.

V. Guilt and innocence in treating patients

A. Often it is difficult for health care professionals to be objective in treating patients who have certain problems that have also been personal problems for the professionals in some way (e.g., a child abuser who needs treatment and a doctor or nurse who is the parent of a small child).

B. Another aspect of this issue arises when professionals have to keep treating patients who continuously abuse their own health (e.g., alcoholics).

C. This issue has become even more of a problem since the advent of AIDS.

D. It is not the job of health professionals to try, judge, or convict any patient of crimes, no matter how heinous. It is their job, rather, to treat sick or injured patients no matter what their background or lifestyle.

E. Professionals need not like such patients or condone what they have done or how they live, but neither must they let their own preconceptions or feelings enter into the quality of their treatment.

VI. Ethical issues in medicine

A. Ethics and behavior control is that aspect of bioethics that deals with general questions concerning the extent to which the behavior of human beings should be controlled by the various technologies available to us.

1. Several specific questions arise in relation to this issue:
   (a) How do we determine what constitutes undesirable or socially unacceptable behavior?
   (b) Which means of behavior control should be considered ethical, and which should not?
   (c) Who should determine when behavior control is to be used?

2. Behavior control is the modification or changing of human behavior—with or without permission and with or without forcible or subtle coercion—by means of various technologies; drugs; psychotherapy; behavior modification techniques (reward or aversive conditioning); Electrical Brain Stimulation (EBS); hypnotism; biofeedback; brain surgery; and incarceration.

3. The major problem here is that any control of behavior involves an encroachment upon or even an elimination of individual freedom; the question, then, is to what extent this should be allowed.

4. There are many ethical issues and problems associated with behavior control.
   (a) Because much behavior control is subtle, we must question whether we have the right to change people's behavior whether they know it or not or whether they consent to it or not.
   (b) Probehaviorists would say that we have this right because we know what normal behavior is, and those in society who can't conform to these norms ought to have their behavior changed.
   (c) Antibehaviorists would say that we do not have this right because we don't know what the norm is, and setting one arbitrarily would be highly dangerous. Individual freedom, uniqueness, and creativity should be prized and protected at all costs.
   (d) There are also questions concerning how far we can carry rewards, bonuses, or punishments when attempting to change or control behavior.
   (e) We must ask ourselves to whom controllers should be responsible.

B. Human experimentation is the use of human beings for experimental purposes, either for their own therapy, for the good of humanity, or to advance scientific knowledge.
   1. Experimentation eventually must be done on human beings because science can only go so far with animal experimentation.
   2. The main question concerns the extent to which human beings can be experimented upon and under what conditions. Another important question concerns the extent to which people should be informed and freely consent to such experimentation.
   3. There are two highly divergent viewpoints on this issue:
      (a) Proponents of experimentation believe that as long as an experiment can advance scientific knowledge or aid humanity in some way, human experimentation is justified.
      (b) Opponents of human experimentation believe that human beings should never be used for experimentation unless protective criteria are met because of the ease with which the rights of people whose freedoms are limited (prisoners, mental patients, and children) can be abused.
   4. Immanuel Kant's Practical Imperative—that each human being must be considered as a unique end in himself or herself and never used merely as a means to someone else's end—can be useful here.
      (a) A person generally should not be experimented on unless the experimental procedure is therapeutic and not harmful.
      (b) A person may be experimented on provided he or she is fully informed and can freely consent to such experimentation, realizing that it may not be therapeutic to himself or herself but good for humanity.
C. Genetics is the area of bioethics that is concerned with the manipulation and control of the human genetic makeup.
   1. The main problem created by genetics is in determining how to use the technology we have acquired for gaining genetic information and manipulating genes, especially when we consider the possibly deleterious effect of genetic manipulation upon individuals, families, and the overall gene pool.
   2. Procedures such as amniocentesis and chorionic villus sampling provide us with information that forces us to make decisions concerning birth control, abortion, and sterilization.
   3. As our technology increases we can correct genetic deficiencies, create life in the laboratory, and clone ideal human beings. This raises questions as to whether we should do any of these things and, if so, to what extent. Also, what effect will this technology have on the human species?
   4. There are two highly divergent viewpoints on genetic experimentation and development.
      (a) Supporters of genetic experimentation and development believe that nothing and no one should stand in the way of scientific advancement and the chance to perfect the human race because the world can only benefit from such improvements.
      (b) Opponents of genetic experimentation and development believe that anything that tampers with the natural life process, interfering with nature's or God's plan, should be prohibited. This includes scientific experimentation in the area of genetics, especially the artificial creation of life.
D. Stem cell research is one of the most controversial types of genetic research.
   1. Stem cells are master cells of the body and can be obtained from both adults and human embryos.
   2. The moral issue with using embryonic stem cells is that the embryo is killed during the procedure.

3. President Bush has authorized federal funds for a very limited use of embryonic cells.

4. Some states have made stem cell research legal and intend to use private funds if the government will not subsidize the research.

E. Rapid progress in biotechnology has outpaced regulation and public awareness of a highly lucrative global industry of body trading: body part buying, selling, retrading and transplanting.

1. There are serious issues about the clandestine nature of body part procurement and the enormous profits generated in the process.

2. Due to lack of regulation there are product health risks to a transplant host including: hepatitis, HIV, made cow disease, bacteria, and other communicable diseases.

3. There is both a lack of information about and a failure to disclose risks about a cadaver's former lifestyle, sexual habits, prior illness, and whether he or she was a smoker, drinker, or drug user.

4. Issues of regulation and transparency must be addressed in the growing enterprise of body trading and tissue banking.

Exercises for Review

1. Investigate and research one of the areas of bioethics not covered in this chapter (for example, organ transplantation), and write or give an oral report on your research following your instructor's guidelines.

2. Outline in detail what you feel are the rights and obligations of doctors, nurses, patients, families, chaplains, and hospitals, and discuss whether these relationships should be paternalistic, radically individualistic, or reciprocal. How do you feel about Veatch's four models? If you were a patient, which model would you choose?

3. To what extent do you think the truth about terminal illness should be told to patients and their families? Why?

4. Describe the difference between "informed consent" and general truth telling, and design an informed consent form for some procedure, experiment, interview, or task you might want people to participate in. Explain in detail what you expect them to do; then describe the methods you would use to help them to understand the project so that they could give their informed consent to it. Explain how you would protect them from exposing their private lives or endangering themselves or their reputations.

5. To what extent and under what circumstances do you feel that people's behavior should be controlled? Do you feel that it is acceptable to control people in such a way that they don't know they are being controlled? Why, or why not?

6. To what extent do you feel that reward, punishment, or other types of forcible or subtle coercion should be used to get people to behave in certain ways?

7. If someone is in a position to control behavior (for example, a teacher or a psychotherapist), to whom should he or she be responsible, and to what degree?

8. To what degree do you believe that human beings can or should be experimented on? Under what conditions would you allow such experimentation? What safeguards or guidelines would you establish and enforce to protect both the subjects being experimented upon and the experimenters? Why?

9. Discuss at length the extent to which you would allow behavior control and experimentation to be performed upon children with or without their parents' permission. Support your position in detail.

10. To what extent do you feel that genetic experimentation and development should be allowed, especially experiments that involve the creation of human life in the laboratory, stem cell research, and the cloning of human beings? Answer in detail, providing evidence and supporting arguments for your position.

11. How do you feel about the issue of moral guilt and innocence as these are perceived by health care professionals when they are treating patients? How do you suggest these professionals treat patients whom they consider to be guilty of terrible crimes or immoralities? What types of patients would you yourself find it difficult to treat, and why? How would you overcome your distaste for or hatred of them? Do you think that all patients deserve the best treatment health professionals can give them, regardless of what they have done or who they are? Why, or why not? Explain in detail.

Views of the Major Ethical Theories on Bioethical Issues

Describe as fully as you can how each of the major ethical theories—Ethical Egoism, Utilitarianism, Divine Command Theory, Kant's Duty Ethics, Ross' *Prima Facie* Duties, and Virtue Ethics—probably would deal with the bioethical issues of the rights and obligations of health care personnel and patients; truth telling and informed consent; confidentiality; behavior control; genetics; and human experimentation. Refer to Chapters 2, 3 and 4 for a description of the ethical theories and to Chapter 9, "The Taking of Human Life," for an example of how you might go about completing this assignment.

Notes

1. Robert Veatch, "Models for Ethical Medicine in a Revolutionary Age," *Hastings Center Report* (June 1972), 6.
2. Ibid.
3. Ibid., 7.
4. John A. Behnke and Sissela Bok, *The Dilemmas of Euthanasia* (Garden City, NY: Anchor Books, 1975), 157–59.
5. Some of these questions are mine, and some were taken from an Ann Landers column in *The Bakersfield Californian* (October 29, 1987), E8.
6. Veatch, "Models of Ethical Medicine," p. 8.
7. Ibid.
8. Ibid., 9.
9. Ibid.
10. See Barney G. Glaser and Anselm L. Strauss, *Awareness of Dying* (Chicago: Aldine, 1965), for the best presentation of the difficulty of maintaining the various types of pretense between the healthy and the professional and the sick and the dying.
11. Thomas A. Shannon, "Stem Cell Research," http://www.americancatholic. org/Newsletters/CU/ac0102. asp, pp. 1–2.
12. *The Bakersfield Californian* (August 10, 2001), Al.
13. Shannon, "Stem cell Research," p. 2.

Research Navigator™
(http://www.researchnavigator.com)

This web site offers three research databases: EBSCO's *Content Select Academic Journal and Abstract Database*, *New York Times* Search by Subject Archive, and *Best of the Web* Link Library. In addition, this site provides helpful advice on how to conduct efficient and productive research from choosing a topic to polishing the final draft. Beginning philosophy students probably will find the *Best of the Web* Link Library the most appropriate place to start their research.

The free access code necessary to employ Research Navigator™ can be found in the Prentice Hall Guide to Evaluating Online Resources. If your text did not come with this guide, please go to *www.prenhall.com/contentselect* for information on how you can purchase an access code.

15

Business and Media Ethics

Objectives

After you have read this chapter, you should be able to

1. Understand what business and media ethics are, and why there is a need for education and training in these areas.

2. Understand how rights, obligations, justice, truth telling, and honesty apply specifically to business ethics.

3. Understand the rights and obligations that exist between employers and employees and between businesses and consumers.

4. Understand some of the ethical issues in the areas of advertising, business, media, the environment, affirmative action, reverse discrimination, corporate greed, and sexual harassment.

5. Understand what constitutes the media and how they affect our lives.

Introduction

Some people argue that, like "military intelligence," the phrase "business ethics" is an oxymoron, and many businesspeople would agree that "all's fair in love and business" or that there is no such thing as ethics in the business world—there is only profit and loss, and the highest goal is to make a profit. They would go on to say that what they do in business has nothing to do with their religious or moral values outside of the workplace. A perfect example of this is the Enron, Andersen fiasco.

These statements are all false and very injurious to the character and reputation of both businesspeople and their businesses. As has been seen up to this point, our everyday lives are fraught with moral decisions, and why should our jobs, where we spend eight hours or more of our days, be exempt from ethical values? The answer, of course, is that they are not. Business ethics, like bioethics, is a specialized area in which an awareness of ethical issues and a systematic approach to solving them are particularly important. As is true of other areas of ethics, business ethics has to do with the establishment and maintenance of vital and significant relationships among human beings—specifically, in this case, among employers, employees, shareholders, businesses, and consumers. As in other areas, ethical principles, such as the five I have argued for—the valuing of life, the striving for goodness and avoiding of badness, the just and fair distribution of good and bad, honesty and truth telling, and individual freedom—apply to business ethics.

The main difference between business ethics and bioethics is that the specific issues, problems, and situations that arise often require a different application of the principles, although the general applications are roughly the same. There is a difference, for example, between a patient signing an informed consent and a builder signing a contract to build a house for a client. In the first situation, the doctor needs the patient's consent so that the patient can undergo some sort of procedure necessary to maintain his or her health and well-being. In the second situation, a businessperson with specialized knowledge and abilities agrees to provide a client with something he or she wants, and the client in turn agrees to pay the builder, for example, a certain amount for doing this. The two situations are similar in that the "contracts" in both cases are an expression of trust, honesty, and mutual agreement executed for the benefit of both parties; they differ, however, in the specific ways in which ethics is applied.

Rights and Obligations in Business

First of all, by *rights* I mean those things to which human beings are entitled by law, morality, or tradition, such as "the right to life" or "the right to be free." By *obligations* I mean some sort of responsibility or duty that people have toward one another—also accorded by law, morality, or tradition—to see that their rights are protected and provided them. I have discussed rights before in dealing with other areas of morality, such as allowing someone to die, suicide, and abortion. I also expressed my conclusion that no rights are absolute—that is, no right is so important that it *always* supersedes all others. All human beings, for example, have a right to life, rights over their own bodies and lives, and also rights to be free, but none of these rights is ever absolute; indeed, they often conflict with one another. Conflicts of rights are not ethically resolved, however, by declaring certain rights to be absolute; rather, these conflicts are resolved by trying to establish some sort of priority system, some *prima facie* rights see Chapter 3 (Ross' *Prima Facie* Duties), and adjusting those rights to each other with reasonable justification and with regard to the attendant circumstances.

Just as the basic rights—the rights to life, justice, honesty and truth telling, privacy, and freedom—apply to life in general, so do they apply in business and the media. However, there also are specific rights or specific applications of the general rights listed above. These rights are the right to have one's own life protected whether one is an employer, an employee, or a consumer; the right to have the opportunity to pursue and qualify oneself for employment without hindrance; the right to establish a business, own property, employ whom one wants, and make a profit; the right to expect agreements and contracts to be executed fairly, whether between employers and employees, businesses and other businesses, business and government, or business and consumers; the right to fairness, trust, honesty, and truth telling at all levels of business dealings; the right to employment security; the right of businesses to try to get consumers to use their products and services; and the right of consumers to choose which products and services they wish to buy.

As far as obligations are concerned, participants in business and media activities are obligated to be honest and tell the truth; to be fair and just in their dealings with others; to be honest and trustworthy in executing and carrying out agreements and contracts; to pay off debts, including interest on money loaned, in a manner agreeable to all parties; to create a safe atmosphere for employees to work in; to make the effort and perform the work for which wages are being paid; to respect one another's privacy, and, finally, to be loyal to employers, employees, shareholders, and customers within reasonable and ethical limits.

Two Ways of Approaching Rights and Obligations in Business

There are two highly divergent ways of approaching the issues of rights and obligations in business; one of these emphasizes competition, and the other emphasizes government control.

The Competitive Approach

The aggressively competitive approach is referred to by a number of names: free enterprise, *laissez-faire*, survival of the fittest, and, by some, the "dog-eat-dog" approach. Supporters of this approach believe that the main obligation in business and in life in general is to "make a buck," that is, to establish and maintain a business without hindrance from the government at any level. The point—whether we are talking about management, labor, or consumers—is to get as large a share as possible of the profits to be made in business, using any method one can. According to this position, the best approach for a local or national economy to take is that of *laissez-faire* (meaning "let people do what they want"), free enterprise, and competition. The theory behind this approach is that existing economic problems will be solved if all participants in business are completely free to compete as aggressively as they can. If there is a demand for certain goods, then businesses that can convince consumers that they can supply those goods at the best quality and the lowest prices should be free to compete with other businesses. In this way, everyone who can survive will profit—successful businesses, government, and consumers.

If small businesses or new businesses can't survive the competition, then they will be eliminated from it, just as the weaker animals in the jungle are killed by those that are stronger. On the other hand, if businesses can make themselves larger and more secure by subsuming or destroying smaller businesses, this is an acceptable part of the competition process. The goal of any state or nation, as seen from this viewpoint, is to allow individuals to compete aggressively with each other for wealth and power because consumers can only benefit from this process, receiving the best products and services at the lowest cost.

Proponents of this position see this as being the most meaningful and, in some cases, the only possible position for a free, democratic society to hold. They feel that whenever state and local government controls are imposed, power becomes centered in government, which tends to feed itself at the expense of individuals, both in business and in society in general.

The Government Control Approach

This approach argues for state or government ownership and control of all business enterprises in the name of and for the good of the people. Although *laissez-faire* may sound good, opponents of this position state that it often puts power and excessive affluence in the hands of a few aggressive people at the expense of the many. Furthermore, wealth is kept in the same hands as families that own big businesses continue to pass them on to their children and grandchildren.

The competitive approach also brings out the most animalistic aspects of human beings, dehumanizing them both because it glorifies the "might makes right—survival of the fittest" jungle ethic, and also because it consigns the have-nots to poverty and hopelessness. It's all well and good to speak of seeing everyone profit from free enterprise, but in fact only a few do so. These people use their control of the supply of goods to control the demand for the goods or to satisfy demand at higher profit to themselves—often offering less quality in the bargain. Furthermore, if small, independent businesses can't and don't survive, then everyone who isn't in control of power becomes a slave to those who are. In other words, what all of this adds up to, according to this view, is that good and bad are distributed unjustly in a *laissez-faire* society, with the haves getting all of the good while the have-nots get all of the bad.

The only ethical and fair way for business to be conducted, according to this view, is to put it in the hands of the government, which then will operate it for the good of all concerned. In this way no one individual or group of individuals will be able to exert control and achieve affluence to the detriment of others. Everyone in such a system will work for the good of all, and a just distribution of good and bad will be made by a central governing body representing all of the people.

Some of the good will be distributed equally; some according to merit; and some by need and ability (see the discussion of these and other methods in Chapters 7 and 8). According to this view, everyone will share—with at least some degree of equality—both the bad and the good emanating from the society's business dealings. For example, if the main business of a country is agriculture and agriculture has a good year, then everyone shares equally in the food distribution and the profits. On the other hand, if it has a bad year, then everyone shares equally in the lack of food and the losses. This is the only fair way. Furthermore, by not stressing aggressiveness and competition, and by providing everyone with a fair and equitable living that is free from poverty and hardship, more time can be spent on civilizing and humanizing the people.

The Moderate Position

The Moderate Position on Business and Media Ethics

It is always difficult to characterize accurately a "moderate position" because unlike extreme positions, moderate ones are spread all along the spectrum between the two extremes. Nevertheless, I will present some generalities that I feel are characteristic of a moderate view. Both extreme positions have strong points to make and, of course, imply or put forth criticisms of each other. It is important to remember, however, that the system that will work best for a society depends upon a great number of factors; it is not just a theoretical matter.

Both extreme positions, and variations or combinations thereof, have had failures and successes in many different societies throughout history. If, for example, a government and its leaders are benevolent and ethical, government control of business and media activities may work well. There is always a problem, of course, of corruption in government, and there is also a problem when governments change and the new one is not benevolent or ethical enough to make a government control system work.

On the other hand, if those running businesses and the media are fair, honest, and otherwise ethical in their dealings with one another and with their employees and consumers, then free enterprise can work also. The danger here, as supporters of government control are quick to point out, is that power, influence, and affluence can end up almost entirely in the hands of the few, and those few can be uncaring and corrupt in their treatment of others. If profit becomes the main or only goal for business, then it becomes easy to leave humaneness behind.

Generally, however, the moderate position seeks to encourage free enterprise and honest competition, with some controls being exerted by employee groups (for example, unions), by consumer groups, and by government where necessary. For example, there may be laws that regulate the absorbing of small businesses by larger ones, or the merging of larger ones, in both cases the goal being to prevent the accumulation of too much power and wealth in the hands of a few to the detriment of society in general.

On the other hand, government should not impose controls upon private businesses except to protect society from dangers that businesses themselves refuse to prevent. In short, freedom should be allowed, but not unlimited freedom. This position also would encourage the development of employee groups to protect workers' rights in employer-employee relationships and the establishment of consumer groups to protect customers from false advertising, risky or dangerous products, and unfair business practices.

What the moderate position advocates is a system of checks and balances to ensure that people have as much freedom in their business dealings as possible while remaining protected from corrupt, unethical, and destructive practices. It goes without saying that the more that businesses, employee groups, and consumer groups monitor and control their own activities from an ethical standpoint, the less government control will be needed.

The moderate position also maintains that both extremes are based upon false assumptions. It is not true, for example, that a democratic society can exist only if completely free enterprise is allowed; there are many societies that are largely democratic but that nevertheless maintain some government and private control of business activities. Neither is it true, however, that the only way to achieve equality and protection for everyone is to allow the government to control business or the media "for the good of everyone." The moderate position tends to try to combine the advantages of both of these extremes while eliminating their disadvantages.

Justice, Truth Telling, and Honesty in Business

Justice

Justice already has been discussed generally in Chapters 3, 7, and 8; however, it is important to examine exactly how this principle applies to business activities. Three types of justice are of concern in business.

      Exchange Justice. Exchange justice[1] involves reimbursement for services rendered or products made or sold. For example, if an object costs $10 and I agree to purchase it for that price, then I owe the businessperson from whom I bought it $10. In another example, if I agree to erect a satisfactory carport for $1,800 and I keep my end of the bargain, then I'm entitled to $1,800. Similarly, if I agree to pay employees $10 an hour each for doing a particular job and they do it for eight hours, then I owe them $80 each. All of these examples demonstrate an exact and just "exchange" of goods or services for some kind of payment.

      Distributive Justice. This type of justice has also already been defined, described, and discussed in a general way in Chapters 7 and 8. When applied specifically to business, however, it has to do with the distribution of profit among owners, managers, employees, customers, and shareholders. Distributive justice raises questions concerning what portion of the gross profit made in any business endeavor should be distributed among all concerned (by means, for example, of higher wages, bonuses, and fringe benefits for employees and managers; greater dividends to shareholders; greater profits to owners; and lower prices and better quality for customers).

      Social Justice. Social justice is concerned with how businesses, the media, and their members should treat consumers and members of society in general. For example, the extent to which business should be willing to protect the public against pollution and other dangers to their property, well-being, and lives is a question of social justice.

Truth Telling

Truth telling, which has been discussed in general in Chapters 8 and 12 and in relation to bioethics in Chapter 14, applies to business in a number of ways: telling the truth in agreeing to render and pay for services and products; not lying when engaged in employer-employee relations; not lying to shareholders about the status of the business; and telling the truth in advertising.

Truth in advertising is a large area of concern in the business world because it involves consumers and, by extension, society as a whole. It is business's obligation to consumers not to lie to them and also not to mislead them through the omission of important facts. For example, car manufacturers may advertise that you need to change your car's oil only every 7,000 miles, but they neglect to tell you that you will have greater need of repairs than if you had changed it every 3,000 miles. Although this is not a direct lie, it does mislead consumers through the omission of important facts.

Honesty

Honesty applies to business and the media in the following ways: keeping agreements and contracts, whether oral or written; admitting errors that have been made in creating products or stories, especially when safety is involved, and correcting those errors wherever possible; giving an honest day's work for pay received; giving appropriate wages for work performed; setting honest prices that allow for a reasonable, but not exorbitant profit; giving the best quality for the price that one can, especially when people's health and lives could be endangered; and, finally, constantly inspecting business and media practices at all levels to ensure that dishonesty and corruption are both discovered and eliminated.

Ethical Issues in Business

As in the area of bioethics, there are many moral issues in business ethics that might be discussed; however, I will concentrate on five areas: advertising; business and the environment; affirmative action and reverse discrimination; sexual harassment, and corporate greed.

Advertising

A large and important part of any business is advertising, for this is the means by which products, services, employees, and the business itself are presented to the public as favorably as possible. As mentioned earlier, advertising is an important area for the application of truth telling and honesty because advertising plays such a large part in our lives at all levels. Surely there is hardly any aspect of our society that does not use advertising to some degree. The government, charities, and even races and religions advertise in order to try to get the public "to buy the product." There are two major approaches to advertising: One states that "anything goes" when it comes to methods of selling products and services, and the other states that advertising always should be honestly presented and properly supported by facts and evidence.

The Anything-Goes Approach. The anything-goes view, which is held by many businesses, states that because advertising does not force anyone to do anything, it is the responsibility of consumers and competitors to be on their guard about the claims made for specific products and services. It is assumed by those who hold to this approach that most people will not check the claims made in advertising, such as that one serving of a breakfast cereal will provide you with all the vitamins you need for the day.

One argument used in support of this approach is that in most advertising, very little harm is done by making somewhat extravagant claims for a product. False advertising endangers no one; it's just part of the "business game," and the stimulation of the economy provided by advertising is good for business, the economy, and, in the long run, for society in general. In a highly competitive society, the important thing is to out-advertise one's competitors so as to create a more successful business by inducing consumers to buy one's product whether they need to or not. Consumers have minds of their own, the argument runs, and it is their responsibility to choose wisely among the products and services they constantly are being offered.

The Truthful Approach. The other view of advertising held by some businesspeople, as well as by consumers, consumer groups, and the government, is that any claims made by any business concerning its products or services ought to be supported or backed up by facts and evidence. According to this approach, businesses have a right to advertise freely but not to lie to the public about their products or services. The argument of the anything-goes proponents that there's no harm done so long as life isn't threatened is highly questionable because constant lying or dishonesty tends to erode significant communication, the trust and faith humans have in one another, and human relationships themselves. Because lying and misrepresentation in advertising contribute to this breakdown, they harm business specifically and society in general.

Two questions are raised by this approach: What actually constitutes lying and misrepresentation, and what guidelines can be presented that will serve to insure establishing ethically proper advertising?

To begin with, no unsafe product or service should be advertised as safe. Of course, products or services that purport to be safe but aren't should not even be put on the market until they have been made safe, especially because some consumers will assume in good faith that they are. This is not to say that no product or service that might be dangerous cannot be advertised and sold. For example, most people know that knives, guns, and scuba-diving gear are potentially dangerous; this doesn't mean, however, that they shouldn't be advertised.

Sometimes, in the case of some products and services, warnings about their use or misuse can be provided. People certainly know that all automobiles can be dangerous if they are misused, but there is a difference between that sort of danger and the kind generated by an automobile whose brakes are likely to fail or whose gas tank might explode in any collision. Such products or services should not be advertised or sold as being safe until they have in fact been made so. There can, of course, be safety problems that were not foreseen by businesses; in such cases, it is the obligation of the business concerned to warn the public immediately and to recall the product or service for repairs or changes that will make it safe.

Second, businesses should not, according to this view, make claims about their products and services that are not true or that are exaggerated or only half true. It's all right to claim that a beauty soap softens and moisturizes skin, and even that it enhances skin beauty if indeed it does these things, but it would be dishonest to say that it removes wrinkles if it doesn't. It is also dishonest to make the claim that a product is used or endorsed by medical doctors or scientists, for example, if it really isn't. In fact, it is even questionable ethics to present television commercials in which actors in white coats purport to be laboratory scientists or doctors when they are no such thing.

Third, all claims and guarantees about a product's or service's nature, effects, and uses should be completely true and should be supported by evidence. This evidence, furthermore, ought to be made readily available to the public. Finally, no one who works in the advertising or public relations departments of a company should be required to make untrue claims about products or services.

Business and the Environment

One of the most compelling problems to have arisen in business ethics in our century concerns the depletion of natural resources through careless overuse and the destruction of the environment. Although people in business should not have to bear total responsibility for these problems, they certainly must accept a large share of it. In fact, now that these problems have become so serious, businesses truly are blameworthy if they fight against viable solutions and don't do what they can to alleviate problems that either are already present or that soon will be. As the case with other problem situations we have discussed, this one provokes two extreme views.

The Primacy of Business. According to this position, it is not business's fault that there are environmental problems; business always has striven simply to give consumers what they want. The ethical responsibility of business begins and ends with business dealings, and it cannot be held responsible for the problems that occur in nature and society. This view also holds that the interference of "nature-loving do-gooders" and government will destroy business, our economy, and finally society itself. If they are not interfered with, science and business will find a way to solve the environmental problems in good time.

Business always has operated on a basis of good faith, and those bad results suffered by employees, the public, and the environment were not intended or foreseen. Moreover, now that they have occurred, business shouldn't have to bear the total responsibility for these health and environmental problems. The solutions to environmental problems that have been proposed by nature groups and the government are extremely expensive ones, and businesses should not have to pay for them out of their profits; furthermore, they should have as long a time as they need to make necessary changes, if indeed changes must be made at all.

The Primacy of the Environment. According to the primacy of the environment view, we have been on such a rampage of rape, gluttony, and waste where the natural resources and the environment are concerned and the only solution is to immediately stop any business practices and activities that are adversely affecting health and the environment. Business, according to the environmentalists, must take the major blame for environmental waste and destruction; therefore, it must use its profits to reverse the damage it has wrought. Furthermore, business—through advertising—has helped to foster the consume-at-all-costs mentality that has been a major factor in creating these problems in the environment. Therefore, it must now attempt to reeducate the public in any way possible, even if this means some loss of profit.

Because business has ignored its responsibilities, government should immediately step into the breach, using fines, imprisonment, the withholding of government contracts, and even business shutdowns to force business to repair the damage it has done. A massive reeducation of businesspeople and the public must be conducted by the government in order to save our environment. Even if businesses are destroyed and the economy is hurt, these actions must be forced upon business in order to alter our present situation before it becomes irreversible.

The Moderate Position on Business and the Environment. Business isn't totally to blame, say the moderates, for the destruction of the environment; rather, both the government and society in general share the blame for waste and destruction. However, none of us—business included—can now afford to ignore the situation; we all must work hard to turn it around and conserve what remains of the environment. Business must change those advertising techniques that serve merely to foster a consumer society, stop all sorts of pollution, and alter its industrial methods so that it begins to work in harmony with the environment.

All of this must be accomplished within a period of time considered reasonable by both business and the environmentalists, and business must pay its fair share of the financial burden out of its own profits. Consumers also must pay a fair share of the costs both through taxes and higher prices, as businesses pass *some* of the share of the cost of environmental protection on to the public.

Neither side should try to profit financially from the situation or to escape from paying its fair share. Constant vigilance with regard to environmental protection should be maintained by businesses themselves, by the government, and by consumer groups. All of us—business included—must recognize that we have an ethical obligation to protect human beings and the environment, both of which are more important in the long run than is power or affluence.

Affirmative Action and Reverse Discrimination

Another serious problem our society faces that relates to business practices is discrimination in the hiring, promotion, and firing of employees. Those most often discriminated against in these areas have been ethnic and religious minorities, women, the handicapped, and the aged. It is common knowledge that prejudice and discrimination against Jews, African Americans, Hispanics, Asian Americans, Native Americans, other minority groups, and women have been going on for hundreds of years. For this reason, I don't feel that it is necessary to describe the associated problems in detail. Instead, I would like to look at the methods that have been used to solve these problems and also at some of the negative effects brought on by these methods.

Definition of Terms. Literally, *prejudice* means the prejudgment of someone or something before one has ever encountered this person or thing. Prejudice often is based upon biased opinions one has been taught, has heard, or has read. *Discrimination*, as the term will be used here, means to differentiate among people in a prejudiced way when hiring, promoting, or firing them. This does not mean that there is anything wrong with "discriminating" among people when choosing one's friends. Nor is there anything wrong with "discriminating" between two well-qualified applicants when an employer is attempting to choose the best person for a job. A problem does arise, however, when that discrimination is based upon people's race, religion, sex, sexual preference, or age rather than on their qualifications for a job or promotion.

Affirmative action is a term that describes the process whereby a society seeks to avoid future discrimination in employment practices and actively tries to correct the problems arising from hundreds of years of past discrimination. *Reverse discrimination* is a term that describes the plight of some, primarily white males, who have in turn been discriminated against when affirmative action programs have been instituted. Reverse discrimination would occur, for example, if a company hired an African-American man or woman who was less qualified than a white person, either because of the person's race or sex. Here again, as in the other problem areas we have looked at, there are two extreme points of view.

The Argument for Discrimination. According to the argument for discrimination, a business's employment practices are its own affair. If employers want to hire white males, then they have a right to do so without interference because they are the owners of their businesses. Furthermore, even if one accepts the notion that there has been discrimination in the past, this is seldom the fault of present employers; therefore, they should not have to correct deficiencies they did not cause. And even if the employers themselves have been guilty of employment discrimination in the past, they shouldn't be forced to hire those discriminated against in order to make amends for their former wrongdoing. In any case, employers definitely should not have to hire less qualified people in order to "integrate" their businesses, nor should they have to provide additional training to people who are unqualified simply in order to make up for past discrimination.

Also, the argument continues, discriminatory practices did not occur only in business; they occurred everywhere. Therefore, there is no reason why businesses should have to make reparations for a practice that was generally accepted only a few years ago. Now that the problem of discrimination in general has been alleviated, people who formerly were discriminated against will have the opportunity to become better qualified. At that point, business can begin to hire them. But it isn't fair to prevent employers from hiring the employees they prefer just because these people are not minority group members. And it isn't fair to ask white or male employees to pay for a problem they never participated in or caused.

The Argument Against Discrimination. Discrimination in employment practices is one of the most insidious kinds because those who have been discriminated against need better jobs and a steady income if they are to advance themselves. Our own generation may not have practiced discrimination—although it is highly questionable to assert that we haven't—but our forebears did; therefore, we, as fellow human beings and good citizens, owe the victims of discrimination some sort of recompense for the immoral actions that have been committed against them. Every effort must be made to put affirmative action into immediate effect. When employees retire, resign, or are fired, they should be replaced—at all levels, including management—by members of those groups that have been discriminated against.

According to this view, quotas, goals, and timetables for affirmative action must be established and adhered to. Training programs must be established to meet the needs of employees who have been discriminated against in the past, and in some cases less qualified applicants may have to be hired or promoted in order to accomplish affirmative action. Reverse discrimination may result from such actions, and this is deplorable, but it is a necessary evil that must be endured if we are to right the wrongs of all the past years. The government should mandate affirmative action employment practices and enforce them fully in all businesses by withholding government contracts and funding, and imposing fines and prison sentences where necessary.

The Moderate Position on Discrimination. According to the moderate position, job discrimination is a complex, controversial problem that must be resolved as equitably as possible. Both extreme positions have strong and valid points to make, but they do go too far. There is no doubt, for example, that affirmative action must be taken at all levels of business in order to right the long-standing wrongs that have been caused by the terrible discriminatory practices of the past 300 years. Employers should have the freedom to hire and promote the best qualified employees; however, they also have a moral obligation at all levels of society to halt the immoral discriminatory employment practices of the past. They should try to do this equitably, avoiding reverse discrimination wherever they can, but that shouldn't mean they have to hire or promote unqualified or less qualified people.

Government, as a representative of all members of society, certainly has an obligation to mandate affirmative action and to attempt to enforce it. It should, however, encourage businesses to set up their own viable programs on a voluntary basis. Government has the right to make fair employment practices a qualification for the receiving of government contracts or funding. However, some of the more stringent measures for obtaining business's compliance—for example, fines and imprisonments—should be imposed only as a last resort.

No one person has an inalienable right to a job in any business, nor does any employer have the obligation to hire or promote any and all persons who apply for employment or who desire promotion. However, employers are obligated to see that equal opportunities exist for all people—regardless of race, religion, sex, handicaps, or age (within reason—one need not hire a 10-year-old, for example)—applying and being seriously considered for jobs in their businesses.

Reverse discrimination can be avoided for the most part if less qualified people belonging to groups that have been discriminated against are not hired over more qualified people from the majority group. Reverse discrimination also can be avoided by setting up training programs that, while largely serving the needs of minority group members, also can train white males who presently lack qualifications. All trainees should be informed that the training must be accomplished satisfactorily, after which full consideration for employment will be given. Sustaining salaries for trainees should be financed partly by businesses and partly by government through public taxation; in this way, everyone pays his or her fair share.

In those cases where reverse discrimination is difficult to avoid, each case must be decided upon an individual basis so as to achieve as fair a decision as is possible. However, when applicants or employees are equally well qualified for jobs and promotions, efforts must be made to hire or promote people from groups that have been discriminated against in the past.

Sexual Harassment

One of the most significant and controversial topics today is sexual harassment, a problem that has existed for a long time, but which only recently has come to light as being unethical. A recent survey conducted by Louis Harris and Associates for the American Association of University Women (AAUW) revealed that sexual harassment at school is an experience common to the vast majority of public school students in the eighth through eleventh grades. The survey discovered that four in five students (81%) have been sexually harassed at some time in their school life and that the majority of both boys (76%) and girls (85%) have been harassed at school.[2] My main emphasis in this chapter is to discuss sexual harassment in the workplace, but if it goes on as early as junior high school for most boys and girls and has for the most part been ignored by school officials, one can only imagine what happens when these same children, both harassers and harassed, grow up and enter the workplace.

Definition of Terms

According to federal law—Equal Employment Opportunity Commission (EEOC)—and, for example, California's Departments of Fair Employment and Housing, sexual harassment is defined as "unwanted sexual advances, or visual, verbal, or physical conduct of a sexual nature." This includes many forms of offensive behavior and includes gender-based harassment of a person of the same sex as the harasser. The following is a partial list of actions deemed as sexual harassment: unwanted sexual advances; offering employment benefits in exchange for sexual favors; making or threatening reprisals after a negative response to sexual advances; visual conduct such as leering, making sexual gestures, displaying of sexually suggestive objects or pictures, cartoons or posters; verbal conduct such as making or using derogatory comments, epithets, slurs, and jokes; verbal sexual advances or propositions; verbal abuse of a sexual nature; graphic verbal commentaries about an individual's body; sexually degrading words used to describe an individual; suggestive or obscene letters, notes, or invitations; and physical conduct such as touching, assaulting, impeding, or blocking movements.[3]

What Constitutes Sexual Harassment Under Federal Law

Under federal law, unwelcome sexual advances, requests for sexual favors, and other verbal or physical conduct of a sexual nature constitute sexual harassment in any of the following circumstances:

1. When submission to such conduct is either explicitly or implicitly made a term or condition of an individual's employment.
2. When submission to or rejection of such conduct by an individual is used as the basis for employment decisions affecting that individual.
3. When such conduct has the purpose or effect of unreasonably interfering with an individual's work performance or creating an intimidating, hostile, or offensive working environment.[4]

Arguments That Sexual Harassment Is Not Immoral

Sexual harassment has been going on for so long that many people think it's just the way things are—the "boys will be boys" attitude. This attitude also implies a double standard for men and women, even though sexual harassment also applies both to women who harass men, vice versa, and to same-sex harassment in the workplace. Many employers and employees, mainly men, see nothing wrong with the kinds of actions and language that sexual harassment includes and would present several arguments in favor of allowing them.

Enlivening the Workplace. Many sexual harassers feel that jokes, comments, sexual "compliments," and other actions or language are ways of enlivening an otherwise boring work situation and atmosphere. Such comments or actions are nothing more than clever repartee or ways of "having fun at the office." No one should get upset at such activities but should instead take them with a grain of salt because they are all in fun. After all, men (mostly) and women have done or said these things for years now. Why should anyone get so worked up over them now?

Women and Men Are Naturally Sexually Attracted to One Another. It's simply natural that men and women should be sexually attracted to one another (the same may be true for attractions to the same sex), and so it also is natural that this sexual attraction doesn't cease merely because people are together at work. Therefore, it should be acceptable for people to express this sexual or romantic attraction at work as well as in other places. The recipients of such expressions should take them as a compliment, not as harassment, and should not feel threatened by them.

Positions of Power Imply Certain Rights. People who have power in the workplace ought to be free to use that power in any way they see fit, especially when dealing with employees, as long as the latter make good salaries and have good jobs. Such employees ought to be willing to acquiesce gratefully when their bosses or others in power request dates, make sexual advances, or even initiate romantic or sexual affairs. Certainly a positive response is not a condition of employment; rather, these advances are like expense accounts: Everyone pads expense accounts and everyone who wants to stay employed and get ahead participates in romantic interludes. If people don't want to accept the conditions imposed by the people who have power over them, then they should look for employment elsewhere or at least not expect to be promoted or retained where they are.

Often Those Being Harassed Ask for or Cause Harassment. People in the workplace, especially women, often "ask for" flirtatious jokes and sexual advances by means of their own attitudes (flirtatious and sexy), the clothes they wear, and their desire to please employers and supervisors and get ahead in the business.

The conclusion of all of these arguments is that employees, especially women employees, make way too much out of common, everyday acts of humor and fun, and that laws governing sexual harassment are ridiculous and put employers and supervisors who were merely bandying about trivial and harmless actions and words into unnecessarily delicate and litigious situations.

Arguments That Sexual Harassment Is Immoral

The bases for all of these arguments that sexual harassment is immoral are that all people deserve to be treated with respect, dignity, and humaneness everywhere, which definitely includes the workplace. Sexual harassment denies individuals all of these rights and often makes their lives in and out of the workplace difficult, humiliating, and even terrifying.

Unfairness of Treatment. Basically it is unfair to hire, promote, retain, or fire people on the basis of their willingness to give or receive sexual favors. People should be judged upon the basis of their intelligence, abilities, conscientiousness, and cooperation, not upon whether they are sexually attractive or well endowed or willing to get involved romantically or sexually with their supervisors. Because these latter attributes or attitudes are not and should not be requirements for doing a good job, people should not be judged on that basis or discriminated against because they do or do not display them.

Creation of a Hostile or Offensive Working Environment. Rather than enlivening the workplace, sexual harassment can create hostile, unpleasant, and offensive environment, one in which it can be extremely difficult for people to get their work done. If people constantly are worried about being bumped, squeezed, or pinched or receiving other unwanted physical or verbal advances, then valuable time and effort that could have been spent doing their jobs is wasted in fending off such advances. Also, such words and actions are both physically and emotionally upsetting and destructive to those who are forced to endure them. This destructive effect does not occur only while people are at work, but also when they are not working; it may adversely affect their personal life as well as their public life.

Positions of Authority Do Not Imply Power over Personal Lives. It is certainly true that people in positions of authority in a business have supervisory and management control over what goes on in the business and therefore over what the people working for them do and how they do it. However, in no way does this control extend to employees' personal lives when they are not at work, and especially not to requiring them to accept dates or sexual advances. This latter type of control is an abuse of power and authority and therefore constitutes unacceptable behavior according to all principles of business ethics. Managers or supervisors engaging in these activities are misusing their authority and they should be removed from their positions.

Attraction Does Not Imply Involvement. It is true that people often are romantically and sexually attracted to each other, but such attraction does not imply coercion of or involvement with others, especially when those others do not wish to be involved. If people who work together are attracted to each other, then they must do everything they can to keep such activities that result from the attraction out of the workplace entirely; also, people should be very careful about getting involved with anyone with whom they work. Sometimes such involvements work out nicely, but other times after a breakup occurs, life on the job becomes miserable. The best advice probably is to avoid getting involved with anyone at work. At any rate, even if people are attracted to others with whom they work, they should not use this attraction as a means of sexually harassing those others.

Harassees Often "Ask for It." This argument often is used by rapists when they are denying they have done anything wrong to their victims. Clearly, even if people wear sexually attractive clothing or flirt or laugh at dirty jokes, they are not asking to be sexually harassed. For example, just because a woman wears low-cut dresses or short skirts or is physically well endowed or attractive does not mean that anyone has the right to sexually harass her, especially when she makes it clear that she resents the harassment. One may not assume anything from her appearance and certainly must not manifest any sexual harassment in the workplace. If people feel that they would like to ask others for a date, then they should contact them when off duty but keep all of this outside the workplace. And of course, if the person contacted does not wish to date, that should be the end of it and not a matter for pressure or coercion at work.

The New Global Economy and the International Business Scene

The twenty-first century has brought unprecedented global change that now structures the dynamic environments in which business is conducted. Radical, rapid, and revolutionary change has given rise to a host of new challenges and among these are ethical problems. In the new global economy, the world's major corporations are multinationals. Multinational corporations are powerful institutions that maintain operations in various "host" countries. Currently there is considerable debate about the kind and character of morality that will govern international business.

Business ethicist Thomas Donaldson observed: "When we leave home and cross our nation's boundaries, moral clarity often blurs. Without a backdrop of shared attitudes, and without familiar laws and judicial procedures that define standards of ethical conduct, certainty is elusive."[5] Whose ethical standards should prevail in global businesses—those of the home country or those of the host country? Should multinational corporations make business investments in countries where civil and political rights are violated? Is it ethical for corporations in developed nations to move plants to developing nations that lack environmental, safety, and other operational standards? How do corporations develop and maintain global integrity? How do multinationals produce codes of corporate conduct that will read consistently in dozens of languages?

One view of the international situation claims that no culture's ethics are better than any others. This view is generally known as cultural relativism but is also referred to as ethical or moral relativism or cultural particularism. We have discussed relativism in Chapter 5. Relativism, you will recall, is the view that there are many standards of morality—not just one. Hence, morality is culturally conditioned and varies from culture to culture in response to unique circumstances.

An opposite point of view is ethical or moral absolutism—also referred to as cultural universalism. Cultural universalists, following the Western enlightenment tradition, take the position that basic truths about the nature of right and wrong actions can be defined objectively. Absolutists believe that moral principles apply to all people independently of place or circumstances and many of these ethical concepts are already universally articulated in internationally accepted documents such as the United Nations Universal Declaration of Human Rights.

Furthermore, it is argued that ethics, properly understood, is a domain unto itself and is therefore independent of particular religious or cultural beliefs.

> Among the most clear-cut ethical principles are the following: that it is ethically wrong to cheat, deceive, exploit, abuse, harm, or steal from others, that we have an ethical responsibility to respect the rights of others, including their freedom and well-being, to help those most in need of help, to seek common good and not merely our own self-interest and egocentric pleasures, and to strive to make the world more just and humane.[6]

Without a system of transcultural values nations with different religious/cultural beliefs remain separated because of fundamental differences and the idea of an integrated global economy is compromised.

How are multinational corporations to navigate between the extreme views of cultural particularism and cultural universalism on the international business scene? Clearly corporations that wish to develop and maintain global integrity must acknowledge and uphold universally recognized ethical principles and human core values. The five ethical principles argued for and reiterated in this chapter—the valuing of human life, the striving for goodness and avoiding of badness, the just and fair distribution of good and bad, honesty and truth telling, and individual freedom—serve well as guiding principles for corporate responsibility on the international scene.

At the same time it is important that international businesses recognize and respect cultural values and local traditions. In this light, ethical principles must be applied in a cultural context. An exercise in good ethical reasoning shows us that while cultural values and local traditions differ, these differences are not necessarily judgments about right and wrong. In fact, honoring cultural differences, within the bounds of ethical frameworks, can enhance both the ways in which people work and how human beings relate to others.

Ethical leadership in business must balance two imperatives: business results and human values. The ongoing movement toward a globally integrated market economy provides a historic opportunity to ask anew the perennial questions that concern the place of moral values in business and economic development. This global situation grants an abundance of opportunities to make business better.

Media Ethics

Introduction

Because of the tremendous explosion of media in the twentieth and twenty-first centuries, more ethical issues have arisen than ever before in history. First of all, we must define exactly what is meant by "media." There are basically two types of media: (1) written or printed media which includes written journalism, such as newspapers and magazines, and photojournalism, or photographs, that accompany written journalism; and (2) electronic media which includes radio, television, computers, and the internet.

The media has become so powerful and pervasive that we now describe many events as *media-driven*, which means the media keeps events alive and at times blows them out of proportion so that they are kept in the public eye. The public's perception of events is often colored by the particular slants the media puts on the reporting of them. Recent examples of media-driven events include the TWA Flight 800 crash; the death of Princess Diana of England; the President Clinton/Monica Lewinsky affair; the airplane crash that killed John F. Kennedy, Jr., his wife, and sister-in-law; the Terri Schiavo case; the Elian Gonzalez controversy over staying in the United States or being returned to Cuba, and the war with Iraq.

Journalism's Ideal

According to Phillip Patterson and Lee Wilkins in their book *Media Ethics: Issues and Cases*, "Each of the traditional professions has laid claim to one of the central tenants of philosophy. Law, ideally is equated with justice; medicine with the duty to render aid; journalism, too, has a lofty ideal: the communication of truth."[7] It would behoove us to return briefly to the chapter "Absolutism versus Relativism," where truth and propositions were discussed. It was pointed out in that chapter that truth and falsity when stated carefully in propositions are absolute; however, the problem is not with the absoluteness of true or false propositions, but rather with seeking and finding the truth or with discovering which propositions are true or false in the journalistic reporting of events.

Truth and How Journalists Obtain Information and Stories

Most journalists get stories by gathering information, and one of the questions that arises is how this information is acquired. Another question which is pertinent is whether it is ethical to lie to get a story either by misrepresenting oneself or otherwise lying to a person from whom the story is to be acquired, or by telling lies in order to make the story more interesting or exciting. Accurate or not, journalists, like lawyers and used car salespersons, are not often held in very high esteem, especially by the newsworthy people they report on (e.g., politicians, sports figures, entertainers), and by the public, who believe journalists are more interested in selling stories and photographs than in telling the truth.

Public Right to Know versus Individual Right to Privacy

Probably the most significant ethical issue in media ethics arises out of the public's right, need, or desire to know and the media's right to report events versus individuals' rights to privacy. Many famous people—politicians, entertainers, sports figures—have had to confront media members, that is, reporters and photographers (newspaper, radio and television) often with dire results. Frank Sinatra, the singer and actor, had many confrontations with reporters and openly expressed his hatred of them. Sean Penn, the actor and director, has had physical fights with many reporters. Princess Diana of England and Dodi Fayed were being hounded by paparazzi (freelance photographers who take pictures of celebrities) as they left a hotel in Paris one evening and were killed in a car accident—presumably trying to outrun the paparazzi. Newspersons were criticized for taking pictures at the scene of the accident rather than helping the fatally injured passengers or sending for help.

Exactly what right to privacy do public figures have? Certainly by virtue of their fame, importance, newsworthiness and public recognizability, they should expect to be approached by news media to be photographed, interviewed, and questioned. In addition, often their desire and demand for publicity are dependent on a continuing relationship with the media. Where do we draw the line between an individual's desire and need for privacy and the right to lead their own lives and the desire or need of the media and the public to know what is happening in their personal and private lives? Many times the media, especially photographers with telephoto lenses on their cameras, catches celebrities in personal and intimate moments. For example, the British duchess, Sarah Ferguson, was caught on film having an affair with a rich American businessman on a beach in the Mediterranean. Also, I remember seeing an attempted TV and newspaper interview of a very sad and unhappy Marilyn Monroe after her miscarriage while she was married to playwright Arthur Miller. She was in an elevator at the hospital trying to leave. When she was confronted with a barrage of questions and flash photography, she started crying and turned her back to the cameras. There is no doubt that many of the celebrities are definitely hounded by the paparazzi until some of them have no private lives at all.

The Clinton/Lewinsky Affair. One of the most significant and annoying media hypes of the twentieth century was the affair of President Bill Clinton with a Whitehouse intern named Monica Lewinsky. The media coverage that went on and on for the better part of two years left no stone unturned in its reporting of the events, to the point where it became almost pornographic on various newscasts. There is no doubt it was big news—to the point where the president was up for impeachment. The issue for most Americans did not seem to be what the president did in his personal life, although no one condoned what he did, but, once caught, the president lied about the affair both on TV and under oath. That he continued to function satisfactorily as president, however, was evident by the polls that gave him high ratings in his job performance, if not in his personal morality. There is no doubt that the whole affair was media-driven to the point where the average American was bored with it, but still every morning and evening we all were subjected to the media overkill.

The Elian Gonzales Event. Another event in which the public was subjected to media overkill was one that should have been resolved immediately, but instead was dragged on for almost a year—to a great extent by the media. Elian Gonzales, a six-year-old boy, left Cuba on a raft with his mother and stepfather but was the only survivor of a storm at sea. He was found floating on an inner tube off the coast of Florida by an American fisherman of Cuban descent. Since his natural father was alive in Cuba, the Immigration Service attempted to send him back to Cuba to be with his father, stepmother, and baby half brother. However, his mother's relatives and other Cuban refugees in Miami wanted to keep him in the United States, so they sought legal means and injunctions to keep him here. Crowds protested outside the house where he was staying. The media assisted in prolonging his deportation by continually photographing Elian and the family so that they were constantly in all the newspapers and on radio and TV broadcasts. Because his Miami relatives wouldn't turn him over to the authorities U.S. Attorney General Janet Reno finally ordered that the house be "invaded" by immigration officials. A photograph taken at an odd angle was carried by most newspapers to "play up" the story—it appeared to show one of the immigration officials with a rifle, hand on the trigger, seemingly aimed at Elian and the fisherman who had rescued him at sea. In reality, the gun was not aimed at them, and the official's finger was on the trigger housing, not on the trigger, but the media's intent to place the U.S. government in the role of autocratic villain was clear. Elian's father and his family eventually came to the United States to take him home, but only after much legal hassling and more media invasion of the family's personal life, and now the public hears no more of him.

Where to Draw the Line

A recent newspaper editorial might suggest where the line could be drawn. A story broke about a politician's alleged personal relationship or affair with a lobbyist who represented several companies and institutions on a national issue over which the politician had a great deal of control. The so-called personal relationship was never denied by either the politician or the lobbyist, but they both denied that their personal relationship had any effect on their professional relationship or dealings. In deciding to print the story, the editor of the paper accompanied it with an editorial in which he stated that the rumors about "the intensely personal relationship" were not the important issue. What anyone, including politicians or lobbyists, do with their private lives was not important in the editor's eyes. What was important was that such a personal relationship with someone who might influence the politician's decisions and dealings with his committee and fellow politicians, the presenting and passage of bills, and the distribution of millions of taxpayer dollars could be considered a conflict of interest. The editor went on to say that those who have chosen to do public service are entitled to their private moments, however, when a politician develops a close personal relationship with someone who is paid to influence the writing of legislation and the shaping of public policy, it is no longer merely a private matter, but one of public concern. Both parties denied all suggestion that there was a conflict of interest. Regardless of the truth or falsity of the article, I think that the editor makes a significant distinction between personal matters in public figures' lives and personal matters that can no longer remain personal but must be considered public.

Ethical News Values

Like other professions, most journalists are honest and ethical, but exactly what would constitute ethical news values? Again, Patterson and Wilkins have come up with elements they believe would be emphasized if news values were constructed from ethical reasoning:

- Dignity: Leaving the subject as much self-respect as possible.
- Reciprocity: Treating others as you wish to be treated (the Golden Rule).
- Sufficiency: Allocating adequate resources to important issues.
- Accuracy: Getting the facts correct, using the right words, and putting things in context.
- Tenacity: Knowing when a story is important enough to require additional effort, both personal and institutional.
- Equity: Seeking justice for all involved in controversial issues; treating all sources and subjects equally.
- Community: Valuing social cohesion equally with individual honor.
- Diversity: Covering all segments of the audience fairly and adequately.[8]

Corporate Greed—Enron

One of the worst scandals and violations of business ethics occurred in 1999–2001 with the Enron Energy Company, in which billions of dollars were hidden from company employees and shareholders, except for the Enron Board and its CEO, managers, and Arthur Andersen, which was Enron's auditing company. In just fifteen years, Enron grew from nothing to be America's seventh largest company, employing 21,000 staff in more than forty countries, but the firm's success turned out to have involved an elaborate scam. The company lied about its profits and is accused of a range of unethical dealings, including concealing debts so they didn't show up in its accounts. Another questionable action involved its relationship with the Arthur Andersen Company which did the auditing for Enron. A significant ethical problem arose when Enron also hired Andersen as a consulting firm. Essentially, the Andersen employees also became employees of Enron, a definite conflict of interest because the independence and integrity of financial auditing organizations are fundamental to the stability and growth of American business and free markets throughout the world. If the conflict of interest wasn't unethical enough, when the scam began to come to light, Arthur Andersen began shredding documents which revealed the relationship and unethical activities between the two companies. As the deception came to light, investors and creditors retreated, forcing the firm into Chapter 11 bankruptcy.

Enron's Code of Ethical Conduct

The irony of all of this is that Enron had a completely printed out code of ethics (or conduct) of over 65 pages! Basically, Enron's ethics code was based on several Boy Scout values:

1. *Respect.* We treat others as we would like to be treated ourselves. Ruthlessness, callousness, and arrogance don't belong here. What actually occurred, however, was a cavalier attitude toward government, investors, employees, and the public who were all seen as dupes for Enron's activities.
2. *Integrity.* We work with customers and prospects openly, honestly, and sincerely. In actuality, the company was totally deceptive and not forthright with those who most needed to know what was going on.
3. *Communications.* We believe that information is meant to move and that information moves people. The company's massive deception made a mockery of this aspect of the code.
4. *Excellence.* We are satisfied with nothing less than the best. We will continue to raise the bar for everyone.[9] This point of the code was belied when Enron's board took the extraordinary step of waiving the firm's code of ethics to permit the kind of deals, off the balance sheet, that hid massive debts from public view, not once but twice, allowing two outside partnerships to be led by an Enron top executive who stood to gain from them.

Some other statements of Enron's so-called ethics are:

1. We have all worked hard over the years to establish our reputation for integrity and ethical conduct. We cannot afford to have it damaged.
2. We believe in offering our employees fair compensation through wages and other benefits. This point was violated by Enron's policy on retirement accounts. When employees received Enron stock in those accounts, they were prohibited from selling it, except for top executives who could dump their shares, and did, as the crisis mounted. Employees saw their retirement savings vanish in the bankruptcy. This certainly was not ethical nor respectful of the employees and their families.
3. Employees of Enron are charged with conducting their business affairs in accordance with the highest ethical standards. An employee shall not conduct himself or herself in a manner which would bring to the employee financial gain separately derived as a direct consequence of his or her employment with the

company. What actually happened is that Enron's CEO and top executives made tremendous profits by dumping their stocks prior to bankruptcy, which other employees could not do.

4. Agreements, whether contractual or verbal, will be honored. No bribes, bonuses, kickbacks, lavish entertainment, or gifts will be given or received in exchange for special price, or privilege. Again this was consistently violated by the company's top executives.

5. Employees will maintain the confidentiality of the Company's sensitive or proprietary information and will not use such information for their personal benefit. The top executives, of course, did just that, profiting from their inside knowledge.

6. Relations with the Company's many customers, stockholders, governments, employees, suppliers, press, and bankers will be conducted in honesty, candor, and fairness.[10]

Why the Code of Conduct Failed

One might ask why, with such an extensive and specific 65 page code of conduct, Enron could have failed so miserably in its dealings with employees, shareholders, and other businesses. A general answer could be that the code was merely eyewash or window dressing for its CEO, managers, and its board of directors. A code of conduct is only as good as it is lived and adhered to by its creators. The fact that Enron's board of directors waived several aspects of the code twice in 1999 is evidence enough that the code was basically a "Don't do as I do, but do as I say" for its employees, except for its top echelon and board members.

Enron provides a textbook example of how not to instill ethics in the workplace. It required employees to sign the code of conduct before joining the company; however, after what emerged in the Enron story, one can see that it was just words without related and appropriate action. The code was completely hypocritical because of the unethical activities of the company in all of its dealings. What Enron did and the consequences therefrom provide the greatest example of how important ethics is in the business world. It is not just another class a business major must take in college, but a living, active, and extremely important activity to any business functioning in today's world. Enron's former CEO and other managers are currently being charged with criminal activity in connection with Enron's unethical activities.

Cases for Study and Discussion

CASE 1 An Engineer Pointing Out Unsafe Car Problems

Susan, a design engineer in a major auto company, receives two reports concerning engine fires and explosions that occurred in hot weather in the company's popular economy car. At the time the engine of this model had been approved and released for production, she had advised the plant that she felt the carburetor and gas lines were constructed so that under excessive heat conditions there could be a gas leak. At that time, she had argued for a modification that would have added about $50 to the cost of producing each engine, but her proposal had been turned down. She had continued to argue for the modification and for special testing, but the standard tests performed on the car did not indicate any danger, and she was told to drop the issue.

Upon receiving the two reports, however, Susan again presses for special testing under excessive heat conditions and urges the company to warn the public and immediately recall all of the cars of this model. By this time, however, such a recall probably will cost the company between $500,000 and $1 million, and Susan again is told to mind her own business or she will be fired.

In the meantime, four more reports of engine fires come in from a desert area in the southwest. The engineer now is convinced that she is right. What should she do? To what extent does she owe loyalty to the company, where she has worked for 15 years and has been promoted several times, and to what extent is she obligated to let the public know the truth? Because the company is removing the responsibility from Susan's shoulders, should she do something about what she knows, or should she just drop the problem? Considering that the company may lose up to $1 million, what are its ethical obligations? What do you think of the way it has handled the entire situation?

CASE 2 Stealing Tools to Make Up the Difference in a Shorter Raise Than Requested

The cost of living in Alderdale, California, has gone up 10 percent during the year, and Steve's union has been negotiating with the management of the plant where he works for a 15 percent raise to cover the present cost of living plus an additional expected increase. The plant, however, has not had a good year, and management and the union decide upon an 8 percent raise, which a majority of the members, not including Steve, agrees to. Steve decides that because he has been shorted 2 to 7 percent of his raise money, he will try to make up for it by taking some expensive tools, some small pieces of equipment, and some supplies home from the plant in order to remodel his workshop at home. He was planning to do this remodeling with some of the raise money anyway, and he feels he was cheated out of this money unfairly because he didn't vote for the raise that was accepted by the union.

Is Steve justified in his actions? Why, or why not? Does management have any obligation to meet the cost of living? Because Steve voted against the smaller raise, is he under any obligation to accept it? Why, or why not? Is he justified in making up the difference between the raise he got and the cost of living by taking things from the plant? Why, or why not?

CASE 3 Switching of an Expensive Speaker with a Less Expensive One

Mike, who is very knowledgeable about stereo components, knows that there are two models made by the Ozato Company: the OC 4000, which sells for $2,000, and the OC 5000, which sells for $3,000. The difference between the two models is that the OC 5000 has a larger, more powerful amplifier-receiver and larger speakers. Because of this difference, Mike buys the more expensive model. A few weeks later, a loose connection causes him to examine the left speaker, and when he takes it apart he discovers that whereas the right speaker is the one designated for the OC 5000, the left speaker is the one designated for the OC 4000. Several of his friends also have the more expensive model, and when he examines those speakers he finds the same situation. To save money, the company evidently has put one more expensive and one less expensive speaker together in each of the expensive models, figuring that the difference in sound may not be very noticeable.

Given that the less expensive speaker was almost the same quality as the more expensive one, was the company right or wrong in making the substitution? Why? What should the company now do about customers who have already bought the OC 5000? Why? Suppose the difference between the two speakers was so minimal that no one ever discovered the switch—would the company then have been justified in having made the switch? Why or why not? Suppose the company offers to replace the less expensive speakers of Mike and his friends with OC 5000s and also offers Mike an additional thousand dollars' worth of stereo equipment if he promises not to say anything more about the switch. What should Mike do in these circumstances? Why?

CASE 4 Doing Public Relations on an Unsafe Car

Myra, 30, is an up-and-coming executive in a large public relations and advertising firm, and she is very close to a big promotion. She is given the assignment by her boss of creating an advertising campaign for the popular economy car described in the first case. Her assignment is to try to make up for some of the bad press the company has been getting because of the six engine explosions that have occurred. Because she is a well-informed person, she knows about the explosions. She tells her boss that she doesn't think their firm ought to take the account, and in any case, she can't in good conscience handle the account unless the car company makes the car safe.

Her boss argues that this is the single biggest account their firm has ever had, and what the auto manufacturer does or doesn't do is not their firm's responsibility; their job is strictly to advertise and promote products and services. He also tells her that if she refuses the account, the promotion she is up for will go to someone else, and he further implies that she may lose her job. What should Myra do, and why? Do you believe that her boss's description of his firm's responsibilities is right or wrong? Why? Do you think he is right in denying Myra her promotion and/or firing her for refusing to handle the account? Why or why not? In this instance, to whom should Myra be loyal: the public? Her firm and clients? Herself? Explain your answer.

CASE 5 Hiring Between an African-American and a Caucasian Woman

Denise, 22, an African-American woman, and Bonnie, 23, a Caucasian woman, are the two top applicants for a computer technician job in a major data-processing center. The center has about 10 percent minority employees and about 30 percent female employees. Both women seem to be equally well qualified except that Bonnie is both prettier and more outgoing than Denise. This particular job doesn't require the person who fills it to meet the public very much, but it takes place in a large office in which almost everyone is Caucasian and in which relations among employees are particularly important because of the constant pressures of the job. If you were the personnel manager, whom would you pick for the job? Why? What should this person's criteria for employee selection be, and in what order of importance should these criteria be placed? Why? To what extent should the personnel manager be concerned about affirmative action or reverse discrimination in this situation?

CASE 6 Pollution Problem in a Factory

The town of Farling, Texas, was almost a ghost town when the Kem Chemical Company decided to establish one of its plants there 10 years ago. Since it moved in, however, the town has grown tremendously, and most people in the town now work at the plant. The only problem is that the chemical waste that the plant emits is gradually polluting the air, the earth, and the water near the town. The company and the town's mayor have both been informed by the government that this pollution must be eliminated as soon as possible. The plant manager tells the mayor that in order to satisfy the government requirements, the company will have to spend about $1.5 million. If this is to be done right away, he says, the company has decided to close this particular plant rather than sink that much money into making the changes. The plant manager also tells the mayor that they can probably stall the government for two years by paying relatively small fines, which the company is willing to do. This will allow the company to spread out the expenses for converting the plant over a longer period as well as permit it to keep the plant open. During this period, of course, the pollution would continue, endangering—according to the government report—the land, water, air, and of course animals, plants, and human beings.

   If the mayor works with the company, he can help them to avoid making immediate changes. If he doesn't, Farling will again become a ghost town and most of its people will lose their jobs. What should the mayor do, and why? Was the government right in investigating and reporting as it did? Why, or why not? Do you feel that the company is doing the right thing in relation to the government, the town, and its mayor? Why, or why not? Is the company obligated to spend some of its profits in order to save its plant and the town? Explore the alternatives and suggest some possible compromises. Assuming that no compromises will work and the mayor has to make his choice, what should he do?

CASE 7 Sexual Harrassment of a Female Police Officer

In an actual case involving the Long Beach, California, Police Department, two female police officers were treated so badly that they sued the City of Long Beach and were awarded over $1 million each for sexual harassment. In the first case, one of the women was having an affair with a higher ranking male police officer (a sergeant) after he told her he was divorcing his wife. When she found out he was lying about his divorce and many other things, she broke off the affair and embarrassed him every time he later made advances. Not only did he use his rank to see that she was treated badly by the whole department, but when she called for backup on a call involving a violent suspect, none of the officers available (and there were several) responded to her call because they sided with him rather than her, thus placing her life at risk. Several times he made it quite clear that he wanted to continue the affair, and when she refused, he told her that her job and life would be made miserable because she wouldn't cooperate.

CASE 8 Sexual Harassment of a Second Female Police Officer

In another actual case also involving the Long Beach Police Department, a female police officer whose husband also was a police officer, was trained and joined the K9 section of the police department, the first and only woman to crack this formerly all-male section of the department. The other police officers constantly verbally humiliated and harassed her and even sent their dogs to attack her when she was acting as decoy. The dogs were supposed to find her and stand guard, but instead the officers involved in the training ordered their dogs to attack. Despite protective padding, she was badly bitten and suffered bruises and contusions.

Both women have required psychotherapy and psychological leaves because of the harassment they received. The K9 officer's life was threatened by phone calls, and her marriage broke up (she also had a small child), and both women left the police department because they could no longer function due to the severe sexual harassment they had received. Even though they were both awarded the large sums of money two years after they initiated their suits, they have not yet received any money because the City of Long Beach is appealing the jury's decision. Both women lost their careers and have found it exceedingly difficult, because of the psychological and emotional trauma brought about by the harassment, to enter any other careers with the exception of low-paying jobs such as part-time waitressing. None of the other police officers involved have been reprimanded or punished in any way; they still hold their jobs. Both officers complained to the chief of police several times, but he did nothing substantive about their complaints—both he and the department psychologist (a female sergeant) told the women that they should expect hazing and that if the job was too tough for them, they should get out and get into another line of work.

Describe your feelings and thoughts about what exactly happened to these two women, who, by the way, evidently were exemplary police officers before harassment drove them out of the department. Do you think the first officer "asked for" what she got by having an affair with a married police officer? Do you think that one case has more merit than the other? Which, and why? What do you think should be done in order to resolve these cases? What should happen to the other police officers and anyone else found guilty of such harassment? Should the women be offered their jobs back? Should they receive retroactive compensation as well as the award of the court? How serious do you think this harassment was? Does this somehow support the belief of many that women should not be allowed to hold such high-stress and formerly all-male jobs? Why, or why not?

CASE 9 Photographs Taken of a Boy Who Drowned

You are a photographer on a local newspaper and have responded to a call on your scanner concerning a possible drowning in a nearby lake. When you arrive on the scene, divers have just brought the lifeless body of a five-year-old boy to the shore where his distraught family is gathered. The family members are grieving openly and you take several pictures. Should you have taken those pictures invading the family's right to privacy to grieve over the little boy? Why or why not? Should you have submitted them to the paper? Why or why not? Next you are the managing editor of the paper and have been called in to decide whether or not to run the photo in the next day's paper. One argument in favor of printing the photos is that it would serve as a warning to readers how dangerous it is to swim in that lake without supervision where there have been several drownings in the last year. Also, such a photo might win a prize for you and the paper. The basic argument against printing it is, of course, that it invades the right of the family to grieve in private. What other arguments are there, pro and con? As editor, what would you decide to do in this situation and why?

Chapter Summary

I. Introduction
   A. Business and the media are specialized areas in which ethics can be applied.
   B. Ethics in business has to do with establishing and maintaining good working relationships among employers, employees, businesses, and consumers.
II. Rights and obligations in business and the media
   A. *Rights* are those things to which human beings are entitled by law, morality, or tradition.
   B. An *obligation* is a responsibility or duty that people have toward one another to see that their rights are protected.
   C. As I have discussed in other chapters, no rights are absolute; conflicts are solved by establishing a priority of rights.
   D. There are a number of rights that relate to business and the media.
      1. There are general rights to life, justice, honesty, truth telling, and freedom.
      2. There is the right to have one's life protected as an employer, an employee, or a consumer.
      3. There is the right to pursue and qualify oneself for employment without unfair hindrance.
      4. There is the right to establish a business, own property, employ whomever you want, and make a profit.
      5. There is the right to expect agreements and contracts to be executed fairly.
      6. There is the right to fairness, honesty, and truth telling at all levels of business dealings.
      7. There is the right to employment security.
      8. There is the right to try to get consumers to use products and the right of consumers to choose which product they wish to buy.
      9. There is the right to information and privacy.
   E. There are a number of obligations related to business.
      1. Participants in business and media activities are obligated to be honest and tell the truth.
      2. They must be fair and just in their dealings with others.
      3. They must be sincere and trustworthy in honoring agreements and contracts.
      4. They must pay off debts in a fashion agreeable to all parties.
      5. They must create a safe atmosphere for employees to work in.
      6. They must give effort and perform work for which wages are being paid.
      7. They must be loyal to employers, employees, and customers, within reasonable and ethical limits.

F. There are two highly divergent approaches to fulfilling rights and obligations in business.
   1. The first is the competitive approach, also called "free enterprise," "survival of the fittest," or the "dog-eat-dog" approach.
      (a) The main objective is to make money in any way one can.
      (b) *Laissez-faire* is the best approach for a local or national economy to take because eventually it solves all economic problems.
      (c) This is the only approach a free democracy can take.
   2. The second approach advocates government control of business.
      (a) Free enterprise puts power in the hands of a few to the detriment of the many.
      (b) Aggression and competition bring out the worst in human beings.
      (c) The only ethical way to conduct business is to put it in the hands of the government, which operates for the good of everyone.
      (d) This system allows everyone to share equally in the good and the bad, eliminating the uneven distribution that exists under free enterprise.
      (e) This approach lessens aggressiveness and competition, allowing more time to be spent on the civilizing of human beings.
G. The moderate position would encourage free enterprise with some controls being exerted by employee groups, consumer groups, and government, so as to provide a system of checks and balances.

III. Justice, truth telling, and honesty in business
   A. There are a number of different types of justice that are of concern in business.
      1. Exchange justice involves reimbursement for services rendered or products made or sold.
      2. Distributive justice involves the distribution of profit among owners, managers, employees, and shareholders.
      3. Social justice is concerned with how businesses and their members treat consumers and members of society in general.
   B. Truth telling applies to business in a number of ways.
      1. Businesspeople must tell the truth when agreeing to render and pay for services and products.
      2. They must not lie in employer-employee relations.
      3. They must not lie to shareholders about the status of the business.
      4. They must tell the truth in advertising.
   C. Honesty applies to business in a number of ways.
      1. Businesspeople must keep agreements and contracts, whether oral or written.
      2. They must admit to errors that have been made during the creation of products, especially where safety is involved, and they must correct those errors wherever possible.
      3. They must give an honest day's work for pay received.
      4. They must give appropriate wages for work performed.
      5. They must set honest prices that allow for a reasonable but not inflationary profit.
      6. They must give the best quality for the price that they can.
      7. They must constantly inspect business practices at all levels to ensure that dishonesty and corruption are discovered and eliminated.

IV. Ethical approaches to advertising
   A. Advertising constitutes a large part of any business.
   B. There are two highly divergent approaches to advertising.
      1. The anything-goes approach argues that advertising does little harm to anyone and is good for business, the economy, and society as a whole.

2. The approach based upon truth telling decrees that businesses have the right to advertise freely but not to lie to the public about their products or services.
    (a) Harm is done by not telling the truth in advertising because lying or dishonesty that is continued over a period of time tends to break down faith and trust in human relations.
    (b) Advertising must neither lie nor misrepresent products or services by omitting important facts.
3. Some questions raised by the issue of truth in advertising are what actually constitutes lying and misrepresentation, and what guidelines can be presented for ethically proper advertising.
    (a) No unsafe product should be advertised as safe.
    (b) Businesses should not make claims about their products and services that are not true or that are exaggerated.
    (c) They should not make false claims about medical endorsement of their products or services.
    (d) All claims and guarantees should be supported by evidence that is readily available to the public.
    (e) No one who works in advertising should have to make claims about products or services that aren't true.

V. Business and the environment
  A. Business should not take total blame for environmental problems, but it bears a large share of the blame.
  B. There are two extreme positions related to this issue.
    1. Some people hold that business should always come first.
      (a) It is not business's fault that environmental problems exist; business has always striven to give consumers what they want.
      (b) Interference by nature-loving do-gooders will ruin business, our economy, and our society.
      (c) If they are not interfered with, business and science will eventually find answers to environmental problems.
      (d) Business always has operated in good faith and could not have foreseen these problems; therefore, why should it shoulder any blame?
      (e) The changes required in order to solve environmental problems are too expensive, and business should not have to suffer this burden.
    2. Some people hold that the environment always should come first.
      (a) We have been ruining the environment, and now the only solution is to halt all destructive activities before it is too late.
      (b) Business must take the major blame for our environmental problems.
      (c) Business, through its use of advertising, has caused the consume-at-all-costs syndrome, which has led to environmental depletion.
      (d) Government should immediately pass legislation so as to ensure a clean environment.
      (e) Government must conduct a massive reeducation of everyone in society, including businesspeople.
      (f) If businesses are destroyed in the process, then so be it—the environment must be saved at all costs.
  C. There is also a moderate view on business and the environment.
    1. Business isn't totally to blame for the destruction of the environment.
    2. The government and society in general share the blame.
    3. Business, government, and society must work together to stop this destruction, recognizing that we all have an ethical obligation to protect human beings and the environment.

VI. Affirmative action and reverse discrimination
    A. There are a number of terms related to this issue.
        1. *Prejudice* means the prejudgment of someone or something from a biased point of view.
        2. To *discriminate* means to differentiate among people in a prejudiced way when hiring, promoting, or firing them.
        3. *Affirmative action* describes the process of trying to avoid present and future discrimination and trying to make up for past discrimination.
        4. *Reverse discrimination* is discrimination practiced against white males in the course of implementing affirmative action.
    B. There are two extreme arguments related to this issue.
        1. Some people argue in favor of discrimination.
          (a) A business's employment practices are its own affair because it is privately owned.
          (b) Even if discrimination has been practiced in the past, this is not the fault of present employers; therefore, they should not be held responsible and be forced to pay for errors that weren't theirs.
          (c) Even if some present employers are guilty of discrimination, they should not be forced to pay for old mistakes.
          (d) Employers definitely should not have to hire less qualified people in order to make up for past errors.
          (e) They should not have to be responsible for training unqualified employees to make them qualified.
          (f) Business is not responsible for discrimination—it exists on all levels of society—therefore, there is no reason why business should have to bear the burden alone.
          (g) If employers are left alone, things eventually will work themselves out in a fair manner.
          (h) Forced hiring of minorities and women will result in reverse discrimination and be unfair to whites.
        2. Some people argue against discrimination.
          (a) Discrimination in business is the most insidious kind of discrimination, and therefore it must be stopped immediately.
          (b) Even though we may not have discriminated in the past (which is difficult to believe), we still owe these wronged people something, as their fellow human beings and as good citizens.
          (c) Every effort must be made to put affirmative action into immediate effect.
             (1) When employees retire, resign, or are fired, they should be replaced with minority-group members.
             (2) Quotas, goals, and timetables for affirmative action must be established and adhered to.
             (3) Training programs must be established for these people immediately.
          (d) Unfortunately, reverse discrimination may take place, but it has to exist in order to right past wrongs.
          (e) Government at all levels should mandate affirmative action and enforce it fully by any legal means available.
    C. There is a moderate position related to this issue.
        1. Business has an obligation to halt immoral discriminatory practices as equitably as it can, but employers shouldn't have to hire or promote unqualified or less qualified people.
        2. Government has an obligation to mandate affirmative action and nondiscriminatory practices and to enforce them.

    3. Society as a whole must also halt its discriminatory practices in all those ways wherein they affect human rights.

    4. Reverse discrimination also should be avoided wherever possible.

VII. Sexual harassment

  A. *Sexual harassment* is defined as "unwanted sexual advances, or visual, verbal, or physical conduct of a sexual nature."

  B. Some people argue that sexual harassment is not immoral.

    1. Actions now deemed to constitute sexual harassment enliven the workplace and are just ways of having fun at the office.

    2. Women and men are naturally sexually attracted to each other.

    3. Positions of power imply certain rights.

    4. Those being harassed often ask for or cause harassment.

  C. Others argue that sexual harassment is immoral.

    1. Sexual harassment constitutes unfairness of treatment.

    2. It creates a hostile or offensive working environment.

    3. Positions of authority do not imply a power over employees' lives.

    4. Attraction does not imply involvement.

    5. No one has the right to assume that people are asking to be harassed, especially when they clearly reject harassment, regardless of the types of clothing people wear or the comments they make.

VIII. The New Global Economy and the International Business Scene

  A. The twenty-first century has brought unprecedented global change that now structures the dynamic environments in which business is conducted.

  B. In the new global economy, the world's major corporations are multinationals. Multinational corporations are powerful institutions that maintain operations in various "host" countries.

  C. Currently there is considerable debate about the kind and character of morality that will govern international business.

    1. One view of the international situation, known as cultural relativism (ethical/moral relativism or cultural particularism), claims that no culture's ethics are better than any others. There are many standards of morality—not just one.

    2. An opposite point of view is ethical or moral absolutism, also referred to as cultural universalism. It holds that basic truths about the nature of right and wrong actions can be defined universally.

  D. Successful multinational corporations must uphold transcultural, universal principles, and human core values that are distinct from religious beliefs and cultural values and, at the same time, respect cultural values and local traditions.

  E. The challenge for ethical leadership in the new global economy is to balance two imperatives: business results and human values.

IX. Media Ethics

  A. Introduction: The media explosion.

  B. Journalism's ideal: The communication of truth.

  C. Truth and how journalists obtain information and stories.

  D. Public right to know versus individual right to privacy

    1. Probably the most significant ethical issue in media ethics.

    2. The Clinton/Lewinsky affair.

    3. The Elian Gonzales event.

    E. Where to draw the line.

    F. Ethical news values.

        1. Dignity for subjects.

        2. Reciprocity (Golden Rule).

        3. Sufficiency: allocating adequate resources.

        4. Accuracy.

        5. Tenacity.

        6. Equity and fairness.

        7. Community: valuing social cohesion.

        8. Diversity: covering everyone fairly and adequately.

X. Corporate Greed—Enron

    A. Enron was one of the worst scandals and violations of business ethics.

    B. Enron's code of ethical conduct.

    C. Enron's ethics and its problems.

    D. Why the code of conduct failed.

Exercises for Review

1. If you have a job, analyze the affirmative action needs and/or programs at your place of business. If you don't work, set up a detailed affirmative action program that might work in any business.

2. How does business ethics differ from bioethics and other specific ethical areas?

3. List in detail what you feel are the rights and obligations in business activities for each of the following groups: businesspeople in general, employers, employees, consumers, and government. Give reasons for your answer.

4. Analyze in detail several advertisements in any of the communications media (newspapers, magazines, radio, TV) and show the degree to which they tell the truth, misrepresent a product or service, warn the public of dangers, omit important information, or make unsupported and unsupportable claims.

5. Write an essay discussing the value or lack of value of competition in business and in other specific areas of society—for example, sports. Do you feel that our society places too heavy an emphasis upon competition? Why, or why not?

6. To what extent do you feel that government controls and regulations of business are necessary? Describe in detail some situations in which government should intervene and some in which it shouldn't, explaining why you think as you do.

7. To what extent should business take precedence over the environment, and to what extent should the environment come first? Explain in detail, giving reasons for your answers.

8. Focus on a specific situation relevant to the business versus environment issue, and analyze what has or hasn't been done to correct the problems involved. Do you agree with what has been done? Why, or why not? What is your general blueprint for how to deal with environmental problems in business?

9. To what extent do you feel it is important for our society to encourage and protect small, independent businesses? How should this be done, and to what degree?

10. To what extent do you believe women should get the same jobs, pay, benefits, promotions, and considerations as men? Why? Discuss the following sayings or phrases: "A woman's place is in the home"; "Women are the weaker sex"; "Women don't need jobs as badly as men do."

11. Have you ever been a victim or perpetrator of sexual harassment, or have you known anyone who has? Describe in detail what happened, how it was handled, what effect it had on

the people involved, and what the conclusion of the incident was. To what extent do you think that such harassment constitutes a problem and is moral or immoral? Support your answer in detail.

Views of the Major Ethical Theories on Business and Media Ethics

Describe as fully as you can how each of the major ethical theories—Ethical Egoism, Utilitarianism, Divine Command Theory, Kant's Duty Ethics, Ross' *Prima Facie* Duties, and Virtue Ethics—probably would deal with the moral issues in business. Be sure to include the cases at the end of the chapter. Refer to Chapters 2, 3, and 4 for a description of the theories and to Chapter 9, "The Taking of Human Life," for an example of how you might go about completing this assignment.

Notes

1. Herbert Johnston, *Business Ethics*, 2nd ed. (New York: Pitman, 1961), 64–65.
2. *Hostile Hallways: The AAUW Survey on Sexual Harassment in America's Schools* (Washington, DC: AAUW, June 1993).
3. State of California, *Sexual Harassment Is Forbidden by Law* (Sacramento, CA: Department of Fair Employment and Housing, December 1992).
4. California Chamber of Commerce, *No Sexual Harassment Allowed* (1993).
5. Thomas Donaldson, "Values in Tension: Ethics Away from Home," in *Business Ethics: Problems, Principles, Practical Applications*, 2nd ed., Keith W. Krasemann (Acton, MA: Copley Publishing Group, 2004), 70.
6. Richard Paul and Linda Elder, *The Miniature Guide to Understanding the Foundations of Ethical Reasoning*, 3rd ed. (Dillon Beach, CA: Foundation for Critical Thinking, 2005), 21.
7. Phillip Patterson and Lee Wilkins, *Media Ethics: Issues and Cases* (New York: William C. Brown, 1991), 17.
8. Ibid., 28–29.
9. Michael Miller, "Enron's Ethics Code Roads Like Fields"; http://columbusbizjournals.com/columbus/stories/2002/04/01/editorial3.html.
10. Business Ethics; http://thesmokinggun.com/enronethics5.shtml, January 20, 2003.

Research Navigator™
(http://www.researchnavigator.com)

This web site offers three research databases: EBSCO'S *Content Select Academic Journal and Abstract Database*, *New York Times* Search by Subject Archive, and *Best of the Web* Link Library. In addition, this site provides helpful advice on how to conduct efficient and productive research from choosing a topic to polishing the final draft. Beginning philosophy students probably will find the *Best of the Web* Link Library the most appropriate place to start their research.

The free access code necessary to employ Research Navigator™ can be found in the Prentice Hall Guide to Evaluating Online Resources. If your text did not come with this guide, please go to *www.prenhall.com/contentselect* for information on how you can purchase an access code.

Chapter
16

Environmental Ethics

Objectives

After you have read this chapter, you should be able to

1. Recognize environmental ethical issues.

2. Understand what lies behind our attitudes toward the natural environment and everything in it (plants, trees, animals).

3. Discern whether we have a moral obligation to preserve and protect nature.

4. Understand and deal with the question "To what extent do animals and plants have rights?"

5. Know and understand the arguments for and against the use and exploitation of the natural environment and everything in it.

6. Recognize the importance of non-Western ethical perspectives for addressing environmental issues.

Key Terms

1. *Speciesism:* A prejudice for one's own species and against other species.
2. *Sentientism:* The theory that only those beings with mental states should be the subject of moral concern.
3. *Wholism:* A conception of nature wherein humans and nature together form a moral community.
4. *Vegetarianism:* The refusal to eat meat, fish, fowl, or any food derived from them and the favoring of a diet of vegetables.

5. *Endangered species:* A species of animals in danger of becoming extinct because of the encroachment of civilization upon the natural environment and careless exploitation by human beings.

Nature and Morality

In recent years, people have come to realize that natural resources and animals, plants, and trees are not boundless but are subject to diminishment, destruction, and loss through careless exploitation, pollution, and the general encroachment of civilization. In the past, despite inklings of this realization in cases such as the near extinction of the American buffalo by white people in the old West through wholesale slaughter, people assumed that natural resources would last forever and were there merely to be used and exploited. Water, air, forests, animals, plants, and minerals were considered to exist in abundance and without end. In recent years, however, with the rise of industrialized, technological, producing, and consuming societies, people have discovered that this just is not so. There indeed are limits to the natural resources of the world, and it is possible to eliminate whole species of animals by means of lack of concern for their survival and willful exploitation.

I refer you to my discussion of the four aspects of morality in Chapter 1, and especially to the second aspect, nature and morality, which has to do with human beings and their relationship to nature. In that discussion, I said that for most modern, "civilized" people, this was a new category, but that in reality it was an ancient idea among primitive human beings who tended to see themselves as being much more closely allied with nature than we do. Even our modern-day concerns often are centered around nature's destruction as that affects our own lives rather than nature having value in and for itself. In this sense, human relations with nature could be subsumed under the social aspect having to do with people in relationship to other people.

However, I also said that many people do consider nature as being valuable in and of itself and insist that we have specific moral obligations toward it and all that it contains, especially those animals that are close to us in nature's order. In this chapter, we will look at both aspects but will concentrate upon nature and morality.

Environmental Ethical Issues

Several environmental ethical issues will be discussed throughout this chapter, and it is important to describe them briefly now.

Waste and Destruction of Natural Resources

As I pointed out, we have assumed that our natural resources will last forever, that our water, air, oil, minerals, earth, plants, and trees will always be there for us to use and will never be depleted. However, in recent times we have discovered that there is a limit to everything, including our natural resources. As we willy-nilly cut down trees for use in wood and paper products, for example, we began to realize that our forests were disappearing. When we had oil shortages in 1973, 1998, 1999, and 2000 and were held hostage by the Arab nations, we began to realize that there was only so much oil in the ground and the sea, and that our pumps would not bring up oil forever. As our rainfall diminished along with our water supply, we began to realize that there was a limit to our water as well, and we simply could not overwater our lawns or let water flow down the drains of our sinks, bathtubs, and toilets or we would actually run out of it.

As each of these realizations hit us, we were shocked that the earth's bounty would not last unless we stopped destroying without rebuilding or replanting and unless we began to conserve our precious natural resources. We simply could not continue cutting down trees without planting new ones to take their place. We also had to recycle paper so that not as many trees would be used up to make it. We had to be careful not merely to let water flow but to restrict our use of it. We couldn't just use and misuse our land by destroying it in digging for oil, coal, and other minerals, and we had to be careful not to exhaust its fertility by continuing to plant in the same soil without protecting it and letting it lie fallow.

Exploiting, Misusing, and Polluting the Environment

We also discovered, probably with what first happened to the air in Los Angeles, California, that heavy industrialization and a tremendous proliferation of automobiles polluted the environment so badly that we found it difficult to breathe, grow things, or even to see on particularly smoggy days. We further discovered that such heavy pollution also destroyed the ozone layer that protects the earth against excessive rays of the sun.

We found further that we could not continue to dump our waste in the ground and in the rivers, lakes, and oceans without dire effects on those bodies of water and their inhabitants. If we drilled for oil in the ocean and sprung a leak or had a spill, we could adversely affect the natural and recreational environments surrounding them, including the plants, animals, or fish within them. As our industrialization and technology increased, so did the toxicity of the waste, and we found ourselves burying in the land or dumping in bodies of water very dangerous and poisonous materials, such as strong chemicals, atomic waste, and other dangerous materials that seriously affected our whole environment as well as us, its inhabitants.

Exploiting, Abusing, and Destroying Animals

One of the most controversial ethical issues concerning the environment is the question of animal rights and whether we have moral obligations toward animals. These issues encompass destroying animals for food or for parts of their bodies (for example, furs, skins, or tusks); hunting them for sport; and using them for scientific and other experimentation.

Hunting and Destroying Animals for Food and Body Parts. Since human beings basically are carnivores—that is, meat eaters—and have been throughout history, destroying animals for food has been and is quite common. In the past, we hunted animals for food and often used their skins or other parts of their bodies for clothes. Primitive people seemed, however, to use only what they needed and did not destroy whole herds of animals just for the sake of killing them. Hunting for food and other necessities is an ancient activity. Hunting and acquiring food and other items were combined, but early human beings seemed to have more respect for animals and the environment than modern ones do.

Several changes have occurred, however, which some people see as eliminating the necessity of using animals for these purposes. First, we have created wonderful synthetic materials—even furs—that eliminate the need for killing animals for their skins. We no longer need whale blubber in order to operate oil lamps because we now have electricity. We no longer need to hunt animals for food because we now raise animals specifically for the food that we eat (creating another ethical issue that we will discuss later). Killing wild animals, then, has become a sport that many enjoy and many others decry because they feel it amounts to murdering animals for excitement and also threatens to cause certain wild animals to become extinct.

Raising Animals for Food. Ethical issues also have arisen with regard to the raising, slaughtering, and eating of animals for food. The demands of modern humans for tastier meats and other animal products, such as eggs, butter, and milk, have caused the food industry to resort to different ways of raising animals for food, some of which cause animals to suffer until they are slaughtered. For example, in the past, animals were raised in the open plains and were allowed to graze, roam, and live in the open air until such time as they were to be slaughtered for food. Nowadays, many animals are raised inside, cooped up in narrow pens, and never allowed outside to graze normally. Some animals never see the sun or breathe the open air, and they are fed food and chemicals that will make them the fattest the soonest without regard for their own likes or dislikes or any concern for their comfort or the pain such conditions or diets may bring.

Some people argue that given what we know about the way animals are raised and about what foods really are good for us, we should stop eating meat at all, thus making the need to raise and slaughter animals for food obsolete. Such people state further that even if we continue to eat meat, we ought to do so sparingly, and, at any rate, we should not use cruel and inhumane methods as we raise animals for this purpose.

Using Animals for Scientific Experimentation. One of the oldest controversies concerning our moral obligations toward animals is whether they should be experimented upon for scientific or medical advancement. Since the antivivisection movement of the nineteenth century protested the cutting into live animals for purposes of scientific research, these protests have expanded to include any experimentation on animals "for the good of humanity." There are strong laws concerning experimenting on human beings, and thus animals must be used, according to science, to test drugs and scientific or medical procedures. Without the use of animals, many of our greatest scientific advancements and cures for diseases (such as heart disease, kidney disease, and diabetes) would never have been made. Opponents of animal experimentation argue that often it is totally unnecessary as well as harmful and fatal to the animals being experimented on. They argue that research should be conducted without the use of either humans or animals.

Endangerment, Decimation, and Extinction of Animal Species. Because of the encroachment of civilization, as when forests are cut down and towns are built, the natural habitats of animals have shrunk significantly or been destroyed. In addition, because of the continuing demand for animal skins, parts, and trophies, whole species have been slaughtered to the point of extreme endangerment or extinction. Animal rights supporters deplore such activities and have called for an end of the hunting of all animals, especially endangered species, and also for the restriction of any activities that will destroy the environments in which animals live and thrive. They argue that every effort must be made to stop all activities that threaten any animal species, and that attempts should be made to restore such environments to their natural states.

Many issues have arisen in our century that deal with the proper stance people should be taking toward the natural environment and all of its inhabitants. The first important question we should address concerning these issues is what lies behind the attitudes that brought the issues to a head. What caused us to see nature as something to be controlled and manipulated for our own use, regardless of the effects on it and all it contains? Why have we arrived at such a state that we have to be concerned about our relationship with the environment and animals?

Our Attitude Toward Nature and What Lies Behind It

Attitudes toward nature have not developed overnight; however, we cannot say that they always have been nor that they always are present in every culture. In the Native American culture, for example, there exists a kind of monistic (oneness) or wholistic view of nature and humanness as being one, not as separate from each other. Native Americans historically and currently see themselves as a part of nature, as closely related to everything natural rather than as something or someone separate from it. They believe that spirits inhabit everything, not just them, and they relate to nature and animals as if they were family. They take only what they need and have a deep respect for all aspects of nature and animals.

Eastern religions, such as Hinduism, Buddhism, and Taoism, also see nature and humans as being one unified whole instead of seeing nature as subordinate to humans or as something to be manipulated and controlled by them. Here again, unlike Western religions, if spirituality is accepted by the religion, it tends to permeate everyone and everything, not just human beings. The whole universe is spiritual, not just humans and God. The Western view, however, has tended to see humans and nature in a dualistic relationship that is sometimes almost adversarial. There are two major sources in Western culture from which this dualism emerged.

Platonic Dualism: The Beginnings of Western Philosophy

Socrates and then Plato both tended to see the external world as the shadow copy of a real world that exists somewhere else in what Plato called the "world of ideas." With these two men, philosophy moved away from the external world, which had been the focus of the pre-Socratic philosophers (the first scientists), to a focus on human beings and their reason, which enabled them to attain the real world of ideas, a world that Plato felt exists outside of or beyond this world. Both Socrates and Plato, then, tended to deemphasize the importance of this world as opposed to the world of ideas where they felt that ultimate truths could be found, but only through human reason. Plato felt that if human beings concentrated on the external world and everything that was in it, they would only be seeing shadow copies of the real world that exists beyond this world. For example, when Socrates asked a question of his students, such as "What is justice?" and they answered, "Justice is how Zeus treated Achilles in a certain situation," he then said, "No. I mean what is justice, 'itself by itself'?" In other words, he felt that somewhere there exists the ultimate true idea of justice from which all just acts are mere manifestations. This dualism enabled the Greeks to think abstractly for the first time in their history, but it also tended to split them away from nature in that they, as reasoning beings, saw themselves as different from and more important than nature and the external world, because they and no other beings in nature could attain the "real" world of ideas that Plato thought actually existed.

Judeo-Christian Teachings in the Bible

The second dualistic view emerges from the early Judeo-Christian tradition, which taught that God is a supernatural, spiritual being who shares His spirituality with human beings. No other being in nature, according to the teachings in both traditions, has any spirituality. Again, this world is viewed as being God's creation and significant, but not the real world that lies beyond in the supernatural world (according to Christianity). In Genesis, Adam is told by God that he has "dominion over the animals of the earth, the birds of the air, and the fish of the sea" and that nature essentially is there for his purposes. Adam is told to "go forth and multiply" and have dominion over everything. This again makes nature and everything in it subservient to human beings and their wishes, implying that nature exists strictly for their use and has little or no value in itself. This may not be the way many worshipers in Judaism and Christianity feel today, but there is no doubt that these teachings have had a definite influence on the attitudes people in the Western world have toward nature.

The Rise of Science and Scientific Progress

It is ironic that the influences just mentioned, although giving rise to an exploitative attitude toward nature, also have made science and scientific progress possible. It is no accident that science has progressed by leaps and bounds in the Western world while being almost nonexistent in the Eastern world. And why not? If nature, and all it contains, is subservient to us, or if we can make it so by harnessing its powers and using it for our own best interest, then why not do so?

As science and technology advanced, nature became more and more subservient to human needs and desires, and the environment and animals were used and exploited without regard to any inherent value they might have. After all, so the attitude went, we are the only beings with intrinsic value; nature has only instrumental value, that is, it is only valuable as it helps us attain whatever goals we believe are important to us.

Industrialization

With the tremendous advancement of science and technology most nations in the West and many in the East have become highly industrialized, requiring a greater use of natural resources and also causing a greater deleterious effect on the environment because of the need for more land, and air, and a greater disposal of waste. For example, given our civilization's need for certain chemicals or chemical products, a chemical plant may be situated in a natural setting on a river, which requires trees to be cut and hills to be leveled, while the plant pours its poisonous waste into that body of water and pollutes the air by belching chemical-laden smoke into it.

Encroachment of Nature by Civilization

As I have suggested, with industrialization, civilization has encroached upon nature. This encroachment also has taken many forms. As we have moved out of crowded cities into the countryside nearby and created suburbs, we have eliminated more and more of the natural environment and replaced it with our own. As we have leveled trees and hills to put in housing developments, shopping centers, and other "civilized" creations, we have shrunk the natural environment and pushed species of plant growth and animals back into narrower areas where they often have not been able to survive because of the elimination of their space, air, water, and food supplies.

All of the preceding have contributed to our attitudes toward the natural environment and all it contains. It remains to be seen whether these attitudes should prevail, or whether they should undergo radical or moderate changes. An examination and analysis of the arguments for and against the use and exploitation of nature will help us to look at both sides of environmental ethical issues.

Arguments for Use and Exploitation of the Natural Environment

Dominion-over-Nature Arguments

A strong set of arguments states that human beings are the highest form of natural creation and, therefore, should have complete dominion over nature and everything that it contains. Nature exists strictly for the use of human beings and has no other purpose for its existence. These arguments come from two sources: religion and science.

Religious Basis for Dominion. As pointed out, Western religions seem to support the stance that people, although related to nature, are yet other and higher than nature by virtue of the spirituality that has been conferred upon them by God. No other beings in nature have such high status as humans; therefore, they do not deserve the same ethical considerations as humans do. It is strictly up to human beings to decide what the value of nature is, since it has no value in and of itself.

Natural Order and Evolution Argument. The other argument that supports humans' dominion over nature is that which focuses on the evolutionary scale and the natural order of things that places human beings at the top of everything. Humans, by virtue of their fantastic brains that are considered (by them) to be the highest achievement of nature and evolution, should obviously have dominion over everything else in the natural world. Humans have shown through their ability to reason and invent that, even though nature towers over them in size, they are capable of harnessing it and all of its aspects by flying; traveling on and staying under water; controlling rivers, streams, and seas; leveling the tallest mountains; cutting down nature's biggest trees; and overcoming nature's most ferocious species of animals. And even though nature does in some respects have more control over humans (as demonstrated by earthquakes, tornadoes, floods, and tidal waves), it is just a matter of time until humans will be able to control these aspects of nature too by being able to predict them and then by either averting them or diminishing their destructive powers.

Human Reasoning versus Nature as Blind and Nonreasoning

The main reason that human beings are at the top of the natural order of things is that they have the capacity for reasoning that the rest of nature does not possess. Inanimate objects and plants have no reasoning ability, and animals have it to only a minor degree, if at all. Because nature is blind and nonreasoning, it is obvious that human beings should have complete dominion and control over it.

Civilization More Important Than Nature

Because the human brain and its reasoning capacity is the highest form in the natural order, then civilization, including its institutions, technology, science, industry, and systems of all kinds, should take precedence over nature. Neither nature nor any of its inhabitants except for human beings is capable of reasoning, analyzing, organizing, using a language, or creating. Therefore, if nature must be destroyed in order to allow human civilization to expand and progress, then it simply must be, as it is less important in all of its aspects.

Moral Rights and Obligations

Because humans are at the top of the religious and natural orders, they and only they are deserving of moral rights and obligations; therefore, we have moral obligations only to ourselves and other human beings and not to nature in any of its aspects. Morality does not exist as far as the rest of nature is concerned but either comes from God or is established by humans for humans; therefore, humans have no moral obligations toward any part of nature, nor does any part of nature have any moral rights. Nature, then, can be used and exploited in any way that humans see fit, for it is merely there for their purposes.

Arguments Against the Use and Exploitation of Nature

Monistic Wholism versus Dominion and Domination

Critics of the dualistic arguments that human beings and nature are separate and that the former have been given dominion over the latter state that, first, religious arguments have either been misinterpreted or are irrelevant. Since nature is part of God's creation, say some religionists, then it also should be treated with respect. Just because there are no souls in nonhumans doesn't mean they have no value whatsoever. Second, having dominion, as given by God, means that humans should treat nature as God treats humans, with respect, mercy, and love. If humans are rulers over the world, then they should be benevolent and care for those beings under their rule who do not have the great human capacity for reason.

Also, some passages in the King James version of the Bible could be interpreted as supporting acting morally rather than destructively or dominatingly toward nature.

The Old Testament. First, in the Old Testament in Genesis, chapter 9, verses 12 and 15, it would seem that God made His covenant with Noah to include not only human beings but also animals:

Verse 12: And God said, "This is the token of the covenant which I make between me and you and every living creature that is with you for perpetual generations."

Verse 15: "And I will remember my covenant, which is between me and you and every living creature of all flesh; and the waters shall no more become a flood to destroy all flesh."

The New Testament. Second, in the New Testament, in Revelation, chapters 7 and 9, God again seems to express some concern for the nature He created:

Chapter 7, verses 2 and 3: And I saw another angel ascending from the east, having the seal of the living God, and he cried with a loud voice to the four angels, to whom it was given to hurt earth and sea, saying, "Hurt not the earth, neither the sea, nor the trees, till we have sealed a hundred and forty and four thousand of all the tribes of the children of Israel."

Chapter 9, verses 3 and 4: And there came out of the smoke locusts upon the earth; and unto them was given power, as the scorpions of the earth have power. And it was commanded them that they should not hurt the grass of the earth, neither any green thing, neither any tree; but only those men which have not the seal of God in their foreheads.

Nonreligionists argue that, first, just because people have evolved as higher beings because of their brains doesn't mean that someday they won't be replaced by a yet higher species. Second, this argument does not mean that nature is inferior to, but rather that it is equal to them in every respect. The proper relationship between humans and nature is not dualistic, but wholistic; that is, human beings are an integral part of nature and nature is an integral part of them. Therefore, instead of being a relationship of "survival of the fittest" or domination of one species over all the rest, this relationship should be a reciprocal and wholistic. The relationship should be one in which all aspects are a part of the whole of nature, to be preserved and protected and to coexist in harmony.

Reasoning Should Not Separate Humans from Nature

Because humans can reason, they should realize that nature is intrinsically valuable and must be nurtured and related to in a meaningful manner. Reason should not cause humans to reject nature, but to prize it; as a matter of fact, having reason endows humans with much more responsibility toward nature and all it contains than other beings in nature who do not possess it. Where animals are concerned, the importance of reasoning should be expanded to include sentientism (having mental states) so that animals can be respected even though they cannot reason. There are also certain criteria put forth by some ethicists that clearly can be used to give rights to animals and require human obligations toward them (see the following section on criteria for animal rights).

Civilization versus Nature. Nature, which contains most human needs and which relates to humans in a vital way, should never be made subordinate to civilization, which is human-constructed. Civilization has its value and importance, but nature should never be seriously endangered or destroyed at the expense of expanding civilization. For example, when builders are contemplating putting up a housing development or other buildings, they should never destroy any part of the natural environment in which they are working. Plant and animal life must be preserved and not destroyed as designing and building take place. Frank Lloyd Wright (1869–1959), the great American architect and advocate of organic architecture, felt that buildings should be designed in such a way that they fit into the natural environment or even seem to emerge from it in an organic way. His famous cantilevered house at Willow Run is a perfect example of this attitude.

Moderate Position

Both of the preceding sets of arguments take extreme positions either for or against the use and exploitation of nature. The arguments for such use and exploitation advocate the total subordination of nature to humans and the free use and exploitation of nature for whatever reasons humans deem acceptable. On the other hand, the arguments against these suggest that nature must be considered as standing on an equal footing with humans and should never be used as a means to human ends (see Chapter 3 and Kant's Practical Imperative). A more moderate position exists between these two extremes, however, one in which nature generally is regarded as being important and significant, but not necessarily on the same footing with humans, and in which it may be used for human means with some care so as not to seriously endanger or destroy it.

This position generally agrees with the wholistic position, seeing nature and humans as being intimately related and requiring that humans treat nature with respect; however, it is not against using nature for the good of humans but insists that this be done carefully, allowing for the preservation and protection of the environment and animals in the process and being careful not to overuse either of these. Perhaps these three positions dealing with humans and their relationship to nature can be best exemplified through a discussion of animal rights and human moral obligations toward animals.

Criteria for Animal Rights

Life and Being Alive

Some might argue that as long as something has life or is alive, then it deserves moral consideration, and people have a moral obligation to protect and preserve life wherever it is found. Critics of this position say that it is much too vague and unrealistic and that it would seem to violate the way nature itself works. A food chain exists in nature in which plants feed on other plants, animals feed on plants, and animals feed on other animals. Nature is able to achieve a balance in this process in which species survive but do not necessarily become extinct because they are not destroyed through overhunting, overeating, or overkilling.

Human beings also make distinctions concerning whether just life and being alive constitute sufficient criteria to preserve life. They have and do follow nature in that they eat plants and animals for their own survival just as the latter do for theirs. Further, humans even allow the killing of their own species in certain instances. Even though these are controversial areas, humans do allow the termination of life in their own species in such cases as abortion, defense of the innocent, capital punishment, just wars, mercy death, and mercy killing (see Chapters 9, 10, 11). If humans allow this in their own species, why not in others as well, especially if it is clearly for the good of the human species? Therefore, the fact that something or someone merely is alive or has life does not in itself seem to constitute a strong argument against terminating that life for this or that good reason.

Having Interests

Joel Feinberg states that "to have a right is to have a claim to something and *against* someone," and goes on to say that only beings who can be said to have interests are capable of claiming such rights.[1] He considers that animals do have interests, even though they can't express them verbally, especially the interest not to suffer pain, and therefore he would argue that animals do indeed have rights.

Attributes of Soul, Mind, and Feelings

Some would argue that rights for moral treatment are based upon whether a being has a soul, a mind, or feelings. The difficulty of proving the existence or nonexistence of a soul creates problems with such a criterion. Furthermore, even if we could prove a soul's existence, why should that be the only claim to moral rights?

As far as mind and feelings are concerned, animals, as sentient beings like humans, have to be described as having both of these merely through our observation of them. It seems obvious that they have sense experiences, although often different from those of humans, and they seem to be able to express sadness, happiness, and anger as well as other emotions and states of consciousness (for example, conscious awareness and response to stimuli).

Reason

Although it is limited, animals do seem to also have an ability to reason, even if only on a rudimentary level. Current language experiments with chimpanzees and gorillas would seem to indicate this. Furthermore, human beings with severe mental impairment can reason at no higher a level than some animals do, and generally we give them rights and feel we have moral obligations toward them; therefore, why do we not also have such obligations toward animals? It would seem that the mere fact of being sentient (having mental states) in itself would elicit from us humans at least the obligation not to inflict pain and suffering on one who is so.

Ways of Dealing with Animal Rights

Vegetarianism

One way of ensuring animal rights is to avoid using animals for food at all and to eat only vegetables. In this way hunting or slaughtering animals for food no longer becomes necessary. There are many kinds of people who call themselves vegetarians—some who will not eat any meat at all, some who will eat only poultry and fish, and some who will not even eat animal products such as dairy and eggs. These latter are called "vegans." Some extremists, such as the Jainists, will not even eat vegetables from plants that have to be killed to yield the fruit or vegetable, such as potatoes. They will themselves not kill plants to eat their food but will wait until food drops from plants or trees or accept food donations from others who will pick them. One vegetarian I know felt comfortable eating only vegetables until he discovered that the pinto bean actually is an embryo of the bean plant!

I am not describing all of this in order to ridicule vegetarians and their ideals, but only to show how difficult it is to attain some consistency as we try to preserve the lives of plants and animals. For example, what is the difference, beyond the health reasons, between eating red meat and eating poultry or fish? Is it any more moral to kill and eat a chicken or a fish than it is to kill and eat a cow or sheep?

Arguments Against Vegetarianism

Some argue that even though animals have interests and rights, those interests and rights are of less importance than those of humans, and therefore we have a right to use them for food, just as animals in nature use other animals and vegetables for food. The moderate view states that with these rights go certain responsibilities not to make animals suffer or feel pain, or not to slaughter whole species and make them extinct, but that humans still are entitled within these moral limitations to kill animals for food.

Sentientism

A second way of dealing with animal rights is to respect the fact that they have mental states that are to some extent akin to those of humans and are therefore deserving of rights. The critics of this argument ask, "What about plants and trees?" Sentientism is too restrictive and ignores the livingness of nonanimals. Don't our forests and fields deserve the same kind of consideration as any other living being? These people generally argue for wholism.

Wholism

Every living thing is deserving of respect according to this view because humans, animals, and plants are part of a natural whole and must learn to live in harmony with one another. This attitude relies heavily upon human beings and their reasoning, especially moral reasoning. The critics of this view argue against the blurring of important distinctions between humans, animals, and plants and state that there is indeed a hierarchy of beings that allows us to deem the rights of certain beings to be more important than others'. For example, animal rights activists are more concerned about animals than they are about plants and feel that animals should be given more consideration than wholism would allow.

Use of Animals for Food

One of the most important issues, because of its prevalency, is the raising and slaughtering of animals for food. Is it moral to kill sentient beings, possessing all of the attributes described previously, and use them for human consumption? There are people who stand on both sides of this issue, and some who are in the middle. What is involved in both the raising and the slaughtering of animals for this purpose?

Ways of Raising Animals for Food

In the past, wild animals were hunted and their flesh was used for food while their skins or other body parts were used for clothes and other items. When humans became more civilized, they began to domesticate animals, such as cows, pigs, sheep, and chickens, and to raise them for food. Animals were raised in the open air on farms or ranches alongside one or both of their parents, allowed to graze in pastures, or fed corn or other grains or foods while sometimes being penned in the open air. This is called the "free range" system of raising animals for food. When the time came for slaughter, the animals generally were put to death as quickly and as painlessly as possible.

However, as the demand for more and better meat and other animal products increased, something called "factory farming" came into use. Animals are raised in very close pens, often in the dark, and few of them ever see their mothers or the light of day. Even though killing animals for food is considered to be immoral by some, under the old system, they at least were treated more or less humanely up to the time of slaughter. An example of what goes on in factory farming can be seen in a description of how calves are raised for the veal that humans eat:

In order to make their flesh pale and tender, these calves are given special treatment. They are put in narrow stalls and tethered with a chain so that they cannot turn around, lie down comfortably, or groom themselves. They are fed a totally liquid diet to promote rapid weight gain. This diet is deficient in iron and, as a result, the calves lick the sides of the stall, which are impregnated with urine containing iron. They are given no water because thirsty animals eat more than those who drink water. Is this cruel treatment morally justified? Should we do this to animals just because we enjoy eating their flesh?[2]

A similar description could be given with regard to the raising of chickens, lambs, or pigs and also to using animals for their products, such as eggs, milk, and cream. Is this moral?

The Vegetarian Position

Because vegetarians oppose using animals for food in any way, shape, or form, such people would be totally against the factory farming way of raising animals, calling it even more decadent and corrupt than raising animals on the open farms as before. To raise and kill animals strictly for our needs is to use living, sentient beings merely as a means to our own ends without even the kindness of letting them have a relatively happy and good life before we kill them.

The Carnivore Position

The carnivore or meat-eating position accepts this approach as a modernized and much more efficient way of giving humans the best quality food possible. Because animals are here basically for our use and have no intrinsic value, then we have no moral obligations toward them, and their suffering has no meaning, since they are less than human. Therefore, any method that brings humans the best quality of meat possible is morally acceptable regardless of how it affects the animals involved.

The Moderate Position

The moderate position might condone using animals for food but decry the factory farming method as cruel. It would state that animals may be used by humans for food but insist on the free-range method of raising them and their painless slaughter as basic requirements for dealing morally with them. It would not, of course, deny the rights of vegetarians, but it would not brand as immoral the eating of meat aside from the cruelty to animals in the process of raising or slaughtering them.

Use of Animals for Experimentation

The use of animals for experimentation has gone on for many years and has resulted in the development of many of the greatest scientific and medical discoveries that have helped people to rid themselves of all kinds of chronic and fatal diseases.

Arguments for Animal Experimentation

Scientists would argue that without the ability to use animals for experimentation, humans would have to be used, to their harm and sometimes fatality. Cures simply would not be found for diseases, nor would training in certain procedures, such as surgeries, be possible. Because by law humans cannot be used for experimentation without their informed consent and without tremendous safeguards being imposed, progress in science and medicine simply would have to come to a standstill if animals could not be used.

They would argue further that animals have much less value than human beings, so it is morally correct to use them for experimentation because what will be discovered will benefit many people and sometimes the whole of humankind. Many of the animals scientists use are merely put to death because no one wants them and they cannot be kept in pounds or animal shelters indefinitely; therefore, why not get some use out of them rather than just kill them? The mere fact that nobody wants them or will take care of them should make it all right to use them to benefit humans.

Arguments Against Using Animals for Experimentation

In the view of animal rights activists, animals are thinking, feeling beings that suffer pain to the same extent and degree as humans. Just because they cannot tell us how much what is being done to them hurts doesn't mean they don't feel the pain. Therefore, it is immoral to put animals through suffering, torture, and painful death just so that humans can make progress in science and medicine. Even though Kant's Practical Imperative was meant to apply to rational human beings, animal rights activists would apply it to animals, giving them the same rights and status as human beings.

Many experiments are absolutely unnecessary to the health and well-being of human beings, and yet experiments continue to put animals through terrible tortures and death, merely in order to satisfy scientific curiosity. For example;

> At the Lovelace Foundation in New Mexico, experimenters forced sixty-four beagles to inhale radioactive strontium 90. Twenty-five of the dogs died; initially most of them were feverish and anemic and had hemorrhages and bloody diarrhea. One of the deaths occurred during an epileptic seizure, and another resulted from a brain hemorrhage. In a similar experiment, beagles were injected with enough strontium 90 to produce early death in fifty percent of the group. . . . It was already known that strontium 90 was unhealthy, and that the dogs would suffer and die. Furthermore, these experiments did not save any human lives or have any important benefits for humans.[3]

Animal rights activists see absolutely no redeeming moral value in such experiments and in fact deem them to be terribly immoral. Even when the outcome of experiments is such as to help scientists fight human diseases, other methods besides using animals merely as a means to our own ends must be found, or scientific progress simply should not be made. It is immoral, in these activists' eyes, to use animals for such purposes regardless of how much it may help mankind.

Moderate Position

The moderate position would not be against using animals for experimentation, but it would insist that, first of all, experiments must be absolutely necessary to the health and well-being of human beings. Animals should never be experimented upon merely to satisfy human curiosity, nor should they ever be used for unnecessary experiments such as that described with the beagles.

Second, every care must be taken to avoid inflicting upon animals more pain and suffering during the experiment than is actually needed. Every effort must be made to keep animals out of pain while experiments are going on, and they should be given almost the same amount of respect that would be tendered toward our fellow humans. With these safeguards in mind, necessary animal experimentation may be done.

Killing Animals for Sport

It Should Be Allowed

An Ancient Activity of Man. Several arguments exist for killing animals for sport. Hunting animals was an ancient activity of men in many of the tribes and cultures of the past and it remains so in cultures of the present. Some would argue that it is a part of manhood to engage in the hunting and killing of animals for food, skins, trophies, or just for the thrill of the hunt.

Controlling Animal Population. Protagonists of this position would argue that killing animals at will is the only way of keeping the animal population under control. As humans have built ranches and farms farther into the natural environment, wild animals often have attacked their crops or their domestic animals that are raised for food or for commercial reasons. Such animals must be trapped and killed so as to preserve civilization. If the hunting of wild animals is not allowed, even the least ferocious of them will destroy crops and domestic animals. Further, they will overrun our farms, ranches, and even our towns and cities, especially where there are suburbs. Therefore, in order to keep the animal population under control, hunting should not merely be allowed but encouraged.

Desire for Animal Meat and Other Body Parts. First, despite the fact that we have all the domestic meat we may wish, many people like to eat wild game, such as duck, venison (deer meat), quail, and pheasant, and they should be allowed to indulge their tastes.

Second, many people like to use the skins of wild animals of all kinds to make clothes, shoes, boots, handbags, floor coverings, and wall hangings. Even though all of these items can be made from synthetic materials or from domestic animals' skins, the more exotic wild skins are often prettier, rarer, and valued more highly. It is one thing, for example, to own a pair of cowboy boots made of cowhide, but another to own a pair made from lizard, crocodile, porcupine, or rattlesnake hides. The higher prices for boots made from these skins attest to their higher value.

Third, it is exciting to be able to have the heads of wild animals one has hunted and killed in the jungles and forests hanging on one's walls to indicate prowess and bravery as a hunter. And it is fun and different to have a wastebasket made of an elephant's foot, carved ivory figures made from its tusks, and coats and capes made from the beautiful skins and furs of real wild animals. Some people play tennis, swim, or ski for sport, so why shouldn't the hunter or fisherman be allowed to pursue his or her own preferred sport?

It Should Not Be Allowed

An Ancient Activity No Longer Required. The very fact that hunting is an ancient activity should indicate that it is not necessarily needed in modern times. We no longer have the need for the meat, skins, or body parts of wild animals. Furthermore, modern civilized males should not need to prove their masculinity at the expense of innocent and often beautiful animals who do nothing to harm them and who should be allowed to roam free as they once did.

The Animal Population Will Control Itself. The major cause of the increase in the animal population is that humans have hunted and killed carnivores such as mountain lions, wolves, and bobcats. These predators used to hunt and eat animals such as deer and rabbits, thereby naturally keeping the animal population under control. If hunting these animals were no longer allowed, then the animals they hunt would become a menace as indeed they have. If this natural control system cannot be, then there must be more humane ways of controlling animal populations other than shooting them for sport.

No Further Need for Wild Game or Body Parts. It is a decadent civilization, antagonists to hunting as a sport would say, that needs to hunt animals for their meat when perfectly good domestic meat exists for human consumption. In addition, to use animals' body parts, such as their skins, when there are perfectly good synthetic, man-made materials we can use for these purposes is indefensible. We can make synthetic fur coats that look as if they are made of real furs and that do not require us to kill animals for them. The days of using wild animal skins and hides are over, or should be, and there is absolutely no need to kill 50 lizards, for example, in order to make a pair of cowboy boots or club to death hundreds of baby harp seals in order to make fur coats for women. It is the height of decadence that members of a civilized world have to continue to hunt and kill beautiful wild animals for these purposes.

The Moderate Position

Killing for Sport Can Be Allowed on a Limited Basis. We must recognize that other sports, such as skiing and swimming, do not involve the killing of innocent animals. This position recognizes the enjoyment some people get from the hunt and will allow hunting for sport on a limited basis as long as animals, especially endangered species, generally are protected and that there are limits on the type, age, and sex of the animal to be hunted. The hunt must be a fair one, allowing animals to try to save themselves. "Shooting fish in a barrel," as the saying goes, should not be allowed, and poachers should be fined or otherwise heavily penalized.

There should be specific seasons set aside by forest rangers and other officials, and rules protecting animals from extinction should be strictly enforced. Also, until the predator population can be expanded, hunting should coincide with the need for control of populations of "huntable" animals. Here again, strict limits must be enforced so as to ensure that there is no extinction of any species.

No Reason to Kill Wild Animals for Meat. Except where hunting is allowed, as described, no hunting outside of established limits should take place for meat or body parts unless it is done by primitive tribes in order to get meat for their villages when no other meat can be acquired.

No Killing Animals for Body Parts and Skins. Again, except where allowed within the limits described, no hunting should take place to acquire animal body parts, such as heads for trophies, skins or furs for clothes and footwear, feet for waste-baskets, or tusks for ivory. In order to help ensure that this type of hunting stops, civilized people should not demand such items and should make a strong effort not to order or purchase them; they should openly declare their opposition to such wasteful and useless hunting. In other words, every effort should be made to restrict hunting to a minimum.

Protection of Endangered Species

People who are not particularly concerned about the extinction of species of animals, especially exotic species, cannot see what all the fuss is about. Why worry about such things? Nature always has allowed various species to become extinct; perhaps it is now occurring by means of the advancement of human beings and their civilization. Why, for example, should people try to preserve the California condor? It is one of the ugliest birds in existence and basically is a carrion or vulturelike bird feeding off the carcasses of dead animals. Why does it matter whether we save such species or even those that are prettier to look at? There are several arguments that animal protectionists bring up regarding endangered species:

1. An irreverence for even a small segment of life affects one's reverence for all life. If one has no consideration for even one species, then he or she is likely not to have consideration for any other, including his own. Protectionists argue that human beings should protect and preserve all viable life in all of its forms, not just human life, as best they can.

2. Most species of animals are beautiful or at least interesting to see and know about, especially in their natural habitats, so they should be available not only for us but also for our children, grandchildren, and great-grandchildren. If we are not

careful about encroaching upon animals' habitats and destroying them in all the ways we can and do, then there will be fewer and fewer species around for us and our kin to experience.

3. All animals seem to contribute in some way to the balance of nature and to the natural food chain. We may not clearly know how everything fits into the overall plan of nature, but we should be careful not to upset the balance any more than we have to. It is one thing for nature to take its course and to make certain species extinct, but whenever it is obvious that humans, not nature, are the cause of destruction or extinction, we should cease what we are doing, or do what we are doing less, so as not to affect nature and its inhabitants adversely.

These are the reasons animal protectionists give for doing our utmost to protect and preserve all species of animals, and especially those that are becoming endangered. Obviously such people would be totally against hunting any of these species and also would tend to want to curtail the progress and encroachment of civilization upon nature wherever it tends to threaten the existence of such species.

Non-Western Perspectives on Environmental Issues

Because environmental issues are global in scope and implications raised by these important issues of concern affect people the world over, it will be worthwhile to briefly note the value of non-Western ethical viewpoints. Asian values offer productive alternatives to rights-based moralities that dominate Western societies. There has been much recent debate concerning Asian values and one is led to assume that there is one distinct set of values common to all Asians. This assumption is surely false and misleading; because Asia covers a huge geographical area and Asian traditions include Daoist, Confucian, Buddhist, Neo-Confucian, Hindu and Jain values. Furthermore, Roman Catholicism is the dominant religion in the Philippines and Islam is widespread in Pakistan and Indonesia. So when we talk of the values of Asia it becomes obvious that there is a plurality of ethical thought systems that could be included for discussion. However, four Asian ethical traditions, two originating in India and two in China, seem especially well suited to addressing environmental issues.

Ethical Traditions of South Asia: Hinduism and Buddhism

The fundamental aim of philosophical thinking in India and the ethical traditions of South Asia is to bring about liberation from all suffering. The immanent worldviews of Hinduism and Buddhism, which stress the oneness and interconnectedness of the natural order present clear alternatives to Western transcendent moral perspectives where human beings stand over/against nature. Also, there is no clear distinction between the sacred and the profane, because philosophy in India is not separated from religious activity. Wisdom in South Asia cultures is wholistic in nature and is manifest as knowledge and compassion. "True wisdom is the harmony of mind and heart."[4] For the Hindu "all is one." As one scholar states: "Oneness is not the one word to describe the essence of Hinduism, but it is as close as we can get to a one-word characterization."[5] This fundamental principle is expressed as the truth that *atman* (the individual soul) is *Brahman* (the world soul). Ignorance of this insight leads to the illusion of a separate existence standing over/against its ground. This failure to apprehend the most basic truth about the nature of self and the nature of the universe constitutes the major reason for bondage, misery and destruction in the world. The goal of Hinduism thus is to gain a discriminatory self-transforming knowledge of reality. Acting in the light of this knowledge has a liberating affect upon all existence.

Right conduct for the Hindu is understood in terms of the concept of *dharma*. This notion is derived from the root *dhr,* meaning "to nourish." The term's etymology may be further traced to the word *rita*—the order of the universe. *Dharma* is action that is selfless and without attachment, thus it promotes the oneness and wholeness of all things. Hindus believe that moral order permeates all existence. This idea is played out in the notion of *karma*—the law of sowing and reaping or the principle of moral cause and effect. How is *rita* "the moral order of the universe" related to human actions and their consequences? Hindu scholar Saral Jhingran tells us that

> the moral quality of our deeds, thoughts and desires not only conditions our future character, but also manipulates the natural world order, so that we are thrown into external circumstances that are most suited to materialize or effect the kind of rewards and punishments which our moral character deserves.[6]

"Right conduct" *dharma* requires that one take responsibility for one's deeds and thoughts in ways that lead to "personal self-realization" *moksha* and at the same time nourishes society and existence itself.

Buddhism shares the basic Hindu cosmology and places emphasis on the interconnectedness of all things. According to Buddhist teaching all things are intimately connected in the sense that they affect everything else. Like the ecological system itself, existence is an intricate, interdependent web within which all cause-and-effect relationships occur. In light of this insight one may conclude that, likewise, all human actions impact all other things. Such a metaphysical scheme frames ethical thinking in terms of global accountability.

Buddhist doctrine also emphasizes the Noble Truth of Suffering. That "life is suffering (*duhkha*)" is the central truth of Buddhism and the Buddha's estimate of the world condition. The goal of Buddhist teaching and practice is to achieve nirvana, liberation from suffering (*duhkha*) and release from the cycle of rebirth. Suffering (*duhkha*) is brought about by ignorance. On the one hand, many wrongly identify existence with being and thus experience *duhkha* as a result of attachments to this world and the things of the world. On the other hand, others misidentify existence with nonbeing and, as a consequence, experience *duhkha* in the rejection of life. Although Buddhism teaches the doctrine of "No Self," which is the denial of the self or ego as a separate and permanent entity, it does not deny self as a concrete, living, dynamic entity. Life on Buddhist terms is a process and is constantly changing, yet every moment holds within itself both being and nonbeing. Right living consists in following the Middle Way—the path between a life of attachment, and the extremes of self-indulgence and greed, and the rejection of life and self-denial or deprivation.

The Middle Way is articulated as The Eightfold Path:

- right view (knowledge)
- right intention (resolve)
- right speech
- right conduct
- right livelihood
- right effort
- right mindfulness
- right concentration

Relative to the above eight points one must negotiate the balance between the extremes of materialism and its attachments and ritualism which denies the value of material existence. Since the goal of Buddhism is to liberate all sentient beings from suffering, right living stresses the primary of the virtue of compassion.

Ethical Traditions of East Asia: Daoism and Confucianism

The grand goal of Chinese thought is to achieve balance and harmony. Both Daoism and Confucianism presuppose a dynamic, aesthetically ordered, *yin-yang* constitutive cosmos. *Yin-yang* originally referred to the shaded and the sunny, and the two notions represent complementary, interpenetrating opposites, reciprocals or counterpoints that move around the still point of the universe and account for change. Examples of *yin* would include dark, female, wet, and soft while illustrations of *yang* are light, male, dry and hard. In a Chinese world harmony and balance are sought between other *yin/yang counterpoints;* heaven and earth, intuition and reason, others and self, and nature and society. Because Daoism is chiefly identified with nature and Confucianism with society, the two are sometimes said to represent the *yin* and *yang* of Chinese thought.

Daoist thought is embodied in the person of Laozi, to whom is attributed the philosophical classic, the *Daodejing*—roughly translated, *The Book of the Way and Virtue.* Although it is doubtful that such an individual actually existed, tradition suggests he was an older contemporary of Kongzi (Confucius) and lived in the sixth century B.C. This book is the Daoist "Bible" and is the chief source for later Daoist writers, such as Zhaungzi (fourth century B.C.). It is the primary source for the entire Daoist cannon. It is also the philosophical basis for the Daoist religion and figures significantly in traditional Chinese medicine, the martial arts and Feng-Shui.

In Daoist thought the key concept is the *dao*—"the way." It refers to the way of ultimate reality. It is also the way of nature and, ethically, it is the way an individual ought to live. In other words, one ought to gear his or her life to the power and rhythms of the *dao.* One ought to live in harmony with nature. Because the *dao* is all pervasive it eliminates the source of all conflict and strife by flowing through and embracing all things. The *Daodejing* teaches that no living being can transgress its natural limits without upsetting the balance of the *dao.* Thus, the Daoist attempts to live in harmony with the underlying patterns that are the source of nature and charge.

Chapter 25 of the *Daodejing* illustrates the harmonious relationships we have been discussing:

> There is a thing confused yet perfect, which arose before
> > Heaven and Earth
> Still and indistinct, it stands alone and unchanging.
> It goes everywhere and is never at a loss.
> One can regard it as the mother of Heaven and Earth.
> I do not know its proper name;
> I have styled it "the Way."
> Forced to give it a proper name, I would call it "Great."
> The Great passes on;
> What passes on extends into the distance;
> What passes into the distance returns to its source.
> And so the Way is great;
> Heaven is great;
> Earth is great;
> And a true king too is great.
> In the universe are four things that are great and the true
> > king is first among them.
> People model themselves on the Earth.
> the Earth models itself on Heaven.
> Heaven models itself on the Way.
> The Way models itself on what is natural.[7]

Unfortunately, ethically unchecked desire leads to the pursuit of excessive wealth, power, and artificial goods. As a result the natural balance is upset and so is the well-being of the individual, society, other creatures and larger biological systems. Natural resources are exploited for personal gain or ravaged in a mad rush to secure corporate profits. Daoist wisdom teaches that such unnatural and excessive desires never lead to a satisfying, fulfilled life and are destructive of the very processes that sustain life.

We have already discussed Confucian ethics in some detail in Chapter 4, "Virtue Ethics." Kongzi (Confucius) was concerned to establish social structures and conventions that would ensure right conduct—conduct that would promote harmony with the *dao*.

Kongzi, in dealing with the human world, attempted to ground his philosophy in the natural order of things. He reasoned that human beings, BY NATURE, are social beings. Human beings, he concluded, are nourished, cared for, and flourish best within the structure of the family as governed by the Five Cardinal Relationships. This notion of the family is extended to the entire nation and all relationships are governed by the virtues *ren*—"humanness," "goodness," "human heartedness," or "humaneness," *li*—"ritual propriety" or "appropriateness" as defined by rites and ritual and *shu*—"reciprocity" or "mutual consideration." By way of the virtue *li*, Kongzi ritualized proper conduct and life, in effect, became a performance designed to further the natural harmony. According to Master Kong, "Achieving harmony is the most valuable function of observing ritual propriety."[8]

The difference in both the focus and emphasis of distinct cultural views with respect to environmental ethics offers opportunities for mutual benefit, learning, and enrichment by opening up the scope of the dialogue. In a world of pluralistic cultural values an expanded field of possibilities makes room for alternative responses to serious environmental challenges that are not easily resolved within the limitations of a single cultural viewpoint.

Conclusion

As has been the case with most of the moral issues I have presented in this book, I have tried to present as fairly as I can the extreme pro and con positions. In some cases I also have presented a moderate position. Perhaps the most important question we are left with, after contemplating the moral issues connected with the natural environment, is to what extent it is possible for a balance to be achieved between civilization and its progress and the natural environment and all it contains. Civilization in and of itself is not a bad thing. Human beings have had magnificent achievements through their civilization; at times they even have worked ingeniously to preserve what is best in nature. People who argue for such preservation feel that human beings must never forget that they come from and are a part of nature and that they must always treat it with respect. To the extent that they do not, they will eventually only hurt themselves as well as all the living beings around them.

Cases for Study and Discussion

CASE 1 Seal Hunting

Every year in order to satisfy the demands for seal fur coats, hundreds, even thousands, of baby harp seals are bashed to death on the ice by groups of villagers for whom the sale of such animal skins is the major industry of their village. What occurs is a bloody massacre of a large part of the seal community. Animal rights activists decry this wholesale slaughter of an animal species that is quite innocent and that does not endanger anyone's life. Such slaughter takes place for the sole purpose of satisfying female vanity throughout the "civilized" world when perfectly good synthetic furs could serve the same purpose. The villagers, on the other hand, make their living basically by killing the baby seals and probably would live in poverty if they didn't have this particular business activity. This issue could be extended to include many other animals as well. If you know of other species involved in such "harvesting," present the problem and answer the following questions for that issue also. Do you think that what the villagers are doing is morally right? Why or why not? Can the needs of the villagers be balanced against the lives of the seals? How? What solution to this problem would you suggest?

CASE 2 Killing Animals for Furs

In an Ann Landers column, an upset woman wrote in because someone had criticized her for wearing a rabbit fur coat. She had been asked, "I wonder how many beautiful rabbits died so you could have that coat?" The woman noticed that her questioner was wearing a down coat and retorted, "Do you think the geese they got the down from which to make your coat are still alive?" Ann Landers stated that most of the fur produced in North America is raised on family farms and added that in her opinion it is no more cruel to kill animals for their fur than it is to kill them for food or their hides. She wondered further whether critics of killing animals for fur would be willing to give up their shoes, belts, handbags, saddles, and luggage and any meat they might eat at meals.[9] What do you think of these statements and questions? Is the killing of animals any more justified for food, hides, or feathers than it is for furs? Why or why not? Support your answers in detail. Does it make any difference whether animals are raised on family farms or trapped in the wild? Why or why not? Is there any way to be consistent or to justify inconsistencies when it comes to the use of animals for food, hides, feathers, or furs? For example, someone wrote a letter to the editor of a newspaper stating that the setting on fire by the Animal Liberation Front of a store that sold animal furs is no more justified than setting a restaurant on fire for killing and cooking chickens. How would you sort out and differentiate these issues? Explain in detail.

CASE 3 Oil Spills

A major oil corporation constantly advertises in newspapers, magazines, and on radio and television about what it is doing to protect the environment and endangered species. At the same time, it is responsible for oil spills caused by carelessness both on land and at sea, which, of course, destroy all kinds of sea life and animals that live there. When such spills occur, unless they happen to hit the newspapers because they cannot be hidden from public view, employees are told to clean up the spills, but not to tell anyone outside of the company or even inside the company who does not already know about it. This, of course, would seem to be hypocrisy of the worst kind. Do you think the oil company should spend more time and money on preventing oil spills than on building shelters for some endangered species? Why or why not? What would make the company less hypocritical? Answer in detail. Should the company keep such spills secret when they are unknown to the public, or do they owe the public the right to have that information as well as the advertisements about what they're doing to protect the environment? Why or why not? Is it all right to keep such spills secret because it's good for business? Why or why not?

CASE 4 Animal Testing and Cosmetics

A certain company that manufactures cosmetics uses rabbits to test the irritancy level of its products to their eyes for purposes of making nonirritating cosmetics for the eyes of women who will use such cosmetics. Large doses of any substance to be used are injected into one eye of the rabbits, while the other eye is left alone for comparison of any damage done. The test is painful, and anesthetics are not used on rabbits. Since large doses have to be used in order to provide a greater margin of safety for possible eventual use on humans, permanent eye damage often occurs. No tests that avoid using animals have ever been developed. Is this type of testing moral? Why or why not? Would the use of rabbits for this purpose be more morally acceptable if they were given painkillers? Why or why not? Since the products are to be used on humans, should the company ask for human volunteers with the same safeguards being required as for other types of human experimentation? Why or why not? Do you think animal experimentation is more morally justifiable if it's done for medical reasons—for example, to find a pain relief medication or cure for certain diseases? Why or why not?

CASE 5 Extinction of Small Fish

A dam was proposed to be built on a certain river in a natural setting that would produce hydroelectric power and create recreational activities, such as boating, swimming, and waterskiing. The only problem, as environmentalists see it, is that there is a certain species of small fish found only in this river that will become extinct if the dam is built. The fish is not used for food or sport; in fact, no one knows what purpose it serves by being in the river. Should the dam be built? Why or why not? Would it make a difference to your answer if the small fish were a good food fish or could be used in some other commercial way, or does its possible extinction constitute a sufficient reason to not build the dam? Explain your answer in detail.

Chapter Summary

I. Key terms
  A. *Speciesism* is a prejudice for one's own species and against other species.
  B. *Sentientism* is the theory that only those beings with mental states should be the subject of moral concern.
  C. *Wholism* is a conception of nature that sees humans and nature together as forming a moral community.
  D. *Vegetarianism* is the refusal to eat the flesh of animals in favor of a diet of vegetables.
  E. An *endangered species* is a species of animals in danger of becoming extinct because of the encroachment of civilization upon the natural environment and because of careless exploitation by human beings.

II. Nature and morality
  A. Human beings have discovered in recent years that natural resources, including animals, plants, and trees, are not boundless but are subject to diminishment, destruction, and loss.
  B. This will affect us with regard to the social aspect of our morality (refer to Chapter 1 for a discussion of the four aspects), but many consider that nature also is valuable in itself.

III. Environmental ethical issues
  A. We cannot continue the waste and destruction of natural resources, but must take action now to conserve and replenish what we take from nature for our own uses.
  B. Neither can we continue to exploit, misuse, and pollute the environment.

C. There also is the ethical issue of animal rights.
1. Many people feel that with our modern products and food availability, we no longer should be destroying animals for food and body parts (fur, skin, tusks).
2. Also, we must be much more humane in the way we raise domestic animals for food.
3. We either should not use animals at all for scientific experimentation, or use them only sparingly and, again, humanely.
4. We must also be more careful to ensure that various animal species are not decimated or made extinct.

IV. Our attitude toward nature and what lies behind it
A. These attitudes have not developed overnight.
B. Platonic dualism and the beginnings of Western philosophy, which essentially saw human beings as being separate from and superior to the external world and nature, tended to split human beings off from nature.
C. Judeo-Christian teachings in the Bible taught that human beings are imbued with a soul whereas the rest of nature is not, and that human beings have dominion over all of nature and should "go forth and multiply."
D. With the advancement of science and technology nature has become, at least from the human point of view, more and more subservient to human beings.
E. Industrialization not only has increased the use of natural resources for its operation but also has polluted the environment through the disposing of waste.
F. Through industrialization, population increases, and the greater need for land and space, civilization has encroached upon nature, destroying more and more of the natural environment.

V. Arguments for use and exploitation of the natural environment
A. There are two types of the dominion-over-nature argument.
1. Religious: Western religions seem to condone this type of dominion citing various statements in the Bible.
2. Natural order and evolution: In this view, human beings are considered to be the highest evolved species in nature, so they should exercise power over the rest of it.
B. Civilization is more important than nature. Because humans constitute the highest evolutionary and religious order, human civilization should take precedence over nature.
C. Humans and only humans are deserving of moral rights and obligations.

VI. Arguments against the use and exploitation of nature
A. Monistic wholism versus dominion and domination. Human beings and nature are parts of a whole and not separated into dominant and subordinate groups.
1. Religious arguments about the superiority of humans have either been misinterpreted or are irrelevant.
2. That humans have evolved to a higher level of intelligence does not mean they automatically are entitled to dominion over nature. Someday they could be replaced by a more advanced species.
3. The proper relationship between human beings and nature is wholistic rather than dominant and subordinate.
B. Reasoning should not separate humans from nature but should unite them both more closely. Reasoning should lead to an acceptance of nature as being intrinsically valuable.
C. Nature, which contains most human needs and which relates to humans in a vital way, should never be made subordinate to civilization, which is human-constructed.

VII. The moderate position
   A. Nature is important and significant but not necessarily on the same footing with humans.
   B. It may therefore be used for human ends but with care so as not to endanger or destroy it.
   C. This position generally agrees with the wholistic position but is not against using nature for the good of humans as long as it is done carefully, allowing for the preservation and protection of the environment.

VIII. Criteria for animal rights
   A. One criterion states that anything that is alive is deserving of moral consideration. Critics would argue against this.
      1. It is too vague and unrealistic, and also it seems to violate the way in which nature itself works (e.g., the natural food chain).
      2. Even human life is not valued merely for its own sake; the taking of human life can be declared to be moral under certain circumstances.
   B. Those who have interests have rights. Therefore, because animals have interests (e.g., to survive, not to suffer pain), they have rights.
   C. Attributes of soul, mind, and feelings. Some would argue that moral consideration is based upon whether or not beings have these attributes.
      1. The difficulty of proving the existence of a soul is a problem with this argument as is the question of why such an attribute should be the only criterion for moral consideration. And who knows whether or not animals have souls? Some religions believe they do.
      2. Animals have both minds and feelings and therefore satisfy this aspect of the criterion.
   D. Proponents would state that animals seem to possess the power of reason, at least at the rudimentary level (e.g., chimpanzees and gorillas can learn sign language) and therefore should be considered as having moral rights.
      1. Some humans have severe mental impairment and can barely reason, if at all. If we have moral obligations toward them, why not toward animals?
      2. It would seem that a creature's having mental states at all (being sentient) would require from us at least the obligation not to inflict pain upon it.
      3. Opponents of animal rights would argue that any mental states that animals may have are so far below those of humans that animals are deserving of little or no moral concern.

IX. Ways of dealing with animal rights
   A. True vegetarians (vegans) do not use animals for food at all.
   B. There are arguments against vegetarianism.
      1. Even if animals have rights, they are less important than the rights of humans, so the latter have a right to use the former for food, just as animals use other animals, according to nature's way.
      2. Sentientism, which states that animals should be morally respected because they have mental states, is criticized because it tends to eliminate nonanimal life-forms such as plants, flowers, and trees.
      3. Advocates of wholism would argue that sentientism and vegetarianism are too narrow and merely single out one aspect of nature for moral concern; they argue that all of nature is deserving of such respect. Critics of wholism, on the other hand, argue that it blurs proper distinctions in the hierarchy of beings in nature.

X. Use of animals for food
   A. Is it moral to kill sentient beings possessing all of the attributes previously described, and use them for food?

B. Ways of raising animals for food.
   1. In the past, domesticated animals were raised in the open air on ranches or farms.
   2. Now, given the greater demand for meat and other animal products (e.g., eggs, milk), factory farming, in which animals often are raised in narrow pens without light and air and often are separated from their mothers, is the method used.
C. The vegetarian is absolutely against raising animals for food; moreover, vegetarians are aghast at the current methods used.
D. The carnivore (meat eater) feels that the main purpose of raising animals is for food and that any method that will give human beings better quality meat more efficiently is certainly acceptable.
E. The moderate position condones using animals for food but does not accept wholesale slaughter, factory farming, or mistreatment of any kind where animals are concerned.

XI. Use of animals for experimentation
   A. There are several arguments for animal experimentation.
      1. Scientists argue that without our ability to use animals for experimentation, humans would have to be used and would be harmed or killed, or no cures for diseases could ever be found.
      2. Because, by law, humans cannot be used for experimentation without their informed consent and the application of strict guidelines, scientific and medical progress would simply come to a standstill without animals.
      3. They argue further that animals have much less value than human beings, so it is morally correct to use the former for purposes of experimentation.
      4. Many of the animals used would just be put to sleep anyway because they are not wanted; therefore, why not have their deaths serve a purpose and help human beings?
   B. Arguments against using animals for experimentation also exist.
      1. Animals are thinking and feeling beings that suffer pain to the same extent and degree as do humans; therefore, it is immoral to make animals suffer and die merely so that humans can make progress in science and medicine.
      2. Furthermore, many experiments are absolutely unnecessary to the health and well-being of human beings and are done simply out of scientific curiosity.
      3. Animal rights activists feel that it is absolutely immoral to use animals for any experiments and that if other means cannot be found, then scientific progress simply will not be able to be made.
   C. There is also a moderate position.
      1. Moderates would not be opposed to using animals for experimentation but would insist that such experiments must be absolutely necessary to the health and well-being of humans and not be done merely in order to satisfy human curiosity.
      2. Care must be taken not to inflict upon animals more pain and suffering during the experiment than is absolutely necessary—every effort must be made to keep animals out of pain while experiments are going on.

XII. Killing animals for sport
   A. There are arguments for killing animals for sport.
      1. Hunting is an ancient activity that is a significant rite of manhood. It was done in the earliest tribes and cultures and should continue on even today.
      2. It is the best way of keeping the animal population under control; if not controlled, animals will destroy our crops, kill our domesticated animals, and encroach upon our cities.

      3. There is a need for wild animal meat and body parts.
- (a) Even though they have all the domesticated animal meat they might need, many people prefer wild game, such as venison and pheasant, and they should be allowed to indulge their tastes.
- (b) Even though clothes and other items can be made from the skins of domestic animals or from synthetic products, the more exotic skins and body parts (snakeskin, elephant tusks, fur) are prettier and rarer, and so valued more highly.
- (c) It is exciting to have the heads of wild animals a hunter has killed displayed on the walls, and it is unique to have such possessions as elephant-foot wastebaskets.

  B. There are also arguments against killing animals for sport.
1. Hunting is an ancient activity that is, however, no longer required. Men originally hunted in order to gain for food and clothing, but now both can be acquired without killing wild animals in order to do so.
2. The animal population will control itself if humans will only allow it to do so. Killing animals such as the mountain lion has eliminated from nature predators that would control other animal populations by hunting and killing them for food.
3. There is absolutely no further need for wild game or body parts, given the plethora of domesticated animal meat and wonderful human-made products, such as synthetic furs, that are now available.

  C. The moderate position seeks a midpoint between the extremes.
1. Killing for sport can be allowed on a limited basis as long as endangered species are protected and other species don't become endangered.
2. There is no reason to kill wild animals for meat or body parts except where and when it is allowed within the limits of (1) above.

XIII. Protection of endangered species
  A. An irreverence for even a small segment of life affects one's reverence for all life.
  B. Most species are beautiful or at least interesting and different, and they should be available not only for us but our children, grandchildren, and great-grandchildren to see.
  C. All animals seem to contribute in some way to the balance of nature and its food chain, and we should be careful not to upset that balance.

XIV. Non-Western perspectives on environmental issues
  A. Because environmental issues are global in scope and implications raised by these important issues of concern affect people the world over, it will be worthwhile to briefly note the value of non-Western ethical viewpoints.
  B. The immanent worldviews of Hinduism and Buddhism, which stress the oneness and interconnectedness of the natural order, present clear alternatives to Western transcendent perspectives where human beings stand over/against nature.
  C. The grand goal of Chinese thought is to achieve harmony and balance.
  D. In Daoist thought the key concept is the *dao*—the way. It refers to the way of ultimate reality, the way of nature and, ethically, the way that one ought to live.
  E. Confucianism attempts to extend the way by establishing social conventions and Kongzi ritualized proper conduct in order that life, in effect, becomes a performance that is designed to further natural harmony.
  F. In a world of pluralistic cultural values an expanded field of possibilities makes room for alternative responses to serious environmental challenges that are not easily resolved within the limitations of a single cultural viewpoint.

Exercises for Review

1. What do the following key terms mean, and how do they relate to environmental ethics: *speciesism, sentientism, wholism, vegetarianism, endangered species?*
2. Do you agree with the author's view that we have come to our destructive attitudes concerning the environment from our backgrounds in Western philosophy and Western religion? Why or why not? If you do not believe that either has had anything to do with these attitudes, then what has caused us to have them? Answer in detail.
3. If you believe that the Judeo-Christian Bible really does not condone the way in which we control, waste, and destroy nature, then present evidence from the Bible or Judeo-Christian teachings that encourages reverence, protection, and preservation of nature.
4. Do you think the only and major reason for preserving and protecting nature is to protect our own good, or do you feel that we have a moral obligation toward nature because it is intrinsically valuable? Present arguments in detail.
5. Present arguments as to why we should protect endangered species. What differences does it really make if certain species become extinct? Doesn't nature itself cause some species to become extinct? What difference does it make if human beings do the same thing? Answer in detail.
6. Which is more important: civilization and progress or the natural environment? Why?
7. Do you believe that animals have rights, and do you believe that we have an obligation to see that these rights are protected? Why or why not? If you argue that they do have rights, what are they, and why?
8. What is your position on vegetarianism, and why? Defend or attack the vegetarian position, giving good reasons and arguments for whichever side you take.
9. Do you believe we should use animals for experimentation purposes? Why, or why not? Take a pro, con, or moderate position, and say why you have chosen it.
10. Do you think it is moral to hunt animals for meat, body parts, or sport? Why, or why not? Give good reasons for your answer.
11. Select an important issue in environmental ethics and analyze it from a Hindu, Buddhist, Daoist or Confucian perspective.

Views of the Major Ethical Theories on Environmental Ethics

Describe as fully as you can how each of the major ethical theories—Ethical Egoism, Utilitarianism, Divine Command Theory, Kant's Duty Ethics, Ross' *Prima Facie* Duties, and Virtue Ethics—probably would deal with the ethical issues related to the environment including the cases at the end of the chapter. Refer to Chapters 2, 3 and 4 for a description of the theories and to Chapter 9, "The Taking of Human Life," for an example of how you might go about completing this assignment.

Notes

1. Joel Feinberg, "The Rights of Animals and Unborn Generations," *Philosophical Environmental Crisis,* ed. W. Blackstone (Athens: University of Georgia Press, 1974), 48–68.
2. James White, ed., *Contemporary Moral Problems,* 2nd ed. (St. Paul, MN: West, 1988), 315.
3. Ibid.

4.   Michael C. Brannigan, *The Pulse of Wisdom: The Philosophies of India, China and Japan,* 2nd ed. (Belmont, CA: Wadsworth/Thompson Learning, 2000), 4.

5.   Ward J. Fellows, *Religions East and West* (New York: Holt, Rinehart and Winston, 1979), 71.

6.   Saral Jhingran, *Aspects of Hindu Morality* (Delhi: Motilal Banarsidass, 1989), 34.

7.   Philip J. Ivanhoe, trans., *The Daodejing of Laozi* (New York: Seven Bridges Press, 2002), 25.

8.   Roger T. Ames and Henry Rosemont Jr., trans., *The Analects of Confucius: A Philosophical Translation* (New York: Ballantine Publishing Group, 1998), 74.

9.   Ann Landers, "For Fur or Food, Killing's the Same," *The Bakersfield Californian* 103 (86) (March 27, 1989), D4.

Research Navigator™
(http://www.researchnavigator.com)

This web site offers three research databases: EBSCO's *Content Select Academic Journal and Abstract Database, New York Times* Search by Subject Archive, and *Best of the Web* Link Library. In addition, this site provides helpful advice on how to conduct efficient and productive research from choosing a topic to polishing the final draft. Beginning philosophy students probably will find the *Best of the Web* Link Library the most appropriate place to start their research.

The free access code necessary to employ Research Navigator™ can be found in the Prentice Hall Guide to Evaluating Online Resources. If your text did not come with this guide, please go to *www.prenhall.com/contentselect* for information on how you can purchase an access code.

Appendixes

Introduction

My own views as to how the various moral issues discussed in this book might be dealt with and resolved are presented in the following appendixes. My views are based upon Humanitarian Ethics, as outlined in Chapter 8, and the eight appendixes coincide with Chapters 9 through 16 in the text.

Neither instructors nor students are in any way obligated to use these appendixes. However, they may find that after considering the issues themselves, it is interesting to get another point of view on the problems beyond those of the eight major ethical theories described in Chapters 2, 3, and 4. Furthermore, they may find it useful to analyze and critically evaluate a series of attempts to deal with and solve these problems.

Readers, of course, should not consider themselves bound by these opinions and theories. Instead, it is my hope that they will serve as a catalyst for exciting and profound discussion of the moral issues that we all find so crucial to our daily lives. Instructors may assign each appendix with its respective chapter, posing various discussion questions for students to deal with; they may hold off assigning the appendixes until after students have formed their own theories and solutions to the issues and problems discussed; or they need not assign the appendixes at all. No matter how they are used, I sincerely hope they will serve some useful educational purpose.

1

Applying Humanitarian Ethics to the Moral Problems of the Taking of Human Life

Suicide

General Discussion of the Problem

In the matter of suicide, four of the basic principles—Value of Life, Goodness, Justice, and Freedom—are or may be directly involved. The Principle of Truth Telling and Honesty is only indirectly involved, if at all. For example, if telling a lie or being dishonest could cause someone to commit suicide, then of course the principle would come into play. In the discussion of the priority of the five principles in Chapter 8, I stated that Life and Goodness should come first, so let us begin our discussion of suicide by examining how they come into play with regard to the suicide issue.

Because life is to be valued, efforts must be put forth, within reason, to avoid or prevent suicides, and certainly nothing should be done to cause them. However, as I have said, the value of life is determined most importantly by the person who holds or lives that life. This does not mean that the rest of society does not have some say in whether a person's life is valuable—obviously it does. Society often feels that it has the right to protect its members from others (by means of laws against murder and rape, for example) and even from themselves (through the prevention or stopping of suicides or self-mutilation wherever possible). But how far may we go in deciding on other people's behalf that they should go on living when they themselves have decided that their lives are no longer of value to themselves and that they therefore should be ended? The Principle of Goodness also comes into play in that we generally hold that life is a good—according to many, the highest good—but we must ask ourselves who, in fact, decides that this is so. A general consensus that life is good is one thing; however, an individual's judgment that his or her own life is good is quite another. Who should be the final decision maker here?

It would seem empirically obvious that as long as people are rational, they should have the final decision over whether their lives are valuable or good and, therefore, whether they should continue or be ended. At this point, the Principle of Individual Freedom enters the discussion in a most significant way. Generally speaking, life should be revered, protected, and valued, but decisions concerning people's own lives or deaths should primarily be left up to them. Note that this in no way means that people have the right to make decisions about anyone else's life or death; it merely means that the freedom to decide whether life is good or valuable rests with the individual holding or living that life.

Conflicts can arise between this principle and the Principle of Justice, however, in that the taking of one's life quite often involves the lives and well-being of other people. Is it fair or just, for example, for a husband and father who decides that his life is not worth living to commit suicide when so doing will obviously adversely affect his wife and children, his parents and relatives, his friends, and his coworkers? Though his life and death in the fullest sense are his own, can one dismiss the fact that because he has established significant relationships with others, his life relates to them in a very important way?

This also involves the Principle of Goodness in a new way in that suicide may deprive the loved ones left behind of some goodness. It is true that this man's life may not have been good for him, but how much badness will now descend on the innocent people around him because of his actions? I see this—the conflict between the Principles of Freedom and Justice—as constituting the major problem to be considered when one is attempting to decide whether suicide is moral or immoral.

Generally, then, I would say that suicide is not in itself an immoral act because decisions about the goodness and value of life must be made freely by each person about his or her own life. However, I feel that efforts must be made to help suicidal people seek other alternatives and that help should be given to them in resolving their problems and improving their lives. I also feel that when others are involved, efforts ought to be made by the suicidal people not to cause harm or badness to these people through their act—in other words, the Principle of Justice should be observed wherever possible.

However, the final decision about each person's own life must rest with the person involved, and severe punishment or incarceration should not be used to prevent people from making their own decisions freely. This does not mean that suicidal people cannot be temporarily hospitalized or given therapy, but punishment or incarceration or blame should not be heaped upon them merely because they have decided to commit suicide.

Discussion of Specific Cases

CASE 1

William's act is a moral one. It might have been preferable if he had accepted the hospice approach to his care, but accepting or refusing medical treatment was his choice, and if he decided that his life should be ended, then I feel he had the right to make that decision. Furthermore, he generally eliminated any conflicts with the Justice principle as far as his family was concerned by discussing his desires with them. Under Humanitarian Ethics, then, he made a moral choice, even though not committing suicide would also have been a moral alternative in this instance.

CASE 2

I believe that Joan's decision to commit suicide was a moral one even though it probably would have been preferable for her to seek further help in making her life more worthwhile to her. However, I respect her feelings about her own life and her decision that, as far as she was concerned, nothing else could be done to help her. She didn't seem to be involving anyone close to her (family or friends) by committing suicide, so the Justice principle doesn't apply too closely. Because she made her decision "calmly," I feel she had thought the situation over carefully and made a choice between continuing what she considered to be a miserable existence and ending that existence. She chose a viable alternative and made a rational choice.

Defense of the Innocent (The Self Included)

General Discussion of the Problem

If one or more human beings unjustly threatened the lives of other human beings, then one is morally justified in defending oneself and others against the aggressor, who has violated the major ethical principle having to do with the value of life. Such aggressors also have violated or are threatening to violate three other principles in that they are depriving their victims of their individual freedom, they are taking away goodness in their victims' lives and replacing it with badness, and they are treating the victims unjustly and unequally because the victims have as much right to exist as they do.

In violating these principles, such aggressors forfeit their right to equal consideration under the five basic principles. Thus, according to the Value of Life principle, their prospective victims or others should attempt to stop them peacefully or by any means short of killing; if no such means are possible, however, then they are justified in killing such aggressors.

Exactly what does "morally justified defense of other innocent people and self" mean, and what criteria are available to indicate when this condition prevails? To begin with, someone's life must *actually* be threatened; that is, there must be as little doubt as possible that an aggressor really intends to kill someone. That a person is insulting, aggravating, obnoxious, or mean is not sufficient reason to take his life. Even if a person steals from you, ruins your business, or slanders your good name, you are not justified in killing him; there must be an actual threat to your or someone else's life as signified by some overt action.

For example, if a man holds a gun on you and asks for your wallet or purse, you may or may not be justified in killing him; but if he says that he will kill you regardless of what you do, then you have every right to kill him first. In any case, you do have the right to defend yourself against robbery or any other kind of lesser threat than death, and if in wrestling a gun from a robber the gun goes off and kills him, that is self-defense because there was an equal chance that either of you could have been killed, and the robber was responsible for bringing a deadly weapon onto the scene in the first place.

People also have the right to defend themselves against any physical violation of their person, such as rape or serious permanent injury, and are permitted to use any means, including killing, in this defense. They always should attempt to use peaceful means first, however, followed by any means short of killing. Once it is determined that a person intends to seriously injure or kill someone, however, then killing the aggressor is justified. Here the phrase "innocent people, including oneself" refers to the would-be victims or the victims of an unjust aggression.

The justification for defense of the innocent and of oneself is that a person who is threatening innocent people with death is violating all five ethical principles; therefore, the innocent have a right to defend themselves against one who has "proved himself morally unequal" through a willingness and desire to violate the ethical bases of all humanity and the lives and persons of others. As I have said before, the innocent have the right to kill in their defense, but they are not obligated to do so.

If people feel so strongly about the Value of Life principle that they cannot take a life under any circumstances, then they may, of course, forfeit their own lives rather than kill another. I am making allowances here for pacifists in Christianity as well as in other religions. It is difficult to say that "true Christians" could be anything other than pacifists after hearing and reading such statements by Jesus as "Love your enemies" and "Turn the other cheek." This would be an admirably consistent view of the Value of Life principle, which few Christians or any other human beings, for that matter, follow very closely. Nevertheless, people certainly ought to have the option of losing their own lives rather than taking the life of another, just as they have the right to commit suicide because only their lives are involved. Therefore, defense of the innocent, including the self, is morally justified as a right but not an obligation under the five basic ethical principles.

Discussion of Specific Cases

CASE 1

In view of the general discussion just presented, I don't believe, under Humanitarian Ethics, that Ed was morally justified in killing the young man. I am not condoning the thief's actions, but I do not feel that the punishment Ed meted out fit the crime of stealing. In the case description, there is no evidence that the thief had the intention or even the capability of doing Ed bodily harm or killing him. Ed might have been justified in firing his pistol over the thief's head or even at his legs, but he was not morally justified in killing him. Since Ed got a good look at the thief, the proper moral approach to this problem would be to give this information to the police and let them deal with the thief.

CASE 2

I believe that Mary was fully justified in trying to protect herself against rape and assault as well as possible death. Under such stressful circumstances, she could not fully judge whether or not the rapist intended to kill her, but she was fully justified in protecting herself against a threat of bodily harm or death. She was not in a position to reason with the man or to use gentler means than killing him to prevent him from attacking her; therefore, I believe her act was morally justified.

CASE 3

I believe that the police officer's act was fully justified because innocent people already had been killed or injured and were still being threatened. The police had tried and pretty well exhausted other means to stop the sniper and bring him under control—all attempts had failed. Therefore, because the sniper had violated four of the five basic principles—life, goodness, justice, and freedom—there was no need to grant him any further ethical considerations, and he could be killed.

War

General Discussion of the Problem

Especially in this century, because of the horrendous potential for total destruction when even small wars are waged, many pacifists have felt that war is totally wrong and that people should allow themselves or their country to be attacked without resisting. Some suggest that if settlements of grievances cannot be made peacefully, then any further resistance to invasion also must be made peacefully. However, most people favor at least "national self-defense," and some go so far as to extend such defense to aggressive acts against other countries who "might" threaten their nation with war, or with anything else for that matter.

Generally speaking, war violates all five ethical principles. It seriously violates the Value of Life principle by killing millions, some of whom are not even combatants in the war; it causes a great deal more badness than goodness in most cases and usually distributes goodness and badness unequally; it almost always necessitates lies and dishonesty by means of propaganda on both sides and in the dealings between or among warring factions; and it always encroaches upon many people's freedom, from the involuntary drafting of civilians to the destruction of property and severe injury affecting millions of unwilling participants. Given such serious violations of the five basic principles, one has cause to wonder if pacifism isn't the best solution to the problem of war.

I believe that many of the requirements that have been set down with regard to justifying the defense of the innocent and self-defense can also be used to justify a limited war. A nation is morally justified in entering into a war if it is unjustly and overtly attacked by an aggressor nation, but only after all peaceful means to settle differences or stop aggression have failed. Few if any other reasons can justify such a destructive process. As the earlier Catholic version—a version with which I agree in part—has it, war should not be conducted for purposes of national prestige, influence, or the desire for territory or power.

In short, the defense of innocent human beings is the only valid reason there can be for going to war. I believe that such a requirement was met in World War II, but not in the wars that followed it. During World War II, Germany, Italy, and Japan were set on a path of power, prestige, and mass killing rarely equaled in history. They were the aggressors, time and time again, and there can be no doubt that they carried out the torture and destruction of millions of innocent human beings. Therefore, I believe that the nations that entered the war to stop these three aggressor nations were justified in so doing.

The situations in Korea and Vietnam were a different matter, however. Both of these conflicts were essentially civil wars of ideology within particular countries, and the United States' part in these wars is rather difficult to justify. The Vietnam War is particularly difficult to justify because the reasons for U.S. involvement in it are muddy and suspiciously involved with national prestige, power, and protection of economic interests. None of the five basic ethical principles would suggest that these constitute sufficient or honorable reasons for going to war. The Iraq war is another war which is questionable. The United States has again become involved in another country's internal affairs. Also, it seems that the basis of the invasion was not called for and based on faulty intelligence.

As for terrorism, Humanitarian Ethics would classify this major cause of the deaths of innocent victims as one of the most reprehensible crimes that groups or countries can commit. First, terrorists generally don't declare war on the people they kill. Instead, they attack without warning and have no regard for the lives of the innocent people who happen to be destroyed by them. In all of the recent terrorist bombings, hundreds of innocent people have been killed. One thinks of the 1972 killing of Jewish athlete hostages at the Munich Olympics, the Pan American plane blown up over Scotland, the World Trade Center bombing in New York City and its later destruction by U.S. commercial planes commandeered by terrorists,, the Oklahoma City bombing, the bombing at the 1996 Atlanta Olympics—all of these activities and many more have resulted in the unwarned and untimely deaths of far too many innocent people. These actions are immoral and unjustified, and when the perpetrators are caught they should be punished severely, including capital punishment or life imprisonment without parole.

Because wars and terrorism are essentially immoral, the sooner all destructive weapons can be eliminated from human culture, the better off humanity will be. Perhaps it is not possible to stop all human beings from fighting one another, but if the most destructive means are no longer allowed to exist, then the intensity of such fighting will be significantly reduced.

I personally feel that firearms of all kinds should be destroyed and that the provision of the Constitution dealing with the right to bear arms ought to be amended to state that "no one has the right to bear arms," including law enforcement personnel. All firearms and explosives, especially the nuclear kind, should be banned throughout the world except for peaceful uses, and some method introduced to ensure that none is ever again manufactured. This is, of course, an ideal for which, I feel, we must continue to strive; in the meantime, the best we can do is to keep attempting to reduce the armaments of war and do everything possible to ban wars themselves until the weapons can be eliminated.

Because war, except in defense of innocent people against clear aggression, is immoral, no one should be required to participate in an unjust war. If people can show by their lives and their actions that they are opposed to violence on a moral basis, they should not have to participate in any war that they consider to be unjust if they can provide logical argument to support their contention. Furthermore, as with self-defense and defense of the innocent, if a person refuses on moral grounds to kill other human beings, even in a just war, then this person's pacifistic viewpoint should be respected without recrimination of any kind.

Discussion of Specific Cases

CASE 1

The large country is, of course, completely unjustified in attacking the small country. It has violated not only all five ethical principles, but also the requirements we have discussed for a just war. The small country is morally justified in conducting war to defend itself and its innocent people; it has made every attempt to resolve the problem in a peaceful way, and the only choices it now has are to succumb to an immoral invasion or to try to ward off such an invasion by defending itself in as moral a way as it can.

CASE 2

The large, aggressive country is, of course, immoral, having violated every one of the five basic ethical principles and the requirements for a morally just war. Furthermore, it is continuing to conduct a campaign of death and destruction of innocent people. The alliance has attempted to negotiate and has failed; therefore, it is morally justified in trying to stop the large, aggressive power from continuing to wage war, especially considering the fact that nuclear weapons are not involved.

CASE 3

It would seem that because the two halves of the small country have some ideological beliefs in common, they ought to make a greater attempt to negotiate a compromise or establish a coalition government. Therefore, their civil war does not seem to be morally justified. Instead of providing money, arms, and supplies, the larger powers, which have vested interests in the country, should do everything they can to encourage peace by assisting with negotiations.

Perhaps they can even supply nonmilitary goods such as medicines, food, and clothes, but they should not supply weapons or military assistance. They have a right to protect their vested interests in the country but not to the extent of waging or helping to wage war. The actions of country B were particularly questionable because it supplied its own armed forces, thus obviously escalating the war. The interference of the two outside powers merely prolongs the war, whereas without outside help the war might peter out, especially if the two outside powers push heavily for negotiation between the two sides.

Capital Punishment

General Discussion of the Problem

Innocent people have every moral right to be protected against those who kill or who seriously threaten to kill others. But how should this protection be gained? It can be gained most conclusively if one who has killed is also killed; in this way, at least, this person cannot kill again. Very little proof exists that killing such a person will prevent others from killing, however. The innocent also can protect themselves by separating such killers from them, whether in mental institutions (if the killer is insane) or in prisons.

The ideal situation would be to somehow correct or change the person who has killed so that we could know with certainty that he or she would never kill again except in self-defense or defense of the innocent; psychology and psychiatry have not been able to effect such a change, however. As a matter of fact, they have had a number of failures with regard to their estimates of the rehabilitation of criminals who have killed, and unfortunately such failures often have resulted in the taking of more innocent human lives.

The major question here, of course, is "Are we morally justified in taking the life of someone who has committed a capital crime?" In previous discussions, I certainly have not accepted the Value of Life principle as an absolute that has no exception, and so I cannot with any consistency say that capital punishment is *never* justified. I have said that people have rights to their own lives, and that no one should take people's lives against their will or free consent. I also have argued for taking life as a last resort so as to protect other innocent lives.

Therefore, would it not also be considered defense of the innocent to take the life of known killers, so that they cannot kill again? There is one major difference between killing another in defense of the innocent and taking the life of one who already has killed. In the first case, we presume that there are no other alternatives—the innocent person either has attempted to avoid killing by peaceful means or has attempted to stop the killer by injury rather than death and has failed, leaving only the choice of "kill or let innocent people be killed." Because, in a capital punishment case, we cannot stop the victim who already is dead from being killed, we can only decide, on the basis of the five basic ethical principles, the best and most moral method of protecting other innocent people from being killed.

What alternatives are available? Most drastic of all, of course, is the alternative of actually killing the person who has killed. As I have stated, this will ensure that this person will not kill again but it is, of course, a violation of the Value of Life principle. However, because the killer already has violated this principle, and probably the other four principles as well, are we not justified in taking his or her life?

We can attempt to rehabilitate such killers so that they will never kill again. This, as I have said, is still very difficult. Our present methods are to incarcerate killers, either in a prison or a mental institution. Sometimes in prison an attempt at rehabilitation is made, the seriousness of the attempt varying from prison system to prison system.

Very often killers are merely separated from the rest of society until they can get paroled for good behavior or until they die naturally or are killed in prison. In mental institutions, efforts sometimes are made to find out what caused such people to kill and various sorts of therapy are tried, some with success and some without. In many cases psychopathic killers have been declared sane and released, only to kill again.

One part of the problem with either of these two alternatives is that there are not enough qualified people to do a thorough job of rehabilitation in either kind of institution. The other part of the problem is that we are not psychologically advanced enough to be able to state unequivocally that people have been "cured" of whatever caused them to kill in the first place, and that now we can be certain they never will kill again. Also, there many sociopaths who can't be cured at all (see "amoral" in Chapter 1). For now, at least, our only moral alternatives seem to be long-term imprisonment, life imprisonment without parole, or death.

It is possible that we may in the future become psychologically advanced enough to be able to state with certainty that people who have killed will never kill again. The way to do this, it seems to me, is to extensively study, both psychologically and physiologically, those who already have killed to find out what can be done to prevent other human beings from becoming killers.

For example, I always have felt that Caryl Chessman, the convicted so-called red-light bandit of California, after he had become more aware of himself as a human being as well as a criminal, was a real loss to the study of crime and the criminal. The present system of imprisonment is not satisfactory in that very little constructive study or rehabilitation is being done, partly because of society's views on the reason for imprisonment (punishment) and partly because of the lack of qualified social and medical scientists and facilities. The parole system is not entirely effective either, as some known killers can be paroled from a life sentence early, thus endangering the lives of innocent people. Neither of these approaches works very well.

I make the following suggestions with regard to improving the situation as it now exists. First, I feel that society is ethically justified in separating killers from innocent people, and that because such people have violated the five basic ethical principles so completely, they have forfeited their right to be seen as the moral equals of those who have not. They have not, however, forfeited all of their human rights. Therefore, I feel that the ethical thing would be for such killers to participate in the decision as to what is to be done with them (within the limitations of protecting others from any of their future actions).

Second, I think that state and federal governments ought to liberally finance extensive studies of convicted killers so as to discover the causes of their actions and with a view toward completely rehabilitating them and also preventing others from becoming killers in the future.

Third, known killers either should be given life imprisonment without parole or should be considered ineligible for parole for 50 years unless they become too sick or incapacitated to kill again or unless it can be stated with absolute certainty for some other reason that they never will kill again. This would provide society with more protection than it currently has, while still allowing killers to live, contributing significantly to the study of humanity.

Fourth, killers should have the alternative of being administered a lethal dose of some painless drug rather than having to spend 50 or more years in prison. In other words, killers themselves should make the choice between long-term imprisonment or death.

There are several precautions to be observed here:

1. It must be known for certain that such killers have killed. If there are any doubts as to this, then they ought to get a minimum of 20 years before they are eligible for parole, during which time they should be given every opportunity to appeal their case and prove their innocence. DNA should be used in every case where it applies to prove innocence or guilt.
2. The killing should either be a premeditated murder or a serious crime of passion, rather than an accidental death or a death caused by minor negligence. There should be penalties for these kinds of killings, too, but they should not be as stringent as those for "capital" crimes.
3. After killers have served 50 years, they ought to be *considered* for parole. If they are in any way still presumed to be dangerous, then parole should not be granted.
4. Every effort must be made to ensure that a killer's choice of death is not coerced in any way and that the chosen death is administered painlessly and mercifully.

I feel that this approach to dealing with killers in our society is much more moral than the haphazard way in which we deal with them now. With this approach, we attempt to observe the Value of Life principle, both for the innocent and for the killer; we attempt to bring about more good than bad by preventing the killers from killing again, by trying to discover the causes of human killing and the means to prevent it, and by protecting the innocent; we attempt to distribute the good justly; we are honest and truthful in allowing killers to decide their fate and making them aware of alternatives; and we try to allow for individual freedom, within limitations, both for the killer and for the innocent.

In the case of particularly heinous or vicious crimes and for serial killers, Humanitarian Ethics is not averse to applying capital punishment or life imprisonment without parole. In no way should any such criminal, if not capitally punished, be made eligible for parole at anytime.

Discussion of Specific Cases

CASE 1

The kidnapper-killer in this case, who survives, provides a very strong argument for not using capital punishment. Despite his terrible crime and all of the damage it caused to the victim and his family, this killer was able to contribute a great deal to society, yet society still was protected from him until he was deemed to be safe to parole. Not every killer is capable of being reformed, of course, but in this case I believe that capital punishment certainly would have yielded more bad than good. Perhaps such killers could be given a choice between a lethal injection, life imprisonment without parole, or a 50-year sentence, and if they chose one of the latter two but killed again in prison or continually caused harm or injury, their choice for the sentence could be revoked, and they then could be put to death.

CASE 2

This man obviously is very dangerous to society. He never should be let out of a penal or mental institution again. If he is truly as mentally ill as he seems to be, then he should be kept in an institution for life without parole; or, if he is judged capable of making a rational decision with regard to life or death, he should be given the alternative of choosing painless execution. In any case, he must never again be released into society.

CASE 3

Here, as in Case 1, this man has learned a great deal about himself, crime, and law while he has been in prison. It seems a shame to destroy all of his knowledge and talent. Wouldn't it be better to give him life imprisonment without parole, a 20-to-50-year sentence without parole (50 if he cannot prove his innocence) or the choice of painless execution rather than to destroy his life? Perhaps he could help to teach or rehabilitate prisoners, or aid scientists in their studies of crime and criminal psychology. But in any case, I do not believe that capital punishment would be justified here.

CASE 4

These crimes are heinous, vicious, and the work of a serial killer, and therefore totally immoral; Humanitarian Ethics would not object to capital punishment in such a case. At any rate, this man must never be let out into society again. If he isn't capitally punished, then he should be given life imprisonment without parole.

APPENDIX

2

Applying Humanitarian Ethics to the Moral Problems of Allowing Someone to Die, Mercy Death, and Mercy Killing

Allowing Someone to Die

General Discussion of the Problem

As long as malicious or criminal neglect or negligence is not involved and as long as patients are not abandoned by health care personnel or their families, I believe that allowing someone to die is an appropriate form of action when dealing with patients who have terminal diseases. In fact, I believe it is just as appropriate as is all-out, aggressive treatment when there is a real chance that such treatment will save someone's life.

Furthermore, I am in total agreement with the hospice approach for care of the dying. In every terminal patient's case, there comes a point when treatment should no longer be concerned with curing and healing. Allowing people to die means that you care for and comfort them, giving them treatment that keeps them out of pain, but you do not heroically

449

try to save them from their inevitable end. For example, if a very old patient dying of terminal cancer goes into cardiac arrest, the ethical medical treatment would be to let the person die rather than try to resuscitate her with heroic procedures such as radical heart surgery or open heart massage. Allowing someone to die at the appropriate time is both medically and morally sound.

What about cases, however, in which human beings are not terminally ill, such as in Cases 1 and 2 below, which deal with deformed newborn babies? In general, when people are not in terminal stages of illness, efforts should be made to cure, heal, or maintain them if they wish to accept treatment. The problem with newborn babies, of course, is that they do not have the ability to accept or refuse treatment, so it would seem that proper medical treatment must be given in order to help them to live.

One cannot, however, give a blanket commandment never to let them die because certainly there may be cases in which deformities are so severe that allowing the baby to die would be appropriate. I think that a baby born without a brain or a spinal cord, for example, should be allowed to die. This, it seems to me, is a clear-cut case, but in other cases, how do you determine what should be done? Do you count the number of deformities? Do you add up their severity? This becomes a very difficult decision, one that depends a great deal upon the specific details of the case. However, I feel that the general ethical tendency should be to try to save such children by means of the appropriate medical care and to give financial and emotional support to the children and their families whenever possible.

Discussion of Specific Cases

CASES 1 AND 2

I feel that both of these cases were handled unethically to some degree. Even though a lifetime of mental retardation is extremely difficult for any child and family to face, I do not feel this provides one with sufficient justification to violate the Value of Life principle. However, neither do I feel that immediate families should have to bear the brunt of all of the difficulties. If society values life, as its members constantly say it does, then total and significant support at all levels must be given such children and their families. The lack of support is what I felt was unethical about Case 2. Society (through the hospital and the judge) overruled the mother and father in this case and then did nothing, or very little, to help them with their situation.

If parents do not feel they can raise a mentally retarded child, with or without a defective heart, then society should provide this child with *significant*, homelike, and human environments. If the family is willing to raise the child, then society should provide every assistance, if needed—financial, emotional, educational, and medical— that it can to ensure that the child's life is as meaningful and significant as it can be. That society is not doing its part in such cases is, of course, no excuse for oversimplifying the problem and letting the child die, but it does lend strength to the parents' argument that allowing the child to die would be better than having it live a minimal life and be unwanted besides. I think that the optimum solution in both cases would be to counsel the parents that the blockage should be removed and to promise to give any and all assistance that they need to raise the child. If they do not wish to raise the child, then the child should become a ward of the state and be given the best care possible. All of this should be financially supported by the state through special tax monies set aside for unfortunate children of all types.

Because this "optimum" solution does not exist, however, we still must ask ourselves whether allowing babies to die in such instances remains a viable alternative. I still maintain that it does not. I feel we must either strive to achieve the optimum solution or stop giving lip service to the value of human life. I can certainly sympathize with the problems faced by these children and their families, and I can only say that society must move toward the proper care and support of human beings in these circumstances.

Time and again, experience has shown that even severely mentally retarded people can live meaningful lives, albeit not at the same level as people who are not mentally retarded. When they are given stimulation, education, love, and friendship, they blossom and thrive and develop. When they are minimally "housed" and cared for, they live unsatisfactory existences, as would the rest of us under the same circumstances. In any case, I do not feel that a person's handicap can justify a violation of the Value of Life principle.

Furthermore, when dealing with this type of problem, most ethicists generally agree with the foregoing. They feel that denying remedial surgery such as that described here would be tantamount to denying grown handicapped people simple appendectomies because their lives are considered meaningless by people without handicaps.

CASE 3

I don't think that a stepfather who has beaten his stepdaughter into a coma should have any further say in what is to be done with her. It seems obvious to me that he wants to keep her alive so that he won't have to be tried for her murder. He has given up all rights over her life by having beaten her half to death.

Mercy Death

General Discussion of the Problem

As I have already mentioned, the hospice alternative—which should be extended to seriously, chronically ill patients in pain—should eliminate most of the need or desire for mercy death. If people are prevented from living lives of misery or suffering, then probably they won't ask to be "put out of their misery." The closer we come to establishing and using a hospice approach, the fewer situations will arise in which someone will request to be mercifully put to death. Therefore, we should work to establish such medical care rather than to establish laws that will allow for mercy death or mercy killing. However, we also must consider those people who are not hospice candidates or who want to die rather than live despite the availability of a hospice. Should we allow mercy death for those people who have rationally chosen it after having been offered all other possible alternatives?

It seems to me that if we *clearly* receive a competent person's request to be allowed to die mercifully and every other alternative (possible cure, the hospice approach, and so forth) has been exhausted, then, in effect, we are being asked to assist in a suicide. Because I have already justified suicide within the five basic principles, the difficulties here have to do with making sure that people are competent and have truly given their consent, and deciding whether we are willing to participate directly in their dying.

The law has established very acceptable criteria for judging when a person is competent or incompetent to make decisions of this sort, and the law generally recognizes a person as competent. We would need to make very sure that people requesting mercy death are not just having momentary fits of depression and that they will not change their minds later on. We would also, under the Principle of Truth Telling or Honesty, want to ensure that everyone involved—the person, the family, health care professionals, clergy, and so on—knew the situation as clearly as possible so that joint, rational decisions could be made concerning the death request and what to do about it.

All of those safeguards described in Evaluation of Safeguards in Chapter 10 shall be followed, and where possible transplantation of organs is involved, no member of any transplant team should have anything to do with the decision-making process.

For some who argue against legalizing mercy death, there may never be enough safeguards to protect human life from being involuntarily taken by the state or by heirs of estates or by doctors who seek organs for transplantation. However, if O. Ruth Russell's essay and book and the safeguards (cited in Chapter 10) do not convince those who are skeptical of mercy death that we should allow such a law, her work and these safeguards at least present very clear ideas as to how we might form a law that would let people choose death if and when they want it.

With proper safeguards, then, and when absolutely sure that the person who wants a mercy death has explored all of the alternatives, is competent to decide, and has freely done so, it seems that all of the basic principles have been met in the same way as they would be in relation to suicide. I do feel, however, that every alternative should be examined first and every effort made to convince the person who is requesting mercy death that there are viable alternatives, such as hospice care. If, after this, the person still requests it, then I believe it ought to be allowed, as long as all of the safeguards that have been described—and more, if necessary—are satisfied. I believe, as I have stated in my discussion of suicide, that people have the right to make rational and competent decisions concerning their own lives and deaths.

Discussion of Specific Cases

CASE 1

I think that the officer would be justified, in this particular case, in shooting the driver to spare him the terrible pain and suffering of burning to death. Because there is absolutely no chance of saving the truck driver—unlike other cases where mercy death might be requested—the officer would be doing the man a great service. He, of course, need not answer the request if he feels that he cannot shoot an innocent man or that, as an officer of the law, he should not use his weapon in this way. But if he were able to do it, I feel he would be justified in giving the man mercy death. Unlike that of a dying cancer patient, the truck driver's suffering can in no way be alleviated; therefore, I feel that the officer would be performing a moral act, and that no court of law should indict him or her for committing such an act of mercy.

CASE 2

I feel that more efforts should have been made to help Robert adjust to his difficulties, at least until his prognosis was more certain. I also think that greater effort should have been given to controlling his pain, and that psychiatric help should have been made immediately available to him and his family, especially the brother who eventually killed him. I believe that the brother did not commit a malicious act, but rather that he was under a great deal of emotional pressure and was acting mercifully.

First, he must have felt very bad about Robert's condition, and, second, knowing his brother as he did, he must have thought he was doing "the least he could do" to end Robert's torment. However, only several days had gone by, and no one can be expected to adjust to such a tragic change in his life in so short a period. Perhaps Robert would never have been able to adjust, but he should have been given more time to find out, as well as much more psychological, sociological, and, if desired, religious assistance in making the adjustment.

I believe that he should have been acquitted (as a young man was in a similar, real-life case) because of the tremendous strain he was under at the time. If he had had psychiatric help in dealing with these pressures, he might have tried to help his brother adjust rather than giving in to his request for mercy death. This is another example of a situation in which medical treatment in itself is not enough—in which treatment must address the mental, emotional, sociological, and spiritual problems of both patients and their families.

CASE 3

Here again, I feel that this couple should have been given mental, emotional, sociological, and spiritual assistance as well as medical help. It is difficult to know whether the hospice approach could have been used to alleviate the wife's suffering in a more effective way than the treatment she had been receiving, but certainly it is the case that much more effort should have gone into relieving her pain and suffering.

Furthermore, her doctors should have recommended that she get psychiatric counseling for herself and also perhaps for her husband. It's difficult to understand why she insisted that her husband give her mercy death and why she herself didn't commit suicide, as she didn't seem to be too physically handicapped to perform such an act. If there had been a legal process, such as the one I have suggested, which she could have gone through in order to have her request for mercy death honored, perhaps many of the couple's needs would have come out into the open. And if they had gotten the assistance they needed, it might have been possible to eliminate the woman's desire to die before her illness overcame her.

Because the question of her mercy death had been discussed for two years previously and for four hours on the day it occurred, I believe we have to assume that the decision to die was a rational one. As I have implied, I believe she should not have burdened her husband with the guilt of having to decide to help her die, but I suppose she had the right to ask him; he also had the right to accept or refuse.

I do not believe, however, that he had an obligation to kill her. Given the circumstances, he should have been acquitted as the brother in Case 2 was. These two cases share two major similarities: (1) The acts, in my opinion, were only questionably moral because all alternatives had not been explored and utilized, and (2) the acts were performed under such strong emotional pressure that the extenuating circumstances of their acts would have to be taken into consideration. In Case 1, there was no alternative other than mercy death except to let the truck driver suffer horribly, and that's why I felt that the officer was justified.

CASE 4

Although Dr. Kevorkian's motives, in his eyes, may be humane, there are some serious moral problems with his actions. First, few of the people he helped to die were terminally ill. Rather, they had chronic diseases that could have been treated and would have responded to pain control, which might have helped patients feel that life was worth living (see the hospice approach to pain control in Chapter 10). Therefore, his actions open the door for clinics or doctors or even unqualified persons, to administer death to any individual who desires it. If people wish to commit suicide, then that is a free choice on their part; I have already said this in Appendix 1.

The second problem that arises is that Dr. Kevorkian is operating outside the law, which means there is no control over what he does or how he does it. There have been cases in the past in which relatives of terminally ill family members have gotten drugs illegally in order to help their family members die. In some cases, the terminally ill people did not die but instead were harmed by the misadministration of drugs. Even though this problem has not arisen for Dr. Kevorkian, because he obviously knows what is necessary to terminate people's lives, without legal controls it certainly could happen to others.

The third problem, related to the second, is determining who will be the terminator of people who want help in dying. Many doctors will not be willing to become known as death givers, especially because their profession urges them to help people to live. It is one thing to allow people to die; it is quite another to actively terminate their lives despite the recent appeals courts rulings (see the difference between allowing to die and mercy death or mercy killing in Chapter 10). Doctors also worry about whether such actions will weaken the trust between patients and their doctors. Are patients who want to fight for life at all costs going to worry that their doctors might terminate their lives, perhaps even without permission? And without legal observation, how will we know if patients really have requested to die? Because of these problems, Humanitarian Ethics cannot approve of what Dr. Kevorkian has done and is doing. I believe it would be better to legalize mercy death, with all of the safeguards I have suggested, than to have Dr. Kevorkian or others operate on their own and outside the law.

Mercy Killing

General Discussion of the Problem

The most difficult moral problems in the area of mercy killing—as well as abortion—arise because people's (or people's potential) consent cannot be obtained. Taking a life under these conditions would have to fall under the purview of ending people's lives against their wills or without their wills being exercised. With mercy killing, then, we must consider the quality of human life as well as its inherent value. I have tried to realistically state the Value of Life principle by including within it the acceptance of death, but this says nothing about what kind of life should be revered, preserved, or protected.

Because the quality of life is an extremely nebulous concept, its definition differing from individual to individual, for the most part it should be defined by the individuals themselves, because they are the ones who have to live their lives and the only ones who really can determine whether their lives are worth living. Some people can live what seems to them to be a meaningful existence with multiple deformities, whereas others would rather die than lose a limb, be paralyzed, or in any other way have their capacity for life decreased.

A larger problem exists, however, when one has to make the decision for someone else, such as in the case of unborn fetuses, newly born deformed babies, or older people who are sick and senile to the point of no longer being mentally competent. For example, a person in her late eighties who needs no artificial life support but who remains in a fetal position during her sleeping and waking hours and has given no one an indication of whether she would rather be dead or alive, presents a moral problem. Allowing her to die is not appropriate here because there is nothing to withdraw but food and drink.

If we decide to mercy kill—that is, "put her out of her misery"—won't we be violating the basic moral principles? Can we determine for this person that the quality of her life is such that it should not be allowed to continue? Who can or should make such a decision? Similarly, can we determine for a newly born baby with serious multiple deformities whether the quality of his life will make it worth living? We can predict the fates of the senile old woman and the seriously deformed child to some extent because we know what has happened to those living under such conditions in the past, but should we be allowed to apply our knowledge and experience to beings who cannot give their permission either for death or for life?

I have already said that allowing someone to die is, in certain situations, medically appropriate and perfectly legal and moral. I also have discussed the fact that after all alternatives have been exhausted, competent individuals may choose mercy death. I have even suggested that a request for mercy death could, with many legal safeguards, be legally authorized. However, mercy killing is different from allowing someone to die because it is a direct act to end someone's life; and it is different from mercy death because people who are to be mercy killed have not requested such an act, nor have they in any way been able to give their permission. And because it is a direct act to kill people against their wills or without their consent, I feel that mercy killing, except in the rarest of circumstances, is an immoral act that should not be performed.

Discussion of Specific Cases

CASE 1

Because of the liberalization of abortion laws that followed the United States Supreme Court decision of 1973, situations similar to this have arisen several times in recent years. It seems that doctors who perform abortions feel that because an abortion has been decided upon in a specific case, if the abortion procedure does not kill the fetus, then the living fetus delivered through the abortion procedure should either be allowed to die or be killed. I believe that this view is morally questionable. I will not at this time go into the morality or immorality of abortion; that will be discussed in the next appendix. However, I believe that any fetus/child that is born alive must be given every chance to live and must not be allowed to die or be mercy killed. California passed a law covering this situation after several questionable deaths of live fetuses had occurred. The law essentially states that any fetus born alive must be medically cared for in the same way as any other baby born alive by means of regular birth procedures. Therefore, because the fetus/baby was born alive, the doctor performed an immoral act in this case by purposely suffocating and killing the living child.

CASE 2

This is an extremely difficult case to deal with. The young woman is almost, but not quite, a brain death case. Such a person could live indefinitely at a minimal level of existence; nevertheless, she is alive and cannot be declared dead by any medical or legal criteria we have. One woman who died at the age of 34 had been in such a coma for 28 years. Such situations must be very hard for the family to bear—and we don't know what the patients know or feel—but these difficulties do not justify the mercy killing of such patients. I think that such patients should be removed from acute care hospitals, taken off artificial life support systems, and placed in a hospice atmosphere.

If heart or kidney failure or pneumonia occurs, then I believe such patients should be allowed to die without any extraordinary measures being taken to keep them alive (for example, CPR, dialysis, penicillin). When such patients can be cared for at home with full support, they should be; when this isn't possible, they should be cared for in hospices. The expense for such care should be borne by the family to the extent it can afford it and by the state past that point. I feel that what the woman's sister did was wrong even though I sympathize with her feelings. I think she probably ought to be arrested and brought to trial but that she probably should be acquitted by reason of temporary insanity.

CASE 3

This is the hardest of all of the cases to deal with, yet I feel that in this case mercy killing was justified. As you will see in the abortion chapter, Tay-Sachs carriers can now be warned of this problem in advance, and the fetus also can be tested in the uterus to see if it has Tay-Sachs disease. However, in this case, the child already was born and had no better chance for survival than the truck driver in the burning truck described in the mercy death section. Because the child could only get worse, suffer more, and die a horrible death, I feel that the father was justified in doing what he did. Now that Tay-Sachs disease can be determined prior to birth through amniocentesis or chorionic villus sampling, however, I feel that such children should not be allowed to be born. The father, of course, has the option of allowing the baby to die, and if this can be done while keeping the baby free from suffering and discomfort, then this would be the more moral action. If it cannot be done, however, I feel the father is justified in mercy killing his child.

Let me add that I don't believe this would be moral in just any case involving a deformed child—but definitely in the case of Tay-Sachs disease.

CASE 4

The main problems in this case are, first, that the husband did not explore all possible alternatives before killing his wife, and, second, that there was no evidence that his wife wanted to die. There are specialized facilities for Alzheimer's patients, but the husband evidently made little or no effort to find such a facility. He did try to get some help for her at home, but there were problems, as there often are with Alzheimer's disease patients, in getting his wife to accept this help. Since the couple was quite well off, it would seem he could have afforded to look for a more highly trained specialist if he could not find an acceptable facility. Many people with Alzheimer's do quite well when placed in a situation with optimal care. As in the Kevorkian cases, the man's wife was not terminally ill, which provides less of a reason to kill her than if she were in the end-stages of cancer, for example. Also, I think that the prosecuting attorney made a very good point that this case might set a precedent in a state where many people are retired, old, and infirm. I think that what the husband did was immoral even though he clearly was suffering emotionally and physically. The reason that the husband was sent to prison, in my opinion, is that he would not plead temporary insanity under the law and showed no remorse for what he had done. I think he should have been prosecuted, as he was, and I think that with the evidence available, his case was handled well. Considering his age and health, I think that commuting his sentence after serving some time was probably the humane thing to do. This case obviously differs from Cases 2, 3, and 4 under the mercy death section because, in all of those cases, the people whose lives were terminated were clearly in favor of being put to death.

3

Applying Humanitarian Ethics to the Moral Problems of Abortion

The Moderate Position on Abortion

Before examining specifically how Humanitarian Ethics deals with and attempts to resolve the complex problem of abortion, I believe it is important to present more clearly and specifically the moderate position on abortion, which Humanitarian Ethics embodies and which was described only briefly in Chapter 11.

The Danger of Abortion

All of the research that has been done yields the conclusion that an abortion performed under normal medical conditions is generally not a dangerous procedure; neither, however, is it a minor procedure. Medically, repeated abortions and abortions in young women can cause later problems, but these problems are not so severe that laws prohibiting abortions are needed in order to protect women from bodily harm and death.[1]

Psychologically, it is quite difficult to generalize about the extent to which either going through an unwanted pregnancy or having an abortion will affect the mental and emotional well-being of a woman. Much less research has been done in this area than in the medical-physical sphere, and the data available about psychological trauma are certainly not as "hard" as the medical data. It would seem that each individual woman facing such a dilemma should be counseled carefully in an effort to discover how both abortion and unwanted pregnancy may affect her.[2] Concerning this aspect of the abortion problem, the more moderate position would tend to be quite permissive in allowing abortions for psychological reasons, whereas the less moderate position would be more restrictive.

The medical danger to the mother's life of going through a pregnancy (discussed in Chapter 11) has certainly been reduced by our medical and technological advances. By the same token, however, some danger does exist, and it should perhaps remain the most serious reason for allowing abortion.

Viable Alternatives to Abortion

The moderates in the abortion controversy definitely feel that there are some viable alternatives to abortion, but that these alternatives often are lacking both in availability and in quality. One alternative, adoption, is viable despite a number of problems, which were discussed in Chapter 11. But institutions offering quality care of unwanted and/or deformed children are definitely few and far between.

Furthermore, even though economics shouldn't be the most important factor in a decision for or against the taking of human life, financial assistance simply doesn't exist in sufficient quantity either to help economically deprived parents to raise unplanned-for children or to establish and support humane, homelike institutions to substitute for parents who can't or won't take on the responsibility. The moderate position suggests that if we support the Value of Life principle, then we have an obligation to provide such financial assistance; not to do so is merely to give the principle lip service. As long as conditions do not improve, abortion will remain for many the most viable alternative.

Rape or Incest

The moderate position generally favors allowing a woman whose pregnancy is a result of rape or incest to have an abortion merely upon her request. She may, of course, also elect to go through with such a pregnancy. The feeling here is that the experience the woman has gone through may be so terrifying and brutalizing that allowing a child of such a union to be born would only extend the trauma. Almost everyone, except for the strongest prolife supporters, believes that abortion under these circumstances should be allowed upon the woman's request.

The Woman's Responsibility

The moderate position does not support the so-called "revenge attitude" directed against women who have become pregnant because they were careless in their use of contraceptives. To moderates, women in this situation merely illustrate the need for intensified contraceptive counseling to prevent such situations in the future. That a woman now is pregnant is the real problem, and recriminations concerning why she did not use contraceptives or why she wasn't more careful have no real value.

The Unwanted Child Argument

Although moderates are aware of the problems that ensue from going through with unwanted pregnancies, they generally feel that the prochoice people oversimplify a complex problem. First of all, there are two aspects of the argument: the interests of the child itself, once it is born, and the interests of society, which may have to bear the financial burden of supporting such children.

Several questions must be raised in relation to the question of unwanted children. First of all, does the fact that the child is unwanted by the natural mother necessarily mean that the child is not wanted by *somebody*? The overabundance of adoptive parents would certainly testify to the existence of many people who want, sometimes desperately, children who may be unwanted by their natural parents. The whole adoption process needs to be simplified, sped up, and made less economically prohibitive. Second, to what extent will the fact that children are not wanted be detrimental to them once they are born? There is no hard evidence to show that children who are unwanted don't become loved and wanted once they are born. There are many children, of course, who are not loved, and some who even are hated, but it is very difficult to predict in most cases what the effect upon children will be.

There is no *necessary* connection between unwanted and being abused after birth. In fact, many abused children were the result of planned pregnancies and were, in many instances, "wanted." Finally, does "being unwanted" mean the same thing as "having no value," and is destroying a conceptus more moral than allowing an unwanted child to be born? All of these questions should be asked, and when they are, the prochoice argument may lose a good deal of its force. This does not mean that consideration shouldn't be given to the possibility of abortion, but such consideration might reveal other alternatives besides abortion. For example, if the negative feelings of a mother toward her conceptus are not strong enough to be called hatred, then perhaps psychological support therapy will help her deal with her feelings and overcome them enough to raise the child well.

The Conceptus as the Mother's Property

As we saw in Chapter 11, according to the prochoice argument the conceptus is the sole "property" of the woman in whose body it resides until birth, or at least until viability. This point of view does, however, present some problems. First of all, although the conceptus certainly is *in* the woman's body, it is not a *part* of her body in the same way that, for example, her finger is. Rather, the conceptus has separate genetic, circulatory, hormonal, and nervous systems; therefore, the mother and the conceptus can be distinguished clearly as two separate organisms. Moreover, how can the conceptus be merely a "woman's property" when it is separate, though dependent, and when it would not exist at all without a man's contribution of sperm? Furthermore, since when can one person "confer" personhood on another—what political or legal code gives this right to anyone?

Finally, if the conceptus is the sole property of the woman until it is born, then whose property is it at birth? Is it no longer the woman's property then? Does it become the property of the state? The whole property argument raises myriad problems. The moderate position would suggest that the woman must give some consideration to the conceptus, regarding it as a separate organism that is potentially a human being and whose potential grows with its development.

The Legal Right to Abortion

On the other hand, can we deny women the legal right to abortion, as the prolife people say we should? Callahan suggests that we can do this only if legalizing abortion poses a threat to peace, security, and the safety of the whole society. One possible danger of legalizing abortion is that this could debase society's ideas of the value of life, which could lead to more extensive violations of the Value of Life principle. This, of course, is essentially the domino argument again, and as we have seen, there is no clear evidence that legalizing abortion has ever led to such a situation. The only possible exception is Hitler's Third Reich, but here the motives for performing abortion, mercy killing, and genocide were quite different from the motives behind most abortions.

Legalizing abortion could also be considered a threat if one could show that the actual practice of abortion has been generally harmful to the lives of those already living; there is, however, no evidence to support this. Finally, one would have to show that real harm, not just predicted or asserted harm, has resulted from legalizing abortion, and no hard evidence exists to indicate that permissive abortion laws have been hazardous to the members of those societies in which such laws exist.[3]

One piece of evidence that might be of use here is Daniel Callahan's careful and extensive worldwide study of countries that have changed restrictive abortion laws to moderate or permissive ones. Callahan's study unquestionably revealed that there is no clear or conclusive evidence to indicate that allowing abortions to be performed has caused the reverence for life in other areas to diminish. On the contrary, in many countries where abortion laws had become moderate or permissive, laws against mercy killing and capital punishment remained in force or became even more restrictive.[4] The moderate position, then, would not oppose the legalization of abortion in general, but it might favor the restriction of abortions later in pregnancy.

Summary of the Moderate Position

Generally, the moderate position would allow and restrict abortions in roughly the same way that Sissela Bok has suggested. Supporters of this position would suggest that pregnant women should be counseled objectively about going through with their pregnancies or having abortions. Too much counseling today is one-sided—the advice a woman receives depends to a great extent upon which agency she happens to call. If, for example, she calls an agency that is essentially prolife in philosophy, she is likely to get the advice to go through with pregnancy; if, on the other hand, she happens to call an abortion clinic, she may be advised to have an abortion. What is needed is objective counseling agencies whose only purpose is to furnish women with as much information and as many alternatives as possible. Such counseling should include

1. A determination of the woman's *true* wishes concerning pregnancy or abortion.
2. Information concerning abortion and birth procedures.
3. Information concerning alternatives to abortion (financial assistance, psychological counseling, day care for children, therapy and care for deformed children).
4. Full contraceptive counseling so that unwanted pregnancies can be avoided in the future.

Furthermore, real, viable alternatives *must* be available if women are to be encouraged to go through with pregnancies and to avoid abortion. Such alternatives should include

1. Financial assistance for pregnancy, child care, child rearing, adoption, and abortion.
2. Good and readily available adoptive situations.
3. Humane and homelike institutions for nonadoptive and/or severely deformed children.
4. Psychological and sociological therapy and assistance.

Most moderates believe that their position accomplishes three major objectives. First, it recognizes and deals with the conceptus's right to life. Second, it recognizes and deals with the freedom of women. Third, it expresses the serious concern of society for unborn life. Finally, it provides maximum freedom for everyone concerned with abortion decisions.

Before we go on to discuss the Humanitarian Ethics approach to abortion, two final points need to be made. First, that abortion decisions should essentially be private rather than public decisions; second, that the final decision to abort or keep the child must be left up to the women who are pregnant, with the exception of some restrictions on late abortions. Women should receive the help and support of all aspects of society when making this very difficult decision, but in the final analysis, the decision is theirs.[5]

The Humanitarian Ethics Approach to the Problem

General Discussion of the Problem

In general, Humanitarian Ethics has an inherent bias in favor of protecting human life, even unborn human life, because the Value of Life principle is of primary importance in this ethical system. This would mean, then, that abortion should be seen as a last resort, an option to be used only when there is strong justification for doing so. However, I tend to agree with the moderate choice position more than with either the strong prolife or the strong prochoice position described in Chapter 11. I believe that if abortions cannot be avoided—and women should try to avoid them to the best of their ability—they should be allowed to have them on request up to the twelfth week. Needless to say, if they have to be performed, they should be done as soon as possible after pregnancy is discovered. Also, I agree with Bok's criteria as to when taking a human life is most serious and also as to when later abortions can be allowed.

I also feel very strongly that, with a few exceptions, the decision for or against abortion must finally rest with the woman who is carrying the conceptus. This does not mean that other opinions cannot or should not be brought to bear, or that information, advice, and counseling cannot or should not be given. What it does mean is that the final decision rests with the pregnant woman unless someone wants to exert some kind of force and constraint to make her have the child—a difficult feat to accomplish, and one that probably would be against all five ethical principles. For example, if a woman is Catholic and decides to have the child even if her own life may be lost, then she made the decision, the Catholic Church did not. On the other hand, if she belongs to a Zero Population Growth organization and decides to have an abortion to help avoid overpopulation, then too it is her decision, not ZPG's.

Prior to the Supreme Court's abortion decision when legislation prevented abortions, many women either tried to abort the fetus themselves or had illegal abortions. This sometimes caused disastrous results not only for the aborted fetuses but also for the women carrying them, and two lives often were lost instead of one.

However, that the final decision is the woman's does not make the decision any less a moral one, involving as it does the life and the quality of life of both the woman and her prospective child; nor should it eliminate a full presentation of alternatives and the information and counseling that go with them. Here again, I strongly advocate pointing out as many considerations as possible and providing as much assistance as we can in order to help the woman make this very crucial decision.

Of course, she really has only two ultimate alternatives—to abort or not to abort—but there are many important considerations that will affect which of these alternatives she chooses. The counseling and information that is offered must be fair, full, and objective on both sides of the issue, so that the woman has enough correct information upon which to make a rational moral decision.

A major difficulty with abortion, as with mercy killing, is that the being about whose life or death someone is deciding cannot give its free or informed consent. Therefore, the Value of Life principle is involved in a most serious and crucial way. Because we do not know what the will of the unborn is except in the strict biological sense—that is, once conceived most conceptuses strive to develop to the stage of birth—we must have the utmost justification before we take such a life. We must show that the other four principles will be met if we decide in favor of aborting the conceptus, and that meeting them far outweighs the value of allowing the conceptus to develop and be born.

The best way of avoiding abortion altogether is, of course, to be meticulous about using the effective contraceptive devices that are currently available, and to work very hard to develop more effective ones that will have minimal detrimental side effects. However, no contraceptive device is completely foolproof, and therefore if one fails or is not used for whatever reason, then we are faced with the abortion problem. There also is voluntary sterilization, which is almost entirely foolproof. This is a good solution provided that the person to be sterilized is sure he or she will never, at any time, want to have children. If this is the case, then voluntary sterilization—no matter how offensive such an operation may be to some people—is much better than having one abortion after another. However, until people are more educated and careful with regard to methods of birth control, we still will be faced with the abortion problem.

In no other area of morality is there a greater need for many real and viable alternatives, with full information, counseling, and assistance to be made available to the pregnant woman. If society wishes to strongly recommend that human life not be taken through abortion, then it must, as the moderate position suggests, provide the greatest amount of medical, physical, financial, and moral support possible.

To respect the life of the conceptus is not to deny that its being unwanted makes it an imposition on a woman (from her point of view) for the nine months she must carry it within her. That the woman (and her partner) may have been careless or promiscuous or thoughtless should have no bearing on the kind of help she is given. A good deal of careful counseling should be given to her in reference to possible future pregnancies and how to avoid them, but the prime consideration in any counseling or assistance should be the lives of the woman and the conceptus. For this reason, all such counseling and assistance should be completely free from blame and recrimination.

It is very easy for some people to demand that a young woman carry an unplanned and unwanted conceptus to term, but it is not so easy if these people have to provide complete assistance to the woman and the conceptus so that she can successfully do so. As I have mentioned before, the information and counseling should present her with *all* of the alternatives—the psychological and medical effects of both abortion and of carrying a child to term, the actual possibilities of the child's being adopted, and the offer to give complete financial assistance and medical care during her pregnancy or during and after her abortion.

She also must be given time without pressure to decide for herself and the conceptus which decision will be the best one, given all of the alternatives and her particular circumstances. A great deal of attention must be paid to the kind of life that the prospective child will have if it is allowed to be born. Even though most children are born normal, sometimes the goodness of their lives is almost nonexistent because of the way they are treated by their inexperienced and unloving parents or by various uncaring personnel in the institutions or foster homes in which they live.

When alternatives and assistance can be provided, the prolife argument for the conceptus gains strength. I feel that every encouragement should be given to the woman *not* to decide to take another human life through abortion, *provided* that she is offered such assistance. All of this may be politically, socially, psychologically, and morally as well as economically expensive, but if the Value of Life principle is worth observing, then whatever sacrifices are needed must be made. They should not only be the sacrifices of the woman—her nine-month unwanted pregnancy is sacrifice enough, and those who wish to protect and preserve human life must alleviate any other sacrifices she may have to make.

We also must respect the fact that the final decision to abort or not to abort is the mother's. If she aborts, her act may be an immoral one, but as always, the decision to act morally or immorally is up to the individual. In this case, we have a duty, once she has made her decision, to help her acquire the best medical care available and to have the abortion performed as soon as possible so that the conceptus will be less rather than more of a developed human life.

Discussion of Specific Cases

CASE 1

This is a classic case of what happens to young unwed mothers. Everyone seems to be interested in what they want, but few really are concerned about what Janice wants. She is getting one-sided rather than objective counseling both from her priest and from the abortion clinic. Her mother is imposing her own religious beliefs on Janice, no matter how gently; her father, on the other hand, seems to be motivated, at least partly, by his own ego in wanting her to become a lawyer. The father of her baby does not want to marry her or to become a father at such an early age, nor does he want her to become a young mother. All the people involved, but especially Janice, are prime candidates for the careful pregnancy-abortion counseling I have suggested.

At this point in her pregnancy (8 weeks), an abortion would fit the Bok criterion of less than 12 weeks and therefore could be allowed. Because Janice is under 17 years old, she should be informed about the hazards for future pregnancies that might ensue from an abortion, but she also should be informed that the risk is not high. In addition, she should be given all the information available about both abortion and carrying a child to term.

A sincere and concerted effort should be made to find out what Janice herself really wants to do about her pregnancy, and everyone involved should try to support her decision in every way they can rather than load her with guilt or recrimination. If she really wishes to go through with her pregnancy, then she should get as much support from this decision as she would for an abortion. Last but not least, she and Bob should have clear and complete contraceptive counseling so that future pregnancies and decisions concerning abortion can be avoided.

CASE 2

Both Mary and her husband seem to be quite sure that they do not want another child, so waiting until the fourth month to have an amniocentesis does not seem to be a wise choice. Because they seem so sure that they really do not want to have a child—even one that is born without deformity—then now, when Mary is only one month pregnant, is the time to have the abortion. If they have doubts about having the abortion, then they should, of course, seek full counseling in order to help them clarify their decision, but they seem to have made up their minds, and because of this, I would say that their decision is moral.

CASES 3 AND 4

Before discussing each of these cases separately, I would like to make a general statement concerning abortion for "fetal reasons," or because the conceptus will be born with deformities. As I have already mentioned, the amniocentesis or chorionic villus sampling procedures make it possible for a prospective mother and father to know if their child will be born with, let us say, Down syndrome and will be mentally retarded for its entire life.

The relationship of such information to the abortion question, of course, is that once a conceptus is discovered to have a deformity, a decision may be made to abort it, thereby avoiding both the difficult mercy-killing decision I described in Chapter 10 and also the kind of life that the prospective child and its family would have to live given its limitation. But the difficult decision to commit a mercy killing is replaced by the difficult decision to perform an abortion. Abortion, after all, ends a human life as surely as does mercy killing, except that in the abortion situation, depending upon at what stage the abortion is performed, the human life would be less developed.

Can abortion be morally justified when it is discovered that the conceptus will be defective or deformed in some serious way? The final decision should still rest with the woman who is carrying it even though the prospective father should be given a chance to voice his opinion. The ideal situation would be to have the ability to eliminate the defect or deformity prior to the child's birth, and some are even now possible.

Even though the woman should of course make the final decision, what facts and opinions should she take into consideration when making her decision? First, she should realize that abortion is the taking of a human life and therefore a violation of the Value of Life principle. Next, she should ask herself if an exception to this principle in her situation is morally justified, and if so, why. She would need appropriate information and counseling as to what her prospective child's limitations would be, and then she would need to determine whether, despite these limitations, she and her family would be able and willing to raise such a child so that their lives and the child's life would be as meaningful as possible.

If the family is unable or unwilling to raise the child, then she would need to consider whether a good adoption could be a certainty and whether such an adoption would bring a meaningful life to the child. She also should determine what help would be available to her if she and her family decided to raise the child, what institutional accommodations could be made, and whether such accommodations would be meaningful and enriching for the prospective child.

I already have discussed the general lack of assistance and of quality institutions and institutional care available today. Furthermore, even though there are parents who are willing to adopt retarded or deformed children, these are very few compared to the number of such children available for adoption. These facts would seem to put the emphasis upon whether or not the mother is willing to give birth to the child, and whether she and the father are willing to raise the child and give it as good a life as they can. As mentioned in Chapter 10, the life of a child with Down syndrome, unless it is enhanced by a willing and loving family (real or institutional), will yield a minimum of satisfaction and excellence for all concerned; therefore, abortion in some cases—after all considerations have been taken into account—could be morally justified.

The severity of the prospective child's deformity should also be a factor in the woman's decision, for the deformities of deafness or blindness, although difficult to bear, are not as debilitating as is extensive mental retardation due to Down syndrome. A mother and her family probably would be able to cope better with the former limitations than with the latter.

At any rate, abortion ought to be allowed after all other choices have been examined and the woman can see no other alternative that would bring goodness and its just distribution to the prospective child and its family. In the final analysis, the goodness of the life of the prospective child and its family should be given the strongest consideration. Everything possible should be done to protect and preserve human life, even incipient human life. However, where the goodness of protecting that life is far outweighed by the goodness of terminating it for the reasons already suggested, then abortion may be justified.

CASE 3

I would say that in the case of Tay-Sachs—considering what we know about the disease, and what happens to infants who are born with it—an abortion even at five months of pregnancy can be more easily justified in a moral sense than going through with the pregnancy. After all, if the child were born, both it and the parents would suffer terribly for the short time the child would live. In Chapter 10, I described how the father of a Tay-Sachs child was driven to mercy killing in order to end the child's and the parents' suffering. I think that abortion is a far better means of dealing with this problem than mercy killing, even though if amniocentesis rather than CVS is used, the conceptus has developed further along than is usually the case in abortions upon request, the very serious deformity of the child and the inevitability of its suffering justify a late abortion.

CASE 4

Lupe and Robert have a very difficult decision to make. They should be given full genetic counseling as well as counseling as to the nature and quality of the alternatives that are available to them and their prospective baby. I believe that in their situation, either going through with the pregnancy or having the abortion would be morally justified depending upon the type of support that is available for them and their child. Because they are young and this is their first child, they ought not to have to raise a child with Down syndrome unless they are willing to do so. I think that we ought to encourage them to do so by giving them complete support in all of its aspects (financial, sociological, emotional, and so on), but I also think that even a late abortion in this case can be morally justified, especially if such support is not available to them and their prospective child.

CASE 5

I do not think that an abortion can be justified for such a reason. It is one thing to abort a conceptus because it has Tay-Sachs disease or Down syndrome, but to abort one because of its sex is capricious, inhumane, and immoral. If Bill and Isabel are even thinking about not wanting another daughter, Isabel should have had an early abortion and then be sterilized. I feel that they would be justified in giving their little girl up for adoption if they had wished to do so, but I would rather see them get intense counseling to help them adjust to having another daughter. I don't believe, however, that the life of a conceptus should count so little that it can be terminated simply because it happens to be the "wrong" sex.

CASE 6

To abort one of the twin conceptuses is as capricious as aborting a conceptus because of its sex, especially because the woman definitely is going to go through with the pregnancy to keep one of the twins. The second twin, if born alive, should be offered up for adoption. In the case of a greater number of multiple births, the same principle would apply unless doctors advise, as they did in an octuplet pregnancy, that none of the conceptuses would survive unless some of them were aborted. However, one woman was carrying septuplets, all were carried to term, and born alive and healthy. The woman wouldn't have the abortion, presumably because of her perceived chance of acquiring money and fame by having octuplets, and she ended up losing all eight fetuses as the doctors had told her she would. This kind of picking and choosing among conceptuses, unless a danger exists either for all of them or to the mother's life, is immoral under Humanitarian Ethics.

Notes

1. See Daniel Callahan, *Abortion: Law, Choice and Morality* (New York: Macmillan, 1970), 31–43, for results of research done all over the world on whether abortion is dangerous.
2. Ibid., 48–84.
3. Ibid., 474–80.
4. See Callahan, Section II, Chapters 5 to 8, for his exhaustive research on the effects of legalizing abortion.
5. Ibid., 493.

4

Applying Humanitarian Ethics to the Moral Problems of Lying, Cheating, Breaking Promises, and Stealing

Introduction

Because one of the five basic ethical principles in Humanitarian Ethics is the Principle of Honesty and Truth Telling, the Humanitarian Ethics position on these issues is that they generally shouldn't be done unless there is strong justification for doing them. As was shown throughout Chapter 12, doing any of them tends to break down the quality of human relationships and the trust that binds people together. If we cannot trust others to tell the truth, be honest, keep promises, and respect our possessions, then how can we maintain vital human relationships with them? In addition, lying, cheating, breaking promises, and stealing more often than not tend to injure individuals, thereby violating the Principle of Goodness. Further, most of the time they are unfair and unjust, violating the Principle of Justice or Fairness. They even can involve the lives of others and deny them freedom; therefore, the Humanitarian Ethics position is in general to oppose them.

Lying

General Discussion of the Problem

For all of the reasons listed in Chapter 12 against lying, Humanitarian Ethics would state that lying generally is immoral. It would allow for exceptions where strong justification could be brought forth, such as when lying could save a human life or prevent serious harm from coming to another human being. Even "little white lies" should be avoided whenever possible because by simply adding some compassion and concern one could tell the truth without harming another. Nowhere more than in lying does the domino argument have validity. It seems that whenever a lie is told it almost always follows that more and more lies are required to bolster the first, which often tends to make matters worse and break down trust even more than just the one original lie.

Aphorism though it may be, honesty is indeed almost always "the best policy." As most of us know, we are highly respected for our truth telling and trustworthiness. Lying can only destroy this delicate reputation we all have. One of the finest statements one can make about another is to say that he or she is an honest person. Because of this and the harm that lying causes to others, it should be avoided.

Discussion of Specific Cases

CASE 1

In applying Humanitarian Ethics to this case, I will answer the four questions I asked at the end of the case description:

1. I feel that the family was wrong in not telling Jesusita the truth about her son. They might have justified delaying telling her if at the time she was in a very critical and unstable condition, but as soon as possible they should have told her. As Dr. Elisabeth Kübler-Ross has stated, the question should not be, "Should I tell the hurtful truth to someone?" but rather "How should I share this important information with the person?" Not telling her the truth in the beginning caused many more problems than if they had told her and given her loving support. We can't assume that we are going to "kill" someone who is seriously ill by telling her the truth. If we tell her gently and with compassion, and if we give her some hope and support, we will do her a much greater service than we do by withholding information and playing all kinds of pretense games with her.

2. If she were my relative, I would tell her that her son had died of a heart attack, while also giving her as much hope as I could by telling her that he had very little pain and that I and the rest of her family still love her and want her to keep trying to live as meaningfully as she can because we will not abandon her but will support and visit her often.

3. I definitely would advise now that she be told the truth in the manner described in answer 2, and I would advise the family to apologize to her, saying that at the time they thought they were doing the right thing, but that now they see that it was the wrong thing to do. If not, the longer the situation goes on, the worse it will get. What

must Jesusita think of her son who used to visit her dutifully but does so no longer for a myriad of reasons that seem to relegate her to last place on his list of priorities?

4. Yes, I feel that the situation would have been much better had she been told the truth from the very beginning and that the situation has been made much worse by not telling her, now requiring an apology and an elaborate explanation. If she had been told the truth from the beginning, all of this could have been avoided.

CASE 2

One way of handling this matter without lying is simply to tell Mike that you won't tell him because you fear for Barbara's and the children's safety. However, if you feel that he might go into a rage when told this and hurt you in some manner, then I would say that a lie would be justified because it seems quite obvious that both Barbara and the children could be seriously harmed and perhaps even lose their lives owing to Mike's drinking and abusive behavior.

CASE 3

Situations such as this one are always difficult to deal with. Many spouses know about their spouses' affairs and can deal with them as long as they are not brought into the open. Some spouses, on the other hand, would prefer to know the truth and why the affair happened and then attempt to resolve the problem. Some spouses could adjust to the information, especially if Tom, in this case, expressed remorse and fully intended not to have another affair. Some spouses cannot adjust, no matter what the adulterer says, and immediately will want to separate or get a divorce. It is important for Tom to know Carol and to try to gauge her reaction to his revealing information about his affair.

As I see it, there are two viable alternatives, given the situation:

1. Tom could simply not tell Carol unless she asks him point blank. This probably would have to be considered as a lie of omission, but if he's sure she does not know and that she will never know, then not telling if not asked is certainly a possibility. This kind of lie of omission is certainly not as bad as not telling someone that there is a cliff at the end of the street so that they drive to the end and go over the cliff and die, but it is still a continuing of the dishonesty that has occurred all along. Further, Tom would have to be definite in his mind that the affair was over, and that he would not enter into more affairs later. If Tom chooses this alternative, then he should get counseling to help him alleviate his guilt so that his behavior will not continue to raise Carol's suspicions. If Carol asks him directly about the affair, then I feel he is obliged to tell her the truth as gently as he can with remorse and promises never to have another affair. He also can offer to seek counseling with or without her.

2. The second alternative is to tell her as gently and compassionately as he can, emphasizing how guilty he feels and expressing sorrow for what has happened and also promising that it will never happen again. Here also he should volunteer for counseling, both with their priest and any other counselor who may help. In telling her, he should avoid graphic details and not volunteer additional hurtful information.

Cheating

General Discussion of the Problem

Cheating is primarily a violation of the Principle of Justice or Fairness and therefore should be avoided unless such an act might save a human life or prevent serious harm to someone. All three of the arguments for cheating are, I feel, grossly invalid and unjustified. To endorse the notion that one needs to cheat in order to survive in a corrupt world only contributes to its continuing corruptness. The "everybody does it" argument was refuted in Chapter 1 in that one can't get an *ought* from an is. Further, honesty does not depend upon whether or not one gets caught. Cheating is cheating regardless of whether or not one is caught. Here again, as in the case of lying, a person who cheats and is known for his or her cheating cannot be trusted, and therefore relationships with that person are impossible.

Discussion of Specific Cases

CASE 1

Mike definitely should not cheat. Regardless of the importance of the grade to his career, he should have made more time for studying his history *all* semester. If he had, then his grade would not be as precarious as it was at the time of the final exam. He also should have allowed for more time to complete his studying for the exam so that he would not now be in a position in which he has to consider cheating. Answers to the three questions following the case description are as follows:

1. It would make no difference to my answer if the test grade were or were not crucial. He has no more justification for cheating simply because the test grade is important. I already have stated how his not being prepared could have been avoided. He might now ask the instructor if he could do some extra credit work in order to improve his grade. This would be an act of honesty; cheating would be dishonest and immoral.
2. As I have already argued, whether or not one is caught does not dilute the immorality of cheating. Cheating is still cheating, even if the only person who knows is the cheater.
3. I already have presented arguments as to why Mike should not cheat. The reader may also refer to the arguments against cheating in Chapter 12, with which I concur.

CASE 2

Dick and Lorraine definitely should not include the right fender in the claim. They could tell the body shop foreman about the right fender and offer to pay for it themselves. The foreman might even give them a discounted price because he has to repair so much of the car already under the rightful claim. Because the damage was not caused by the other car, they would be both cheating and lying if they included it in the claim. It is fallacious to argue that the insurance company has great monetary assets because of all of the premiums it collects and that therefore it is okay to cheat it. Again, cheating is cheating whether you cheat a rich person or company or a poor one. Also, the "everybody does it" argument has already been refuted. It doesn't matter what their friends do or how many of them do it; what Dick and Lorraine would be doing is still immoral. I have already dealt with the argument of being or not being caught and its irrelevancy to the act of cheating.

CASE 3

What Mark did was definitely immoral. He actually forged a letter in order to further his own interests—he cheated in trying to get his book published. How does he know, for example, that the letter had that much to do with his book's being accepted by the publisher? At any rate, he should have been honest and taken his chances as all authors must while working to make his book the best it could be. How he could assume that what he had done would never be discovered is unbelievable to me.

I think the publisher had every right to pull Mark's book off the market although he could have published it with an apology from Mark, perhaps even with a case study of what Mark did and his explanation of why he did it and why he now knows he was wrong. However, the publisher has to ensure that the book makes a profit, and if no teachers would adopt it for their classes because of bad publicity, then it could prove to be a financial disaster for the publisher.

Not everyone would agree with me, but I think a dimension of intensity is added to a moral wrong if the person who commits it is especially expected to avoid it because of his or her profession or livelihood. I think that it is especially abhorrent for Mark as an ethicist and a teacher of ethics to so blatantly and directly commit an obvious moral wrong. A person who has studied and who teaches ethics, although no more perfect than any other human being, must try much harder not to commit an immoral act.

If the book were otherwise excellent and had something special to offer that other ethics books did not, then I might consider using it if the author did what I have described with regard to confessing to his ethical error somewhere in the book itself. However, I probably would not use it, given his terrible breach of trust with his colleagues and students of ethics.

Breaking Promises

General Discussion of the Problem

Humanitarian Ethics generally rejects the idea that breaking promises can be moral for all of the reasons listed in Chapter 12 in the arguments against it. People who break their promises cannot be trusted, making it very difficult to have a meaningful relationship with them. We all like to know that if a person promises to do or not do something, we can count on him or her to keep that promise. If someone breaks a promise even once, then we cannot have a significant relationship with that person.

Promises may be broken only for good reasons, again such as to save someone from harm or death. In order to break a promise, one must have an exceedingly important reason to do so; otherwise, promises should be kept.

Discussion of Specific Cases

CASE 1

No promise is ever too trivial for one to keep, and in this case keeping the promise was very important to Janice. That she made it a condition for her marrying Bernie also adds to its importance. I think all promises are important, but those made in connection with something as important as marriage are even more important, because breaking them tends to destroy an important relationship. It is quite possible to break only one promise or a few promises in one's life, but in my experience, one broken promise, like a lie, often leads to other broken promises. In other words, the domino theory is especially pertinent with regard to this moral issue.

CASE 2

Such promises as David made to Harold should not be made. It is unfair of Harold to demand such a promise of David, and David should not have made such a promise if he had no intention of keeping it. Harold could have asked him to help and protect Doris in any way he could, but he had no right to demand that David promise to marry her. David, too, could have promised to take care of Doris as best as he could but not to marry her unless he wanted to anyway. One should try to keep reasonable promises one has made, of course, whether or not anyone else knows about them.

Sometimes a promise is made only under conditions of unusual duress, and if David's was made under such conditions, he could be justified in breaking it rather than marry someone he doesn't love. A lot would depend on the circumstances. If the circumstances were extenuating, then one honest way David could handle breaking his promise would be to tell Doris what happened and ask to be released by her from the promise while still offering to continue to be her friend.

CASE 3

Because Wanda had an agreement with Sandy, what she did was not a moral act. We shouldn't lie to children any more than to adults. We may not reveal to children everything that we know or are doing, but when asked specific questions, we should answer honestly but gently. Wanda is of course also entitled to her own life as an adult and does not have to govern her every action by what Sandy thinks, feels, or wants; however, she should deal with Sandy as fairly and honestly as possible. If Wanda's relationship with Howard is a serious one, which it seems to be, then what Wanda does will eventually affect Sandy's life and cannot be merely relegated to Wanda's right to privacy. Wanda could have conducted her affair more discreetly and not at her home, which would have avoided Sandy's discovery. However, that Sandy actually asked her mother about the affair makes it all the more essential that Wanda be truthful with her. She of course need not and should not be graphic, but she can tell Sandy in a nice way about her feelings for Howard and give Sandy a chance and the time to relate to the situation without being confronted with it. I feel that it's important to be as honest with children as we can be, because if adults lie or break promises, children will assume that these actions are acceptable.

I feel that Wanda's reasons for not telling Sandy and for reacting with anger are understandable but neither helpful nor really justifiable. As I said earlier, she should have attempted to be honest with Sandy, especially when she promised to and also because Sandy had asked her a direct question that required an honest answer. Rather than respond to Sandy's anger with her own anger, she should have apologized to her and explained why she didn't act as she said she would in this instance. She then could have gone on to explain her relationship with Howard more fully so that Sandy would understand better how her mother felt and where Sandy would fit into the situation.

Stealing

General Discussion of the Problem

In most societies, people are entitled to what they have earned or inherited honestly, and no one has the right to take such possessions from them. People generally assume that their belongings are safe and that other people can be trusted not to steal them. Stealing primarily violates the Principle of Justice or Fairness, but also the Principles of Honesty and Truth Telling and Individual Freedom. Therefore, in Humanitarian Ethics, stealing is in general considered to be immoral. It is not fair, of course, to steal someone's fairly acquired earnings, possessions, ideas, or even reputation. Stealing also is dishonest even though it may be allowed in some extenuating situations. By stealing someone's possessions, material or otherwise, the thief limits that person's freedom. For example, if a couple has saved all year in order to go on a vacation and someone steals all of their money, then their freedom to enjoy that vacation has been denied. Therefore, the general view of stealing—like that of lying, cheating, and breaking promises—is that it is immoral unless strong justification can be brought forth, as when one justifies stealing in a disaster situation because it prevented the starvation of innocent people.

Discussion of Specific Cases

CASE 1

The theft of anything that is important to the owner is not a trivial wrong. This case presents beautifully the distinction between what is legal and what is moral as discussed in Chapter 1. Whether or not titles are protected by law, the moral principles previously described should be observed. That Victor has used this title for seven years and that his book has made it famous belies the title's theft. In addition to the outright stealing of the title, the publisher and the authors obviously are "cashing in" on the book's popularity, which certainly is unfair and unjust. That neither the publisher nor the authors even answered Victor's complaints reveals not only a blatant disregard for the seriousness of the situation but also a breach of good manners (see Chapter 1 on manners in their relationship to morals).

Victor cannot merely assume that they stole his title on purpose, but it certainly seems to be implied that what happened was not merely an error on the part of either the publisher or the authors. For example, if the publisher had done this without the authors knowing it, then, of course, they wouldn't have been guilty. Because neither party responded to Victor's complaint, he could only presume that all parties knew what they were doing. Once a book has been published, there is not much anyone can do, but the parties responsible could have written Victor and said that any revised edition would use a different title and apologized for stealing his. What hurts here, as with the forged letter of recommendation in Case 3 under the section on cheating, is that teachers of ethics are supposed to know the difference between what is legal and what is moral, and therefore immoral actions on their part are even more reprehensible than those taken by people who have not been formally trained in ethics.

CASE 2

I believe that Katia is justified in stealing during the wartime, emergency-type situation she was in. It would be better if some sort of rationing or control could be set up so that all survivors could receive equal shares, but such situations are not always feasible. Therefore, I believe that she would be justified in taking only what is needed. She certainly would not be justified in looting so as to acquire luxury items. When times were better, Katia could even offer to compensate the people whose house she had broken into.

Stealing during peacetime is of course a different matter. Usually there are many agencies of both the state and federal governments that Katia could turn to, and only if all of these avenues had been fully explored and exhausted could stealing be condoned at all. It isn't impossible that such a situation could occur, but most people can acquire some help, and even begging should be tried before one resorts to stealing.

CASE 3

Stealing such items is immoral. One can understand how people felt during such riots and how their anger and frustration could have surfaced. However, even if their society were corrupt and even though it certainly suppressed and segregated them, they could not justify stealing things that did not belong to them, especially when most of the stolen goods were luxury items. These were not items needed for simple survival as was the food in Case 2, and therefore it cannot be condoned or justified.

CASE 4

I do feel that Anne and Eric were guilty of theft. If they had felt that the will was unfair, then they should have sat down with the designated heirs and tried to get the will changed so as to be more equitable to their side of the family. Legally, of course, people may leave their estate to whomever they want; however, this does not always ensure justness or fairness. If after discussing the matter with the designated heirs Anne and Eric received no satisfaction, they could then have announced that they were going to contest the will. At least they would have been honest and open and aboveboard in their actions. What they did was certainly highly questionable—getting Margaret, who was more or less mentally incompetent, to change her will and then operating "under the table." On the face of it, they had no right to change Leroy's will unless they proceeded honestly and forthrightly. I feel also that they should have taken into consideration the effects of their actions—not just the immediate effects of gaining more money, but all of the hard feelings and loss of friendship that their actions caused. It would seem that friendship of long standing held very little importance for them.

5

Applying Humanitarian Ethics to the Moral Problems of Human Sexuality

General Discussion of the Problem

Before discussing specific sexual activities and the moral considerations surrounding them, it is important to see how the five basic principles relate to human sexuality. The Value of Life principle should not be, and very seldom is, involved in matters of private sexuality; however, any act that is life threatening may be considered immoral unless people choose it for themselves, which is a rarity (for example, cardiac patients who choose to risk their lives in order to have sexual relations). The Principle of Goodness is definitely involved in human sexual relationships in that sexual activity should cause pleasure and avoid pain, should strive for excellence, and should encourage harmony and foster creativity among all concerned.

There should always be a strong attempt to be honest and tell the truth in all aspects of any type of human relationship, but especially in matters of sexuality. Frankness and openness in the discussion of sexuality and sexual problems must also be encouraged. One of the absurdities in our culture is the obvious lack of education in or teaching about sexuality. There are, after all, experts available who have written books and who can supply clear empirical evidence and valid arguments concerning how to engage in meaningful sexual activity. Such information should be made available to all people at various stages of their development so that they can lead lives that are as full and rich as possible. Every effort should be made to distribute goodness and to be fair and just to all concerned, but especially toward the people immediately involved in the relationship.

Finally, in matters of private sexuality, individual freedom should be the guiding principle as long as the rights of the people immediately involved in the relationship are also observed. Humanitarian Ethics would consider rape, child molestation, sadism performed on unwilling victims, or any other kind of forced or coercive sexuality to be immoral, and it would consider any other human sexual activities performed between or among consenting adults to be moral as long as it can be shown that no direct harm comes to others because of these activities.

In other words, my ethical system is generally in agreement with the liberal point of view, which considers pornography, homosexuality, prostitution, masturbation, non-monogamous marriages, and sex outside of marriage, except for adultery, to be private sexual matters that should not be legislated against. As for "unnatural" sexuality, I would condone all forms of it that are performed by consenting adults except for bestiality.

Because I do not have a specific case to discuss with regard to each aspect of human sexuality presented in Chapter 13, before going into a discussion of these cases I feel that I should describe the Humanitarian Ethics point of view on sexuality in general.

First, I feel that both nonmonogamous and group marriages are moral as long as the five basic principles are carefully observed—especially in relation to any children involved—and all people in these types of marriages have agreed to be involved. If no one outside of them is harmed (other than that the group's style of living is not to a person's taste), then there seems to be nothing immoral about these marriages in themselves. Such arrangements are of a private nature pertaining only to those who have freely entered into them. Because people and their tastes and feelings differ so widely, voluntary experimentation may be allowed to take place so long as it is in consonance with the five basic principles.

Second, there is no evidence that masturbation leads to any harm either to the masturbater or to anyone else. It is, of course, generally prohibited as a public act under indecent exposure laws. However, assuming that it is a private act involving only one person, because it brings pleasure to that person without harming anyone else, and because it can help that person to find out about and to be at ease with his or her own body, then it should not be considered an immoral act.

Third, as far as so-called sexual perversion or unnatural sex acts are concerned, I would say that, except for bestiality, as long as these are private sexual matters entered into by consenting adults and they bring no harm to anyone else, then they should be considered to be moral. In other words, many sexual activities—such as oral sex, anal sex, sadism and masochism, homosexual sex, and group sex—should be allowed under the Principle of Individual Freedom as long as none of the other four principles is violated. What adults freely consent to do in their private sexual relationships—as long as it does not harm anyone else—cannot be considered immoral under the five basic principles. In such relationships, the decision about what is perverted or unnatural must be left to the people involved. Of course, people must recognize that several of these types of sexual activities are at high risk as far as developing AIDS and other Sexually Transmitted Diseases (STDs) goes and therefore should practice safer sex in order to protect one another.

Bestiality—that is, sex acts between human beings and animals—is offensive to most, but not all human beings. Because offensiveness to taste should not in itself be a determining factor, and because adults are consenting in such acts, should bestiality, like other private sex acts, be morally allowed? One factor here is that animals cannot consent, cannot resist, and probably are unwilling participants in such acts. My basis thus far for considering any private sexual activity to be moral has been that the participants are consenting adult human beings. Because animals do not fall into this category—and even though they are not human beings, they would be denied their freedom and forced into a sexual act they cannot consent to—then bestiality could be considered to be immoral under the five basic principles.

Some people consider it hypocritical to raise animals to be killed for food without moral qualms, yet do consider sexual activities with animals, even though they probably won't even be harmed, to be immoral. Whether killing animals for food is immoral or not, however, I would still say that bestiality should not be considered as moral, certainly not on the same basis as other acts undertaken by freely consenting adults.

Fourth, I believe that as long as prostitution occurs between or among consenting adults, it is moral. In this regard, I am in favor of the "social acceptance and governmental control" argument presented as the last argument for prostitution in Chapter 13.

Discussion of Specific Cases

CASE 1

It is my general feeling that premarital sex should be left entirely up to the individuals involved, providing that proper contraceptive precautions are taken so that the moral predicaments of abortion and the births of unwanted children, as well as the contraction of AIDS and other STDs, can be avoided. There is no legal or overriding moral requirement that people be legally married before they engage in sexual activity, but to my way of thinking there certainly should be a clear agreement—possibly even a personal contract— as to what people involved in such a relationship can expect from each other. Safe sex should be practiced so as to ensure mutual protection.

Furthermore, as long as the five basic principles (most often four, because the Value of Life seldom is an issue in sexuality) are practiced by people involved in premarital sex, there would seem to be no need for any moral or legal sanctions against it. As I have mentioned, this type of sexual activity usually is referred to as "fornication" in the Bible, where it is considered to be immoral, but it need not be immoral as long as the people involved are consenting, free, honest, just, truthful, and good toward each other.

For example, if two single people consent to have sexual relations without any commitments or ties being implied—solely for the pleasure that they hope can be derived from their sexual relationship—I can see nothing overtly wrong with such a relationship. It is important for the people to be honest and truthful with each other so that one person is not led to think that the relationship means more than it does; it would be immoral for one person to lie to another about this matter in order to get the other to engage in a sexual relationship. As long as both people understand the situation, however, I can see no reason why immorality need *necessarily* be involved.

People should be aware that sex is one of the most intimate of human relationships—one that can often lead to a greater commitment than is anticipated at the beginning of a relationship, so that either member of the relationship may be hurt by expecting more from it than was originally agreed upon. However, this is a risk that both parties take, and if they have any intimation that such a situation may develop, then perhaps the person who could get hurt should avoid this type of relationship. This possibility certainly can be discussed in advance, and once a person knows himself or herself well enough, he or she should know whether such a situation should be avoided. However, merely because people may get more deeply involved than they originally planned to do is not enough reason to make all such relationships immoral.

Evidence and arguments are not conclusive enough to assert that this type of relationship, by and in itself, is detrimental or immoral to any human who might enter into it. Nor—because this is a matter of private sexual relations—should what other people think have any necessary bearing upon whether or not such a relationship is entered into. The reactions of other people would certainly be one of the considerations people might want to make before engaging in such activity, especially if they cannot take criticism or any form of ostracism that they might receive from others in a culture that has frowned on premarital sexual relations for many years. But if people in such a relationship feel that they are not being immoral and can handle the reaction of others, then there should be no difficulty in having such a relationship.

In view of this, I obviously feel that Tom and Barbara, the two college teenagers, are not doing anything immoral. They seem to have arranged everything in such a way (contraception and a clear agreement) as to avoid serious difficulties as much as possible. For this reason, and because we are talking about a private sexual relationship that, as far as we can tell, will not directly harm anyone, I feel that their decision is moral.

CASE 2

I tend to take a liberal point of view in terms of homosexuality also. There is no conclusive proof that homosexuality is a sickness, an abnormality, or a form of perversity. Moreover, there is no conclusive proof as to whether it is physiologically or culturally caused or merely a chosen sexual lifestyle. Given these ambiguities, we seem to be talking about private rather than public sexual matters, and the Principle of Individual Freedom should take precedence as long as the other principles are not violated and other people are not harmed (except by possible offense to their taste). The same principles and concerns apply here as in other marriage- or nonmarriage-type relationships, such as practicing safe sex to avoid AIDS and other STDs. There is nothing in the relationship between Richard and Walter that poses harm to anyone outside the relationship. People around them might not want such a relationship or might not want to associate with them, but that is their privilege. Because the two men are not harming anyone, however, I would say that their relationship is moral.

CASE 3

I see nothing immoral in the relationship between Sarah and Ben. They are both adults, and they obviously have entered freely into their live-in arrangement. The financial situation certainly is a factor, and it's too bad that our laws are structured so as to discourage legal marriage for people of this age, but even if they didn't want to marry for other reasons, what business is that of anyone? Their children certainly do not have to accept the relationship, but these are matters of taste and should not be allowed to interfere with the important life decisions of others when no harm to anyone is involved. I believe that what Ben and Sarah are involved in is a private matter between two freely consenting adults and, for this reason, that it is a moral act.

CASE 4

Although adultery seldom violates the Value of Life principle, it does seem to involve a violation of the principles of Justice (in that it is an unfair and unjust treatment of another person: the other member of a marriage relationship) and Honesty or Truth Telling (in that it usually involves cheating on someone and not telling the truth about one's sexual affairs). It also can be said to violate the Principle of Goodness in that although it may bring pleasure to the two people involved in the adultery, it often causes extreme displeasure, unhappiness, and pain to the spouse who is being deceived and may infect him or her with AIDS or other STDs. Moreover, it obviously causes disharmony in the marriage relationship by destroying the unity of the family, perhaps resulting in separation and/or divorce, and often affecting innocent children who are members of the family unit. The adulterer or adulterers are exercising their own freedom, but at the cost of the freedom and rights of others. For all of these reasons, adultery is immoral and should be avoided.

The approach that should be used (but seldom is) when an adulterous temptation arises is to have an open and frank discussion with one's marriage partner about any problems before an adulterous relationship is entered into. Instead, most tempted unhappy marriage partners go ahead with an adulterous relationship or relationships until they are regularly practicing adultery. Because their mates have not been told and do not know about their affairs ("What they don't know won't hurt them"), the adulterers feel that the marriage is being maintained.

In addition to the fact that at least three basic principles are being violated, the unity and possible harmony and creativity of their marriage is constantly being undermined and, at least for one spouse, actually is destroyed. Very often the innocent marriage partner suspects, or even knows, but chooses to ignore what is happening. In this situation, however, nothing really is solved, and both partners continually live a lie. As mentioned in my justification for the Principle of Honesty or Truth Telling, if human relationships are to be meaningful and significant, they must be based upon people telling each other the truth wherever possible and being honest with each other to the greatest degree possible. Once this basis is undermined, any human relationship will be weakened and eventually destroyed. Tempted spouses ought to admit their temptation to their mates, stressing that no adulterous act has yet been committed and that they feel the need to enter into a new human relationship that will very probably damage their marriage; then they should offer to openly and frankly discuss their marital problems with the idea of avoiding the adulterous relationship.

If the situation is brought into the open *before* any overt action has been taken, and before any real commitments have been made to anyone other than the marriage partner, several alternatives are possible:

1. Both marriage partners can attempt to solve their marital problems, trying to discover why the adulterous act has been contemplated, with the idea of making up somehow for whatever is lacking in their marriage.
2. They can openly agree to and accept the practice of adultery with safe sex practices for *both* partners (as there should be no double standard) but continue their marriage under these conditions.
3. They can terminate their marriage either by separation or divorce if neither the first nor the second alternative can be worked out. In any of the three cases, however, the principles of Justice and Honesty or Truth Telling will have been observed, because whatever agreements are made will have been entered into with the full knowledge of both partners.

It is for these reasons and under these criteria that I feel that what Eric did was immoral; indeed, I feel that adultery in general is immoral unless it is agreed upon by all parties concerned because it tends to violate all of the basic ethical principles except for the Value of Life principle.

CASE 5

In the matter of pornography, I agree with the liberal viewpoint. In Chapter 13, I discussed the public implications of pornography, stating that as long as no one is forced to engage in or view any activity that he or she feels is obscene, then pornography is a private matter. I also discussed the fact that there is no conclusive evidence that viewing or engaging in pornographic activities has any harmful effect upon others or on the people engaging in such activities; in fact, there is evidence to the contrary. Therefore, if a person wishes to read or collect pornographic literature, art, or objects, or to view or participate in pornographic activities, and provided others are not forced to do the same, then that person should be allowed to do whatever he or she wants.

There should be no attempt to ban or eliminate such activities or objects, but children and unwilling adult participants should be protected from any outward display of pornography. For example, the outside of a store that carries pornographic books should stress that minors are not allowed and should not display such books outside. In this way, those who wish to read and purchase such books may do so, but those who do not may avoid the bookstore altogether. Otherwise, matters of pornography should be left up to the individual, and the Principle of Individual Freedom should take precedence.

It would seem in this case that the owners of the pornographic stores and theater have complied with all of these criteria; therefore, I think that in this situation, pornography is a private sexual matter. No further laws should be enacted against these owners, and what they are doing should not be considered to be immoral.

6

Applying Humanitarian Ethics to Moral Problems in Medicine (Bioethics)

General Discussion of the Problem

The five basic ethical principles apply to bioethical issues in the same way as they apply to the other moral issues I have discussed thus far. In fact, all five of these principles come into play in almost all bioethical situations, as we have seen in our discussions of death and dying, abortion, and just distribution of scarce medical resources. Generally, in bioethics, we should value life but accept death as inevitable; strive for goodness at all times, mainly for patients and secondarily for families and others; be just and fair in our treatment of patients, families, and health care personnel despite any preconceptions we may have concerning their "guilt" or "innocence"; try to establish and maintain honest and truthful relationships and significant human communication; and allow for as much individual freedom as is possible within the limits of the other four principles.

    As for the rights and obligations of health care professionals and patients and families, I would favor the reciprocal approach, with either the collegial or contractual model, because it maximizes freedom, equality, and justice, encouraging a free exchange of ideas. According to this approach, decisions are made collegially or contractually with everyone having equal input, and the best interests of the patient are the main focus of discussion and decision making. In terms of truth telling and informed consent, I favor the moderate position. I feel that patients should be kept as informed as they wish to be and that they should be given information as they want and need to know it. In short, they should provide the guidelines for truth telling and informing. There are times when informed consent is necessary for tests and other procedures, and in such cases all information should be carefully gone over in person by the doctor, and all the patient's questions should be fully and clearly answered.

There are also other considerations involved in truth telling. First, most medical situations involve some ethical decisions, and doctors should not make such decisions alone. They need, rather, to be willing to share their expertise and their concern for and jurisdiction over their patients with other health care professionals, support professionals (such as social service workers and the clergy), and, of course, patients and their families themselves. Second, professionals must recognize that they are in their profession to serve patients and their families, not the other way around. Third, studies have shown that at some point most patients who are seriously ill and/or dying recognize the seriousness of their situation and want to know how they stand. In such cases, doctors should share the truth without destroying all hope, and they should do this with compassion for patients and their families rather than regard them as numbers or personified diseases. Fourth, professionals should use all available means of communication— eye contact and touch, as well as oral and written language. Finally, professionals must realize that they can't make a blueprint for truth telling approaches; methods will differ in relation to the patients, the families, and the situations. If patients and families wish or need to deny the truth, and if this denial is not destructive, then they should be allowed their temporary illusions. If they want to know part or all of the truth, then they should be allowed that, too. Generally speaking, however, I am in favor of being honest with patients and their families.

Behavior Control

The Moderate Position. A more moderate position than the two views described in Chapter 14 states that behavior modification is justified provided that an individual is free and competent to consent to such modification (for example, people who join Weight Watchers or Alcoholics Anonymous). As long as these conditions are met, behavior controllers in all areas are justified in furnishing people with safe, ethical means and methods of accomplishing what they want to. According to this position, it is questionable whether a person incarcerated in a prison or a mental institution is ever free or competent to make such decisions, especially where the change is strongly desired not by the person but by the institution or society at large.

The Humanitarian Ethics Approach. I agree with the moderate position in the area of behavior control. It seems to me that people who want to change their behavior should be allowed to do so in ethically permissible ways, which are not destructive to themselves or others. For example, brain surgery is justified if there is operable physiological brain disease or injury, but generally it should not be used to correct psychological problems that are not physiologically based because brain tissue cannot be replaced once it has been removed.

Of course, in some cases behavior is violent, destructive, vicious, or murderous and must be controlled. Here again, every ethically permissible method can generally be used provided that subjects are not seriously injured or made ill by the behavior control procedures, although some "harm" may be necessary for the protection of innocent people. For example, life incarceration for a murderer might be considered harmful to the murderer, but that harm is outweighed by the danger to innocent people of releasing him.

I personally prefer conditioning techniques based upon rewards to aversive techniques. Perhaps in some situations, such as when dealing with people who have committed serious crimes, some aversive conditioning (for example, a long period of incarceration, or solitary confinement) will need to be used. Generally, however, the reward approach is preferable unless subjects freely agree to aversive conditioning.

An example of reward conditioning is the method used by Weight Watchers. Everything is done to reinforce members' staying on a diet and maintaining or losing weight, but nothing is done if weight is gained except to encourage members to keep trying to lose it. I also feel that no behavior control techniques for which side effects are not clearly known should be used except under extraordinary circumstances.

Finally, I feel that people who work as behavior controllers should be well qualified both medically and ethically. Moreover, they should be well versed in all methods of behavior control and should be willing to use the method that best suits the patient and the situation. For example, if patients need psychotherapy of some sort, they should have it; if they need certain psychotherapeutic drugs, they should have them; if they need operant conditioning, then they should have that, too. Generally, then, controllers or therapists should always consider first what is in the best interest of their patients, except when the latter could pose a serious danger to other innocent people.

Human Experimentation

The Moderate Position. From the moderate point of view, experimentation can be done on human beings, but only within strict guidelines. Any people to be experimented upon must be competent adults, and they must be fully informed both in person and in writing of all the risks, side effects, and benefits of the experimentation. It also can be allowed as a last resort for therapeutic reasons provided that the people experimented upon are fully informed and freely consent, and that the risk or pain is no greater than for any other procedure prescribed for their particular disease or injury. Such experimentation may even take place upon children, provided parental consent has been given. In such cases, however, it may be advisable to have a judge hear the case in order to provide the child with further protection.

Great care must be taken when an experiment has no benefit for the subject but, rather, is being done in order to "benefit humanity" in general or to advance knowledge. Subjects of such experiments must be fully consenting, competent adults; risks must be minimized; subjects should be free from coercion; and subjects must be fully informed about the experiment. Mental incompetents and children should not be experimented upon for these reasons.

The moderate position also accepts experimentation on incarcerated subjects, but only if they freely consent and are fully informed, just as they would be if they weren't incarcerated. They must not, in any case, be used as unknowing guinea pigs. Special bioethics committees should be established whenever and wherever *any* human experimentation is to be done, and all applications for human experimentation must be screened carefully before being approved.

Membership on such committees should not be limited to medical personnel but should also include ethicists, religious and nonreligious members, and other informed laypeople such as lawyers, sociologists, and psychologists. In such situations, the protection of subjects should have first priority. That is why experimentation that seeks to enhance the therapeutic well-being of subjects is generally more acceptable than experimentation for "the good of humanity" or for the advancement of scientific knowledge. If such protection cannot be given, then experimentation must not be done.

The Humanitarian Ethics Approach. I generally favor the moderate position in relation to human experimentation. I feel that human experimentation can be done on freely consenting adults who are fully and clearly informed, especially when it is to be done for their own therapeutic well-being, but I also feel that it can be done for the benefit of others and for scientific advancement as long as the stated conditions are met.

Generally, however, I feel that prisoners should not be experimented upon. Subjects of experiments should be completely free from coercion, and people who are incarcerated obviously don't have this freedom. I also feel that children should not be experimented on unless it is for their own therapeutic good, and that it should be done only as a last resort, after nonexperimental therapies and procedures have all been tried to no avail. For example, if a child has a cancer upon which none of the usual therapies has been successful and if the child will die unless remission is attained, and if there is an experimental therapy that is not overly painful and that has some promise of success, then it may be tried. I also feel that any experiments to be done on children for any reason ought to be presented before a judge so that parents and doctors won't have to bear the whole burden of decision making and so that another, perhaps more objective, opinion may be obtained, thereby further safeguarding children's rights, health, and lives.

In any type of human experimentation, great care must be taken to see that coercion, either forcible or subtle, is fully eliminated. Finally, I am definitely in favor of clearing any and all human experimentation through the type of bioethics committee described in Chapter 14.

Genetics

The Moderate Position. Genetic experimentation and development should be allowed within careful guidelines. Amniocentesis, CVS, and genetic counseling have helped people to make important decisions about pregnancy, childbearing, abortion, and sterilization, and as long as such matters are left to individual choice, they are ethically valid.

Other advances, however, must be made more carefully. Radical experimentation, such as cloning or the creation of life in a laboratory, should not proceed until we know with some certainty what its effects upon the human species will be. Limited experimentation can be done in these areas; for example, the creation and cloning of animal life in order to increase food production would be justified and encouraged. The correction of genetic defects in conceptuses or in parents is also an area worthy of investigation and development. Even a limited creation of human life or cloning may later be authorized, but only after its effects are known and safe guidelines have been established.

The Humanitarian Ethics Approach. I also favor the moderate position here. I feel that we should learn as much as we can about our genetic makeup, but that we must have carefully drawn guidelines and safeguards in order to ensure that we know what the effects of applying genetic knowledge will be *before* we proceed with such techniques. I definitely am in favor of procedures such as amniocentesis and CVS and believe in full and complete counseling both before and after the birth of children in families where genetic problems are suspected or evident. I believe that genetic counselors play a very important role in this area and that they must be well qualified and suited for their jobs.

In addition, I believe that when we have the ability, we should encourage the correction of genetic defects in the conceptus, just as we now encourage such correction after the birth of children with genetic problems. Also, the correction or alteration of defective genes in adults should be encouraged when and if it becomes possible. I believe that we should proceed *very* carefully with the laboratory creation of human life and especially with the cloning of human life. I do feel that controlled experimentation can proceed in these areas, however. We already have made progress with artificial insemination and fertilized ovary implantation, so the creation in the laboratory of normal human life—to provide children for childless couples, for example—would seem to be a next and viable step. However, all of this experimentation should be kept on a small, individualistic, humanistic, and ethical level.

Discussion of Specific Cases

CASE 1

The doctor seemed either to be very callous where Richard's feelings were concerned or to be unable to stop himself from expressing his own frustrations that he was no longer able to help his patient. I believe that he was right in telling Richard the truth, but that he should not have done it so coldly and brutally, without offering Richard any hope. If he had listened carefully to Richard's questions, he would have known that Richard needed some hope, even if it only involved some medication to alleviate discomfort and pain.

To tell Richard that nothing more could be done was false (consider the hospice approach to care for the dying), and it eliminated all of Richard's hope not just for a cure, but for being cared for as a significant human being. Once he had seen the extent of Richard's distress, the doctor could have prescribed the medication, telling Richard he couldn't promise any startling changes but also telling him that he would continue to look into other drugs and therapies for him. Finally, the doctor could have asked Richard about his pain, his ability to eat and sleep, and so on, really listening to him and trying to resolve or ease these difficulties for him.

CASE 2

I don't believe that counselors have the right to withhold any information that parents really desire and certainly none that they ask for. If parents don't ask for certain information, I don't feel that the counselors have the obligation to volunteer such information unless it will have some serious implication for the prospective child's health and well-being. A child's sex definitely does not fall into this category, so if parents did not specifically ask for this information, counselors are not obligated to reveal it. However, if parents do seek this information, then counselors are obligated to reveal it.

The only thing counselors can do if they discover that a couple will seek an abortion for such a questionable reason is to counsel them against the abortion. Counselors should make it clear that the child will otherwise be healthy and that late abortions, besides being more risky than earlier ones, are morally questionable because of the extent to which the fetus has developed. However, if the parents still wish to seek an abortion, and the law allows it, there is nothing more that the counselors can do. I stated in Appendix 3 that I feel that the parents are not ethically justified in aborting the fetus because of its sex, but despite this, I do not feel that counselors can withhold the truth if counselees directly ask for it.

CASE 3

The experimenter is in quite a quandary here because if he tells his subjects, the experiment will be ruined, but if he doesn't he will be invading their privacy, which should be guaranteed regardless of whether they are patients in or outside of an institution. In fact, as patients these people should be protected even more. There is, however, a third alternative, and that is to tape the patients without telling them, but not to use the tapes in any way unless patients agree to it. Patients should be informed clearly in person and in writing as to how the tape will be used, and they should be allowed to see it, after which they should have the right to refuse to have the tape used at all.

If this is their desire, then the tape must be immediately erased or destroyed so as to acquiesce in the patients' wishes. If patients will allow the tape to be used, then they ought to have the right to specify the purposes and limitations for its use; this also ought to be done in writing, and clear indications should be given as to how the tape may or may not be used. If this alternative is utilized, then tapes must be made totally secure until patients can give or refuse permission for their use. If this security cannot be guaranteed, then either the patients' permission must be acquired prior to taping or the experiment simply cannot be conducted. In all cases of experimentation, subjects' rights should come before the experiment, the desires of experimenters, or the advancement of science.

CASE 4

As I have already stated, I don't believe that experiments should be done upon children—with or without their parents' permission—unless it is therapeutic for them and only when it is a last resort to save their lives. I think it is even more unforgivable to experiment upon children in institutions, especially when those children are mentally retarded. There are acceptable cures for children who suffer from dysentery, and infecting otherwise healthy children with dysentery is completely unjustified, both medically and ethically.

The coercion of allowing only those children into the institution whose parents would agree to experimentation is also highly unethical and should not be permitted. A case such as this one makes it easy to see why it is important to require a court opinion prior to experimentation with children. If such a case had to be brought before a judge, it is very unlikely that the experiment would be allowed. In no way should the desire for experimentation be allowed to supersede the protection of the rights, bodies, and lives of children.

CASE 5

I believe, as I have already stated, that a controller or therapist *generally* owes first allegiance or responsibility to the patient rather than to society, government, or an institution; therefore, in this situation, I feel that the therapist's first responsibility is to John, and that he must begin therapy by finding out what John really wants. This, of course, would require some preliminary therapy sessions.

If John really is happy as a homosexual, then the therapist should help him to adjust to his homosexuality; if, however, he would be happier being heterosexual or even bisexual, then the therapist's responsibility is to help him to change his behavior and adjust to his new sexual orientation. The important thing is that the therapist not force John into some sort of mold, preconceived either by the therapist or society; rather, he should help John to change his behavior once it has been discovered what John really wants.

CASE 6

As I mentioned earlier, I generally am not in favor of brain surgery to control behavior, unless the behavior problem is physiologically based. It would seem to me that all other alternative therapies should be exhausted before the question of brain surgery ever arises. If there are no viable alternatives, then there is a question as to whether Mary should be subjected to a medical procedure with such great attendant risks and unknown effects. Related to this is the question of whether or not Mary really is in a position—given that she is in a mental institution—to freely give an informed consent to such a procedure.

I believe that if all alternatives have been exhausted, including electrode implantation in the brain (the electrode could be removed if it didn't work, or if it caused dangerous side effects), then the decision would first have to be made as to whether Mary was mentally competent to decide to have brain surgery.

I feel that several psychologists and psychiatrists, outside the institution where Mary is housed, should examine her and present their opinions before a judge qualified to hear competency cases. If Mary is adjudged to be mentally competent after a careful legal hearing, and if she is fully informed and aware that she may become very passive and suffer memory loss, then I feel she has a right to such surgery. I believe that no coercive methods should be used. The important thing for Mary to understand is the effect the surgery will have on her. Perhaps she could even be shown several brain-surgery patients who have had the type of surgery she would undergo. In any case, she should not be promised that her violent episodes will cease or that she will be released from the institution.

CASE 7

This is a very serious moral dilemma. The fairest way of resolving the issue is to put a prisoner on the list, under whatever criteria apply to patients in general, and let him have the transplant when it becomes available in the normal sequence of events and according to tissue match providing he has been convicted of only one misdemeanor or minor felony. Humanitarian Ethics would accept this egalitarian way of dealing with transplants. However, in this case, where the criminal has been caught three times or where a criminal is guilty of a major felony, such as murder, rape, torture, mayhem, child molesting, and so forth, Humanitarian Ethics would be opposed to his name's being entered on the waiting list for a transplant. In the case cited, this drug dealer could be out on the streets again in four years to push more drugs—the heart transplant, at the expense of an innocent patient in need of it, would have made it possible.

APPENDIX

7

Applying Humanitarian Ethics to Moral Problems in Business (Business and Media Ethics)

The Humanitarian Ethics Approach

General Discussion of the Problem

As in bioethics, the five basic ethical principles generally should apply in the area of business. One of the common ethical mistakes made in our society is to somehow separate business dealings from our moral activities. That is, we may generally believe that it is wrong to lie, cheat, and steal, but may somehow view these behaviors as being acceptable when done in the world of business. There is, of course, no logical or moral basis for such a separation.

In approaching business activities, therefore, people must value, protect, and preserve human life; strive for goodness in business and avoid badness and harm; strive to be just and fair in distributing the good and bad arising out of business activities; be as honest and truthful as they can in all of their business dealings, including agreements, contracts, advertising, and labor negotiations; and allow for as much individual freedom as possible for employers, employees, and consumers, within the limits of the other four principles. These principles have as much meaning and application here as they have in dealing with any of the other moral issues or problems presented in this book.

In general I tend to support the moderate positions on discrimination and the environment and also the truthful approach in advertising described in Chapter 15. I feel that advertising should be based, as much as possible, on honesty and truth telling unless this principle would seriously conflict with the other principles—for example, if it would unnecessarily cost people their lives. It would seem that honesty and truth telling generally are the best policies to follow in business, as they are in other areas of our existence.

I also tend to lean more toward protecting and preserving the environment than allowing business to grow larger and more powerful because using up resources as if they will never run out and destroying our living environment have a more serious immediate and long-range effect upon our lives and health than does the state of our economy. This policy does not have to mean the end of business; all it means is that business will now have to be conducted in harmony with our environment rather than in disregard of it. As I have mentioned, this policy will be expensive, and it may mean that economic progress will have to be slowed somewhat; however, we all should be willing to make the sacrifices necessary to preserve our world, our lives, and the lives of future generations.

I also lean toward a strong affirmative action program, not only in business but also in all aspects of our society. I feel strongly that reverse discrimination should be avoided as much as possible, but for a while, anyway, I think it must remain a necessary evil in some situations. My reason for this position is that although we have made strides as a nation toward righting wrongs resulting from discriminatory practices in the past, the immorality of racial, religious, and sexual prejudice has gone on for so long that gargantuan efforts now will be needed to eliminate it. I feel that if we are strong in our resolve to make the necessary changes in this area, we can do so in a way that will avoid, for the most part, the additional harm of reverse discrimination.

As for rights and obligations, as I have mentioned in earlier chapters, no rights are absolute, but some do take precedence over others: the right to have one's life preserved and protected, for example. The rights of everyone involved in business activities should be established and carried out generally in accordance with the five principles and their priorities as described in Chapter 8. Conflicts of rights must be resolved not by arbitrarily establishing absolutes but rather by applying the basic ethical principles to specific situations, taking into consideration the particularities of that situation and the people involved in it.

Obligations, too, are to be established in accordance with the five basic ethical principles, and they must be fulfilled, whenever possible, in consonance with the Principle of Justice. Rights and obligations in any business should be clearly stated for everyone involved—employees, consumers, and employers—and they should be monitored and followed to the best of everyone's ability. In other words, in business—as in other aspects of our lives—being ethical or moral is all-important, and it must have priority over production, consumption, competition, and expansion. If everyone in business has this attitude, then we cannot help but create a better life for ourselves, not only economically, but in an overall human way as well.

Discussion of Specific Cases

CASE 1

This case is a good example of a situation in which production and profit in business take precedence over safety. Manufacturers often are loath to increase the cost of production in order to make their products safer; they would rather take the risk that no harm will result from this—that the product will be "safe enough." Obviously, as this case illustrates, this attitude often results not only in a threat to people's health and lives, but also in a higher cost in the long run to the manufacturers, in terms both of good public relations and of money.

This car company compounded its original mistake by ignoring the fact that the mistake was costing lives, making no effort to rectify it once it was discovered. Furthermore, the company even threatened to penalize the employee who was trying to rectify the problem. In this situation, public health and well-being should have been the main priority, not profit and loss. The design engineer was right in diligently attempting to correct the safety error, and for the car manufacturer to consistently penalize her for her ethics rather than reward her is a perfect example of misplaced values.

Susan's first ethical obligations were to the protection of innocent lives and to her own sense of right and wrong rather than loyalty to a company that was unethical in its actions toward others. By these unethical actions, in fact, the company nullified any obligations its employees might have had to be loyal to it; one need not and indeed should not be loyal to an organization that is unethical.

The engineer should have quit or allowed herself to be fired and then reported what she knew to public authorities. This action would have provoked an investigation, stopped production of the car until proper corrections were made, and forced the manufacturer to recall cars already sold so that their safety problems could be corrected. It obviously behooves every company to be exceptionally prudent when the safety of consumers is concerned, and in the long run such a policy will cost companies less. The research engineer cannot shirk her own ethical responsibility just because the company has removed direct responsibility from her because the lives of innocent people are involved here. Losing her job may be a hardship, but she really has no other choice if she wishes to act ethically.

CASE 2

Steve's decision is wrong because he is ignoring an agreement he made when he entered his union to abide by majority decisions in negotiations. It also is unethical to steal from one's business even if the company is insured against loss of tools and equipment and even if a worker thinks that the company can afford the loss because it makes so much money. Because a majority of Steve's coworkers and fellow union members approved the contract, he has no right to violate it unilaterally. Evidently, management and the union worked out what they both felt was a fair and just increase considering that the plant had lost profits in the last year.

Assuming that both sides negotiated in good faith, then Steve also must abide by the decision in good faith; his only other alternative is to resign and look for work elsewhere.

Under the circumstances, Steve has no basis for stating that he was cheated out of his raise unfairly. Management does, I feel, have an obligation to help its workers meet the cost of living wherever it can do so, but this company seems to have done its best by coming within 2 percent of the cost of living increase. In short, all of the parties involved, except Steve, seem to have done the best they could under the circumstances. What Steve did, however, was definitely unethical.

CASE 3

No business is ethically justified in selling products or services that differ in content from what is advertised. It is ethically wrong for a company to switch major parts of its product in order to save money, and when such a practice is discovered, whether done inadvertently or deliberately, immediate restitution must be made without attempts to cover up, use bribery, or employ any other stalling tactics.

Because the price difference is $1,000, the customers are entitled to the superior equipment that the higher price calls for—any other arrangement would be unethical. Whether the company is caught or not has absolutely nothing to do with the ethics of the situation; even if it knows it will never be caught, its basic policy should be to give consumers the right equipment for a fair price. Mike should, of course, refuse the bribe for not revealing what the company has done, no matter how enticing that bribe may be. Rather, he should report his discovery to the proper authorities and do everything he can to ensure that the company corrects all discrepancies and makes good its original claims.

CASE 4

As in the case of the research engineer for the car company, Myra has done the ethical thing up to this point and should persevere in her line of action. Her boss's version of what is and is not ethical in public relations and advertising serves only expediency; it is erroneous both logically and ethically. Advertising firms have an ethical obligation to tell the truth and to make sure that the products and services they are advertising are not dangerous, regardless of how large the account is. Because Myra cannot in good conscience create a campaign to promote a car that is endangering the lives of innocent people, she should not be required to do so. She certainly should not be coerced into doing so by being threatened with the denial of a just promotion.

As I have already said, the advertising firm should have a policy against representing unethical firms such as the car manufacturer, but even if it does decide to represent them, its employees should not be forced to violate their consciences by having to participate in such lies and misrepresentations. Like the research engineer, Myra owes her first loyalty to the people whose lives are endangered and also to her own conscience; she does not owe any loyalty to an organization that is not only being unethical but also is trying to coerce her into acting unethically. The position in which both Myra and Susan, the engineer, find themselves is very difficult—it is not easy to give up one's livelihood and job security—but how can they be happy in the long run, working for firms that are so obviously unethical and that have such a total disregard for the rights and lives of others?

CASE 5

Because Denise and Bonnie are equally qualified, and because they both are women—which helps to fulfill one aspect of affirmative action—the decision to be made is how the difference between their personalities and their races should affect which one of them is hired. That Bonnie is more outgoing does not relate directly to the job, and its importance in terms of keeping office personnel happy is far outweighed by the mandate of affirmative action. If the two women were white, perhaps the more outgoing personality might be a factor in hiring, but it seems a factor of minimal importance in this situation.

My feeling is that, under these circumstances, the personnel manager should hire Denise. I don't feel that Bonnie could claim reverse discrimination because Denise is as well qualified as she is. It is also probably true that Bonnie, despite affirmative action, still has a better chance than Denise of finding a job elsewhere. Obviously, I feel that the personnel manager should be very conscious of affirmative action and reverse discrimination in making this decision, especially because the percentage of minority and women employees at the center is so low. I feel that the first criterion for hiring should be that the prospective employee has the qualifications for the job; once that criterion has been met, however, I feel that affirmative action should have the greatest influence on the choice, at least until the ratio of minorities and women has been raised to an acceptable level.

CASE 6

I feel that every effort should be made by all parties to effect a series of compromises that will save the people and the environment, the town, and the company—in that order. I definitely think that the government, as the representative of all people, does have a right— indeed, an obligation—to investigate businesses and communities so as to avoid destruction of the environment. The government's report obviously is very important to everyone in this area, and all parties should accept the following as their goals: to clean up the environment as soon as possible; to keep the town economically alive by maintaining the plant, even if at a reduced capacity until necessary changes can be made; and to allow the company to reap a reasonable profit from the plant's operations. Representatives of the company, the townspeople and their representatives (mayor, city council), and the federal government should meet together to see what can be done to accomplish the stated objectives.

The company must be willing to pay its fair share of the costs, but it should not be overburdened. The townspeople also must bear some of the burden, perhaps through higher taxes or the foregoing of raises for workers at the plant for one year. The government also should help financially by offering either low-interest government loans or part payment for the changes that the plant must undergo.

I feel that the mayor would be wrong in entering into collusion with the plant manager to stall environmental changes at the expense of the health and welfare of the entire community. I believe that the problem ought to be brought into the open so that the townspeople can be made aware of it and can help to solve it in some way. I also feel that the company that owns the plant ought to consider more than just a loss of profits in its decision making. After all, the company is contributing not only to the economic well-being of a town but also to the destruction of its environment and the possible ill-health of its people. The company also should consider the goodwill it can gain by maintaining the plant, even if it sustains some loss of profit. Instead of taking the either-or position, the company ought to present choices as to what can be done, and it should ask for help and cooperation from all involved parties.

The company must—as must everyone who is involved in this situation—accept the long-range necessity of protecting and preserving the environment; otherwise, there may not be a plant or many people around in years to come. I feel that all aspects of the situation are important, but I feel that the environmental aspect should be given first priority by all parties. If the plant maintains its rigid position and will take only the stalling route the manager has suggested to the mayor, I feel that the mayor has no choice but to refuse to go along with it.

Perhaps now that the town is better established, there will be time to encourage new, less environmentally destructive businesses to set themselves up in Farling. In any case, I feel that a decision to increase the danger to the health and well-being of the people and the environment would be the wrong decision for the mayor to make, even if it is the only way of saving the town economically. After all, if people have their health and lives, they can still move somewhere else and get other jobs; if, on the other hand, they are sick or dying, then the economics of the situation definitely becomes unimportant.

CASE 7

I think what happened to the first officer was abominable. True, she made a foolish mistake in having an affair with a higher-ranking officer, but she did think that he loved her and she believed him when he said that he was divorcing his wife. Once she found out that he was not committed to her and just wanted to have sex with her, having no intention of divorcing his wife, she had every right to break off the affair and to have that be the end of it. Nothing she did deserved the treatment she received after breaking up with him. Despite an error in judgment, she should have been left alone by that officer once she said she wanted to end the affair, and in no way should she have received any harassment on her job. She definitely should have been able to count on backup while doing her police duties, regardless of what had gone on with the sergeant. Officers, especially the sergeant, should have been reprimanded, transferred to a different precinct, and perhaps even demoted, including those who did not back her up when she needed it.

CASE 8

The second officer certainly was unfairly treated because of her sex and should not have been discriminated against because she is female. She had successfully completed the difficult training that qualified her for the K9 corps and therefore should have been allowed to perform her duties without harassment, humiliation, or dehumanizing language and actions. That she was put in danger of being seriously injured when not only one but two male officers purposely gave their dogs the wrong commands is absolutely unacceptable and thoroughly unethical. Here again, I think that the officers responsible for her harassment should have been severely reprimanded, demoted, and transferred, and perhaps even should have had their jobs terminated because of their irresponsible behavior.

I think that both women should be offered their jobs back after the offenders have been removed from the precinct and should be paid full retroactive compensation whether they take their jobs back or not. I also think that any psychological therapy treatments should be paid for by the City of Long Beach. I also feel that they should receive the awards of their civil suits as soon as possible. These two are the worst cases of sexual harassment I have ever heard about. I'm sure that there are others equally bad or worse, but such actions must not be allowed to take place in any type of employment situation according to Humanitarian Ethics.

CASE 9

I feel that the photographer probably shouldn't have taken the photograph unless it was for his own private file. I don't think it should've been printed in the paper because it was definitely an invasion of the family's private grieving over their young relative. It might interest you to know that this was based on an actual event. The photographer, of course, took the picture, and the managing editor was convinced by his staff to print it for the purpose of warning the community about the dangers of drowning. The paper received 500 letters attacking the printing, and 100 readers discontinued their subscriptions to the paper based on what they perceived to be a definite invasion of the family's right to grieve privately.

8

Applying Humanitarian Ethics to Environmental Ethics

Environmental ethical issues have become quite significant and controversial in the last 20 years or so. When I was growing up in Los Angeles in the 1930s and 1940s, there was no concern about the diminution of resources. We believed that our natural resources would last us forever. The air in Los Angeles was clean and pure, water was clear and delicious, and trees were plentiful. I don't need to describe what has happened since then all over our nation and the world, much less in Los Angeles, the smog capital of the world. Civilization and society have taken their toll on all aspects of our environment—animals, bodies of water, plants and trees, air, and land—to the extent that all human beings must realize that if the environment is not protected, the world as we know it will not exist for us, our children, or future generations.

However, problems with the environment have occurred as a result of those scientific and technological advances that have made life better and more rich for human beings, and there is a battle going on between making progress and maintaining and even developing a beautiful natural environment and staying healthy in the process. In addition, many companies make their profit from the natural environment, such as lumber companies, chemical companies, mining firms, scientific research firms, and fur trapping organizations. It would seem that the best way to approach this ethical issue would be to seek a balance between protecting the environment in all of its aspects and allowing for the advancement of civilization and progress within reason.

As you might expect from the way in which Humanitarian Ethics has proceeded in the previous appendixes, it tends to favor the moderate position, which is to maintain the environment in its beauty and vitality, protect endangered species, and respect the lives of other living creatures (whether animals or plants and trees) and yet to allow for progress, scientific advancement, and scientific research for the betterment of all human beings.

Protection of the Environment: Recycling and Waste Disposal

Every effort must be made to protect and preserve the environment and yet allow for progress to continue to be made and businesses to flourish. These are not always easy tasks to accomplish, however. We obviously cannot continue on with the willy-nilly, irresponsible destruction of the environment: laying waste to our forests and land; polluting our rivers, streams, and lakes; and burying waste that will not disintegrate and toxic chemicals that will destroy our lands, waters, and population.

Recycling

One of the most important actions that we can take is to recycle our products and to use recycled materials in business. Where I once had two trash cans, I now have nine for the separation of various recyclable products. We need to make an even greater effort to recycle and to use recycled products so that we will not continue, for example, to decimate the trees throughout our land in order to get paper and paper products. Cities, city councils, and state governments must provide for pickup and disposal of recyclable products.

Toxic Waste Disposal

We also must regulate the disposal of toxic wastes; otherwise, we ourselves and our children and grandchildren will not survive. Science and technology must come up with new ways to safely destroy such wastes without having to bury them in our land, dump them in our bodies of water, including our oceans, or let them escape into the atmosphere. There should be ways to accomplish this, and we must continue to develop them. I see no way around the governmental regulation of all of these things, and government must be reasonable and moderate in allowing businesses and people to flourish without destroying the environment.

Animal Rights

Humanitarianism believes that animals have rights because they are sentient and mental beings to varying degrees, but it does not put animals ultimately on the same level as human beings. It believes that animals may be used for food, but not wastefully, and that they should not be killed in any way that gives them great pain. It favors free range over factory farming or at least careful concern for animals' well-being and treatment. It respects the vegetarian point of view but does not believe that people are immoral in any way if they choose to eat animal flesh as long as animals are not cruelly treated in the process. It also takes the view that since animals are killed for food, their skins and other parts can also be used as needed, but it is opposed to using endangered species either for food or for body parts.

Animal Experimentation

Humanitarian Ethics believes that animals can be used for experimentation as long as they are treated humanely and not caused pain or needless suffering. Cures for diabetes, polio, heart disease, and many other diseases would never have been discovered without animal experimentation. This does not give researchers the right to torture or mutilate animals in any way, however, and there should be strict rules regulating this and safeguards against allowing animals to suffer pain. Any experiments also must be significant and not trivial or useless, as with the beagles and the strontium 90 testing. Given such rules and safeguards, it would seem that rather than being put to sleep, unwanted animals could be used for fitting experimental purposes.

Killing Animals for Sport

Although I do not like to hunt or fish, I do not oppose allowing other people to do so, provided that they follow rules and regulations that protect animals and fish from becoming endangered or extinct. If hunting or fishing is indeed an ancient custom or ritual, then an unsportsmanlike approach to killing animals or fish should not be allowed. However, careful licensing, regulation, and quotas should be in effect to protect animals and fish and yet also allow for the control of their overpopulation. The killing of exotic endangered animals for food and body parts should not be allowed, and laws protecting them should be duly enforced.

Discussion of Specific Cases

CASE 1

The issues presented in the case of the baby harp seals or any other animal-harvesting situation are very controversial and difficult to resolve. In the first place, I am opposed to killing animals for furs when there are perfectly good synthetic furs available that are just as beautiful as real furs. I don't think that people who wear fur coats that were made years ago should be looked down upon in any way, but I think we should stop using materials such as ivory, furs, or exotic skins unless they are acquired from animals who die naturally or who are hunted on a limited basis under strict quota regulation and licensing.

Perhaps a quota system could be applied to the harp seals, but only to adults. Just as fawns are protected from deer hunting, so also should other baby animals be allowed to grow up before being harvested. It should also be required that the harp seals be killed in the most painless way possible. Further, every effort should be made to find another industry for the people in that area so that they will not be deprived of their livelihood once the killing of the harp seals has been restricted or stopped.

CASE 2

Many of these distinctions seem to fall under the heading of "split-hairs." I would favor using parts of the animals that have been killed for food for clothing or shoes and accessories, thereby using natural animal resources efficiently. As I stated in Case 1, I see no reason for people to kill animals in order to gain furs, hides, or feathers unless the animals already have died or have been killed for food. Obviously, I think that killing animals for food is not unethical, whereas killing them merely for hides, furs, feathers, or body parts is. That is the distinction I find so important. Again, I stipulate that the killing of any wild animals should be done as humanely as possible and regulated by quota and licensing so as to avoid the endangerment of species. Therefore, I oppose raising animals just for their hides, furs, feathers, or body parts.

CASE 3

As I described in Chapter 15 on business ethics, industry has a powerful obligation to protect the environment to the greatest extent possible. Constant research should be done and safety procedures enacted to prevent such calamities as oil spills and to find effective methods of neutralizing and controlling spills when they do occur. This should be an oil company's first priority. It also is admirable to protect and preserve our natural environment and animal and plant species from destruction by the technology of oil drilling or strip mining, for example, but these actions should be real and extensive, not just the building of a pipe here and there for a fox to hide in. Any and all destruction to the environment should be reported along with the causes and efforts being made to resolve whatever problem has occurred. Keeping the public informed is much better for a company's image than having people find out about the destruction of the environment after the fact. Advertisements and commercials that describe what the company is doing to preserve and protect the environment are fine so long as they're not distracting the public from the company's mistreatment of the environment.

CASE 4

First of all, other tests that do not use animals or humans should be developed. It is difficult to understand why, given all of the scientific knowledge about chemistry, such experiments still have to be conducted. I believe it is hard to justify experimenting upon animals or humans merely for cosmetic reasons when pain and destruction are involved. I do feel that experimenting upon animals for significant medical developments, as I stated earlier in this appendix, is justified as long as these experiments are not trivial but benefit human beings. If it is absolutely necessary to test an important cosmetic on animals, then testing should be done painlessly, and such tests that might result in the loss of eyesight, for example, should be avoided. A company could also ask for human volunteers, as long as the same protections and strict rules and regulations are followed that exist for human experimentation in general.

CASE 5

One of the most difficult balances we have to achieve is that between preserving the environment and allowing scientific and technological progress. As I have said before, it is a balance that has to be achieved to the best of our abilities. We cannot stop the construction of necessary things such as dams, roads, or hospitals simply because they will encroach upon the environment or a certain animal species. We can, however, make sure that we do our best to prevent excessive damage to the environment. The famous twentieth-century architect Frank Lloyd Wright set a good example. When designing a house or other building, he tried to fit it into its natural environment as much as possible, trying, for example, to maintain the forest around it. We should continue this practice. First of all, the project to be built must really be necessary to the well-being and progress of society (not the fourteenth shopping center in a two-mile area, for example). Second, everything must be done to protect the environment or the animal species in the area. Many approaches are possible, such as moving endangered animal species to safer environments, or trying to leave intact as much of the natural environment as possible so that the species will not be destroyed by the project. It would seem that moving this fish to a safer environment would be more acceptable than blocking the building of the dam.

Supplementary Reading

ADDLESON, KATHRYN P. *Impure Thoughts: Essays on Philosophy, Feminism, and Ethics*. Philadelphia: Temple University Press, 1991.

ADLER, MORTIMER J. *The Time of Our Lives: The Ethics of Common Sense*. New York: Holt, Rinehart and Winston, 1970.

ALMOND, BRENDA, AND DONALD HILL, eds. *Applied Philosophy: Morals and Metaphysics in Contemporary Debate*. New York: Routledge, 1991.

ALSTON, WILLIAM P., AND RICHARD B. BRANDT. *The Problems of Philosophy*, 2nd ed. Boston: Allyn and Bacon, 1974.

ALVAREZ, A. *The Savage God: A Study of Suicide*. New York: Random House, 1972.

AMATO, JOSEPH A. *Ethics: Living or Dead? Themes in Contemporary Values*. Tuscaloosa, AL: Portals Press, 1982.

ANNAS, GEORGE J., et al. *Informed Consent to Human Experimentation: The Subject's Dilemma*. Cambridge, MA: Ballinger, 1977.

APPLEBAUM, PAUL, et al. *Informed Consent: Legal Theory and Clinical Practice*. New York: Oxford University Press, 1987.

ARENDT, HANNAH. *On Violence*. New York: Harcourt Brace Jovanovich, 1969.

ARRINGTON, ROBERT L. *Rationalism, Realism, and Relativism: Perspectives in Contemporary Moral Epistemology*. Ithaca, NY: Cornell University Press, 1989.

ARTFIELD, ROBIN. *The Ethics of Environmental Concern*. New York: Columbia University Press, 1983.

ASCH, S. E. *Social Psychology*. Upper Saddle River, NJ: Prentice Hall, 1952.

ASSITER, ALISON. *Pornography, Feminism, and the Individual*. Concord, MA: Paul and Co., Publishers, 1991.

ATIYAH, PATRICK S. *Promises, Morals, and Law*. New York: Oxford University Press, 1981.

ATKINSON, RONALD et al. *Sexual Latitude: For and Against*. New York: Hart, 1971.

ATTFIELD, ROBIN. *The Ethics of Environmental Concern*. New York: Columbia University Press, 1983.

AUNE, BRUCE. *Kant's Theory of Morals*. Princeton, NJ: Princeton University Press, 1980.

AYD, FRANK J., JR., ed. *Medical, Moral and Legal Issues in Mental Health Care*. Baltimore: Williams and Wilkins, 1974.

AYER, A. J. "The Principle of Utility." In *Philosophical Essays* by A. J. Ayer. New York: St. Martin's Press, 1955.

BAIER, KURT. *The Moral Point of View*. Ithaca, NY: Cornell University Press, 1958.

BAIRD, ROBERT M., AND STUART E. ROSENBAUM, eds. *Pornography: Private Right or Public Menace*. Buffalo, NY: Prometheus, 1991.

BAIRD, ROBERT, AND STUART E. ROSENBAUM, eds. *Animal Experimentation: The Moral Issues*. Buffalo, NY: Prometheus, 1991.

BAKER, ROBERT, AND FREDERICK ELLISTON, eds. *Philosophy and Sex*, rev. ed. Buffalo, NY: Prometheus Books, 1984.

BANDURA, A. *Principles of Behavior Modification*. New York: Holt, Rinehart and Winston, 1969.

BARBER, BERNARD et al. *Research on Human Subjects: Problems of Social Control in Medical Experimentation*. New York: Russell Sage Foundation, 1973.

BARNETT, RANDY. "Restitution: A New Paradigm of Criminal Justice." In *Assessing the Criminal*, eds. Randy Barnett and John Hagel. Boston: Ballinger, 1978.

BARNHART, J. E., AND MARY ANN BARNHART. "Marital Faithfulness and Unfaithfulness." *Journal of Social Philosophy* 4 (10–15) (April 1973).

BARNSLEY, JOHN H. *The Social Reality of Ethics: The Comparative Analysis of Moral Codes*. London: Routledge and Kegan Paul, 1972.

BARROW, ROBIN. *Utilitarianism: A Contemporary Statement*. Brookfield, VT: Ashgate Publishing, 1991.

BARRY, BRIAN. *The Liberal Theory of Justice*. London: Oxford University Press, 1973.

BARRY, VINCENT, AND WILLIAM SHAW. *Moral Issues in Business*, 4th ed. Belmont, CA: Wadsworth, 1989.

BARTELL, GILBERT D. *Group Sex: A Scientist's Eyewitness Report on Swinging in the Suburbs*. New York: Peter H. Wyden, 1970.

BATCHELOR, EDWARD, JR., ed. *Homosexuality and Ethics*, rev. ed. New York: Pilgrim Press, 1982.

BATTIN, M. PABST, AND DAVID J. MAYO, eds. *Suicide: The Philosophical Issues*. New York: St. Martin's, 1980.

BATTIN, M. PABST. *Ethical Issues in Suicide*. Upper Saddle River, NJ: Prentice Hall, 1982.

BATTIN, MARGARET P., AND RONALD MARIS. *Suicide and Ethics: A Special Issue of Suicide and Life Threatening Behavior*. New York: Human Science Press, 1984.

BAYER, RONALD. *Homosexuality and American Psychiatry: The Politics of Diagnosis*. New York: Basic Books, 1980.

BAYLES, MICHAEL D. *Reproductive Ethics*. Upper Saddle River, NJ: Prentice Hall, 1984.

BAYLEY, JAMES E. *Aspects of Relativism: Moral, Cognitive, and Literary*. Lanham, MD: University Press of America, 1992.

BEARDSLEY, ELIZABETH L. "Determinism and Moral Perspectives." *Philosophy and Phenomenological Research* 21 (1960): 1–20.

BEAUCHAMP, TOM L. *Case Studies in Business, Society, and Ethics*. Upper Saddle River, NJ: Prentice Hall, 1983.

BEAUCHAMP, TOM L., AND LEROY WALTERS, eds. *Contemporary Issues in Bioethics*. Encino, CA: Dickenson, 1978.

BEAUCHAMP, TOM. *Philosophical Ethics: An Introduction to Moral Philosophy*. New York: McGraw-Hill, 1982.

BECK, ROBERT N., AND JOHN B. ORR. *Ethical Choice: A Case Study Approach*. New York: Free Press, 1970. (See Part II, Section 8.)

BECK, ROBERT N., AND JOHN B. ORR. *Ethical Choice: A Case Study Approach*. New York: Free Press, 1970. (See Part II, Section 7.)

BEDAU, HUGO, ed. *The Death Penalty in America*, 3rd ed. New York: Oxford University Press, 1982.

BEECHER, HENRY K. *Experimentation in Man*. Springfield, IL: Charles C. Thomas, 1959.

BEECHER, HENRY K. *Research and the Individual: Human Studies*. Boston: Little, Brown, 1970.

BEECHER, HENRY K., et al. "A Definition of Irreversible Coma." *Journal of the American Medical Association* 205 (August 1968): 85–88.

BEHNKE, JOHN A., AND SISSELA BOK. *The Dilemmas of Euthanasia*. Garden City, NY: Anchor Books, 1975.

BELL, ALAN P., et al. *Sexual Preference: Its Development in Men and Women*. Bloomington: Indiana University Press, 1981.

BELL, J. BOWYER, AND BARTON WHALEY. *Cheating and Deception*. New Brunswick, NJ: Transaction Publications, 1991.

BELL, ROBERT R. *Premarital Sex in a Changing Society*. Upper Saddle River, NJ: Prentice Hall, 1966.

BENTHAM, JEREMY. *Principles of Morals and Legislation*. Many editions (1789).

BEROFSKY, BERNARD, ed. *Free Will and Determinism*. New York: Harper & Row, 1966.

BERTOCCI, PETER A. *Free Will, Responsibility and Grace*. Nashville: Abingdon Press, 1957. This is a discussion of the problem from a Christian perspective.

BERTOCCI, PETER A. *Sex, Love, and the Person*. New York: Sheed and Ward, 1967.

BIER, WILLIAM C., ed. *Human Life: Problems of Birth, of Living and of Dying*. New York: Fordham University Press, 1977.

BIRK, LEE, et al. *Behavior Therapy in Psychiatry: A Report of the American Psychiatric Association Task Force on Behavior Therapy*. New York: Jason Aronson, 1974.

BOGOMOLNY, ROBERT L., ed. *Human Experimentation*. Dallas: Southern Methodist University Press, 1976.

BOK, SISSELA. "Ethical Problems of Abortion." *The Hastings Center Studies* 2 (1) (January 1974): 33–52.

BOK, SISSELA. *Lying: Moral Choice in Public and Private Life*. New York: Random House, 1989.

BOK, SISSELA. *Secrets: On the Ethics of Concealment and Revelation*. New York: Pantheon Books, 1982.

BOND, E. J. *Reason and Value*. New York: Cambridge University Press, 1983.

BOSCO, JAMES J., AND STANLEY S. ROBIN, eds. *The Hyperactive Child and Stimulant Drugs*. Chicago: University of Chicago Press, 1977.

BRADLEY, FRANCIS H. *Ethical Studies*. London: Oxford University Press, 1876.

BRANDT, RICHARD B. *Utilitarianism and Rights*. New York: Cambridge University Press, 1992.

BRECHER, EDWARDS, ed. *The Consumers Union Report: Licit and Illicit Drugs*. Boston: Little, Brown, 1972.

BRINKLEY, LUTHER J. *Contemporary Ethical Theories*. New York: Citadel Press, 1961.

BROAD, R. A. *Punishment Under Pressure: The Probation Service in the Inner City*. Bristol, PA: Taylor and Francis, 1991.

BROADIE, SARAH. *Ethics and Aristotle*. New York: Oxford University Press, 1991.

BRODIE, JANINE. *Abortion Politics*. New York: Oxford University Press, 1992.

BRODY, BARUCH, ed. *Suicide and Euthanasia*. Norwell, MA: Kluwer Academic Publications, 1989.

BROOKS, ROBERT E. *Free Will: An Ultimate Illusion*. Portland, OR: Circa Press, 1987.

CALLAHAN, DANIEL, AND SIDNEY CALLAHAN, eds. *Abortion: Understanding Differences*. New York: Plenum, 1984.

CALLAHAN, DANIEL. *Abortion: Law, Choice and Morality*. New York: Macmillan, 1970.

CALVIN, DEWITT. *Environment and the Christian: What Can We Learn from the New Testament*. Grand Rapids, MI: Baker Books, 1991.

CAMERON, PAUL. "A Case Against Homosexuality." *Human Life Review* 4 (Summer 1978): 17–49.

CAMPBELL, C. A. *In Defense of Free Will: With Other Philosophical Essays*. New York: Humanities Press, 1967.

CAPLAN, ARTHUR L. et al., eds. *Concepts of Health and Disease*. Reading, MA: Addison- Wesley, 1981.

CARNANA, CLAUDIA M. *Abortion Debate*. Brookfield, CT: Millbrook Press, 1992.

CARR, CALEB. *The Lessons of Terror*. New York: Random House, 2002.

CEDERBLOM, JERRY, AND WILLIAM BLIZEK, eds. *Justice and Punishment*. Cambridge, MA: Ballinger, 1977.

CHANDRASEKHAR, S. *Abortion in a Crowded World*. Seattle: University of Washington Press, 1974.

CHORON, JACQUES. *Suicide*. New York: Free Press, 1951.

CHRISTENSEN, F. M. *Pornography: The Other Side*. Westport, CT: Greenwood, 1990.

COHEN, MARSHALL et al., eds. *The Rights and Wrongs of Abortion*. Princeton, NJ: Princeton University Press, 1974.

COHEN, MARSHALL, et al., eds. *Equality and Preferential Treatment*. Princeton, NJ: Princeton University Press, 1977.

COLKER, RUTH. *Abortion and Dialogue: Pro-Choice, Pro-Life, and American Law*. Bloomington: Indiana University Press, 1992.

COOPER, DAVID E., AND JOY A. PALMER. *Environment in Question: Ethics and Global Issues*. New York: Routledge, 1992.

COPPENGER, MARK. *Bioethics: A Casebook*. Upper Saddle River, NJ: Prentice Hall, 1985.

CORTESE, ANTHONY J. *Ethnic Ethics: The Restructuring of Moral Theory*. Albany, NY: State University of New York Press, 1990.

COWELL, FRANK A. *Cheating the Government: The Economics of Evasion*. Cambridge, MA: MIT Press, 1990.

COWLES, JANE. *Informed Consent*. New York: Coward, McCann, and Geoghegan, 1976.

COZIC, CHARLES, AND STACY TIPP. *Abortion: Opposing Viewpoints*. San Diego: Greenhaven, 1991.

CROSBY, JOHN F. *Sexual Autonomy: Toward a Humanistic Ethic*. Springfield, IL: Charles C. Thomas, 1981.

CULVER, CHARLES M., AND BERNARD GERT. *Philosophy in Medicine*. New York: Oxford University Press, 1982.

CUNDIFF, DAVID. *Euthanasia Is Not the Answer*: *A Hospice Physician's View*. Totowa, NJ: Humana, 1992.

CUNNINGHAM, ROBERT L., ed. *Situationism and the New Morality*. New York: Appleton-Century-Crofts, 1970.

DANIELS, NEIL M. *The Morality Maze: An Introduction to Moral Ecology*. New York: Prometheus, 1991.

DANNECKER, MARTIN. *Theories of Homosexuality*. New York: Gay Men's Press, 1981.

DECKER, JOHN F. *Prostitution: Regulation and Control*. Littleton, CO: Rothman, 1979.

DEDEK, JOHN F. *Contemporary Medical Ethics*. Mission, KN: Sheed, Andrews, and McMeel, 1975.

DELGADO, JOSÉ M. R. *Physical Control of the Mind: Toward a Psychocivilized Society*. New York: Harper & Row, 1969.

DESJARDINS, JOSEPH R., AND JOHN J. MCCALL, eds. *Contemporary Issues in Business Ethics*. Belmont, CA: Wadsworth, 1985.

DESPELDER, LYNNE A., AND ALBERT L. STRICKLAND. *The Last Dance*, 2nd ed. Palo Alto, CA: Mayfield, 1987. Chapter 12.

DOBIHAL, EDWARD F., JR. "Talk or Terminal Care," *Connecticut Medicine* 38 (July 1974): 364–67.

DOBZHANSKY, THEODOSIUS G. *The Biological Basis of Human Freedom*. New York: Columbia University Press, 1960.

DONALDSON, THOMAS, AND PATRICIA H. WERHANE, eds. *Ethical Issues in Business*. Upper Saddle River, NJ: Prentice Hall, 1979.

DONNELLY, JOHN, ed. *Suicide: Right or Wrong*. Buffalo, NY: Prometheus Books, 1989.

DORE, CLEMENT. *Moral Skepticism*. New York: St. Martin's Press, 1991.

DUMONT, RICHARD G., AND DENNIS C. FOSS. *The American View of Death*: *Acceptance or Denial?* Cambridge, MA: Schenkman, 1972.

DURKHEIM, E. *Suicide*. New York: Free Press, 1951.

DUSTER, TROY. *The Legislation of Morality: Law, Drugs and Moral Judgment*. New York: Free Press, 1970.

DUVAL, EVELYN RUTH, AND REUBEN HILL. *Why Wait till Marriage?* New York: Association Press, 1965.

DWORKIN, ANDREA. *Pornography*: *Men Possessing Women*. New York: NAL-Dutton, 1991.

DYNES, WAYNE R. *Homosexuality and Religion and Philosophy*. New York: Garland, 1992.

DYNES, WAYNE R. *Homosexuality: Discrimination, Criminology, and the Law*. New York: Garland, 1992.

DYNES, WAYNE R., AND STEPHEN DONALDSON, eds. *Homosexuality and Government, Politics, and Prisons*. New York: Garland, 1992.

ECK, MARCEL. *Lies and Truth*. New York: Macmillan, 1970.

EDEL, ABRAHAM. "Two Traditions in the Refutation of Egoism." *Journal of Philosophy* 34 (1937): 617–28.

EDWARDS, JONATHAN. *Freedom of the Will*. Ed. Paul Ramsey. New Haven: Yale University Press, 1957. This is a good presentation of Calvinistic predestination.

EDWARDS, REM B., AND GLENN C. GROBER. *Bioethics*. New York: Harcourt Brace Jovanovich, 1988.

EGONSSON, DAN. *Interests, Utilitarianism, and Moral Standing*. New York: Chartwell Bratt, 1990.

ELLIS, ALBERT. *The Art and Science of Love*. New York: Lyle Stuart, 1965.

ELLISON, CRAIG, ed. *Modifying Man: Implications and Ethics*. Washington, D.C.: University Press of America, 1977.

ENNIS, BRUCE, AND LOREN SIEGEL. *The Rights of Mental Patients*. New York: Avon Books, 1973.

EWING, ALFRED C. *The Morality of Punishment*. London: Routledge and Kegan Paul, 1929.

EZORSKY, GERTRUDE, ed. *Moral Rights in the Workplace*. Albany, NY: State University of New York, 1987.

FAGOTHEY, AUSTIN. *Right and Reason*, 8th ed., rev. Milton A. Gonsalves. St. Louis: C. V. Mosby, 1985.

FALIKOWSKI, ANTHONY. *Moral Philosophy*. Upper Saddle River, NJ: Prentice Hall, 1990.

FARBEROW, NORMAN L., AND EDWIN S. SCHNEIDMAN. *Clues to Suicide*. New York: McGraw-Hill, 1959.

FARRER, AUSTIN. *The Freedom of the Will*. New York: Charles Scribner's Sons, 1958.

FEIFEL, HERMAN, ed. *The Meaning of Death*. New York: McGraw-Hill, 1959.

FEINBERG, JOEL, AND HYMAN GROSS, eds. *Philosophy of Law*, 3rd ed. Belmont, CA: Wadsworth, 1986.

FEINBERG, JOEL. *Doing and Deserving*. Princeton, NJ: Princeton University Press, 1970.

FEINBERG, JOEL. *Freedom and Fulfillment*: *Philosophical Essays*. Princeton, NJ: Princeton University Press, 1992.

FEINBERG, JOEL. *The Problem of Abortion*, 2nd ed. Belmont, CA: Wadsworth, 1984.

FINNIS, JOHN. *Fundamentals of Ethics*. Washington, DC: Georgetown University Press, 1983.

FISCHER, JOHN M., AND MARK RAVIZZA. *Ethics: Problems and Principles*. San Diego: Harcourt, Brace, Jovanovich, 1992.

FLETCHER, JOSEPH. *Moral Responsibility: Situation Ethics at Work*. Philadelphia: Westminster, 1967.

FLETCHER, JOSEPH. *Morals and Medicine*. Boston: Beacon Press, 1954.

FLETCHER, JOSEPH. *Morals and Medicine: The Moral Problem of the Patient's Right to Know the Truth*. Princeton, NJ: Princeton University Press, 1979.

FLETCHER, JOSEPH. *Situation Ethics: The New Morality*. Philadelphia: Westminster Press, 1966.

FLETCHER, JOSEPH. *The Ethics of Genetic Control: Ending Reproductive Roulette*. New York: Prometheus, 1988.

FRANKENA, WILLIAM K. "Ethics and the Environment." In *Ethics and Problems of the 21st Century*, ed., Kenneth Goodpaster and K. M. Sayre. Notre Dame, IN: University of Notre Dame Press, 1979.

FRANKENA, WILLIAM K. *Ethics*, 3rd ed. Upper Saddle River, NJ: Prentice Hall, 1974.

FRAZER, ELIZABETH, et al. *Ethics: A Feminist Reader*. Cambridge, England: Blackwell Publishers, 1992.

FREUD, SIGMUND. *Collected Papers of Sigmund Freud. Sexuality and the Psychology of Love*, Vol. 8. New York: Collier Books, n.d.

FREY, R. G. *Interests and Rights: The Case Against Animals*. Oxford: Clarendon Press, 1980.

FROMER, MARGOT J. *Ethical Issues in Sexuality and Reproduction*. St. Louis: C. V. Mosby, 1983.

FUMERTON, RICHARD A. *Reason and Morality: A Defense of the Egocentric Perspective*. Ithaca, NY: Cornell University Press, 1990.

FURROW, BARRY R., et al. *Bioethics: Health Care, Law, and Ethics*. Anaheim, CA: West Publishers, 1991.

GARDNER, R. F. R. *Abortion: The Personal Dilemma*. New York: Pyramid Books, 1974.

GARLAND, DAVID. *Punishment in Modern Society: A Study in Social Theory*. Chicago: University of Chicago Press, 1990.

GARLING, TOMMY, AND GARY EVANS. *Environment, Cognition, and Action: A Multidisciplinary Approach*. New York: Oxford University Press, 1992.

GAUTIER, DAVID P., ed. *Morality and Rational Self-Interest*. Upper Saddle River, NJ: Prentice Hall, 1970.

GELLNER, ERNEST. *Relativism and the Social Sciences*. New York: Cambridge University Press, 1985.

GIBSON, MARY. *Workers' Rights*. Totawa, NJ: Roman and Allanheld, 1983.

GILLIGAN, CAROL. *In a Different Voice*. Cambridge: Harvard University Press, 1982.

GINSBERG, M. *Essays in Sociology and Social Philosophy*, Vol. 1. London: Heinemann, 1956.

GIRVETZ, HARRY K., ed. *Contemporary Moral Issues*, 2nd ed. Belmont, CA: Wadsworth, 1968.

GLASER, BARNEY G., AND ANSELM L. STRAUSS. *Awareness of Dying*. Chicago: Aldine, 1965.

GLOVER, JONATHAN. *Causing Death and Saving Lives*. Harmondsworth, Middlesex, England: Penguin Books, 1977.

GLOVER, JONATHAN. *Utilitarianism and Its Critics*. Ed. Paul Edwards. New York: Macmillan, 1990.

GOLDMAN, A. "Abortion and the Right to Die." *Personalist* 60 (1979).

GONSALVES, MILTON A. *Fagothey's Right and Reason: Ethics in Theory and Practice*, 8th ed. St. Louis: Times/Mirror Mosby, 1985.

GRAY, IAN, AND MOIRA STANLEY. *Punishment in Search of a Crime: Americans Speak Out Against the Death Sentence*. New York: Avon Books, 1989.

GREENWALD, ROBERT A., et al. *Human Subjects Research: A Handbook for Institutional Review Boards*. New York: Plenum, 1982.

GRISEZ, GERMAIN G. *Abortion: The Myths, the Realities, and the Arguments*. New York: Corpus Publishing Division of World Publishing Company, 1970.

GROSS, BARRY R., ed. *Reverse Discrimination*. Buffalo, NY: Prometheus, 1977.

GROSS, HYMAN. *A Theory of Criminal Justice*. New York: Oxford University Press, 1979.

GRUMMON, DONALD L., AND ANDREW M. BARCLAY, eds. *Sexuality: A Search for Perspective*. New York: Van Nostrand, 1971.

GRUPP, STANLEY E., ed. *Theories of Punishment*. Bloomington: Indiana University Press, 1971.

GUERNSEY, JOANN B. *Capital Punishment*. Minneapolis: Lerner Publications, 1991.

HALL, ROBERT E., ed. *Abortion in a Changing World*, 2 vols. New York: Columbia University Press, 1970.

HAMILTON, MICHAEL, ed. *The New Genetics and the Future of Man*. Grand Rapids, MI: William B. Eerdmans, 1972.

HANIGAN, JAMES. *What Are They Saying About Sexual Morality?* Ramsey, NJ: Paulist Press, 1982.

HARDING, CHRISTOPHER, AND RICHARD W. IRELAND. *Punishment*: *Rhetoric, Rule, and Practice*. New York: Routledge, 1989.

HARE, R. M. *Applications of Moral Philosophy*. Berkeley: University of California Press, 1972.

HARGROVE, EUGENE, C., ed. *Animal Rights—Environmental Ethics Debate: The Environmental Perspective*. Albany, NY: State University of New York Press, 1992.

HARRIS, C. E., JR. *Applying Moral Theories*, 2nd ed. Belmont, CA: Wadsworth Publishers, 1992.

HART, H. L. A. *Punishment and Responsibility*. New York: Oxford University Press, 1968.

HAWKINS, GORDON, AND FRANKLIN ZIMRING. *Pornography in a Free Society*. New York: Cambridge University Press, 1991.

HAY, ROBERT D. et. al., eds. *Business and Society*. Cincinnati: South-Western, 1976.

HICK, JOHN. *Philosophy of Religion*, 3rd ed. Upper Saddle River, NJ: Prentice Hall, 1983.

HILTON, BRUCE, et. al., eds. *Ethical Issues in Human Genetics*. New York: Plenum, 1973.

HOCHBERG, GARY M. *Kant: Moral Legislation and Two Senses of "Will."* New York: University Press of America, 1982.

HOFFMAN, W. MICHAEL, AND JENNIFER MILLS MOORE, eds. *Business Ethics*. New York: McGraw-Hill, 1984.

HOFFMAN, W. MICHAEL, et al. *Business, Ethics, and the Environment: The Public Policy Debate*. Westport, CT: Quorum Books, 1990.

HOLMES, ARTHUR F., ed. *War and Christian Ethics*: *Classic Readings on the Morality of War*. Grand Rapids, MI: Baker Books, 1991.

HOLMES, HELEN B., et al., eds. *The Custom-Made Child? Women Centered Perspectives*. Clifton, NJ: Humana, 1981.

HOOK, SIDNEY, ed. *Determinism and Freedom in the Age of Modern Science*. New York: Collier Books, 1958.

HOOK, SIDNEY, ed. *Human Values and Economic Policy*. New York: New York University Press, 1967.

HORAN, DENNIS J., AND DAVID MALL, eds. *Death, Dying and Euthanasia*. New York: University Publications of America, 1980.

HOSPERS, JOHN. *An Introduction to Philosophical Analysis*, 2nd ed. Upper Saddle River, NJ: Prentice Hall, 1967.

HOSPERS, JOHN. *Human Conduct*: *An Introduction to the Problems of Ethics*, 2nd ed. New York: Harcourt, Brace, Jovanovich, 1982.

HUMPHRY, DEREK, AND ANN WICKETT. *The Right to Die*: *Understanding Euthanasia*. New York: Harper & Row, 1986.

HUMPHRY, DEREK. *Final Exit*. Secaucus, NJ: Carol Publishing, 1991.

HUMPHRY, DEREK. *Jean's Way*. New York: HarperCollins, 1986.

ITZIN, CATHERINE, ed. *Pornography*: *Women, Violence, and Civil Liberties*: *A Radical View*. New York: Oxford University Press, 1992.

IYER, RAGHAVAN. *Utilitarianism and All That*. Santa Barbara, CA: Concord Grove, 1983.

JACOBS, JONATHAN. *Virtue and Self-Knowledge*. Upper Saddle River, NJ: Prentice Hall, 1989.

JAMES, WILLIAM. *The Will to Believe and Other Popular Essays in Philosophy*. New York: Longmans, Green, 1912. The essay "The Dilemma of Determinism" presents James's theory of indeterminism.

JOHNSON, VIRGINIA E., AND WILLIAM H. MASTERS. *Human Sexual Response*. Boston: Little, Brown, 1966.

JOHNSTON, HERBERT. *Business Ethics*, 2nd ed. New York: Pitman, 1961.

KANE, R. *Free Will and Values*. Albany, NY: State University of New York Press, 1985.

KANT, IMMANUEL. "The Supreme Principle of Morality." In *The Range of Ethics*, eds. Harold H. Titus and Morris Keeton. New York: Van Nostrand, 1966.

KANT, IMMANUEL. *Fundamental Principles of the Metaphysics of Morals.* Trans. H. J. Paton. New York: Harper & Row, 1957.

KARP, L. E. *Genetic Engineering: Threat or Promise?* Chicago: Nelson-Hall, 1976.

KELLY, PAUL. *Utilitarianism and Distributive Justice: Jeremy Bentham and the Civil Law.* New York: Oxford University Press, 1990.

KIRKENDALL, LESTER A. *Premarital Intercourse and Interpersonal Relationships.* New York: Julian Press, 1961.

KLASSEN, ALBERT D., et al. *Sex and Morality in the U.S.: An Empirical Enquiry Under the Auspices of the Kinsey Institute.* Hanover, NH: University Press of New England, 1989.

KLAWANS, HAROLD L. *Informed Consent.* New York: New American Library, 1988.

KLEIN, MARTHA. *Determinism, Blameworthiness, and Deprivation.* New York: Oxford University Press, 1990.

KLUCKHORN, CLYDE. "Ethical Relativity: Sic et Non." *Journal of American Philosophical Association Fifty-two* (November 1955).

KOHL, MARVIN, ed. *Beneficent Euthanasia.* Buffalo, NY: Prometheus Books, 1975.

KORNER, STEPHEN. *Kant,* rev. ed. New Haven, CT: Yale University Press, 1982.

KRASEMANN, KEITH W. AND WERHANE, PATRICIA H., eds. *Contemporary Issues in Business Ethics: The Callista Wicklander Lectures.* Lantham, MD: University Press America, 2006.

KRASEMANN, KEITH W., ed. *Quest for Goodness: An Introduction to Ethics,* 2nd ed. Boston: Pearson, 1999.

KRASEMANN, KEITH W., ed. *Business Ethics: Problems, Principles, Practical Applications,* 2nd ed. Acton, MA: Copley Publishing Group, 2004.

KÜBLER-ROSS, ELISABETH. *On Death and Dying.* New York: Macmillan, 1969.

KUPPERMAN, JOEL J. *Character.* New York: Oxford University Press, 1991.

LABBY, DANIEL H., ed. *Life or Death: Ethics and Options.* Seattle: University of Washington Press, 1968.

LACK, SYLVIA, AND RICHARD LAMERTON, eds. *The Hour of Our Death.* London: Geoffrey Chapman, 1975.

LAMERTON, RICHARD. *Care of the Dying.* Westport, CT: Technomic Press, 1976.

LEBACQZ, KAREN. *Genetics, Ethics, and Parenthood.* New York: Pilgrim, 1983.

LEISER, BURTON. *Liberty, Justice and Morals,* 3rd ed. New York: Macmillan, 1979.

LEONI, BRUNO, ed. *Freedom and the Law.* Indianapolis: Liberty Fund, 1991.

LEOPOLD, ALDO. "The Land Ethic." In *A Sand County Almanac.* New York: Oxford University Press, 1966.

LEVY, DONALD. "Perversion and the Unnatural as Moral Categories." In *The Philosophy of Sex,* ed. Alan Soble. Totowa, NJ: Littlefield, Adams, 1980.

LINTON, RALPH. "The Problem of Universal Values." In *Method and Perspective in Anthropology,* ed. R. F. Spencer. Minneapolis: University of Minnesota Press, 1954.

LONDON, PERRY. *Behavior Control,* 2nd ed. New York: New American Library, 1977.

LUBS, HERBERT A., AND FELIX DE LA CRUZ. *Genetic Counseling.* New York: Raven Press, 1977.

LUKER, KRISTIN. *Abortion and the Politics of Motherhood.* Berkeley: University of California Press, 1984.

LUNNEBORG, PATRICIA. *Abortion: A Positive Decision.* Westport, CT: Greenwood, 1992.

MACINTYRE, ALASDAIR. *After Virtue,* 2nd ed. Notre Dame, IN: University of Notre Dame Press, 1984.

MACLAGAN, W. G. "Punishment and Retribution." *Philosophy* 14 (1939): 281–98.

MANNING, RITA C. *Speaking from the Heart: A Feminist Perspective on Ethics.* Vantage, NY: Rowman, 1992.

MAPPES, THOMAS A., AND JANE S. ZEMBATY, eds. *Biomedical Ethics,* 2nd ed. New York: McGraw-Hill, 1986.

MAPPES, THOMAS A., AND JANE S. ZEMBATY. *Social Ethics: Morality and Social Policy,* 3rd ed. New York: McGraw-Hill, 1987.

MARKS, EMERSON R. *Relativist and Absolutist: The Early Neoclassical Debate in England.* Westport, CT: Greenwood Press, 1975.

MAY, WILLIAM W. *Business Ethics and the Law: Beyond Compliance.* Iowa Falls, IA: P. Lang Publishers, 1992.

MAY, WILLIAM. *Moral Absolutes, Catholic Traditions, Current Trends, and the Truth.* Shoreview, MN: Marquette, 1989.

McCARY, JAMES L. *Human Sexuality: Physiological and Psychological Factors of Sexual Behavior.* New York: Van Nostrand, 1967.

McDONALD, DOUGLAS C. *Punishment without Walls: Community Service Sentences in New York City.* New Brunswick, NJ: Rutgers University Press, 1989.

McGEE, ROBERT W., ed. *Business Ethics and Common Sense.* Westport, CT: Greenwood, 1992.

McKEON, RICHARD, ed. *Introduction to Aristotle.* New York: The Modern Library, 1947.

McWHIRTER, DAVID P., et al. *Homosexuality—Heterosexuality: Concepts of Sexual Orientation.* New York: Oxford University Press, 1990.

MEDLIN, BRIAN. "Ultimate Principles and Ethical Egoism." *Australasian Journal of Philosophy* 35 (1957): 111–18.

MEILAND, JACK W., AND MICHAEL KRAUSZ, eds. *Relativism: Cognitive and Moral.* Notre Dame, IN: University of Notre Dame Press, 1982.

MELDEN, A. I., ed. *Ethical Theories,* 2nd ed. Upper Saddle River, NJ: Prentice Hall, 1967.

MENNINGER, KARL. "The Crime of Punishment." In *Taking Sides,* ed. Stephen Satris. Guilford, CT: Dushkin Publishing Group, 1988.

MILGRIM, STANLEY. *Obedience to Authority.* New York: Harper & Row, 1974.

MILL, JOHN STUART. *Utilitarianism: With Critical Essays.* Ed. Samuel Gorovitz. Indianapolis: Bobbs-Merrill, 1971.

MILLER, NATHAN. *Stealing from America: A History of Corruption from Jamestown to Reagan.* New York: Paragon House Publishers, 1992.

MILLER, RICHARD W. *Moral Differences: Truth, Justice, and Conscience in a World of Conflict.* Princeton, NJ: Princeton University Press, 1992.

MILUNSKY, AUBREY. *The Prevention of Genetic Disease and Mental Retardation.* Philadelphia: W. B. Saunders, 1975.

MOORE, G. E. *Principia Ethica.* New York: Cambridge University Press, 1959.

MORRIS, HERBERT. "Persons and Punishment." In *Understanding Moral Philosophy,* ed. James Rachels. Belmont, CA: Dickenson, 1976.

MUNN, ALLEN M. *Free-Will and Determinism.* Toronto: University of Toronto Press, 1960. This book discusses freedom and determinism from the point of view of physics and physical science.

MURPHY, JEFFRIE G., ed. *Punishment and Rehabilitation,* 2nd ed. Belmont, CA: Wadsworth, 1985.

NARVESON, JAN. *Morality and Utility.* Baltimore: Johns Hopkins University Press, 1967.

NEUBECK, GERHARD, ed. *Extra-Marital Relations.* Upper Saddle River, NJ: Prentice Hall, 1969.

NIELSEN, KAI. "Why Should I Be Moral?" In *Problems of Moral Philosophy,* 2nd ed. Ed. Paul W. Taylor. Belmont, CA: Dickenson, 1972.

NOONAN, JOHN T. JR., ed. *The Morality of Abortion: Legal and Historical Perspectives.* Cambridge, MA: Harvard University Press, 1970.

O'BRIEN, WILLIAM V. *War and/or Survival.* Garden City, NY: Doubleday, 1969.

O'CONNELL, JOHN P., ed. *The Catholic Encyclopedia,* Holy Bible. Chicago: Catholic Press, 1954.

O'NEILL, GEORGE, AND NENA O'NEILL. *Open Marriage: New Life Style for Couples.* New York: M. Evans, 1972.

OLASKY, MARVIN N. *Abortion Rites: A Social History of Abortion in America.* Wheaton, IL: Good News, 1992.

OLSON, ROBERT G. *The Morality of Self-Interest.* New York: Harcourt Brace Jovanovich, 1965.

OPPOSING VIEWPOINTS SERIES. *Homosexuality: Opposing Viewpoints.* San Diego: Greenhaven Press, 1993.

OPPOSING VIEWPOINTS SERIES. *Suicide: Opposing Viewpoints.* San Diego, CA: Greenhaven, 1992.

OUSTERHOUDT, ROBERT G., ed. *The Philosophy of Sport: A Collection of Original Essays.* Springfield, IL: Charles C. Thomas, 1973.

OUTKA, GENE, AND JOHN P. REEDER, JR., eds. *Religion and Morality.* Garden City, NY: Anchor Press/Doubleday, 1973.

PATON, HERBERT J. *The Categorical Imperative*: *A Study in Kant's Moral Philosophy*. Chicago: University of Chicago Press, 1948.

PATTERSON, PHILLIP AND LEE WILKENS. *Media Ethics: Issues and Cases*. New York: Wm. C. Brown, 1991.

PETCHESKY, ROSALIND P. *Abortion and Woman's Choice*: *The State, Sexuality, and Reproductive Freedom*. Brookfield, CT: Northeastern University Press, 1990.

PETTIT, PHILLIP. *Judging Justice*. London: Routledge and Kegan Paul, 1980.

PIERCE, CHRISTINE, AND DONALD VANDEVEER, eds. *AIDS: Ethics and Public Policy*. Belmont, CA: Wadsworth, 1987.

PINES, MAYA. *The Brain Changers: Scientists and the New Mind Control*. New York: Harcourt Brace Jovanovich, 1973.

POLLARD, PATRICK. *André Gide: The Homosexual Moralist*. New Haven, CT: Yale University Press, 1992.

PRESIDENT'S COMMISSION FOR THE STUDY OF ETHICAL PROBLEMS IN BIOMEDICAL AND BEHAVIORAL RESEARCH. *Deciding to Forego Life Sustaining Treatment*. Washington, DC: Government Printing Office, 1983.

PRIOR, WILLIAM J. *Virtue and Knowledge*: *An Introduction to Ancient Greek Ethics*. New York: Routledge, 1991.

QUINN, PHILIP L. *Divine Commands and Moral Requirements*. New York: Oxford University Press, 1978.

RACHELS, JAMES. *The End of Life*: *Euthanasia and Morality*. New York: Oxford University Press, 1986.

RAMSEY, PAUL. *Fabricated Man: The Ethics of Genetic Control*. New Haven, CT: Yale University Press, 1970.

RAMSEY, PAUL. *The Just War: Force and Political Responsibility*. New York: Charles Scribner's Sons, 1968.

RAMSEY, PAUL. *The Patient as Person*. New Haven, CT: Yale University Press, 1970.

RAND, AYN. *The Virtue of Selfishness*. New York: New American Library, 1964.

RANDALL, RICHARD S. *Freedom and Taboo*: *Pornography and the Politics of a Self Divided*. Berkeley: University of California Press, 1989.

RAVIN, NEIL. *Informed Consent*. New York: Putnam, 1983.

RAWLS, JOHN. *A Theory of Justice*. Cambridge, MA: Harvard University Press, 1971.

REED, ROBERT D., AND DANEK S. KAUS. *Pornography: How and Where to Find Facts and Get Help*. Ed. Diane Parker. Saratoga, CA: R and E Publications, 1993.

REEVE, C. D. *Practices of Reason*: *Aristotle's Nichomachean Ethics*. New York: Oxford University Press, 1992.

REGAN, TOM, AND PETER SINGER, eds. *Animal Rights and Human Obligations*. Upper Saddle River, NJ: Prentice Hall, 1976.

REGAN, TOM, ed. *Earthbound: New Introductory Essays in Environmental Ethics*. New York: Random House, 1984.

REGAN, TOM, ed. *Matters of Life and Death*. New York: Random House, 1980.

REGAN, TOM, ed. *New Introductory Essays in Business Ethics*. New York: Random House, 1984.

REGAN, TOM. *The Case for Animal Rights*. Berkeley: University of California Press, 1983.

RESCHER, NICHOLAS. *Distributive Justice*. Indianapolis: Bobbs-Merrill, 1966.

ROBINS, MICHAEL H. *Promising, Intending, and Moral Autonomy*. New York: Cambridge University Press, 1984.

ROBITSCHER, JONAS B. "The Right to Die." *The Hastings Center Report* 2 (September 1972): 11–14.

RODMAN, HYMAN, et al., eds. *The Abortion Question*. New York: Columbia University Press, 1987.

ROLLIN, BERNARD E. *Animal Rights and Human Morality*. Buffalo, NY: Prometheus, 1981.

ROLSTON, HOLMES III. *Philosophy Gone Wild: Environmental Ethics*. New York: Prometheus, 1989.

ROSENSTAND, NINA. *The Moral of the Story*. Mountain View, CA: Mayfield, 1994.

ROSOFF, ARNOLD J. *Informed Consent: A Guide for Health Care Providers*. Rockville, MD, 1981.

ROSS, ELISABETH K. *On Death and Dying*. New York: Macmillan, 1969.

ROSS, ELISABETH K. *Questions and Answers on Death and Dying*. New York: Collier Books, 1974.

ROSS, SIR WILLIAM DAVID. *Kant's Ethical Theory*. New York: Oxford University Press, 1954.

ROSS, SIR WILLIAM DAVID. *The Foundations of Ethics*. Oxford: Clarendon Press, 1939.

Ross, Sir William David. *The Right and the Good*. New York: Oxford University Press, 1930.

Rossman, Parker. *Hospice*. New York: Association Press, 1977.

Rubin, Eva R. *Abortion, Politics, and the Courts: Roe vs. Wade and Its Aftermath*. Westport, CT: Greenwood, 1982.

Rudovsky, David. *The Rights of Prisoners*. New York: Avon Books, 1973.

Runkle, Gerald. *Ethics: An Examination of Contemporary Moral Problems*. New York: Holt, Rinehart and Winston, 1982.

Russell, O. Ruth. "Moral and Legal Aspects of Euthanasia." *The Humanist* 34 (July–August 1974): 22–27.

Russell, O. Ruth. *Freedom to Die: Moral and Legal Aspects of Euthanasia*. New York: Human Sciences Press, 1975.

Ryan, Alan. *Utilitarianism and Other Essays*. New York: Penguin, 1987.

Sagan, Carl, and Ann Druyan. "Is It Possible to Be Pro-Life and Pro-Choice?" *Parade Magazine* (April 22, 1990): 2–8.

Sartre, Jean-Paul. *Being and Nothingness: An Essay on Phenomenological Ontology*. Trans. Hazel E. Barnes. New York: Washington Square Press, 1964. This book presents Sartre's special point of view on existentialist freedom.

Saunders, Cicely. "St. Christopher's Hospice." *Death: Current Perspectives*. Ed. Edwin S. Schneidman. Palo Alto: Mayfield, 1976.

Scheff, David. "Playboy Interview with Derek Humphry." *Playboy* (August 1992): 49–144.

Scherer, Donald, and Thomas Attig, eds. *Ethics and the Environment*. Upper Saddle River, NJ: Prentice Hall, 1983.

Schrag, Peter. *Mind Control*. New York: Pantheon Books, 1978.

Scriven, Michael. *Primary Philosophy*. New York: McGraw-Hill, 1966.

Scruton, Roger. *Kant*. New York: Oxford University Press, 1982.

Sellars, Wilfred, and John Hospers, eds. *Readings in Ethical Theory*. New York: Appleton-Century-Crofts, 1952.

Sen, Amartya, and Bernard Williams, eds. *Utilitarianism and Beyond*. New York: Cambridge University Press, 1982.

Shannon, Thomas A. *Bioethics*, 3rd ed. Mahwah, NJ: Paulist Press, 1987.

Shaw, William H. *Business Ethics*. Belmont, CA: Wadsworth, 1991.

Shearer, Lloyd. "Porno and Crime." *The Bakersfield Californian*, "Parade" (December 10, 1978), 17.

Shilts, Randy. *And the Band Played On*. New York: St. Martin's Press, 1987.

Shuman, Samuel I. *Psychosurgery and the Medical Control of Violence: Autonomy and Deviance*. Detroit: Wayne State University Press, 1977.

Shwayder, D. S. "The Sense of Duty." *Philosophical Quarterly* 7 (1957): 116–25.

Siegel, Harvey. *Relativism Refuted*. Norwel, MA: Kluwer Academic Publishers, 1987.

Silk, L., and D. Vogel, eds. *Ethics and Profits*. New York: Simon and Schuster, 1976.

Singer, Peter. "Is Racial Discrimination Arbitrary?" In *Moral Issues*, ed. Jan Narveson. New York: Oxford University Press, 1983.

Singer, Peter. *Animal Liberation*, 2nd. ed. New York: Avon Books, 1990.

Sjoberg, Gideon, ed. *Ethics, Politics, and Social Research*. Cambridge, MA: Schenkman, 1967.

Skinner, B. F. *Beyond Freedom and Dignity*. New York: Knopf, 1971.

Skinner, B. F. *Science and Human Behavior*. New York: Macmillan, 1953.

Skinner, B. F. *Science and Human Behavior*. New York: Macmillan, 1973.

Slote, Michael. *From Morality to Virtue*. New York: Oxford University Press, 1992.

Smart, J. J. C. *Outlines of a Utilitarianism System of Ethics*. London: Cambridge University Press, 1961.

Smart, J. J. C., and Bernard Williams, eds. *Utilitarianism for and Against*. New York: Cambridge University Press, 1973.

Smith, George P., III. *Genetics, Ethics, and the Law*. New York: Associated Faculty Press, 1981.

SNOEYENBOS, MILTON, et al., eds. *Business Ethics*. Buffalo, NY: Prometheus, 1983.

SOMERVILLE, JOHN. "Democracy and the Problem of War." In *Moral Problems in Contemporary Society*, ed. Paul Kurtz. Upper Saddle River, NJ: Prentice Hall, 1969.

STEINBOCK, BONNIE, ed. *Killing and Letting Die*. Upper Saddle River, NJ: Prentice Hall, 1980.

STERBA, JAMES. *The Demands of Justice*. Notre Dame, IN: University of Notre Dame Press, 1980.

STEVENS, REX. P. *Kant on Moral Practice*: *A Study of Moral Success and Failure*. New Orleans: Mercer University Press, 1981.

STEWART, ROBERT M., ed. *Readings in Social and Political Philosophy*. New York: Oxford University Press, 1986.

STODDARD, SANDOL. *The Hospice Movement*: *A Better Way of Caring for the Dying*. Briarcliff Manor, NY: Stein and Day, 1978.

STOLZ, STEPHANIE et al., eds. *Ethical Issues in Behavior Modification*. San Francisco: Jossey-Bass, 1978.

STONE, CHRISTOPHER. *Should Trees Have Standing?* Los Altos, CA: Kaufman, 1974.

STRAWSON, GALEN. *Freedom and Belief*. New York: Oxford University Press, 1991.

SULLIVAN, ROGER. *Kant's Moral Theory*. New York: Cambridge University Press, 1989.

SUMNER, L. *Abortion and Moral Theory*. Princeton, NJ: Princeton University Press, 1981.

SUMNER, W. G. *Folkways*. Boston: Ginn, 1934.

SWANTON, CHRISTINE. *Freedom*: *A Coherence Theory*. Indianapolis: Hackett Publishing, 1992.

SZASZ, THOMAS S. "The Ethics of Suicide." *The Antioch Review* (Spring 1971): 7–17.

SZASZ, THOMAS. *The Manufacture of Madness*. New York: Harper & Row, 1977.

TANNEN, DEBORAH. *That's Not What I Meant*. New York: Ballantine, 1986.

TANNEN, DEBORAH. *You Just Don't Understand*. New York: William Morrow, 1990.

TAYLOR, BRON R. *Affirmative Action at Work: Law, Politics, and Ethics*. Pittsburgh: University of Pittsburgh Press, 1991.

TAYLOR, PAUL W. "Social Science and Ethical Relativism." *Journal of Philosophy* 55 (1958): 32–43.

TAYLOR, PAUL, W., ed. *Problems of Moral Philosophy*, 2nd ed. Belmont, CA: Dickenson, 1972.

TAYLOR, RICHARD. *Having Love Affairs*. Buffalo, NY: Prometheus, 1982.

TAYLOR, RICHARD. *Virtue Ethics*: *An Introduction*. Interlaken, NY: Linden Books, 1991.

TAYLOR, TELFORD. *Nuremberg and Vietnam*: *An American Tragedy*. Chicago: Quadrangle Books, 1970.

THOMASMA, DAVID C., AND GLENN C. GRABER. *Euthanasia: Toward an Ethical Social Policy*. New York: Continuum, 1990.

TITUS, HAROLD H., AND MORRIS KEETON. *Ethics for Today*. New York: Van Nostrand, 1973. Chapters 7 and 11.

TITUS, HAROLD H., MARILYN S. SMITH, AND RICHARD NOLAN. *Living Issues in Philosophy*, 8th ed. Belmont, CA: Wadsworth, 1987.

TOOLEY, MICHAEL. *Abortion and Infanticide*. New York: Oxford University Press, 1983.

TRIBE, LAURENCE, ed. *Abortion: The Clash of Absolutes*. New York: Norton, 1992.

TRUSTED, JENNIFER. *Free Will and Responsibility*. New York: Oxford University Press, 1984.

UHR, LEONARD M., AND JAMES G. MILLER. *Drugs and Behavior*. New York: Wiley, 1960.

VANDEN HAAG, ERNEST, AND JOHN P. CONRAD. *The Death Penalty*: *A Debate*. New York: Plenum, 1983.

VANNOY, RUSSELL. *Sex Without Love*: *A Philosophical Exploration*. Buffalo, NY: Prometheus, 1980.

VAUX, KENNETH. *Biomedical Ethics: Morality for the New Medicine*. New York: Harper & Row, 1974.

VEATCH, ROBERT, AND EDWARD WAKIN. "Death and Dying." *U.S. Catholic* (April 1972): 7–13.

VELASQUEZ, MANUEL G. *Business Ethics*. Upper Saddle River, NJ: Prentice Hall, 1982.

VILLANI, JIM, ed. *Environment: Essence and Issue*. Youngstown, OH: Pig Iron Press, 1992.

VLASTOS, GREGORY. "Justice and Equality." In *Moral Concepts*, ed. Joel Feinberg. New York: Oxford University Press, 1970.

VON HIRSCH, ANDREW. *Doing Justice*: *The Choice of Punishment*. New York: Farrar, Straus, and Giroux, 1976.

WAELDER, ROBERT. "Psychiatry and the Problem of Criminal Responsibility." In *Criminal Law*, ed. Richard Donnelly, et al. New York: Free Press, 1961.

WALKER, RALPH C. *Kant*. New York: Methuen, 1982.

WALL, GEORGE B. *Introduction to Ethics*. Columbus, OH: Charles E. Merrill, 1974. Chapter 2.

WALLACE, JAMES D. *Moral Relevance and Moral Conflict*. New York: Cornell University Press, 1988.

WARNER, RICHARD. *Morality in Medicine*. Sherman Oaks, CA: Alfred, 1980.

WARNOCK, MARY. *Existentialism*. New York: Oxford University Press, 1970.

WASSERSTROM, RICHARD A. *War and Morality*. Belmont, CA: Wadsworth, 1970.

WASSERSTROM, RICHARD A., ed. *Morality and the Law*. Belmont, CA: Wadsworth, 1971.

WASSERSTROM, RICHARD, ed. *Today's Moral Problems*, 3rd ed. New York: Macmillan, 1985.

WEISS, ANN E. *Bioethics: Dilemmas in Modern Medicine*. Hillside, NJ: Enslow, 1985.

WERKMEISTER, WILLIAM H. *A Philosophy of Science*. Lincoln, NE: University of Nebraska Press, 1965. Chapter 12 contains a discussion of freedom in relation to the laws of nature.

WERTENBAKER, LAEL TUCKER. *Death of a Man*. New York: Random House, 1957.

WHITE, JAMES E. *Contemporary Moral Problems*, 2nd ed. St. Paul, MN: West, 1988.

WHITE, THOMAS J. *Business Ethics: A Philosophical Reader*. New York: Macmillan, 1993.

WILLIAMS, BERNARD. "The Idea of Equality." In *Moral Concepts*, ed. Joel Feinberg. New York: Oxford University Press, 1970.

WILLIAMS, CLIFFORD. *Free Will and Determinism: A Dialogue*. Indianapolis: Hackett Publishing, 1980.

WILLIAMS, GLANVILLE. *The Sanctity of Life and the Criminal Law*. New York: Knopf, 1957.

WILLIAMSON, WILLIAM P. "Prolongation of Life or Prolonging the Act of Dying." *The Journal of the American Medical Association* 202 (October 1967): 162–63.

WILSON, GARY W. *Free Will*. New York: Oxford University Press, 1982.

WILSON, LASCELLES A. *Ethics: Its Impact in Real Estate*. New York: Vantage, 1992.

WINFIELD, RICHARD D. *Freedom and Modernity*. Albany, NY: State University of New York Press, 1991.

WINOCUR, MARK. *Einstein, a Portrait*. Corte-Madera, CA: Pomegranate Artbooks, 1984.

WOOD, ALLEN W. *Kant's Moral Religion*. Ithaca, NY: Cornell University Press, 1970.

ZAITCHIK, ALAN. "Viability and the Morality of Abortion," *Philosophy and Public Affairs* 10 (1) (1981): 18–24.

ZWERDLING, DANIEL. *Workplace Democracy*. New York: Harper & Row, 1979.

Glossary

Abortion: The termination of a pregnancy prior to birth. A *spontaneous abortion*, or *miscarriage*, is one that is not purposely caused by the potential mother or anyone else. An *induced abortion* is one that is caused by someone, usually a doctor or midwife. A *self-induced abortion* is caused by the pregnant woman without the aid of a doctor. A *therapeutic abortion* refers to abortion done for some medical reason, but this term usually is used interchangeably with induced abortion. An *illegal abortion* is one that is against the law, and a *legal abortion* is one that is in accordance with the law (abortions presently are legal in the United States). Generally there are other types of abortion: uterine aspiration, hysterotomy, and saline abortion (sometimes called amniocentesis abortion).

Absolute: Perfect in quality and complete; not to be doubted or questioned—positive, certain, unconditional; not limited by restrictions or exceptions. This term usually is applied to beings (for example, God), but most importantly to truth. *Absolutism* is the theory that morality is absolute rather than relative; that is, that there are absolute moral truths to which we must adhere and which particular situations, people, or places do not affect. *Near or almost absolute* are terms coined by the author of this book to describe basic principles in ethics.

Abstinence: The act of foregoing or abstaining from something. As the term is used in this text, it means not engaging in sexual activities as one way of avoiding AIDS or STDs.

Acquired Immune Deficiency Syndrome (AIDS): A disease transmitted by various types of sexual activity, other means of ingesting bodily fluids, and injecting drugs with infected needles. The virus effectively destroys the infected person's immune system, making him or her susceptible to such diseases as Kaposi's sarcoma (a type of cancer) and pneumocystic carinii (a form of pneumonia).

Ad Hoc Committee: A committee formed to deal specifically with a single issue or problem—for example, the *ad hoc* committee on brain death, or irreversible coma.

Adultery: Sexual relations between a married person and a person other than the spouse. This is also known as *extramarital sex*.

Aesthetics (Esthetics): In philosophy, the study of values in art or beauty. Related to ethics because it involves values, although here the values apply to art or beauty.

Affective: That aspect of human beings that involves emotions and feelings.

Affirmative Action: That action taken so as to eliminate racial, religious, sexual, age, and handicap discrimination in employment practices.

Agent: A term in philosophy that means "one who performs an act or action."

Allowing Someone to Die: The medical practice of deciding when treatment is no longer curing and healing and when artificial or extraordinary means of life support are to be discontinued. *See also* Euthanasia.

Amniocentesis: A test that is performed by withdrawing fluid from the amniotic sac and subjecting it to various tests through which any of about 200 birth defects can be detected in a conceptus (fetus). This test also can determine other characteristics, such as sex. The term also can mean a form of abortion in which fluid is withdrawn from the amniotic sac and replaced with a saline, prostaglandin, or glucose solution that causes the uterus to contract and premature labor to begin. *See also* Amniotic Sac *and* Abortion.

Amniotic Sac: The sac containing fluid in which the conceptus floats during the entire period of gestation unless aborted.

Amoral: Indifferent to morality. This term applies only to some adult human beings, such as the severely mentally disturbed, those who have had prefrontal lobotomies, certain criminal types, and those with no moral education. Amoral also can mean "not knowing the difference between right and wrong" and "feeling no remorse or regret for the immoral actions one has taken."

Analects: The writings of Confucuious.

Analytic Ethics: *See* Metaethics.

Appropriate or Inappropriate Care: How to treat patients based upon what is appropriate or inappropriate, rather than using the terms *ordinary means* or *extraordinary means*.

Behavior Control: The alteration or manipulation of human behavior by various techniques, such as behavior modification, psychotherapy, drugs, brain surgery, and so on.

Behaviorism: A materialistic theory of human nature, developed originally by John Watson and further developed by B. F. Skinner, which states that human beings essentially are their behavior and that there is no such thing as mind, soul, spirit, or self but only body and brain, which react to external stimuli.

Beneficent: That which is good or which causes or brings about goodness, such as a beneficent act, which is a good act. The Principle of Beneficence is another name for the Principle of Goodness. *See also* Good or Right *and* Principle of Goodness or Rightness.

Bestiality: Sexual relations between human beings and animals.

Bioethics: Literally "life ethics." Essentially, ethics having to do with medicine and medical aspects of human beings, such as human experimentation, abortion, mercy killing, and truth telling, among others.

Bisexual: Human beings who have sexual relations with either the opposite sex or their own sex. *See also* Homosexuality *and* Heterosexuality.

Brain Death: Refers to irreversible or irreparable brain damage as determined by four criteria established by an *ad hoc* committee at Harvard Medical School in 1968: (1) unreceptivity and unresponsitivity, (2) no spontaneous movements or breathing, (3) no reflexes, and (4) a flat EEG. *See also* Electroencephalogram (EEG).

Capital Punishment: Usually punishment either by death or by a long jail sentence for having committed capital crimes such as premeditated murder, kidnapping, or torture and mutilation.

Cardinal Virtues: *See* Virtue.

Care Ethics: A theory sometimes called feminist ethics, established by psychologist Carol Gilligan, who states men and women are different when it comes to ethical decision making.

Categorical Imperative: The key principle of Immanuel Kant's ethics, which states essentially that an act is immoral if the rule that would authorize it cannot be made into a rule for all human beings. *See also* Universal.

Cheat: To deceive by trickery; to swindle; to mislead; to act dishonestly or practice fraud.

Chemotherapy: Any therapy involving the introduction of chemicals into a person's body.

Chorionic Villus Sampling (CVS): A tool, like amniocentesis, that can be used to diagnose genetic defects in a fetus as early as the ninth week of pregnancy. A flexible catheter, inserted vaginally, is guided by ultrasound along uterine walls and extracts fetal cells from the threadlike projections (villi) on the chorion (outermost embryonic layer). Some studies have revealed that CVS may cause limb deformities in the fetus.

Cloning: A scientific technique, still in the experimental stages, by which a second human being or animal can be created from the cells of one already living. The new human being, for example, will be exactly like the one from whom he or she was "cloned" and will be called the first person's "clone."

Cognitive: That aspect of human beings that involves rationality and reason.

Collegial Model: A model under the reciprocal approach to doctor-patient relationships in which the patient and everyone having to do with the care of the patient are considered to be part of a team. All team members have significant input into how the patient should be cared for.

Conceptus: A term coined by Daniel Callahan in his book *Abortion: Law, Choice and Morality,* meaning "that which has been conceived." By using this term, one avoids the confusion of using the words *zygote, embryo,* and *fetus* to describe the conceptus at different stages of gestation because *conceptus* can be used from conception until birth. This term also eliminates the emotional connotations of calling unborn human life by the terms *child, baby, organism,* or *vegetating matter.*

Conditioning: A term used in behaviorism to describe the process by which human beings are caused to behave in certain ways, often as a "controller" wants them to behave. The term first was used by Pavlov in relation to the conditioned reflex and later by B. F. Skinner in his theory of operant conditioning.

Consequentialism: Ethical theories that are concerned with the consequences of actions or rules. The traditional philosophical name for this is *teleology* (from the Greek *telos,* meaning end or purpose). Examples of consequentialist theories are all forms of ethical egoism and utilitarianism.

Consistent: Compatible, not self-contradictory; harmonious; conforming to a set of rules or principles. *See also* Contradictory, Self-Contradictory.

Contractual Model: A model under the Reciprocal Approach to patient care that establishes an oral or written contract between doctor and patient. *See also* Reciprocal Approach.

Contradictory, Self-Contradictory: Inconsistent, contrary; for example, two statements so related that if one is true the other must be false. ("I am a human being" and "I am not a human being" are contradictory statements.) *Self-contradictory* refers to a proposition that contradicts itself, such as "A circle is a square." *See also* Consistent.

Cost-Benefit Analysis: Also called "end-justifies-the-means" approach. The idea that one should strive to achieve the greatest benefits derived from the least possible cost expended. This is a possibility with any form of utilitarianism when "the greatest good for the greatest number" approach is stressed. Many ethicists question whether this approach is moral. *See also* End-Justifies-the-Means Approach.

CVS: See Chorionic Villus Sampling.

Declaration Pursuant to the Natural Death Act of California: A legalized "living will" type of document. This declaration is a part of California's Natural Death Act, which was signed into law on January 1, 1977, and revised in 1992. It purports to allow patients to state legally how they wish to be medically treated when they are dying or in other ways severely debilitated. *See also* Living Will *and* Durable Power of Attorney for Health Care.

Deontology: See Nonconsequentialism.

Determinism: Universal causation; the theory that everything in the universe has a cause. *Hard,* or *strong, determinism* states that freedom or free will is not compatible with universal causation. *Soft,* or *weak, determinism* states that everything is caused but that some causes originate with human beings; therefore, freedom or free will is compatible with universal causation. Many theories of determinism arise out of the fields of the natural and physical sciences, the social sciences, and religion. *See also* Predestination *and* Fatalism.

Developmental View: That view of the beginning of human life, held by Daniel Callahan and others, which states that human life begins at conception but develops gradually through various stages until it reaches full human status. According to this view, the conceptus's biological and moral significance increases with its development.

Diagnosis: The medical examination of patients in order to discover what is wrong with them. The results of such examinations are also called "the doctor's diagnosis."

Dialysis, Hemodialysis: The medical procedure whereby people who have no kidney function can be kept alive by having the wastes removed from their blood. Dialysis machines sometimes are referred to as "artificial kidneys."

Domino Argument: Also called the "slippery slope," "the wedge," and "the camel's-nose-under-the-tent" argument, this essentially argues that if human beings allow one thing to be declared legal or moral, this will cause a flood of bad things to follow. For example, if we legalize abortion, then mercy killing and infanticide are sure to follow. Like a row of dominoes, if you push over the first one, the rest will fall over in turn.

Down Syndrome: A type of congenital moderate to severe mental retardation that can occur in pregnancies of women of any age but most often in those 35 or older.

Durable Power of Attorney for Health Care: A legal document by means of which people can appoint an attorney-in-fact to make health care decisions for them in the event that they become incompetent to do so.

Duty Ethics: The name sometimes attributed to Immanuel Kant's system of ethics because of his stress upon performing a moral act out of a sense of duty, not inclination.

Eclectic: Selecting what is best from different systems or sources; having a wide range of tastes, desires, or likings. *See also* Synthesis.

Ectopic Pregnancy: A pregnancy that occurs in the fallopian tubes in which the ovum never moves down into the uterus. This is one of the two reasons for which the Roman Catholic church will allow abortion; the other is cancer of the uterus.

Egoism: That theory which is concerned with self-interest. *Psychological egoism* exemplifies the scientific, or descriptive, approach to morality, describing how human beings are thought to behave. *Strong psychological egoism* states that human beings *always* act in their own self-interest. *Weak psychological egoism* states that human beings *often* act in their own self-interest. Psychological egoism differs from *ethical egoism* in that the latter exemplifies the philosophical-normative approach to ethics. *Individual ethical egoism* says, "Everyone ought to act in my self-interest." *Personal ethical egoism* says, "I ought to act in my own self-interest but I make no claim concerning what others should do." *Universal ethical egoism* says, "Everyone ought to act in his or her own self-interest."

Electroencephalogram (EEG): A test by which a record of brain waves can be acquired from electrical impulses produced by the brain; it is often used to confirm the results of other diagnostic techniques that indicate that a patient's brain has been severely or irreversibly damaged. *See also* Irreversible Coma.

Embryo: A term describing the conceptus between the second and the eighth weeks of gestation and development. *See also* Conceptus *and* Fetus.

Emotive Theory: That theory of morality which holds that morality is not based upon reason, and that moral statements simply mean (1) that the people uttering them are stating their approval or disapproval of someone or something or (2) that they are trying to evoke such approval or disapproval or actions of a certain type in others. *See also* Intuitionism.

Empirical: Reasoning from experience and sense observation, as opposed to the "ideological" approach, which has to do with reasoning from among ideas in the mind. The empirical approach to knowledge is a cornerstone of scientific investigation.

End-Justifies-the-Means Approach: A problem for those consequentialist theories, especially utilitarianism, that present the idea that as long as the end or consequences are good, then any means used to attain that good are justified, regardless of the morality of the means or any motives. *See also* Cost-Benefit-Analysis.

Engineering Model: A model under the Paternalistic Approach to patient care, in which the doctor is a scientific engineer and the patient a machine. *See also* Paternalism, Paternalistic Approach *and* Priestly Model.

Ethical: *See* Moral.

Ethical Egoism: *See* Egoism.

Ethical Monism: The theory which states that there is only one intrinsic good or value in life; that is, only one thing that is good in itself and worth having for its own sake. For example, hedonism states that pleasure or happiness is the only intrinsic good or value.

Ethical Pluralism: That theory which states that there is more than one intrinsic good or value in life.

Ethics: From the Greek *ethos*, meaning character. In this book *ethics* is used interchangeably with *morality* except that in philosophy *ethics* means the study of morality. There are two approaches to ethics: the *scientific*, or *descriptive*, as used by the social sciences (for example, psychological egoism), and the *philosophical*, which includes the normative, or prescriptive, and metaethics (*see also* Normative, or Prescriptive, Ethics *and* Metaethics). When used in its ordinary sense, however, *ethics*, like *morality*, means "the values by which human beings live in relation to other human beings, nature, God, and/or themselves." *See also* Moral.

Euthanasia: A Greek word originally meaning "a good death" or "death with dignity." To many people, however, this term refers to murder. *See also* Allowing Someone to Die, Mercy Death, *and* Mercy Killing.

Extramarital Sex: Sex outside of marriage. *See also* Adultery.

Extraordinary, or Heroic, Means: Any means used to treat a sick person or dying patient that is out of the ordinary, or heroic; that which will not cure or heal a patient but will only prolong his dying. This term originally was coined by Pope Pius XII, who said that *extraordinary* would have to be defined according to particular persons, places, and times. *See also* Ordinary Means.

Falsity: Applies only to propositions. A proposition is false if it describes a state of affairs that was not, is not, or will not be actual. *See* Proposition *and* State of Affairs *and* Truth.

Fatalism: The view that all events are irrevocably fixed and predetermined so that they cannot be altered in any way by human beings—the future is always beyond their control. *See also* Predestination *and* Determinism.

Fetus: A term describing the conceptus between the eighth week of gestation or development and the time it is born. *See also* Conceptus *and* Embryo.

Free Love: The idea that anyone can freely engage in sex with anyone else within or outside of marriage as long as no coercion or force is used. *See also* Group Marriage.

Freudianism: Named after Sigmund Freud, the nineteenth-century founder of modern psychology. It is, among other things, a theory that states that human beings are driven by inner drives and unconscious motivations to behave in the way they do. *See also* Determinism.

Gene Pool: The reproductive elements of all mating individuals, which comprise a "pool" from which the genes of the next generation are drawn.

Genetics: The biology of heredity; the study of heredity and its variation.

Genetic View: A view of the beginning of human life that says it begins at conception; that is, as soon as the genetic makeup of a conceptus is established. *See also* Developmental View.

Genocide: The deliberate and systematic destruction of a racial, political, or cultural group.

Gestation: The period of development of the conceptus from conception until birth; also called pregnancy. *See also* Conceptus *and* Embryo *and* Fetus *and* Zygote.

Good or Right: As defined in this book, that which has pleasure or happiness in it, involves excellence, creates harmony, and encourages creativity. A person can be said to be *good*, whereas an action can be said to be *right*.

Group Marriage: A communal type of living in which legally or nonlegally married couples and/or single people live together. Sexual relations in such a group may be monogamous or "free."

Hedonism: The theory that pleasure or happiness is the one intrinsic good or value in life; that an action is moral if it brings the greatest amount of pleasure or happiness with the least amount of pain or unhappiness. This is a basic tenet of the ethical theories of Epicurus (egoism) and Jeremy Bentham and J. S. Mill (utilitarianism).

Heterosexuality: The love or sexual orientation of a man for a woman or a woman for a man; the most approved and accepted form of sexuality and love in the Western world.

Homosexuality: Generally, the love and/or sexual orientation of a man for a man or a woman for a woman; commonly used to mean love and/or sexual relationships only between or among men. *Lesbianism* is used to describe love and/or sexual relationships between or among women.

Hospice Approach to Care for the Dying: *Hospice* literally means "a place of rest and refuge for strangers or pilgrims." The hospice approach to care for the dying was initiated at St. Christopher's Hospice in London by Dr. Cicely Saunders; there are now about 100 hospices all over England and many throughout the United States. The aim of the hospice approach is to provide comfort and care for the dying. Those involved in this approach have conducted advanced research on pain control and have provided a much more humane environment for dying patients and their families. Whenever possible, this approach stresses home care.

Human Being: A member of the species *homo sapiens*. The term *potential human being* is sometimes applied to a human life from shortly after conception to about the twelfth or thirteenth week of development, after which the human life is called *actual*. This definition is not hard and fast, however, as some do not define a life as a human being until birth. *See also* Person, Personhood.

Humanism (Humanistic Ethics):   *Humanism* means many things, but in this text it refers to a nonreligious view of life essentially based upon atheism or agnosticism and advocating a morality that excludes religion or religious belief.

Humanitarian Ethics: A system of ethics originated by the author that advocates five basic principles and a synthesized act-rules, consequentialism-nonconsequentialism approach to morality (sometimes referred to as *mixed deontology*) that can include any moral system—religious or nonreligious—as long as the five basic moral principles are observed.

Immoral: That which is bad or wrong, such as a bad person or a wrong action; used interchangeably in this book with *unethical*.

Incest: Sexual relations between persons who are so closely related by blood that their marriage is illegal or forbidden by custom—usually those between fathers and daughters, mothers and sons, or brothers and sisters.

Incipient Human Life: Life that is not yet born; life during almost the entire period of gestation. *See also* Conceptus.

Inclinations: Those things that human beings are inclined to do usually by habit or emotions. Immanuel Kant opposed inclinations to duties, stating that in order for it to be truly moral, an act had to be done out of a sense of duty, not from inclination.

Indeterminism: The theory that there is a certain amount of chance and freedom in the world, that not everything is caused, and that there is a real pluralism in reality. The opposite of *determinism*.

Informed Consent: Usually refers to a formal written consent form that patients give to health care professionals allowing them to conduct tests, procedures, or experimentation upon patients with patients' complete and "informed" knowledge and consent.

Intravenous (IV):   Literally "within or into a vein." Refers to fluids pushed into the veins of human beings (for example, blood transfusion, glucose, or medications of various sorts).

Intuitionism: Morality based upon feelings or emotions rather than upon reason or rules; this also is known as *subjectivism*. Act nonconsequentialism is the best example of such a theory. Sayings such as "If it feels good, do it" and "Do your own thing" exemplify this approach to morality.

In Utero: Within the uterus.

Irreversible Coma: *See* Persistent Vegetative State (PVS).

Justice: Generally moral rightness, equity, fairness. There are four types of justice: *exchange justice*, which has to do with equal exchange of remuneration for products or services; *distributive justice*, which has to do with the distribution of good and bad based upon merit or desert, need and ability, or according to the equality of human beings; *social justice*, which has to do with the obligation to be just and fair to all members of society or to society in general; and *retributive justice*, which is based upon the "eye for an eye, tooth for a tooth" philosophy. *See also* Reward and Punishment.

Killing: To put to death, slay, or deprive of life.

Laissez-faire: The doctrine that government should not interfere with business.

Larceny: The felonious taking and removing of another's personal property with the intent of permanently depriving the owner. *Grand larceny* is stealing on a grand scale (e.g., a car); *petit* (or petty) *larceny* constitutes minor theft (e.g., stealing apples from a grocery store). *See also* Stealing.

Law of Nature: A term used to describe events in nature that occur consistently and without exception—for example, the law of gravity.

Lesbianism: *See* Homosexuality.

Leukemia: A form of cancer of the blood.

Lie: An intentionally deceptive message in the form of a statement; a piece of information deliberately presented as being true; anything meant to deceive or give a wrong impression. A *white lie* is a falsehood not meant to injure anyone and considered by many to be of little import.

Living Will: A will by which healthy and competent people can inform their relatives and others of how they want to be treated or not treated when they are too sick or incompetent to decide such things as whether to start or discontinue life-support systems, submit to surgery, and so on. It is not a legal document. *See also* Declaration Pursuant to the Natural Death Act of California *and* Durable Power of Attorney for Health Care.

Manners: The socially correct way of behaving; also, the prevailing systems or modes of social conduct of a specific society.

Masochism: The deriving of pleasure—including sexual pleasure—from being hurt, abused, or mistreated.

Mercy Death: Distinguished from mercy killing in that mercy death is a termination of life expressly requested by a dying patient who is competent to do so; distinguished from allowing someone to die in that a direct act (such as the administering of a massive overdose of drugs) is taken to end the patient's life. This also is known as *physician assisted suicide*. *See also* Allowing Someone to Die *and* Euthanasia *and* Mercy Killing.

Mercy Killing: A direct act taken to end someone's life with the motive of being merciful. The means include the administering of poison or a massive overdose of drugs, shooting, and so on. Mercy killing is distinguished from mercy death in that the former is done without the person's express consent; it is distinguished from allowing someone to die in that it is a direct act of termination. *See also* Allowing Someone to Die *and* Euthanasia *and* Mercy Death.

Metaethics: The second type of ethics under the philosophical approach. The word comes from the Greek, and means "beyond or above ethics." In metaethics, also known as *analytic ethics*, the language and logic of ethics and ethical systems are studied, defined, and discussed, usually without the intent of setting up any kind of alternative ethical systems or of prescribing human behavior, as in *normative ethics*. *See also* Ethics *and* Normative, or Prescriptive, Ethics.

Metastasis: The spreading of bacteria or body cells (especially cancer cells) from one part of the body to another.

Missionary Position: The customarily accepted heterosexual position for sexual intercourse in which the man is on top of the woman.

Monogamy: Having only one spouse; the major form of marriage (legal or nonlegal) practiced in the Western world.

Moral: That which is good or right, such as a good person or a right action. Used interchangeably in this text with *ethical*.

Moral Import: That which contains moral importance or significance. For instance, the proposition "Human beings should not kill other human beings" has moral import, whereas "The house is green" does not. *See also* Proposition.

Morality: From the Latin *moralis*, meaning "customs or manners." In this book it is used interchangeably with *ethics* except when *ethics* is used specifically to note that area of philosophy that constitutes the study of morality. In the author's working definition, morality, or ethics, refers to how humans relate to or treat one another in order to promote mutual welfare, growth, and meaning while striving for good over bad and right over wrong. *See also* Ethics *and* Moral.

Moratorium: A temporary suspension of something; for example, certain scientific experiments.

Murder: The unlawful and immoral killing of one person by another, especially with malice aforethought. *See also* Killing, *and* Mercy Death, *and* Mercy Killing.

Nichomachean Ethics: The system of ethics established by Aristotle in the fourth century B.C., named after his son Nichomachus.

Nonconsequentialism: Ethical theories based not upon consequences but upon some other moral standard (usually considered "higher" by the nonconsequentialist); referred to in traditional philosophy as *deontology* (from the Greek, loosely meaning "ought"). Examples of such theories are Kant's Duty Ethics and the Divine Command Theory.

Nonmoral: That which is completely out of the sphere of morality. Animals, plants, and inanimate objects are essentially nonmoral.

Normative, or Prescriptive, Ethics: The first type of ethics under the philosophical approach. This also is known as *prescriptive ethics* because it is interested in setting up norms or value systems that *prescribe* how human beings ought to behave. All ethical systems, such as Ethical Egoism, Utilitarianism, *Virtue Ethics*, and Kant's Duty Ethics, are normative.

Objective: Outside of or external to human beings rather than within them. For example, objective values would be those outside of humans as opposed to those within them. *See also* Subjective.

Obligations: Responsibilities that human beings have toward one another by law, morality, or tradition to see that their just rights are protected and accorded them. *See also* Right.

Oncology, Oncologist: *Oncology* is the branch of medicine dealing with tumors, especially cancerous tumors; an *oncologist* is a doctor who specializes in this branch of medicine.

Ordinary Means: Distinguished from extraordinary, or heroic, means of medical treatment of patients; refers to the appropriate treatment that would not be unusual or beyond what should be done for any particular patient given his or her specific illness, disease, or stage of dying. *See also* Extraordinary Means.

Oxymoron: A figure of speech that contains a seeming contradiction, such as "make haste slowly."

Paradigm, Paradigmatic: A *paradigm* is a pattern or model; *paradigmatic* means *patternlike* or *model-like*.

Paternalism, Paternalistic Approach: A type of human relationship in which one person is dominant (for example, the doctor) and one submissive (for example, the patient). In medicine, it is characterized by the Engineering and Priestly Models.

Persistent Vegetative State (PVS):   A state that results from damage to the cerebral or neocortex, which controls the cognitive functions. Can also be called *irreversible coma* or *cortical* or *cerebral death. See also* Brain Death.

Person, Personhood: That point at which a human being can be considered to possess a personality and be able to enter into meaningful human relationships—usually after birth and after some socialization; not clearly defined for those who are at various stages of minimal human being-ness (comatose and severely retarded people). *See also* Human Being.

Physician-Assisted Suicide: When a doctor helps a person to commit suicide. *See also* Mercy Death.

Polygamy: Having more than one spouse. Less commonly, *polyandry* means having more than one husband, whereas *polygamy* means having more than one wife. *Bigamy* means having two spouses. Generally, polygamy is not legally or morally approved of in the Western world.

Pornography: Generally considered to be any form of literature, art, film, or live display that is intended to incite lewd and lascivious feelings without any redeeming social, literary, or artistic value. *Kiddie porn* refers to pornographic material depicting children. *Snuff porn* refers to pornographic material depicting murder.

Practical Imperative: Another name for Immanuel Kant's maxim that no human being should be treated merely as a means to someone else's end but, rather, that all human beings should be treated as unique ends in themselves.

Predestination: A religious version of determinism that states essentially that because God knows all, He also has foreordained everything to happen the way it has from the beginning. Human beings are completely determined by a supernatural power. *See also* Determinism *and* Fatalism.

Premarital Sex: Sexual relations that occur prior to marriage or without marriage; referred to in the Bible as *fornication.*

Prescriptive Ethics: *See* Normative or Prescriptive Ethics.

Priestly Model: The model in the doctor-patient relationship, under the Paternalistic Approach, in which the doctor is priest and the patient is parishioner. *See also* Engineering Model *and* Paternalism, Paternalistic Approach.

Prima Facie Duty: Literally, a duty "at first glance"; that is, all other things being equal, we ought to do it. This term, introduced by Sir William David Ross, means that some duties and obligations must come before others. For example, Ross believed that to avoid doing harm to someone is more important than to do good.

Principle of Goodness or Rightness: The ultimate principle of any moral system because *moral* and *ethical* mean *good* or *right*. This principle requires us to do three things: first, to promote goodness over badness; second, to cause no harm or badness; and third, to prevent badness or harm. *See also* Good or Right.

Principle of Individual Freedom (Equality Principle):   The principle that states that human beings ought to be free to pursue their own values and morality as long as these do not seriously conflict with or violate the other four basic moral principles (Value of Life, Goodness, Justice, and Truth Telling or Honesty).

Principle of Justice or Fairness: The principle that states that it is not enough to do good and avoid bad, but that some effort must be made to distribute the good and bad resulting from our actions. *See also* Justice *and* Punishment *and* Reward.

Principle of Truth Telling or Honesty: The principle that states that human beings always ought to strive to tell the truth or be honest except when this would interfere with or seriously violate the principles of Goodness, Value of Life, and Justice. This principle must be abided by if there is to be meaningful communication and human relationships.

Prochoice or Abortion on Request: The position that abortion should be allowed at any time merely upon the woman's request or demand.

Procreation: Creating children mainly through human sexual intercourse although artificial insemination and laboratory, or test-tube, babies also may be included.

Prognosis: Prediction of the course and end of a disease and the outlook based upon this prediction.

Prolife or Right to Life: The position that unborn conceptuses have an absolute right to life superseding all other rights, such as the woman's right to decide whether or not to go through with pregnancy.

Promise: A declaration that one will or will not do something; a vow. *Breaking a promise* is failing to conform to or acting contrary to or violating a promise.

Promulgate: To set forth or lay out something—for example, a set of ethical principles or a moral system.

Proponent: One who supports a particular point of view, position, or argument.

Proposition: A meaningful statement that asserts or claims something about reality and that has the characteristic of being either true or false. There are four types of propositions: *analytic*, such as "All triangles are three-sided"; *internal*, such as "I have a headache"; *external*, or *empirical*, such as "I see a table here before me"; and *moral*, such as "Human beings should not kill other human beings."

Proselytize: To try to convert someone from one point of view to one's own or to another.

Protective Isolation: In medicine, protecting patients and nonpatients from contagion. *Reverse isolation* is the means used to protect patients from coming into contact with infections from the outside environment.

Psychological Egoism: *See* Egoism.

Punishment: The act of penalizing someone for a crime, fault, or misbehavior; a penalty for wrongdoing. There are three basic theories of punishment and reward: (1) retribution, or deserts theory, which states that we ought to give people what they deserve, regardless of the consequences; (2) utilitarianism, or results, theory, which states that we ought to punish or reward only if it brings about good consequences; and (3) restitution, or compensation, theory, which states that proper reward or punishment is valid only when the victim is compensated for wrongs or harm done to him or her. *See also* Justice *and* Reward *and* Principle of Justice or Fairness.

PVS: *See* Persistent Vegetative State.

Qualifying Rule: Rather than making an exception to a rule, one can qualify a rule so that the exception applies to all humanity. For example, "Never kill" can be qualified to read, "Never kill except in self-defense or defense of the innocent."

Radical Individualism: In health care, the approach that patients have absolute rights over their own bodies and lives and therefore may reject all recommendations of health care personnel (especially doctors). *See also* Paternalism, Paternalistic Approach, *and* Reciprocal Approach.

Rawls, John: Put forth his theory of justice, that life, liberty, and property are given to human beings by a just society.

Reciprocal Approach: In health care, the approach that decisions should not rest only with the doctor or only with the patient but must instead be made in a reciprocal way. This approach consists of the collegial and contractual models. *See also* Paternalism, Paternalistic Approach, *and* Radical Individualism.

Relativism: The opposite of *absolutism* in that those who hold this point of view believe that there are no absolutes in morality, but rather that morality, is relative to particular cultures, groups, or even individuals, and further that everyone must decide upon his or her own values and ethics because there are no absolutes.

Reverse Discrimination: That type of discrimination and prejudice which works against the majority (usually young white males). In business employment practices, this usually occurs as part of the effort to eliminate discrimination against minorities.

Reverse Isolation: *See* Protective Isolation.

Reversibility Criterion: An ethical principle that states that one should test the morality or immorality of an action by putting oneself in the other person's place, by reversing the situation in question. The Golden Rule ("Do unto others as you would have them do unto you") is one example of this criterion. Kant used this criterion in his system along with the criterion of *universalizability*.

Reward: Something given or received for worthy behavior, usually on the basis of merit, desert (what people deserve), or ability. *See also* Justice *and* Principle of Justice *and* Punishment.

Right: That which is due to anyone through law, morality, or tradition, such as the right to life or the right to freedom. *See also* Obligations.

Sadism: Enjoyment, including sexual enjoyment, gained from administering pain or hurt to another. *See also* Masochism.

Sanction: Authoritative permission or approval for some course of action; for example, a religious sanction of an action makes it moral for those who belong to that religion.

Sexually Transmitted Disease (STD): Any disease, such as chlamydia, syphilis, gonorrhea, herpes, and AIDS, which can be transmitted by sexual activity.

Situation Ethics: The theory invented by Joseph Fletcher which says that there are no moral rules or guides other than Christian love—what is moral in any situation is the loving thing to do in that situation. *See also* Relativism *and* Utilitarianism (specifically *act utilitarianism*).

Situationism: The theory that one's actions are governed strictly by the situation rather than by rules or principles. All act approaches to morality are situational.

State of Affairs: An occurrence or situation that either is or is not actual; the occurrence or situation in reality, as distinguished from our judgment or claims about it. States of affairs are either actual or not actual, never true or false. *See also* Proposition *and* Truth.

STD: *See* Sexually Transmitted Disease (STD).

Stealing: Taking something without right or permission, generally in a surreptitious way. *See also* Larceny.

Stem Cell Research: Research using master cells of the body obtained from both adults and human embryos.

Subject: As used in this book, one who is to be experimented upon.

Subjective: Coming from within human beings rather than outside of them. *See also* Objective.

Subjectivism: *See* Intuitionism.

Suicide: The act or instance of intentionally killing oneself. *See also* Killing *and* Mercy Death.

Synthesis: A bringing together of the best of a series of divergent ethical systems. A reasonable synthesis is a bringing together of the best of all the systems or theories of ethics coupled with an attempt to eliminate their difficulties or faults. *See also* Eclectic.

Tay-Sachs Disease: A fatal disorder that is genetic in character and that is usually found in the infant offspring of Eastern European Jews.

Teleology: *See* Consequentialism.

Tenable: Capable of being held; workable, defensible. *See also* Viable.

Terrorism: War deliberately waged against civilians.

Triage: In medicine, a disaster that requires decisions as to who will be treated first or at all; an emergency situation in which hospital facilities are taxed beyond their capabilities.

Truth: As applied to propositions, a proposition is *true* if it describes a state of affairs that was, is, or will be actual. *Truth* in this sense is absolute, not relative. *See* Falsity *and* Proposition *and* State of Affairs.

Unethical: *See* Immoral.

Unity in Diversity: The theory that attempts to resolve the absolutism-relativism controversy by stating that human beings are similar and also different; therefore, we should strive for a unity within such diversity. This can be accomplished if we allow for freedom and diversity while accepting certain unifying principles; for example, allowing people freedom as long as they do not harm other people in the process.

Universal: Applicable to all human beings, situations, times, and places. A moral rule that is *universalizable* is one that can be applied to all human beings without self-contradiction. *Universalizability* is a principle in Kant's ethical system that is embodied in the Categorical Imperative, which states that a moral rule that cannot be universalized, or made applicable to all human beings, is not a true moral rule. *See also* Categorical Imperative *and* Absolute.

Universal Causation: *See* Determinism *and* Indeterminism.

Utilitarianism: A normative ethical theory originally established by Jeremy Bentham and John Stuart Mill that advocates bringing about good consequences or happiness to all concerned— sometimes stated as "the greatest good for the greatest number." *Act utilitarianism* states that one should perform that act which will bring about the greatest amount of good for all concerned. *Rule utilitarianism* states that one should always establish and/or follow that rule or those rules which will bring about the greatest amount of good for all concerned.

Value of Life Principle: The first moral principle, which states that human life should be preserved, protected, and valued; sometimes referred to as the Sanctity of Life Principle. In this book it means a reverence for life and an acceptance of death.

Vegan: A person who will eat no flesh of animals or animal products, including dairy products.

Vegetarianism: Similar to vegan except some flesh may be eaten (e.g., fish or chicken).

Viable: Capable of working, such as a moral system. Also, in connection with pregnancy and abortion, a fetus that is able to exist outside of the mother's womb (usually after 28 weeks of gestation). *See also* Tenable.

Virtue: The quality of moral excellence, righteousness, responsibility; a specific type of moral excellence or other exemplary quality considered to be meritorious. For example, the cardinal or natural virtues are justice, prudence, fortitude, and temperance.

Virtue Ethics: A moral theory that had its beginnings with Aristotle and which is based not upon consequences, feelings, or rules, but upon human beings developing a moral or virtuous character by doing what an ideal good or virtuous person would do.

Zero Population Growth (ZPG):   A situation in which a man and a woman together produce no more than two children, one to replace each of them when they die, thereby ensuring no increase in the population.

Zygote: The term used to describe a conceptus immediately after the joining of the sperm and the egg; the fertilized ovum. *See also* Conceptus *and* Embryo *and* Fetus.

Index